THE TEMPLETON GUIDE

Colleges
THAT ENCOURAGE
Character
Development

Character

is

destiny.

—Heraclitus

THE TEMPLETON GUIDE

Colleges
THAT ENCOURAGE
Character
Development

A RESOURCE

FOR PARENTS,

STUDENTS,

AND EDUCATORS

EDITED BY THE
JOHN TEMPLETON FOUNDATION

TEMPLETON FOUNDATION PRESS
PHILADELPHIA

TEMPLETON FOUNDATION PRESS
Five Radnor Corporate Center, Suite 120
100 Matsonford Road
Radnor, Pennsylvania 19087
http://www.templeton.org/press

Library of Congress Cataloging-in-Publication Data

Colleges that encourage character development : a resource for parents, students, and educators / edited by the John Templeton Foundation.
    p.   cm. – (The Templeton guide)
    Includes index.
ISBN 1-890151-28-9 (pbk. : alk. paper)
1.Universities and colleges—United States Directories. 2. Universities and colleges—United States Evaluation. 3. Moral education (Higher)—United States Directories.
I. Templeton Foundation. II. Series.
L901.C79 1999
378.73—dc21   99-38958
                                                                                      CIP

Printed in Canada

To order call 800-621-2736

CONTENTS

EDITORIAL STAFF

Project Director   Arthur J. Schwartz, Ed.D.
                      John Templeton Foundation

Executive Editor   Pamela M. Bond

Research Director   Jon C. Dalton, Ed.D.
                      Director, Institute on College Student Values
                      Florida State University

Research Staff   Anne T. Kaiser, Coordinator
                      David M. Cayton, Greg J. Joiner,
                      Leah Ewing Ross

Contributing Editors Tracie A. Barnard, Therese Boyd,
                        Valerie Gittings, Robert Hochschild,
                        Greg J. Joiner, Joanne M. Kaldy,
                        Julie Ann Maggio, Melissa F. McCall,
                        Vivian R. McLaughlin, Rachel R. Sivyer,
                        Linda Triemstra, Mary Wachs

Managing Editor   Laura G. Barrett

Designer   David Skolkin

Typesetter   Angela Taormina

Printer   Webcom, Inc.

THE REVEREND MARTIN LUTHER KING JR. once said, "Intelligence plus *character* — that is the goal of a true education." Keeping the spirit of Dr. King's wisdom alive, *Colleges That Encourage Character Development* recognizes and profiles exemplary programs, presidents, and higher-education institutions that inspire students to lead ethical and civic-minded lives.

Recent national studies suggest that the vast majority of Americans share a common set of core values: honesty, self-control, perseverance, respect, compassion, and service to those less fortunate. Americans also agree that the college years are an ideal time to engage the minds, hearts, and hands of our young people to learn about and practice these virtues. But which college programs encourage character development? We believe that in this guidebook you will find clear and persuasive answers to this important question.

DEFINING
CHARACTER

Rooted in the Greek word *charakter*, the term "character" has come to mean the constellation of strengths and weaknesses that form and reveal who we are. Our character does not consist of a single statement or a random act but of those qualities and dispositions that we practice consistently — both good and bad. Assessing our character means taking an inventory of our dominant thoughts and actions. As Aristotle once said, "We are what we repeatedly do."

Character is not engraved by age six — or even sixteen. We can change and improve our character. However, like a comfortable pair of shoes, selfishness, laziness, dishonesty, and irresponsibility are easy to slip into. But the uplifting message of character development is that we can acquire a good and sound character — one that is durable yet evolving. All it takes is hard work and commitment. Just as a mountain is constantly being reshaped by weather patterns, our character is reshaped by the different choices we make and the virtues we choose to practice. In much the same way, *our choices develop our character — and our character determines our choices.*

A popular definition of character is "what we do when no one is looking." We often think that a person's character is "tested" in response to various temptations and challenges ("No! I won't cheat, even if nobody is looking.") Other definitions emphasize character as the capacity to draw a line where none exists. Indeed, people of good character are usually described as having strong principles such as truthfulness and fairness. As Mark Twain once wrote, "In matters of opinion, swim with the fish; but in matters of principles, stand firm like a rock."

DEVELOPING CHARACTER
IN THE COLLEGE YEARS

Parents are a young person's first and most significant character educators. Whether modeling the Golden Rule, emphasizing how important it is to be honest, or showing concern for those less fortunate, most parents try their best to teach their sons and daughters the essential lessons of character.

Although developing good values is certainly a lifelong process, the college years are critical to forming a strong and steady character. Students are now cognitively and emotionally ready to develop or refine an *internalized* set of ideals and standards that they cannot betray or violate ("I can't lie. "I must do whatever I can to help others."). These standards and beliefs serve as powerful guides to their conduct. During the college years, students begin to rely on their own moral compass — a set of virtues and principles that enable them to do the right thing despite pressures to do the contrary ("I am not a binge drinker. It's just not the kind of person I want to be or the way I want to live.").

A great many college students strive to live lives of good character. They are honest and hard working, and they care deeply about those less fortunate. Other students do not yet show consistent patterns of good character, but nonetheless they are searching for the kind of person they want to become. Recognizing this, college educators play an important role in reinforcing and strengthening the ideals and moral values that students already hold. They provide and encourage meaningful opportunities for college students to learn about, reflect on, and practice the virtues of personal and civic responsibility.

In his landmark study, *College: The Undergraduate Experience in America*, Ernest Boyer eloquently captured the belief that at the very heart of a higher education is not the cultivation of skills or the learning of certain branches of knowledge but the formation of good character:

> Education for what purpose? Competence to what end? At a time in life when values should be shaped and personal priorities sharply probed, what a tragedy it would be if the most deeply felt issues, the most haunting questions, the most creative moments were pushed to the fringes of institutional life. What a monumental mistake it would be if students, during the undergraduate years, remained trapped within the organizational grooves and narrow routines to which the academic world sometimes seems excessively devoted.

Boyer reminds us that we must never forget that education in its fullest sense is inescapably a moral enterprise — a continuous and conscious effort to guide students to know and pursue what is good and worthwhile.

JOHN M. TEMPLETON JR., M.D.
President
John Templeton Foundation

ARTHUR J. SCHWARTZ, ED.D.
Director, Character Development Programs
John Templeton Foundation

Colleges That Encourage Character Development contains 555 profiles of exemplary programs, presidents, and colleges and universities that inspire students to lead ethical and civic-minded lives. It has been designed for students, parents, and educators who know deep in their hearts that *character matters.*

Although the John Templeton Foundation does not recommend any single character-development curriculum, formula, or approach, we have published this guidebook to stress how important it is for each college and university in the United States to establish its own unique set of character-development practices, expectations, and outcomes. In short, this guidebook celebrates the belief that character development can and does occur within a wide diversity of higher-education settings.

High-School Students and Their Families

It is important to know that our selection process was highly competitive. If a school or program is not profiled in this guidebook, this does not mean that the college or university has no interest in character development or that it does not provide excellent opportunities for students to explore and strengthen their values, beliefs, and convictions. We encourage college-bound students and their families to contact the admissions office of the school in which they are interested and find out what character-development programs and activities the institution has in place.

High-School Counselors

High-school guidance and college admissions counselors across the United States help more than one million students each year identify and select the college they will attend. Many counselors are actively involved in their school or community's character-education programs and understand that the old adage "character is destiny" contains an essential truth. We hope that counselors will make this guidebook available to students and their families and help them understand how to use it as a resource during their college selection process.

College Administrators, Trustees, Faculty, and Alumni

College trustees and officials, faculty members, and alumni have a special understanding that during the college years young people frequently seek to define or redefine for themselves a set of ethical and civic commitments. This guidebook profiles some of the best practices in higher education that inspire students to lead ethical and civic-minded lives. We hope that educators will use this comprehensive resource in discussions with colleagues to determine what their institutions can do to increase their commitment to educating students for moral leadership.

Colleges That Encourage Character Development is divided into three major sections: 405 exemplary programs listed in 10 categories, 50 presidents, and 100 colleges and universities that inspire students to lead ethical and civic-minded lives. The programs, presidents, and institutions selected are listed alphabetically by school name, not according to any ranking or rating. Our goal was to highlight these outstanding examples of character-development programs at colleges and universities.

Exemplary Programs

The Exemplary Programs section consists of 405 programs divided into 10 categories:

✦ FIRST-YEAR PROGRAMS: 60 college programs that offer students the tools to develop a moral compass to navigate between increased personal freedom and new responsibilities

✦ ACADEMIC HONESTY PROGRAMS: 35 college programs that effectively communicate the values of honesty, trust, respect, responsibility, integrity, and fairness in the classroom

✦ FACULTY AND CURRICULUM PROGRAMS: 45 college programs that offer opportunities in the classroom for students to examine, reflect on, and articulate a set of moral ideals and commitments

✦ VOLUNTEER SERVICE PROGRAMS: 60 college programs that provide opportunities for students to learn through serving others in their communities and in the world

✦ SUBSTANCE-ABUSE PREVENTION PROGRAMS: 35 college programs that place character development at the heart of their alcohol- and drug-abuse prevention efforts

✦ STUDENT LEADERSHIP PROGRAMS: 40 college programs that help students develop the competencies, conscience, and compassion required of leaders in a civil society

✦ SPIRITUAL GROWTH PROGRAMS: 40 college programs, not all church-related, that provide opportunities for students to develop a coherent vision of moral integrity that connects belief to behavior

✦ CIVIC EDUCATION PROGRAMS: 40 college programs that encourage students to develop the skills and habits of mind to become active, well-informed, responsible citizens in a democratic society

✦ CHARACTER AND SEXUALITY PROGRAMS: 20 college programs that help students to learn, appreciate, and apply the core virtues of self-control, respect, responsibility, and integrity in their relationships

✦ SENIOR-YEAR PROGRAMS: 30 college programs that help seniors reflect on, connect, and attach meaning to their undergraduate experience

In some cases, it is obvious that these activities directly foster and encourage character development (e.g., Academic Honesty Programs, Volunteer Service Programs). However, the uniqueness of this guidebook is that it identifies the *character dimension* of college programs that might not immediately appear to encourage developing such virtues as self-control, respect, and courage.

For example, the 60 First-Year Programs do more than help students adjust to new surroundings; they provide critical-thinking skills that enable them to address the ethical and behavioral challenges of contemporary college life. Most significantly, these programs foster the development of good character by encouraging first-year students to commit themselves to high standards of academic and personal behavior.

The Substance-Abuse Prevention Program category is another example of how college programs focus on the character dimension of education. Virtually all colleges and universities have in place programs that aim to reduce binge drinking and drug use. However, the 35 programs profiled in this guidebook place character development at the *heart* of the issue. They extend beyond mere enforcement of campus rules to include campus and community activities that strive to change perceptions, expectations, and behaviors about alcohol and other drug use. At the core of these efforts are professionally designed and often student-led activities that equip young people with the skills to resist participating in peer cultures and community practices that lead to binge drinking and drug use.

As part of each of the 405 Exemplary Program profiles, we provide the name and contact information for the college official or faculty member who coordinates or directs that particular program. We encourage readers to contact these men and women to learn more about their successes and continuing challenges. Most important, we hope that these profiles inspire college-bound students and their families to find out what character-development programs are offered at the college or university they are considering attending. Admissions officers need to know about this interest in learning more about the school's commitment to character development.

Presidential Leadership

Colleges That Encourage Character Development profiles 50 college and university presidents who are setting the standard in higher education for what a leader can do to establish priorities and programs that help prepare students for lives of personal and civic responsibility.

It is a sad but undeniable fact that too many students graduate from college without ever talking to the college president. It used to be different. A century ago, the college president frequently taught a capstone course to seniors to challenge students to develop a lifelong commitment to the virtues of personal and civic responsibility. Indeed, these courses often asked the student to address the core question: *What sort of life do I want to live?*

Today, we realize that it is not feasible for college presidents to teach a capstone course to every graduating senior. But a college president still can visibly demonstrate a personal commitment to establishing character development as a high priority for his or her institution. Serving as a catalyst, college presidents can provide the necessary resources and support to initiate a wide variety of character-development activities on their campuses. Presidents also can provide national leadership to promote the importance of character development in higher education. In addition, college presidents can model in their own actions those aspects of character and integrity that students should emulate.

By recognizing these men and women, we hope that they become *beacons of inspiration* for college administrators across the United States who are interested in learning about ways to establish character development as a priority for their institutions.

For parents and educators — or other alumni — who graduated from one of these 50 institutions, we encourage you to contact your alma mater and tell the president how much you personally appreciate his or her commitment. Most important, we hope that you will enjoy learning in these pages how critical presidential leadership can be to establishing character development as a high priority on a college campus.

The Templeton Honor Roll

In 1989, the John Templeton Foundation established the *Honor Roll for Character-Building Colleges* to recognize institutions that emphasize character development as an integral part of the undergraduate experience. To date, more than 350 colleges and universities have been named to one or more *Honor Rolls*. Continuing this tradition of affirming excellence, we recognize 100 *Templeton Honor Roll* schools in this guidebook. Although their particular missions, practices, and perspectives may differ, each of these institutions exhibits a strong and inspiring campus-wide ethos that articulates the expectations of personal and civic responsibility in *all* dimensions of college life. In many cases, the *Templeton Honor Roll* institutions have received numerous awards or recognition for their programs that help students learn about and practice the core values of honesty, compassion, and personal responsibility.

It has been a significant challenge to capture in words the inspiring campus-wide ethos that is common to all of the 100 *Templeton Honor Roll* colleges and universities. We encourage readers to contact a college featured in the *Honor Roll* to find out more about its commitment to character development. We certainly hope that these profiles will jump-start a lively conversation in homes and in schools about the importance of character development in selecting a college or university.

Glossary

The glossary in the back of this guidebook offers easy-to-understand definitions of the words and terms commonly used to describe campus-based character-development programs. Terms such as "binge drinking," "*in loco parentis*," and "service learning" are explained in simple and straightforward language. We hope that the glossary will help to increase knowledge and awareness of many terms used today by college students and educators.

Resource Directory of Higher-Education Organizations That Encourage Character Development

This guidebook also includes a directory of organizations in higher education that research, support, or advance one or more dimensions of character development as an essential aspect of the undergraduate experience. We encourage you to contact these organizations to find out more about their mission and activities.

THE JOHN TEMPLETON FOUNDATION was established in 1987 by international investment manager John Marks Templeton. The Foundation works closely with educators, scientists, theologians, medical professionals, and other scholars throughout the world to support over 100 programs serving three chief purposes: to encourage character development in schools and colleges, to encourage an appreciation for the benefits of freedom, to stimulate serious and scientific research on the relationship between spirituality and health.

The Foundation's College and Character: A National Initiative is an effort to support institutions of higher education in the United States that provide meaningful opportunities for college students to learn about, reflect upon, and practice the virtues of personal and civic responsibility. The Initiative seeks to foster widespread dialogue and activities within the higher education community about the importance of character development. The Foundation also seeks to provide useful information to college-bound students, parents, policy makers, and the general public on how colleges and universities are responding to this challenge. The Initiative currently has five major areas of activity: Grantmaking, Public Education, Building Strategic Relationships, Conferences and Meetings, and Research.

For more information about College and Character: A National Initiative, please contact Arthur J. Schwartz, Ed.D., Director of Character Development Programs at the John Templeton Foundation (610-687-8942), or visit our website at www.collegeandcharacter.org.

The John Templeton Foundation encourages you to contact us with constructive ideas and tangible suggestions to improve future editions of this guidebook. It remains our goal to provide generations of students, parents, and educators with a useful resource that profiles the many different kinds of programs that colleges and universities have established to encourage character development.

PURPOSE

The 405 exemplary programs profiled in the Exemplary Program section of the guidebook are divided into 10 categories: First-Year Programs, Academic Honesty Programs, Faculty and Curriculum Programs, Volunteer Service Programs, Substance-Abuse Prevention Programs, Student Leadership Programs, Spiritual Growth Programs, Civic Education Programs, Character and Sexuality Programs, Senior-Year Programs

Collectively, these 10 categories represent a rich tapestry of best practices on college campuses that encourage character development. Although strategies, approaches, and objectives may differ, these 405 exemplary programs focus on fostering such virtues as honesty, self-control, respect, and compassion.

SELECTION CRITERIA*

✦ A clear vision and statement of purpose

✦ Significant and stable institutional resources

✦ Strong character-development dimension

✦ Active involvement of institutional leaders

✦ Evidence of positive impact

✦ Impact on a significant percentage of students

✦ Integration of program into the core curriculum

✦ A campus-based office or center that provides program information, recruitment, and training

✦ External recognition or honors

✦ Procedures to assess effectiveness

---

* Programs profiled in this guidebook did not have to meet every criterion in order to be strongly considered.

Exemplary first-year programs offer students
the tools to develop a moral compass by which to
navigate between their increased personal freedom
and their new responsibilities. Effective programs
do more than help students adjust to new surroundings
— they provide critical-thinking skills required to
address the character challenges of contemporary
college life. Most significantly, such efforts foster
the development of moral character by encouraging
students to develop a commitment to high standards
of academic and personal behavior.

ALVERNIA COLLEGE

400 ST. BERNARDINE STREET
READING, PA 19607
610.796.8200
http://www.alvernia.edu/

UNDERGRADUATES: 1,300

For program information, please contact:
DONNA J. KLINIKOWSKI
klinido@alvernia.edu

"The main objective of the first year program was responsibility: for oneself, school work, on-campus activities, towards others."

—AN ALVERNIA FIRST-YEAR STUDENT

Alvernia College is a Catholic co-educational college sponsored by the Bernardine Sisters of St. Francis. The first-year College Success Program (CSP) prepares students for a life of charity joined with knowledge. Class work is designed to expand academic proficiencies and provide the basis for character development.

✦ Enabling students to take responsibility for their lives, beginning with academic success and personal achievement, is the first objective. Learning how a college campus functions and reviewing study and testing techniques are critical steps on this path to intellectual competence in addition to competence with physical and manual skills.

✦ Responsibility toward self and learning to manage emotions are emphasized by topics including wellness, stress management, alcohol and drug awareness, and spirituality.

✦ Students extend their responsibility toward others and strive for interpersonal competence through their choices regarding diversity, and other relationship issues. Civic responsibility enters with students' introduction to sources for their community-service requirement.

Full-time faculty, administrators, and student development professionals teach sections of the course and design co-curricular activities to complement classroom topics. CSP encourages students to become professionally competent and socially responsible, while developing moral integrity and spiritual fullness.

ARIZONA STATE UNIVERSITY

TEMPE, AZ 85287
480.965.3097
http://www.asu.edu/

UNDERGRADUATES: 40,000

For program information, please contact:
LESLIE A. CHILTON, Ph.D.
leslie.chilton@asu.edu

Personal responsibility is the primary focus of the course "Academic Success at the University: UNI 100," taught at Arizona State University in Tempe. This theme runs throughout the one-semester course as students are encouraged to take responsibility for their academic career and all aspects of their new life in college.

✦ CAREER PORTFOLIO. In a preview of life after college, UNI 100 students assemble a career portfolio, which includes a study of their values, their first visit to a career fair, and their first resumé.

✦ HEALTH COMPONENT. Students receive counseling in health issues of alcohol, body image, and eating disorders. A powerful aspect of the health unit is a dramatization of date rape, which reveals the complexities and misunderstandings of this crucial campus issue.

✦ CULTURAL AWARENESS. Moving beyond the staple lesson that "stereotyping is bad," the cultural awareness unit encourages students to study their own stereotyping activities and trace the origins. In conclusion, students write a personal paper about a critical cultural experience from their own lives.

UNI 100 tackles the barrage of unexpected issues associated with attending college by helping students learn about utilizing campus resources, knowing their options, getting in contact with their values, and helping them grasp the importance of strategizing time, studies, and career planning. A program designed to make the frequently difficult transition from high school to the university more understandable, UNI 100 can help the student successfully complete the step from one world to the next.

BEAVER COLLEGE

450 SOUTH EASTON ROAD
GLENSIDE, PA 19038-3295
215.572.2900
http://www.beaver.edu/

UNDERGRADUATES: 1,600

For program information, please contact:
JEFF EWING
ewing@beaver.edu

Shaping individuals into strong leaders distinguishes Beaver College. Established in 1895, this coeducational college in suburban Philadelphia begins the process of cultivating leadership through its First Year Programs. Three distinct components of the program work together to help first-year students adjust to college life and achieve their goals:

✦ THE NEW STUDENT ORIENTATION assists students in transitioning to life in a college community. Current students hone their leadership skills by helping new students adjust. The orientation program offers workshops on topics such as diversity, alcohol and drug abuse, and relationships. The community-service component of the orientation program has received an Innovative Program Award from the National Association of Student Personnel Administrators Region II.

✦ THE FRESHMAN SEMINAR PROGRAM builds on the New Student Orientation Program. It helps new students adjust to the academic and social challenges of college life by offering them a variety of informational seminars on diverse and unusual topics. Classes are small and emphasize interactive discussions and collaborative activities. Outside of class, peer mentors meet with students to discuss issues of time management and self-discipline and encourage first-year students to participate in on-campus activities, including those involving community outreach.

✦ THE FIRST YEAR ADVISOR works with new students to develop a strong sense of identity, responsibility for self and others, commitment to personal goals, and self-direction in learning. As he or she works with students, the advisor stresses honesty in academics, communication, and self-reflection.

By engaging students in leadership roles early on, Beaver succeeds in its mission to develop strong leaders who will accept and face future challenges and responsibilities.

BENEDICTINE COLLEGE

1020 N. SECOND ST.
ATCHISON, KS 66002
913.367.5340
http://www.benedictine.edu/

UNDERGRADUATES: 800

For program information, please contact:
TONY GILLET
913.367.2420

Recognizing that students arrive at Benedictine College from diverse cultural and academic backgrounds, the college has developed a first-year program that welcomes them to the community and encourages them to build relationships vital to their success at Benedictine from the first weeks on campus. The program also provides an introduction to the type of Benedictine, residential, liberal arts environment students enjoy.

✦ RAVEN ORIENTATION KAMP. Attended by all new students, this week-long program reinforces the value and dignity of the individual within a community. From their first days on campus, it is imperative that students know they are a part of something larger than themselves and that they are responsible for themselves and for each other. Focusing on character development and the value of college, ROK includes skits performed by upper-class student leaders addressing topics such as alcohol and drug use, date rape, roommate issues, academic honesty, and parent-student relationships.

✦ B.C. COLLOQUIUM. This required, one-credit-hour course, taken during the first semester of enrollment, includes readings, lectures, classroom discussions, and experiential activities. Group projects consist of six to eight students with one or two faculty/staff facilitators. Students also tour the two sponsoring religious communities and learn about the Benedictine heritage and commitment to hospitality, work, and prayer. For international students, a cross-cultural orientation integrates the topics of culture shock, customs, the academic culture, classroom conventions, and interpersonal relationships. For all students, the course explores important topics such as understanding of self, responsibility to others, communication and conflict, commitment, and service.

Both components of the Benedictine College first-year program strive to enable students to better understand and practice the virtues of personal and civic responsibility.

BLUFFTON COLLEGE

280 WEST COLLEGE AVENUE
BLUFFTON, OH 45817
419.358.3000
http://www.bluffton.edu/

UNDERGRADUATES: 1,000

For program information, please contact:
JOHN KAMPEN, Ph.D.
kampenj@bluffton.edu

"The Freshman Seminar helped me to learn more about myself and my identity. Had I not taken this course I would not be who I am today."

—A BLUFFTON FOURTH-YEAR STUDENT

Bluffton College, a liberal arts college, has sought to "prepare students of all backgrounds for life as well as vocation, for responsible citizenship, and for service to all peoples." Inaugurated in 1995, the First-Year Seminar goes beyond conventional college skills and challenges first-year students to wrestle with the questions of how we come to be who we are.

As the foundation course in Bluffton's general education curriculum, the seminar begins a progression through a values-oriented curriculum. The First-Year Seminar begins with readings during the summer prior to the fall semester; proceeds through orientation and the opening convocation; and continues on to form the basis of the curricular agenda for students. During the fall semester, First-Year Seminar themes are integrated into Bluffton's weekly forum series, inviting the campus community into a conversation of identity and life's purpose. The following activities characterize the First-Year Seminar:

✦ Organized and led by full-time faculty members, sections of 20 students reflect on issues of family, faith, race, gender, and class by reading literature, writing essays, and viewing films.

✦ Students keep journals for each session to nurture reflection, analysis, and creative response.

✦ A custom-made book of readings reflects the values orientation of the college and the general education program.

✦ Weekly meetings of all faculty members teaching the course encourage attention to values.

✦ Identity exploration lays the foundation for a self-conscious service orientation that is developed in later courses.

Shaped by the peace church tradition and a desire for academic excellence, Bluffton College integrates the values and the faith of the college into all facets of the curriculum.

BRIDGEWATER COLLEGE

BRIDGEWATER, VA 22812
540.828.8000
http://www.bridgewater.edu/

UNDERGRADUATES: 1,200

For program information, please contact:
W. STEVE WATSON, Ph.D.
swatson@bridgewater.edu

"Personal development with an ethical emphasis is what the college believes education should be all about."

—A BRIDGEWATER ALUMNUS

Developing whole individuals is the sole purpose of the Personal Development Portfolio (PDP) program at Bridgewater College, a liberal arts college in the Shenandoah Valley of Virginia. PDP has been the most direct implementation of Bridgewater's mission to graduate individuals who are equipped to become leaders and live ethical, healthy, useful, and fulfilling lives with a strong sense of personal accountability and civic responsibility. PDP 150, the first-year program, requires students to set personal goals in each of eight personal dimensions: academics, citizenship, cultural awareness, esthetics, ethical development, leadership, social relationships, and wellness. PDP 150 integrates the entire educational experience by fully incorporating convocation programs, lyceum (art) programs, leadership workshops, service-learning requirements, career counseling, and wellness seminars into the curriculum.

PDP 150's emphasis on character development is evident in the following:

✦ Beginning in the first year, students are required to participate in community-service projects.

✦ Ethical development, cultural awareness, and citizenship are explicitly emphasized in the curriculum and in senior evaluations.

✦ Leadership seminars are integrated into the portfolio program to promote servant leadership.

✦ Faculty advisors serve as models for character development.

Bridgewater has emphasized its support of the PDP program and especially PDP 150 in all its activities. Ethical living, personal accountability, civic responsibility, and high standards of integrity become more than rhetoric when implemented in personal student plans; their standards are required and modeled by faculty and expected of students for graduation.

Brooklyn College

2900 BEDFORD AVENUE
BROOKLYN, NY 11210
718.951.5771
http://www.brooklyn.cuny.edu/

UNDERGRADUATES: 11,500

For program information, please contact:
KATHLEEN A. GOVER
kgover@brooklyn.cuny.edu

 In 1995, Brooklyn College of the City University of New York (CUNY), a four-year, nonresidential institution, inaugurated the Freshman Year College. The Freshman Year College emphasizes student services by offering block programming, accelerated summer programs, tutorial assistance, service learning, orientation to academic integrity, mandatory counseling at registration, interdisciplinary collaboration, and outreach in high school and the community. Some highlights are:

✦ **13-course Core Curriculum.** These mandated courses, including fields such as classics, philosophy, history, and the arts, as well as five courses in science and mathematics, emphasize critical thinking and provide a common intellectual foundation for advanced study.

✦ **Block Programming.** This component ensures that groups of first-year students share at least three classes, promotes integration into academic life, structures student time, and advocates participation in the independent study groups. It also provides tutorial assistance to ease the transition into college study.

✦ **Transformations.** A new concept in faculty development, this component includes a faculty seminar that serves as the think tank for the program, university-wide conferences with national authorities, explorations of new technologies, and interdisciplinary collaboration between faculty. Transformations won the 1998 Hesburgh Award.

✦ **Freshman Orientation.** Led by student volunteers recruited among campus leaders, these small groups stress the importance of academic integrity and mutual respect in relations between the sexes and between diverse ethnic and cultural groups.

Surveys show 73% student satisfaction with the program; 84% of faculty express willingness to continue teaching in it.

California State University–Fresno

5241 NORTH MAPLE AVENUE
FRESNO, CA 93740
559.278.2324
http://www.csufresno.edu/

UNDERGRADUATES: 14,800

For program information, please contact:
PATRICIA B. HART, Ed.D.
patricia_hart@csufresno.edu

"The University 1 class provides an insightful combination of school and people skills that are needed to succeed in a four-year university."
—A CALIFORNIA STATE–FRESNO SECOND-YEAR STUDENT

The development of personal and community responsibility, mutual respect, and shared values are hallmarks of California State University–Fresno, a comprehensive, four-year public institution. University 1, a three-unit First-Year Experience course, fosters a successful transition into the academic community as well as the larger community. Integrating student development and academic rigor, this course leads students to a holistic understanding of the value of an education and its role in creating a healthy society.

Content areas include academic study skills, career planning, library resources, information competence, diversity, time and financial management, health and wellness, ethics and responsibility, critical thinking, and lifelong learning. Students reflect on the concept and patterns of change, as well as the implications of change for the future. Students also recognize how change and patterns of change are influenced by a variety of factors: personal, family, cultural, environmental, historical, and social.

The Cultural History Research Project, which incorporates team building, problem solving, diversity, and writing, provides the experience of working in groups to facilitate exploration of diverse cultural heritages. The project emphasizes the roles, responsibilities, and respect for others that are required to achieve a common goal.

University 1 encourages students to take responsibility for their educational development, for contributing to the development of others, and for honoring values and commitments in their private and public behavior. Faculty, staff, and students exchange ideas on what it means to be a responsible member of the academic and social communities.

CALIFORNIA STATE UNIVERSITY–NORTHRIDGE

18111 NORDHOFF STREET
NORTHRIDGE, CA 91330-8267
818.677.2099
http://www.csun.edu/

UNDERGRADUATES: 21,800

For program information, please contact:
MERRI C. PEARSON
Merri.c.pearson@csun.edu

For students who are deaf or hard of hearing, the National Center on Deafness (NCOD) on the campus of California State University–Northridge (CSUN) is a bridge of independence—both to the university and the world beyond. Founded in 1972, NCOD is considered to be the largest mainstreamed program in the U.S. and is internationally recognized for its excellence and pioneering programs, which empower students to achieve social and academic success. This process begins with NCOD's eight-day Fall Orientation program, which introduces new students to the numerous services provided by NCOD and CSUN.

Aspects of orientation that help students build character include:

✦ Establishing contact with support personnel

✦ Learning how NCOD services network with CSUN's services

✦ Building lifelong friendships

✦ Teaching cooperation and understanding diversity

✦ Providing positive role models in deaf and hard-of-hearing group leaders and coordinators

✦ Dealing with the challenges and responsibilities of living independently

✦ Developing leadership skills

Beyond Fall Orientation, NCOD provides students with counselors who are dedicated to helping them participate in extracurricular activities and develop leadership skills. Skill building is achieved through retreats planned and facilitated by staff and students to promote growth through experiential exercises.

Easing the transition for deaf and hard-of-hearing first-year students is the primary mission of NCOD.

CASTLETON STATE COLLEGE

CASTLETON, VT 05735
802.468.5611
http://www.castleton.edu/

UNDERGRADUATES: 1,500

For program information, please contact:
THOMAS S. EDWARDS, Ph.D.
edwardst@sparrow.csv.vsc.edu

"Connecting you with the faculty, students, and all of the resources available, the First-Year Seminar treats you as a complete person. What a great way to begin your college career."

—A CASTLETON FIRST-YEAR STUDENT

For students at Castleton State College, a small, residential, liberal arts college, easing the transition to the academic community is the focus of an innovative First-Year Seminar (FYS) program. Through their efforts, faculty and staff introduce students to "the life and values of the college," providing each individual with opportunity to grow academically, socially, and personally.

Each new student is enrolled in a First-Year Seminar, a specially designated section of a traditional academic course limited to eighteen students. In the context of teaching in disciplines ranging from sociology and psychology to calculus and history, First-Year faculty emphasize the acquisition of effective academic skills. But academic life extends beyond the classroom, as does the First-Year Seminar program. Program highlights include:

✦ Close advising relationships with faculty, staff, and students from across the campus who serve as mentors beginning with summer registration and extending throughout the first year;

✦ Summer reading and writing assignments, as well as opportunities for community service during orientation;

✦ Weekly "Common Hours" presentations by college staff that range from workshops on e-mail or time management techniques to presentations on cultivating healthy relationships;

✦ Cohort classes enrolling the same groups of students offer peer support and study groups;

✦ *Castleton Connects,* a newsletter providing information for the families of new students.

A college is a living community, and Castleton's First-Year Seminar program provides a model for how students, faculty and staff can come together to practice inquiry, exploration, and character development.

CENTRAL METHODIST COLLEGE

411 CENTRAL METHODIST SQUARE
FAYETTE, MO 65248
660.248.3391
http://www.cmc.edu/

UNDERGRADUATES: 1,200

For more information, please contact:
JOHN J. CARTER, Ph.D.
jcarter@cmc.edu

The choices and challenges of civic and personal responsibility are the primary focus of the First-Year Program at Central Methodist College (CMC). The program's curricular component, CMC 109, engages students in a semester-long examination of the problems and choices associated with becoming a person of character in our society. Supported by a dedicated first-year academic advising and monitoring program, First-Year Seminars:

✦ work from a common syllabus emphasizing critical-thinking skills, character development, and issues of civic and personal responsibility;

✦ group students with similar academic interests or majors together;

✦ provide senior student mentors drawn from the college's capstone course, HU 409, to augment the faculty seminar leaders;

✦ feature an opening lecture by the college's president in which she defines the institution's mission as a character-building college. This sets the tone for a series of small-group breakfast sessions between the president and each seminar section in which the themes of character building and issues of community values and practices are woven together in an open discussion format.

The First-Year Program enhances opportunities for success through an integration of curriculum and support services. The program optimizes retention and academic success among first-year students while engaging them in a critical exploration of the problems and choices associated with becoming persons of character. The First-Year Program reflects Central's commitment to the ideal that the centerpiece of a liberal arts education should be a critical examination of the values of civic and personal responsibility that define our communities and our relationships with others.

CLAFLIN COLLEGE

700 COLLEGE AVENUE, NE
ORANGEBURG, SC 29115
803.535.5349
http://www.claflin.edu/

UNDERGRADUATES: 900

For program information, please contact:
SHARON FRINKS
sfrinks@clafl.claflin.edu

Development of the whole student at Claflin College, a church-affiliated institution, begins early, with a program called "Freshman College," a mixture of mandatory courses, assembly and lyceum events, and dynamic mentoring sessions. The program is designed to serve the college's overarching mission of developing leaders of strong moral fiber through a curriculum that is academically rigorous and emphasizes social and cultural development as well as personal and civic responsibility. Professor and program director Sharon Frinks speaks of Freshman College with great pride. "It is gratifying to see young people blossom into responsible individuals with strong moral and civic values and to realize that the program had something to do with this." The program develops character in young people by implementing several initiatives:

✦ EDUCATION 101—THE FRESHMAN YEAR EXPERIENCE. This mandatory orientation course underlines the need for civic and personal involvement while requiring every student to complete a community-service project.

✦ SPIRITUAL VALUES AND IDEALS. A Christian-living approach is emphasized through mandatory attendance at Assembly and Cultural Enrichment (ACE) events and programs, Religious Emphasis Week, and the Granville Hicks Lecture and Staley Distinguished Christian Scholar series.

✦ STUDENT OUTREACH FOR ACADEMIC RETENTION (SOAR) CENTER. SOAR takes a proactive role in the overall development of the student, nurturing and mentoring students to blossom as leaders.

Claflin's Freshman College has been featured in the media and has received endorsements from organizations such as the Knight-Ridder Foundation. Evaluations of the program have been positive, and it is clear that Claflin is helping young people develop into exemplary lifelong leaders and citizens of high moral character.

THE COLLEGE OF NEW JERSEY

PO BOX 7718
EWING, NJ 08628-0718
609.771.2202
http://www.tcnj.edu/

UNDERGRADUATES: 5,900

For program information, please contact:
NINO SCARPATI
scarpati@tcnj.edus

Ideals of service, excellence, diversity, and community define the mission of The College of New Jersey, a public, liberal arts institution. TCNJ's FYE program (First-Year Experience) provides a strong foundation for undergraduate education by challenging students to translate these ideals into action. Students directly examine their responsibilities to self and others through an academic and student life program that includes:

✦ "ATHENS TO NEW YORK." An interdisciplinary core requirement, taught by full-time faculty in residence-hall classrooms, addresses four basic questions: what it means to be human; what it means to be a member of a community; what it means to be moral, ethical, or just; and how individuals and communities respond to differences.

✦ SERVICE LEARNING. The service-learning component of FYE provides a compelling context for new students to confront complex social problems and act as responsible members of a community. They are challenged to understand community service in the context of social justice. Students taking the "Athens to New York" course must complete a minimum of ten hours of service learning.

✦ RESIDENCE LIFE. FYE students learn and practice the rights and responsibilities of community living by completing *Community Living Agreements*. Civic responsibility is further developed through "Leadership Legacy," a yearlong, leadership training program.

The FYE program has been presented at numerous national and international higher education conferences and is recognized as an exemplary student-development program by national organizations in higher education.

COLLEGE OF THE HOLY CROSS

COLLEGE STREET
WORCESTER, MA 01610
508.793.2011
http://www.holycross.edu/

UNDERGRADUATES: 2,700

For program information, please contact:
DAVID DAMIANO, Ph.D.
ddamiano@holycross.edu

College of the Holy Cross, a private, Jesuit, liberal arts institution, has developed a First-Year Program (FYP) designed to break down the barriers between classroom learning and residential life. Students who enroll for the Holy Cross FYP live in the same residence hall and together explore ways of developing character, leadership skills, and a supportive living environment. The array of yearlong FYP seminars, capped at 15 students per course, are taught by 8 to 10 faculty members, representing a wide range of academic areas. There are several distinct character-building aspects to the Holy Cross FYP:

✦ RESIDENTIAL LIFE. Students periodically hold "Town Meetings" when pressing issues arise. Faculty are invited to such meetings and participate in students' discussions of residential self-governance. Students are encouraged to host friends to demonstrate an alternative model of residential campus life.

✦ FYP CURRICULAR THEMES. The core theme of the FYP is "How then shall we live?" At the outset of each FYP, the participating faculty members meet to particularize that year's theme. Faculty subsequently craft new FYP courses, drawing on their own academic disciplines while addressing the new FYP theme and overall philosophy.

✦ CO-CURRICULAR ACTIVITY. Students and faculty design co-curricular events, lectures, and field trips. Some of the events are open to the Holy Cross community or to the surrounding community.

FYP students have consistently gone on to become campus leaders, and an extensive assessment by the sociology department at Holy Cross suggests that the program far exceeds its goals. Students who participated in the program are top-notch leaders with decision-making skills that help create a better life on campus and beyond the college gates.

COLLEGE OF THE OZARKS

POINT LOOKOUT, MO 65726
417.334.6411
http://www.cofo.edu/
UNDERGRADUATES: 1,500

For program information, please contact:
LARRY COCKRUM, Ph.D.
cockrum@cofo.edu

"Organizing new students into 'families' during orientation makes the transition from home to college much easier. I still call the students in my 'family' brothers and sisters."

—A COLLEGE OF THE OZARKS THIRD-YEAR STUDENT

College of the Ozarks believes that character in young people is best developed from an education that involves the mind, heart, and hands. C of O, a four-year, coeducational, liberal arts institution, has been called "Hard Work U" by the *Wall Street Journal* to describe the college's longstanding practice of providing a rigorous academic environment; requiring students to work on campus in lieu of paying tuition; and discouraging debt. The College provides a Christian education to young men and women, especially those who have limited financial resources. Character Camp, a two-week orientation, is designed for new students to begin the process of acquiring the values of maturity and responsibility through service to others. Character Camp requires new students to work in groups on service projects both on and off campus. Some specific aspects of Character Camp include:

✦ Using character case studies to learn about character and ethics;

✦ Completing an Outward Bound–type course in which faculty and staff advisors emphasize trust and responsibility;

✦ Attending an Etiquette Banquet where faculty members teach the importance of high personal and social standards;

✦ Signing an Honor Code card.

As a small institution, C of O expects students to realize their potential so that they may move beyond their initial constraints to become concerned citizens and leaders, lifelong learners, and men and women of responsibility.

THE DEFIANCE COLLEGE

701 NORTH CLINTON AVENUE
DEFIANCE, OH 43512
800.520.4632
http://www.defiance.edu/
UNDERGRADUATES: 800

For program information, please contact:
BRUCE BUSBY, Ph.D.
bbusby@defiance.edu

Defiance College, a private, liberal arts college, prides itself on the integration of learning and serving. The First-Year Program helps new students become citizens of the Defiance community by extending the influence of the teaching faculty beyond the walls of the traditional classroom. Recognizing the special nature and power of the faculty-student relationship, this program coordinates the energies and resources of the faculty in key first-year courses in order to support new students in their pursuit of the college's learning objectives. The First-Year Program includes three central components:

✦ **FRESHMAN SEMINAR: BUILDING COMMUNITY.** Freshman Seminar is an open forum for discussion of issues related to the student's entrance into the college community and development of a sense of belonging and group responsibility.

✦ **SURVEY OF WESTERN CIVILIZATION: EXPLORING OUR HERITAGE.** The Western Civilization Survey provides an interdisciplinary study of the values and historical issues that link us to our shared past. These two courses encourage the students to perceive themselves as unique individuals who are nevertheless participants in the shared human experience.

✦ **FACULTY IN RESIDENCE: INTEGRATING THE ACADEMIC LIFE WITH STUDENT LIFE.** The Faculty in Residence Program brings teaching faculty into the residence halls and the student center. Faculty provide information sessions on alcohol abuse, lead study sessions, and provide academic counseling one on one in the residence halls. The program also funds faculty who wish to meet with students for meals in the school cafeteria.

Together these components help students understand the college as a community of learning, their new responsibilities as citizens within this community, and the importance of their contributions to their new community.

EASTERN COLLEGE

1300 EAGLE ROAD
ST. DAVIDS, PA 19087
610.341.5803
http://www.eastern.edu/

UNDERGRADUATES: 1,200

For program information, please contact:
LAURIE SCHREINER, Ph.D.
lschrein@eastern.edu

Eastern College is a private Christian college that teaches that personal and civic responsibility is one's natural response to a just and loving God. Within this context, Eastern's required first-year program uses a model focused on building relationships and community and expands it through components in service learning, integrated advising, and wellness programs. This intentional focus on students' holistic development results in a more significant and meaningful college experience.

Five key aspects of "Living and Learning in Community" promote personal and civic responsibility:

✦ The service-learning component enables students to connect with others, with themselves, and with issues and values larger than themselves.

✦ An overarching theme of the program is stewardship—of one's time, material goods, body, and mental resources.

✦ Students read and discuss Viktor Frankl's account of life in a Nazi concentration camp. In the process, they grapple with issues of justice, suffering, freedom, and individual worth, leading to a critical reflection of their own key values.

✦ Strong emphasis on issues of justice helps students understand the broader global context.

✦ Students write personal success plans based on their strengths and challenges, thereby increasing self-awareness and a sense of personal responsibility.

The director of this program, Dr. Laurie Schreiner, is an expert on factors that influence student success in college. As a result of her work, Eastern's first-year program has received a "dissemination of proven reforms" grant from the U.S. Department of Education. Through this grant, "Living and Learning in Community" has become a model for other colleges throughout the U.S.

EASTERN MENNONITE UNIVERSITY

1200 PARK ROAD
HARRISONBURG, VA 22802
540.432.4000
http://www.emu.edu/

UNDERGRADUATES: 1,000

For program information, please contact:
PATRICIA S. HELTON
heltonp@emu.edu

Students at Eastern Mennonite University, a private, liberal arts institution under the guidance of the Mennonite Church, are challenged to answer Christ's call to a life of nonviolence, witness, service, and peace building. A requisite First Year Experience (FYE) course reinforces and gives life to the challenge through these components:

✦ DISCUSSION GROUPS. The FYE groups of 10 to 12 students provide a built-in group of familiar faces and encourage a feeling of belonging.

✦ FACULTY, ADMINISTRATOR, AND STAFF PERSONNEL. These EMU professionals serve as leaders of the small groups. This allows the student to have at least one person who becomes a personal advocate for the confusing adjustment period and who is a good role model for the character traits promoted by the institution. Some faculty and students develop ongoing mentor/mentee relationships.

✦ GROUP SERVICE PROJECT. Many students discover an area of interest while completing the three required hours of service and continue participation on an individual basis. Others use the service area as a springboard for ongoing academic study.

✦ PROFESSIONAL EXPERTS. Diversity/mediation, sexuality issues, and career counseling are addressed by visiting experts who meet with each group for training and exploration. These leaders nurture personal growth such as acceptance of diverse racial/cultural backgrounds, acquisition of a positive self-image in relationships, and determination of a career direction based on skills and interests.

Assessment by students and group leaders is obtained at the close of the course. This information has been consistently helpful in improving and strengthening the course during the eight years of its existence. The overall vision remains to make FYE a bridge between high school and college and to accelerate the maturation of students so that they become valuable global citizens.

GORDON COLLEGE

255 GRAPEVINE ROAD
WENHAM, MA 01984
978.927.2300
http://www.gordon.edu/
UNDERGRADUATES: 1,500

For program information, please contact:
DAVID AIKEN, Ph.D.
daiken@faith.gordon.edu

 Gordon College, a four-year, non-denominational Christian, liberal arts institution, strives to graduate men and women of intellectual maturity and Christian character who are committed to the concept of servanthood and prepared for leadership roles in diverse contexts worldwide. The First-Year Seminar, held in small groups, helps students make the transition from secondary to undergraduate education. The central focus of this two-semester, four-credit course is forming character through understanding and appreciating diverse worldviews.

In weekly meetings, students reflect on a wide range of readings and write response papers in which they creatively and critically analyze issues. Some readings stress both tolerance and diversity, such as Chaim Potok's novel *The Chosen*. Others, such as Alan Paton's novel *Cry, The Beloved Country* and Martin Luther King Jr.'s *Letter from a Birmingham Jail*, expound on and illustrate how to maintain integrity in the face of social injustice and personal temptation. Other aspects of the seminar that stress character development include:

✦ CHURCH TRADITIONS. This project requires students to become familiar with specific Christian beliefs and practices with which they were previously unfamiliar.

✦ SPIRITUAL AUTOBIOGRAPHY. This student composition, written in several drafts, is one example of assignments that assist students in assessing their spiritual and moral development and in setting goals for further growth.

✦ CLASS DISCUSSIONS. All participants are expected to take a leadership role by preparing responses to specific questions on the readings for the day.

Gordon is committed to high standards of education within a faith-based framework. The FYS has developed into an increasingly rigorous and effective program that assists students, during a vulnerable year of transition, in forming a mature, dynamic, and responsive worldview while attaining a strong sense of stewardship as Christians.

GREENSBORO COLLEGE

815 WEST MARKET STREET
GREENSBORO, NC 27401
336.272.7102
http://www.gborocollege.edu/
UNDERGRADUATES: 1,000

For program information, please contact:
TIFFANY MCKILLIP FRANKS
frankst@gborocollege.edu

"The First Year Programs offered me many opportunities to expand my leadership roles on campus, discover what college has to offer, make new friends, and come into my own."

—A GREENSBORO FIRST-YEAR STUDENT

At Greensboro College, a private, liberal arts, United Methodist–related institution, personal responsibility and a commitment to integrity and character are cornerstones to the educational experience. First-year program activities include:

✦ NEW STUDENT ORIENTATION. In all orientation programs, Greensboro emphasizes the importance of personal responsibility and accountability. "On Your Honor," for example, is a special session in which students officially join the Greensboro community by pledging to uphold certain standards of good conduct and character.

✦ PRECIS. All first-year students participate in this relationship-building experience, which is held in the North Carolina mountains prior to the start of the semester. The objective is to provide a supportive foundation on which students can build as they encounter challenges during their first year. Sessions focus on the importance of responsible decision making and the relationship between choices and consequences.

✦ FIRST-YEAR SEMINAR. During the seminar students are introduced to the value and importance of volunteerism and service. Key character-building topics are addressed, including dealing effectively with conflict; developing a multicultural understanding and sensitivity; setting goals that build on values, interests, and responsibility as students.

✦ CO-CURRICULAR ADVISING AND PORTFOLIO PROGRAM. This program assists new students in developing a plan for involvement in community service and other college activities.

The First-year programs and support systems work together to ensure that students develop a positive character that will help them be successful students and responsible citizens.

HIGH POINT UNIVERSITY

833 MONTLIEU AVENUE
HIGH POINT, NC 27262
336.841.9000
http://www.highpoint.edu/

UNDERGRADUATES: 2,900

For program information, please contact:
MORRIS G. WRAY, Ph.D.
mwray@highpoint.edu

"I participated in the academic enrichment program and the week-long orientation program. Both experiences increased my determination to succeed in the classroom and to leave High Point University better than I found it."

In order to encourage character formation and academic success among entering students, High Point University has designed two separate but complementary first-year programs, each of which is intended to meet the personal needs of entering students and encourage moral development. Collectively, these programs have received several national recognitions, including the 1997 National Student Retention Award. Program directors for both the academic enrichment program and the first-year orientation program have been recognized as Outstanding Freshman Advocates by the Houghton Mifflin Company.

✦ **THE ACADEMIC ENRICHMENT PROGRAM.** Approximately 50% of the entering first-year students are required to complete a mandatory academic enrichment program during the summer or during their first regular semester, and some are required to attend the summer session in order to validate their admission to the university. Others are required to complete the academic enrichment program based on their academic performance during the fall semester. Graduation rates for cohorts of students who have been required to attend the summer session have historically raised graduation rates for their class as a whole.

✦ **THE FRESHMAN ORIENTATION PROGRAM.** During four mandatory general sessions, entering students consider the idea that the university is "a purposeful (academic), open, just, disciplined, caring, celebratory community" (Ernest L. Boyer). Following the introductory lectures, students break into 24 orientation groups to discuss these concepts under the leadership of teams of faculty and student mentors. At the matriculation ceremony during the last general session, students receive three documents, suitable for framing, that summarize the goals of orientation and that encourage good citizenship on campus and beyond.

HOPE COLLEGE

HOLLAND, MI 49423
616.395.7000
http://www.hope.edu/

UNDERGRADUATES: 2,900

For program information, please contact:
MAURA M. REYNOLDS
MReynolds@Hope.edu

The First-Year Seminars (FYS) offered at Hope College, a private, liberal arts institution, provide an intellectual transition for new college students. Taking an active role in at least one FYS course during their first semester at Hope is a requirement of all students. These seminars emphasize different ways of knowing, seeing, and evaluating rather than specific content or knowledge. They are discussion-driven and focus on exploring questions for which there is no single, clear answer. As one student reported in an end-of-the-semester evaluation, "We learned to discuss instead of argue." Additional goals of the seminars include:

✦ Enhancing listening and speaking skills;

✦ Developing the ability to work and interact with others productively;

✦ Encouraging students to learn from each other as they work together to explore a topic;

✦ Asking students to articulate their own perspectives and to consider perspectives different from their own.

The significant institutional resources provided to the FYS exemplifies Hope's commitment to first-year students. All of the instructors are full-time faculty members who also serve as academic advisors to the students. The FYS faculty are funded to attend summer workshops and receive course development stipends. The FYS faculty also receive four teaching credits for this two-credit course, allowing FYS to be one-third of their teaching load in the fall semester.

Initiative taking and independent action, humility and intellectual courage, moral and spiritual discernment are habits and virtues valued at Hope College; First-Year Seminars aim to socialize students in the importance and practice of these values from the beginning of their time on campus.

JAMES MADISON UNIVERSITY

800 SOUTH MAIN STREET
HARRISONBURG, VA 22807
540.568.3788
http://www.jmu.edu/
UNDERGRADUATES: 13,500

For program information, please contact:
LEE WARD
wardwl@jmu.edu

"I want to be at the point where I have complete confidence in myself and not be afraid to try to learn and grow. The first-year programs at JMU helped me do that."

—A JMU SECOND-YEAR STUDENT

James Madison University, a public institution founded in 1908, recently reconfigured its first-year programs to reflect a stronger commitment to student learning and success. Under the coordination of the Center for Leadership, Service, and Transitions, cornerstone programs include:

✦ SUMMER ORIENTATIONS. In July, a day-long program enables students to meet with peer mentors, a freshman advisor, and a faculty member within their major to connect with people and offices that help them throughout the year. A four-day program in August with 125 upperclass students and faculty advisors prepares students for the challenges of balancing freedom with increased responsibilities.

✦ FRESHMAN READING PROGRAM. First-year students read an assigned book over the summer and participate in small group discussions in the fall.

✦ CONVOCATION. This student-designed event focuses on high standards of academic achievement, personal growth, and involvement in the life of the campus and community. It eschews the traditional faculty processional in favor of student-to-student interaction and an invitation from peers to walk across a symbolic transitional bridge.

✦ FIRST-YEAR INVOLVEMENT CENTER. Run by the Office of Residence Life, this program offers intentional learning experiences in the residence halls and provides information about academic support, leadership opportunities, mentoring programs, roommate concerns, home visits, and other issues.

At the heart of JMU's programs is an effort to motivate students to engage in purposeful activities, both in and out of class. By quickly helping students learn how to learn, JMU invites all first-year students to pursue their goals within the supportive and nurturing community that is the hallmark of the institution.

KALAMAZOO COLLEGE

1200 ACADEMY STREET
KALAMAZOO, MI 49006
616.337.7000
http://www.kzoo.edu/
UNDERGRADUATES: 1,300

For program information, please contact:
ZAIDE PIXLEY, Ph.D.
pixley@kzoo.edu

 The intentional weaving together of hands-on involvement, experiential learning, and mentorship within the context of a rigorous academic life is the hallmark of the First-Year Experience at Kalamazoo College. Dr. Zaide Pixley, director of the program, writes, "The First-Year program at Kalamazoo is a team effort, involving faculty and other staff. Almost everyone on our campus helps first-year students get connected and make the best possible start." Activities include:

✦ WEEK-LONG ORIENTATION PROGRAM focuses on intercultural understanding, social responsibility and leadership. Students, faculty, and staff meet together in small groups to discuss the values and honor system of the college. Students engage in volunteer activities and hands-on projects.

✦ FIRST-YEAR SEMINARS emphasize critical thinking and writing and are taught in disciplines across the curriculum. All seminars include projects that foster intercultural understanding, encourage collaboration, and deepen a collective awareness of the college's honor system.

✦ FIRST-YEAR FORUMS teach the history and traditions of Kalamazoo, focus on personal and civic responsibility, highlight volunteer opportunities, and address issues of intercultural understanding,

✦ PORTFOLIOS help students reflect on the meaning of their experiences and link their growth as students to a variety of learning experiences.

The adjustment from home and high school to college and campus life can be challenging. The FYE program at Kalamazoo helps students make this adjustment more gracefully, take active roles in their education, explore new experiences, address issues of community and responsibility, and thus develop true maturity.

LEE UNIVERSITY

1120 NORTH OCOEE STREET
CLEVELAND, TN 37311
423.614.8500
http://www.leeuniversity.edu/

UNDERGRADUATES: 2,800

For program information, please contact:
SUZANNE HAMID
Shamid@leeuniversity.edu

Lee University seeks to develop in students the knowledge, appreciation, and understanding that will prepare them to become responsible adults. Toward this end, the Office of First-Year Programs plans and executes a comprehensive program designed to help new students adjust to university life. "Gateway to University Success" conveys the central objectives and purposes of the First-Year Experience. Facilitated by a team of faculty, administrators, and peer leaders, the Gateway Program introduces new students to essential academic skills, the application of critical-thinking skills, and a personal Christian worldview to life decisions. Activities within the program focus on three distinct areas: prematriculation, new student orientation, and extended orientation.

The centerpiece of the Gateway Program is a two-hour, credit course (GST 101, Gateway to University Success) in which the following topics are discussed:

+ Applying thinking skills in life-related areas such as time management, career planning, and money management;

+ Humanism, nihilism, and theism;

+ Awareness of the social aspects of campus life;

+ Managing relationships with faculty, peers, and roommates;

+ Christian stewardship and sexuality.

The Office of First-Year Programs incorporates its mission to integrate faith with the demands and responsibilities of citizens.

MARIST COLLEGE

290 NORTH ROAD
POUGHKEEPSIE, NY 12601
914.575.3000
http://www.marist.edu/

UNDERGRADUATES: 4,100

For program information, please contact:
EDWARD J. O'KEEFE, Ph.D.
jzc9@maristb.marist.edu

"The self-management program enabled me to motivate myself toward achieving my goals."

—A MARIST THIRD-YEAR STUDENT

Personal and civic responsibilities are integral to education at Marist College, a private, liberal arts institution. The Self-management Program teaches students to examine how their own feelings, behaviors, and thoughts are central to personal development and achievement in all aspects of life.

Edward O'Keefe and Donna Berger, Marist educators and authors of *Self-management for College Students: The ABC Approach,* initiated the program with the college's Academic Learning Center in 1989. Their ABC philosophy places responsibility for personal and societal change on the individual. The program emphasizes that we create the societal conditions of which we are a part and that one's own affect (A), behaviors (B), and cognitions (C) are the common denominator through which all areas of personal development and change are understood and managed.

Through a common ABC core, students learn to identify and change ABCs in order to improve motivation, time management, self-esteem, communication skills, and interpersonal relationships. Students also learn to identify and change habits that may lead to interpersonal conflict and prejudice. Classroom activities requiring students to practice or model self-management skills include: conducting an interview with a professor and delivering a class presentation, which is videotaped and critiqued; completing values-clarification and related goal-setting exercises; developing and following time schedules reflective of personal values and goals; and role playing problem-solving strategies using self-management principles.

This nationally recognized program has been featured in local and national publications and on local television. Program developers have presented at numerous local, national, and international conferences such as the Freshman-Year Experience, The Society of Teaching and Learning, and the Professional and Organizational Development Network in Higher Education.

Maryville College

502 E. LAMAR ALEXANDER PARKWAY
MARYVILLE, TN 37804
423.981.8000
http://www.maryvillecollege.edu/

UNDERGRADUATES: 950

For program information, please contact:
PEGGY COWAN, Ph.D.
cowan@maryvillecollege.edu

"The Freshman Program helped me realize that I had more responsibility for myself, my environment, and my community."

—A MARYVILLE COLLEGE SECOND-YEAR STUDENT

Environmental, individual, and civic responsibility are fundamental themes for the Freshman Program at Maryville College, a private, liberal arts college affiliated with the Presbyterian Church (USA). By engaging students in application of academic skills to concrete life situations, the program challenges students to take responsibility for their environment, their society, and themselves. Activities include:

✦ MOUNTAIN CHALLENGE. This team-building event encourages group problem solving, leadership skills, creative thinking, and taking responsibility for others by confronting students with obstacles that they must negotiate as a group.

✦ PERSPECTIVES ON THE INDIVIDUAL. In this fall seminar, students explore their identity; reflect on vocation; make connections among physical, vocational, psychological, and spiritual well-being; and connect lifestyles and ethical decision making to fundamental beliefs.

✦ PERSPECTIVES ON THE ENVIRONMENT. This January seminar helps students examine the impact on the Southern Appalachian environment of the Cherokee, European settlers, and contemporary society and then develop their own environmental ethic.

✦ PERSPECTIVES ON THE AMERICAN COMMUNITY. In this spring seminar, students explore American institutions that enable diverse groups to live together within the U.S., recognize the tension between protecting individual rights and promoting the common good, and wrestle with the interplay of personal and civic responsibility.

The Freshman Program allows students to apply what they have learned in the classroom. These classes introduce themes that are revisited in later core courses and lays the foundation for a liberal arts education that supports Maryville College students in developing informed ethical judgment, a commitment to service and global citizenship, and a sense of responsibility for the common good.

Maryville University of St. Louis

13550 CONWAY ROAD
ST. LOUIS, MO 63141-7299
314.529.9299
http://www.maryville.edu/

UNDERGRADUATES: 3,000

For program information, please contact:
BEBE NICKOLAI
nickolai@maryville.edu

Maryville University is committed to helping students develop a reasonable, decent, and civilized philosophy of life in an academic environment that encourages responsible interaction, personal growth, and development of character. Its liberal arts core serves as the foundation for students who are exploring the values that will inform their decisions as leaders in their communities. One core course is the first-year seminar, "Dialogues: Texts on Community and Justice."

This two-semester course offers students the opportunity to engage in dialogues about community and justice while exploring books, essays, and works from the visual and performing arts. Students read texts from a variety of disciplines, including the humanities, social sciences, arts, and sciences. Guest speakers address these classes regularly on topics that will broaden students' perspectives. Every spring students complete a unit on the Holocaust and visit the St. Louis Holocaust Museum. In 1999 the tour was led by a Holocaust survivor.

The readings for the class address justice and civic responsibility. Students study justice and responsibility in the government with readings from Lao-Tsu, Machiavelli, Rousseau, Jefferson, and Arendt. Students study justice in the community and their own civic responsibility with readings from Frederick Douglass, Thoreau, Gandhi, Martin Luther King Jr., and John Kenneth Galbraith. Students write reflective journal entries on the readings, speakers, and other activities. Students are also encouraged to do community service and often choose to do a class project that serves the community.

In the first-year seminar, students broaden their perspectives and learn to value the perspectives of others. They become more aware of some of the injustices in society and consider their own responsibility for creating a more just society.

MOUNT SAINT MARY'S COLLEGE

12001 CHALON ROAD
LOS ANGELES, CA 90049
310.954.4000
http://www.msmc.la.edu/

UNDERGRADUATES: 1,700

For program information, please contact:
JANE LINGUA, Ph.D.
msmc.la.edu

"Freshman Seminar was far more than a basic orientation; it gave me an opportunity to explore my personal goals and gain a sense of direction."

—A MOUNT SAINT MARY'S SECOND-YEAR STUDENT

Mount St. Mary's College offers a values-based liberal arts education for women. Founded in 1925, the college has a special mission to educate women for participation and leadership in society. This goal begins with an array of first-year programs that are both challenging and motivational. Cornerstone first-year programs include:

✦ FRESHMAN SERVICE PROJECT DAY. Each year, all first-year students participate in a service project. In 1999, first-year students and 10 faculty members painted murals, removed graffitti, and cleaned classrooms and the exteriors of three Los Angeles elementary schools.

✦ LEADERSHIP PORTFOLIO. Each first-year student at MSMC develops a Leadership Portfolio. In addition to including material about volunteer service activities, students are asked throughout the year to assess their personal growth and character development.

✦ FRESHMAN SEMINAR CLASS. This required class focuses on making healthy and responsible choices. Combining small group discussions and journal writing, the Freshman Seminar Class encourages students to establish a personal commitment to responsible and healthy behavior.

✦ SOCIAL ACTION CLASS. MSMC students also take a Social Action Class in which they volunteer in a distressed community and learn about the underlying social issues that confront such communities.

A student's first-year education at MSMC is filled with discipline and purpose. As they acquire new skills, knowledge, and values, students begin to develop the commitment to service and leadership that defines the goal of an undergraduate education at Mount Saint Mary's College.

NEW MEXICO HIGHLANDS UNIVERSITY

NATIONAL AVENUE
LAS VEGAS, NM 87701
505.425.7511
http://www.nmhu.edu/

UNDERGRADUATES: 1,700

For program information, please contact:
MERYL KRAVITZ, Ph.D.
m_kravitz@venus.nmhu.edu

New Mexico Highlands University, a comprehensive, public institution, helps students make the transition from high school to college through a required class called the Freshman Leadership Course. Combining classroom studies, community service, and field trips, students learn how to take responsibility for their education, clarify their values, and resolve ethical dilemmas. In addition, the course features segments on study skills, time management, using the library and online resources, and analytical thought. The course is taught in several sections by 24 NMHU faculty members, each of whom are selected for their willingness to mentor students beyond the first semester. "The [Freshman Leadership Course] is about helping students change from being passive high school students to college students who proactively take charge of their education," said one of the course instructors, Lynn deMartin. Several aspects to the course help build character in NMHU students:

✦ CLASSROOM STUDIES. Each course has a unique theme stemming from the instructor's discipline, ranging from education to multiculturalism.

✦ COMMUNITY SERVICE. Students are required to provide four hours of community service during the semester. Projects have included helping construct an animal shelter and visiting with the elderly.

✦ INITIATIVE GAMES. An array of interactive and experiential exercises help students develop leadership, decision-making, and teamworking skills.

After completing the course, participants reported that they were better prepared for both the academic and nonacademic demands of being a university student. NMHU students emerge from their Freshman Leadership studies as more responsible and mature citizens who have a better chance of excelling in college and beyond.

NORTH CAROLINA STATE UNIVERSITY

BOX 7925
RALEIGH, NC 27695
919.515.5838
http://www.ncsu.edu/

UNDERGRADUATES: 25,000

For program information, please contact:
THOMAS CONWAY, Ph.D.
thomas_conway@ncsu.edu

North Carolina State University (NCSU) offers incoming students First-Year College (FYC), a unique, comprehensive program. Within the scientific-oriented environment of NCSU, students may begin their academic lives without declaring a major during their first year. Professional advisors help students select challenging courses with the objective of keeping their choice of major and career options open. The program's integrity relies on the personal, in-depth attention given to each student and on the challenge to students to take charge of their education.

Establishing meaningful relationships with mentoring adults and student leaders lays the groundwork for further development of character and personal values. Some of the programs that accomplish this goal include:

✦ MENTORING. First-year mentoring is conducted by the advisor, who also teaches MDS 101/102, a year-long course designed to engage students in the learning process, advance critical-thinking skills, and enable the informed selection of a major.

✦ FACULTY INVOLVEMENT. The FYC Faculty Fellows Program encourages faculty relationships and places faculty mentors in small-group interaction with students. Faculty gather together to provide support to students by hosting exam-week meals and entertainment.

✦ PARENT PARTICIPATION. FYC supports and enables family-student interaction by encouraging contracting among family members and advisors, sponsoring parent orientation, writing newsletters, hosting an annual coffee for parents to meet advisors, and including parent volunteers in career networking for FYC students.

First-Year College is the hub in a wheel of partnerships that build community and present students with seamless, rather than segmented, access to information and support. Within NCSU's comprehensive and dynamic learning environment, students can explore their values, define their goals, and develop the character to lead.

PORTLAND STATE UNIVERSITY

PO BOX 752
PORTLAND, OR 97207-0751
http://www.pdx.edu/

UNDERGRADUATES: 14,000

For program information, please contact:
CHARLES WHITE, Ph.D.
whitecr@irn.pdx.edu

"The first-year program at PSU encouraged me to become an individual who thinks before he acts."

—A PORTLAND STATE FOURTH-YEAR STUDENT

Portland State University, a comprehensive public university, in 1996 designed University Studies to increase student learning on campus. University Studies operates on these four fundamental goals for students: inquiry and critical thinking, ethical issues and social responsibility, communication, and understanding of the human experience.

A key experience of the program is Freshman Inquiry (Frinq), an interdisciplinary, team-taught course that is a first-year requirement. Led by faculty and peer mentors, students learn:

✦ Group process skills and their application to academic discourse and community building. Students strive to learn about each other as a diverse community of learners and set ground rules of appropriate behavior that serve to create an environment of trust and respect. Opportunities through Student Affairs activities on campus and service projects in the city are included in course assignments.

✦ Inclusion of issues of diversity and multicultural themes across the curriculum. Courses address educational equality, free speech, political action, and historical issues. Related assignments encourage inquiry and critical thinking about these topics.

✦ Community-based learning as a requirement of University Studies. Hands-on learning begins in most Frinq courses, where students tutor and teach life skills in community centers for new immigrants, pack potatoes for donation to food banks, or research and practice political action skills.

Portland State has become a national model that colleges and universities can use to respond to the changing needs of our communities and country. Most important, PSU has demonstrated that it puts students and their development as moral and educated citizens as a top priority.

Prescott College

220 GROVE AVENUE
PRESCOTT, AZ 86301
520.778.2090
http://www.prescott.edu/

UNDERGRADUATES: 400

For program information, please contact:
JULIE MUNSELL
520.778.2090, ext. 2239

"You have such a sense of accomplishment after completing the program. You have this feeling of shared experience not only with the other incoming students, but with all students over the years who completed the program."

—A Prescott senior

Wilderness Orientation at Prescott College, a private, liberal arts institution, is a three-week backcountry expedition that immerses all new students in the college's educational philosophies of self-direction and experiential learning. Part seminar in small group living and wilderness travel, and part introduction to the deeper meaning possible in educational experiences, the program helps students find a balance between self-fulfillment, service to others, and sensitivity to the natural environment. Upper-class students, faculty, staff, and alumni plan and participate in Wilderness Orientation, helping new students learn the history and importance of the program, which has been a core Prescott experience since the College's inception in 1966. Character-building aspects of the program include:

✦ **Values Clarification.** During a three-week stay in remote Arizona backcountry with minimal gear and amenities, students develop a new perspective on personal goals and priorities. The daily challenges of group expeditionary travel help students develop qualities such as compassion, patience, generosity, and acceptance.

✦ **Service Learning.** This increasingly emphasized component of the program gives students opportunities to work with local ranchers, land-management agencies, and other groups and individuals involved in environmental issues.

Of incoming students, 99% report that they are significantly more prepared for their educational journey as a result of the program. Every office and department is involved with Wilderness Orientation, a unified effort that helps illustrate the Prescott motto, "The Southwest is our classroom." Students completing this unusual orientation program in the wild not only have a greater sense of responsibility for the earth, but a better understanding of themselves and how to be productive and positive members of a group.

Rhodes College

2500 NORTH PARKWAY
MEMPHIS, TN 38112
901.843.3000
http://www.rhodes.edu/

UNDERGRADUATES: 1,400

For program information, please contact:
DOUGLAS HATFIELD, Ph.D.
hatfield@rhodes.edu

"'Search' not only showed us how cultures in the past grappled with great moral questions, but it also facilitated our own search for the answers to these questions."

—A Rhodes College fourth-year student

At Rhodes College, "The Search for Values in the Light of Western History and Religion" academic program challenges students to embark on a continuing inquiry into the development of beliefs about issues of value and character over time. Students see how in every historical era humans have grappled with fundamental questions, such as:

✦ What does it mean to be a human being and how is human life different from other kinds of life?

✦ What is the most meaningful (satisfying) life for a human to live?

✦ What kinds of lives do (should) humans live in relationship with one another?

✦ How do humans relate to powers and forces divine, natural, and human, which are larger than themselves and which impinge on their lives?

✦ What are the possibilities for individual freedom and what are the connections between freedom and responsibility?

Students see how these questions have been asked and answered, and are given opportunities to ask their own versions of these questions and to move toward the articulation of their own values. One aim of the program is to encourage students to see that what they have done in the course is not an end in itself but the beginning of a life-long project of self-reflection and renewal.

The Search Advisory Council tries to help students see that the search is not just "internal" but has implications for how they actually live their lives in the world. Each year about one-fourth of the students in the program are appointed to this Council. Appointment is an opportunity for service on behalf of other students, the teaching staff of the course, and prospective students and their parents.

SAINT AUGUSTINE'S COLLEGE

1315 OAKWOOD AVENUE
RALEIGH, NC 27610-2298
http://www.st-aug.edu/

UNDERGRADUATES: 1,600

For program information, please contact:
CAROLYN E. KNOWLES
cknowles@es.st-aug.edu

*"The Learning Community Program helped me
to transition well to Saint Augustine's. Overall, I have
grown tremendously during my first year of college."*
—A SAINT AUGUSTINE FIRST-YEAR STUDENT

The Learning Community Program's motto, "It Takes a Community to Educate a Student," describes Saint Augustine's College's unique approach to promoting the virtues of personal and civic responsibility. This Episcopal-related, historically Black, private, liberal arts institution exercises a holistic approach to education, focusing on academic, spiritual, social, physical, and financial well-being. The program emphasizes the following concept-centered programs:

✦ TRANSITIONING. Learning Community Camp develops critical-thinking, problem-solving, and computer skills, and a sense of community with peers, faculty, staff, and administrators.

✦ SKILL BUILDING. The Learning Course provides the philosophy of Process Education (trademarked by Pacific Crest) and teaches students an interdisciplinary approach to learning.

✦ MENTORING. The Learning Community Hour provides one-on-one mentoring between faculty and students, identifies students in need of supplemental instruction, tutoring, or counseling, and encourages participation in cultural and civic programs.

✦ INNOVATIVE TEACHING. Faculty Mentors Summer Institute introduces contemporary teaching strategies, incorporates technology in the classroom, teaches assessment of students' academic and social-development needs, and addresses sensitivity, relationship development, and support techniques.

Alumni, corporate, and educational leaders also contribute time, talent, and financial support as members of the Executive Council. This collaborative effort not only helps students successfully matriculate and graduate but brings the Learning Community Program's motto to life, as the entire community works together to educate each individual student.

ST. FRANCIS COLLEGE

PO BOX 600
LORETTO, PA 15940
814.472.3100
http://www.sfcpa.edu/

UNDERGRADUATES: 1,500

For program information, please contact:
JAY HILFIGER, Ph.D.
jhilfiger@sfcpa.edu

*"The First-Year Experience was a positive influence for
me. The requirements helped me adjust to college life,
meet people with different backgrounds, and have diverse
learning experiences in many different fields of study."*
—A ST. FRANCIS FIRST-YEAR STUDENT

Helping students understand moral and intellectual decision-making is a major goal of the Freshman-Year Experience at St. Francis College, a Catholic, coeducational liberal arts institution. The Experience also promotes the Franciscan values of humility, generosity, respect for others, service to the needy, ethical behavior, and reverence.

The program provides first-year students a set of common experiences, both in and out of the classroom, including:

✦ THE SUMMER READING PROGRAM. All incoming students read a book that deals with moral questions and attend a small group discussion during orientation. The author or another guest with relevant experience may visit campus to further discuss the book's topic.

✦ ORIENTATION WEEK PROGRAMS. Topics include Franciscan values, racial/sexual prejudice, and acquaintance rape.

✦ CONVOCATIONS. Notable guest speakers, performers, and others pay a visit to campus. Sometimes professors plan topics that complement courses and provide time to students for relevant class discussions.

✦ FRESHMAN COLLOQUIA. This program emphasizes active learning, in classes of no more than 17 students. Examples in recent years have included "Banned in Boston, Not in Loretto," dealing with censorship and its consequences, and "Studying the Holocaust: An Introduction to the Behavior of Victims, Bystanders, and Perpetrators," focusing on persuasion and moral decision-making.

The advising component of the first-year program won the 1997 Outstanding Advising Program Award from the National Academic Advising Association. Advisors first meet their students during summer orientation sessions, then work with each student throughout the first year, for example, helping with schedules, adjustment to college life, and career goals.

Saint Louis University

221 NORTH GRAND BOULEVARD
ST. LOUIS, MO 63103-2097
800.758.3678
http://www.slu.edu/

UNDERGRADUATES: 6,200

For program information, please contact:
ELEONORE STUMP, Ph.D.
stumpep@slu.edu

"We are all connected to each other in a great community, and we dream of changing the world. The great part about Micah House is that we make contacts that will help us to accomplish this."

—AN SLU FIRST-YEAR STUDENT

Innovative residential, service, and learning concepts come together at Saint Louis University, a private, liberal arts, Jesuit institution, through the following initiatives:

✦ **MICAH HOUSE.** This program, which takes its name from the biblical prophet who spoke out against social injustice, has four primary aims: to foster leadership; to offer interdisciplinary courses covering issues of peace and justice; to enable students to serve alongside the poor and disadvantaged; and to foster a sense of community through living together in a residence hall. The Freshman-Year Project admits high-school seniors to Micah House each May, and The Companions Project admits students already enrolled at SLU. Interdisciplinary study and reflection are complemented by speakers, retreats, social events, and service projects that students can continue throughout their college careers.

✦ **FIRST-YEAR TASK FORCE.** This group, made up of faculty representatives, a student representative, and additional persons under the direction of cochairs Dr. Eleonore Stump and Father J. J. Mueller, was appointed to examine the experience of SLU's first-year students and make recommendations for strengthening it. The group recognized Micah House for providing students with the opportunity to develop the Jesuit ideal of "living for others."

An SLU education integrates thought and action, values and facts, compassion and fulfillment. Faculty members supplement the multidisciplinary core curriculum through mentoring, focusing on issues such as adjusting to university life, the tension between responsibility and freedom, and where to find support systems on campus. Together, these initiatives make the first-year experience effective and comprehensive by helping SLU students create lives that are rich and fulfilling.

Samford University

800 LAKESHORE DRIVE
BIRMINGHAM, AL 35229
205.726.2011
http://www.samford.edu/

UNDERGRADUATES: 2,900

For program information, please contact:
AMANDA W. BORDEN, Ph.D.
awborden@samford.edu

The mission of Samford University is to provide a nourishing Christian environment that will encourage students to establish challenging academic, social, and spiritual goals for their lives. Through the Freshman-Year Experience (FYE), first-year students are mentored to develop a vision of a future for themselves based on their own unique characteristics. The FYE Program instills the virtue of personal responsibility in new students through the following programs:

✦ **S.U.ccess Program.** First-year students who believe they need assistance with their academic course work are paired with an adult mentor on campus. Through weekly meetings, the mentor encourages, affirms, and assists the student with securing resources to help attain success.

✦ **Co-Nexus Core Curriculum.** All first-year students share this 22-credit core curriculum. The Co-Nexus program places great emphasis on developing problem-solving skills and teamwork.

✦ **Horizons 101.** This orientation class deals with such issues as building self-esteem, study skills, drug abuse, and selection of a major and career.

✦ **Connections.** All first-year students meet for a preschool weekend retreat. Upperclassmen discuss first-year issues, and a faculty member discusses academic issues and questions the students may have. Also, a faculty member or administrator pairs with each group of students for a half-day of community-service work.

Students who participate in these programs are equipped to select a major of study, make decisions and solve problems that they may encounter, and locate the appropriate person or persons to provide assistance to them. First-year students at Samford are provided with the guidance and encouragement they need to become all that God created them to become.

Seattle Pacific University

3307 THIRD AVENUE WEST
SEATTLE, WA 98119
206.281.2000
http://www.spu.edu/

UNDERGRADUATES: 2,600

For program information, please contact:
JOYCE ERICKSON, Ph.D.
jqericks@spu.edu

Research shows that most university students don't see a connection between general education requirements and their everyday lives. The Common Curriculum at Seattle Pacific University links the liberal arts and real-life issues through the disciplines of intellectual inquiry. The Common Curriculum is designed to help students:

✦ Develop skills in writing, speaking, critical thinking, and information literacy as a foundation for higher learning. Students learn the value and power of education in character formation as evidenced in the campus-wide reading of *The Narrative of Frederick Douglass.*

✦ Understand and shape their identity as responsible human beings created in the image of God. One-third of the first-year course load requires engagement in personal and community responsibility.

✦ Develop the disciplines of intellectual inquiry that will sustain them in their studies and as they explore their chosen vocation. Students participate in community service through a common civic-service project.

The University Core sequence of the Common Curriculum explores key human questions in three classes titled "Character and Community," "The West and the World," and "Belief, Morality and the Modern Mind." The senior capstone course integrates learning from the Common Curriculum with learning from a major discipline chosen by each student. Particular attention is paid to questions of faith and ethical action as they relate to the practice of disciplinary inquiry or professional practice. Through these and other sequences of required courses, students are taught critical thinking, self-understanding, and personal discipline, along with a love of God, neighbor, and learning. In so doing, the Common Curriculum helps define an SPU education as one that builds on the qualities of heart, mind, and action.

Simpson College

INDIANOLA, IA 50125
515.961.6251
http://www.simpson.edu/

UNDERGRADUATES: 2,000

For program information, please contact:
JIM THORIUS
thorius@simpson.edu

"The First Year Program allowed me to meet the people that were going to be shaping my future. I immediately saw a serving attitude and a giving heart."

—A SIMPSON COLLEGE FIRST-YEAR STUDENT

The First-Year Program at Simpson College, a private, liberal arts college, is a broadly inclusive program structured to help new students adapt to what is universally recognized as a stressful and vulnerable time in their lives. The theme of the First-Year Program is "The Responsible Self in Community." Through a variety of activities, first-year students are challenged to think about their obligations and responsibilities to the communities of which they are a part.

The program uses a multifaceted approach, including a focus on the following: adjustment issues; critical-thinking skills through enrollment in a liberal arts seminar; the practice of responsible citizenship and leadership; diversity; involvement in self-governance; and community service. The program extends throughout the first year, in effect continuously challenging students to develop as good campus citizens. It provides a variety of opportunities for students to practice the virtues of personal and civic responsibility. Significant character-building components include:

✦ Faculty-, staff-, and student-led workshops and convocations

✦ Community-service projects

✦ Classroom discussions entitled "Honest Conversations about Community"

Each of these components provides a vehicle for making students aware of the mission and values of the college and of their role as responsible members of the community. Students are also encouraged to become involved in the life of the campus early in their college career. Freshman Council and first-year residence-hall governments provide significant involvement in the governance and operation of each first-year living area.

Southeast Missouri State University

CAPE GIRARDEAU, MO 63701
573.651.2000
http://www.semo.edu/

UNDERGRADUATES: 8,200

For program information, please contact:
KAREN A. MYERS, Ph.D.
kamyers@semovm.semo.edu

"The FLighT Program steers students toward success in their first year while easing the transition from the comforts of home to the uncertainty of college."

—A SOUTHEAST MISSOURI FIRST-YEAR STUDENT

Southeast Missouri State University has evolved into a comprehensive state university with more than 150 academic programs. The First-year Learning Team (FLighT) Program was implemented to create a seamless learning environment. FLighT programs consist of a cluster of three courses, centered on a particular theme or area of interest, such as Music, Biology, International Studies, and Adolescent Development. These clusters of approximately 25 students are small learning communities that with the help of a peer mentor assist in the academic and social transition to college life.

Areas of focus for the FLighT Program include:

✦ HOUSING. Residence halls play an important role in the FLighT program, although students are not required to live on campus to participate. Resident FLighT students are housed together, they have a specially selected Community Advisor, and they receive academic and social support.

✦ COMMUNITY SERVICE. Each FLighT is required to commit to a service-learning project in an effort to enhance campus community and broaden the student's sense of personal and civic responsibility.

✦ SPECIAL TOPIC SEMINARS AND TRIPS. The FLighT Program offers first-year students the opportunity to learn inside and outside the classroom, with workshops on stress management and self-defense, and trips to concerts, museums, and the municipal zoo. Participation provides FLighT students opportunities to live the University motto, "Learn, Experience, Succeed."

Southeast students are encouraged to develop a sense of personal responsibility as they adapt to college life. The fundamental foundation of the FLighT Program rests in the belief that students develop holistically and that the University must be attentive to not only academic development, but to emotional and spiritual growth as well.

Southwest Missouri State University

901 SOUTH NATIONAL AVENUE
SPRINGFIELD, MO 65804
417.836.5000
http://www.smsu.edu/

UNDERGRADUATES: 14,000

For program information, please contact:
MONA CASADY
mjc671f@mail.smsu.edu

"SMSU's First-Year Program has helped to develop my character not only by strengthening my academic abilities, but also by encouraging me to become a well-rounded student who participates in campus activities."

—A SOUTHWEST MISSOURI FIRST-YEAR STUDENT

Developing character as well as personal and civic responsibility is at the core of IDS 110, Introduction to University Life, at Southwest Missouri State University. Required of all new students, IDS 110 emphasizes the holistic development of the student. Teachers (faculty, staff, administrators, and graduate assistants) for this course come from 52 departments or units on campus. Peer leaders provide the younger students with role models for appropriate academic, leadership, and personal behaviors. Components of the course include:

✦ Before classes begin, new students and their families are required to attend the Freshman Convocation, where a nationally known speaker addresses a public affairs theme. Students are required to read a book written by the speaker to prepare for the convocation, as well as for IDS 110 class discussions and writings that will follow.

✦ Presentations provide IDS 110 students with information on health and safety issues (alcohol, drugs, sexual conduct, STDs, and AIDS), as well as diversity awareness.

✦ Salute to Veterans Convocation is a special community-wide program that brings together the University community (students, faculty, administrators, and staff) with the surrounding community.

✦ Members of the Campus Ministers' Association speak on topics that support character development, values clarification, personal responsibility, and morality. Participation in a religious organization of choice is encouraged.

In addition, students are required to participate in community-service projects and interact in class discussions and write position papers to develop critical-thinking, problem-solving, and values-clarification skills. Through these efforts, first-year students at SMSU develop a foundation of knowledge, skills, and understanding to maximize their performance in college and success in life.

TEXAS A&M UNIVERSITY

COLLEGE STATION, TX 77843
409.845.3211
http://www.tamu.edu/

UNDERGRADUATES: 34,000

For program information, please contact:
RODNEY P. MCCLENDON
rpm@tamu.edu

"I came to Texas A&M knowing exactly what I wanted to do. Through the ExCEL class, I gained the tools to accomplish my goal."

—A TEXAS A&M SECOND-YEAR STUDENT

ExCEL (Excellence uniting Culture, Education, and Leadership) is a comprehensive student-success program designed for, but not exclusive to, first-year students in the ethnic minority at Texas A&M University. ExCEL's mission is to assist these students and their parents in making a smooth transition from high school to college and to help ensure the students' successful matriculation and graduation from Texas A&M. Students are encouraged to identify and preserve their cultural heritage and use that awareness to attain academic, professional, and civic "ExCELlence."

ExCEL consists of two programs:

✦ ExCEL CONFERENCE. Held the weekend before the fall semester, ExCEL Conference consists of motivational speakers, workshops on academic and student life, discussions facilitated by Team Leaders (peer mentors), and social activities. Several components of the ExCEL Conference address personal and civic responsibility.

✦ ExCEL PLUS. This year-long credited seminar course covers topics ranging from study skills and time management to interview skills, personal pride, ethical leadership, and social etiquette. The seminar is designed to develop well-rounded students on the academic, personal, professional, and social levels and is open to any first- or second-year student.

To date, ExCEL has helped over 1,700 students and their parents successfully make the transition to Texas A&M. ExCEL students have held top leadership positions in campus organizations and most have returned to serve as ExCEL Team Leaders. They have gone on to medical, law, and professional schools, and are serving as Big Brothers and Big Sisters in their communities. Through their commitment to their respective communities, these students have shown that ExCEL has made a positive difference in their lives.

TRINITY COLLEGE

300 SUMMIT STREET
HARTFORD, CT 06016
860.297.2000
http://www.trincoll.edu/

UNDERGRADUATES: 2,100

For program information, please contact:
DIANE MARTELL
Diane.Martell@mail.trincoll.edu

Trinity College is a community united in a quest for excellence in liberal arts education. Its paramount purpose is to foster critical thinking, free the mind of parochialism and prejudice, and prepare students to lead personally satisfying, civically responsible, and socially useful lives. Trinity's First-Year Program supports this mission by promoting the intellectual life of students in and outside the classroom. The program is designed to enhance the intellectual, civic, social, developmental, and spiritual aspects of the lives of new students.

✦ THE FIRST-YEAR SEMINARS provide new students with a small, stimulating discussion-based course during their first semester. Students are encouraged to challenge the instructor, other students, and themselves in the exchange of beliefs and ideas. Each seminar is designed to provide rigorous instruction to students in critical thinking and writing, areas that are vital to students' academic success and character development.

✦ FIRST-YEAR MENTORS are academically successful upperclass students who work alongside the instructor in each First-Year Seminar. In addition to providing academic support to students, Mentors bring the issues of personal and civic responsibility into the residence halls. Mentors act as role models on how a college student should behave in regards to studying, academic honesty, alcohol usage, and respect for one's neighbor and hall community.

✦ THE FIRST-YEAR ORIENTATION PROGRAM incorporates educational programs on personal responsibility relating to alcohol use, sexual behavior, and cross-cultural understanding into the four-day orientation program that all new students are required to attend.

Trinity's first-year students are provided with a unique educational and residential experience that encourages them to be both critical thinkers and responsible members of the college community.

UNITED STATES NAVAL ACADEMY

121 BLAKE ROAD
ANNAPOLIS, MD 21402-5000
410.293.1000
http://www.usna.edu/

UNDERGRADUATES: 4,000

For program information, please contact:
MAJOR CAROLINE SIMKINS-MULLINS
mullins@nadn.navy.mils

"During Plebe Year, we not only learn about courage, honor, and commitment, we practice and strengthen these values daily."

—A USNA THIRD-YEAR MIDSHIPMAN

The U.S. Naval Academy prepares young men and women to become professional officers in the Navy and Marine Corps by helping its midshipmen to develop "morally, mentally and physically and to imbue them with the highest ideas of duty, honor and loyalty." In support of this mission, the first-year program lays down the foundation from which midshipmen can build their character and develop a sense of commitment of service to their country through the following components:

✦ Honor training

✦ Human relations training

✦ Integrity-development seminars

✦ Distinguished guest lecturers

✦ Core courses focusing on ethics in government, naval heritage, and naval leadership

✦ MAG (Midshipman Action Group), a volunteer civic organization run by midshipmen

A revealing response from a first-year student's visit to the Holocaust Museum shows the significant impact of this experience: "I learned an important moral lesson . . . the need for character and integrity. This inner sense of morality must . . . have the ability to stand bravely alone, even in the face of certain death." MAG is an exceptional example of how midshipmen embody the ideals of civic responsibility—during the last two years, they contributed 35,000 hours to community projects in education, environment, and social services.

By encouraging the character dimension of education through its program components and emphasizing the ability to distinguish right from wrong and the strength and moral courage to do the right thing, the Naval Academy's first-year program promotes personal and civic responsibility in its future military leaders.

UNIVERSITY OF ARKANSAS AT LITTLE ROCK

2801 SOUTH UNIVERSITY AVENUE
LITTLE ROCK, AR 72204-1099
501.569.3127
http://www.ualr.edu/

UNDERGRADUATES: 10,500

For program information, please contact:
THEA M. HOEFT, Ed.D.
tmhoeft@ualr.edu

Learning how to learn is at the foundation of the First-Year Experience Program (FYE) offered by the University of Arkansas at Little Rock (UALR). FYE helps students connect their coursework to the idea that all learning carries the duty to share what is learned. To achieve this objective, the FYE program provides the following character-building courses:

✦ PERSONAL AWARENESS. This three-hour course features writing assignments that foster the development of strong character. Students write essays describing their service-learning projects and assessing the results of their work. Students volunteer at local schools, healthcare facilities, and community-based businesses. In serving on these projects, students learn to make and keep commitments and to share their learning and expertise. Additionally, students write essays assessing their curiosity, industry, cooperation, and integrity—all essential characteristics of "Master Students."

✦ LEARNING COMMUNITIES. Groups of students enroll in thematically linked clusters of core courses, allowing them to remain together as they pursue common themes within different courses. For example, students in one PEAW section have also enrolled in a section of Composition and a section of Ethics. Students in these linked courses write papers focused primarily on the ethical responsibilities of teachers and students.

Program evaluations confirm that students develop civic and personal responsibility. Pre- and postprogram surveys show that many students experience a significant change in attitude as they begin to recognize the personal, academic, and professional benefits of public service. By the end of their first semester, many FYE students have successfully developed personal service plans to help them achieve short- and long-term goals and have become concerned, responsible members of the UALR community.

University of California, Santa Barbara

SANTA BARBARA, CA 93106
805.893.8000
http://www.ucsb.edu/

UNDERGRADUATES: 16,000

For program information, please contact:
BRITT J. ANDREATTA, Ph.D.
andreatta-b@sa.ucsb.edu

"I think that the Freshman Experience Course was very valuable and will enhance the rest of my college education and life."

—A SANTA BARBARA FIRST-YEAR STUDENT

Students at the University of California, Santa Barbara (UCSB), are encouraged to participate in intensive scholarly activities while developing integrity, both personally and as members of the community. The Freshman Experience Course, Interdisciplinary Studies 20 (INT 20), is a three-unit course that encourages first-year students to take an active role in their own education and in creating the community in which they want to live. Students benefit by participating in four different areas:

✦ EXPLORING ISSUES. Leadership development, eating disorders, binge drinking, and being an active ally for underrepresented communities are just some of the topics explored.

✦ ATTENDING EVENTS AND PROGRAMS. Students explore the history, culture, and experiences of a community of which they are not individually a member, such as a different ethnicity, class, gender, or sexual orientation.

✦ PARTICIPATING IN ACTIVITIES. UCSB offers a variety of activities specifically designed to help students develop a variety of academic and career-based skills and goals.

✦ LEARNING ABOUT HIGHER EDUCATION. Students learn about the roles faculty and students play in shared governance; the importance of research; the roles and responsibilities the university has to society at large and the local community; and opportunities available for directed personal, academic, and professional development.

Cosponsored by both Academic and Student Affairs divisions, INT 20 is taught by teaching assistants and staff members from the entire campus community. This collaborative team ensures that UCSB students achieve scholastic excellence, learn about important issues, and explore their personal values in order to develop into leaders with a strong sense of personal integrity and commitment to their community.

University of Mary Hardin-Baylor

PO BOX 8426
900 COLLEGE STREET
BELTON, TX 76513
254.295.4475
http://www.umhb.edu/

UNDERGRADUATES: 2,600

For program information, please contact:
BECKY BRADLEY
bbradley@umhb.edu

The University of Mary Hardin-Baylor is a Christ-centered, coeducational liberal arts institution. Christian principles and beliefs form the basis of the educational environment that includes the Department of Student Advising and Retention. In addition to promoting learning and character development, Mary Hardin-Baylor encourages obedience to the Great Commission expressed in Matthew 29:18–20. The Department of Student Advising and Retention dedicates its personnel and programs to this UMHB purpose by giving first-year students a personalized, one-on-one, life-enhancing experience that will impact each one spiritually, academically, mentally, and physically.

✦ ADVISING, the cornerstone that establishes relationships with students, parents, and coworkers built on trust and Christian values, is conducted by three role-model advisors.

✦ TAKE-CHARGE FRESHMEN take responsibility for their educational destiny; individualize a schedule balanced with reading, writing, hands-on and physical activity classes; and maintain contact with an advisor.

✦ PEER ACADEMIC SUPPORT COUNSELORS, MENTORS, AND TUTORS are exemplary academic and spiritual role models; provide continued emotional support, encouragement, and friendship; demand accountability; build self-confidence and self-esteem; and recommend other resources on campus.

✦ SUCCESS IN ACADEMICS is a first-year seminar requiring studies, reflection papers, and projects to earn credits for goal setting, time management, business affairs, study skills, personal and spiritual growth, community involvement, and campus pride. The instructor is also the student's advisor.

The Student Advising and Retention Department, along with all campus resources, works to provide experiences and support for first-year students as they prepare for careers, continue their personal growth and development, and learn to serve the communities in which they live.

UNIVERSITY OF NEVADA–RENO

RENO, NV 89557
775.784.4865
http://www.unr.edu/

UNDERGRADUATES: 9,000

For program information, please contact:
BARBARA KING
bking@unr.edu

"The weekly meetings of the Rural Assistance Program (RAP) are a time for me to relax and escape the pressures of the week. I feel secure in knowing that people are willing to help, listen and care for me any time I may need it."

The University of Nevada–Reno, a land-grant institution founded in 1874, demonstrates in philosophy, academic offerings, and a wide variety of student services that the diverse undergraduate student population plays a significant role in the success of the institution. The Rural Assistance Program (RAP) was initiated in 1990 to encourage enrollment and support the perseverance of students from the extensive rural areas of Nevada by emulating the strong community experience from which they came. The key components of the RAP program are:

✦ Freshman-Year Experience Course

✦ Intensive mentoring

✦ Individualized career exploration

✦ Participation in the weekly RAP meetings and activities

Academic success and character development are paramount to RAP. Students sign a contract committing them to taking personal responsibility for their college success. Through the supportive community spirit of the RAP club, students are encouraged to become mentors and to get involved in community service. RAP motivates students to learn about personal values, motivation, leadership, and ethics. Students are involved in the learning process through individualized surveys, inventories, class discussions, group projects, and presentations.

In 1997 this unique program was selected as one of six Exemplary Programs in American colleges and universities by the National Association of Student Personal Administrators (NASPA).

Through the guidance, challenge, and support of the Rural Assistance Program, students from small Nevada towns become ambassadors confidentially negotiating, participating in, and contributing to the University community.

THE UNIVERSITY OF NORTH CAROLINA AT ASHEVILLE

ONE UNIVERSITY HEIGHTS
ASHEVILLE, NC 28804-8510
828.251.6600
http://www.unca.edu/

UNDERGRADUATES: 3,100

For program information, please contact:
SARAH J. BUMGARNER
Sbumgarner@unca.edu

 The University of North Carolina at Asheville (UNCA) has a First-Year Experience Program that supports the University's liberal arts mission with its strong commitment to the development of the student as a whole individual and a contributor to society. First-Year Experience courses help students take the first steps in developing skills that will help them become life-long learners, engaged in a world full of freedoms and responsibilities. Activities include:

✦ BULLDOG DAY: A TIME OF SERVICE. This orientation event involves more than 100 faculty and staff and over 500 students working side by side in community-service projects. Students get to know their professors and learn firsthand what it means to be part of a larger community.

✦ ACADEMIC CONTEXT. All First-Year Experience course goals are met within an academic context. Several courses satisfy general education requirements while others are interdisciplinary special topics such as principles of biological evolution, writing and critical thinking, and work, learning, and life.

✦ FIRST-YEAR SEMINARS. Topics of the seminars are designed to complement and support activities taking place in First-Year Experience courses on campus and in the community. The academic and social experiences become integrated by providing an environment in which learning is a shared responsibility extending beyond the classroom.

Starting with Bulldog Day, UNCA students begin to understand the connection between academic experiences, community service, related career options, and the central role of humane values in thought and action. First-Year Experience courses enable students to see themselves as part of a larger community and ask them to reflect on the consequences of their choices. The result is a richer intellectual experience and a richer life experience.

UNIVERSITY OF OKLAHOMA

NORMAN, OK 73019
405.325.0311
http://www.ou.edu/

UNDERGRADUATES: 16,200

For program information, please contact:
BECKY BARKER, Ph.D.
rreed@ou.edu

The University of Oklahoma is proud of its tradition of preparing students to avidly pursue academic excellence, leadership, and community service. This is evident in OU's first-year programs, which encompass three unique opportunities for new students to make a successful transition to college life:

✦ CAMP CRIMSON is a precollege camp experience that offers incoming students an introduction to campus life in a casual, interactive setting. Some of the Camp's unique programs include "Keeping It Real," a forum on race relations and diversity, and the Interactive Theatre Company, which presents vignettes in which student actors address realistic college situations.

✦ NEW SOONER ORIENTATION introduces OU to new students through numerous activities, including Academic Success, Campus Resources, and Recreation and Health. During this four-day orientation, students learn to face the personal responsibilities they now have as adults. Resident Advisors hold several meetings during New Sooner Orientation to ensure that students understand their responsibilities.

✦ THE GATEWAY TO COLLEGE LEARNING course includes major units in volunteer work, physical and mental health, multicultural diversity, substance abuse, effective decision-making and problem-solving skills, and values-clarification exercises. The volunteer component of Gateway has been instrumental in making a difference in the community. Students have volunteered their time to Special Olympics, Habitat for Humanity, environmental clean-up projects, and tutoring programs at local schools.

OU's first-year programs ensure that students develop understanding, tolerance, and self-confidence during their college experience so that they can become mature, responsible, and independent men and women who will be leaders in their communities and role models for others.

UNIVERSITY OF OREGON

1217 UNIVERSITY OF OREGON
EUGENE, OR 97403-5256
541.346.3036
http://www.uoregon.edu/

UNDERGRADUATES: 17,300

For program information, please contact:
JACK BENNETT, Ph.D.
jbennett@oregon.uoregon.edu

"The Freshmen Interest Groups helped me to succeed academically and socially. This program is beneficial to all students who want to make the transition to college easier."

—A UNIVERSITY OF OREGON THIRD-YEAR STUDENT

The University of Oregon, a major research university, seeks to provide academic coherence and social involvement as a part of a student's university experience. The Freshman Interest Program (FIGs) offer first-year and transfer students the opportunity to take thematically linked classes that often include a faculty taught college-experience seminar and always include returning student mentors. The FIG program addresses issues both in and out of the classroom and involve the teaching faculty, student leaders, and the new students.

✦ The faculty, especially those involved in teaching a college experience seminar, ensure that meaningful intellectual and social interaction with teaching faculty is a reality.

✦ Returning student mentors meet weekly for the first five weeks with the FIG students, often continuing their relationships beyond the first term. The student mentors lead by example rather than precept, as they model attitudes and behaviors of self-control and moderation. The job of the student mentor is critical to the success of the program.

✦ New students contribute through their participation, helping others learn what issues are important to them as they become part of the UO community. Students are afforded opportunities to address issues of academic integrity, participation in the university community, and issues of citizenship and responsibility.

New FIG initiatives include utilizing grant monies to encourage faculty collaboration across disciplines and working to increase the number of year-long FIG experiences for new students. The FIG learning communities help students embody the principles of the Carnegie Report—being purposeful, just, open, caring, disciplined, and celebrative.

University of San Francisco

2130 FULTON STREET
SAN FRANCISCO, CA 94117-1080
415.422.5555
http://www.usfca.edu/

UNDERGRADUATES: 4,700

For program information, please contact:
KUNI HAY
hayk@usfca.edu

P.E.A.C.E. (People of color Enhancing Achievement in College Environment) Partners Mentoring Program is a student-coordinated program at the University of San Francisco that assists new students of color with their cultural, educational, academic, and social transition to the college environment. Students expand their understanding of the University as an institution and learn to develop activities, programs, and services that will actualize their goals.

✦ **Mentor Program.** This program emphasizes the importance of community-based operations where mentors and mentees exist as a large community of support while retaining their individual mentor/mentee relationships. The P.E.A.C.E. program serves as a springboard from which the student mentors and mentees can develop relationships with diverse sectors of the University.

✦ **Advocates Program.** The second component of the P.E.A.C.E. program matches continuing students of color with alumni of color. This prepares students for life after college. This two-tier system conveys the importance of generational connection.

As supplements to the Mentor and Advocate Programs, the P.E.A.C.E. Partners program provides numerous opportunities for students of color to succeed in the college environment. Some of these opportunities include monthly luncheons with faculty members, community-service commitments, cultural and educational events, and career and study skills workshops. Mentors and mentees are encouraged to participate in and utilize all activities and services provided by the program.

Beginning with their first year, students witness the University of San Francisco's commitment to the highest standards of learning and scholarship in the American, Catholic, Jesuit tradition seeking knowledge, love, and dissemination of truth.

University of Virginia

PO BOX 9017
CHARLOTTESVILLE, VA 22906
804.924.3200
http://www.virginia.edu/

UNDERGRADUATES: 12,400

For program information, please contact:
SYLVIA V. TERRY
svt@virginia.edu

"UVA's Peer Advisor Program is the primary reason why this university has the highest success rate and retention among African-American students in the nation. The program allows our culture to shine as we venture into the bright daybreak of success." —A UVA FIRST-YEAR STUDENT

The motto of the University of Virginia's Office of African-American Affairs' Peer Advisor Program is "Lending a Helping Hand." Lending that hand, however, goes far beyond this public, comprehensive university's mission of assisting first-year African-American students with their transition to college life. The Peer Advisor Program seeks to build character and shape the lives of the students it serves. Sylvia V. Terry, program director, has received institutional and national recognition for her work and points out the value of peer advising by highlighting the positive differences that student advisors make in their advisees' lives: "Students use Peer Advisors not only for information, but for direction-setting as well. Rather than seeing the upperclassmen as authority figures, freshmen see them as supporters, cheerleaders, and role models."

The program has several tiers:

✦ **Peer Advisors.** Upperclassmen are assigned a number of students with whom they work on an individual and group basis throughout the academic year. Peer Advisors are not only role models, but also facilitators, helping students to discuss or confront issues of relationships, identity, sensitivity, negotiation, work ethics, and responsible social behavior.

✦ **Programming and Publications.** Publications such as *Harambee, For Women Only,* and *For Men Only,* academic sessions, newsletters, and a home page provide students with orientation, recognition, and forums on such topics as relationships, spirituality, stress management, and motivation.

✦ **Direct Outreach.** Personal appointments, e-mail communication, and personalized notes and letters complement the program's other efforts.

The program works hand-in-hand with the entire UVA community to provide support and encouragement for its students by building bridges, forging partnerships, and setting positive examples.

Valparaiso University

KRETZMANN HALL
VALPARAISO, IN 46383-6493
888.GO.VALPO
http://www.valpo.edu/

UNDERGRADUATES: 3,000

For program information, please contact:
MARK R. SCHWEHN, Ph.D.
mark.schwehn@valpo.edu

The creative relationship between faith and learning is a central theme of the Freshman Program at Christ's College. This interdisciplinary honors college at Valparaiso University is dedicated to cultivating intellectual, moral, and spiritual virtues. Every fall semester, approximately 80 first-year students have the opportunity to study selected great Western and non-Western works of humankind in history, literature, art, philosophy, and religion. Both students and teachers experience the learning process as a joint venture through small classes held in a discussion-based atmosphere.

The Freshman Program is distinguished by the following character-building activities:

✦ First-year students write and perform an original full-length play with music, addressing themes such as justice, forgiveness, and leadership. This unique project helps students experience collaboration, trust, humility, charity, civility, honesty, collegiality, and friendship.

✦ First-year students publicly debate international issues such as human rights, freedom of speech and religion, and political ethics in an annual series of Oxford Union–style debates.

✦ The "Dimensions of Leadership" seminar acquaints self-selected first-year students with leadership theory, problems, and issues, and their own promise as leaders.

✦ First-year students engage in numerous service activities that help develop leadership and citizenship qualities. CC students regularly emerge as leaders in the arts, religious life, student government, residential life, and many other areas.

A focus on integrative scholarship at Valparaiso fosters a collaborative learning environment in which the virtues of intellectual excellence and service to others are actively pursued. Through academic study and fruitful discussion, students learn the value of patience, humility, prudence, courage, and charity.

Virginia Polytechnic Institute and State University

BLACKSBURG, VA 24061
540.231.6000
http://www.vt.edu/

UNDERGRADUATES: 21,000

For program information, please contact:
GERRY KOWALSKI, Ph.D.
Kowalski@vt.edu

"VPI's First-Year Experience provided a diverse living environment in which we were able to develop strong bonds."

—A VPI SECOND-YEAR STUDENT

Virginia Polytechnic Institute and State University (VPI)'s size does not prevent VPI from demonstrating an individualized concern for the success of all its students. This philosophy becomes evident in VPI's WING program, a First-Year Experience in a coeducational environment. The WING program creates a more seamless learning environment for incoming students, providing them with assistance as they acclimate to the University environment.

Cornerstone activities of the WING program include:

✦ The First-Year Experience is mandatory for program participation. All students take a two-credit course that includes a large group lecture and small discussion sections. During the weekly lectures, faculty and administrators speak on topics relevant to first-year transitions. The small group sessions, limited to 15 students per group, are led by Student Assistants (SAs) to discuss weekly topics in detail.

✦ Group projects and presentations for the first-year course include the profiling of a campus-based organization and creation of new activities by first-year students.

✦ SAs augment the efforts of the Resident Advisor staff by providing ongoing mentoring and peer support. They also live alongside the WING participants. During the second semester, SAs meet individually with students to review academic goals and progress.

The WING program has enjoyed considerable success with first-year students. WING students experienced higher academic achievement levels, greater degrees of involvement in campus activities, and greater interaction with faculty. Similarly, WING residents report a deeper sense of community on a variety of levels, including cohesiveness, stimulation, input, and involvement. Clearly, VPI has created a first-year program that exemplifies a strong community that lives and learns together.

Viterbo College

815 NINTH STREET SOUTH
LA CROSSE, WI 54601
608.796.3000
http://www.viterbo.edu/

UNDERGRADUATES: 1,700

For program information, please contact:
DEBRA MURRAY
damurray@mail.viterbo.edu

"I learned from my PCC instructor that college can be like a rollercoaster ride. Going up the track can be a struggle, but once you reach the top you can't wait to see what's over the next hill."

—A VITERBO SECOND-YEAR STUDENT

Learning truth, building unity, and spreading hope play an important part in Viterbo College's mission to prepare students for leadership and service rooted in human dignity and respect for the world. Viterbo introduces these themes in PCC ("Person, College and Community"), a first-year experience course that helps students explore character issues. PCC has three sections designed to teach personal and community-based values:

✦ **PERSON.** First-year students begin the course by answering questions designed to help them determine who they are, what they value, and to what and whom they are committed. Each first-year student examines personal issues and goals, identifies an area in need of change, and implements a personal change plan.

✦ **COLLEGE.** Students are introduced to the philosophical and religious roots of Viterbo College, learn about the Franciscan Sisters of Perpetual Adoration (FSPA) and the traditions and values of the Order, and engage in service activities that incorporate the Franciscan heritage. Specific activities designed to build community include Cope Course, an outdoor challenge activity, which requires team planning and work to complete the course.

✦ **COMMUNITY.** Students examine case studies of community problems and utilize ethical decision-making processes to develop strategies to address hypothetical problems. Service learning is a required component of the course and provides students with the opportunity to learn firsthand about a community's problems.

Through PCC, Viterbo provides students with a values-based foundation that teaches them to recognize and cherish their personal values, prepares them to live within a community, and helps them experience the peace that comes from helping others.

Wartburg College

222 NINTH STREET NW
WAVERLY, IA 50677-0903
319.352.8200
http://www.wartburg.edu/

UNDERGRADUATES: 1,500

For program information, please contact:
VICKI EDELNANT
edelnant@wartburg.edu

"First-Year Council is an exceptional organization. It builds character, enhances decision-making skills, and takes the initiative to plan activities for the first-year students."

—A WARTBURG COLLEGE FIRST-YEAR STUDENT

Students at Wartburg College learn to express faith and learning through leadership and service. Through programming and examples set by the entire campus community, first-year students quickly realize that caring for one another is expected and practiced on this campus. Some examples of first-year programs offered at Wartburg include:

✦ **OUTDOOR CHALLENGE EDUCATION COURSE.** Using an outdoor ropes course, students learn about teamwork, cooperation, and problem-solving skills.

✦ **CASE STUDY DISCUSSIONS.** Students are encouraged to anticipate problems and practice creative responses to challenges they will face living in a residence-hall community.

✦ **WEDNESDAY NIGHT WORKSHOPS.** Students discuss the challenges of adjusting successfully to college life, such as time and money management. Students are also encouraged to get involved, matching their talents with leadership opportunities.

✦ **INTER-DISCIPLINARY SOCIAL SCIENCES COURSE.** Students are challenged to articulate and grapple with their values. They examine obstacles such as sexism, racism, and classism, and discuss what it takes to make it today, both as an individual and as a community.

The institutional emphasis on leadership, service, and ethics is apparent from a student's first contact with campus. During orientation students participate in a service project. Books chosen for discussion during orientation, such as *Amazing Grace: The Lives of Children and the Conscience of the Nation* and *The Control of Nature,* reflect faculty eagerness to spark discussions of ethical issues. Faculty, student life staff, administrators, and upperclass student role models all work together to set a tone for new students at Wartburg which will encourage them to become contributing members of a caring community.

WASHINGTON STATE UNIVERSITY

PULLMAN, WA 99164
509.335.6000
http://www.wsu.edu/

UNDERGRADUATES: 16,000

For program information, please contact:
JEAN M. HENSCHEID, Ph.D.
henschj@mail.wsu.edu

Students taking responsibility for their own learning and collaborating to enrich the learning of their peers are central to the undergraduate experience at Washington State University. In keeping with this philosophy, the University's Freshman Seminar Program forms small learning communities in which new students negotiate, compromise, and research collaboratively on academic and social issues. Small groups of first-year students "co-enroll" for a minimum of two courses, including required entry-level courses and a Freshman Seminar. In these biweekly seminars, students learn to think critically, work with each other, access computer-based resources, and communicate with representatives from the campus and local communities, including librarians, instructional faculty, business owners, and social-service providers.

These first-year seminars have a twofold, character-building impact:

✦ **AUTHENTIC RESEARCH EXPERIENCE.** Each seminar group completes a major project that includes formulation of a research question, data collection, analysis, and presentation. Students present their findings to the campus and local communities at a major exposition near the end of every semester.

✦ **POSITIVE OUTCOMES.** The people who are objects of these studies can, and have, used these findings to inform their decision making on a range of issues, such as local radio programming, flood control, and increasing student involvement in the political process.

Students who participate in the Freshman Seminar earn better grades, are retained at the University at a higher rate, and demonstrate a higher level of academic confidence than nonparticipants. Equally important, they report a sense of belonging, accomplishment, and responsibility. These students are developing skills that are helping them make a difference today, and will help them do so for years to come.

WESTMINSTER COLLEGE

NEW WILMINGTON, PA 16172
724.946.8761
http://www.Westminster.edu/

UNDERGRADUATES: 1,400

For program information, please contact:
DAVID TWINING, Ph.D.
twinindc@Westminster.edu

"The Inquiry course challenged me, dragged me out of Plato's proverbial cave, and forced me to begin looking at the world as it truly is."

—A WESTMINSTER SECOND-YEAR STUDENT

As part of a new curriculum adopted several years ago, Westminster College launched a First-Year Program designed to provide all first-year students with a set of core experiences that challenge and engage students to confront questions that have traditionally been at the center of a liberal arts education. At the heart of the program are two courses, titled Inquiry I and II, which focus primarily on four questions: What do we know? What is the nature of humankind? What is the good and how can humans attain it? What should we make our ultimate concern?

Inquiry II specifically examines "ways of acting." The course investigates how humans have structured their families, economics, political lives, and religious and social organizations. A special concern of the course is understanding how culture shapes a group of individuals, and how individuals change and adapt their culture.

Westminster's faith heritage and affiliation with the Presbyterian Church (USA) provide an appropriate vantage point for examining these enduring questions. Students are expected to evaluate their own belief systems in the process of understanding others and developing a more mature and informed philosophy of life.

ACADEMIC HONESTY PROGRAMS

Academic honesty (or integrity) is the fundamental understanding that a person of character does not lie, steal, or cheat, especially in relationship to academic work. These principles may be supported in daily campus life by policies, enforcement procedures, sanctions, and educational programs that communicate the values of honesty, trust, respect, responsibility, and fairness. Although traditions, institutional missions, and student and faculty characteristics vary throughout the academy, exemplary academic honesty programs affirm and promote fundamental principles and standards for all members of the campus community.

ALLEGHENY COLLEGE

MEADVILLE, PA 16335
814.332.3100
http://www.alleg.edu/
UNDERGRADUATES: 1,800

For program information, please contact:
DAVE MCINALLY
dmcinall@alleg.edu

"Allegheny's Honor Code is central to its students' academic experience. Professors and students work together to increase knowledge of and appreciation for the Code."

—AN ALLEGHENY FOURTH-YEAR STUDENT

Personal integrity is the foundation of the honor program at Allegheny College, a private, liberal arts institution in northwest Pennsylvania. Developed by students in 1960 and administered by students since then, the Honor Code places the highest value on honesty and integrity in all matters, particularly academic work. This value is created and maintained through a variety of methods:

✦ All exams are unproctored and designed to emphasize original written work; students may complete exams in a variety of private locations.

✦ Twelve student representatives serve on the Honor Committee, accepting responsibility for educating students about the Honor Code and for preliminary investigation of alleged violations.

✦ Students sign the Honor Pledge on every piece of work submitted for academic credit.

✦ Students are informed of the Code through numerous publications and personal contacts before matriculating at Allegheny. The matriculation ceremony includes an address from the Honor Committee Chair, and all new students take the pledge for the first time in the presence of their parents and the entire faculty. The student body reaffirms its commitment to the Code through a student-wide referendum conducted every three years.

By teaching honesty and integrity as personal values that should be understood and taken to heart by every Allegheny student, the Honor Code provides an effective structure for regulating academic honesty. Its most enduring value, though, lies in the important lessons students learn about integrity and personal character—lessons that they will carry into all of life's settings.

BLUFFTON COLLEGE

280 WEST COLLEGE AVENUE
BLUFFTON, OH 45817
419.358.3000
http://www.bluffton.edu/
UNDERGRADUATES: 1,000

For program information, please contact:
JOHN KAMPEN, Ph.D.
kampenj@bluffton.edu

Bluffton College, a church-affiliated, liberal arts institution, has incorporated honesty and integrity into the essence of the school through its Honor System, which has been a significant part of campus life since the college's early years. As Bluffton grew, students and faculty determined a need for increased overt emphasis on academic integrity, good citizenship, and responsibility to one another. In response, the Honor System was developed, patterned after an honor code at Princeton University that was brought to Bluffton in 1913 by Professor H. W. Berky, who recognized the compatibility of such a system with the college's emphasis on honesty and self-reliance. Students at that time committed to live under such a system—a commitment that has continued in the student body for 85 years.

All aspects of Bluffton's academic honesty program demonstrate the great amount of trust placed in the students by the faculty:

✦ Students are reminded of the Honor System each time they take an exam or write a research paper.

✦ No monitors are present in classrooms during tests or exams.

✦ Students are asked to write and sign the following pledge on every examination paper: "I am unaware of any aid having been given or received during this examination." If a student cannot conscientiously sign this pledge, the course instructor is notified.

✦ Plagiarism is considered a serious violation of the Honor System. Reported offenses are normally resolved though the campus judicial system.

Although the honesty program applies specifically to the academic area, its spirit is meant to pervade all aspects of campus life. An integral part of the Bluffton community, the Honor System helps prepare students for a life based on personal responsibility and integrity.

BRANDEIS UNIVERSITY

415 SOUTH STREET
PO BOX 9110
WALTHAM, MA 02254-9110
781.736.3000
http://www.brandeis.edu/

UNDERGRADUATES: 3,000

For program information, please contact:
JEFFREY W. GRODEN-THOMAS
thomas@din.cc.brandeis.edu

"Brandeis will be an institution of quality, where the integrity of learning, of research, and of writing will not be compromised."
—BRANDEIS' FOUNDING PRESIDENT ABRAM SACHAR IN 1948

"Truth even unto its inner most parts," the motto of Brandeis University, a private, liberal arts institution, is the basis for the school's commitment to foster a community that supports the ideals of honesty and integrity. The academic integrity initiatives at Brandeis include the following:

✦ Each year, the University distributes, campus-wide, "Getting It Right: A Guide to Academic Integrity for the Brandeis Community," a brochure that addresses the significance of academic honesty issues.

✦ The first night new students are on campus, the Dean of Student Affairs delivers a strong caution about the risks of dishonest behavior, both in and out of the classroom.

✦ Students and staff work together to produce an annual program on academic integrity, mandatory for all new students, that includes student and faculty presentations and educational workshops.

✦ Because Brandeis subscribes to a peer-judgment system, students are selected annually to the University Board of Student Conduct, which takes an active role not only in addressing and determining outcomes for student conduct cases, but also in providing preventative measures to academic dishonesty.

✦ Examination bluebooks include the University's honesty statement and a signature block.

At Brandeis, every member of the community shares the responsibility for protecting the academic integrity of the institution. Brandeis' academic honesty initiatives play an important role in the development of students, helping to ensure that they pursue their academic goals with the utmost of integrity and respect for the campus community.

BRIDGEWATER COLLEGE

402 EAST COLLEGE STREET
BRIDGEWATER, VA 22812-1599
540.828.8000
http://www.bridgewater.edu/

UNDERGRADUATES: 1,200

For program information, please contact:
WILLIAM E. ABSHIRE, PH.D.
wabshire@bridgewater.edu

Personal honor, integrity, and respect for the word of another are the bases of the Bridgewater College Honor Code. Reflecting the ethos of Bridgewater, a Christian liberal arts college, the Code focuses on developing student character, rather than just punishing the lack of it. Key aspects of the Code include the following:

✦ A brochure containing the Honor Code is mailed to incoming students, who, along with their parents, attend an Honor System presentation during summer orientation.

✦ The Code is discussed at an annual assembly of the student body, and a representative of the Honor System introduces the program to each new student as part of the required first-year Personal Development Portfolio program.

✦ Framed statements about personal honor are displayed in all Bridgewater classrooms, and faculty are encouraged to include a statement about the Code on syllabi, speak about the Code and Honor System in first class sessions, remind students of the Code at test time, and include matters of personal honor in course work.

✦ The Honor Council, which began 50 years ago and is overseen by Student Government, is composed of 12 students who deal aggressively with academic lying, cheating, and stealing. Two faculty members serve as Council advisors, and faculty, staff, and administrators provide any information and documentation requested as part of an investigation.

✦ Honor System announcements and results of inquiries are posted on a bulletin board in the Campus Center building, and results of Council investigations are posted campus-wide and printed in the campus newspaper.

In a recent survey, the majority of students favored retaining Bridgewater's Honor Code, a system that enables students to practice civic responsibility on campus and in their wider world – strong indication that the college's efforts to stress the importance of academic integrity is not only effective, but also beneficial.

CALVIN COLLEGE

3201 BURTON STREET, SE
GRAND RAPIDS, MI 49546
616.957.6000
http://www.calvin.edu/

UNDERGRADUATES: 3,900

For program information, please contact:
DEAN WARD, Ph.D.
Ward@calvin.edu

Calvin College, a church-affiliated, liberal arts school, has woven its Academic Writing Program into the entire curriculum, creating an effective venue for faculty to nurture academic integrity. English 101, Written Rhetoric, is the cornerstone of the program and is required of all students. In this course, students are exposed to two institutional documents:

✦ *The First Faith and the Teaching of Writing* sets forth the school's philosophy and includes the following statements:

We witness the power and the beauty of written communication, its potential for perpetrating as well as exposing falsehood, for degrading as well as inspiring, for creating chaos as well as nurturing order.

We see writing as something that goes on in the real world, not as an artificial exercise that goes on only between student and teacher. After confronting a realistic rhetorical situation, writers must evaluate their aims and audience, and ask: Is my aim consistent with my Christian commitments?

We believe that we are training students for leadership in the community, as a means to redeeming our culture. They must therefore believe in and train them to become adept in clear, honest, ethical public argument.

✦ *Policy on Plagiarism* establishes the following viewpoint: "Plagiarism is not only legally but morally wrong" and is "inimical to values and ideals of a Christian educational institution." Calvin's approach to plagiarism does not focus on illegality but on corruption of integrity.

Calvin's aim is that students not only will make appropriate moral choices as they write college papers but also will prepare for the moral acuity and ethical practice that they should exercise in their professional writing. The Writing Program applies the ethical vision of both *Policy on Plagiarism* and *Faith and the Teaching of Writing.* That vision is at the heart of Calvin College's identity—an identity proudly maintained by both faculty and students.

COLLEGE OF THE OZARKS

POINT LOOKOUT, MO 65726
417.334.6411
http://www.cofo.edu/

UNDERGRADUATES: 1,500

For program information, please contact:
KENTON C. OLSON, Ph.D.
olson@cofo.edu

"Even though we're known as Hard Work U, my experiences here lead me to believe that we could also be called Honest U."

—AN OZARKS FOURTH-YEAR STUDENT

College of the Ozarks, a coeducational liberal arts school called "Hard Work U" by the *Wall Street Journal,* is unique among U.S. institutions of higher education in that it charges no tuition, requires all students to work on campus, and discourages debt. A five-fold mission stressing not only academics but also vocational, cultural, patriotic, and spiritual growth underscores the college's philosophy of educating the whole person. The development of character and responsibility in its students has been an integral part of the purpose of the school since its founding in 1906, and academic integrity is one of its most basic tenets. Two distinct elements of College of the Ozarks' academic honesty efforts are:

✦ **CHARACTER CAMP.** Prior to enrolling for classes, all Ozarks students participate in a special, two-week orientation that focuses on character development and covers plagiarism, cheating, and other issues related to academic integrity.

✦ **HONOR INDUCTION BANQUET.** All new students attend the banquet, where they sign an Honor Code card stating, "I agree to be an honest, trustworthy, caring and responsible citizen. I will uphold these values in others and myself."

Because of its serious commitment to education, College of the Ozarks insists upon rigorous academics and high expectations inside the classroom that will prepare students to be lifelong learners as well as men and women of maturity and responsibility. Lying, stealing, and cheating are absolutely not tolerated inside the classroom, just as they would not be tolerated in the outside world. Through its character development initiatives, the College of the Ozarks helps its students to become individuals of integrity, honesty, and honor.

CONNECTICUT COLLEGE

270 MOHEGAN AVENUE
NEW LONDON, CT 06320
860.447.1911
http://www.conncoll.edu/

UNDERGRADUATES: 1,600

For program information, please contact:
LINDA VAN DOREN
cmwoo@conncoll.edu

Connecticut College, a private, liberal arts institution, views its unique Honor System as a crucial component of the campus community that provides students with both freedom and responsibility. When students sign the college's Certificate of Matriculation, or Honor Code Pledge, they accept the responsibilities that the student body has established and agree to live within them. Every member of the Connecticut College community is expected to participate in upholding the Honor Code in order to maintain an atmosphere of fair academic competition and mutual respect of individual rights.

The Honor System is carried out through:

✦ **RESPONSIBILITIES OF THE STUDENT.** First, students must be aware of the regulations of the college and behave accordingly. Students who break any of these rules must turn themselves in to the chair of the Judiciary Board and be accountable for their actions. Second, students who become aware that someone else has committed an infraction should remind the individual to report himself or herself to the Judiciary Board Chair.

✦ **RESPONSIBILITIES OF THE JUDICIARY BOARD.** The Judiciary Board is responsible for hearing cases of suspected infractions of the Honor Code and arriving at an appropriate verdict and decision based on the evidence presented.

Academic honor is of prime importance in maintaining the high standards of scholarship in the Connecticut College community. Although all matriculated students are already honor bound, the following pledge must be written and signed on every examination: "I promise to neither give nor receive any aid on this examination." Steps such as this help to ensure that Connecticut College students continue to uphold the institution's Honor System, thus securing for future students the same freedom and responsibility they enjoy.

HAMPDEN-SYDNEY COLLEGE

COLLEGE ROAD
HAMPDEN-SYDNEY, VA 23943
804.223.6000
http://www.hsc.edu/

UNDERGRADUATES: 1,000

For program information, please contact:
LEWIS H. DREW, Ph.D.
lewisd@hsc.edu

"The Code isn't just a set of rules; it's a way of life. We hold ourselves to high standards in all aspects of our lives."

—A HAMPDEN-SYDNEY THIRD-YEAR STUDENT

Hampden-Sydney College, a private, liberal arts school for men founded in 1776, remains committed to its original statement of purpose: "To form good men and good citizens in an atmosphere of sound learning." The heart of the College's Honor Code is individual responsibility.

Components of Hampden-Sydney's Honor Code include:

✦ **THE COLLEGE'S CANDIDATE'S GUIDE.** Written by students and provided to all prospective students, the guide stresses the devotion of Hampden-Sydney students to the principles embodied in the Honor Code.

✦ **STUDENT COURT.** Through the faculty, College trustees delegate authority for the operation and enforcement of the Honor Code to the students. Thus it is a student-run system, with the Student Court having the full authority to suspend or expel a student from the college for violating the Code.

✦ **HONOR CONVOCATION.** The president of the College addresses new students in an Honor Convocation their first night on campus, speaking about the spirit of the Honor Code and about the ways in which its principles are inextricably connected to the College's mission.

✦ **SMALL-GROUP DISCUSSION.** Immediately following the Honor Convocation, the ten students serving on the Student Court, all elected by their fellow students, lead small groups in discussion of the precepts of the Honor Code and the mechanics of the system. Every new student is required to sign a statement that he commits to living under the Honor Code.

Hampden-Sydney College's Honor Code is part of an institutional effort to create an environment in which students developmentally learn to balance freedom and responsibility and become accountable for their actions, on their way to becoming self-disciplined men.

HAVERFORD COLLEGE

370 LANCASTER AVENUE
HAVERFORD, PA 19041-1392
610.896.1000
http://www.haverford.edu/

UNDERGRADUATES: 1,100

For program information, please contact:
HELENE POLLOCK
hpollock@haverford.edu

LEWIS AND CLARK COLLEGE

0615 S.W. PALATINE HILL ROAD
PORTLAND, OR 97219-7899
503.768.7188
http://www.lclark.edu/

UNDERGRADUATES: 1,900

For program information, please contact:
MICHAEL FORD, Ph.D.
mford@lclark.edu

Haverford College, a liberal arts and sciences school founded in 1833, follows a student-run Honor System based on the belief that students can take responsibility for establishing and maintaining standards for their own behavior. The college's Honor Code, which is the foundation of the Honor System, is not a list of rules, but rather a philosophy of conduct governed by honesty, integrity, and understanding. Components of Haverford College's Honor System include:

✦ **HONOR PLEDGE CARD.** Upon admission, all new students must sign a card that states: "I hereby accept the Haverford Honor Code, realizing that it is my responsibility to uphold the Honor Code and the attitudes of personal and collective honor upon which it is based."

✦ **STUDENT RESPONSIBILITY.** Students are expected to take full responsibility under the Honor Code for their conduct and integrity in all academic work, including all homework assignments, papers, and examinations, and to confront those who do not. In return, they are trusted with a greater degree of freedom in their academic pursuits.

✦ **UNMONITORED TESTS.** Take-home and unproctored examinations are a routine part of the Haverford experience.

✦ **THE HONOR COUNCIL.** Consisting of 16 elected students (four from each academic-year class), the Council fosters awareness of the Honor Code and helps to resolve questions and issues concerning the Code throughout the academic year. First-year students are introduced to the Code through group discussions with their Honor Code representatives.

Haverford's Honor Code makes it possible for members of a diverse student body to live together, interact, and learn from one another in ways that protect both personal freedom and community standards. It also creates a climate of trust, concern, and respect among students, faculty, and staff—a climate that allows learning to flourish.

Lewis and Clark College, founded in 1867, is a private, church-affiliated institution that strives to comprehensively and consistently address issues of student conduct in both classroom and cocurricular settings. Over the years, this educational community has made positive strides in modifying policies, updating the Student Code of Conduct, and revising judicial systems to make them more effective.

Lewis and Clark takes the following steps to promote and safeguard its academic integrity policy:

✦ References to the policy are included in admission materials and the student handbook, The Pathfinder, clearly states that matriculation signals acceptance of the policy.

✦ The policy is printed in a variety of locations, including in a handout for new students, in the Student Code of Conduct, in the College Catalog, and on the inside cover of bluebooks.

✦ Resident Assistants, Resident Directors, Student Life staff, and faculty members are knowledgeable of policy definitions and related procedures.

✦ A copy of the policy is included with materials given to first-year students, and the policy is personally presented by the Chair of the Honor Board.

✦ Statistics of cases adjudicated are published annually in the Academic Integrity Policy and Procedures brochure.

Lewis and Clark College believes that each member of the community is responsible for the integrity of his or her own academic performance. In addition, because each act of dishonesty harms the entire community, all members are responsible for encouraging the integrity of others, by their own example, by confronting individuals they observe committing dishonest acts, and by discussing such actions with a faculty member or academic dean. The principles of mutual respect, academic integrity, and responsible decision making lead in only one direction—toward personal and academic excellence.

LYON COLLEGE

2300 HIGHLAND ROAD
BATESVILLE, AR 72503
870.793.9813
http://www.lyon.edu/

UNDERGRADUATES: 500

For program information, please contact:
BRUCE JOHNSTON, Ed.D.
bjohnston@lyon.edu

An effective honor system sets forth a way of living rather than a set of rules. The purpose of the honor system at Lyon College, a church-affiliated, liberal arts institution, is to instill in students, through positive peer pressure and the force of intellectual reason, the value of integrity and the importance of doing their own work.

Aspects of Lyon's academic honesty system include the following:

✦ Prior to enrolling, students receive several essays that reflect on the reasons that Lyon has an honor system.

✦ Students may not register for classes before signing Lyon's Roll of Honor, which signifies their support for the honor system. Faculty members also sign the Roll of Honor.

✦ Course syllabi contain a statement about the honor system as the responsibility of each person at the College. Each course is taught with the honor system as a significant element.

✦ Each piece of academic work submitted for a grade is signed with the word "pledged," indicating that the student is submitting it under the honor system.

✦ The Honor Council, composed of 12 students elected by their peers, orients new students to the honor system and adjudicates alleged violations.

✦ The Freshman Advising Program includes an academic course that features the honor system as a significant dimension of the Lyon Experience.

✦ Students are responsible for proctoring tests themselves, are permitted to take their tests wherever they choose, and often are able to self-schedule their tests and examinations.

All members of the Lyon College community are required to abide by the honor system and to confront anyone they believe may have violated it. Lyon students learn through experience that few things in life are more valuable than knowing they are trusted and that their word is their bond.

METHODIST COLLEGE

5400 RAMSEY STREET
FAYETTEVILLE, NC 28311
910.630.7000
http://www.methodist.edu/

UNDERGRADUATES: 1,400

For program information, please contact:
RICHARD WALSH, Ph.D.
rwalsh@methodist.edu

"The Methodist College Honor Code helps create a bond of trust between students and professor that allows us to work freely together to reach our academic and career goals."

—A METHODIST THIRD-YEAR STUDENT

Methodist College, a private, church-affiliated, liberal arts institution, operates under an Honor Code that provides guidelines for academic integrity for faculty and students, encouraging them to respect the work of others as well as their own. The Honor Code was established in 1986 at the request of the Student Government Association in light of student allegations that widespread cheating was taking place. During a full academic ceremony implementing the new Honor Code, students signed an honor book indicating their agreement to abide by the code. In subsequent years, each entering student signed the honor book as part of an academic ceremony, which took place on the first day of the orientation class required of all new students. It is no longer feasible to have only one orientation class, so the matter is now taken up in sections. The emphasis remains, however, on the importance of honesty and respect. To this end, all academic work bears not only the students' names but also their signatures and the word "pledged" to indicate that they are abiding by the Honor Code.

Finding that its entering students are less and less cognizant of the character and virtue required of one participating in an academic community, the College has had to work harder to instill a sense of honor among students. Thus, the School of Business has recently included an ethics component in each one of its classes, particularly the "Introduction to Business" course.

Through its student-initiated Honor Code, Methodist College lives out its motto, *"Veritas et virtus,"* inculcating in its students a love of truth, both as a quest for knowledge and as a matter of personal honesty.

MILLSAPS COLLEGE

1701 NORTH STATE STREET
JACKSON, MS 39210
601.974.1000
http://www.millsaps.edu/

UNDERGRADUATES: 1,200

For program information, please contact:
KEVIN RUSSELL
russeka@millsaps.edu

"Our Honor Code wasn't imposed upon students by the Administration; rather, it emerged out of students' genuine desire to strengthen the values of our community."

—A MILLSAPS THIRD-YEAR STUDENT

Millsaps College, a private, church-affiliated, liberal arts institution, is dedicated to the pursuit of scholarly inquiry and intellectual growth in an environment of personal honesty and mutual trust. Through their Honor Code, students at Millsaps affirm their adherence to the basic ethical principles needed in such an environment. Millsaps' Honor Code permeates campus life in a number of ways:

✦ All entering students must sign the Honor Code as part of the application for admission.

✦ A formal signing ceremony is held during Freshman Orientation, and the signature pages are bound into the Honor Book, which is part of the college's permanent archives.

✦ In every class, the Honor Code and its implications are discussed on the first day as part of the syllabus.

✦ Each assignment or examination submitted is pledged as being the individual's own work. In most classes, professors do not proctor examinations except to be available to answer questions.

✦ Both faculty and students are obligated to report violations of the Code to the Honor Council, which is composed of faculty and students from every academic-year class.

✦ Since the Honor Council is student-organized and student-led, the students themselves have primary responsibility for hearing cases, weighing the evidence, and recommending sanctions.

Students and faculty at Millsaps are committed to the concept of academic integrity and take their responsibilities to each other and to the Honor Code very seriously, fully embracing the philosophy that an Honor Code is not simply a set of rules and procedures governing academic conduct, but an opportunity to put personal responsibility and integrity into action.

MOUNT HOLYOKE COLLEGE

COLLEGE STREET
SOUTH HADLEY, MA 01075-1488
413.538.2000
http://www.mtholyoke.edu/

UNDERGRADUATES: 1,900

For program information, please contact:
BEVERLY DANIEL TATUM, Ph.D.
btatum@mtholyoke.edu

A private, liberal arts school for women founded in 1837, Mount Holyoke College abides by an Honor Code that governs both social interactions and academic performance. All members of the college community choose to live by this simple but powerful statement: "I will honor myself, my fellow students, and Mount Holyoke College by acting responsibly, honestly, and respectfully in both my words and deeds."

Because the Honor Code is such an integral part of Mount Holyoke life, it is supported in numerous ways:

✦ Before students arrive on campus, they receive a copy of the Honor Code, which is published in the Student Handbook.

✦ Before classes begin, during orientation, students participate in a special ceremony in which they publicly sign the Honor Code.

✦ A student who observes another student in a clear violation of academic responsibility is obligated to maintain the integrity of the honor system by making the violation known to the instructor or to the Dean of the College.

✦ Students can choose the time they will take each final exam. The exams are proctored by other students.

✦ Violations of the Honor Code that are not academic in nature are adjudicated by a nine-member student judicial board. The judicial board is advised by the Dean of Students.

Mount Holyoke's honor system, which derives its strength from the honesty and self-discipline of every student and from the faith of the faculty and the administration in the student body, promotes individual freedom tempered by responsibility to the community. Students under the Honor Code grow to understand, through course work, collaborative learning, and living together, that honor is achieved through diligence, commitment, and courage.

MUHLENBERG COLLEGE

2400 CHEW STREET
ALLENTOWN, PA 18104-5586
610.821.3100
http://www.muhlenberg.edu/

UNDERGRADUATES: 1,900

For program information, please contact:
CAROL SHINER WILSON, Ph.D.
lwilson@muhlenberg.edu

Muhlenberg College, a private, church-affiliated, liberal arts institution, insists that its students conduct themselves honestly in all academic activities. Believing that academic honesty is a matter of individual and institutional responsibility and that each member of the community is harmed when standards of honesty are violated, the College has established standards of academic conduct. As prerequisite for matriculation and registration each semester, students must pledge to adhere to the Academic Behavior Code, thereby accepting their share of the responsibility for maintaining the institution's standards of academic integrity. Furthermore, on all work submitted for a grade, students are required to write and sign a pledge indicating their compliance with the code.

Both students and faculty are responsible for the success of Muhlenberg's Academic Behavior Code:

✦ Students are expected to be familiar with and adhere to the Code. Students foster compliance by urging any student suspected of violating the Code to discuss the matter with the appropriate faculty member.

✦ Faculty members are expected to be familiar with the Code. At the beginning of each semester, they must identify the procedures to be used for classroom exams and other assignments in their courses.

✦ Faculty members are expected to implement the Code at all times. Should this not be the case, students may direct their concerns to the appropriate department head.

When violations of the Code occur, faculty and staff engage the accused in serious conversation regarding the alleged violation. Such conversations enable students to reflect upon their personal integrity and give the College an opportunity to stress the importance of fairness to others and honesty with oneself. In this and in many other ways, Muhlenberg seeks to incorporate the practice of academic integrity into the very fabric of each student's life.

NORTHWESTERN UNIVERSITY

1801 HINMAN AVENUE
EVANSTON, IL 60204-3060
847.491.3741
http://www.nwu.edu/

UNDERGRADUATES: 7,700

For program information, please contact:
DAN GARRISON, Ph.D.
d-garrison@nwu.edu

At Northwestern University, a private, comprehensive institution, academic integrity is based on respect for individual achievement that lies at the heart of academic culture. The Undergraduate Academic Conduct Committee, composed of students, faculty, and an administrator, recommends institutional policy and informs members of the community about their rights and obligations under the university's principles of academic integrity.

Northwestern distributes to all students eight cardinal rules of academic integrity:

✦ KNOW YOUR RIGHTS. Do not let other students in your class diminish the value of your achievement by taking unfair advantage. Report any academic dishonesty you see.

✦ ACKNOWLEDGE YOUR SOURCES.

✦ PROTECT YOUR WORK. In examinations, do not allow your neighbors to see what you have written; you are the only one who should receive credit for what you know.

✦ AVOID SUSPICION. Do not put yourself in a position where you can be suspected of having copied another person's work or of having used unauthorized notes in an examination.

✦ DO YOUR OWN WORK. The purpose of assignments is to develop your skills and measure your progress. Letting someone else do your work defeats the purpose of your education

✦ NEVER FALSIFY A RECORD or permit another person to do so.

✦ NEVER FABRICATE DATA, citations, or experimental results.

✦ ALWAYS TELL THE TRUTH when discussing your work with your instructor.

Northwestern's faculty members and students make up a community of scholars in which academic integrity is a fundamental commitment—a commitment that is renewed every day.

Presbyterian College

503 SOUTH BROAD STREET
CLINTON, SC 29325
864.833.2820
http://www.presby.edu/

UNDERGRADUATES: 1,100

For program information, please contact:
J. DAVID GILLESPIE, Ph.D.
dgillesp@cs1.presby.edu

"Since the Honor Code at Presbyterian is student run, professors and students have a mutual respect for it, leading to a trust that one cannot find on many campuses."

—A PRESBYTERIAN THIRD-YEAR STUDENT

Presbyterian College, a private, church-affiliated, liberal arts institution, proves wrong the common view that students at a small college where "everyone knows everyone" might find it burdensome to enforce upon others the requirements of the institution's Honor Code. Beyond their obligation to refrain from violating the Code, students, like faculty and staff, are pledged to report the confirmed or suspected violations of others and, in fact, Presbyterian students initiate a substantial proportion of the charges of Code violation, usually through a report to the professor in whose class the alleged violation has taken place. Additionally, students serving in judicial capacities have proven to be at least as inclined as their faculty counterparts to impose the normal penalty upon a finding that the Code has been broken. Eighteen students—nine seniors, six juniors, and three sophomores—along with six faculty members serve on the Judicial Council. The Council Chair, a senior, selects new members from a list of students who apply to serve.

The College's Honor Code tangibly benefits the quality of community life at Presbyterian. As the College points out in its catalog, "The commitment to honor has its rewards: taking tests or writing papers with the expectation that everyone will do his or her own work; leaving doors unlocked; leaving books or personal property unattended; and rescheduling tests because of conflicts. But along with these privileges [also come] responsibilities: a respect for the ideas, values, and property of others [and] a readiness to subordinate one's own interests to the interests and well being of the whole . . . community." These are values that Presbyterian instills in its students to carry with them as established practices for a lifetime.

Princeton University

PRINCETON, NJ 08544
609.258.3000
http://www.princeton.edu/

UNDERGRADUATES: 4,600

For program information, please contact:
JANINA MONTERO, Ph.D.
janimont@princeton.edu

Princeton University, a private, comprehensive institution, was founded in 1746; its Honor System was established in 1893 and has become an integral part of the code by which the campus community lives. Students have a two-fold obligation: individually, they must not violate the code, and as a community, they are responsible to see that suspected violations are reported.

Princeton's Honor System is fostered and enforced in a variety of ways:

✦ A letter explaining the Honor System is sent by the chair of the Honor Committee to each newly admitted student, who then signs a statement expressing willingness to abide by the Honor System. Final entrance to the University is contingent upon the committee's receipt of this statement.

✦ Status as a student in good standing and graduation from Princeton are contingent upon continued participation in the Honor System.

✦ The Honor Committee consists of three current class presidents, three past class presidents, and three undergraduates selected by application from the student body at large. Two additional undergraduates are selected from the student body at large to serve as alternates.

✦ Under the Honor System, students assume full responsibility for honesty in written examinations, which are not supervised.

✦ On each examination paper, students write out and sign the following statement: "I pledge my honor that I have not violated the honor code during this examination."

Princeton's Honor System was established by the undergraduates more than 100 years ago and has been in effect without interruption since that time. Its success is due to the generations of students who have respected it and by common agreement have given it the highest place among their obligations as members of the Princeton community.

RHODES COLLEGE

2000 NORTH PARKWAY
MEMPHIS, TN 38112
901.843.3000
http://www.rhodes.edu/

UNDERGRADUATES: 1,500

For program information, please contact:
KATHERINE OWEN RICHARDSON, Ph.D.
owen@rhodes.edu

"The Honor Code not only stands as a symbol to remind students of their obligations as members of the Rhodes community but also as a guide for living beyond the college years."
—A RHODES THIRD-YEAR STUDENT

Students at Rhodes College, a small, private, liberal arts institution, find within the school's honor system a moral ideal by which to guide their actions: the ideal of absolute honesty to oneself and to others in all aspects of life. The objective of the honor system is the student's spiritual, moral, and intellectual development, which is nurtured by the freedom and responsibility inherent in the honor system. All members of the Rhodes community are required to uphold the Code and to report suspected violations.

Students play a vital role in safeguarding academic honesty at Rhodes:

✦ Students elect an Honor Council, comprised of representatives from each of the four academic-year classes, which is charged with enforcing the Honor Code.

✦ The Honor Council presents academic-honesty information to first-year and transfer students during orientation, at which time a formal ceremony is held. Students sign their names in a leather-bound volume beneath the statement: "I pledge that I will neither lie, cheat, nor steal as a member of the Rhodes community and that I will report any such violations that I may witness."

✦ Upon completion of course work, students pledge: "I have neither given nor received aid on this work, nor have I witnessed any such violation of the Code."

The honor system, instituted at Rhodes well before the turn of the century, is a tradition, an inheritance, and an opportunity: a tradition because it is and has been a valued possession of Rhodes students since the early days of the school; an inheritance because each entering class receives it from the previous class as a gift to be proud of and respected; and above all, an opportunity because it allows the fullest possible expression of individual life in harmony with community life.

ST. OLAF COLLEGE

1520 ST. OLAF AVENUE
NORTHFIELD, MN 55057
507.646.2222
http://www.stolaf.edu/

UNDERGRADUATES: 2,900

For program information, please contact:
STEVE MCKELVEY, Ph.D.
mckelvey@stolaf.edu

"The Honor Code brings ethics to the forefront. It implies respect and trust, and that I have integrity. It says something about the integrity of the whole school as well."
—A ST. OLAF FOURTH-YEAR STUDENT

The Honor System at St. Olaf, a private, church-affiliated college, expresses an agreement between the student body and the faculty that the students will be responsible for honest conduct during written examinations. For St. Olaf's students, every examination becomes an opportunity to practice the virtues of personal responsibility.

The Honor System is clearly visible in campus life:

✦ As part of new student orientation, the Dean of Students provides students with information on the Honor System.

✦ All tests, quizzes, and examinations of any kind are taken under the auspices of the Honor System.

✦ Every examination bears a statement with two clauses. "I pledge my honor that during this examination I have neither given nor received assistance, and that I have seen no dishonest work." A student's failure to sign this pledge indicates that in the student's opinion the system was violated during the examination. In such cases, the matter is turned over to the Honor Council.

✦ The student-elected Honor Council is made up of three senior students, two juniors, one sophomore, and one first-year student, as well as one nonvoting faculty adviser. Faculty agree to honor the findings of the Honor Council. For members of the Honor Council, the act of investigating possible honor-code violations, hearing testimony from witnesses, and sitting in judgment of those accused provides a powerful lesson in civic responsibility.

Not only by conducting themselves honestly, but also by bringing forth information concerning any unethical behavior on the part of others, students maintain the high level of academic honesty at St. Olaf's.

TEXAS A&M UNIVERSITY

COLLEGE STATION, TX 77843
409.845.3211
http://www.tamu.edu/
UNDERGRADUATES: 34,000

For program information, please contact:
KIM NOVAK
klm@stulife2.tamu.edu

"The Code reminds students that honor and integrity are more than words; they're a way of life."
—A TEXAS A&M FIRST-YEAR STUDENT

The Code of Honor at Texas A&M University, a public, comprehensive school, is an institutional effort to unify the aims of all its students toward a high level of ethics and personal dignity. The Code functions as a symbol to all "Aggies," promoting loyalty to truth and confidence in one other. Simply stated, "Aggies do not lie, cheat, or steal, nor do they tolerate those who do." The University publishes separate educational brochures for students and faculty that explain the idea of academic integrity, describe actions that violate the concept, and outline the University's Scholastic Dishonesty Process, which is established to address alleged violations. The steps of the process are as follows:

✦ The instructor meets with the student suspected of the violation and determines if a violation was committed.

✦ If an instructor determines that no violation occurred, the case is dismissed. If an instructor decides that a violation has occurred, appropriate sanctions would be recommended to the department head.

✦ If the student decides to appeal the sanction decided upon by the instructor, the case is brought before the department head. At this point, the department head may decide to either dismiss the case or uphold the sanction.

✦ An appeal of the department head's decision is forwarded to the dean. The dean may review the case with or without a hearing. Again, the decision may be dismissed, upheld, or lessened.

✦ Appeals of the dean's decision are brought before the appropriate Appeals Panel, whose decisions are final.

Although Texas A&M has this process in place, it continues to work with students and faculty on what it believes is the best method of handling violations of academic integrity: preventative measures that will avoid them altogether.

UNITED STATES AIR FORCE ACADEMY

USAF ACADEMY, CO 80840-5025
719.333.4904
http://www.usafa.af.mil/
UNDERGRADUATES: 4,100

For program information, please contact:
LIEUTENANT COLONEL JOHN H. HERD
HerdJH.34CWC@USAFA.AF.MILs

"Tell the truth, live the truth, be the truth," says Medal of Honor recipient Paul S. Bucha. The United States Air Force Academy's Honor Code establishes a minimum standard that all cadets must uphold. Integrity development at the Academy is designed to push cadets beyond the minimum to the highest level of honorable conduct and includes these initiatives:

✦ HONOR CODE. Each cadet takes the Honor Oath: "We will not lie, steal, or cheat, nor tolerate among us anyone who does. Furthermore, I resolve to do my duty and to live honorably, so help me God."

✦ ACADEMICS WITH HONOR. To address academic integrity, faculty members distribute and discuss the Academic Honesty Policy at the beginning of each course, reminding cadets about the issues of fairness, honesty, and integrity in the submission of work.

✦ HONOR EDUCATION PROGRAM. Cadets receive honor education during all four years at the Academy. The program's 42 lessons, which sometimes feature guest speakers, include material on honor principles, honor system administration, application, and case studies.

✦ HONOR BOARD. Cadets accused of violating the Honor Code are subject to a trial by jury of their peers. Cadets administrate the entire judicial process and decide upon the guilt or innocence of the accused.

✦ HONOR PROBATION PROGRAM. Although disenrollment is the presumed sanction for all Honor Code violators, the Commandant may order a probationary period, which gives violators the opportunity to perform in a manner that removes doubts about their qualifications to be USAF officers with the highest degree of integrity.

The United States Air Force Academy is committed to instilling in its graduates a sense of honor essential to leadership. The system enables cadets to learn and develop integrity so that it becomes an essential part of their character.

UNITED STATES MILITARY ACADEMY

606 THAYER ROAD
WEST POINT, NY 10996
914.938.4041
http://www.usma.edu/

UNDERGRADUATES: 4,000

For program information, please contact:
COLONEL GEORGE B. FORSYTHE
zb8085@usma.edu

"The Honor Code at West Point creates a rapport and trust between the faculty and the cadets that frees up the classroom for its true purpose."

—A WEST POINT THIRD-YEAR STUDENT

The mission of the United States Military Academy, America's oldest service academy, is to develop leaders of character. At West Point, all three programs comprising the Cadet Leader Development System—Academic Program, Military Program, and Physical Program—stress the Honor Code. This integrated approach to character development is known worldwide. For the past 13 years, the Academy has hosted the National Conference on Ethics in America, which brings together students from colleges and universities throughout the United States to discuss character development on college campuses. The USMA's academic integrity program includes:

✦ The Honor Code, "A cadet will not lie, cheat, or steal, or tolerate those who do," governs all aspects of cadet life. From the first day at West Point, cadets are expected to live by the Code and to confront and, if necessary, report other cadets who violate it.

✦ Academic courses are designed to produce graduates who can engage in moral discourse, examine moral implications of situations, analyze ethical responses to moral problems, and promote ethical conduct within their organizations.

✦ Faculty members lead seminars with cadets on topics of professional ethics, thus connecting academic and professional development.

✦ Faculty members also mentor, coach, and advise cadets involved in intercollegiate sports and extracurricular activities; matters of integrity are an important part of their service in this role.

In some professions the cost of dishonesty is measured in dollars—in the Army, the cost is measured in human lives. The United States Military Academy expects its graduates and cadets to commit to a lifetime of honorable living; the successful defense of the nation relies on that.

UNITED STATES NAVAL ACADEMY

121 BLAKE ROAD
ANNAPOLIS, MD 21302
410.293.1000
http://www.USNA.edu/

UNDERGRADUATES: 4,000

For program information, please contact:
LCDR BRIAN GOODROW
goodrow@nadn.navy.mil

In preparing young men and women to become professional officers, the United States Naval Academy focuses on moral, mental, and physical development. The Academy seeks to instill in the midshipmen the highest ideals of duty, honor, and loyalty. In pursuit of this, it has established the Academic Integrity Program, which spans all four years of the students' education. Providing unique challenges and training each year, the program serves as a means for midshipmen to build character and develop a commitment to doing what is right.

The Academic Integrity Program includes:

✦ THE HONOR CONCEPT OF THE BRIGADE OF MIDSHIPMEN. Developed and enforced by the midshipmen themselves, the Honor Concept stipulates that they are persons of integrity and that they stand for what is right.

✦ THE HONOR EDUCATION PROGRAM. The four-year training program on the Honor Concept includes explanation and discussion of expectations and standards, as well as case studies.

✦ CORE VALUE TRAINING. Leaders of the training are distinguished guest speakers who address their personal and professional experiences in relation to the Navy's core values of honor, courage, and commitment.

The Naval Academy exists to prepare young men and women who want to dedicate themselves to making the ultimate civic contribution: service to their county. Thus the two overarching themes continually reinforced in the Academic Integrity Program—the ability to distinguish right from wrong, and the strength and moral courage to do the right thing—are meant not only to affect their midshipman experiences, but also to shape their future service to the nation.

University of California, Davis

DAVIS, CA 95616-8678
530.752.1011
http://www.ucdavis.edu/
UNDERGRADUATES: 18,800

For program information, please contact:
JEANNE M. WILSON, J.D.
jxwilson@ucdavis.edu

"Our academic integrity policies at UC–Davis provoke students to reflect on their own ethics and values. We hope students realize that following community standards develops their own sense of personal integrity."
—A UC-DAVIS PROFESSOR

The office for Student Judicial Affairs (SJA) at the University of California, Davis, a public, comprehensive institution, promotes academic integrity by enforcing the Code of Academic Conduct, publishing and disseminating standards for ethical academic behavior, conducting educational programs, and facilitating student learning through the disciplinary process. SJA's educational approach to discipline encourages the moral development of students who break the rules, fostering skills for making ethical decisions and helping them to avoid similar breaches in the future.

SJA also provides leadership opportunities for student members of the Campus Judicial Board (CJB) in outreach education, in the disciplinary process, and as peer educators:

✦ CJB students plan and carry out a variety of publications, presentations, and events each year, culminating in an annual Integrity Week program.

✦ CJB students help draft the "Campus Judicial Report," a summary of new referrals and resolved cases, which is published weekly in the campus newspaper.

✦ In formal disciplinary hearings, CJB students serve not only as members of the student-faculty decision panels but also as advisors or advocates for referred students and the referring faculty alike.

✦ CJB members work directly with students in several capacities outside the adversarial hearing process.

Through its varied activities, UC–Davis's Student Judicial Affairs provokes students to reflect on their own ethics and values and to commit to making decisions in the future that will be consistent with community standards and their own personal integrity.

University of Maryland College Park

COLLEGE PARK, MD 20742
301.405.1000
http://www.umd.edu/
UNDERGRADUATES: 34,000

For program information, please contact:
GARY PAVELA, Ph.D.
gpavela@oz.umd.edu

The University of Maryland College Park, a public, comprehensive institution, has a nationally known academic integrity program that has been featured in the *Washington Post, Reader's Digest, Chronicle of Higher Education,* and many other publications. The University's commitment to student ethical development is reflected in the creation of the new Office of Judicial Programs and Student Ethical Development.

Maryland's academic integrity program is manifested in both curricular and co-curricular activities:

✦ Hundreds of students participate in "Academic Integrity Week" each year, which includes a free showing of a pertinent feature film, such as *Quiz Show,* followed by presentations and discussions by prominent faculty members.

✦ Academic programs in Computer Science and Engineering contain special sections on academic integrity and applied ethics, which are developed and taught by staff members in the Office of Judicial Programs and Student Ethical Development. Evaluations have been highly favorable, and the special sections are now being expanded to other classes.

✦ An interactive web page has been created (www.umd.edu/ Ethics) that is designed to promote ethical dialogue in and out of class, through specially designed "Socratic Questions," featured student answers, and pertinent "Principles" statements, for example, "The Ten Principles of Civility in Cyberspace" and "The Ten Principles of Academic Integrity."

At the University of Maryland College Park, the academic integrity program is designed to do far more than deter academic dishonesty. The intent of the Office of Judicial Programs and Student Ethical Development, in cooperation with the Student Honor Council, is to help every Maryland student understand education as a lifelong process that is enriched by the development of a sense of civic and ethical obligation.

University of Miami

PO BOX 248025
CORAL GABLES, FL 33124
305.284.2211
http://www.miami.edu/

UNDERGRADUATES: 8,000

For program information, please contact:
WILLIAM W. SANDLER, JR.
wsandler@miami.edu

The Undergraduate Honor Code at the University of Miami, a private, comprehensive institution, was established to protect the academic integrity of the school, to encourage consistent, ethical behavior among students, and to foster a climate of fair competition. The Honor Council consists of 22 student representatives from the University's undergraduate schools and colleges.

The Honor Council uses a multifaceted approach to help students better understand the need to maintain academic integrity:

✦ All prospective applicants are required to complete a short essay explaining the importance of honor and academic integrity and describing the role those values have played in their lives.

✦ An Honor Council representative explains the Honor Code to all first-year students during an orientation program.

✦ The Council conducts a number of flyer and poster campaigns during the academic year to remind students about their individual responsibility to uphold the Code.

✦ Throughout the year, Honor Council members staff information tables at various schools and colleges on campus, giving members an opportunity to interact with students and distribute promotional material.

✦ The Honor Council conducts an "Academic Awareness Week" to encourage the entire university community to discuss issues related to honor and academic integrity.

The Honor Council takes seriously its responsibility to educate the University community about the benefits of maintaining integrity and honor in all academic endeavors. In fact, Honor Council members at Miami spend more time executing public awareness initiatives than in conducting hearings—hallmarks of an effective program well on its way to creating a legacy of academic integrity.

The University of North Carolina at Chapel Hill

CHAPEL HILL, NC 27599-2200
919.962.2211
http://www.unc.edu/

UNDERGRADUATES: 15,300

For program information, please contact:
GERALD ANDRADY
gandrady@email.unc.edu

"The Honor Code at Carolina goes a long way toward ensuring the validity of the degrees that we earn, while at the same time giving us the opportunity to monitor ourselves."

—A UNC FOURTH-YEAR STUDENT

For a century, students at The University of North Carolina at Chapel Hill, a public, comprehensive institution, have embraced the principles of self-governance in matters of academic and social conduct. The University's Honor System, representing a common bond between students, faculty, and administration, rests on a solid foundation of trust. Students may expect that their academic work will be accepted as authentic and that their word will be taken as truth.

Under the Honor Code, students carry the responsibility to:

✦ Conduct all academic work within the letter and spirit of the Honor Code.

✦ Sign a pledge on all graded academic work certifying that no unauthorized assistance has been received or given in the completion of the work.

✦ Comply with faculty regulations designed to reduce the possibility of cheating.

✦ Maintain the confidentiality of examinations by divulging no information concerning an examination to another student yet to write that same examination.

✦ Report any instance in which reasonable grounds exist to believe that a student has given unauthorized aid in graded work.

By accepting such responsibility, students earn the many practical rewards of the Honor System. They are secure in the knowledge that personal welfare and property are protected, and they are left to make the very personal decisions about their own conduct. They also enjoy an environment of trust that fosters the free exchange of ideas so necessary to an education of the highest quality.

University of Notre Dame

NOTRE DAME, IN 46556
219.631.5000
http://www.nd.edu/
UNDERGRADUATES: 7,900

For program information, please contact:
SR. ANNA MAE GOLDEN, Ed.D.
amgolden@hcc-nd.edu

"The Honor Code is beneficial because it explicitly states what is acceptable and what is unacceptable and gives students responsibility for their own ethical behavior."
—A NOTRE DAME SECOND-YEAR STUDENT

Students, faculty, and administrators at the University of Notre Dame, a church-affiliated, comprehensive institution, come together to learn, to work, and to grow in moral character. Central to the concept of community at Notre Dame is a belief in the importance of the honorable behavior of individuals and of the body as a whole. The Academic Code of Honor formally recognizes the ability of students to take responsibility for their ethical behavior. Under the Code, faculty strive to engender an atmosphere of trust in the classroom, and all students are expected:

✦ To sign a pledge to the community to uphold the Code's tenets in all academic affairs as a precondition for admission to the University.

✦ To become familiar with the Code and appreciate the reasoning behind it, such as the emphasis placed on a moral as well as an academic education, personal integrity, and community responsibility.

✦ To perform academic work honestly.

✦ To make the ethical and moral commitment not to act dishonestly and not to tolerate academic dishonesty on the part of other students. If aware of a likely violation of the Code, students must take responsible action.

Some students also participate in investigating and determining innocence or guilt in Academic Code of Honor cases by serving on Department Honesty Committees. The Code depends on the ethical spirit of each student to care enough to warn a friend or a fellow student, even if a stranger, to abandon dishonesty for the individual's own sake and for that of the community. Encouraging good will and fostering student pride, the Code of Honor is a valuable educational tool for exercising the power of community and for expressing the Christian values of Notre Dame.

University of South Carolina – Columbia

COLUMBIA, SC 29208
803.777.7000
http://www.sc.edu/
UNDERGRADUATES: 15,900

For program information, please contact:
DENNIS A. PRUITT, DL.D.
dpruitt@gwm.sc.edu

The University of South Carolina–Columbia, a public, comprehensive institution, was founded in 1801 to create a learning environment filled with the finest quality of human behavior, such as mutual respect, integrity, and selflessness. The Carolinian Creed, which serves as a social honor code for USC students, establishes the University's values for governing peer relationships. It does not define violations, nor does it provide specific remedies or punishments (thus the choice of the word *creed* rather than *code*). The Creed provides a common vocabulary, one that is meant to inspire and instruct, not to punish or persecute. The Creed suggests that individual virtue is its own reward.

THE CAROLINIAN CREED. The community of scholars at the University of South Carolina is dedicated to personal and academic excellence. Choosing to join the community obligates each member to a code of civilized behavior. As a Carolinian:

✦ I will practice personal and academic integrity;

✦ I will respect the dignity of all persons;

✦ I will respect the rights and property of others;

✦ I will discourage bigotry, striving to learn from differences in people, ideas, and opinions;

✦ I will demonstrate concern for others, their feelings, and their need for conditions which support their work and development.

Allegiance to these ideals obligates each student to refrain from and discourage behaviors that threaten the freedom and respect that all USC community members deserve.

Instead of focusing on minimal expectations for behavior or on a list of things students should not do, the Carolinian Creed focuses on understanding, appreciating, and living the values of civility, compassion, empathy, and openness—values that help mold USC students into citizens of character and integrity.

UNIVERSITY OF VIRGINIA

PO BOX 9017
CHARLOTTESVILLE, VA 22906
804.982.3200
http://www.virginia.edu/

UNDERGRADUATES: 12,400

For program information, please contact:
HONOR COMMITTEE
804.924.7602

"By simply refraining from lying, cheating, and stealing, UVA students enjoy a community of trust in which they are taken at their word."

—A UVA GRADUATE

The University of Virginia, a comprehensive, public institution, was founded in 1819 by Thomas Jefferson. In 1842, as a gesture of confidence in the students, Professor Henry St. George Tucker offered a resolution that they sign a statement on each test: "I do hereby certify on my honor that I have derived no assistance during the time of this examination from any source whatsoever." The resolution was meant to govern conduct in the classroom only, but the students so strongly wished to be measured by their own standards that since that time the Honor System has been completely student-run.

In the past three decades, changes have helped the Honor Committee more effectively reach students:

✦ In 1969, the System was revised to cover honor violations wherever a student represented him/herself as a student of UVA.

✦ In 1977 the student body ratified a written constitution for the Honor Committee.

✦ In 1980, students were given the right to choose a trial panel comprised of randomly selected students and elected committee members.

✦ In 1987, the Honor Committee created an investigative panel to serve as a check on the thoroughness of investigations and the validity of investigators' decisions.

✦ In 1990 the student body approved a referendum giving students the option of choosing a random student panel.

✦ The fall of 1993 saw the beginning of a new investigation process. Random student investigators were eliminated, and Honor Advisors began investigating all cases.

As the University of Virginia evolves, the System will continue to adjust to reflect the opinions and needs of the student body, while upholding the principles originally brought to the school by Thomas Jefferson.

VILLANOVA UNIVERSITY

800 LANCASTER AVENUE
VILLANOVA, PA 19085
610.519.4500
http://www.vill.edu/

UNDERGRADUATES: 7,100

For program information, please contact:
JOHN IMMERWAHR, Ph.D.
Jimmerwa@email.vill.edu

The purpose of Villanova University, a private, church-affiliated institution, is twofold: to develop independent, active learners; and to develop moral, spiritual students. Cheating, plagiarism, and other forms of academic dishonesty are completely incompatible with the school's character and vision. To combat the influence of a broader culture that values grades over substance, Villanova has begun a long-term effort to create a climate of academic integrity on campus.

Aspects of the academic integrity policy, which was developed by both faculty and students, include the following:

✦ All students receive a brochure on academic integrity, which includes the university's Honor Code, and an academic integrity quiz that is used by faculty to spark discussion on the topic.

✦ Resident assistants and new-student orientation counselors receive training on academic integrity principles.

✦ During new-student orientation, students pledge to abide by the Honor Code.

✦ Bluebooks include a preprinted integrity statement that students must sign before handing in the assignment.

✦ Most of the control is in the hands of the faculty. If a professor feels a violation has occurred, normally the penalty stands.

✦ Students may appeal penalties to a panel consisting of students and faculty drawn from the Board of Academic Integrity. Faculty members may testify at hearings, but they are not required to do so.

When students attend Villanova, they join an academic community founded on the search for knowledge in an atmosphere of cooperation and trust. The intellectual health of the campus community depends on this trust and draws nourishment from the integrity and mutual respect of each of its members.

VIRGINIA WESLEYAN COLLEGE

1584 WESLEYAN DRIVE
NORFOLK/VIRGINIA BEACH, VA 23502-5599
757.455.3200
http://www.vwc.edu/

UNDERGRADUATES: 1,500

For program information, please contact:
STEPHEN MANSFIELD, Ph.D.
Smansfield@vwc.edu

Virginia Wesleyan College, a private, liberal arts institution, believes that all members of the campus community, including students, should embrace the concept of academic integrity. The school's Honor Code states, in part, that the "responsibility for safeguarding honor and trust belongs to the entire academic community; therefore, students need to assume increasing measures of responsibility for honorable behavior in themselves and others as they advance academically."

The Honor Code is promoted in a number of ways:

✦ It is introduced to new students on the day they matriculate, at an Honor Convocation ceremony, which parents are also invited to attend.

✦ The president of the College gives the Convocation address joined by student members of the Honor Council, who elaborate on the concept of honor in an academic setting.

✦ As part of the Honor Convocation ceremony, all new students are asked to sign an Honor Code commitment card.

✦ The Honor Code is incorporated into the required Freshman Seminar Course, which involves an Honor Council simulation that engages students in an interactive introduction to the Code and its administration.

✦ Faculty members routinely include statements about academic integrity and responsibility in their syllabi and discuss the subject as part of the expectations for the course.

As a liberal arts college, Virginia Wesleyan is committed to the values of citizenship and social responsibility, which are essential to any community of scholars, and relies on its students to play a vital role in upholding the standards of integrity.

WAKE FOREST UNIVERSITY

1834 WAKE FOREST ROAD
WINSTON-SALEM, NC 27109
336.758.5000
http://www.wfu.edu/

UNDERGRADUATES: 3,900

For program information, please contact:
E. CLAYTON HIPP, JR.
Hippec@wfu.edu

Wake Forest University, a private, comprehensive institution, believes that the honesty, trustworthiness, and personal integrity of each student are integral to the life and purposes of the campus community. Specifically, that means that students are expected not to deceive any member of the community, not to steal from one another, not to cheat on academic work, not to plagiarize academic work, and not to engage in any other forms of academic misconduct. The essence of the Honor Code is that each student's word can be trusted and that any dishonest act is an offense against the whole community.

The importance of the Honor Code is reinforced in a variety of ways:

✦ Prospective students are required to sign a statement indicating their willingness to abide by the principles of the honor system.

✦ During first-year orientation, new students are exposed to the Honor System at a formal ceremony at which administrators, faculty, and students discuss the tradition of honor on campus. Students then recite the Honor Statement, sign a Book of Honor, and receive a symbolic lapel pin, which signifies their support of the Honor System.

✦ In the future, entering students will receive an interactive compact disc, which will provide both substantive and practical advice regarding the Honor System and its significance to the campus community.

✦ "Honor and Ethics" has been named the institutional theme of the 2000–2001 academic year.

By adhering to the principles outlined in the Honor Code, students at Wake Forest are freed of the many constraints that become necessary in the absence of honorable conduct and can devote themselves to the unfettered pursuit of their common and individual interests.

Washington and Lee University

LEXINGTON, VA 24450
540.463.8400
http://www.wlu.edu/

UNDERGRADUATES: 1,700

For program information, please contact:
DAVID HOWISON, Ph.D.
dhowison@wlu.edu

A strong thread woven through the many aspects of campus life, the commitment to honorable behavior creates an atmosphere of trust that fundamentally affects all relationships among the academic community at Washington and Lee University, a small, private, liberal arts institution. In accordance with W&L's belief in student autonomy, students are granted the privilege of overseeing the administration of the Honor System. The Student Executive Committee, a group of students elected annually by their peers, is charged with defining dishonorable acts; investigating and judicially managing honor hearings; writing and revising the Honor System policy and procedures manual; and reporting directly to the Board of Trustees on the administration of the Honor System. The sole penalty for an Honor System violation is dismissal from the University.

Under the Honor System, students enjoy a variety of benefits, including:

✦ The faculty grants flexibility in the scheduling of most final examinations, and all are taken without supervision. Take-home closed book examinations are a common occurrence.

✦ The pledge, "On my honor, I have neither given nor received any unacknowledged aid on this assignment," is accepted as the student's promise that the work submitted is his or hers alone and that no unfair advantage has been taken of peers by cheating.

✦ Students' dedication to honorable behavior engenders a strong bond of trust among them and between them and the faculty, providing the basis for the faculty member's commitment to accepting a student's word without question.

The Honor System has been a uniquely defining feature of W&L for more than a century. The morals of thousands of students have been shaped by it, graduates continue to be guided by it in their professional lives, and current students remain committed to this distinctive and challenging ideal.

FACULTY AND CURRICULUM PROGRAMS

Whether in formal or informal learning environments, outstanding faculty provide opportunities for students to examine, reflect on, and articulate a set of moral ideals and commitments. Courses in every discipline have the potential to raise important moral issues. Exemplary programs support faculty efforts across the curriculum to introduce questions of ethics and character into their courses. These programs also enable students to encounter how the great ideas of civilization inform our understanding of today's issues.

ALVERNO COLLEGE

3401 SOUTH 39TH STREET
MILWAUKEE, WI 53234
414.382.6000
http://www.alverno.edu/

UNDERGRADUATES: 2,200

For program information, please contact:
AMY SHAPIRO, Ph.D.
amy.shapiro@alverno.edu

Alverno College, a liberal arts college for women, is nationally recognized for its ability-based, outcome-oriented curriculum. Alverno students must demonstrate a firm grasp of their specific academic discipline as well as master eight critical "abilities": communication, analysis, problem solving, valuing, social interaction, global perspectives, effective citizenship, and aesthetic responsiveness. The "valuing" aspect of the curriculum is implemented by faculty members from each discipline division at the college, who comprise the college's Valuing Department and are charged with overseeing the pedagogy associated with the "ability." Members of the department also create or revise criteria related to mastery outcomes and assessment tools. A requirement to graduate is the ability to demonstrate valuing at four developmental levels as defined by the Valuing Department.

The "valuing ability" is a process by which students explore the importance of values within a number of different contexts, including:

✦ The relationship between values and actions. Students examine how values influence actions and behaviors.

✦ Values in one's profession. Students research, study, and observe the values prevalent in their future professional field or within their major or minor.

✦ The sources of values. Students are challenged to examine the sources of their values as well as the values held by others. This ability is especially critical when confronting conflicts in which students can react from a position of perspective-taking and understanding.

Alverno's "ability-based curriculum," an integral part of the curriculum since 1973, is designed to help students learn specific disciplines while learning how to do something with what they know. At Alverno, knowledge and its application are inseparable. Consequently, an Alverno education places a strong emphasis on active and experiential learning.

CALIFORNIA UNIVERSITY OF PENNSYLVANIA

250 UNIVERSITY AVENUE
CALIFORNIA, PA 15419-1394
724.938.4000
http://www.cup.edu/

UNDERGRADUATES: 5,000

For program information, please contact:
HENRY A. HUFFMAN, Ed.D.
huffman@cup.edu

Integrity, civility, and responsibility have been identified as the core values at the California University of Pennsylvania (CALU). In January of 1995, CALU created the Character Education Institute as a resource to faculty, staff, and administrators as they carry out their role as character educators.

While all segments of the University have an opportunity to make a contribution to the moral development of students, initial efforts have concentrated on the curriculum and faculty. During the last three years, the University's commitment to examining values through the curriculum has included:

✦ A new general-education plan requiring students in all majors to select a three-credit course from the values menu;

✦ A position paper entitled, "Emphasis on Values: California University Position Paper," written by two professors to facilitate discussion of the University's core values in the curriculum;

✦ A Values Seminar. In response to the University's identification of three core values, the Philosophy Department offers a Values Seminar.

✦ Guest lecturers. The University brings guest lecturers to the campus to discuss the role of the university in moral development. Speakers have included Stephen Carter, Sidney Callahan, Sanford McDonnell, and Stephen Covey.

✦ A character education curriculum. The College of Education has developed a character education curriculum that is integrated into existing required courses. The content is taught through guest lecturers provided by the director of the University's Character Education Institute.

Through the Character Education Institute, students who attend CALU learn integrity, civility, and responsibility. The programs, resources, and counseling services provided by the Character Education Institute help students integrate moral values into every aspect of their lives.

CALVIN COLLEGE

3201 BURTON STREET SE
GRAND RAPIDS, MI 49546
616.957.6000
http://www.calvin.edu/

UNDERGRADUATES: 3,900

For program information, please contact:
FRANK ROBERTS, Ph.D.
Robefr@calvin.edu

"Spending a semester in Honduras challenged me to critically think about the root causes and systemic solutions to hunger and injustice."

—A CALVIN COLLEGE THIRD-YEAR STUDENT

By committing substantial resources—financial, professorial, and administrative—to off-campus programs, Calvin College, a private, liberal arts institution, has demonstrated its belief that these programs build moral character and foster personal and civic responsibility.

Calvin College's off-campus programs are designed to provide students with coherent, comprehensive, and authentic learning experiences that have deep and long-lasting effects on their spiritual and moral development. Semester-long programs send students all over the world, to Great Britain, Hungary, Honduras, Spain, China, and New Mexico, among others. A program in Ghana is anticipated for 2000. Month-long opportunities are also provided during the January term.

The goals of off-campus programs are to apply Christian beliefs in a new context and provide opportunities not available on campus.

Students who participate in off-campus programs develop a cross-cultural consciousness. Dislocated from their own culture and forced to live as a stranger among unfamiliar people, students can achieve a deeper self-understanding. Such experiences also help students develop a deeper appreciation and respect for their host culture. Finally, students experience first-hand what it feels like to be an "outsider" or part of a minority group, which in turn makes them very sensitive to issues of justice and the need for compassion.

Calvin College is convinced that there is no better way to encourage moral and civic development than to provide programs that give students the opportunity to live in another cultural setting.

CARSON-NEWMAN COLLEGE

1646 RUSSELL AVENUE
JEFFERSON CITY, TN 37760
423.475.9061
http://www.cn.edu/

UNDERGRADUATES: 2,000

For program information, please contact:
WILLIAM M. MCDONALD, Ed.D.
mcdonald@cncacc.cn.edu

In keeping with Dr. Ernest L. Boyer's admonition to ensure that students expand "beyond their private interests, [and] learn about the world around them, [and] discover how they can contribute to the common good," in 1992 Carson-Newman, a church-related, liberal arts college, established a "residential college" model for small private institutions. The Ernest L. Boyer Laboratory for Learning has partnered students with faculty and staff leaders and created cocurricular residential teams designed to expand learning beyond the classroom.

The Boyer Lab involves both institutional leaders and students in two teams:

✦ THE RESIDENTIAL TEAM. Composed of at least three students, one faculty, one administrative staff, and the Resident Director of each residence hall, these five teams of Residential Fellows serve as a liaison both between departments and between faculty, students, and staff. Each month, the Residential Teams plan programs to focus on issues related to life and academics. The Teams also plan cocurricular activities, such as visiting museums, attending concerts, and bringing speakers to campus.

✦ THE STEERING TEAM. This larger body of the combined Residential Fellows and Program Directors coordinates the work of the entire program across campus.

Established in the spirit of Dr. Boyer's philosophy, the Boyer Lab demonstrates to student leaders effective ways to help classmates and fellow hall residents connect classroom teaching to life-development issues. Programming implemented by the Boyer Lab integrates human relationships with personal identity, eases the natural tension between social responsibility and individuality, and explores the challenges of composing a set of personal values that fits with a coherent life philosophy in a world of economic concerns, environmental stewardship, and pragmatic realities.

CENTRAL METHODIST COLLEGE

411 CENTRAL METHODIST SQUARE
FAYETTE, MO 65248
660.248.3391
http://www.cmc.edu/

UNDERGRADUATES: 1,200

For program information, please contact:
J. KEITH KEELING, Ph.D.
kkeeling@cmc.edu

Close relationships between faculty members and students at Central Methodist College are primary for preparing leaders of character for society. Students and alumni alike cite the quality of their overall learning experience as significant in equipping them for lives of service and contribution. CMC faculty focus on "character development as a dimension of a strong liberal arts education and professional preparation for a life of service" by integrating a commitment to values in the following ways:

✦ Courses currently include a first-year seminar on character development which is taught by students' advisors; a senior capstone focusing on service and a life of character; and Wellness for Life, addressing physical, social, emotional, and spiritual health. Texts include *A Call to Character* and *The Moral Compass.*

✦ Each year the faculty select a common reading for use in classes and as the subject of forums and convocations. Recent choices include Shelby Steele's *The Content of Our Character* and Stephen Carter's *Integrity.*

✦ The current general-education requirement is being revised around "Character Core," a set of four courses addressing the meaning of character and its application to people's lives and society. These courses include the first- and senior-year courses, religion, and literature.

✦ Issues of character formation are addressed in courses and majors across the curriculum: ethics, business, pre-law, the sciences and health-related fields, the social sciences, music and the arts, teacher education, and communication.

Character is modeled in the interactions among all members of the CMC community. Through small classes and a high degree of personal attention from faculty and staff, students are guided in developing and refining their own personal credos and principles of living.

COLORADO STATE UNIVERSITY

1005 W. LAUREL STREET
FORT COLLINS, CO 80523
970.491.1101
http://www.colostate.edu/

UNDERGRADUATES: 18,600

For program information, please contact:
DAVID A. MCKELFRESH, Ph.D.
davemac@lamar.colostate.edu

Founded in 1870 as a public, land-grant institution, Colorado State University provides a comprehensive educational experience designed to engage students in dialog on local, national, and global issues, and to encourage them to participate in activities that strengthen their moral reasoning skills. The Ethics Workshop was designed to challenge students regarding character development issues. Over the past 10 years it has evolved into a highly successful experience for students, faculty, and staff. The program bridges theory and practice and has become an excellent vehicle for empowering participants to engage each other in discussion regarding character and contemporary moral and ethical issues. In addition, the program:

✦ Enables students to better understand and practice the virtues of personal and civic responsibility through lecture, discussion, role play, and demonstration. Students are challenged to consider several moral dilemmas, as well as review their own past behaviors.

✦ Impacts a large number of students. Hundreds participate each year through student leadership training and development sessions, specially selected academic classes, student paraprofessional training, and University student conduct referrals.

✦ Has a positive influence on students, as evidenced by their positive evaluation of the program. No student who has attended the Ethics Workshop has been back in the campus judicial system.

✦ Led to the development of a required semester-long ethics class for master's candidates in the Student Affairs in Higher Education program.

The Ethics Workshop is one of Colorado State's character-building cornerstones and has received external recognition through national associations and publications. The program helps participants to uncover and clarify personal values, move across cultural boundaries, and operate ethically in our increasingly complex, global society.

Concordia College

901 8TH ST. SOUTH
MOORHEAD, MN 56562
218.299.3004
http://www.cord.edu/
UNDERGRADUATES: 2,900

For program information, please contact:
ERNEST L. SIMMONS, JR., Ph.D.
simmons@cord.edu

As a liberal arts college of the Evangelical Lutheran Church in America, Concordia College is committed to fostering spiritual, intellectual, physical, social, and emotional growth in students. The Program on Faith and Learning is intended to assist faculty to connect their religious faith, including the requisite moral values and character concerns, to their academic work.

✦ The goal of the Program on Faith and Learning is not to impose a singular value system on any academic field, but rather to create a learning environment in which the academic learning (reasons) and Christian tradition (faith) can creatively interact.

✦ The Program's purpose is to keep the questions and issues of faith and learning alive on campus and to assist faculty in connecting matters of faith with the teaching of their discipline.

✦ Among other activities, the Program conducts a summer workshop for faculty on Christian Faith and the Liberal Arts; brings in guest speakers; and has established summer study grant opportunities.

✦ The Program assists faculty teaching core courses to introduce faith and value issues. Ultimately, the program will result in student character formation through contact with faculty.

Christian colleges like Concordia assist a student's identity-forming process by cultivating an environment in which faith and learning are kept in a dynamic relationship. Therefore, helping faculty articulate their faith through their discipline is Concordia's chosen method of instilling a strong sense of faith. Through the Program on Faith and Learning, Concordia College fulfills its mission of "sending into society thoughtful and informed men and women dedicated to the Christian life."

Eastern Mennonite University

1200 PARK ROAD
HARRISONBURG, VA 22802
540.432.4000
http://www.emu.edu/
UNDERGRADUATES: 1,000

For program information, please contact:
WILLIAM J. HAWK, Ph.D.
hawkw@emu.edu

Preparing ethically informed leaders for global citizenship serves as a guiding aspiration of Eastern Mennonite University. The University expects all graduates to complete a "global village" core curriculum which requires students to participate in a significant cross-cultural experience, usually outside the U.S. The Honors Program prepares the most talented students for global citizenship by heightened learning expectations in specific areas.

✦ **SEMINARS.** First-year honors students participate in a "Ruling Ideas" seminar in which the best faculty from the University explore the dominant paradigms of their discipline. In their senior year, honors students construct personal "worldview" papers under faculty guidance in a "Worldview Seminar."

✦ **COLLOQUIA.** Elective colloquia offer in-depth explorations into various topics, such as the ethical and religious witness of Dietrich Bonhoeffer; music and life; and self, mind, and spirituality. Each colloquium opens a window on how persons committed to the values of peace and justice should live in the global village.

✦ **MENTORING.** Each honors student develops a mentoring relationship with a faculty member where ethical, intellectual, and spiritual guidance takes place. Mentoring meetings cover topics from the student's current experience to the large questions of career, life direction, and personal faith commitment.

✦ **ENCOUNTERS.** Honors students and faculty convene weekly for social interaction and to discuss issues of the day. In addition, some honors encounters feature guest or campus speakers who raise issues of global citizenship.

Honors students at EMU bring formal learning together with informal mentoring and encounters. To these they add the global village curriculum, the expertise of a major, and a cross-cultural experience. Honors students graduate as informed global citizens who go on to make significant contributions through service to others.

EMORY UNIVERSITY

1380 OXFORD ROAD NE
ATLANTA, GA 30322
404.727.6123
http://www.emory.edu/

UNDERGRADUATES: 6,000

For program information, please contact:
STACIA BROWN
sbrown06@emory.edu

"With the new program in Ethics, students have great opportunities to explore Emory's place in Atlanta, and to build a strong relationship with that community."

—AN EMORY UNIVERSITY THIRD-YEAR STUDENT

Emory University's identity is captured by the words of Chancellor Billy Frye: " . . . an excellent institution that is at once powerful in its intelligence, moral in its sensibilities, global in its perspective, and distinctive in its cast." The Center for Ethics in Public Policy and the Professions forms a crucial locus of commitment in the University's embodiment of this identity. Each year, the Center for Ethics sponsors several nationally known scholars to lecture at Emory and engage with faculty around ethical issues.

In addition, the annual Faculty Ethics Seminar offers an opportunity for sustained attention to ethics. The Seminar invites all University faculty to participate in ethical practices and to engage in ethical theory. This melding of theory and practice models education for character development through the following:

✦ **INTERPERSONAL DIALOG.** The seminar is interdisciplinary and interprofessional. Therefore, one can interact with persons different from oneself.

✦ **SERVANT LEADERSHIP.** Faculty members themselves lead the seminar in service to the community and seminar members learn a great deal about teaching through the experience of being students to their faculty colleagues. They are equipped as leaders who reach beyond the safe confines of their own disciplines to engage the deep and expansive questions of ethics, morality, and virtue.

✦ **KNOWLEDGE IN COMMUNITY.** The seminar builds on the long-standing tradition of the University as a community of scholars in dialog and offers the possibility of ongoing connections at the conclusion of the seminar.

Faculty dedicate significant time and energy to the seminar. They develop increased competence and confidence in addressing the ethical issues related to their field, their research, and the professions for which they prepare their students.

FRANCISCAN UNIVERSITY OF STEUBENVILLE

1235 UNIVERSITY BOULEVARD
STEUBENVILLE, OH 43952
740.283.3771
http://www.franuniv.edu/

UNDERGRADUATES: 1,600

For program information, please contact:
JOSEPH ALMEIDA
Jalmeida@franuniv.edu

"When people ask why I believe something, I now have rational, well-thought-out answers to back up my beliefs."

—A FRANCISCAN UNIVERSITY FOURTH-YEAR STUDENT

Cicero on old age, Aristotle on friendship and politics, the early Church leaders on justice. Franciscan University students become acquainted with these and many other great authors through the four-year Great Books Honors Program. Franciscan University established the Great Books Honors Program to familiarize students with some of the most important writings of Western civilization. This series of eight four-credit seminars is an alternative way for students to satisfy the University's core requirements. The Honors Program includes:

✦ **SEMINARS.** In the first year, the program starts with classical thought, including works by Plato, Aristotle, and Euripides. The students conclude their senior year with great writers of the nineteenth and twentieth centuries such as Tolstoy, Keats, C. S. Lewis, and Pope John Paul II.

✦ **VALUE-BUILDING EXERCISES.** Students in the Honors Program answer questions that help them determine for themselves who God is and what their place in the world is. They learn about basic qualities of character such as honesty, friendship, and love, and they incorporate these ideals into their personal lives.

✦ **CURRICULUM-WIDE INVOLVEMENT.** Faculty from as many as eight academic departments, including Classics, Theology, and Philosophy, teach in the program. This provides a rich variety of perspectives as professor and students immerse themselves in the best recorded works on human and Christian wisdom.

Students in the Great Books Honors Program develop critical-thinking skills and ethical foundations as they research, analyze, and vigorously critique ideas they encounter. They become part of a community of scholars who engage in direct examination of moral virtues through the medium of literature.

Georgia College & State University

MILLEDGEVILLE, GA 31061
912.445.5001
http://www.gcsu.edu/

UNDERGRADUATES: 4,400

For program information, please contact:
DEBORAH VESS, Ph.D.
dvess@mail.gac.peachnet.edu

"I have enjoyed my IDST classes. These classes have exposed me to different disciplines, ideas, and cultures."

—A GC&SU THIRD-YEAR STUDENT

As the public liberal arts university of Georgia, one of the goals of Georgia College & State University is to provide a curriculum that emphasizes character education. GC&SU created the Interdisciplinary Studies (IDS) program to enhance student awareness of and empathy toward modern ethical dilemmas in the university, workplace, home, and in society.

The mission of the Interdisciplinary Studies program is to enable students to synthesize and to integrate the diverse array of information encountered in the curriculum. Students develop a critical appreciation of various disciplinary perspectives and methodologies with respect to problems of contemporary and historic interest. These goals are accomplished in various ways:

✦ All students are required to take at least two of nine courses in the IDS program. A team of faculty across the disciplines joins to teach classes such as Ethics in Society, Communication and Society, and Global Issues. These courses introduce students to a variety of ethical problems such as plagiarism, date rape, and political compromise.

✦ Symposia are held every semester in conjunction with the IDS core courses. The IDS program brings in nationally or internationally renowned speakers and guest artists who cover such topics as "The Ethics of Cloning."

✦ The IDS director organizes faculty development workshops. Faculty who attend these workshops explore pedagogical techniques, such as creative writing in IDS courses and technology in the classroom. The IDS program also regularly sends faculty to outside workshops and institutes.

Students who are involved in the IDS program develop problem-solving and critical-thinking skills. Students emerge from these courses better prepared for challenges of the complex world in which they live.

Greensboro College

815 WEST MARKET STREET
GREENSBORO, NC 27401-1875
336.272.7102
http://www.gborocollege.edu/

UNDERGRADUATES: 1,100

For program information, please contact:
PHILIP A. ROLNICK, Ph.D.
rolnickp@mail.gborocollege.edu

"My participation in the Ethics Across the Curriculum Program has been one of the most challenging and rewarding experiences of my career at Greensboro College."

—A GREENSBORO COLLEGE FOURTH-YEAR STUDENT

The vision and purpose of Greensboro College's Ethics Across the Curriculum (EAC) Program is to promote the study, exploration, discussion, debate, and living of ethical principles at Greensboro College and in its broader sphere of influence. The academic study of ethics directly helps students address the issues not only of personal and civic responsibility, but also the classical "cardinal virtues" of practical wisdom, courage, and justice, and the "theological" virtues of faith, hope, and love. The EAC Program is two-pronged:

✦ CAMPUS-WIDE EAC PROGRAM. All students are required to take ethics classes, such as Introduction to Ethics, with Old and New Testament courses as prerequisites of all ethics courses. This is to ensure that students have formed a basis of the current ethical situation through an informed, historical study of the formative texts of Judaism and Christianity.

✦ MAJOR/MINOR-SPECIFIC ETHICS COURSES. The Ethics minor also requires the study of Old and New Testament as a foundation. Business Ethics is required for all Business majors. Advanced Seminar is a required capstone course. Finally, students may choose Special Topics courses, such as Ethics in Film.

An important strategy of the EAC Program has been to provide faculty with intensive training in the history of ethical thought. Faculty have become involved through summer seminars, a course on ethical writings, and a symposium series. Another important aspect of the EAC Program is the Student Ethics Committee (SEC), composed of volunteer undergraduates and appointed seniors, which plans and executes a large portion of program events. Students who attend Greensboro College have many opportunities to build a strong foundation of ethical beliefs that they can implement in their lives.

GROVE CITY COLLEGE

100 CAMPUS DRIVE
GROVE CITY, PA 16127
724.458.2100
http://www.gcc.edu/

UNDERGRADUATES: 2,300

For program information, please contact:
GARY S. SMITH, Ph.D.
gssmith@gcc.edu

Founded in 1876 Grove City College is an independent Christian college of liberal arts and sciences. One of the institution's guiding spirits, J. Howard Pew, stated that the College's "prime responsibility is to inculcate in the minds and hearts of youth those Christian, moral and ethical principles without which our country cannot long endure." To that end, ethical absolutes and Christ's moral teachings guide the College's efforts to develop intellect and character in the classroom, as well as in the chapel and cocurricular activities, and are central to The Civilization Series.

The Civilization Series is a three-year, six-course interdisciplinary sequence that advocates preservation of America's heritage of individual freedom and responsibility. Focusing on the origin, development, and implications of civilization's seminal ideas, the Series examines history, theology, philosophy, politics, literature, art, and music and fosters intellectual, moral, and spiritual development by:

✦ Evaluating cultural, economic, political, and social structures and policies in light of Christian principles;

✦ Helping students develop a biblical worldview that directs their private and public lives;

✦ Emphasizing the importance of religious, political, and social freedoms;

✦ Discussing the connection between the ethical standards and practices of a society and the moral commitments and character of individuals.

The Civilization Series was recently recognized in two national publications. *The National Review College Guide* states that "[the Series] reflects Grove City's solid grounding on . . . traditional values" by promoting "moral, spiritual, and social development consistent with a Christian commitment to truth, morality and freedom." *Choosing the Right College: The Whole Truth about America's Top Schools* commends Grove City for insuring that every student receives an education that is intellectually coherent and morally grounded.

HEIDELBERG COLLEGE

310 E. MARKET STREET
TIFFIN, OH 44883
419.448.2000
http://www.heidelberg.edu/

UNDERGRADUATES: 1,300

For program information, please contact:
JAN J. YOUNGER, Ph.D.
jyounger@heidelberg.edu

"Heidelberg's Honors Program is designed to foster excellence. For me, it has created fantastic opportunities and experiences I would never have experienced outside the program."

—A HEIDELBERG COLLEGE THIRD-YEAR STUDENT

Challenging students to consider the choices they make and to understand the context in which they make those choices is a hallmark of the Heidelberg College Honors Program. Called "The Life of the Mind," the program empowers the College's most outstanding academic students to explore their abilities within a supportive community. The program strives for the development of depth of character in each student. This is achieved through:

✦ **A Unique Curriculum.** The heart of the Honors Program is found in the curriculum, which is centered on the four personae of the mind—Scholar, Scientist, Artist, and Citizen. The progression of seminars from the 100 level, which focuses on commitment to the integrity of scholarship, toward the 400 level, which highlights commitment to the responsibilities of citizenship, is designed to stress the importance of personal leadership and civic responsibility.

✦ **Service Learning.** The habit of service, which may have the most enriching and life-lasting effect on students, is encouraged. Students are expected to prepare for their service-learning projects and to reflect on ways the project affected them.

✦ **National Speaker's Forum.** In over 20 seminars the faculty engage students in reflection and discussion of interdisciplinary material, moral and ethical issues, needs of society, and the joys of the Life of the Mind.

In keeping with Heidelberg College's mission, the Honors Program curriculum is distinguished by its quality and commitment to fostering student growth through the integration of learning and life experiences.

Huntington College

2303 COLLEGE AVENUE
HUNTINGTON, IN 46750
219.356.6000
http://www.huntington.edu/

UNDERGRADUATES: 900

For program information, please contact:
JOHN PAFF
jpaff@huntington.edu

At Huntington College, all academic disciplines—the arts, humanities, and sciences—are viewed as living, breathing expressions of God's creative work. As a Christian college, Huntington is not a refuge from the contemporary world, but an arena for encounter with that world and creative response to it. The comprehensive Character Throughout Curriculum Program teaches students to develop cognitive skills for the formation of ethical judgments, and to become responsible individuals who positively influence moral reasoning and acting within the community. The program has three aspects:

✦ THE COLLEGE LIFE CLASS. Incoming students study values and decision-making in this 10-week seminar held at the beginning of each fall term. Meeting in small groups, students are helped to make positive choices about lifestyle standards and interpersonal relationships.

✦ THE SENIOR CAPSTONE COURSE. Before graduation, all students take this course, which focuses on socially responsible Christian responses to societal problems. Within the context of a predetermined theme, students have the opportunity to enrich the campus community as they work together to conduct research, solve problems, explore ethical questions, and make public presentations.

✦ THE SPIRITUAL FORMATION PROGRAM. Students are afforded many opportunities each week to participate in religious services, including two traditional chapel services, a weekly student-led evening worship service, weekly small group discussions, and monthly convocations. Faculty and staff are involved as well, and guest lecturers are brought in frequently.

As a result of their experiences in the Character Throughout Curriculum Program, Huntington College students are prepared to address issues in uncommon depth. They leave college with the confidence to question prevailing opinion and the academic preparation to provide leadership in a morally needy world.

Indiana University Bloomington

2931 EAST TENTH STREET
BLOOMINGTON, IN 47405
812.855.4848
http://www.indiana.edu/

UNDERGRADUATES: 31,000

For program information, please contact:
DAVID H. SMITH, Ph.D.
smithd@indiana.edu

The Poynter Center is charged with fostering the examination and discussion of ethical issues in American society. David H. Smith, the Center's director, writes, "Ethics courses taught by ethicists certainly have their place, but we believe it is more important and more effective for faculty members from many fields to teach ethics relevant to their own courses." To this end the Center has sponsored numerous programs to enable faculty members to incorporate the teaching of ethics into their curricula, including the following:

✦ With funding from many sources, including the Lilly Endowment, the National Endowment for the Humanities, and FIPSE, the Center has conducted seminars on professional ethics, bringing together religious leaders, academics, and professionals to explore ethical issues in health care, the media, the military, and business.

✦ The Poynter Center spearheaded the effort to organize the Association for Practical and Professional Ethics, dedicated to the encouragement of interdisciplinary scholarship and exemplary teaching in practical and professional ethics.

✦ Grants from the Lilly Endowment have also allowed the Poynter Center to continue its outreach to Indiana colleges and universities. Faculty teams come to Bloomington for an intensive workshop that helps them to design ethics curricula for their home campuses.

✦ "Teaching Research Ethics" (TRE), originally funded by FIPSE, and then with financial support from 10 major research universities and a workshop fee, is an annual workshop for teaching research ethics for scientists who train graduate students.

Hundreds of faculty members from colleges and universities have taken part in Poynter Center workshops and projects. The Poynter Center, an established leader in ethics education, is hard at work trying to lose itself in a crowd of its own making.

Iowa Wesleyan College

601 NORTH MAIN
MT. PLEASANT, IA 52641
800.582.2383
http://www.iwc.edu/

UNDERGRADUATES: 850

For program information, please contact:
JERARD NAYLOR
iwcrsi@iwc.edu

Community service and civic responsibility describe the ideals at Iowa Wesleyan College, a private, liberal arts college in the Methodist tradition. Through the Real World Learning Curriculum, students are actively engaged in a multidimensional education. Real World Learning consists of three fundamental phases, each providing students with the skills to succeed in a rapidly changing world:

✦ **Life Skills.** Communication, problem-solving, and value-building are at the heart of an Iowa Wesleyan education. These principles are taught in every class, so that students can realize their full potential as thinking, communicating, and socially effective human beings.

✦ **Field Experience.** Through internships, clinicals, and practice in nearly every major across the curriculum, students may complete a minimum of six hours of field experience in their chosen field of study. They gain professional experience and networking opportunities in real career settings.

✦ **Service-Learning.** Established in 1968, the Responsible Social Involvement (RSI) program requires students to complete 160 hours of service-learning. Through RSI, students are instilled with the obligation to reimburse society for the heritage they have enjoyed. Students also serve on most faculty committees, participate in self-governance through Student Senate and Student Court, and actively plan campus events through the Student Union Board.

The majority of Iowa Wesleyan graduates report that their RSI experience was a critical, life-changing experience in their total college encounter. RSI forces every student to "live into" a world outside the campus—and often outside their cultural environment. Because Real World Learning combines the heart of the liberal arts with the muscle of career preparation, students who graduate from Iowa Wesleyan College emerge well rounded and well prepared.

King's College

133 NORTH RIVER STREET
WILKES-BARRE, PA 18711
570.208.5900
http://www.kings.edu/

UNDERGRADUATES: 1,700

For program information, please contact:
MARGARET MONAHAN HOGAN, Ph.D.
mmhogan@kings.edu

The commitment of King's College to provide students with intellectual, moral, and spiritual preparation for satisfying and purposeful lives is evident in the College's Recovering the Moral Dimensions of Collegiate Education program. Integrating serious ethical study and reflection within the various academic programs, it transforms the public and personal dimensions of students' lives through moral reflection. Students, as well as faculty and administrators, are empowered to be wise stewards of the resources of the world and to be agents of peace and justice in their generation.

The goal of the program is student development that is both theoretical and practical. To that end, two stages of the program are currently in place: faculty development and student (moral) development.

✦ Faculty development is achieved through intensive, directed study of both the major traditions in ethics and contemporary ethical issues, such as assisted suicide in the medical context. The program fosters regular dialog within the College on ethical dimensions in the academic fields by sponsoring programs for the faculty to enable them to address, more effectively, ethical concerns in their disciplines.

✦ The moral development program strives to fulfill its charge by arranging lectures, roundtable discussions, and seminars on timely ethical topics; assisting in the development of reflective service learning projects; and developing discipline-specific ethics modules for upper-level courses.

Recovering the Moral Dimensions of Collegiate Education serves as a resource and agent for regular College reflection on moral life. The program's purpose is to transform King's College into an ethical body both in public and private life. King's College students and faculty can then join with their community to make a difference in the world.

LaGrange College

601 BROAD STREET
LAGRANGE, GA 30240
706.812.7260
http://www.lgc.peachnet.edu/
UNDERGRADUATES: 900

For program information, please contact:
BOB THOMAS
rthomas@lgc.edu

"The freedom I have had in choosing my own work assignments and doing personal study has taught me the value of ethics within my educational experience."

—A LAGRANGE COLLEGE FOURTH-YEAR STUDENT

Founded in 1831, LaGrange College is the oldest private, Methodist-affiliated liberal arts college in Georgia. The faculty, staff, and president have adopted the following mission statement: "LaGrange College is called through The United Methodist Church to challenge the minds and inspire the souls of students by improving their creative, critical and communicative abilities in a caring and ethical community."

The goal of LaGrange College is to become a Servant Leadership institution. This spiritual-based approach to leadership views the leader as servant and measures results by the positive impact brought to those being led. The College has elected to embark upon a four-year initiative that will weave the principles and concepts of Servant Leadership into the fabric of the culture of LaGrange College.

✦ The first step is to determine the constituents' highest priority needs and then strive to meet those needs, in part by listening and by gaining the trust of those served. A Servant Leadership institution must constantly be open to the concerns of those served; therefore, the discernment process is ongoing.

✦ The second element of the process is to create a learning environment focused on Servant Leadership and to empower the faculty, staff, and students to develop appropriate programs. This will arm the members of the College community with the knowledge and spirit of Servant Leadership and motivate them to reach their highest potential.

As these elements are put into practice, faculty, staff, and students will understand that the entire campus must exhibit Servant Leadership. By meeting the goals of this initiative, LaGrange College will develop the necessary organization to raise both its capacity to serve and its performance as servants.

Louisiana College

1140 COLLEGE DRIVE
PINEVILLE, LA 71359
318.487.7011
http://www.lacollege.edu/
UNDERGRADUATES: 1,000

For program information, please contact:
GERRY C. HEARD, Ph.D.
heard@andria.lacollege.edu

"The Values program has caused me to ask myself why I believe what I believe and to realize that issues are often not black and white, but gray."

—A LOUISIANA COLLEGE FOURTH-YEAR STUDENT

Louisiana College is a private, liberal arts institution with a Christian perspective that seeks to provide students with an environment of excellence promoting their improvement and growth. The College offers a program designed to inform students about the nature of values and to encourage them in the development of their own value systems. The six courses in the program enable students to learn about the part that values play in individual lives, social issues, and the various professions and academic disciplines.

The program seeks to assist the student in achieving the following goals:

✦ To become more aware of how values function in an individual's life and how they change as that person matures and enters different stages of life;

✦ To adopt consciously one's own value system and acquire skills in making value decisions;

✦ To learn about the meaning of Christian values and how they differ from other value systems;

✦ To recognize traditional values in American society and compare them with values from other cultures;

✦ To learn more about value issues that arise in academic areas and within the vocations and institutions of American society and to develop constructive responses to these issues.

The courses utilize team teaching and interdisciplinary teaching along with a variety of methods such as the use of case studies and small group discussions. The introductory course is required of all students and concentrates on studying the nature and development of values and acquiring skills in decision-making. Students often say that the courses in the program are especially beneficial in enabling them to structure their own personal value system and improve their ability to make moral decisions.

MALONE COLLEGE

515 25TH STREET NW
CANTON, OH 44709
330.471.8100
http://www.malone.edu/

UNDERGRADUATES: 1,600

For program information, please contact:
JOHN CHOPKA
jchopka@malone.edu

Through Christian liberal arts education, Malone College seeks to develop students who exhibit moral character, conscience, and spiritual health. Malone's Evangelical Friends tradition values involvement in society while emphasizing justice, compassion, and peace, the basis for civic action and service. Malone's commitment to biblical, evangelical faith encourages the formation of a Christian worldview and the integration of Christianity with the life of the mind. Malone's faculty represents a range of Christian traditions and denominations, sometimes with diverse theological opinions, so that students are provided with an understanding of the depth and breadth of Christian thought. Moral character and Christian values are seen as foundational to students' ability to engage meaningfully with others in the contexts of their vocations and service.

Character development is pursued through:

✦ A comprehensive General Education program, focused on the theme of stewardship, that is, the responsible use of talents and resources;

✦ Intentional efforts to involve students in the lives of others, through a required first-year experience called "Into the Streets," a multicultural experience, and optional mission trips and off-campus programs;

✦ An active chapel program and opportunities for spiritual growth.

The concept of stewardship that unifies the General Education program is clarified in four areas: Stewardship Under God, Stewardship and Skills, Stewardship and the Sciences, and Stewardship and Society. The overall education experience at Malone helps students forge connections between what they are learning and how they are living. Supported with an active residence-hall life, athletic programs, and other opportunities, the educational experience at Malone attempts to build "rock-solid" individuals whose understanding of a Christian worldview gives way to genuine expression of Christian values and moral character.

METHODIST COLLEGE

5400 RAMSEY STREET
FAYETTEVILLE, NC 28311
910.630.7000
http://www.methodist.edu/

UNDERGRADUATES: 1,900

For program information, please contact:
JENNIFER ROHRER-WALSH
jrwalsh2@aol.com

"It was truly an honor to participate in the Student Lyceum sponsored by the Faculty Collegiality and Development Group."

—A METHODIST FOURTH-YEAR STUDENT

Methodist College, a private four-year liberal arts college, is strongly committed to nurturing the moral character of its students. The College's Faculty Collegiality & Development Group, a volunteer group, enhances students' characters through discussions, curriculum, lyceums, and calendar awareness. The Group also provides the campus forum for discussing interdisciplinary teaching, student-teacher ratios, academic standards, and the honor code.

Many projects have been influenced by the Faculty Collegiality & Development Group, including:

✦ Discussions inspired the Honors Program to add a character component actualizing the college motto: *"Veritas et virtus."* Students in the Honors Program are exposed to the liberal arts tradition and experience an esprit de corps as a class. They integrate social issues with their curriculum, perform community service, and join their course professors at cultural events.

✦ The annual B. F. Stone Endowed Lyceum, orchestrated by the Faculty Collegiality & Development Group, has featured faculty presentations on such subjects as *Hamlet* and self-image, American medical practices and ethics, and public safety versus individual freedom. Increased student interest led to the creation of a student lyceum.

✦ The Faculty Collegiality & Development Group is responsible for creating and publicizing the campus calendar of events. In particular, the establishment of an MC Marquee at strategic campus locations has resolved scheduling conflicts and encouraged faculty and students to respect one another's time and plan responsibly.

The Faculty Collegiality & Development Group remains committed to enhancing the educational, social, and moral development of Methodist College's students.

Millsaps College

1701 NORTH STATE STREET
JACKSON, MS 39210
601.974.1000
http://www.millsaps.edu/

UNDERGRADUATES: 1,200

For program information, please contact:
KEVIN RUSSELL
russeka@millsaps.edu

"Since enrolling at Millsaps, I have been constantly challenged by my professors to be an 'active' participant in my education."

—A MILLSAPS COLLEGE SECOND-YEAR STUDENT

Virtually every college has a "core" curriculum. Millsaps College, a private, church-affiliated, liberal arts institution, has developed a core curriculum that clearly stands out from the rest. For more than 30 years, Millsaps has molded and shaped its course offerings to give students a framework for their entire education. Required of all students, the Millsaps Core is a distinguishing attribute of this college.

Components of Millsaps College's Core Curriculum include:

✦ All students are required to complete the 10 Core courses, taught by interdisciplinary faculty teams to provide differing perspectives and points of view. These courses instill seven basic liberal arts abilities: reasoning, communication, quantitative thinking, historical consciousness, aesthetic judgment, global and multicultural awareness, and value and decision-making.

✦ Core 1, "Introduction to Liberal Studies," sets a learning framework for students by helping them analyze their core beliefs. Students develop a nurturing relationship with their Core 1 faculty member and small study group.

✦ Core 10, taken in the senior year, is designed to synthesize three years of study in relation to the student's chosen major and future plans. Students reflect on "where they have been," "where they want to go," and "how they will make a difference." In this capstone course, students write a paper integrating their studies into a final reflection of their learning experience.

Each course at Millsaps, regardless of discipline, emphasizes active and participatory learning and the development of writing and thinking skills. Guided by the College's student-developed honor code, students and faculty thrive in an environment that is grounded by trust and disciplined learning.

Northeastern Illinois University

5500 NORTH ST. LOUIS AVENUE
CHICAGO, IL 60625-4699
773.794.3060
http://www.neiu.edu/

UNDERGRADUATES: 7,500

For program information, please contact:
RON GLICK
r-glick@neiu.edu

Northeastern Illinois University is a comprehensive, state-supported commuter institution dedicated to teaching, research, and public service. Northeastern prides itself on excellent classroom instruction delivered by highly qualified faculty in an environment where technology is the key to a well-rounded education. In 1987 Northeastern piloted the substance-abuse prevention strategy of Curriculum Infusion, where faculty across disciplines integrate prevention content seamlessly into their classes. The program is especially significant for a commuter university where substantial numbers of students can only be reached in the classroom.

✦ Curriculum Infusion allows faculty, an influential group, to become a major component of the campus effort to prevent abuse of alcohol and other drugs. A core group of faculty, serving as a dissemination team, has learned to effectively disseminate the strategy through workshops, consultation, and development.

✦ Students examine a critical area of personal responsibility in the context of their course learning. They may write about and research issues related to alcohol and other drugs in an English course, study the effects of drugs in a science course, and observe the negative impact of drugs on the community in a political science course.

Curriculum Infusion stresses active student participation in the learning process through discussion, role play, and small group presentations. As many as 35 Northeastern faculty have integrated prevention into a variety of courses emphasizing active student learning and encouraging students to reflect on attitudes and behavior in relation to alcohol and other drugs. Students at Northeastern have many opportunities to examine their responsibility to self, others, and the community.

Northwestern State University

COLLEGE AVENUE
NATCHITOCHES, LA 71497
800.383.2208
http://www.nsula.edu/

UNDERGRADUATES: 7,700

For program information, please contact:
MARGARET E. COCHRAN, Ph.D.
cochran@nsula.edu

Established in 1987 by the Louisiana Board of Regents for Higher Education, the Louisiana Scholars' College at Northwestern State University serves as the state's sole public four-year, selective-admissions honors college in the liberal arts and sciences. The integrated, multidisciplinary curriculum is designed to expose students to the "great ideas" of the Western intellectual tradition and encourage them to enter an extended debate with student and faculty colleagues over the issues that have shaped our culture.

Cornerstone activities include:

✦ FACULTY INVOLVEMENT. The original Faculty Study Group that created the Honors' College identified several features of the Honors' College that remain in place today: an emphasis on personal and civic responsibility, faculty and student interaction, and a core sequence of courses titled "Texts and Traditions."

✦ HONOR CODE. Upon entering the College all students sign the College's Honor Code. The key features of the code are discussed regularly by the core faculty.

✦ CAPSTONE COURSE. The topic for the senior capstone course, chosen democratically by the rising senior class in collaboration with the faculty, typically involves an issue of contemporary concern.

✦ SENIOR THESIS. Students work individually with one or more faculty mentors to produce a senior thesis representing new scholarship in their discipline.

By encouraging students to question one another and to base their opinions on evidence rather than emotion, the Honors' College has been very successful in producing critical thinkers and problem-solvers. The College also resists the tendency to offer an education that ignores the importance of values and ethical principles. Approximately two-thirds of the students who graduate from the Honors' College go on to a professional school.

Olivet College

OLIVET, MI 49076
616.749.7000
http://www.olivetnet.edu/

UNDERGRADUATES: 900

For program information, please contact:
DONALD TUSKI, Ph.D.
dtuski@olivetnet.edu

The faculty at Olivet renewed their commitment to character development in 1993 by developing the Olivet Plan, a vision of education that affirms the importance of individual and social responsibility. In 1997 the faculty was instrumental in developing and adopting the Olivet College Compact, a set of principles that defines what it means to be a responsible member of the Olivet community. In addition, Olivet has put into place several exemplary faculty and curriculum programs that foster development:

✦ SELF AND COMMUNITY COURSE. A required year-long course for all students, the curriculum has been designed by faculty to help students explore their personal character, spiritual and philosophical issues, and family life in a rapidly changing and complex society. This course is the first step students take toward an Olivet education that focuses on character and competence.

✦ PORTFOLIO PROGRAM. A distinctive part of an Olivet education, the Portfolio Program provides an opportunity for students to graduate with something tangible in their hands—a portfolio filled with polished samples of their capabilities, accomplishments, and creative ideas. Students include in their portfolios examples of volunteer service and classroom assignments that focus on character development activities.

✦ CHARACTER EDUCATION RESOURCE CENTER. The center serves the college community and youth-serving organizations in the nearby surrounding regions. Among its many programs, the center sponsors an ongoing lecture and symposium series, "A Responsibility Matters," and a quarterly publication that focuses on character development issues at all levels of education.

Faculty at Olivet College are committed to providing the necessary resources and support to challenge students to develop the skills, perspectives, and strength of character to contribute to the common good.

OREGON STATE UNIVERSITY

CORVALLIS, OR 97331-4501
541.737.1000
http://www.orst.edu/

UNDERGRADUATES: 11,100

For program information, please contact:
COURTNEY CAMPBELL, Ph.D.
pese@orst.edu

"My involvement with PESE has enriched my understanding of the relationship of science and ethics and given me insight into the role values and personal integrity play in my life."

—AN OREGON STATE UNIVERSITY FOURTH-YEAR STUDENT

Oregon State University is committed to providing high-quality educational programs in the sciences, liberal arts, and selected professions. The Program for Ethics, Science, and the Environment supports multidisciplinary education and scholarship to assist the University and local communities in understanding and resolving value conflicts raised by scientific inquiry, biotechnology, and natural resource use. The ability to make informed and responsible decisions can be enhanced by the methods of self-examination and self-criticism that are at the core of ethical inquiry.

These objectives are realized through a variety of educational and research programs, including:

✦ An applied ethics certificate offered to undergraduate students. This interdisciplinary course provides students the opportunity to integrate ethics with various preprofessional interests, particularly in the environmental sciences and natural resources, and health and medicine.

✦ Workshops on ethics for local high-school students and civic organizations. The Program has joined with businesses and civic organizations in the Corvallis community to coordinate a workshop for high-school students on "ethical issues in the workplace and society."

✦ A biweekly student-faculty discussion forum. Students are challenged to assume responsibility in areas of sustainable lifestyles and personal ecology.

✦ A newsletter, with articles written by professors and religious leaders. The articles express varying views on critical moral issues, from cloning to environmental responsibility.

Since the initiation of the Program for Ethics, Science, and the Environment, enrollment in ethics courses at Oregon State University has doubled, as have the number of disciplines offering courses in ethics education.

PACE UNIVERSITY

ONE PACE PLAZA
NEW YORK, NY 10038
212.346.1200
http://www.pace.edu/

UNDERGRADUATES: 9,000

For program information, please contact:
KARLA JAY
kjay@fsmail.pace.edu

"Women's & Gender Studies at Pace has really helped me to grow as a person. What I have learned through this program will continue to be a part of my life long after I have graduated."

—A PACE UNIVERSITY FOURTH-YEAR STUDENT

At Pace University, the motto is *"Opportunitas,"* and both students and faculty take opportunity seriously. The Women's & Gender Studies Program at Pace seeks to enhance the college experience for its diverse student body by bringing issues relating to gender, race, class, and sexual orientation into the classroom. Courses explore economic and social issues and the intersections of gender with ethnic, racial, and sexual differences. Part of Pace's mission is to examine the assumptions underlying traditional disciplines and subjects of study.

Because feminism sprang from a philosophy of the "personal as political," students are encouraged to learn about the problems of women, children, and minorities around the world. An emphasis on justice, compassion, and outreach is reinforced through service-learning and internship programs in which students work with individuals and nonprofit institutions.

✦ Students attend lectures on international and national issues, human rights, and violence against women and men. Recent programs have discussed women and religion and the institution of marriage.

✦ Students can choose to work in cultural institutions, such as archives and museums, where they learn the ways in which nonprofit institutions benefit local communities. They may also perform service-learning for credit by working in battered women's shelters, settlements, and other community organizations.

By including faculty, staff, administrators, and students in the Women's Studies program, Pace has set up a model of achievement through cooperation. Graduates report that what they have learned in the Women's Studies program has served them well. They maintain a close connection with the program, even after graduation, because they learned to see the world in a completely different way.

Point Loma Nazarene College

3900 LOMALAND DRIVE
SAN DIEGO, CA 92106
619.849.2200
http://www.ptloma.edu/

UNDERGRADUATES: 2,200

For program information, please contact:
MAXINE WALKER, Ph.D.
maxinewalker@ptloma.edu

Building civic and personal responsibility for moral social reform is an essential focus of the Wesleyan Center for 21st Century Studies at Point Loma Nazarene College, a private, Christian liberal arts institution in the Wesleyan tradition. Programs include collaborative research, conversation among selected faculty and student scholars, craftsmanship in Wesleyan models for practice, collaborative writing for publication, special chapels, and seminars and symposia on vital cultural topics so that faculty and students can understand and fulfill their transformational role in the world. Numerous academic centers for Christian studies and professional societies have endorsed and commended the Wesleyan Center for its cultivation of strategies to influence the academy, church, and contemporary society.

The Wesleyan Center is involved with activities such as:

✦ Student seminars on "Science & Religion" and "Christians & Social Responsibility." These seminars are voluntary and require a competitive essay to participate.

✦ Collaborative faculty/student research on cultural issues;

✦ Student membership in the Society for the Study of Psychology and Wesleyan Theology;

✦ Faculty/student partnerships in conference planning and presentations. Future conferences include: "Companions & Apprentices," "Building Religious Bridges to Peace," and "Grace and the Creative Imagination."

Point Loma Nazarene College and the Wesleyan Center work collaboratively with students, faculty, and spiritual-development personnel on a myriad of topics. Indicative of the Wesleyan Center's influence on the campus is the number of faculty/student initiatives that have evolved independently and are then linked with the Wesleyan Center, which assists with resources, planning assistance, and a presentation format. These initiatives, both guided and organized by the Wesleyan Center, create a campus environment where responsibility in the personal, social, and natural worlds is creatively nurtured.

Ramapo College of New Jersey

505 RAMAPO VALLEY ROAD
MAHWAH, NJ 07430
201.529.7500
http://www.ramapo.edu/

UNDERGRADUATES: 4,800

For program information, please contact:
MICHAEL R. EDELSTEIN, Ph.D.
medelste@ramapo.edu

On the threshold of the 21st century, there is no more vital role for higher education than preparing students to live sustainably, assuring access to the resources necessary for life on this earth. Sustainability provides a new context for the traditional discussion of civic responsibility. Ramapo College of New Jersey serves as a model for how a campus can embrace the goals of ecoliteracy. The Institute for Environmental Studies oversees a variety of programs, all with direct student involvement, relating to the importance of sustainable practices:

✦ Student coordinators conduct a series of regional environmental conferences, providing outreach to a network of interested citizens, academics, communities, and institutions.

✦ Students manage the Alternative Energy and Environment Center, maintain the organic gardens, and operate various educational outreach programs, held in the Solar Schoolhouse.

✦ Students in the Sustainable Communities course work to make the campus more sustainable, including improving energy savings and recycling and composting food wastes from the cafeteria.

✦ Ramapo has implemented ecoliteracy throughout the curriculum and environmental education training for K-12 teachers through workshops.

✦ Students in the Environmental Assessment course conduct an actual impact assessment of a real community problem.

✦ Study abroad programs allow students to learn the issues surrounding ecotourism in Costa Rica, regional problems in the Aegean Sea, and park management and land-use conflicts in Western America.

Through such experiences, Ramapo students confront the difficult dilemmas of their time and move beyond pat answers toward complex problem-solving. At the nexus of the Environmental Studies program is the personal responsibility each person faces to have the minimum adverse impact on the earth while offering the maximum positive benefit to society.

Roanoke College

221 COLLEGE LANE
SALEM, VA 24153-3794
540.375.2500
http://www.roanoke.edu/

UNDERGRADUATES: 1,700

For program information, please contact:
HANS ZORN, Ph.D.
zorn@roanoke.edu

Part of the mission of Roanoke College is to develop in its students a capacity for responsible leadership so that they may make significant contributions to society. To further this goal, all Roanoke students participate in the college's General Education Program, consisting in a core sequence of General Studies courses in addition to distribution courses designed to provide breadth of knowledge and courses in their chosen major field of study.

✦ The General Studies Core teaches students to read critically, express themselves clearly, think with discrimination, and act responsibly.

✦ After a two-semester writing sequence, students take three Civilization courses exposing them to the central ideas and events that have shaped and continue to shape the world.

✦ All second-year students take "Values and the Responsible Life," dealing with key moral, religious, and intellectual values, and taught by faculty from the Religion and Philosophy Department. This course addresses value questions from a normative standpoint, examining major Western and world perspectives and relating these values to contemporary social and personal issues.

✦ A senior symposium is taught by the Humanities, Mathematics and Science, and Social Science faculties. This course requires students to synthesize what they have learned in their General Studies courses and in their major to address a topic of common interest.

The Roanoke College General Education Program encourages students to reflect on their own values in a critical, disciplined way, to understand the values of others, and to apply values responsibly. Roanoke graduates find themselves well placed to articulate a system of ethical or religious values and to take their places as citizens in a free society.

Saint Anselm College

100 SAINT ANSELM DRIVE
MANCHESTER, NH 03102
603.641.7000
http://www.anselm.edu/

UNDERGRADUATES: 1,900

For program information, please contact:
KEVIN STALEY, Ph.D.
kstanley@anselm.edu

"The goal of the Humanities Program is not just to introduce students to artistic and political genius from antiquity to the present, but also to encourage us to ask the most penetrating questions about what it means to be a human being." —A RECENT SAINT ANSELM GRADUATE

A Catholic liberal arts college in the Benedictine tradition, Saint Anselm was founded in 1889. Today, the 40 monks who live at the college imbue the college with the contemplative ethos so much a part of the Benedictine tradition. In the early 1970s, when so many colleges were abandoning core curriculum requirements, Saint Anselm faculty developed an interdisciplinary, two-year Humanities Program titled "Portraits of Human Greatness."

✦ YEAR ONE: ARCHETYPES. During the first year at Anselm, students study nine archetypes or ideal-types, such as the warrior, the prophet, and the teacher. Twice each week, a professor from one of the academic departments delivers the Humanities Lecture. Seminars, with 20 students or less, are held twice a week to examine the archetype or ideal and to help students understand, evaluate, and discuss lectures and readings. Each archetype includes historical and literary figures ranging from the Ancient Greeks and Hebrews through the European Middle Ages.

✦ YEAR TWO: INDIVIDUAL PORTRAITS. During the second year, students study 12 individuals from the Italian Renaissance to the present. Each individual has far-reaching social, cultural, or political significance. In recent years students have studied the lives of Michelangelo, Martin Luther, and Dorothy Day.

In short, the goal of the Humanities Program is to study composite pictures of people, real and fictional, who reveal what it means to be human and to act humanely. With the help of the faculty, Saint Anselm students learn to discern patterns within the choices made by these figures. Understanding these patterns of behavior become the foundation for students to explore their own behavior as well as the values and the virtues they want to embody.

Saint Joseph's College

HIGHWAY 231
RENSSELAER, IN 47978
219.866.6000
http://www.saintjoe.edu/
UNDERGRADUATES: 900

For program information, please contact:
TIMOTHY MCFARLAND, Ph.D.
timm@saintjoe.edu

"The Core Curriculum has opened my mind to a wonderful range of disciplines outside my major, including psychology, history, and philosophy."
—A SAINT JOSEPH'S FOURTH-YEAR STUDENT

Civic, personal, and global responsibility are thoroughly incorporated into the holistic education at Saint Joseph's College, a private, liberal arts institution. The Core Curriculum is a four-year program of general education in which all students and approximately 80% of the faculty participate. Centered on the theme of Christian Humanism, the Core Curriculum provides an intellectual challenge through courses in the liberal arts and sciences. It also includes various assessment strategies that appraise intellectual and affective development throughout the students' four years. Unique features of the program include the following:

✦ Students are offered ongoing opportunities for service in the local community. A number of students and faculty have traveled to other parts of the world for volunteer projects.

✦ Students and faculty share a common learning experience, which often continues outside the classroom.

✦ Development seminars to help the faculty involved in the program are presented on a regular basis.

✦ Students are challenged to see the interdependence among academic disciplines and peoples throughout the world.

✦ The third-year "Intercultural Studies" component expands students' horizons and perspectives.

The shared experiences engender a true sense of "academic community" among students and faculty. Since the program's inception in 1969, the lives of thousands of students have been transformed, so that they see themselves and their roles in the world very differently. Students have learned to recognize the value commitments at the foundation of their respective majors, to appreciate the interdependence of various fields of knowledge, and to understand their own responsibility for making the world a better place.

Saint Mary's College

NOTRE DAME, IN 46556-5001
219.284.4584
http://www.saintmarys.edu/
UNDERGRADUATES: 1,500

For program information, please contact:
PATRICK E. WHITE, Ph.D.
pwhite@saintmary's.edu

Saint Mary's College, a Roman Catholic institution for women in the liberal arts tradition, founded the Center for Academic Innovation (CFAI) to reaffirm and nurture the personal responsibility of faculty and students for the vitality of the college community and for the civic community beyond. Under the direction of Dr. Patrick White, defining programs, such as Student Independent Study and Research (SISTAR), the CFAI Fellows, and Novice Mentor Partnership, support a model of intellectual development that is at once collaborative, value-based, intellectually rigorous, and practical:

✦ SISTAR. Students work with faculty, not as assistants but as full partners in their own research, giving both faculty and students ownership of their work and responsibility for growth.

✦ CFAI FELLOWS. Faculty receive support for research and study, and their work must be given back to the community in sharing ideas and results. One CFAI Fellow team, for example, helped faculty at Saint Mary's learn how to use portfolios to improve teaching.

✦ NOVICE MENTOR PARTNERSHIP. New faculty are paired with mentors outside their departments, enabling them to connect both to the cohort of their entering group and to that of their senior mentors. This enables the school to communicate and explore its values, as well as articulate the goals of the faculty at Saint Mary's.

Through its many programs and its receptivity to new ideas, the CFAI combats the narrow self-involvement and careerism that sometimes limits development of students and faculty. Constantly attentive to serving emerging needs for student, faculty, and administrator development, the Center attends to the special values of community, service, and leadership that are at the heart of Saint Mary's College.

Salem College

PO BOX 10548
WINSTON-SALEM, NC 27108
336.721.2621
http://www.salem.edu/

UNDERGRADUATES: 1,000

For program information, please contact:
ANN MCELANEY JOHNSON, Ph.D.
McElaney@salem.edu

Civic and personal responsibility are a fundamental focus of the learning experience at Salem College, a private, liberal arts institution founded in 1772. Salem's rigorous academics are complemented by a challenging, integrated program developed by President Julianne Still Thrift, the "Salem Signature," which is dedicated to preparing young women for leadership. Each academic year offers specific elements of the program:

✦ First-year students take an intensive two-semester reading, discussion, and writing course that explores issues of personal growth, multiculturalism, environmental responsibility, and leadership. Students begin a journal they will keep throughout the four years at Salem.

✦ Second-year students spend at least 30 hours working with a community-service agency and meet each week with a teacher in a Reflection Group to discuss the implications of their volunteer experiences. They also participate in group community-service projects, such as working in homeless shelters or soup kitchens.

✦ Third-year students serve internships directly related to their career interests. They work throughout the U.S., Europe, and Asia, gaining experience that helps them find jobs in their chosen fields, while learning the cultural and social dynamics of a different environment.

✦ Fourth-year students participate in a senior seminar, "Values in Leadership for Life," which helps them interpret and consolidate their college experiences in order to move into a successful future.

Salem assesses the program's influence through individual student portfolios, reflections, and input from the campus faculty and administrators. The Salem Signature, an academic experience offered by no other college, enables students to learn more about themselves and to take their places as leaders in an ever-changing world.

Santa Clara University

500 EL CAMINO REAL
SANTA CLARA, CA 95053
408.554.4000
http://www.scu.edu/

UNDERGRADUATES: 4,200

For program information, please contact:
JEROME FACIONE
jfacione@scu.edu

"Santa Clara University provides opportunities for students to be an integral part of the community."
—A Santa Clara third-year student

Santa Clara University is dedicated to providing an education that emphasizes moral and spiritual as well as intellectual and aesthetic values, with a commitment to academic excellence, freedom of inquiry and expression, and the search for truth.

The Markkula Center for Applied Ethics of Santa Clara University is the natural outgrowth of an institution committed to moral debate and consideration in all fields and professions. The Center has developed a character-education program that integrates ethics into schools and organizations. The programs offered by The Center, which build a personal understanding of values and teach educators, students, and other leaders to become ethical role models, include:

✦ Ethics Camp. Teachers, counselors, and administrators from elementary, middle, and high schools learn to be ethical role models and to incorporate ethics into the classroom at this weeklong camp and retreat. Returning to their classrooms, they are better prepared to be effective role models and help students make a commitment to live as ethical individuals.

✦ Student Reflection Leaders Program. The Markkula Ethics Center and the Center for Student Leadership offer a yearlong course to raise students' moral awareness and sensitivity using the perspectives of facts, emotions, social issues, ethics, and spirituality.

✦ Leadership through Ethical Action and Development (LEAD). Undergraduates at SCU are trained to teach ethics in school and recreational settings, lead group activities in ethics workshops, and mentor students in local schools.

✦ Student Performers Involved in Character Education (SPICE). In partnership with SCU's Theatre Department, the Markkula Ethics Center trains a group of drama students to perform skits about everyday moral dilemmas young people face (such as parental relations, sex, academic integrity) in local schools.

Spring Arbor College

SPRING ARBOR, MI 49283
517.750.1200
http://www.arbor.edu/

UNDERGRADUATES: 2,500

For program information, please contact:
JOHN NEMECEK
jnemecek@arbor.edu

The Family Life Education major at Spring Arbor, a Christian liberal arts college, is designed for students interested in strengthening families. Students develop the knowledge and skills needed to prevent problems in families or to intervene when a problem arises. The major is offered at various sites throughout the state of Michigan through the School of Adult Studies. Required courses within the Family Life Education major which focus on dimensions of character development include:

✦ ADULT DEVELOPMENT AND LIFE PLANNING. Students review adult development, including moral and faith development. Students are challenged to examine their own growth in these areas by developing a personal mission statement reflecting their core values.

✦ MARRIAGE AND FAMILY. Students learn about marriage and family within a positive context and as an important place for developing virtues and values.

✦ VALUES: PERSONAL AND SOCIAL. This capstone course applies classic perspectives on values to behavior. The student's mission statement from the first course is reviewed and refined.

Since the Family Life Education major began in 1991, more than 800 students have completed the program. Over 70% of these students indicate that the program has stimulated significant personal growth. The program was also recently featured by Focus on the Family, a national organization that supports families through radio broadcasts and a monthly magazine.

Sweet Briar College

US 29 NORTH
SWEET BRIAR, VA 24595
804.381.6100
http://www.sbc.edu/

UNDERGRADUATES: 750

For program information, please contact:
LAURA STAMAN
staman@sbc.edu

"The 'Learning the Land' program was a wonderful way for me to meet members of the faculty, as well as to learn about our college's natural treasures."

—A SWEET BRIAR SECOND-YEAR STUDENT

Nationally recognized for its science programs, Sweet Briar College, founded in 1901 as a private, liberal arts school for women, educates students to be responsible and responsive members of a world community. Preparing women for careers in math, engineering, and the sciences is more than an issue of equity at Sweet Briar: it is the college's priority. "Learning on the Land" is an orientation program organized by Sweet Briar faculty, staff, and upperclass students to challenge incoming students to explore important moral and environmental issues using the entire campus as a classroom.

Some of the cornerstone activities include:

✦ DIGGING UP SWEET BRIAR'S PAST. English and archeology professors lead students on a dig to learn about the college's natural resources and landmark history. The dig includes learning about Sweet Briar House, a structure that expresses cultural ideals stretching back to the Italian Renaissance.

✦ EXPLORING THE ENVIRONMENT. A theater professor creates sound and movement improvisations to explore the relationship between humans and nature. A professor of philosophy also explores whether women experience the environment differently—and if so, how?

✦ DESIGNING WITH NATURE. An environmental studies professor explores Sweet Briar's land to help students better understand the patterns that exist in nature and in ourselves.

✦ EXPLORING SWEET BRIAR'S HORTICULTURAL TREASURES. The campus is home to a number of interesting flowers and gardens. A professor of chemistry acquaints students with the college's horticultural treasures and explores the medicinal uses of native plants.

Sweet Briar is committed to educating women of character who can contribute their talents and skills to any community through a deep appreciation of the natural world.

United States Military Academy

606 THAYER ROAD
WEST POINT, NY 10996
914.938.4041
http://www.usma.edu/

UNDERGRADUATES: 4,000

For program information, please contact:
COL. GEORGE B. FORSYTHE
zb8085@usma.edu

*"As Chairperson of the Cadet Honor Committee,
I have the support of a dedicated faculty who are deeply
committed to supporting the Cadet Honor Code and
graduating leaders of character."*

—A U.S. MILITARY ACADEMY FOURTH-YEAR CADET

The mission of the U.S. Military Academy, America's oldest service academy, is to develop officer leaders of character. At West Point, character development spans three programs that comprise the Cadet Leader Development System: Academic, Military, and Physical Programs. This comprehensive approach to character development has been in place at the U.S. Military Academy for over 150 years.

✦ Cadets and faculty are expected to be persons of character in every setting. The Cadet Honor Code, "A cadet will not lie, cheat, or steal, or tolerate those who do," governs all aspects of cadet life. From their first day at West Point, cadets agree to live by the Honor Code and are expected to confront and, if necessary, report other cadets who violate the Honor Code.

✦ Courses within the academic curriculum explicitly address character development so that West Point graduates are officers who can engage in moral discourse, analyze ethical responses to moral problems, and promote ethical conduct within their organizations.

✦ Beyond the classroom, faculty members lead seminars with cadets on topics of professional ethics, such as honor and respect, thus connecting academic and professional development.

✦ Faculty members also mentor, coach, and advise cadets involved in intercollegiate sports and extracurricular activities. Matters of integrity are an important part of their service in this role.

West Point's integrated approach to leadership and character development is known worldwide. West Point graduates understand the civic responsibilities associated with the officer's role in society, especially those responsibilities that emanate from the U.S. constitutional system of government, the subordination of the military to civilian authority, and the role of the Army in national security.

University of Notre Dame

NOTRE DAME, IN 46556
219.631.5000
http://www.nd.edu/

UNDERGRADUATES: 7,800

For program information, please contact:
ALFRED STASHIS, JR.
stashis.2@nd.edu

*"People enter the ACE program because they want to
make the world a better place. They learn how to teach,
and they leave with experience and a charge to continue
the mission."*

—A NOTRE DAME GRADUATE

The 1990s have witnessed a growing awareness of the strengths of American Catholic schools. At the same time, many leading Catholic educators recognize that the declining numbers of men and women choosing religious vocations, many of whom in the past served Catholic education as teachers and administrators, is creating a need for talented young people to teach and lead the 8,500 Catholic schools across the nation.

In 1993, in an effort to respond to this call, the University of Notre Dame forged the Alliance for Catholic Education (ACE) with the U.S. Catholic Conference's Department of Education, the National Catholic Education Association, and the University of Portland. ACE seeks to develop a corps of highly motivated educators to meet the needs of the nation's most under-served elementary and secondary schools by recruiting, training, placing, and supporting them as teachers in nine Southern states.

ACE teachers undergo an intensive teacher-training program designed and administered by the University of Portland and the University of Notre Dame. Graduate-level course work is integrated with an immersion in teaching. Upon completion of two years in the ACE program, participants have fulfilled the requirements for a master's degree in education.

Demand for ACE teachers across the country outpaces the program's capacity. This continuing demand is perhaps the best testimony to the overall effectiveness of the ACE teachers in the schools and communities in which they serve. Roughly two-thirds of the program's graduates have decided to pursue careers in education, giving Notre Dame every confidence that, in addition to providing a needed presence in the lives of our children, ACE is shaping talented new leaders for the future of education.

VALPARAISO UNIVERSITY

VALPARAISO, IN 46383
888.GO-VALPO
http://www.valpo.edu/
UNDERGRADUATES: 3,000

For program information, please contact:
MARK R. SCHWEHN, Ph.D.
mark.schwehn@valpo.edu

"The greatest asset of Christ College is the unparalleled dedication of its faculty to the guidance of each student's personal, professional, and scholarly development."
—A VALPARAISO FOURTH-YEAR STUDENT

Christ College, the Honors College of Valparaiso, an independent Lutheran institution, is a community of faculty and students that enriches Christian intellectual life through independent thought and collaborative inquiry. Faculty members are prominent in national conversations about the role of church-related higher education. Dean Mark R. Schwehn, author of *Exiles from Eden: Religion and the Academic Vocation in America,* is a widely recognized authority on Christian higher education. Providing honors-level, interdisciplinary study, Christ College offers a curriculum that emphasizes liberal arts and the humanities:

✦ The first-year curriculum integrates the study of great books in history, literature, art, philosophy, and religion. The "Dimensions of Leadership" seminar acquaints first-year students with leadership theory, practices, problems, issues, and their own promise as leaders.

✦ Third/fourth-year seminars that address character formation and ethical development include "Ethical Reflection and Modern Literature," "Love and Friendship," and "Character and Destiny."

✦ The Senior Colloquium provides a capstone experience in which students refine their understandings of their spiritual, moral, and vocational journeys through autobiographical narrative.

✦ Valparaiso University's honor code, established in 1944 by students with the full support of the faculty, ensures academic integrity among students and fosters a lifelong habit of intellectual honesty.

Dedicated to the cultivation of intellectual, moral, civic, and spiritual virtues in its students, Christ College nurtures their formation as men and women of exemplary character.

VANDERBILT UNIVERSITY

2201 WEST END AVENUE
NASHVILLE, TN 37240
615.322.7311
http://www.vanderbilt.edu/
UNDERGRADUATES: 5,900

For program information, please contact:
GAY WELCH, Ph.D.
gay.h.welch@vanderbilt.edu

At a time when public perceptions separate "the university" from "the real world," Vanderbilt University, a private institution, seeks to involve the entire community in a continuing conversation that connects students' classroom learning with larger societal issues. Through Project Dialogue, a variety of programs, including small group discussions, art events, and speakers, address the wide-ranging interests of students. Although the contents and formats among the four undergraduate schools are diverse, the focus is similar: to include public moral discourse in the very definition of academic excellence.

Project Dialogue consists of four main objectives:

✦ To encourage students to reflect on their opinions, carefully considering their sources as well as their relation to the spirit of service and citizenship at Vanderbilt.

✦ To give students the opportunity to consider others' views in a safe environment. Learning about someone who is "different" through personal experience offers insights not easy to gain secondhand, often leading to the awareness that difference does not have to divide.

✦ To instill in students a broader understanding of the connections between knowing and doing and between truth(s) and goodness to equip them to better serve society.

✦ To empower students as they identify issues, develop programs, and educate one another. In so doing, they enact the leadership and civic virtue Vanderbilt strives to impart.

All aspects of Project Dialogue encourage students to find the common ground between the necessarily limited experience of undergraduate education and the vast possibilities of the larger community—and to explore that territory with integrity.

Wheaton College

501 EAST COLLEGE AVENUE
WHEATON, IL 60187
630.752.5000
http://www.wheaton.edu/

UNDERGRADUATES: 2,250

For program information, please contact:
ALAN JACOBS, Ph.D.
alan.jacobs@wheaton.edu

"The Faith and Learning seminar for new faculty is social, intellectual, and practical. Almost on a weekly basis, I incorporate into my own classroom something that I read as part of the faculty seminar."

—A WHEATON PROFESSOR

Although Wheaton College has had a faculty development program for the past 25 years, this highly selective Christian liberal arts college has recently revised and strengthened the program. The new Faith and Learning initiative for faculty includes the following cornerstone activities:

✦ FOUNDATIONS FOR INTEGRATING FAITH AND LEARNING. This seminar for new faculty considers the contemporary issues that need to be informed by faith. Eight senior faculty serve as mentors and introduce new faculty to Wheaton's distinctive mission and purpose. The faculty participating in the seminars are asked to complete a faith and learning paper as a condition for receiving tenure at Wheaton. The papers are designed not only to demonstrate the ability to think integratively about faith and one's discipline but, more directly, the papers serve as a resource for senior seminars and other forums in each academic department.

✦ ENRICHING SEMINARS FOR SENIOR FACULTY. This summer seminar offers faculty the opportunity to read and critique "Faith and Learning" essays written by Wheaton professors as well as those from the broader community of evangelical scholars.

Along with institutional support and grants, the Wheaton alumni association has taken on funding of the Faith and Learning initiative. The program is so vital to the entire college community because of the belief that Wheaton students will be better equipped to integrate issues of faith and learning as faculty develop the teaching tools to think creatively about these questions.

William Penn College

201 TRUEBLOOD AVENUE
OSKALOOSA, IA 52577
515.673.1001
http://www.wmpenn.edu/

UNDERGRADUATES: 1,200

For program information, please contact:
JOHN OTTOSSON
ottossonj@wmpenn.edu

Education at William Penn College, a church-affiliated institution, is grounded in the themes of leadership development, lifelong learning, ethical practice, and service to others. The William Penn College Leadership Core is designed to provide students with a solid foundation for their future roles as leaders through a series of prescribed courses that emphasize the intellectual, spiritual, physical, and moral makeup of productive citizens. Each course in the sequenced curriculum addresses one of the basic requirements for leadership development: inquiry and critical analysis, communication, numerical reasoning, technological proficiency, historical consciousness, scientific reasoning, values formation, aesthetic appreciation and experience, international and multicultural understanding, or leadership and management skills. The Core program's key elements set it apart as a unique curriculum:

✦ A required first-year course introduces students to the Leadership Core, and participants design and build the first entry into their Leadership Portfolios.

✦ Several Leadership Core classes require a service project, such as working with Habitat for Humanity, volunteering to assist the elderly, and tutoring homeless children during the school year and providing a camp for them in the summer months.

In addition, student-life activities offer extensive leadership opportunities. The Student Government Association oversees all other student organizations on campus, allocating funds on the basis of competitive requests. This students-leading-students structure allows the organizations to serve as incubators for future leaders.

The Leadership Core's required course sequence, the stress placed on character development, the myriad participatory experiences for future leaders, and the emphasis on learning through service combine effectively to provide William Penn students with a distinctive and invaluable preparation for the future.

XAVIER UNIVERSITY

3800 VICTORY PARKWAY
CINCINNATI, OH 45207
513.745.3000
http://www.xu.edu/

UNDERGRADUATES: 3,900

For program information, please contact:
WILLIAM MADGES, Ph.D.
madges@admin.xu.edu

*"My Ethics, Religion, and Society classes open my eyes
to social injustice, provide a framework to analyze issues,
and inspire me to take informed action."*

—AN XAVIER THIRD-YEAR STUDENT

To foster in students the desire to be "persons for others" is a major educational goal at Xavier University, a private, coeducational institution grounded in the liberal arts tradition. To help achieve this goal, the University established the E/RS (Ethics/Religion and Society) Program, a four-course program based in the core curriculum that provides students with substantive opportunities for the ethical and religious analysis of socially significant issues, as well as for the development of a worldview that is oriented to responsible moral action. The E/RS Program addresses the whole person:

✦ INTELLECTUALLY, through courses that examine questions concerning the purposes of life, the nature of society, and the process of moral decision-making;

✦ MORALLY, through the Ethics as an Introduction to Philosophy course, in which students ponder the meaning and practice of justice in society; and

✦ SPIRITUALLY, through the core Theological Foundations, which explore the significance of the Jewish, Christian, and other religious traditions as resources for addressing the pressing ethical, social, and political issues of our time.

Students are also encouraged to complete area minors, several of which deal with issues of social justice, including peace studies, women's and minorities' studies, and environmental studies. Learning semesters are available to immerse students in the social conditions of a different culture, be it urban Cincinnati or disadvantaged communities in Nicaragua or Nepal. In recognition of its excellence, the E/RS Program has received grants from the McGregor Foundation and the National Endowment for the Humanities. Small classes, mentoring relationships with faculty, and varied opportunities for service all allow Xavier students to explore values and move toward becoming significant contributors to the betterment of society.

VOLUNTEER SERVICE PROGRAMS

Character development is more than teaching students to know what is good — it provides opportunities for students to do what is good. Volunteer service programs enable students to contribute and learn through a volunteer activity. Outstanding programs include opportunities for students to recognize that they have learned something significant through their service experience and that what they have learned is important for life.

ALVERNIA COLLEGE

400 ST. BERNARDINE STREET
READING, PA 19607
610.796.8200
http://www.alvernia.edu/

UNDERGRADUATES: 1,300

For program information, please contact:
ELLEN ENGLER
engleel@alvernia.edu

"Alvernia has shown me the meaning of service."
—AN ALVERNIA THIRD-YEAR STUDENT

The phrase, "To Learn, To Love, and To Serve," embodies the spirit of Alvernia College's academic, spiritual, and moral filament. Service to the community has been an integral part of this private, liberal arts institution of Franciscan heritage since the College was founded in 1958. Alvernia's goal is to encourage students to make a difference in society. To that end, the College requires students to complete 40 hours of community service in order to graduate.

✦ Core curriculum provides several courses where students are exposed to the virtues of civic and personal responsibility. Assignments often address responsible behaviors.

✦ First-year students are given the opportunity to participate in a service activity during new student orientation.

✦ Students pursuing a career in community service may receive a Volunteer Management Certificate.

✦ Courses including a service-learning component carry a free fourth credit for students who take advantage of that component.

Alvernia recently introduced "The Community Classroom" course, whose first class opted to form a partnership with Dayspring Homes, a local organization dedicated to providing a Christian environment for people with special needs. Dayspring trains college students to serve as mentors and companions to the clients. The College will soon be offering Principal's Service Scholarships to local high schools. The principals of these schools will nominate students who have a record of community service during high school; those students chosen will be rewarded financially to continue as leaders in service at Alvernia College.

Each year, Alvernia College students volunteer over 20,000 hours of service, a figure that speaks to the institution's goals of fostering a community of faith and devotion to service, particularly to the materially and spiritually disadvantaged.

AZUSA PACIFIC UNIVERSITY

901 EAST ALOSTA
AZUSA, CA 91702-7000
626.969.3434
http://www.apu.edu/

UNDERGRADUATES: 2,500

For program information, please contact:
JOY BIANCHI BROWN
jmbbrown@apu.edu

Service, community, scholarship, and Christian values serve as the four cornerstones of Azusa Pacific University's mission. Azusa's Office of Community Service Learning was established in 1994 with a Council of Independent Colleges grant to give more academic credibility to the service that students were already required to perform in order to graduate. Through service, students at this private, liberal arts institution can begin to make connections between their actions, their education, and their faith.

The Office of Community Service Learning serves several functions:

✦ It acts as a liaison between the community and the University to match needs with the knowledge, resources, and commitment to meet those needs.

✦ It assists faculty with the logistics of integrating classroom learning with outside experience to actively engage students in attaining knowledge through service experiences.

✦ It instills leadership skills in students, who manage its activities and learn through serving. Faculty work with them to promote pedagogy and assist with any logistical details of their service-learning projects.

Each professor is assigned a Service Learning Advocate, a student coordinator who provides orientation, training, and placement in service sites for their students, and helps the professor find ways to best integrate service into the curriculum.

Institutional leaders at APU strive to produce graduates who will be mature in their faith, concerned for their world, actively involved in their community, and dedicated to life-long learning. The Office of Community Service Learning assists in inspiring students to live lives of continual awareness and involvement in the world around them. Students leave APU with a sense of belonging and commitment that they keep for the rest of their lives.

BENTLEY COLLEGE

175 FOREST STREET
WALTHAM, MA 02154-4705
617.891.2000
http://www.bentley.edu/

UNDERGRADUATES: 4,100

For program information, please contact:
ROBERT E. KOULISH, Ph.D.
rkoulish@bentley.edu

Bentley is the only business school in the U.S. with a cross-disciplinary service-learning program and an extensive scholarship and work program at the undergraduate level. The Bentley Service Learning Center (BSLC) teaches students that community involvement outside the classroom contributes significantly to what they have learned within it.

Components of the Bentley Service Learning Center include:

✦ CITY YEAR SERVE-A-THON. All first-year students are required to participate in a service-learning project. To that end, Bentley students work in collaboration with the group City Year on projects in the local community.

✦ BANKBOSTON/BENTLEY COLLEGE FORUM. This annual event brings together business executives, community representatives, and Bentley students, faculty, and staff to explore the relationship between business and community.

✦ JUNIOR ACHIEVEMENT (JA). This unique program enables Bentley students to volunteer in local elementary and secondary schools, teaching children the business and economic concepts of the world today.

✦ AMERICA READS. This federal program encourages states and communities to form literacy partnerships among local schools, libraries, and youth groups.

✦ BENTLEY IMMIGRATION ASSISTANCE PROGRAM. Specially trained students assist area immigrants toward formalizing their citizenship to the United States.

✦ THE SCHOLARSHIP PROGRAM. First-year students with a demonstrated interest in community service are eligible for this program, which awards $5,000 annually to students who wish to enhance their community awareness, leadership, and interpersonal skills.

Bentley endeavors to inculcate in their students a sensitivity to diversity in all its types (cultural and intellectual), as well as the capacity to be collaborative while maintaining a strong sense of personal responsibility.

BOISE STATE UNIVERSITY

1910 UNIVERSITY DRIVE
BOISE, ID 83725
208.385.1011
http://www.idbsu.edu/

UNDERGRADUATES: 13,300

For program information, please contact:
PEG BLAKE, Ph.D.
pblake@boisestate.edu

Boise State University, a public, liberal arts institution, prizes commitment to community service. This dedication is best exemplified by the leadership and conviction of President Charles Ruch, who says, "It's absolutely critical that we provide opportunities for students which enable them to give back to the community that supports them in so many ways."

Boise State engages in community service and leadership through several programs, including:

✦ STUDENT CITIZENSHIP PROGRAM. This program focuses primarily on establishing service-learning courses and encouraging faculty to offer a fourth-credit option to foster citizenship through involvement in academically based community service.

✦ VOLUNTEER SERVICES BOARD. Through this student-run organization students are provided with the opportunity to gain career experience and personal growth through volunteering.

✦ STUDENT ORGANIZATIONS. In order to receive financial support from the University Student Government, organizations are required to engage in community service.

✦ ACADEMIC TENURE. Faculty seeking tenure are required to demonstrate their commitment to community service at Boise State. BSU faculty participate in community life as leaders and members of local organizations and projects such as the Red Cross, Idaho Suicide Prevention Hotline, and the community homeless shelter.

Each year, an increasing number of students, faculty, and staff get involved with service learning. Annual events such as the University's Volunteer Fair, where local organizations are invited to campus to recruit students, exhibit Boise State's commitment to service and the community. That commitment is further exemplified by the University's expansion of its service-learning credit program, which requires students to complete 40 hours of community service linked to the course, keep a journal, and attend bimonthly reflection sessions that help them learn from their experiences.

Brown University

45 PROSPECT STREET
PROVIDENCE, RI 02912
401.863.2234
http://www.brown.edu/

UNDERGRADUATES: 6,000

For program information, please contact:
PETER HOCKING
peter_hocking@brown.edu

Brown University's Swearer Center for Public Service considers active community participation and social responsibility to be central concerns of this institution's private, liberal arts education. This approach reflects Brown's public trust both to prepare its students for meaningful engagement in the American democracy and to be of service to the world at large. Over the past decade, the Center has evolved to reflect the notion of a powerful intersection between service, vital community, and social change, where the theory of the classroom meets the practice of living in the world.

Activities of the Swearer Center include:

✦ **Short-Term Service.** One-day projects involve individual students, student organizations, residence-hall units, and other special-interest student groups in work with community agency partners.

✦ **Language and Literacy.** Swearer Language and Literacy programs fill gaps in existing services, collaborating with other service providers whenever possible. Students work with special-needs populations including immigrants, parenting teens, low-income and minority communities, senior citizens, the developmentally disabled, the Deaf, and adults in need of basic education skills.

✦ **Youth Education.** The Kids' Project matches college students with local elementary-school students to help meet a variety of academic and social needs.

✦ **Community Health.** The Domestic Abuse Advocacy Project places volunteers in local women's shelters and in the Providence District Court as advocates for survivors of abuse.

The Swearer Center encourages students to expose themselves to the complexity of social problems as they build relationships within communities. While the Center's definition of service includes many approaches, it is grounded in a community-development model of respect, cooperation, and partnership.

California State University– Chico

FIRST AND NORMAL STREETS
CHICO, CA 95929-0722
530.898.6116
http://www.csuchico.edu/

UNDERGRADUATES: 12,500

For program information, please contact:
NAN TIMMONS
ntimmons@csuchico.edu

Community Action Volunteers in Education (CAVE) is a community-service program located on the California State University – Chico campus. A nationally recognized, nonprofit, volunteer organization serving the community since 1966, CAVE administers 23 programs that provide volunteer services to children, elderly, special populations, and other community agencies and state facilities.

Activities of CAVE include:

✦ **Kids Program.** The Project Pals Program allows students to act as Big Brothers/Big Sisters to children in kindergarten through 8th grades. The volunteer serves as a positive role model for the child, offering support and companionship.

✦ **State Facilities Program.** The Napa Program provides students the opportunity to interact with adults in psychiatric hospitals. Students are provided with a unique opportunity to learn more about mental illness while the patients experience special activities and contact with the community.

✦ **Adult Literacy Program.** Students tutor adults who are interested in improving their reading, writing, and comprehension skills, many of whom are English-as-a-second-language learners.

✦ **Seniors Program.** The Friendship Circle Program is designed to provide socialization among students and residents of local convalescent hospitals and/or retirement homes. Under the supervision of a CAVE staff member, groups of volunteers visit residents on a weekly basis.

✦ **The Volunteer Connection Program.** This referral service connects people who are looking for volunteer opportunities in the community with social-service agencies who need volunteers.

CAVE's goal is to provide Cal State – Chico students with meaningful service-learning programs while servicing a broad base of community needs. CAVE's motto is "Life is for Learning," and each year between 1,800 and 2,000 CAVE volunteers provide more than 155,000 hours of community service.

CALVIN COLLEGE

3201 BURTON STREET, SE
GRAND RAPIDS, MI 49546
616.957.6000
http://www.calvin.edu/

UNDERGRADUATES: 3,900

For program information, please contact:
GAIL GUNST HEFFNER
gheffner@calvin.edu

The Service Learning Center at Calvin College, a private, liberal arts institution, is the hub for student and faculty involvement in the local community. Their motto—"Serving to Learn, Learning to Serve"—underscores their belief that Calvin students learn through participation in organized service in the larger community.

Students at Calvin participate in service learning in the community through academically based service, performed within the context of a course in the college's curriculum. Such activities encourage students to connect theory and practice.

The goals for service learning at Calvin College include:

✦ To learn to relate to others as bearers of God's image—including the poor, the sick, and the old.

✦ To bridge social and economic barriers between people.

✦ To understand the broader context and causes of the needs that exist.

✦ To discover and develop a personal vision and capacity for service in a broken world.

By being involved in academically based service learning, Calvin students are able to see the connections between course content and "real" issues in the larger culture. They observe faculty members as role models while addressing pressing issues, and they increase their capacity to work for justice and mercy. Students learn that their decisions and their actions have an impact on others and that they can make a positive difference in the world. Service learning helps students see the value of partnership in addressing needs and building on strengths in the local community. It helps them learn to work *with* and not *for* the community.

CENTENARY COLLEGE

2911 CENTENARY BOULEVARD
SHREVEPORT, LA 71104
318.869.5100
http://www.centenary.edu/

UNDERGRADUATES: 700

For program information, please contact:
DIAN TOOKE
dtooke@centenary.edu

"It was a true honor for me to be involved in Service Learning. 'Leadership, listening, and learning' are three words that best describe the honorable experience that I had."

—A CENTENARY THIRD-YEAR STUDENT

Centenary College, a private, religious institution, recognizes that education rarely takes place in isolation; instead, it occurs within a community. The very idea of a college as a community of learners emphasizes the communal nature of education. As students become educated within the apparent seclusion of the College, they in fact incur a substantial obligation to the local community, which also has played an important role in making their education possible.

As a means of increasing students' awareness of this obligation, Centenary has integrated a community service-learning component into its curriculum. As part of that service-learning program, all students must complete a 30-hour-minimum service-learning project. They also must maintain a journal focusing on their service experience and attend seminars that provide the opportunity for guided reflection. Neither academic credit nor wages are earned for the service-learning requirement. The primary beneficiary of the service project shall be the local community, not Centenary itself.

Service learning is one of three components of The Centenary Plan, which all students must complete prior to graduation. Students must also participate in an experiential learning project in the areas of career development and intercultural living. The Plan weaves reality into the growth process of students' own intellectual and moral development. Through experiential learning, continual analysis, and reflection, Centenary offers students the opportunity to develop a lifelong commitment to service and to the community.

CHRISTOPHER NEWPORT UNIVERSITY

1 UNIVERSITY PLACE
NEWPORT NEWS, VA 23606-2998
757.594.7100
http://www.cnu.edu/

UNDERGRADUATES: 4,700

For program information, please contact:
CHERYL HARRISON-DAVIDSON
Cherylhd@cnu.edu

"My volunteer experience was very useful. It gave me a better understanding of myself and others, as well as helped me choose my career path."

—A CHRISTOPHER NEWPORT THIRD-YEAR STUDENT

At Christopher Newport University, a comprehensive, public liberal arts institution, the Praxis Project exemplifies a collaborative effort among faculty, students, community-service agencies, and United Campus Ministries. Praxis offers an opportunity to earn class credit for participation in valuable community service. Designed for students to experience how their involvement can make a difference, Praxis offers hands-on, practical experience in a variety of settings.

The basic features of the Praxis Project are:

✦ Campus ministers offer selected faculty the possibility of including a service-learning component in their regular curriculum and provide a list of negotiated nonprofit placement sites.

✦ Faculty include Praxis as an option in their course syllabi, often in lieu of another research requirement or exam, and specify how students are to integrate their service experience with their course work and what course-work credit they will receive for completing Praxis.

✦ Students complete a requisite number of service hours (usually 16–20) during the semester, attend two 90-minute reflection groups at prearranged times, and fulfill their instructor's academic requirements.

✦ Community-service agencies place students in direct contact with persons in need, train and supervise students, and maintain a record of their service during the semester.

The unique aspect of Praxis is its emphasis on the integration of action and reflection on service to the community in the context of the regular college curriculum. In addition to their optional service commitment and faculty-directed academic requirements, students must meet at least twice during the semester with a peer group and a mentor for the purpose of reflecting on their own growth. This process often elicits questions of meaning and responsibility.

THE COLLEGE OF NEW JERSEY

PO BOX 7718
EWING, NJ 08628-0718
609.771.1855
http://www.tcnj.edu/

UNDERGRADUATES: 6,800

For program information, please contact:
NINO SCARPATI
scarpati@tcnj.edu

Service learning is an integral component of The College of New Jersey's nationally recognized First-Year Experience (FYE) program, an innovative partnership between the College and over 30 local social-service agencies. This public, liberal arts institution provides service-learning efforts so that students may understand one's responsibility to self and others and examine the broader purpose of an undergraduate education.

The College's FYE program highlights the importance of integrating academic and student life experiences. To this end, all first-year students enroll in the Interdisciplinary Core course, "Athens to New York," taught by full-time faculty in residence-hall classrooms. The course is based on four questions: What does it mean to be human? What does it mean to be a member of a community? What does it mean to be moral, ethical, or just? How do individuals and communities respond to differences in race, class, ethnicity, and gender? A 10-hour service-learning experience reflecting the themes of the course is also included.

Students share a common living experience that incorporates the elements of community upon which the College's residential program is built. Each residence-hall wing offers support by a volunteer Faculty Fellow who is involved in a specific curriculum of student programming and activities.

Through the FYE program The College of New Jersey has developed numerous partnerships that provide over 40 sites, offering a wide variety of service options for students to participate in with children, teens, senior citizens, and people with disabilities. The service-learning component moves students from a prevailing attitude of charity to an overriding concern for civic responsibility and justice.

COLLEGE OF ST. MARY

1901 SOUTH 72ND STREET
OMAHA, NE 68124
402.399.2400
http://www.csm.edu/

UNDERGRADUATES: 1,000

For program information, please contact:
CARLYNN HARTMAN-KURTZ
chartman-kurtz@csm.edu

College of Saint Mary (CSM) is dedicated to educating women in an environment that calls forth potential and fosters leadership. A key value in this Roman Catholic, liberal arts college's educational mission is "compassionate service to others," based on the tradition of its founders, the Sisters of Mercy. CSM has traditionally served students of limited means by providing them with the opportunity to help others. The College's strategic plan calls for 100% of students, faculty, and staff to participate in service learning. While specific needs have changed over time, the welfare of women and children continues to be the major societal issue addressed.

Activities of CSM's Service-Learning Program include:

✦ **SPIRIT OF SERVICE.** Students, staff, and faculty volunteer their services in this day-long event to best meet community needs.

✦ **ACADEMIC INTEGRATION.** Faculty are encouraged to integrate service learning into the curriculum.

✦ **SMART (SCIENCE, MATH AND RELATED TECHNOLOGY).** This after-school program brings elementary girls from local disadvantaged neighborhoods to campus for hands-on activities in math/science/technology.

✦ **VOLUNTEER OUTREACH CENTER.** The Center operates as a clearinghouse for community volunteer opportunities and encourages faculty to integrate service learning into course content.

At CSM, students are oriented to the community agency, and then asked to reflect on their experience. This process challenges each student to think critically about the underlying need for a service intervention. It also challenges the student to consider how the need for service might be prevented or met at a systemic level. Students involved in service learning at CSM enhance their understanding of real-world complexity—they recognize and develop a spirit of service as part of their education.

COLORADO STATE UNIVERSITY

FORT COLLINS, CO 80523-0015
970.491.1101
http://www.colostate.edu/

UNDERGRADUATES: 18,600

For program information, please contact:
VICTORIA KELLER
vkeller@vines.colostate.edu

The mission of Colorado State University's (CSU) Office for Service Learning and Volunteer Programs (SLVP) is to build partnerships between the campus and local community. SLVP designs and implements meaningful service projects that address community-defined needs, contribute to student learning, and encourage student leadership.

Activities of the SLVP include:

✦ **SERVICE INTEGRATION PROJECT.** Faculty develop and foster service learning as a valuable teaching strategy.

✦ **MAKE A DIFFERENCE DAY.** This annual project links service work with learning about the environment.

✦ **SERVICEBANK.** A database matches students, faculty, and staff with both volunteer and service-learning opportunities according to their skills and interests.

✦ **CANS AROUND THE OVAL.** Canned foods is collected for a local food-distribution center during this annual event, held in conjunction with World Food Day.

✦ **SHELTER TO SHELTER.** Students, faculty, and staff join the local arts community to build and sell artwork to benefit local homeless shelters.

✦ **POUDRE RIVERFEST.** Students join community members each fall to clean an adopted section of a local river.

✦ **CAMPUS CLUB.** Student volunteers and local children, ages 6–11, are paired together as buddies and meet as a group to complete service projects and participate in recreational activities.

At CSU, a public, liberal arts institution, service learning represents an opportunity for students to learn about others and themselves. SLVP makes it clear to Colorado students that if they are selected to work with a service-learning project, they must be committed to exploring these issues, thus maximizing the benefits of participation in service learning.

CORNELL UNIVERSITY

ITHACA, NY 14853
607.255.2000
http://www.cornell.edu/
UNDERGRADUATES: 13,300

For program information, please contact:
MARCIA L. HARDING
mlh15@cornell.edu

"This year has brought the discussion about the role of higher education in fostering character development. This dialog has focused Cornell's efforts to address the University's responsibility to its community."

—A CORNELL FOURTH-YEAR STUDENT

Cornell's Public Service Center (CPSC) was founded in 1991 to support, expand, and institutionalize the public-service initiatives that connect academic study with real-world experiences. The Public Service Center champions the conviction that the Cornell University experience confirms service as essential to active citizenship. To fulfill this commitment, the Public Service Center promotes faculty and student engagement in service and social action, using service-learning theory as the basis.

CPSC supports student programs and projects that are guided by the following principles:

✦ Service should be thoughtfully organized.

✦ The community being served should have the primary responsibility to define needs and control the services provided.

✦ Students should have primary control over what is learned, and structured time should be provided for the participants to reflect on the service experience.

✦ Mutuality and reciprocity should be essential qualities in the relationship among participants.

Service Learning at Cornell, a private, liberal arts institution, takes an educational approach to build bridges between academic study and community. Programs are informed by a student-development perspective that encourages activities that meet students at their own level of service and educational competencies. Academic instruction (lectures, readings) is combined with community-based experiences. Students' level of social awareness and commitment is increased gradually through service activities that require more complex analytical (intellectual) and technical skills. As a result, Cornell students develop the ability to understand and solve problems in a more complex way; to imagine and respect different perspectives; and to relate to and appreciate different people and cultures.

DARTMOUTH COLLEGE

HANOVER, NH 03755
603.646.1110
http://www.dartmouth.edu/
UNDERGRADUATES: 4,300

For program information, please contact:
JAN TARJAN
jan-roberta.tarjan@dartmouth.edu

Dartmouth College, a private, liberal arts institution, demonstrates a long-established concern for the moral development of students. In 1951 the Trustees created the William Jewett Tucker Foundation "for the purpose of supporting and furthering the moral and spiritual work and influence of Dartmouth College." The leadership of Dartmouth is deeply committed to the development of moral character as part of education, and continues to support the modern-day Tucker Foundation.

Dartmouth's commitment to service learning is manifested by the following Foundation activities:

✦ **AMERICORPS.** Twenty-two student leaders serve through the AmeriCorps Education Award Program, learning leadership skills while cohering in a nationwide service corps.

✦ **BIG BROTHER, BIG SISTER.** Nearly 200 students maintain one-on-one Big Brother, Big Sister relationships with local children.

✦ **BOOKBUDDY.** Sixty students maintain literacy-mentoring relationships through the BookBuddy program.

✦ **SURFER GUIDES.** Dartmouth students provide computer and internet training to local school systems.

Approximately 60 students participate annually in 10-week-long service initiatives across the U.S. and abroad. Other students participate in shorter "break trips" to locations such as Kingston, Jamaica, and the rural U.S. The Lombard Fellowship program supports students who want to pursue intensive work on social problems during the year following graduation.

The Tucker Foundation coordinates community-service programs that help more than 1,000 students annually participate in more than 35 regular programs of community service. DarCorps, a twice-annual day-of-service event, involves another 450 students. All local service combined involves 38% of the student body and provides approximately 33,000 hours of service, noted as a main source of support for many community-service agencies in the region.

The Defiance College

701 NORTH CLINTON STREET
DEFIANCE, OH 43512
800.520.4632
http://www.defiance.edu/

UNDERGRADUATES: 800

For program information, please contact:
JAMES T. HARRIS, Ph.D.
jharris@defiance.edu

To further its new mission statement adopted in 1995, The Defiance College, a private, church-affiliated, liberal arts institution, has committed itself to an integrated Service Learning Program in which all traditional graduates will have completed at least four service-learning experiences throughout their major course work, plus a senior-level culminating experience.

One example of how this approach has an impact beyond The Defiance College campus can be found in the field of Teacher Education, which has been identified as one of five flagship academic programs. By incorporating service-learning pedagogy into the Teacher Education programs at Defiance, future teachers will be trained to disseminate the tools, techniques, and practices of service learning into the elementary and high-school classrooms throughout the local region.

At the Neighborhood Learning Centers (NLC), students considering Education as a major can experience real life while fulfilling a service-learning requirement.

✦ Students primarily serve as tutors and mentors for at-risk elementary students. This requires a commitment of four hours per week each semester.

✦ Student tutors serve as role models for basic decorum: hanging up coats, cleaning up after snacks, pushing chairs in at the table, and walking quietly in the hall.

✦ Through their experience at NLC, student tutors quickly realize that they must have self-control and a great deal of patience, skills all educators must possess.

The Defiance College is committed to service learning as a method of experiential learning through which students engaged in community service meet community needs. Students discover their own abilities for critical thinking and group problem-solving, their sense of social responsibility, and the skills they need for effective citizenship.

DePauw University

313 SOUTH LOCUST STREET
GREENCASTLE, IN 46135
765.658.4800
http://www.depauw.edu/

UNDERGRADUATES: 2,200

For program information, please contact:
STUART LORD
slord@depauw.edu

The Grover L. Hartman Center for Civic Education and Leadership, founded in 1995, is home to DePauw University's nationally recognized community-service and leadership-development programs. The Hartman Center's programs are dedicated to developing a life-long volunteer ethic in DePauw students by providing them with the opportunity to develop leadership skills and awareness of civic issues through direct service to the community.

Activities of the Hartman Center include:

✦ **WINTER TERM IN SERVICE.** Teams of students and faculty serve in developing communities in the U.S. and abroad during DePauw's January winter term.

✦ **BONNER SCHOLARS PROGRAM.** Select students volunteer an average of 10 hours per week in a community-service placement.

✦ **SAFE PLACE SUMMIT FOR YOUTH.** Local residents meet with DePauw students, faculty, and staff to discuss issues facing the community and to formulate solutions.

✦ **MAKE A DIFFERENCE WEEK.** This week of community service involves over 9,000 volunteers from DePauw and the local community.

✦ **COMMUNITY PLUNGE.** First-year students can participate in this single-day work project in the community.

✦ **MOTIVATING THE MOTIVATED.** Selected students attend a weekend leadership seminar featuring workshops by DePauw faculty and nationally prominent speakers.

The Hartman Center's student-run programs require that students be responsible for planning and coordinating events that involve hundreds—even thousands—of students and community members.

In addition to learning practical skills and self-discipline, students also focus on issues of social justice. Hartman Center volunteer programs require participation in reflection sessions to reinforce the students' direct service experience.

EARLHAM COLLEGE

801 NATIONAL ROAD WEST
RICHMOND, IN 47374-4095
765.983.1200
http://www.earlham.edu/

UNDERGRADUATES: 1,100

For program information, please contact:
THERESA LUDWIG
ludwigte@earlham.edu

Earlham College's Service Learning Program (SLP) is designed to encourage civic responsibility through community service. Working in conjunction with the student-run Earlham Volunteer Exchange (EVE), SLP volunteers view service as an integral part of their learning experience.

In collaboration with EVE, the SLP sponsors the following activities:

✦ BONNER SCHOLARS PROGRAM. Sixty students are given the opportunity to engage in service on a weekly basis in the local community.

✦ SERVICE LEARNING THEME HOUSE. This residential living/learning house is for students focusing on service and community issues.

✦ EARLHAM'S AMERICA READS INITIATIVE. America Reads is a nationwide program that helps to ensure all third-graders can read independently.

✦ AMERICORPS BONNER LEADERS PROGRAM. Ten students have the opportunity to serve as part-time volunteers in partnership with local community organizations.

✦ NEW STUDENT WEEK SERVICE PROJECT. As part of new student orientation, all first-year students, along with the residential life staff and faculty advisors, participate in a two-hour service project in the community.

✦ TEST MIDDLE SCHOOL PARTNERSHIP IN EDUCATION. Earlham students are paired with local sixth-graders to encourage them to aspire toward higher education.

✦ GREAT HUNGER CLEAN-UP. This nationwide service-a-thon raises funds for the hungry and homeless and encourages student participation in volunteer activities.

More than 60% of Earlham students engaged in volunteer activities during the recent academic year, reflecting the College's commitment to community service and to the Quaker values of honesty, responsibility, and integrity.

ELON COLLEGE

2700 CAMPUS BOX
ELON COLLEGE, NC 27244
800.334.8448
http://www.elon.edu/

UNDERGRADUATES: 3,700

For program information, please contact:
JOHN H. BARNHILL
barnhill@elon.edu

Elon College, a four-year, coeducational, private college founded in 1889 by the United Church of Christ, attracts students from 40 states and 22 foreign countries. At the core of the academic offerings are the Elon Experiences, five programs that involve virtually every student in service, leadership, study abroad, internships, and research. The Elon Experiences reflect important values of the College—an ethic of service to others, an appreciation for cultural diversity, and a commitment to civic responsibility.

The Kernodle Center for Service Learning and "Elon Volunteers!" provide the College community the opportunity to develop an ethic of service by connecting campus and community through service experiences. More than 67% of Elon students provided more than 40,000 hours of service during the most recent academic year.

The following service organizations are represented on campus:

✦ BACCHUS. Students are educated about mature management of alcohol, and the "Safe Rides" program provides Elon students with responsible drivers.

✦ CIRCLE K. This campus organization promotes leadership and service in the community through such programs as Habitat for Humanity.

✦ S.C.A.L.E. The Student Coalition for Action in Literacy Education targets various age groups; the Peacock Program offers student mentors to minority youth.

Until the mid-1970s, Elon was a small college that primarily served in-state students, but in the last 25 years the College has undergone a dramatic transformation. Today, Elon enjoys a growing national reputation for its diverse programs and commitment to active and experiential learning, drawing service-minded students from the entire Eastern seaboard.

Franciscan University of Steubenville

1235 UNIVERSITY BOULEVARD
STEUBENVILLE, OH 43952
740.283.3771
http://www.franuniv.edu/

UNDERGRADUATES: 1,600

For program information, please contact:
LISA FERGUSON
lferguson@franuniv.edu

Putting faith into action is at the heart of Franciscan University of Steubenville's Works of Mercy Program, which provides students with opportunities to reach out to the poor, the needy, and the marginalized. Franciscan University's service-learning program derives its name from the traditional Christian corporal works of mercy, such as feeding the hungry, sheltering the homeless, and visiting the sick. This program enables a student to integrate academics, faith, and service so that he or she becomes a responsible citizen.

A Works of Mercy sampling includes:

✦ **Urban Mission Ministry.** Along with members of the local community, student groups volunteer for such service projects as a food pantry, soup kitchen, homeless shelter, and holiday outreach events.

✦ **Prison Outreach.** Students reach out to inmates through group sharing, pastoral care, and enrichment programs at a local correctional facility.

✦ **Nursing Home Outreach.** Students spend two hours each week listening, sharing, and developing personal relationships with nursing-home residents, who often become like family.

✦ **Mentoring Project.** Students mentor at-risk toddlers to teen inner-city children, taking them on field trips and to visit the elderly.

✦ **St. John's Villa.** Students plan and carry out activities and special events with mentally and physically disabled residents of this facility.

All 15 Works of Mercy give students the chance to give something back to the community. They can also put into practice the leadership theory they learn in the classroom and through the Leadership Project, Franciscan's leadership training seminar. At Franciscan, students discover Christ in the face of the poor and learn to live St. Francis' ideal: "Go out and preach the gospel, and, if necessary, use words."

Furman University

3300 POINSETT HIGHWAY
GREENVILLE, SC 29613
864.294.2000
http://www.furman.edu/

UNDERGRADUATES: 2,600

For program information, please contact:
BETTY J. ALVERSON
betty.alverson@furman.edu.

Furman University, founded in 1826, is a nonsectarian, liberal arts university. For 33 years, Furman's Collegiate Educational Service Corps (CESC) has been a leading advocate for human service. In the beginning, only a handful of students assisted in six local agencies, but CESC now involves more than half of the University's 2,600 students in 93 programs throughout the Greenville region.

Students administer the program, through which they volunteer as tutors in local schools, run errands for wheelchair-bound cancer patients, and deliver leftovers from the University's dining hall to soup kitchens and homeless shelters. CESC has become so successful that seven colleges have recently visited Furman to learn how to establish a similar program.

Additional programs sponsored by CESC include:

✦ **Adopt a Grandparent.** Students volunteer one hour per week to a local nursing home, where they participate in activities with the elderly.

✦ **Book Buddies.** Students are paired with local elementary-aged children and read with them weekly.

✦ **Child Haven.** Students volunteer in this daycare center for abused and neglected children that strives to create a stable, loving environment for each child.

✦ **Loaves and Fishes.** Students deliver and assist in serving food to local homeless shelters.

Through CESC, students develop practical skills. They learn to be creative and resourceful while planning or participating in a project or recruiting volunteers. As one student recently remarked, "I've gained so much in terms of leadership experience and in organizational and people skills."

As a liberal arts college, Furman strives to develop the whole person—intellectually, physically, socially, spiritually, and emotionally. With its emphasis on service and human dignity, CESC is an excellent complement to Furman's academic mission.

George Mason University

4400 UNIVERSITY DRIVE
FAIRFAX, VA 22030-4444
703.993.1000
http://www.gmu.edu/

UNDERGRADUATES: 14,000

For program information, please contact:
LYNN LEAVITT
lleavitt@gmu.edu

George Mason, founded in 1957 as a public university, promotes positive change and civic responsibility in student life through its mission embodied in the Center for Service and Leadership (CSL). By combining academic study, leadership development, and direct community service, CSL encourages students to think critically about their service to and leadership in multiple communities. GMU students identify personal and academic learning goals at the onset of their volunteer experience and can participate in CSL activities.

Leadership development and service-learning opportunities are in a variety of formats, including credit-bearing courses, conferences, workshops, seminars, retreats, and one-on-one consultations. CSL serves as the central point of contact for the University on leadership development and service-learning initiatives and involvement. The Center maintains a collection of resources for students, faculty, and staff to use.

CSL emphasizes skills such as time management, goal setting, interpersonal communication, ethical decision-making, conflict resolution, understanding/appreciating diversity, and stress management/balance, which are taught in leadership courses and practiced in service initiatives/projects. Student clubs and off-campus organizations offer students additional leadership positions to practice what they have learned.

In 1998 approximately 586 George Mason students, through service-learning initiatives, provided over 23,000 volunteer hours to local community organizations. These figures do not begin to reflect the large number of GMU students who provide community service through faith-based and extracurricular programs at the University. Programs such as the Hunger Banquet, Hunger and Homelessness Action Week, Community Service Fair, AIDSWalk, and Holiday Spirit introduce students to issues in the local community and world, and move them toward a life of volunteer service.

Georgia College & State University

CLARK STREET
MILLEDGEVILLE, GA 31061
912.445.5004
http://www.gac.peachnet.edu/

UNDERGRADUATES: 4,400

For program information, please contact:
KENDALL M. STILES
kstiles@mail.gcsu.edu

At Georgia College & State University, a unique service-learning opportunity exists in the Involved in Volunteer Efforts program (GIVE). The GIVE program serves as a volunteer clearinghouse, empowering students to make a difference by linking them to the needs of the local community. Opportunities to learn and serve locally provide GCSU volunteers with the unique opportunity to enhance their education beyond traditional classroom learning. Through reflection on service experiences, volunteers are challenged to make an inner journey of personal growth and an outer journey of commitment to community concerns.

GIVE's goals and objectives include:

✦ Matching volunteer interests and skills with community partners' needs;

✦ Linking students and student organizations with one-time and ongoing service opportunities;

✦ Enhancing students' education beyond the traditional classroom experience;

✦ Making a difference in lives through the spirit of volunteerism;

✦ Using students' hearts and hands instead of their pocketbooks;

✦ Performing 70–80% of service in the local community.

The mission of GIVE is to promote, support, develop, and facilitate meaningful learning experiences for the campus community through service. Out of this mission emerged GIVE'rs, a group with a representative from each student organization or campus program who sponsors or participates in community-service events. Working together, these representatives form a network to increase participation and foster friendships. Currently, more than 40 student organizations and programs comprise the GIVE'rs corps—a good indication that GCSU students actively support and participate in service to the community.

GETTYSBURG COLLEGE

GETTYSBURG, PA 17325-1484
717.337.6000
http://www.gettysburg.edu/

UNDERGRADUATES: 2,200

For program information, please contact:
GRETCHEN C. NATTER
gnatter@gettysburg.edu

"Service learning has helped me to understand that solving smaller problems leads to tackling the larger ones. The awareness I developed through my four service-learning projects . . . will last my whole life. Now I am devoted to service." —A GETTYSBURG FOURTH-YEAR STUDENT

Gettysburg, founded in 1832, is a church-affiliated, liberal arts college. In keeping with the institution's mission to educate young people to think critically and to act compassionately, the Center for Public Service organizes and supports community service by members of the College community. In this context, the Center strives to accomplish three goals that assist students in becoming responsible citizens:

✦ To respond to community needs as identified by community members (community action);

✦ To develop in students the requisite knowledge, skills, and commitment for a lifetime of effective engagement with social issues (service learning);

✦ To connect community needs with academic scholarship in a way that expands students' intellectual development and provides effective assistance to off-campus communities (curriculum development).

Gettysburg's Center for Public Service is staffed full-time by a director and associate director who work closely with 16 student program coordinators. Working in teams, the program coordinators provide opportunities and support (including orientation, training, and reflection) for other students to become involved in the community in areas such as literacy, Latino migrant farm-worker issues, adult education, youth mentoring, environmental issues, hunger and nutrition, homelessness and housing, and health advocacy.

During the last academic year, approximately half of Gettysburg's students participated in volunteer programs facilitated through the Center for Public Service. In surveys administered through the College's institutional research office, approximately 78% of seniors reported involvement with the Center. Through such activities, the Center for Public Service provides a proactive environment for students to learn through service to others.

JOHN BROWN UNIVERSITY

2000 WEST UNIVERSITY STREET
SILOAM SPRINGS, AR 72761
501.524.9500
http://www.jbu.edu/

UNDERGRADUATES: 1,400

For program information, please contact:
STEPHEN BEERS
sbeers@adm.jbu.edu

"Working with Student Ministries has helped me grow spiritually, emotionally, and intellectually." —A JBU FOURTH-YEAR STUDENT

To best understand the Service-Learning Program at John Brown University, it is necessary to first consider the purpose of the university at large. The founder's dream was to develop a college that nurtured improvement in three areas: the head (intellectual growth and competencies development), the heart (fostering compassion and healthy conscience), and the hand (the development of a service lifestyle). Thus the University's motto from its inception has been to develop the Head, Heart, and Hand.

John Brown's Service-Learning Program furthers that purpose through the following activities:

✦ CAUSE LEADERS. Student leaders provide fellow students with moral and ethical leadership as they meet the local community's service needs through 16 ministries.

✦ INTERNSHIPS. Students work for local organizations such as Boys & Girls Club and Camp Barnabus, a retreat for mentally and physically disabled children.

✦ WORLD AWARENESS WEEK. In this annual event, guest speakers are brought on campus to open students' eyes to the problems of the world.

✦ DAY OF CARING. To encourage students to consider service as a part of their development, JBU sponsors this annual day of community projects during new student orientation.

Significant evidence of service learning permeates JBU, from the well-integrated internship program (65% of the majors) to campus ministries volunteer opportunities (50% of the student body). These programs provide educational experiences dedicated to helping students to increase their understanding of the communities in which they will work and live. Such efforts help to instill compassion for all people through educational experiences.

JOHNSON & WALES UNIVERSITY

8 ABBOTT PARK PLACE
PROVIDENCE, RI 02903-3703
401.598.1000
http://www.jwu.edu/

UNDERGRADUATES: 7,600

For program information, please contact:
JUDITH E. TURCHETTA
401.598.1266

Johnson & Wales, a private, liberal arts university, made a strong commitment to the Feinstein Community Service Learning Center (CSL) in September 1996 with the inclusion of CSL options into all University programs. Johnson & Wales also supported the creation of a 10-hour theoretical course that imparts CSL's philosophy to all students during their first year. At the same time, the University adopted a policy requiring that students complete a CSL experiential component, in conjunction with a course or practicum experience.

The Feinstein CSL oversees activities that enable students to become contributing members of society. Skills acquired in the classroom are utilized while students volunteer their services in nonprofit community-service agencies.

The Community Service Center encourages students to:

✦ Understand the relationship between community service-learning theory and action;

✦ Apply course content to real-life situations;

✦ Reflect upon their own talents/roles within the surrounding community;

✦ Recognize and address social problems on the personal, political, and/or legislative levels;

✦ Develop civic leadership skills that will follow them into their adult personal and professional lives.

Students who participate in CSL programs generally make a 10-week commitment, investing approximately 10 to 20 hours per term at a specific agency where projects are similar to those concepts taught in the course through which the student has chosen the volunteer option. Through their participation in CSL, students strengthen their understanding of civic responsibility through hands-on experience with complicated social issues that might otherwise remain intangible to them.

KANSAS STATE UNIVERSITY

ANDERSON HALL
MANHATTAN, KS 66506
http://www.ksu.edu/

UNDERGRADUATES: 17,000

For program information, please contact:
CAROL PEAK
cpeak@ksu.edu

Kansas State, founded as a land-grant institution in 1863, is a public, comprehensive university. The Community Service Program (CSP) at Kansas State assists the entire University in meeting the needs of the local community, particularly rural areas. The program is based on two important assumptions: First, Kansas State students are caring individuals who will generously contribute to their communities if meaningful opportunities are made available within the context of their higher-education goals. Second, the institution has a responsibility to organize meaningful service opportunities for students that respond to local needs, particularly those of small rural places whose needs are often unrecognized.

The CSP works both directly and indirectly to support service learning and citizenship education on the KSU campus through several activities, including:

✦ KANSAS SUMMER TEAMS. Interdisciplinary groups of students are placed in communities throughout Kansas, where they complete community-service projects.

✦ THE INTERNATIONAL SUMMER TEAMS. Interdisciplinary groups of students travel to communities throughout the world where they complete community-service projects.

✦ CSP TUTORS. Students provide academic assistance to local K through 12th graders.

✦ AMERICA READS TUTORS. Students provide literary assistance to local K through 6th graders.

✦ CORPORATION FOR NATIONAL SERVICE GRANT. Through this grant, the CSP works with faculty to integrate service learning into existing courses.

The purpose of Kansas State's Community Service Program is to provide meaningful service as part of students' education experience. CSP activities, combined with course-based service-learning initiatives, are structured to help students encounter important societal issues. Students are supported in this learning experience through orientation sessions, reflection activities, and faculty mentoring.

LYNCHBURG COLLEGE

1501 LAKESIDE DRIVE
LYNCHBURG, VA 24501-3199
804.544.8100
http://www.lynchburg.edu/

UNDERGRADUATES: 1,700

For program information, please contact:
CAROLYN EUBANK
eubank@admvax.lynchburg.edu

Lynchburg College is a private, coeducational college established in 1903 in covenant with the Christian Church (Disciples of Christ). Lynchburg has embraced service as a vital component of the learning experience since its beginning. Students are afforded numerous opportunities for service at Lynchburg, including:

✦ S.E.R.V.E. Through "Students Engaged in Responsible Volunteer Experiences," nearly 500 students, faculty, and staff volunteer more than 15,000 hours annually to over 200 college and community organizations, such as the Battered Women's Shelter, Adult Literacy Corps, and Special Olympics.

✦ SEMESTER OF SERVICE. This program is sponsored by the College's Center for Community Development and Social Justice. Students from colleges across the nation study the effects of poverty in rural and urban settings

✦ BELLE BOONE BEARD GERONTOLOGY CENTER. This college organization sponsors the Adult Health & Development Project, an interdisciplinary experiential/service-learning project, which pairs students with local senior citizens.

✦ HUNGER AWARENESS WEEK. The College's Hunger Task Force oversees this event, which includes preparing and serving meals to the homeless, weighing wasted food in the dining room and publicizing the results, and arranging the Hunger Banquet, where participants are randomly selected for meals representing those typical of affluent and third world nations.

Recently, Lynchburg College President Charles Warren wrote: "In this complex and rapidly changing world, our mission is to develop the whole person—as critical thinker, principled leader, and community servant." That mission is realized by student participation in Lynchburg's service-learning activities.

LYNN UNIVERSITY

3601 NORTH MILITARY TRAIL
BOCA RATON, FL 33431-5598
561.994.0770
http://www.lynn.edu/

UNDERGRADUATES: 1,600

For program information, please contact:
JOAN SCIALLI, Ed.D.
joan@gate.net

The Christine E. Lynn School of Nursing at Lynn University, a private, coeducational institution, parallels the University's mission of developing academic programs reflecting the importance of global transformations. At the Lynn School, the RN to BSN Program is designed for registered nurses who desire to obtain a bachelor of science degree in Nursing. A major component of the program is the integration of education and service. As students learn, they also provide service to the local community.

In order to graduate from the RN to BSN Program, students are required to design and implement a service-learning project that not only builds on their talents and interests but also fulfills local health needs as identified by the student and community agencies. During the course of their service project, students collaborate with consumers, health-team members, and community leaders; develop communication, technological, and critical-thinking skills; and formulate recommendations to improve health care based on program assessment.

Recent service projects completed include:

✦ Creation of a teaching tool for Haitians with active tuberculosis, which includes an instructional flip chart and cassette tape recording (later adopted by the local Public Health Department).

✦ Implementation of a Universal Newborn Hearing Screening Program, which led to the student's appointment to a state committee on the subject.

The belief that RN to BSN students are adult learners who bring a wealth of life experience and knowledge to the institution serves as the foundation of the Lynn School of Nursing's service-learning efforts. As students design and implement their own service projects, each has a unique, personalized learning experience. Such experiences propel students toward a life of service to the community.

MARQUETTE UNIVERSITY

MILWAUKEE, WI 53201-1881
414.288.7302
http://www.marquette.edu/
UNDERGRADUATES: 7,300

For program information, please contact:
JENNI BUGNI
jenni-bugni@marquette.edu

Marquette, founded in 1881, is a church-affiliated university with a history of community-service involvement. The University's Jesuit mission is to develop leaders in service to others. Through its programs of access, outreach, and service, Marquette seeks to instill in its students a spirit of service, especially to those most in need.

The Center for Student Development and Community Service was established to enhance the total educational experience of each student. The programs coordinated by the Center provide opportunities for students to engage in quality cocurricular experiences and to reflect on their life-long goals in relation to the world beyond Marquette's campus.

The Center's activities include:

✦ **BEST BUDDIES OF MARQUETTE.** College students and adults with mild to moderate mental retardation become friends through participation in group outings and one-on-one activities.

✦ **FOUNDATIONS FOR FRIENDSHIP.** This project promotes student community service to encourage fellowship and unity between Marquette and Milwaukee.

✦ **STUDENTS ENHANCING EDUCATION (SEE).** This organization works to enhance education in urban Milwaukee by providing positive young adult role models to inner-city children.

✦ **ADOPT.** Student organizations receive assistance through the Center in arranging one-day community-service projects or in adopting a local agency.

The community-service learning programs at Marquette help students develop a better understanding of themselves, their relationship to others, and their role in society. In the past four years, academic classes integrating service learning have grown to more than 35 courses with over 500 student participants. Clearly, few students leave Marquette without becoming involved in serving the community.

MARYVILLE COLLEGE

502 EAST LAMAR ALEXANDER PARKWAY
MARYVILLE, TN 37804
423.981.8000
http://www.maryville.edu/
UNDERGRADUATES: 1,000

For program information, please contact:
LINDA CLARK
lyclark@knoxnews.infi.net

Maryville, founded in 1819, is a church-affiliated, liberal arts college. The Maryville College Student Literacy Corps involves 60 students directed by a 12-person student board. The vision and purpose of the Literacy Corps is best summarized in its mission statement: "The Maryville College Student Literacy Corps is dedicated . . . to trying to promote awareness of the importance of literacy, both within our campus community and the community outside. Our utmost concern is to provide opportunities and services for those seeking a better way of life through education."

In the academic component of Literacy Corps, the students investigate, define, and analyze the complex issues surrounding literacy education in America; in the experiential component, students participate in tutor training sponsored by the Literacy Corps and work as tutors in collaboration with community literacy educators.

In the immediate community beyond the campus, the Corps serves and learns at three primary sites:

✦ **MCFAMILIES.** Students provide educational services to local teen mothers and their children.

✦ **BLOUNT COUNTY JAIL.** Students tutor incarcerated men and women who are working to become productive members of society.

✦ **BLOUNT COUNTY CHILDREN'S HOME.** Students provide one-on-one tutoring to children in state protective custody.

One Student Corp member described the learning experience as follows: "Through teaching others, MC students reinforce their own academic learning. But they also learn important life lessons: understanding human motivation, appreciating the diversity of the human experience, comprehending the complexity of life in our pluralistic, capitalistic society." At Maryville College, graduates develop sound values through outstanding examples of service.

MICHIGAN STATE UNIVERSITY

EAST LANSING, MI 48824-0590
517.355.1855
http://www.msu.edu/

UNDERGRADUATES: 33,300

For program information, please contact:
MARY EDENS
edensm@pilot.msu.edu

"Service Learning engages students through active learning in diverse populations. Students build a consciousness to the universal ethical values and become competent and committed citizens."

—AN MSU FOURTH-YEAR STUDENT

Michigan State, founded in 1855, is a comprehensive, land-grant, public university. Michigan State's Service-Learning Center (SLC) connects University students with community agencies and helps to recruit, train, orient, supervise, and evaluate students for those agencies. The SLC also provides support services to academic departments by coordinating openings in community-based programs and by interviewing and preparing students to find meaningful placements.

The SLC has three categories of placements: service learning, integrated with classes or independent study; civic and career development for preprofessional students in medicine or public-service careers; and cocurricular community service through local organizations.

Opportunities for MSU students include:

✦ **MSU COOL/ACTION.** The Campus Outreach Opportunity League introduces students to community service in two different programs: "Into the Streets" and Alternative Breaks.

✦ **SPECIAL NEEDS EDUCATION.** This program provides MSU students with an opportunity to gain experience working with children and young adults with special needs.

✦ **COMMUNITY NUTRITION.** Students educate preschool youth, teenagers, senior citizens, and needy families regarding nutrition and assist local agencies in implementing food projects or services.

✦ **SERVICE-LEARNING INTERNSHIPS.** These internships are designed to give a meaningful educational experience to students in their chosen field of study.

Students report that service learning increases their motivation to learn, to pursue their dreams, and to engage in civic endeavors. For many students, that motivation continues after graduation; thus other communities reap the benefits of caring individuals interested in helping the needy.

OHIO UNIVERSITY

ATHENS, OH 45701-2979
704.593.1000
http://www.ohiou.edu/

UNDERGRADUATES: 16,200

For program information, please contact:
MERLE GRAYBILL
graybill@oak.cats.ohiou.edu

"I like to keep busy, and volunteering is an opportunity to meet and work with many different types of people. You learn more about yourself personally when you're helping others. It's an amazing and very rewarding experience."

—AN OU FOURTH-YEAR STUDENT

Founded in 1804, Ohio University, a public, comprehensive institution, prizes community involvement among its undergraduates. The University's Center for Community Service functions as a connecting point for students, faculty, staff, and community-based organizations interested in volunteer and community service. The Center helps students and community members find service opportunities that integrate activities, promote collaboration, and meet the varying needs of students, faculty, and community.

The Center sponsors many programs, including:

✦ **SERVICE LEARNING.** The Center works in partnership with the University's Center for Teaching Excellence to help faculty incorporate community service into the curriculum.

✦ **NATIONAL SERVICE/AMERICORPS.** The Center serves as the lead agency in Ohio AppalCORPS, a collaborative program designed to improve the reading skills of third-graders and to increase the number of local youth in higher education.

✦ **VOLUNTEER MOBILIZATION.** The Center, in partnership with Rural Action, Inc., mobilizes student and community volunteers to meet pressing community needs.

✦ **UNIVERSITY-COMMUNITY ACTION NETWORK (U-CAN).** The Center supports student groups with an interest in providing service to the region.

Ohio University's formal commitment to incorporate service learning into its curriculum came in 1991 when OU sent a team of faculty and staff to Campus Compact's Institute on Integrating Service with Academic Study. Service-learning activities on OU's campus have proven to be an excellent mechanism for supporting community revitalization while educating OU students for effective citizenship.

OHIO WESLEYAN UNIVERSITY

61 SOUTH SANDUSKY STREET
DELAWARE, OH 43015
740.368.2000
http://www.owu.edu/

UNDERGRADUATES: 1,900

For program information, please contact:
SUE PASTERS
smpaster@cc.owu.edu

"I am proud to be one of the recipients of OW's community-service scholarships."

—AN OW SECOND-YEAR STUDENT

Ohio Wesleyan, founded in 1842, is a church-affiliated, liberal arts university. For over 150 years OW has challenged its students, faculty, administration, and staff to "willingly meet the responsibilities of citizenship in a free society." The University's Division of University Chaplaincy and Community Service Learning provides quality programs for students to gain hands-on experience while offering service to others. Each program exposes the participant to challenging experiences. The Division strives to develop thoughtful and committed citizens through community service.

Activities of OW's Division of University Chaplaincy and Community Service Learning include:

✦ THE COLUMBUS INITIATIVE. This program matches students with children and youth from the inner-city in tutoring and mentoring relationships.

✦ THE SCIOTO/RIVERVIEW PROJECT. This program stresses learning about other cultures, creative expression, and the arts by providing a chance for incarcerated youth to spend time with college students.

✦ BIG PAL/LITTLE PAL. Students are paired with local middle-grade students in mentoring relationships.

✦ SECOND SERVINGS. To glean food that would otherwise be wasted and redistribute it to area charitable organizations to feed the hungry are the goals of the Second Servings program.

Ohio Wesleyan's ethos of service-learning integration supports the University's Statement of Aims, which says the University "attempts to develop in its students qualities of intellect and character that will be useful no matter what they choose to do in later life." Through community service, Ohio Wesleyan students not only gain satisfaction by a job well done, they also gain values that last a lifetime.

PALM BEACH ATLANTIC COLLEGE

PO BOX 24707
WEST PALM BEACH, FL 33416-4708
561.803.2100
http://www.pbac.edu/

UNDERGRADUATES: 1,600

For program information, please contact:
LISA BOLLING
bollinga@pbac.edu

Palm Beach Atlantic is a church-affiliated, liberal arts college. The Workship program—combining the concepts of work and worship—has been a part of the College since its beginning in 1968. Each student is required during his or her undergraduate career to give 45 hours of community service each academic year. A primary goal of the Workship program is that students learn the value of servanthood through meeting the needs of others.

Students may meet the requirements for community service in one of the following ways:

✦ Regional projects send groups of students into the global community during weekends and school breaks.

✦ Group projects allow students to serve in a designated area of the community.

✦ Individual assignments enable students to work in specific fields, which may be related to their areas of study. Students may choose from among hundreds of nonprofit agencies, churches, and schools or they may create their own placements.

✦ Club/class opportunities, coordinated by a faculty member, allow campus clubs and academic classes to participate in special Workship projects together.

✦ Samaritan Gardens is a special program that encourages students to serve as interns living in a designated apartment complex while providing specific opportunities for community service in an assigned ministry. Workship graduate students act as campus supervisors for the interns.

The original concept of Workship, which will soon record over one million hours in community service, was based on Judeo-Christian teaching that a person should treat others as he or she would want to be treated. Workship allows students to step out of the classroom and into the community, instilling in them a lifelong commitment to serving those in need.

Providence College

549 RIVER AVENUE
PROVIDENCE, RI 02918
401.865.1000
http://www.providence.edu/

UNDERGRADUATES: 4,600

For program information, please contact:
DANA FARRELL
Dfarrell@providence.edu

The Feinstein Institute for Public Service was established in 1993 when Providence College, a church-affiliated, liberal arts college, was named the recipient of a substantial grant from Rhode Island philanthropist Alan Shawn Feinstein to develop an innovative academic program that would integrate community service with academic study. The core programs of the Institute include a major and minor in Public and Community Service Studies. Built on the pedagogical model of service learning, the program emphasizes that nearly all of the courses students complete integrate service in an intentional way.

To fulfill its mission of providing Providence students with an educational experience that will prepare them to become builders of human communities and responsible citizens of a democratic society, the Feinstein Institute seeks to:

✦ Provide students with an understanding of how to be productive citizens in a democratic society;

✦ Stimulate an understanding of, and appreciation for, community;

✦ Make positive contributions to the larger community by offering students opportunities for learning through community service.

The Feinstein Institute champions community service as one of the key responsibilities of a citizen in a democracy. For this reason, the Institute attempts to link the service experiences of students to broader questions about the responsibilities of individuals to the communities of which they are a part. The educational vision of the Institute upholds the unique Catholic tradition of the Dominican Order, which asks all persons to bear witness to the human and social dimensions of their religious faith, and which expresses the mission of Providence College and Alan Shawn Feinstein's dream of educating the young about the importance of compassionate service.

Purdue University

WEST LAFAYETTE, IN 47907
765.494.4600
http://www.purdue.edu/

UNDERGRADUATES: 29,000

For program information, please contact:
JOHN G. POMERY, Ph.D.
pomeryj@mgmt.purdue.edu

At Purdue University, a public, comprehensive institution, undergraduate engineering students face a future in which they will need more than just a solid technical background. They must be able to interact effectively with people of varying social, educational, and technical backgrounds. Likewise, community-service agencies must now rely to a great extent upon technology. The Purdue Engineering Projects in Community Service (EPICS) provides a service-learning structure that enables these two groups to work together and satisfy each other's needs. Teams of undergraduates in Engineering are matched with community-service agencies requesting technical assistance. Under the guidance of Engineering faculty, the EPICS project teams work closely with their partner community-service agencies to design and build the necessary systems. The resulting systems have a lasting impact on the community-service agencies and the people they serve.

Recent EPICS projects include:

✦ HOMELESSNESS PREVENTION NETWORK. Students designed and implemented a centralized database, allowing agencies to coordinate their services, trace clients, and assemble accurate and confidential reports.

✦ THE WABASH CENTER CHILDREN'S CLINIC. Students developed computer-controlled and electromechanical toys as well as play areas for children with disabilities.

✦ PURDUE AGRICULTURAL RESEARCH CENTER, AND DEPARTMENT OF FORESTRY AND NATURAL RESOURCES. Students provided engineering design and construction services for a wetland constructed to treat contaminated agricultural runoff.

Through EPICS, students learn valuable lessons, including the role of a partner, or "customer," in defining an engineering project; the necessity of teamwork; the difficulty of managing and leading large projects; the need for skills and knowledge from many different disciplines; and the art of solving technical problems.

RICE UNIVERSITY

6100 MAIN STREET
HOUSTON, TX 77005-1892
713.527.8101
http://www.rice.edu/

UNDERGRADUATES: 2,800

For program information, please contact:
HEATHER SYRETT
heathers@ruf.rice.edu

 As a private, comprehensive university, Rice supports the Community Involvement Center (CIC), offering students, faculty, and staff opportunities to serve in the local, national, and international communities. Intense international service projects during spring breaks and in the summer are available, as well as programs solely to introduce incoming students to the social needs of the greater Houston area.

Activities of the CIC include:

✦ RICE STUDENT VOLUNTEER PROGRAM. RSVP, the University's largest student service organization, encourages participation in the community through service. RSVP includes five committees (Children, Education, Environment, Health, and Hunger & Homelessness).

✦ BEST BUDDIES. This program matches students with disabled individuals at the local Center for the Retarded in one-on-one relationships through group trips and events.

✦ OPERATION SUCCESS. Started by a Rice student, this group organizes volunteers to mentor and tutor high-school students in academic subjects as well as to prepare them for standardized tests.

✦ ESL TUTORING PROGRAM. The English as a Second Language Tutoring Program trains Rice students, faculty, and staff to work with University employees and international students.

✦ JUNIOR ACHIEVEMENT. Students volunteer to teach business skills and concepts to elementary students in at-risk or inner-city schools to demonstrate that what they learn in school is relevant to daily life.

By introducing students to service during their first year and facilitating reflection activities on these experiences, Rice instills the idea of responsible citizenship. As Rice students involve themselves more deeply in service, they gain a greater commitment to the individuals or groups they serve and the issues they address. That sense of personal responsibility translates into lasting commitment to community service.

RUTGERS, THE STATE UNIVERSITY OF NEW JERSEY

65 DAVIDSON ROAD
PISCATAWAY, NJ 08854-8097
732.932.1766
http://www.rutgers.edu/

UNDERGRADUATES: 10,700

For program information, please contact:
MICHAEL SHAFER, Ph.D.
mshafer@rci.rutgers.edu

At this public, liberal arts university founded in 1766, Rutgers' Walt Whitman Center for the Culture and Politics of Democracy considers service an essential activity for responsible citizens. The Center develops and promotes program models that strive to enable individuals to serve others while fostering an understanding of the meaning of democratic citizenship. Through service learning, the Center encourages individuals to view citizenship as a way of linking the self with others in a web of common values and common pursuits.

In collaboration with the Whitman Center, Rutgers' Citizenship and Service Education (CASE) program serves as a model of how to combine service and learning across the undergraduate curriculum. CASE courses link academic studies in a wide variety of fields with community service.

✦ COURSE DEVELOPMENT. CASE works with professional schools, academic departments, and individual faculty to develop new service-learning courses and to convert existing courses to the CASE format.

✦ TRAINING. CASE offers general and placement-specific training to CASE students and volunteers, provides on-site supervision, and conducts final evaluations.

✦ COMMUNITY PARTNERS. CASE actively recruits Community Partners to accommodate the expanding range of students' community-service interests and solicits Community Partner input about community needs.

✦ TECHNICAL ASSISTANCE. CASE provides technical assistance to service-learning programs at educational institutions across the U.S. and oversees specific areas in the management of community-service programs.

CASE offers New Jersey communities an important window on the University and a means to develop Rutgers' resources to meet community-identified needs.

St. John Fisher College

3690 EAST AVENUE
ROCHESTER, NY 14618
716.385.8000
http://www.sjfc.edu/

UNDERGRADUATES: 1,600

For program information, please contact:
ANNE GEER
geer@sjfc.edu

"Volunteering gives me a feeling of satisfaction and achievement. My service work has shown me that by becoming involved with others I better understand myself."

—A ST. JOHN FISHER THIRD-YEAR STUDENT

To reward high-school students who have demonstrated a commitment to community service, St. John Fisher College has established the Fisher Service Scholars Program. This unique program presently enrolls 71 students and, when fully implemented in the fall of 2000, will enroll 144 students.

Service Scholars enter this church-affiliated, liberal arts college after nomination by community leaders or high-school administrators on the basis of their involvement in community service. These students commit to more than 700 hours of community service during their college years. Students begin their year in a "Leadership Through Self-Development" course and enroll in a service-learning seminar every subsequent semester.

Highlights of the Service Scholars Program include:

✦ The Service Scholars have a higher combined grade-point average than any other group of students on campus, despite the fact that their academic profile is not as high as most students.

✦ Faculty benefit by participation in the program, which has allowed them to collaborate interdepartmentally and participate in faculty development and research.

✦ Service Scholars' retention rate is outstanding. Of the initial cohort of students, only two have left the College.

Service Scholars will provide more than 11,000 hours of service in the Rochester community this year. When the Service Scholars Program is fully implemented, nearly 15% of Fisher's student body will be involved, as either scholars or scholar alternates. Fisher Service Scholars commit 100 hours per semester to community service in addition to carrying a full academic course load and maintaining other commitments. Their ability to manage these competing demands helps them to understand the virtues of personal responsibility and prepares them for a lifetime of service to the community.

St. John's University

8000 UTOPIA PARKWAY
JAMAICA, NY 11439
718.990.6161
http://www.stjohns.edu/

UNDERGRADUATES: 13,900

For program information, please contact:
STEPHEN C. BICSKO
bicskos@stjohns.edu

"People that have never done service before—I see them go to hospitals and love it. I will continue to do this after I graduate. It is what I do."

—A ST. JOHN'S FOURTH-YEAR STUDENT

St. Vincent De Paul spent his life caring for the poor and abandoned. One of the groups inspired by Vincent's works—the Vincentian Fathers—founded St. John's University in 1870, which seeks to minister to the poor and to those most in need of assistance.

This church-affiliated university has initiated a Service-Learning Program that combines academic goals with community service, inviting faculty members to challenge students to achieve academic goals in an experiential, hands-on setting. At the same time, students learn first-hand how to meet the genuine needs of different groups and individuals. The University sees both outcomes as part of its mission.

Activities of St. John's Service-Learning Program include:

✦ SHERIDAN HEALTH CENTER. Students assist social workers with the homebound meal program and coordinate an exercise program for seniors.

✦ MARY IMMACULATE HOSPITAL. Students visit patients/residents and their families to provide emotional and spiritual support in time of crisis.

✦ AIDS CENTER OF QUEENS COUNTY. Students provide case management, support groups, legal services, counseling, child care, and fundraising for local residents with HIV and AIDS.

✦ ST. JOHN'S UNIVERSITY COLLEGE BOUND PROGRAM. Students provide supportive services to junior and senior high-school students who have the potential to pursue a college education but need assistance to finish secondary school.

St. John's Service-Learning Program is intended to promote the development of community, applied academic experience, and a dialog between faith and culture. Through their involvement in service learning, students recognize the problems of the real world, and know how to put Vincentian spirituality into action.

ST. MARY'S UNIVERSITY

ONE CAMINO SANTA MARIA
SAN ANTONIO, TX 78228-8503
210.436.3011
http://www.stmarytx.edu/

UNDERGRADUATES: 2,600

For program information, please contact:
JUDY M. GEELHOED
Judyg@stmarytx.edu

St. Mary's, founded in 1852, is a private, church-affiliated university that houses the Service Learning Center, which offers opportunities for students to respond to today's complex social realities by reaching out to the community. Through reflection, students are helped to integrate personally the principles of justice and peace inspired by the Gospel values and Catholic social teaching in the Marianist tradition. Service learning is defined by the institution as "an instructional method intended to help students learn and develop through participation in supervised, community service activities and their own critical reflection on their service experiences."

Through the following programs, St. Mary's students grow in civic and personal responsibility:

✦ THE SUMMER SERVICE PROGRAM. Students serve 20 hours a week with a local service agency, study the social justice doctrine of the church, and live and reflect together on campus.

✦ IMMERSION PROGRAMS. The University supports programs where students experience an intensive service opportunity for a short period of time, from weekends with the homeless in San Antonio to three-week programs in community development in Mexico.

✦ FIRST-YEAR PERSONAL & ACADEMIC DEVELOPMENT. All first-year students are given a presentation in their personal and academic development course, which provides the groundwork to involve them in service through the University.

Through the Center, St. Mary's encourages significant leadership opportunities for students. Community-service work-study students are particularly cognizant of the fact that they are responsible for meeting the needs of those they are serving. Also, the Center offers workshops as well as a Not-for-Profit Career Fair to help St. Mary's students examine how they will integrate their dedication to service into their professional lives.

SAN FRANCISCO STATE UNIVERSITY

1600 HOLLOWAY AVENUE
SAN FRANCISCO, CA 94132
415.338.1381
http://www.sfsu.edu/

UNDERGRADUATES: 20,700

For program information, please contact:
GERALD S. EISMAN, Ph.D.
Geisman@sfsu.edu

Community service learning at San Francisco State, a public, comprehensive university founded in 1899, integrates academic study with community service and provides opportunities for structured reflection. Interest in service learning arises from an awareness of a growing disparity between the undergraduate curriculum and the marketplace; and the realization that this disparity has fostered the disengagement of today's youth from larger social issues and civic concerns.

The goals of San Francisco State University's Office of Community Service Learning are:

✦ To enhance the educational experience of students by encouraging faculty to incorporate community service-learning pedagogy into the institution's undergraduate curriculum;

✦ To expand the number of courses incorporating community service learning so that over a five-year period almost all undergraduates will have the opportunity to take at least one community service-learning course before graduation;

✦ To provide service of value to Bay Area community agencies and organizations by building upon University community partnerships through the development of service-learning internship opportunities for students;

✦ To develop mechanisms to ensure the institutionalization of community service learning as an ongoing part of the curriculum and the life of the University.

For students at San Francisco State University, community service learning contributes to civic and moral understanding and to the development of individual and collective social responsibility. For faculty, community service learning offers opportunities for interdisciplinary collaboration and the chance to become involved in public service and action-oriented research. And, finally, for community agencies and organizations receiving San Francisco State students, community service learning represents an opportunity to strengthen their capability to meet community needs and to contribute to the education of San Francisco State students.

SETON HALL UNIVERSITY

400 SOUTH ORANGE AVENUE
SOUTH ORANGE, NJ 07079-2689
973.761.9000
http://www.shu.edu/

UNDERGRADUATES: 4,900

For program information, please contact:
JOSEPH MARBACH, Ph.D.
marbacjo@shu.edu

Seton Hall, founded in 1856 as a private, church-affiliated comprehensive university, houses the Institute for Service Learning, which was established in 1997 to support the implementation of service-learning activities on campus. The Institute creates and develops seminars to introduce faculty to the theory and practice of service learning, works with faculty as they craft courses that involve service learning, and works with local community leaders to establish service learning and nonprofit management relationships.

Recognizing the University's unique service capability, the Institute mobilizes students and faculty to serve the nonprofit community. Three major components of this initiative are:

✦ THE STUDENT COMMUNITY ASSISTANCE PROGRAM, which provides nonprofit agencies with the opportunity to receive management and technical assistance from Seton Hall students;

✦ THE RESEARCH COMPONENT, which provides research services from the Seton Hall academic community to nonprofit agencies;

✦ THE INFORMATION CENTER FOR NONPROFITS, which includes a newsletter and a series of seminars that make accessible the latest scholarly research.

The Institute for Service Learning also works with Seton Hall's Division of Volunteer Efforts (DOVE) and the Nonprofit Sector Resource Institute of New Jersey (NSRI) in developing appropriate placements for students. NSRI is dedicated to addressing the educational and research needs of New Jersey's nonprofits by building a bridge between the nonprofit community and Seton Hall University.

Seton Hall University has made a commitment to service throughout the undergraduate curriculum. All first-year students are required to complete a 10-hour community-service activity organized through Freshman Studies and DOVE. Through the activities of the Institute the University emphasizes the importance of service, civic responsibility, and experiences beyond the classroom for Seton Hall graduates.

SOUTHWEST MISSOURI STATE UNIVERSITY

901 SOUTH NATIONAL
SPRINGFIELD, MO 65804
417.836.5000
http://www.smsu.edu/

UNDERGRADUATES: 14,000

For program information, please contact:
DEBRA MCDOWELL, Ph.D.
dsm259f@mail.smsu.edu

Southwest Missouri State, founded in 1905, houses the Citizenship and Service Learning (CASL) program, which serves as the vehicle through which the institution enacts its statewide public affairs mission.

Welcoming the 21st Century, this public, comprehensive university's master plan through the year 2000, states that SMSU's mission is to promote opportunities for students to develop focused, disciplinary knowledge; to cultivate critical thinking and judgment; and to encourage a campus-wide commitment to foster competence and responsibility in the common vocation of citizenship. CASL fulfills this mission with a voluntary program intended to strengthen the University's bond with the community and to provide Southwest Missouri students with opportunities to practice citizenship.

CASL, a form of experiential education, connects classroom learning with service learning in the community. Students perform at least 40 hours of service related to the course content, which benefits external social-service agencies, and receive an additional credit hour for the learning they demonstrate as a result of their volunteer work.

SMSU's Citizenship and Service Learning program benefits students by helping them to:

✦ Apply theoretical concepts to real-life work and develop independence;

✦ Gain insight into how government agencies and nonprofit organizations can work together to improve communities;

✦ Contribute to the quality of life in their communities;

✦ Test their career choices through work experience related to their area of interest.

Southwest Missouri State University's Citizenship and Service Learning program promotes service learning as an effective pedagogical method that develops educated students who work voluntarily to benefit the local community. Service-learning students exemplify an outstanding engaged citizenry for SMSU's entire student population.

SPALDING UNIVERSITY

851 SOUTH FOURTH STREET
LOUISVILLE, KY 40203
502.585.9911
http://www.spalding.edu/

UNDERGRADUATES: 1,100

For program information, please contact:
MICHAEL DAY
Mday@spalding.edu

Founded in 1814, Spalding is dedicated "to providing experiential learning experiences grounded in community service consistent with Spalding's mission of promoting peace and justice." The Service-Learning Program enables students to integrate theory and skill learned in the classroom with concrete application emphasizing social responsibility and moral development.

Activities of Spalding University's Service-Learning Program include:

✦ **COURSE-BASED SERVICE LEARNING.** These courses strive to integrate service into theoretical work to meet academic objectives.

✦ **ACADEMIC PROGRAM-BASED SERVICE LEARNING.** Some majors are required to combine service with course work.

✦ **STUDENT ORGANIZATION-BASED SERVICE LEARNING.** Student clubs and organizations plan and conduct service to the community.

✦ **"TEAMVERSITY."** This service-learning projects partners Spalding students with local middle-school students in an academic enrichment program.

Spalding's Service-Learning Program addresses personal and civic responsibility. Reflection activities are central to service-learning courses, where under the direction of faculty members students are introduced to aspects of social systems analysis. Students are also guided in critical analysis of how they can impact society and their responsibility in their community, both as citizens and as future members of their chosen career. All participants—the population "being served," Spalding students, agency members, and faculty—are considered to be simultaneously learner and teacher, servant and service-recipient. Consequently, an inherent equality among the participants and an overt sense of mutual care and responsibility permeate student life at Spalding University's Service-Learning Program.

STANFORD UNIVERSITY

STANFORD, CA 94305
415.723.2300
http://www.stanford.edu/

UNDERGRADUATES: 6,600

For program information, please contact:
TIM STANTON
cr.tks@forsythe.stanford.edu

As Stanford University's most visible commitment to community and public service, the Haas Center for Public Service offers students the opportunity to acquire service experience in local, regional, national, and international contexts. At this private, comprehensive university founded in 1891, the Haas Center serves as a focal point for students, faculty, and staff interested in public and community service. The Center maintains and coordinates volunteer, internship, and community-research opportunities for undergraduate and graduate students in the San Francisco Bay Area. Through the "study-service connections" initiative, the Center's staff assists students and faculty seeking to integrate service-based learning with academic study, and administers a Public Service Scholars honors research program.

Working with Stanford faculty, students, and staff, the Center's program staff:

✦ Develops and supports a growing range of service-learning courses across the curriculum;

✦ Implements a student development program that gives every student the chance to build leadership skills and knowledge of the best practices of service;

✦ Collaborates with local communities to help meet immediate needs through direct service.

The Haas Center for Public Service promotes, organizes, and supports public and community service by members of the Stanford community. By cultivating partnerships with local, state, national, and international organizations, the Center engages students in a wide variety of service activity—government service, policy research, and community development. Through service involvement, students develop a spirit of giving and sharing while expanding their understanding of social problems and their ability to solve these problems. By encouraging student initiative and leadership, the Center helps Stanford students gain knowledge and skills necessary for effective citizenship in a democratic, multicultural society.

Susquehanna University

514 UNIVERSITY AVENUE
SELINSGROVE, PA 17870-1040
570.374.0101
http://www.susqu.edu/

UNDERGRADUATES: 1,700

For program information, please contact:
CHRISTOPHER WOLFGANG
Cwolfgan@roo.susqu.edu

Susquehanna University, founded in 1858, is a selective, residential university that champions the means for students to achieve academic excellence, leadership, and service to others. The mission of the University's Center for Service Learning and Volunteer Programs is to assist in the coordination of service-learning opportunities for students and faculty.

Center activities include:

✦ THE PROJECT HOUSE SYSTEM. Founded in 1976, this undertaking consists of 14 student-initiated community-service projects. Selected students live together in University-owned houses. The combination of group living and a commitment to community service allows students to grow and develop.

✦ THE SERVICE SCHOLAR PROGRAM. Established as a self-sustaining program to increase student participation in community service, Service Scholars work 700 hours for two to three years and receive a stipend. At the completion of their service they receive a postservice educational benefit in the form of tuition remission.

✦ THE SERVICE LEARNING RESOURCE CENTER. The Center acts as a clearinghouse for service-learning program information and opportunities. By 1999/2000, the Resource Center will also house a library for postundergraduate service opportunities, such as AmeriCorps and Teach for America.

Susquehanna students practice the virtues of civic responsibility through the University's service-learning curriculum. The Spanish for the Social Services course enables students to work with the Hispanic community, such as with Pine Meadows, a local, low-income housing development.

Susquehanna University's mission is to be a respected community in which able students are prepared for productive and reflective lives. Susquehanna establishes a strong liberal arts education for each student, with particular emphasis on the development of personal values and an awareness of global opportunities.

Syracuse University

201 TOLLEY ADMINISTRATION BUILDING
SYRACUSE, NY 13244
315.443.1870
http://www.cwis.syr.edu/

UNDERGRADUATES: 10,400

For program information, please contact:
PAMELA KIRWIN HEINTZ
pkheintz@syr.edu

"Thank you for all the volunteers you sent our way this semester. Without your help, our program could not be successful! We depend on students from Syracuse University to help us out."

—TUTORING PROGRAM COORDINATOR

Founded in 1870, Syracuse is a private, comprehensive university dedicated to academic excellence and community service. In 1994 the University's Center for Public and Community Service (CPCS) was established with a three-year grant from the Carrier Corporation.

CPCS's mission is to support, facilitate, and recognize public and community service as a fundamental part of the teaching and learning experience for Syracuse students, faculty, and staff members. CPCS works with numerous public-service organizations in the local community. The Center:

✦ Supports faculty and staff in integrating service-learning experiences into academic course work.

✦ Creates new opportunities and supports ongoing academic and campus activities that foster public and community service on the local, national, and international levels.

✦ Furnishes information for all those seeking service opportunities.

✦ Assists others in locating preservice training, ongoing support, and thoughtful evaluation of service experiences.

✦ Assists students, faculty, staff, and members of the community, both local and beyond, to support and evaluate service opportunities that meet the needs of the community.

Syracuse University's Center for Public and Community Service constitutes an integral part of the institution's efforts to create a unique volunteer service culture within a major research university. The Center reflects the University's guiding values of Quality, Caring, Diversity, Innovation, and Service. Through the Center's activities, these values permeate every aspect of Syracuse's campus culture, thereby enhancing its tradition of service and social responsibility.

TUSCULUM COLLEGE

PO BOX 5093
GREENEVILLE, TN 37743
423.636.7300
http://www.tusculum.edu/

UNDERGRADUATES: 1,100

For program information, please contact:
JOHN REIFF, Ph.D.
jreiff@tusculum.edu

Tusculum College, a private, church-affiliated college of arts and sciences, underwent major changes in curriculum, governance, and mission ten years ago when it dedicated itself to the cultivation of the "civic arts"—the knowledge, skills, and attitudes necessary for effective and responsible citizenship. Numerous courses in the curriculum explore issues of individual, community, and civic responsibility.

Before graduation from Tusculum, students must validate nine competencies that the College believes are integral to its mission. Six of these competencies are Foundational, involving such abilities as writing, critical analysis, and public speaking. The other three are gathered under the rubric "The Practice of Virtue":

✦ Civility requires students to interact with others in productive and respectful ways, contributing to discussion and problem-solving.

✦ Self-Knowledge requires students to demonstrate an understanding of their own fundamental ethical values and the ways that their desires and goals position them to make contributions within civic contexts.

✦ Ethics of Social Responsibility requires students to demonstrate the ability to understand ethical issues arising from the interdependence of individuals and community, and to seek the common good.

In planning, carrying out, and reflecting on their service experience, students demonstrate these three competencies. Faculty members write up recommendations for validation that become part of students' portfolios.

Tusculum students often begin service-learning courses unconvinced that the experience will be valuable but afterwards report that they have grown in unexpected ways. As a result of Tusculum's unique curriculum, that growth continues after students leave the College, thus benefiting communities in need across the world.

UNIVERSITY OF DAYTON

300 COLLEGE PARK
DAYTON, OH 45469
937.229.1000
http://www.udayton.edu/

UNDERGRADUATES: 6,700

For program information, please contact:
TIME BETE
bete@udayton.edu

For nearly 150 years, the very heart of a University of Dayton (UD) education has been learning combined with service. The University's mission statement says that it is dedicated to "educating the whole person and to linking learning and scholarship with leadership and service." Dayton challenges its students to be servant leaders who render public service to improve the communities in which they live.

University-sponsored service-learning initiatives include:

✦ **CAMPUS MINISTRY.** UD has one of the largest campus ministry programs in the U.S., and it has a 30-year tradition of providing voluntary service opportunities for students.

✦ **PLUNGE EXPERIENCES.** This past spring some 125 UD students weighed the rewards of a spring break vacation against serving and building community—and they chose service.

✦ **CHRISTMAS ON CAMPUS.** Each December the University cancels classes and transforms the campus into a winter wonderland called "Christmas on Campus." UD students, faculty, and staff gather with more than 1,200 underprivileged children and others from the Dayton area.

✦ **COMMUNITY LEADERSHIP AND SERVICE PREPARATION (CLASP).** The Provost's Office supports this faculty initiative, which sponsors varied service-learning projects for both faculty and students, including a certificate program in community service, preparing students for volunteer stints with such organizations as the Peace Corps.

✦ **THE INSTITUTE FOR NEIGHBORHOOD AND COMMUNITY LEADERSHIP.** This on-campus office works closely with neighborhood development organizations in Dayton on economic and human development issues.

In preparing graduates for the information age, the University of Dayton enhances student development in the knowledge, skills, and religious convictions that enable them to work with others and address those critical issues, in large part through its service-learning initiatives.

UNIVERSITY OF MARYLAND BALTIMORE COUNTY

1000 HILLTOP CIRCLE
BALTIMORE, MD 21250
410.455.1000
http://www.umbc.edu/

UNDERGRADUATES: 8,500

For program information, please contact:
JOHN S. MARTELLO, PH.D.
martello@umbc.edu

In his acclaimed essay, "The New American College," the late Ernest Boyer, former President of the Carnegie Foundation for the Advancement of Teaching and founding Chair of the Shriver Center National Advisory Board, challenged the American academy to return to its roots and to reconfigure its purpose in terms of a new "scholarship of service." The Shriver Center at the University of Maryland Baltimore County (UMBC), a public, comprehensive university, is one of the few institutions within American higher education which is committed to working out the details of Boyer's vision.

Founded in 1993 in honor of Robert Sargent Shriver, Jr., and Eunice Kennedy Shriver, the Center addresses the social needs of greater Baltimore and links the theory of the classroom to the realities of urban life in the U.S. This multifaceted mission makes the Shriver Center the prototype for urban education in the 21st century.

The Shriver Center's mission is:

✦ To focus the resources of the colleges and universities of greater Baltimore on urban issues.

✦ To engage faculty, students, and the community in strengthening existing programs and in developing new initiatives to improve urban life.

✦ To help students deepen their sense of civic responsibility and discover the relationship of formal learning to contemporary issues.

✦ To broaden the meaning of scholarship to include research, teaching, and the application of knowledge.

The Center's programs emphasize the practical, theoretical, and moral dimensions of all social problems. Through Shriver Center placements, students establish mutually beneficial partnerships between the University and the community. Such service placements enable UMBC students to develop practical and professional skills, as well as acquire first-hand knowledge of the complex problems confronting urban America today.

UNIVERSITY OF MICHIGAN

ANN ARBOR, MI 48109
734.764.1817
http://www.umich.edu/

UNDERGRADUATES: 24,000

For program information, please contact:
JEFFREY P. HOWARD
jphoward@umich.edu

The University of Michigan, Ann Arbor, founded in 1817, is a national leader in service-learning initiatives. For more than 20 years, students at this comprehensive, public institution availed themselves of the service-learning opportunities offered through the Office of Community Service Learning (OCSL). In 1997 the Center for Community Service and Learning was established, enlarging upon the efforts made by the OCSL. Today, the Center involves students and faculty in community service and academic study, and publishes the *Michigan Journal of Community Service Learning*.

One of the Center's major initiatives is Project SERVE. Campus programs sponsored through Project SERVE include:

✦ **COMMUNITY PLUNGE.** This daylong service project is designed to introduce first-year students to community service learning.

✦ **VOLUNTEER FAIR.** Each fall, SERVE sponsors a Volunteer Fair so that students can meet with representatives from campus and community service organizations that need volunteers.

✦ **INTO THE STREETS.** This national initiative is designed to introduce students to thoughtful community service.

✦ **ACTING ON THE DREAM.** A one-day service project celebrating the life and work of Martin Luther King, Jr., with students, faculty, and staff working together on projects related to multicultural understanding and societal justice.

✦ **SERVE WEEK.** This weeklong celebration fosters unity through collaborative action and a shared commitment to service in the community.

Each year more than 5,000 students participate in service-learning activities. Another 3,000 students volunteer in community service. More than 75 courses at the University of Michigan involve students in service learning. These numbers prove that both the University and its students are committed to service learning and to meeting the needs of the local community.

UNIVERSITY OF NOTRE DAME

NOTRE DAME, IN 46556
219.631.5000
http://www.nd.edu/

UNDERGRADUATES: 7,800

For program information, please contact:
KATHLEEN MAAS WEIGERT, Ph.D.
kathleen.m.weigert.2@nd.edu

Notre Dame, founded in 1842, is a church-affiliated, comprehensive university. Notre Dame's service-learning (SL) program is inspired by the University's mission, which reads in part: "The aim is to create a sense of human solidarity and concern for the common good that will bear fruit as learning becomes service to justice."

The mission of the Center for Social Concerns constitutes a living model of Gospel values and Catholic social teachings through educational experiences. As Notre Dame students, faculty, staff, and alumni embrace the complex realities of social issues, spiritual and intellectual awareness continue this vision long after the college experience ends.

To achieve its mission, the Center offers students many educational and related service opportunities, including:

✦ ACADEMIC COURSES AND SEMINARS. The Center coordinates a variety of academic courses and cocurricular seminars that not only integrate experiential and service learning, but also focus on such issues as poverty, justice, and peace.

✦ EXPERIENTIAL AND SERVICE-LEARNING PLACEMENT. Students are placed in service positions in conjunction with related academic course work.

✦ SERVICE AND SOCIAL ACTION GROUPS. The Center functions as a home and resource for more than 30 student groups recruiting volunteers in such areas as literacy, the environment, and disability services.

Programs sponsored by Notre Dame's Center for Social Concerns provide mutually beneficial links between the University and the larger community. Through these programs, students are brought into contact with alumni, clergy, laypersons, and other students involved in a variety of clubs, agencies, and organizations. In many instances, student participants are inspired and motivated to offer their gifts and talents, both as students and later as alumni, to the larger Church and international community.

UNIVERSITY OF OKLAHOMA

NORMAN, OK 73019
405.325.0311
http://www.ou.edu/

UNDERGRADUATES: 16,200

For program information, please contact:
LARRY K. MICHAELSON, Ph.D.
lmichael@ou.edu

The University of Oklahoma, founded in 1892 as a public, comprehensive institution, houses the Integrated Business Core (IBC), a partnership between the University's Price College of Business and First Fidelity Bank of Oklahoma City. Through the IBC program, students are exposed to material from three business disciplines simultaneously: Legal Environment of Business, Principles of Marketing, and Principles of Organization and Management, along with an Entrepreneurship and Community Service Practicum. Students develop a business plan in which profits from their venture provide needed resources to chosen service projects.

The IBC strives to achieve the following objectives:

✦ To enable students to develop a cross-discipline view of business organizations;

✦ To provide opportunities for students to increase their communication skills in a work-like setting;

✦ To allow students to use analytical tools and business concepts to solve a wide range of unstructured problems; and

✦ To require students to create and manage two significant enterprises: a start-up company and a community-service project, through which they learn to use their business education as a means of providing financial resources for community service organizations.

The IBC program provides community-service opportunities in two ways. In recent semesters students have averaged 15 community-service hours in IBC-organized activities. The program also cultivates community service through the profits of the students' start-up business ventures. IBC students experience a great deal of personal satisfaction from being able to provide needed material and financial resources to community service organizations.

Many OU students continue their service work long after graduation, proof that this unique program not only prepares students to become successful business people, but also proactive, concerned citizens.

University of Rhode Island

330 MEMORIAL UNION
KINGSTON, RI 02881
401.874.1000
http://www.uri.edu/

UNDERGRADUATES: 11,000

For program information, please contact:
SABRINA ALBAN
sabrina.alban@uri.edu

The Feinstein Center for Service Learning is dedicated to providing service-learning and volunteer opportunities to students throughout their educational experience at the University of Rhode Island (URI), a public, comprehensive institution founded in 1892.

The Feinstein Center offers resources to URI faculty, staff, and off-campus agencies, such as the Clearinghouse for Volunteers. For over 20 years, the University has supported the Clearinghouse for Volunteers' initiatives, which have included hundreds of community projects in which thousands of URI students have provided much-needed services to the citizens of this state. The Clearinghouse, together with the University Year for Action (UYA), promote well-developed relationships with community agencies throughout Rhode Island and more recently have supported international service-learning programs.

The Feinstein Center integrates service learning in academic endeavors in several ways:

✦ Staff members work with faculty to help integrate service learning into their curriculum and to promote partnerships between academic departments and community agencies.

✦ The Center is moving toward a special designation in the University Catalog that will help students identify classes with a service-learning component.

✦ Four focus areas of the institution guide the Center's development of new service-learning opportunities: Health; Marine and Environmental Studies; Children, Families, and Communities; and Enterprise and Advanced Technologies.

The Feinstein Center for Service Learning, together with URI, puts volunteer and service-learning opportunities in the path of students because they know how valuable such experiences can be. Students gain leadership ability, become more analytical about themselves and their relationship to others, and dedicate themselves more easily to serving the community. Such results guide the Feinstein Center, thereby enhancing the education students receive at the University of Rhode Island.

University of Virginia

PO BOX 9017
CHARLOTTESVILLE, VA 22906
804.982.3200
http://www.virginia.edu/

UNDERGRADUATES: 12,400

For program information, please contact:
CINDY FREDRICK
cf7f@unix.mail.virginia.edu

"Volunteers from Madison House have greatly enriched my life through their love and encouragement and even more importantly through their compassion."

—A BENEFICIARY OF MADISON HOUSE

The University of Virginia, founded in 1819 by Thomas Jefferson, is a public institution. Madison House, an independent, nonprofit organization serving as the University's student volunteer center, organizes service programs to address the needs of the community as well as the educational and personal-growth objectives of students. The service programs achieve their mission by:

✦ Cooperating with community organizations to meet the educational, service, companionship, and referral needs of community members;

✦ Empowering and training student leaders to recruit, train, and support student volunteers; and

✦ Providing students with a meaningful volunteer experience that allows them to gain a greater perspective and understanding of the community and themselves.

Madison House embodies hands-on civic involvement. Student program directors, the heart and soul of the program, each manage a volunteer site for which they recruit, train, supervise, and evaluate student volunteers. Madison House creates an essential link for University students to experience many of the needs that exist in their community. By providing well-established programs and by coordinating a wide range of volunteer opportunities, Madison House allows students to give back to their community in ways that often parallel their own personal interests.

Through weekly volunteer service, students cultivate a true sense of compassion. For many volunteers, community service begins as an extracurricular activity but becomes a way of life. By offering positions of leadership, Madison House provides motivated student volunteers a means of taking on even greater responsibility, thereby developing future service leaders outside the University of Virginia.

University of Wisconsin– Eau Claire

105 GARFIELD AVENUE
EAU CLAIRE, WI 54701
715.836.2637
http://www.uwec.edu/

UNDERGRADUATES: 10,000

For program information, please contact:
ROBERT E. BURNS, PH.D.
burnsre@uwec.edu

The University of Wisconsin at Eau Claire, a public, comprehensive institution, requires all candidates for the baccalaureate degree to complete 30 or more hours of approved service-learning activity. This requirement encourages students to serve their community, to apply their knowledge gained in the classroom to real-world experiences, and to enhance their critical-thinking skills.

Service-learning activities may be incorporated into courses or they may be extracurricular. To qualify as service learning, these activities must challenge students to apply their academic knowledge and skills to meet community needs.

Students can meet the service-learning requirements in one of three ways:

✦ **Credit Option—Academic Major.** Students in some majors (such as Education, Nursing, and Social Work) will automatically fulfill the service-learning requirement through course work required for their major.

✦ **Credit Option—Selected Course.** Approximately 90 courses throughout the University have service-learning components. Projects conducted within these classes may fulfill the service-earning requirement.

✦ **Noncredit Option.** Most students will not meet the service-learning requirement through formal course work. In this instance, a student may fulfill the requirement—without receiving course credit—through volunteer work with an on-campus group or off-campus community organization.

An impetus for the creation of the University's service requirement was to foster diversity awareness. Students are encouraged to work with community organizations that attempt to meet local needs that typically are not met through usual market forces (e.g., Habitat for Humanity, social services through a variety of nonprofit organizations, and environmental causes through public interest groups). These service activities awaken Eau Claire students to real-world issues that they themselves will face as responsible citizens.

Vanderbilt University

2201 WEST END AVENUE
NASHVILLE, TN 37240
615.322.7311
http://www.vanderbilt.edu/

UNDERGRADUATES: 5,900

For program information, please contact:
MARK BANDAS, PH.D.
mark.bandas@vanderbilt.edu

Vanderbilt University, founded in 1873, is a private university that serves as home to the Mayfield Living/Learning Program. Mayfield staff believe that important out-of-the-classroom learning can be achieved through the active engagement of students in service to others through collaboration with other students, faculty, staff, and community leaders.

Through the Mayfield program, students pursue a self-directed, out-of-the-classroom, residential, structured learning experience. Groups of 10 students of the same gender prepare a proposal with the assistance of a faculty advisor for a yearlong program of learning. A committee of faculty, academic deans, student affairs deans and staff members, and representatives from the residence-hall student government reviews these proposals. Selected groups are then assigned to one of 20 Mayfield lodges, among the most desirable residence-hall assignments at Vanderbilt.

Each Lodge must fulfill program requirements, including:

✦ The maintenance of monthly reports citing student participation and progress on proposals;

✦ Student attendance at programs on community development and/or service learning, weekly meetings, lectures with faculty and other staff;

✦ The completion of Quality of Life surveys and other research instruments as requested; and

✦ Regular meetings or dinners with advisors and participation in educational programs sponsored by other lodges.

The goal of Vanderbilt University's Mayfield Living/Learning Program is to help students see the values in service to others in a comprehensive and reflective way. While serving others is good, it is a greater good to serve others with understanding and personal insight. Consequently, Mayfield participants incorporate reflection into the structure of their projects, and they seek out training on social and group dynamics and other special skills relevant to their particular project.

Virginia Polytechnic Institute and State University

BLACKSBURG, VA 24061
540.231.6000
http://www.vt.edu/

UNDERGRADUATES: 21,000

For program information, please contact:
MICHELE JAMES-DERAMO
deramo@vt.edu

Virginia Tech, founded in 1872, is a public, comprehensive university. The Service Learning Center at Virginia Tech promotes the integration of community service with academic study in order to advance student learning and civic involvement.

Programs include:

✦ COMMUNITY PARTNERSHIPS. The Center works in collaboration with organizations such as the Christiansburg Institute and the the Downtown Merchants of Blacksburg to revitalize public spaces important to community life.

✦ DISTANCE AND SERVICE LEARNING IN THE SCIENCES. This National Science Foundation–funded program uses the Internet to link undergraduate science majors with youth in rural areas to enhance science curriculum in schools.

✦ SERVICE-LEARNING EXTENSION PROJECT. This project between the Center and Virginia Cooperative Extension develops service-learning activities at sites statewide.

✦ STEP (SERVICE TRAINING FOR ENVIRONMENTAL PROGRESS). STEP targets third-party technical support to communities and civic groups addressing environmental concerns.

✦ VIRGINIA TECH COMMUNITY LITERACY CORPS. This America Reads initiative matches federal work-study students as reading tutors with students at local schools.

✦ VTOPS. This umbrella program includes a variety of academic mentoring activities that instill confidence in children's learning abilities.

While the Center primarily assists faculty wanting to incorporate a service component into their courses, it also offers a resource library pertaining to service learning, a Listserv and on-line forum to discuss service learning at the University, as well as training and technical support. The Service Learning Center exhibits Virginia Tech's commitment to graduating responsible students who understand the importance of service to one's community.

Yale University

PO BOX 208234
NEW HAVEN, CT 06520-8234
203.432.9300
http://www.yale.edu/

UNDERGRADUATES: 5,400

For program information, please contact:
PAMELA BISBEE-SIMONDS
Pamela.Bisbee-Simonds@yale.edu

Yale University, a private, liberal arts institution, houses Dwight Hall, a community committed to pursuing public service and social justice. Founded in 1886 by undergraduates as the Young Men's Christian Association at Yale to serve the poor in New Haven, Dwight Hall was incorporated 12 years later as a nonprofit educational and religious student organization devoted to service, and is independent of Yale financially and by governance, yet interdependent.

The concerns that brought the Hall into existence continue today. The issue of Yale's relationship to New Haven remains crucial, as does the University's responsiveness to the needs of its students. Although Yale does not offer an institutionalized academic service-learning program, Dwight Hall provides significant experiential learning for undergraduates who participate in the 65 student-run community service and advocacy programs under its umbrella, and through extensive leadership and volunteer trainings through the Hall.

Two current programs connect Dwight Hall to its roots, inspiring and preparing students for a lifetime of involvement.

✦ THE LEADERSHIP INSTITUTE strives to encourage student skills that lead to effective social change through group leadership.

✦ THE MAGEE FELLOWSHIP was founded in 1986 in honor of John Magee, Class of '06, who served as the first chaplain of the Episcopal Church at Yale. The Fellow's role is to provide moral and religious guidance to students involved in Dwight Hall programs.

Developing students' understanding of personal and civic responsibility has been a part of Dwight Hall's mission since its founding as a religious organization. Initially, Dwight Hall was explicitly Christian. As diversification at the University grew, the Hall evolved into a more secular institution. Nevertheless, it is deeply committed to doing good works, both on campus and in the community.

SUBSTANCE-ABUSE PREVENTION PROGRAMS

An increasing number of colleges and universities
are designing comprehensive alcohol- and
substance-abuse prevention programs that place
character at the heart of the issue. These programs
extend beyond mere enforcement of campus rules
to include activities that focus on changing perceptions
and behaviors regarding alcohol and drug abuse.
At the core of these efforts are professionally
designed and often student-led initiatives that equip
students with skills to resist participating in peer
cultures and community practices that lead to
binge drinking and drug use.

BETHANY COLLEGE

BETHANY, WV 26032
304.829.7000
http://www.bethany.wvnet.edu/
UNDERGRADUATES: 800

For program information, please contact:
GREGORY S. WELLS
g.wells@mail.bethanywv.edu

"I never drank in high school, but I started my first semester in college. Then Vision was formed. I decided that alcohol wasn't necessary, and I didn't want to let anyone down, including myself."
—A BETHANY SECOND-YEAR STUDENT

Bethany College, a four-year liberal arts college affiliated with the Christian Church (Disciples of Christ), values intellectual rigor and freedom, diversity of thought and lifestyle, attention to personal growth within a community context, and responsible engagement with public issues. Under the guidance of Gregory Wells, Director of Student Support Services, the VISION program at Bethany fits within those values in that its mission focuses on the concept of personal and civic responsibility.

✦ Through the education of its members and the strength in its numbers, the program helps students find the courage they need to make responsible personal decisions about the use of alcohol and other drugs.

✦ Through helping create and manage chemical-free alternatives, such as campus dances, "ghost story night," community Christmas caroling, and an on-campus coffeehouse, members learn about the personal commitment and self-discipline required in being responsible to others.

✦ Through creating and publishing 20/20 Vision, a campus-wide educational newsletter, members recognize the importance of providing accurate, timely, and useful information to others.

✦ Through making personal presentations in schools in surrounding counties, members take active steps to help shape, strengthen, and reinforce the values of younger students who are facing imminent decisions about alcohol and other drugs.

This program is based on the vision of a safer and happier future for the next generation. Participants understand that the vision won't be fulfilled unless they take personal responsibility to see that it does.

CENTRAL MICHIGAN UNIVERSITY

MOUNT PLEASANT, MI 48859
517.774.4000
http://www.cmich.edu/
UNDERGRADUATES: 16,000

For program information, please contact:
MARK MINELLI, Ph.D.
mark.j.minelli@cmich.edu

Central Michigan University, a public institution, has received numerous national awards for its substance-abuse prevention programs. The National Collegiate Alcohol Awareness Week committee repeatedly recognizes CMU's program as one of the ten best in the country. The Center for Advancement of Public Health has also recognized CMU's programs as exemplifying "Promising Practices" in substance-abuse prevention. Credit for these awards, suggest CMU officials, ought to go to the many student groups on campus dedicating their time to reducing high-risk drinking among their peers. Eta Sigma Gamma, BACCHUS/GAMMA, Pride, and SADD have worked together to educate students about responsible use as well as healthy alternatives to alcohol use. The University's cornerstone activities include:

✦ SOCIAL NORMS CAMPAIGN. The campaign educates students about the misperceptions of alcohol abuse. One of the purposes of the campaign is to support a student's choice not to use alcohol.

✦ PRESIDENTIAL LEADERSHIP. Dr. Leonard Plachta, president of CMU, has made alcohol reduction and prevention a top priority of his administration. In collaboration with the Dean of Students, he holds quarterly meetings to address concerns, strategies, and assessment issues.

✦ PROGRAM EVALUATION. CMU conducts ongoing data collection and analysis on student use and abuse patterns of alcohol and other drugs. The state-of-the-art evaluation component enables CMU to measure program impact and make adjustments in methods, strategies, and focus.

CMU's commitment to reducing alcohol and other drug abuse and misuse has made a difference. The percentage of students who drink is decreasing. Although challenges remain, Central Michigan University has made great strides in educating students about the harmful effects of alcohol misuse.

COLLEGE MISERICORDIA

301 LAKE STREET
DALLAS, PA 18512
570.674.6400
http://www.miseri.edu/

UNDERGRADUATES: 1,100

For program information, please contact:
DARCY BRODMERKEL
dbrodmer@miseri.edu

"The program has taught me about choices. Because of it, I realized I don't have to drink to have a good time—but if I do, I need to be responsible."
—A MISERICORDIA FOURTH-YEAR STUDENT

Emphasizing civic and personal responsibility, the Alcohol and Other Drug Awareness Program at College Misericordia, a Roman Catholic liberal arts school, reflects the values of the college's founding Sisters of Mercy. These values, which Misericordia considers critical to character development, include mercy, service, justice, and hospitality. Program activities focus on responsible decision-making. Throughout the program, students consider the variety of ways that drinking and drug use can adversely affect their academic and career goals, as well as the communities in which they live. Rather than telling students not to drink, the program encourages moderation and self-control. Character-building opportunities include:

✦ Activities sponsored by the school's chapter of BACCHUS (Boosting Alcohol Consciousness Concerning the Health of University Students), which often benefit the community, such as donations to the local chapter of MADD (Mothers Against Drunk Driving);

✦ Self-screening assessments to gain objective feedback on level of high-risk behaviors;

✦ Wellness housing for students who choose to live a substance-free lifestyle;

✦ Good Samaritan Policy, encouraging students to help peers engaged in at-risk behaviors;

✦ Campus Peer Associates Program, whereby trained students talk with their peers;

✦ DAW/N (Drug and Alcohol Awareness) Weekend, providing the opportunity for reflection on one's use/abuse of alcohol and other drugs.

Misericordia's Program helps students gain a greater sense of self-control and establish an appropriate support network that focuses on the development of healthy lifestyle choices.

COLLEGE OF SAINT BENEDICT

ST. JOSEPH, MN 56374
320.363.5601
http://www.csbsju.edu/

UNDERGRADUATES: 1,900

For program information, please contact:
DOROTHY SOUKUP BENDER
dsoukup@csbsju.edu

"A main focus of the 'Lalla-no-booza' event is to involve as many student clubs and organizations as possible. This says to students, 'It's not just the Health Advocates who choose a healthy lifestyle; it's the athletes, the musicians, anybody; it can be you.'"
—A ST. BENEDICT SECOND-YEAR STUDENT

Responsibility for self and community are fundamental elements of the interdisciplinary model of development for students at the College of Saint Benedict, a private, church-affiliated, liberal arts institution for women. By approaching alcohol and drug prevention from a holistic perspective, staff and faculty are able to influence students, as well as engage them in a process that will affect lifelong decision-making. Students are challenged to examine their alcohol and drug use in light of their personal values systems and the potential risks associated with their behavior.

✦ HEALTH ADVOCATE PROGRAM. This peer-educator program promotes wellness, healthy choices, and responsibility.

✦ LALLA-NO-BOOZA. Each fall students gather for a five-day event to promote having fun and socializing without the use of chemicals.

✦ HEALTH AND WELLNESS LEARNING COMMUNITY. St. Benedict's residential life program provides an environment for students wishing to make healthy life choices to live with others holding similar value systems.

✦ SEXUALITY AND SPIRITUALITY, THE SACRED CONNECTION. This course encourages identification of personal values and beliefs as integral to self-knowledge and decision-making.

The College of Saint Benedict was included in the 1997–98 *Promising Practices: Campus Alcohol Sourcebook* and has received a three-year Bush Foundation Grant to further develop the concept of Healthy Learning Communities. Faculty and staff in health education, residential life, and counseling continue to collaborate in programming that encourages students to realize the impact their actions have, not only on their own lives but also on the lives of others.

THE COLLEGE OF ST. ROSE

432 WESTERN AVENUE
ALBANY, NY 12203-1490
518.454.5111
http://www.strose.edu/

UNDERGRADUATES: 2,600

For program information, please contact:
GRAHAM KNOWLES
knowlesg@mail.strose.edu

"As 'Hooray Players,' we try to educate our peers on social issues through role-playing in the hope that we can eliminate ignorance about alcohol abuse from our campus."

—A ST. ROSE THIRD-YEAR STUDENT

In keeping with its mission of challenging students "to explore and clarify their values, and to contribute actively as caring individuals to the larger community," The College of St. Rose, a private school of liberal arts and sciences, has established an Office of Alcohol and Other Drug Prevention Services. This multifaceted prevention program incorporates media advocacy, peer education, and extensive collaboration between students, faculty, and the administration. The program has a two-prong peer education component:

✦ THE HOORAY PLAYERS. This student-run education group uses role-playing to inform the audience about a variety of complex issues, including alcohol, sexuality, and gender roles. The fact that no script is used allows the group's members to adapt spontaneously, remaining flexible and genuine in their portrayal of any scenario. At the climax of each scene, the action is stopped and the audience is encouraged to interact with the players, who stay in character.

✦ C.H.O.I.C.E.S. (Chemical Health: Owning Individual Choices and Educating Students). Much like the high-school S.A.D.D. (Students Against Drunk Driving) program, this group provides educational opportunities and attempts to reduce the number of alcohol- and other drug-related problems.

The Office of Alcohol and Other Drug Prevention also sponsors campaigns such as National Collegiate Alcohol Awareness Week and houses a library on the topic of substance abuse. The program was awarded a FIPSE grant in 1992, was recognized by the 1996–97 *Promising Practices* publication, and was given a second-place Neighborhood of the Year Award by Neighborhoods USA. The program's use of student-to-student communication not only permits greater acceptance of the message of prevention, but also allows opportunities for leadership development among the student body.

COLLEGE OF THE HOLY CROSS

1 COLLEGE STREET
WORCESTER, MA 01610
508.793.2011
http://www.holycross.edu/

UNDERGRADUATES: 2,800

For program information, please contact:
ANN-MARIE MATTEUCCI
amatteu@holycross.edu

"Students for Responsible Choices aims to educate the campus community about drugs and alcohol. We present programs in the residence halls and sponsor alcohol-free activities, but it is our position as role models that makes us most effective." —A HOLY CROSS FOURTH-YEAR STUDENT

College of the Holy Cross, a church-affiliated, liberal arts institution, is dedicated to supporting intellectual growth while offering opportunities for spiritual and moral development. To foster that development, the Alcohol and Drug Education Program, directed by Jacqueline Latino, challenges the attitudes, behaviors, and unhealthy norms that lead to abusive drinking and drug use. Drawing on all available resources, including students, faculty, administrators, alumni, and parents, the program tackles head-on the problems associated with substance abuse. Highlights include:

✦ STUDENTS FOR RESPONSIBLE CHOICES are trained to educate peers about alcohol and other drug issues, assist them in making informed choices, and provide leadership through modeling of appropriate behavior. Each week one member writes an article in the college newspaper regarding alcohol and drug issues. The students have also produced a 30-second public service announcement targeting abusive drinking, which aired on local television stations, and a training video on how to confront someone who is drinking excessively.

✦ THE ALCOHOL AND OTHER DRUG REFERRAL PROGRAM, for students who violate school policies or who are referred by a concerned faculty or staff member, provides information about the effects of alcohol and drugs on self and on others.

The Office of Alcohol and Other Drug Education at Holy Cross aims to work with students to identify life plans that are affected by the decisions they make in college and to empower the students themselves to create a climate of change around the issue of substance abuse. The target of all these efforts is the same: a safer and more caring environment for all members of the school community.

GEORGE MASON UNIVERSITY

4400 UNIVERSITY DRIVE
FAIRFAX, VA 22030-4444
703.993.1000
http://www.gmu.edu/

UNDERGRADUATES: 14,000

For program information, please contact:
NANCY SCHULTE
nschulte@gmu.edu

George Mason University, a public institution that enjoys a growing reputation as an innovative educational leader, strives to eliminate substance abuse on campus through educational initiatives and counseling. George Mason's Drug Education Services (DES), in existence since 1988, is coordinated by Nancy Schulte, who recently chaired a national symposium on college alcohol practices and published "What Can You Do?" a booklet outlining the symposium recommendations. She has been named advisor of the year by both George Mason University and the national office of BACCHUS/GAMMA and has been featured in numerous publications, local television, and national broadcasts. Under her direction, DES:

✦ Offers information on substance-abuse prevention to parents and new students during summer orientation. Orientation leaders model appropriate behavior and relate community standards to incoming students through small-group discussions and peer theater.

✦ Presents programs to first-year classes, as well as other academic classes, student organizations, and residence halls. The focus of these programs is to improve attitudes regarding personal health and concern for the welfare of others.

✦ Trains peer educators who present programs in the campus community and in the local public school systems.

✦ Distributes the Alcohol 101 interactive CD-ROM to appropriate classrooms and processes related pre- and post-tests.

DES has been recognized the past seven years by the Inter-Association Task Force on Alcohol and Other Substance Abuse Issues as one of ten outstanding institutions for year-round prevention programming. It was also cited in *Promising Practices* as a model comprehensive prevention program. With plans for reinforcing strict policies and providing students greater opportunities to socialize on campus, DES continues seeking new ways to raise the quality of campus life.

LA SIERRA UNIVERSITY

RIVERSIDE, CA 92515-8247
909.785.2000
http://www.lasierra.edu/

UNDERGRADUATES: 1,600

For program information, please contact:
LENNARD JORGENSEN, Ph.D.
ljorgens@lasierra.edu

Students making the transition from high school to university tend to be vulnerable in their values clarification during the first year of college. La Sierra University, a private, liberal arts school, addresses potential problems through Mountain High Retreats for first-year students. The retreats rely heavily on social cognitive learning theory (modeling) to transmit good values and provide an effective alternative to the negative influences young adults often encounter. Designed specifically to help develop internalized personal and civic responsibility, the retreats offer:

✦ **FAMILY SUPPORT GROUPS.** Peers help peers, creating a powerful venue for honesty, trust, and clarification. Students who finish the three-day retreat frequently express how helpful the family support groups have been to them in making commitments to remain true to themselves.

✦ **PEER PRESENTERS.** Students are able to transmit information on values to other students more effectively than older adults because of the natural sense of trust that exists among peers.

✦ **KEYNOTE SPEAKERS.** Upperclassmen deliver high-powered keynote addresses with the goal of motivating students into accepting good values. The speeches are also a means by which the students can observe peers filling significant leadership roles.

In addition to witnessing the excitement the upperclassmen enjoy by being leaders at the retreat, the students learn that standing up for their Christian value system can be done with respect for others' values. They also learn that giving and receiving unconditional support on moral, social, emotional, and academic levels enriches and gives meaning to life. Through participating in the retreat, young adults can practice resisting negative peer pressure in the specific areas of alcohol and drugs—a lesson they can take with them through life.

LEHIGH UNIVERSITY

27 MEMORIAL DRIVE WEST
BETHLEHEM, PA 18015
610.758.3000
http://www.lehigh.edu/

UNDERGRADUATES: 4,000

For program information, please contact:
MADDY EADLINE
mcw@lehigh.edu

With support from the Robert Wood Johnson Foundation, Lehigh University has established a three-prong approach to its substance-abuse prevention efforts, focusing on programs, promotion, and policy. Titled Project IMPACT, at the core of this effort is a university-wide call for more responsibility on the part of all stakeholders. The following initiatives are but some of the university's cornerstone activities:

✦ **NONALCOHOL SOCIAL EVENTS.** A newly established social policy requires a dramatic increase in the number of nonalcohol social events on campus, many of them sponsored by fraternities and sororities.

✦ **HOMECOMING FORMAL FOR ATHLETES.** Lehigh athletes organized a "Hard Bodies–Soft Drinks" formal that brought together 400 students and members of the athletic departments. This activity exemplifies the efforts by students-athletes to change perceptions that they are heavy drinkers.

✦ **SUBSTANCE-FREE HOUSING.** Over the past several years there has been a dramatic increase in the number of students who opt for substance-free residential housing.

✦ **TOWN/GOWN ACTIVITIES.** A University staff member serving as a community liaison canvases the nearby neighborhoods, talking to students and community members about the University's activities to reduce the secondhand effects of alcohol misuse.

✦ **WORK SMART/PLAY SMART.** Lehigh has established a Play Smart publication and website that offer updates on nonalcoholic activities and events on campus and in the community.

At the heart of Lehigh's substance-abuse prevention activities is a coordinated effort to bring together the campus and community to enforce all alcohol-related policies. Lehigh faculty, administrators, and trustees continue their efforts to confront the issue of binge drinking and connect it to the goals and ideals of character development.

LYON COLLEGE

2300 HIGHLAND ROAD
BATESVILLE, AR 72503
870.793.9813
http://www.lyon.edu/

UNDERGRADUATES: 500

For program information, please contact:
DIANE ELLIS
dellis@lyon.edu

Campus life at Lyon College, a church-affiliated, liberal arts institution, is infused with a strong sense of community, affording students a great measure of personal freedom and requiring an equal measure of responsibility. It is no surprise, then, that the alcohol education program at Lyon is designed and conducted by a student organization, P.A.R.T.Y. (Promoting Alcohol Responsibility Through You). The Director of Counseling, Diane Ellis, acts as advisor to the group. The primary education component of the program is a series of three student-led sessions called Peers, Tears, and Cheers:

✦ **PEERS** addresses the positive and negative impact that fellow students have on decision-making about alcohol. Strongly emphasized is the fact that individuals often put more pressure on themselves than do their peers. Peers illustrates the different types of drinkers, including the binge drinker.

✦ **TEARS** outlines the various legal consequences of underage alcohol consumption and of drunk driving, the emotional consequences of drinking, and the on-campus consequences of school policy violations.

✦ **CHEERS** focuses on appropriate hosting and on activities that can be done without alcohol. It also stresses the fact that facing one's problems rather than hiding from them is much less painful in the long run.

The Peers, Tears, and Cheers program was recognized by the U.S. Department of Education with a presentation at the Fifth National Forum on Substance Abuse Issues in 1992 and was selected in 1996 for inclusion in *Promising Practices: Campus Alcohol Strategies*. Evaluations of the program have consistently rated it as good or excellent, and—most important—students have said that the program has given them skills they can use in responsible decision-making.

Marshall University

400 HAL GREER BOULEVARD
HUNTINGTON, WV 25755
304.696.3170
http://www.marshall.edu/

UNDERGRADUATES: 9,000

For program information, please contact:
CARLA LAPELLE
lapelle@marshall.edu

"The Volunteer Project is a great opportunity for students to have a fun time with peers without having to deal with the social pressures of drugs and alcohol."

—A MARSHALL GRADUATE

Marshall University, a public institution, strives to develop programs that will be recognized for their excellence. Toward this goal, strong emphasis is placed on high-quality teaching and interaction with the individual student. Just such interaction occurs in the Volunteer Project, begun in 1996 in an effort to increase volunteerism among students and to foster attitudes consistent with non-drug use. Students involved in the Volunteer Project, directed by the coordinator of Student Health Education Programs, have painted facilities at a Boy Scout camp, sponsored a toy drive for the Huntington City Mission, and staffed a Ronald McDonald House, among many other activities. When students work together to plan and accomplish a community service, they:

✦ Learn life skills that are important as prevention strategies;

✦ Gain an increased awareness of their strengths and weaknesses;

✦ Find their assumptions about the disenfranchised, disabled, and disadvantaged challenged;

✦ Develop an awareness of their own boundaries and limitations and recognize opportunities to push beyond these;

✦ Place themselves in situations where the difference between the reassuring, normative messages about campus drinking and the full spectrum of human turmoil connected to alcohol and other drugs is blatant.

Volunteer Project was named a Program of Excellence in *Promising Practices: Campus Alcohol Strategies.* The increase in student volunteerism has begun to change the perception of college students as "party animals" to that of reliable, compassionate young adults.

Newbury College

129 FISHER AVENUE
BROOKLINE, MA 02146
617.730.7000
http://www.newbury.edu/

UNDERGRADUATES: 900

For program information, please contact:
KRISTIN GEARIN
k.gearin@newbury.edu

"'Winners Choose Not to Use' is an encouraging program. My experience with it helps me to avoid peer pressure and not to accept the attitude that doing drugs and alcohol is being cool."

—A NEWBURY COLLEGE SECOND-YEAR STUDENT

Newbury College, a private, liberal arts school, has been a pioneer in providing career-relevant education. In 1992, supported by a FIPSE grant, Newbury applied its innovative style to an institution-wide substance-abuse prevention effort. The initiative includes an outreach program, "Winners Choose Not to Use," directed specifically toward Newbury athletes. Coordinated by Newbury's Center for Counseling and Health Education, all elements of the campaign emphasize student responsibility to self and community and convey the message that substance use and athletic achievement are mutually exclusive.

✦ "The Healthy Profile," printed on all Newbury sports programs, features a model student athlete's photograph, academic achievements, career goals, and reasons for avoiding the abuse of alcohol and other drugs. This brings a powerful message to all athletes and spectators. The profile also serves to recognize students who make a public commitment to Newbury's non-use philosophy and invites nominations of other students for future editions. A copy of the Healthy Profile is mounted and presented to the featured athlete at the year-end awards ceremony.

✦ Athletes can also participate in the "Winners" program through nonalcoholic events, such as the Super Bowl Bash and the annual March Midnight Madness.

✦ Volunteer community service, such as assisting in a neighborhood cleanup each semester and hosting basketball clinics for area youth organizations, boosts team spirit and promotes a sense of working together to achieve a higher purpose.

The "Winners Choose Not to Lose" banner is hung at every major athletic event, including all Newbury-sponsored tournaments and year-end banquets, integrating the message into this important part of campus life and creating a strong "prevention presence" throughout the entire year.

Northeastern Illinois University

5500 NORTH ST. LOUIS AVENUE
CHICAGO, IL 60625-4699
773.583.4050
http://www.neiu.edu/

UNDERGRADUATES: 7,500

For program information, please contact:
RONALD L. GLICK
r-glick@neiu.edu

Northeastern Illinois University, a comprehensive, state-supported commuter institution, incorporates substance-abuse prevention into the curriculum to help students develop a strong internal sense of personal responsibility. The school's approach is to integrate prevention seamlessly into the curriculum in a process that promotes active student involvement in the learning process. Students are encouraged to consider the prevention information carefully and apply it to the decisions they make about their own behavior and about how they will relate to others.

✦ The question of personal responsibility is addressed directly in a number of courses; for example, a philosophy class may consider driving under the influence, or a sociology class may consider the special risks for women that are associated with binge drinking. A biology course may include a unit on fetal alcohol syndrome.

✦ Teacher education courses prepare future teachers to integrate prevention into the middle- and high-school classes they will teach. These students are especially urged to consider their own behavior in relation to alcohol and other drugs as they take responsibility for positively affecting the sense of self-control and wellness of their future students.

The University has stated that the most important facets of its mission are to offer high-quality programs to a broad spectrum of students and to foster student growth and development. By making the topic of substance abuse an integral part of the curriculum, the University accomplishes both.

Ohio University

ATHENS, OH 45701
740.593.1000
http://www.ohiou.edu/

UNDERGRADUATES: 16,000

For program information, please contact:
MICHAEL BUGEJA, Ph.D.
bugeja@ohiou.edu

Founded in 1804, Ohio University uses the principles of character education, along with a focus on health and wellness, to increase awareness about high-risk drinking and to foster holistic education. A variety of programming through the Office of the President and Division of Student Affairs, as well as other units, includes:

✦ "Your PATH at Ohio," a character- and community-building program that emphasizes personal accountability, trust, and honor, and expands on Ohio University's core values of respect, civility, and diversity. Michael Bugeja, creator of the PATH program, fosters dialog about PATH principles and other ethical concepts through seminars, class visits, and public presentations.

✦ "A Community of Values" program, directed specifically at first-year students in an annual convocation, emphasizes learning, involvement, and commitment—values that promote PATH principles throughout the school year.

✦ The Binge Drinking Prevention Coalition, an organization that influences the campus community by disseminating proactive messages and encouraging healthy choices and responsible alcohol use. Made up of students, administrators, faculty, and community members, the coalition creates and models a caring environment that emphasizes the importance of responsible, safe policy and law-abiding behavior. The coalition is part of and contributes to the "Community of Values" program coordinated through the Division of Student Affairs.

The faculty, administration, and staff of Ohio University believe that incoming students who "make a habit" of learning—and commit to that—will travel their own unique PATH to success.

PACE UNIVERSITY

ONE PACE PLAZA
NEW YORK, NY 10038
212.346.1200
http://www.pace.edu/

UNDERGRADUATES: 9,000

For program information, please contact:
LAURA SMITH
lsmith@fsmail.pace.edu

In recognition of its need to design fresh ways to serve its diverse, nontraditional, urban student body, Pace University, a private institution, has taken a comprehensive wellness approach to student services. Through its "Discover You, Discover Pace, Discover the World" program, Pace addresses the students' physical and emotional well-being, their needs for community and support, and the development of their personal goals, aspirations, and values. Specific programming efforts are cooperative ventures by "out-of-classroom educators," representatives from Student Development, Residential Life, Multicultural Affairs, the Counseling Center, Career Services, and the Health Care Unit, among others.

Substance abuse is targeted in the "Discover You" phase, which also involves projects dealing with other wellness topics, such as sex and stress management. Spectrum is a comprehensive series of campus-wide wellness programs, including events related to National Collegiate Alcohol Awareness Week and "Love on the Rocks," an interactive workshop that examines the relationship between alcohol use and making decisions about sex. Spectrum's presentations are coordinated by Dr. Laura Smith, who also chairs the Wellness Task Force.

For students who have difficulty attending wellness presentations scheduled outside the classroom, Bridges, a new initiative, brings Spectrum programming inside the classroom. It provides academic departments with a menu of classroom presentations that can be requested when a faculty member calls in sick or when a guest speaker might supplement course material.

Pace believes that this comprehensive, multifaceted approach to wellness issues is ultimately the most effective means of combating substance abuse and improving the lives of individual students and campus life in general.

THE PENNSYLVANIA STATE UNIVERSITY

201 OLD MAIN
UNIVERSITY PARK, PA 16802
814.865.7611
http://www.psu.edu/

UNDERGRADUATES: 35,000

For program information, please contact:
WILLIAM ASBURY
wwal@psu.edu

From agricultural college to world-class university, the story of The Pennsylvania State University is one of an expanding mission of teaching, research, and service. Responding to underage and excessive drinking on campus, this public, comprehensive university is working to improve responsibility among its students. Believing that strong peer engagement is vital to the success of prevention, treatment, and education programming, the school trains peer counselors and integrates them into programs. The school's campaign against substance abuse is multifaceted:

✦ THE ALCOHOL INTERVENTION PROGRAM (AIP) uses peer counselors and an addiction specialist as the first line of education and treatment defense for those referred for liquor-law violations.

✦ THE CENTER FOR COUNSELING AND PSYCHOLOGICAL SERVICES (CAPS) treats alcoholism and drug abuse through group and individual therapy. CAPS programs have been cited at national meetings as models of intervention activities.

✦ THE COMMISSION FOR THE PREVENTION OF ALCOHOL AND OTHER DRUG ABUSE (CPATODA) focuses on the religious and spirituality issues related to alcohol use.

✦ THE LATE-NIGHT WEEKEND PROGRAM, from big-band dancing to talent competitions, draws thousands of students to Penn State's HUB student union. Late-Night Weekend is almost entirely student supported.

✦ LIFE HOUSE, a special-interest housing option, offers substance-free living space to students committed not to use or possess alcohol, tobacco, or other drugs inside the house.

Penn State does not expect to eliminate alcohol but instead to modify student behavior by accelerating the maturing process. Thus it asks upperclassmen to tell newcomers: "We've been there. Your new freedom is great, and part of that freedom is to choose whether to drink. You also have plenty of nonalcoholic options. Know your options and choose well."

RAMAPO COLLEGE OF NEW JERSEY

505 RAMAPO VALLEY ROAD
MAHWAH, NJ 07430
201.684.7500
http://www.ramapo.edu/

UNDERGRADUATES: 4,700

For program information, please contact:
ALBERT FRECH, Ph.D.
afrech@ramapo.edu

As a progressive school with a vigilant eye to the future, Ramapo College of New Jersey endeavors to move from a traditional campus drinking culture to one in which positive social, academic, and personal development is expected and visibly acknowledged and rewarded. The prevention program at this public, liberal arts college includes the following elements:

✦ Student involvement in peer education, outreach, and volunteerism promotes a visible model of citizenship, especially through activities that tackle the problem of substance abuse.

✦ Alcohol and other drug education, infused throughout the academic departments and the cocurriculum, addresses the association of substance abuse with date violence, assault, incivility, and academic underachievement. It also raises for public discussion the issues of decision-making ethics, consequences of students' actions to themselves and to others, and ways in which the students' individual decisions can support or undermine the community in which they live.

✦ Health and wellness programming provides a mechanism for teaching team cooperation, respect for one's body and mind, and the need for self-management and control.

All policies are developed and all programming designed to teach responsible choices and set clear standards for behavior. Training for faculty and staff, alcohol-free activities, and substance-free residence areas enhance Ramapo's prevention program. And the prevention program contributes vitally to the school's strides toward its goal of helping students develop the solid foundations of knowledge, skills, abilities, and values required to be productive members of tomorrow's society.

SAINT LOUIS UNIVERSITY

221 NORTH GRAND BOULEVARD
ST. LOUIS, MO 63103-2097
314.977.2222
http://www.slu.edu/

UNDERGRADUATES: 6,500

For program information, please contact:
SHAWN SWINIGAN
sswiniga@lan.slu.ed

"The Alcohol Awareness program has helped to provide students here with the tools to make their own decisions on major issues."

—A SAINT LOUIS FOURTH-YEAR STUDENT

The mission of Saint Louis University, a private, church-affiliated institution, is the pursuit of truth for the greater glory of God and for the service of humanity. Following a similar philosophy, the mission of the school's Alcohol Awareness Program is to educate the campus community about the need to recognize and intervene in substance-abuse situations and to promote responsible alternatives to alcohol. The program uses a variety of methods to reach the students.

✦ Alcohol Awareness Week features events with strong emotional impact, such as a candlelight service organized by the Greeks, at which a former student and fraternity member related his experience with a close friend who drank excessively and died in an automobile accident as a result.

✦ Training for Intervention Procedures (TIPS) sessions are offered during Welcome Week for first-year students. A series of continuing sessions is incorporated into Residence Life's Community 101 program as part of the required seminars for residents, especially first-year students.

✦ Weekly workshops hosted by the Counseling Center focus on the effects of binge drinking and the benefits of responsible alcohol use. Most of the students who participate are referred to the Counseling Center for first-time minor infractions of residence-hall guidelines relating to the use of alcohol on campus.

The ultimate goal of the Alcohol Awareness Program is to lead students to ethical and moral decision-making, equipping them to live full and responsible lives with a sense of civic commitment and a desire to help others.

Saint Michael's College

WINOOSKI PARK
COLCHESTER, VT 05439
802.654.2000
http://www.smcvt.edu/

UNDERGRADUATES: 2,000

For program information, please contact:
AARON KUNTZ
akuntz@smcvt.edu

Saint Michael's College, a church-affiliated school of liberal arts and sciences, welcomes students who believe that thinking about—and talking about—larger issues, such as God, responsibility to others, and the question of a soul should be an integral part of education. A continuous conversation regarding alcohol and drug use, then, centers on information-sharing mixed with knowledgeable assistance to help members of the campus community live healthy lifestyles and have a positive impact on others. Saint Michael's puts its resources into expanding that segment of its student body that chooses to abstain from or moderate its use of alcohol and other drugs:

✦ **G.R.E.A.T.** (Growing Recognition of the Effects of Alcohol on Thinking) housing, which was profiled in *Promising Practices: Campus Alcohol Strategies,* establishes living space for individuals who sign a contract not to abuse alcohol or other drugs and to abstain from drinking in their residence.

✦ **Friday Knight Dry,** the culminating event of Alcohol Awareness Week, provides alternative, drug-free events to the campus community.

✦ **The Decisions Program,** a three-tiered process that outlines the behavioral expectations of student athletes, reinforces healthy behavior, and helps them to be better role models and leaders on campus.

✦ **The Wilderness Program** allows students to evaluate their responsibility to a larger social group and encourages them to pledge their commitment to healthy physical experiences without alcohol and drug use.

The greatest strength of Saint Michael's substance-abuse prevention efforts is the interwoven nature of the programming, which the school believes has allowed for significant improvement in campus culture. The efforts to stem the problems associated with alcohol and other drugs continue in a spirit of persistence and of hope.

St. Xavier University

3700 WEST 103RD STREET
CHICAGO, IL 60655
773.298.3000
http://www.sxu.edu/

UNDERGRADUATES: 4,100

For program information, please contact:
HOLLY GIBSON HERGAN
hergan@sxu.edu

St. Xavier University, a Catholic liberal arts school founded by the Sisters of Mercy, proactively educates its community about the risks associated with substance use, particularly alcohol. The Career and Personal Development Center works closely with Student Activities, Residence Life, and Academic Affairs to offer multifaceted programming:

✦ "Alcohol 101," an individualized, interactive CD-ROM (developed by the University of Illinois at Urbana-Champaign and the Century Council), is offered as a cocurricular workshop for new students enrolled in a required one-credit college success seminar. The program's scenarios are designed to help students recognize when they or their peers are at risk.

✦ During Alcohol Awareness Week (October) and Alcohol Awareness Month (April), public-service radio announcements and flyers, posters, and articles are used to highlight alcohol-related problems. The Student Activities Board hosts "mocktail parties" to generate enthusiasm for functions that exclude alcohol, makes arrangements for free transportation from off-campus events at which alcohol is served, and provides free nonalcoholic beverages for designated drivers. Student leaders volunteer to be "Dead for a Day" by wearing T-shirts stating, "I died last night in a drunk-driving incident," and remaining silent for the day. The Career and Personal Development Center offers several "Alcohol 101" workshops for the St. Xavier community. A "Self-Quiz" is posted throughout the campus to heighten awareness of signs of alcohol abuse.

Valuing the mission of the Catholic tradition, which is to see that the Christian mind may achieve "a public, persistent, and universal presence in the whole enterprise of advancing higher culture," St. Xavier University guides its students into making informed decisions about the use of alcohol.

Southern Illinois University Carbondale

CARBONDALE, IL 62901-6802
618.536.4441
http://www.siu.edu/

UNDERGRADUATES: 18,000

For program information, please contact:
BARB ELAM
delam@siu.edu

Promoting core values through multiple systems and strategies in a comprehensive approach is an ongoing process at Southern Illinois University Carbondale, a public, comprehensive institution. SIUC is committed to providing leadership in prevention programs intended to develop the whole person; thus the school employs both intensive individual approaches and overall systems methods to affect the campus ecology. A required semester course for athletes, for instance, addresses their total development through a variety of topics, including substance use and self-care.

Wellness Program Coordinator Barb Elam has gained a national audience for her promotion of caring and active participation as a means of effecting personal and social change. Facets of the Wellness Program include:

✦ MOTIVATIONAL INTERVIEWING. Individual meetings with students provide models of empathy, connectedness, and responsibility in health change process.

✦ COMMUNITY PARTICIPATION AND SERVICE. Students provide service in large-scale events with high visibility to other students, including forums for local high-school youth, and are trained to offer life-skills discussions to their peers.

✦ RECOGNITION. The Positive Lifestyle Award Program rewards constructive health efforts made by the students.

✦ PLEDGES. Students sign agreements to avoid risky health behaviors and to take responsibility for seeking alternatives.

✦ STUDENT-TO-STUDENT SOCIAL MARKETING PROJECT. CORE Institute-Marketing classes design socially responsible media campaigns for college students to reduce binge drinking.

SIUC has been recognized by the Promising Practices Project, Department of Education, nationally and regionally, for advancing ideals in the field of prevention. The Wellness Program has made a vital difference in the life of the student body.

Southwest Missouri State University

901 SOUTH NATIONAL AVENUE
SPRINGFIELD, MO 65804
417.836.5000
http://www.smsu.edu/

UNDERGRADUATES: 14,000

For program information, please contact:
TERRI OEHM
tso177t@mail.smsu.edu

"Many students experiment with harmful substances in college. The Natural High Club's adventures and values demonstrate that you can achieve a high without the negative health effects."

—AN SMSU FOURTH-YEAR STUDENT

Southwest Missouri State University, a public, metropolitan institution serving a unique combination of urban and rural environments, claims a single purpose: to develop educated persons. The University is committed to the creation of a teaching and learning environment that maximizes the student's opportunity to become such a person. That is why SMSU students who are concerned about the problem of substance abuse can be found not only studying in classrooms and residence halls, but also clinging to rocks and jumping out of airplanes. Sponsored by the Taylor Health and Wellness Center and Campus Recreation, the SMSU Natural High Club encourages students to take personal responsibility for their decisions about alcohol use and offers healthy, adventurous alternatives to drinking. Club members learn to safely expand their personal boundaries and limitations through positive risk-taking and community service. Program highlights include:

✦ Extreme adventures in a substance-free environment—rock climbing, skydiving, hot-air ballooning, spelunking, and rappelling;

✦ A safer spring break whitewater-rafting trip;

✦ Operation CPR, a one-day mass CPR training session;

✦ Campus and community-wide events working with local shelters and community youth programs.

Through participation in the program, students derive important benefits, such as gaining organization and leadership skills and learning to respect others' ideas, values, and beliefs.

At SMSU, outdoor adventures, community service, and positive peer support have all proven to be effective means of promoting healthy lifestyles and making a commitment to personal and civic responsibility.

STATE UNIVERSITY OF NEW YORK AT ALBANY

1400 WASHINGTON AVENUE
ALBANY, NY 12222
518.442.3300
http://www.albany.edu/

UNDERGRADUATES: 10,000

For program information, please contact:
M. DOLORES CIMINI, Ph.D.
dcimini@uamail.albany.edu

The University Counseling Center at SUNY-Albany has for 28 years organized the Middle Earth Assistance Program, a peer assistance and education initiative that serves the campus community and surrounding region. The primary mission of the Middle Earth program is to help students meet their educational goals and cope with emotional, social, and other life issues. Cornerstones of the Program include:

✦ THE MIDDLE EARTH PLAYERS. A group of undergraduates communicate the personal and social risks associated with high-risk drinking and drug use by improvising scenes to portray realistic situations concerning alcohol or other drugs. At the climax of each scene, the action is stopped, and the audience is encouraged to explore their thoughts and feelings regarding the conflict or dilemma.

✦ PEER ASSISTANCE HOTLINE. In addition to providing anonymous and confidential advice and support, the hotline also has five- to eight-minute prerecorded informational and self-help tapes. At the end of each tape a peer counselor comes on the line to answer any questions a student may have or to discuss the topic. The hotline received more than 1,000 contacts in 1997–98.

✦ PEER COUNSELING AND PEER EDUCATION COURSE. The objectives of this popular course combine theory and principles of peer counseling with "training" to practice the skills discussed in class. Students work with experienced peer educators in the context of a service agency located on campus.

The Middle Earth Assistance Program has been recognized for its service by the Psychological Association of Northeastern New York, and the New York State Office of Alcoholism and Substance Abuse Services has included the program among a select group of innovative prevention initiatives.

STATE UNIVERSITY OF NEW YORK COLLEGE AT ONEONTA

ONEONTA, NY 13820
607.436.3500
http://www.oneonta.edu/

UNDERGRADUATES: 5,000

For program information, please contact:
COLLEEN BRANNAN
brannace@oneonta.edu

"The College's programs aren't just about preventing substance abuse. They're about educating students to understand community norms, adopt positive behaviors, and develop a sense of personal and civic responsibility."
—A SUNY-ONEONTA FOURTH-YEAR STUDENT

The development of students' personal and community responsibility was the basis for establishing the Community Coalition: Forum on Alcohol and Other Drug Prevention at the State University of New York College at Oneonta, a public comprehensive college of the liberal arts and sciences. The Community Coalition brought together more than 130 concerned individuals—students, representatives from area colleges, community leaders, school-district representatives, and business owners—to share ideas about preventing substance abuse and providing alternative youth activities. In addition to fostering in students a broader understanding of the far-reaching impacts of alcohol- and other drug-induced behavior, the forum sparked collaboration among the participants on five initiatives. With the support of the students, colleges, and community, planning is under way for:

✦ Enhancing enforcement, to help students understand that policies benefit all members of the community;

✦ Developing a cooperating tavern model, to work collaboratively with business owners in reducing negative alcohol-related behaviors;

✦ Communicating social norms more effectively, to ensure that both the students and the community understand their responsibilities to each other;

✦ Involving students in policy changes to help them develop leadership skills in an area that directly affects their lives;

✦ Mentoring students in the importance of their part in combating negative alcohol and drug-related behaviors locally and in society as a whole.

The Community Coalition is just one component of a comprehensive alcohol- and drug-prevention strategy at the College at Oneonta. All the programs encourage students to understand the extensive benefits of making healthy choices.

Texas Christian University

2800 SOUTH UNIVERSITY DRIVE
FORT WORTH, TX 76129
817.257.7000
http://www.tcu.edu/

UNDERGRADUATES: 7,200

For program information, please contact:
ANGELA D. TAYLOR, Ph.D.
a.d.taylor@tcu.edu

"My time at TCU has helped me learn that I must take responsibility for myself."

—A TCU THIRD-YEAR STUDENT

A private, church-affiliated institution, Texas Christian University operates on the premise that free inquiry is best protected in the context of a representative democracy. The Alcohol and Drug Education Center at TCU, under the direction of Dr. Angela Taylor, promotes the ideal of personal and civic responsibility by educating students about healthier lifestyles and responsible decision-making regarding the use of alcohol and other drugs:

✦ Students who commit alcohol/drug violations on campus must attend a one-on-one counseling session with the program specialist, who holds a master of science in counselor education. After an evaluation, the student must complete a group session that addresses the dangers of alcohol and drugs and promotes responsible choices.

✦ The ADE Center provides opportunities for students to take on leadership roles in the area of prevention. These opportunities take the form of student employment, participation in student organizations, and national certification as peer educators.

✦ The ADE Center offers a Wellness Resource Library, available to the entire TCU community, which contains more than 500 books and videos that address the problems of addictions and dependencies, as well as other health issues.

The TCU Alcohol and Drug Education Center has received awards from BACCHUS and GAMMA. The Center promotes the concepts of prevention and personal responsibility by hosting campus-wide events that entertain while they inform, such as a "mocktail" bar during Howdy Week, "Safe Spring Break" week sponsored by BACCHUS and GAMMA, and Red Ribbon Week. Distribution of promotional items that address wellness issues and the accessibility of counselors to all students are also among the many weapons TCU uses to combat substance abuse.

University of Arizona

PO BOX 210066
TUCSON, AZ 85721
520.621.2211
http://www.arizona.edu/

UNDERGRADUATES: 26,000

For program information, please contact:
CAROLYN COLLINS
collins@health.arizona.edu

The University of Arizona is recognized as a leader in the field of substance-abuse prevention. Through its office of Campus Health Service, and with the support of institutional resources and federal funding, the University has put together a comprehensive approach to substance-abuse prevention that includes the following cornerstone activities:

✦ SOCIAL NORMING AND MEDIA CAMPAIGN. Utilizing student surveys, the campaign focuses on changing the perception that almost all students at U of A drink heavily. A weekly advertisement in the campus newspaper states that 69% of university students do not engage in heavy drinking, even when attending a party. The university has also established a highly successful poster campaign to inform students that they do not have to "drink up to fit in."

✦ DIVERSION PROGRAM. This six-hour referral program for students, in cooperation with Greek and residential-life programs, explores decision-making skills and character development issues.

✦ PARENT INVOLVEMENT. During first-year orientation the University talks to students and parents about alcohol-related issues with a focus on encouraging students to make responsible decisions.

✦ OFFICE FOR EVALUATION AND RESEARCH. The Coordinator for Evaluation and Research works with the Campus Health Service staff to collect and disseminate data on issues related to alcohol use by students.

The University's commitment to health and prevention services is showing tangible dividends. From 1995 to 1998, there has been a 29% decrease in heavy drinking by U of A students. There has also been a decrease in DUIs and reports of injuries related to heavy drinking. University officials remain committed to decreasing heavy drinking by promoting healthy behaviors and activities.

UNIVERSITY OF IOWA

114 JESSUP HALL
IOWA CITY, IA 52242
319.335.3500
http://www.uiowa.edu/

UNDERGRADUATES: 18,500

For program information, please contact:
JULIE M. PHYE
julie-phye@uiowa.edu

"I believe binge drinkers should be held accountable for their actions. But the binge drinkers are not the only ones with the power to stop binge drinking. This is a campus and community problem."

—A UI FIRST-YEAR STUDENT

At the core of the University of Iowa's substance-abuse prevention programs is The Stepping Up Project, a nationally recognized community and campus effort to reduce binge drinking. More than 60% of UI students engaged in some form of binge drinking in 1997. UI President Mary Sue Coleman recognizes that substance abuse is a serious campus and health problem. "We know that students who drink to get drunk are less likely to succeed academically," she states. The Project's cornerstone activities to change the culture of high-risk drinking include:

✦ NORMING CAMPAIGN. In its fourth year, the focus of this campaign, titled "Absolute Reality," is to give the campus community the facts about high-risk drinking and its effects.

✦ ALCOHOL-FREE GREEK HOUSES. All UI fraternities and sororities have eliminated alcohol from socials at their houses. The Greeks took this initiative on their own, realizing that it was time for these organizations to return to their mission of community service, academic excellence, and brotherhood.

✦ ALCOHOL-FREE TAILGATING. The University has designated one lot at the football games "alcohol free."

✦ COMMUNITY OUTREACH. Realizing that 36% of all UI first-year students were binge drinkers in high school, the University has established an outreach program to county high schools. Working with the youth organization United Action for Youth Agency, college and high-school students work together to plan Friday nights for nonalcohol-related social activities.

UI President Coleman is highly involved in each of these initiatives. She remains a strong supporter of The Stepping Up Project and its mission to raise the standards of personal and civic responsibility related to high-risk drinking.

UNIVERSITY OF MIAMI

PO BOX 248025
CORAL GABLES, FL 33124
305.284.2211
http://www.miami.edu/

UNDERGRADUATES: 8,000

For program information, please contact:
CRISTIE CARTER
cap@miami.edu

"In accomplishing each goal we set as peer educators my knowledge grows, reflecting upon the obstacles I face and my means for overcoming them."

—A UNIVERSITY OF MIAMI SECOND-YEAR STUDENT

Character is at the core of the program of the Center for Alcohol and Other Drug Education at the University of Miami, a private research institution that operates both law and medical schools. The Center's purpose reaches beyond the creation and enforcement of campus alcohol and drug policies to include fostering personal and social responsibility in a variety of ways:

✦ PEER EDUCATION. BACCHUS Peer Educators and GAMMA (Greeks Advocating the Mature Management of Alcohol) organize such events as National Collegiate Alcohol Awareness Week, Safe Spring Break, and a Drinking and Driving Candlelight Vigil. They also host substance-free campus activities, present peer-education programs, perform community service, create a forum for open dialog on alcohol issues, and strive to promote responsible choices.

✦ PIER 21 (Prevention, Intervention, Education, Referral). Students are referred to PIER 21 either through the discipline system or through self-referral. At "educational sessions," students are asked to examine their own behaviors and are challenged to take the responsibility of making positive choices.

✦ CAMPUS ALCOHOL AND OTHER DRUG PREVENTION COALITION. The Coalition brings together faculty, staff, and students to address the campus culture, assesses what currently is being done, and makes recommendations for initiatives.

✦ CAMPUSES ADDRESSING SUBSTANCE ABUSE (CASA). In conjunction with other institutions, the University of Miami received a FIPSE grant in the early 1980s to create a consortium of colleges and universities in the South Florida area.

A dedication to fostering personal and social responsibility creates an environment where students can develop the skills to make healthy lifestyle choices, as well as the skills to become positive contributors to society.

University of Rhode Island

330 MEMORIAL UNION
KINGSTON, RI 02881
401.874.1000
http://www.uri.edu/

UNDERGRADUATES: 11,000

For program information, please contact:
FRAN COHEN
franc@uri.edu

"Substance Abuse Services is one of the most highly respected offices on campus. The energy, dedication, and passion expressed by the employees and advisors is inspirational to me."

—A URI FIRST-YEAR STUDENT

The University of Rhode Island, the principal public research institution in the state, is committed to providing undergraduate programs to promote students' ethical development. Emphasizing personal responsibility for choices and minimizing harm through awareness and education are key factors in the school's substance-abuse education and prevention efforts. Specific strategies include:

✦ **Workshops** held in residence halls, classes, and Greek houses help students analyze how personal choices and actions affect a community environment.

✦ **Ram Choices,** a peer-mentoring/education program, addresses pressures unique to student athletes.

✦ **True Stories,** an art exhibit featuring stories of URI students describing their experiences with alcohol and other drugs, inspires students to analyze their own patterns of substance abuse.

✦ **Peer Education Training,** a three-credit course focusing on substance abuse and sexual-assault prevention, offers students the knowledge and skills needed to work effectively with their peers.

✦ **Judicial Alcohol and Drug Education,** a mandatory program for judicial offenders, helps students examine personal responsibility as well as possibilities for behavior change.

✦ **URI Students Against Drunk Driving** (S.A.D.D.) reminds students of the personal accountability involved and the impact of impaired driving on the community.

URI and its Substance Abuse Services have received national attention, including coverage in *U.S. News and World Report* and *Promising Practices: Campus Alcohol Strategies.* The major payoff for the program, though, has been the improvement in the lives of the students it has reached.

University of Vermont

85 SOUTH PROSPECT STREET
BURLINGTON, VT 05405
802.656.3480
http://www.uvm.edu/

UNDERGRADUATES: 7,500

For program information, please contact:
RICK CULLITON
rcullito@zoo.uvm.edu

The University of Vermont is one of 10 universities that have been awarded a five-year grant from the Robert Wood Johnson Foundation to address high-risk drinking. The project involves identifying the many factors on the campus, in the surrounding community, and in the state that contribute to the problem. Cornerstone activities include:

✦ **Policy and Enforcement.** The Faculty Senate has revised the academic calendar to avoid beginning the school year with two three-day weekends, stressing the University's focus on academic rigor and not alcohol use.

✦ **Substance Use Reduction Education (SURE).** Some students are required to attend these classes in order to remain in good academic standing with the University.

✦ **Healthy Lifestyles Campaign.** In an effort to highlight the many ways that college students make good decisions about healthy living, the Coalition to Create a Quality Learning Environment publishes a biannual newsletter and has developed a web page to better communicate activities and efforts.

✦ **Substance-Free Residence Halls.** Students choose these substance-free living spaces and make an explicit commitment to remain free from the influence of alcohol and other drugs when they are in the residence hall.

✦ **OPT.** Short for "Options," this student-initiated group wants to be part of a campus community that doesn't have alcohol at the center of its culture. OPT recently received the President's Award for outstanding student organizations.

At the heart of these activities is a concerted effort on the part of the University of Vermont to be clear about the expectations and standards of conduct related to alcohol use. Clearly, changing the environment that has contributed to alcohol abuse in the past has become a priority for the University.

VALDOSTA STATE UNIVERSITY

1500 N. PATTERSON ST.
VALDOSTA, GA 31698
912.333.5800
http://www.valdosta.edu/

UNDERGRADUATES: 8,500

For program information, please contact:
BRIGITTE PIRSON LACY
bpirson@valdosta.edu

Valdosta State University, a public, multipurpose institution, strives to create an environment conducive to learning both in and out of the classroom. The Office of Alcohol and Other Drug Education (AODE) attempts to reach students in a variety of ways to effectively convey its antisubstance-abuse message. The office emphasizes personal responsibility and healthy choices in outreach efforts that include Alcohol 101, "On Campus . . . Talking about Alcohol," resident assistant training, newspaper articles, and presentations to classes and other organizations. Campus-wide events such as the National Collegiate Alcohol Awareness Week, Safe Spring Break Fair, and Red Ribbon Week bring key campus and community resources together. The AODE office also sponsors two organizations that depend on student leadership:

✦ **KARMA** (Knowledge, Awareness, Respect, Maturity, and Achievement), the VSU Peer-Education Program. Students are trained to give presentations on a variety of health-related topics to classes, residence halls, Greek organizations, and other student groups and organizations. KARMA students also present programs to local elementary and high schools.

✦ **NATURAL HIGH,** a collaborative effort among the offices of AODE, Campus Recreation, and Housing and Residence Life. This student-run organization provides fun and creative activities that promote positive lifestyle choices.

The AODE office provides free assessments and referrals for anyone experiencing a substance-abuse problem, as well as services for those with friends and family members who are addicted to alcohol or other drugs.

An intercampus Substance Abuse Task Force, composed of key campus professionals, meets regularly to make recommendations for improvement of programs and services. In short, VSU uses every means at its disposal to encourage healthy lifestyles and optimize learning opportunities.

VITERBO COLLEGE

815 NINTH STREET SOUTH
LA CROSSE, WI 54601
608.796.3000
http://www.viterbo.edu/

UNDERGRADUATES: 1,700

For program information, please contact:
ANNE ELLEFSON
amellefson@mail.viterbo.edu

Viterbo College, a Catholic, liberal arts school founded by the Franciscan Sisters of Perpetual Adoration, offers a person-centered, values-based community. Working toward Viterbo's stated mission to "prepare students for leadership and service rooted in the values of human dignity and respect for the world," the school's substance-abuse prevention services strive to reduce the negative impacts of alcohol and other drugs and to provide students with meaningful leadership and service opportunities. The college's chosen strategies for substance-abuse prevention include policy implementation, curriculum infusion, community involvement, and alternative activities. The recognized cornerstone of these efforts is the student organization, Connect.

Connect members collaborate to identify problems and implement solutions. Recurrent themes in all program activities include individual responsibility for choices, the benefits of abstinence and moderation, and the importance of helping other community members. Members demonstrate their principles by delivering challenging messages to their peers through presentations that they develop themselves and tailor for diverse audiences. In addition, the Connect Program sponsors a variety of other events to combat drug and alcohol abuse:

✦ Prevention presentations in all first-year seminar courses;

✦ Weekly coffeehouse activities;

✦ A campus-wide Alcohol Awareness Week;

✦ Informal one-to-one interactions with peers;

✦ Presentations in residence halls and for athletic teams;

✦ Regular public-awareness campaigns.

In conjunction with the academic departments, residence life, athletics, and campus clubs, the Connect Program is a powerful tool in helping students to develop leadership skills, build personal character, and use personal interests for the good of the college and civic community.

WAKE FOREST UNIVERSITY

BOX 7305 REYNOLDA STATION
WINSTON-SALEM, NC 27109
http://www.wfu.edu/

UNDERGRADUATES: 3,900

For program information, please contact:
MARY GERARDY
beil@wfu.edu

"A couple of us who lived in substance-free housing during our first year at the University wanted to continue living in substance-free housing. Wake Forest helped us to start a theme house program so we could do just that."

—A WAKE FOREST FOURTH-YEAR STUDENT

Wake Forest University, a private institution with historic church ties, is committed to fostering healthy lifestyles. Recognizing that students have been bombarded since childhood with messages encouraging the consumption of alcohol and other drugs and that many bring established patterns of drinking with them to college, Wake Forest uses a comprehensive approach to encourage responsible decision-making. The University's approach includes these elements:

✦ A letter from the president to all incoming students and their parents outlining Wake Forest's commitment to reducing the incidence of risky drinking behaviors on campus, and a follow-up session for parents during orientation that offers candid information about alcohol issues;

✦ An interactive orientation program with peer health educators for first-year students (during orientation);

✦ Peer health-education classes, which train students to provide educational programs for their fellow students;

✦ Student Athlete Mentoring, which arranges peer mentors for members of sports teams;

✦ JUST THE FACTS, a social norms poster campaign, which increases students' awareness of actual as opposed to perceived behavior related to alcohol use on campus;

✦ Alcohol education programs for Greek organizations;

✦ Substance-free residence-hall option for students;

✦ Parental notification of alcohol-abuse cases;

✦ Creation of a conference (The DrinkThink) dedicated to finding solutions to alcohol problems on college campuses.

Believing that substance abuse is one of the most serious problems faced by higher education today, Wake Forest steadfastly continues its efforts to reach students and make a difference.

WEST VIRGINIA UNIVERSITY

PO BOX 6009
MORGANTOWN, WV 26506
800.344.9881
http://www.wvu.edu/

UNDERGRADUATES: 15,000

For program information, please contact:
MARY COLLINS
mcollin7@wvu.edu

"The relaxed atmosphere, free food, and activities of 'WVUp All Night' make it a great way to end a hard week of classes and studying. It's a chance to do something different besides the same old weekend routine of jamming into a crowded bar or party." —A WV FOURTH-YEAR STUDENT

Because of its strong commitment to providing a safe and healthy campus environment, West Virginia University, a land-grant, research institution, has undertaken an innovative initiative in the ongoing battle against alcohol and substance abuse among students. The weekend program, WVUp All Night, has been featured in the national and international media, including ABC's *Good Morning America* and the BBC.

WVUp All Night offers an attractive alternative to bars, nightclubs, and house parties. Free food (including a midnight breakfast bar) and free entertainment attract an average of 2,000–4,000 first-year through graduate-level students each Thursday, Friday, and Saturday night to the Mountainlair student union. Educational programs, often in a peer panel or game show–type format, are included in WVUp All Night programming. Topics include safe sex, alcohol and substance abuse, general safety issues, and domestic violence. WVUp All Night creates a safe, fun place for students to gather, increasing a sense of university community. The program also provides an academic computing lab and study lounges.

Since the inception of WVUp All Night, the University has dropped off *Princeton Review*'s list of the top 10 party schools, police and hospital incidents are down on nights the program takes place, and WVU's Department of Public Safety and the residence-hall staff have also reported a decrease in incidents. WVUp All Night has captured the attention of others who are engaged in the battle against alcohol abuse, including several colleges and universities, a senator's office, and a city police department.

WESTMINSTER COLLEGE

NEW WILMINGTON, PA 16172
724.946.8761
http://www.westminster.edu/
UNDERGRADUATES: 1,600

For program information, please contact:
NEAL EDMAN
nedman@westminster.edu

"Inquiry gave me the opportunity to question the foundation of my beliefs. I do not think my education would have been complete without it."
—A WESTMINSTER FIRST-YEAR STUDENT

Development of the individual—intellectually, spiritually, and socially—is the primary purpose of Westminster College, a private, liberal arts institution. Accordingly, Westminster's substance-abuse program is a multifaceted endeavor that integrates classroom and cocurricular efforts:

♦ **PEERS** (Peers Educating and Encouraging Responsibility among Students) Program. Interactive workshops presented by student educators focus on the value of individuality, personal value systems, and self-esteem.

♦ **THE WELLNESS PROGRAM.** Required of all first-year students, this program offers information-sharing using the "Alcohol 101" interactive CD-ROM. Through this technology, students are challenged to assess not only their own drinking behaviors, but those of others.

♦ **THE BINGE DRINKING TASK FORCE.** A 30-member team of students, faculty, administrators, and representatives of the New Wilmington community meet regularly to combat binge drinking among students.

♦ **THE HAPPY BUS.** Volunteers from fraternities and sororities work as designated drivers of a van for students to safely commute to and from campus, fostering a sense of personal responsibility for the safety of others.

♦ **THE DOWN UNDER.** At the college's nonalcoholic pub, students learn the value of personal interaction, enjoyable socialization, and recreation without the use of alcohol.

Westminster College, which also offers individualized counseling and assessment at the Counseling Services and Student Health Center, is committed to building support networks, character, and values systems that supply students with a firm foundation upon which they can find the strength to say no, and the compassion to help others do the same.

STUDENT LEADERSHIP PROGRAMS

Almost all colleges and universities aspire to
prepare students for positions of leadership
both inside and outside the campus community.
A growing number of college programs are
dedicated to providing high-quality educational
experiences for students to develop the
competencies, conscience, and compassion
required of leaders in a civil society.

ASBURY COLLEGE

1 MACKLEM DRIVE
WILMORE, KY 40390
606.858.3511
http://www.asbury.edu/

UNDERGRADUATES: 1,300

For program information, please contact:
MARK TROYER
mark.troyer@asbury.edu

Asbury College, a Christ-centered, liberal arts institution, focuses on intentional leadership development through the LEAD-ON! program. Students begin their college journey with "First Serve," a community-service project during orientation, and complete their time at Asbury with a reception focusing on the learning and development that have taken place over their four years.

Development of character and competence is woven into the program in the following ways:

✦ Workshops such as "Moral Dilemmas and Decision Making" and "Making Service and Outreach Part of Your Life" are offered each semester and are open to the entire student body. Additional workshops focus on the character of leaders throughout history.

✦ Leadership development "cocurriculum" culminates in the coordination of a service event focused on making a difference in the community.

✦ Personal reflection sessions, hosted in cooperation with the Education Department, examine the impact of community-service events on a student's life.

✦ Integrative leadership papers including personal action plans are required in the Introduction to Leadership course.

✦ Leadership and service requirements must be met for upperclassmen to qualify for apartment-style residences.

✦ Challenge Course, an adventure-based ropes course, helps LEAD-ON! reach approximately 1,500 local community members, including corporate groups, youth groups, and adult nonprofit organizations by offering team-building and leadership training.

LEAD-ON! helps students understand themselves, gain skills in working with others, and make improvements in their community. The diverse training opportunities and "real world" experiences of LEAD-ON! challenge students to grow in leadership that emphasizes service, integrity, faith, and competence.

AUSTIN COLLEGE

900 NORTH GRAND AVENUE
SHERMAN, TX 75090
903.813.2000
http://www.austinc.edu/

UNDERGRADUATES: 1,200

For program information, please contact:
SHELTON WILLIAMS, Ph.D.
saistype@aol.com

"More than wealth and recognition, I want to make a contribution to society. Being a leader is wanting to do something, not simply to be something."

—AN AUSTIN THIRD-YEAR STUDENT

Austin College, a church-affiliated, liberal arts school, serves as home to the Leadership Institute, a four-year comprehensive program that structures experiences in leadership within the context of the established curriculum. A combination of academic and practical pursuits, the program is based on a set of fundamental values—respect, responsibility, and selflessness—and reinforces the belief that good decisions are based on a solid understanding of those values. The Leadership Institute annually offers 15 first-year and up to five second-year students $10,000 scholarships to study leadership, ethics, policy studies, and communication throughout their college careers.

Components of the Leadership Institute include:

✦ VOLUNTEER SERVICE. Leadership students make a commitment to service that enhances classroom work and allows them to put into practice what they learn in the Institute.

✦ MENTOR PROGRAM. In this one-on-one learning experience, each student is matched with a mentor from a local professional or community organization. The program broadens students' understanding of the work environment and teaches them how to prepare for the demands of the 21st century.

✦ INTERNATIONAL STUDY. An Institute requirement, international study is an excellent means of expanding a worldview, enhancing personal growth, and putting knowledge and skills into action. Students see their own culture from an outside, perhaps more objective, viewpoint.

The Leadership Institute helps students realize that those who lead must first learn to serve. It also provides a broad education that includes an international perspective, enables students to build close associations with recognized leaders and mentors, and—above all—fosters a strong sense of ethics to guide their decision-making.

BIRMINGHAM-SOUTHERN COLLEGE

ARKADELPHIA ROAD
BIRMINGHAM, AL 35254
205.226.4620
http://www.bsc.edu/

UNDERGRADUATES: 1,400

For program information, please contact:
JEANNE JACKSON
jjackson@bsc.edu

"The program challenged me to integrate leadership theories with a commitment to civic responsibility. I found the complexities of leadership much like trying to solve Rubik's cube. BSC helped me to solve the puzzle."
—A BSC FOURTH-YEAR STUDENT

In October 1998, the Center for Leadership Studies and the Office of Service Learning at Birmingham-Southern College, a church-affiliated, liberal arts school, combined to form the Hess Center for Leadership and Service. The merger of these two vital programs demonstrates BSC's commitment to educating socially responsible leaders for the 21st century. The goals of the Hess Center are to:

✦ Provide experiential leadership and service programs.

✦ Emphasize the importance of moral and civic imagination by providing leadership and service opportunities locally, nationally, and internationally.

✦ Provide resources on leadership and service for institutions of higher education, communities of faith, and service organizations.

Through academic courses, community-service projects, reflection sessions, and public-speaking opportunities, students master four fundamental competencies: self-understanding, a theoretical knowledge of leadership through academic study, commitment to social responsibility, and the ability to communicate personal convictions.

Special recognition at graduation is given to students who complete all of the requirements of the College's Distinction in Leadership Studies program, a community-service initiative that provides students with an understanding of their personal leadership strengths and weaknesses as well as a comprehensive, interdisciplinary review of leadership theories.

More than 50% of BSC students are involved directly in the Leadership Studies and Service Learning programs. No matter what form their participation takes, all BSC leadership and service students are united in their sincere commitment to improving their communities.

BLACKBURN COLLEGE

700 COLLEGE AVENUE
CARLINVILLE, IL 62626
http://www.blackburn.edu/

UNDERGRADUATES: 600

For program information, please contact:
GEORGE BANZIGER, Ph.D.
gbanz@mail.blackburn.edu

"The Leadership Program has been a big help to me because by understanding the various ways of effective leadership I feel I will become a successful teacher."
—A BLACKBURN SECOND-YEAR STUDENT

A commitment to building student character is clearly revealed in the routine of campus life at Blackburn College, a church-affiliated, liberal arts institution. All students participate in Blackburn's Work Program, spending 10 to 20 hours per week in jobs ranging from campus support services to administrative and academic assistantships. Because the Work Program is entirely student-managed, graduates leave Blackburn with not only an academic degree, but also experience in personnel management, teamwork, conflict resolution, and ethics in the workplace.

As an academic complement to the Work Program, Blackburn offers an innovative Leadership Program that allows students to graduate with the degree of their choice plus a Leadership Certificate. The Leadership Program helps students develop practical leadership competencies as well as conceptual understanding, gives them an opportunity for guided reflection of their campus work experience, and instills a sense of appreciation for the contributions of all workers.

Students gain a conceptual understanding of leadership through three curricular offerings: "Leadership, the Human Dynamic"; "Constructive Resolution of Conflict"; and "Theory and Practice of Leadership."

A capstone experience in the leadership program is the successful performance of a leadership role, such as managing others in the work program, directing a student performance, mentoring young people, or leading a community-service project.

The integrated learning of curricular and cocurricular elements that takes place in Blackburn's Leadership Program develops skills, abilities, and constructive attitudes that apply universally and last a lifetime.

BUENA VISTA UNIVERSITY

610 WEST FOURTH STREET
STORM LAKE, IA 50588
712.749.2400
http://www.bvu.edu/

UNDERGRADUATES: 1,300

For program information, please contact:
JULIE KEEHNER
keehnerj@bvu.edu

"My involvement with leadership activities has given me an appreciation for service learning and provided me with the skills to become both a productive citizen and a volunteer activist."

—A BUENA VISTA FOURTH-YEAR STUDENT

While many schools provide training for students who have already assumed leadership positions, Buena Vista University, a church-affiliated, liberal arts institution, has chosen a different strategy. The Leadership Development Program at Buena Vista provides training for all its students, preparing them for leadership challenges they have not yet considered. Fostering civic responsibility and citizenship, the program includes the following components:

✦ SERVICE LEARNING. Participants plan and participate in service projects. Past projects have included working in a soup kitchen, a maximum-care facility for the elderly, and a home for severely emotionally and physically challenged children; sponsoring a carnival for needy children in the community; and serving as mentors for adolescents.

✦ CAREER DEVELOPMENT. During their third year, students participate in a series that focuses on "life after BVU," which includes a program on the importance of service and civic responsibility, and presentations that highlight volunteer opportunities.

✦ YOUTH LEADERSHIP. During their final year, participants provide leadership programs for local youth organizations and high-school classes, helping students develop such skills as time management, motivation, and goal setting. In addition, they present programs on issues related to the transition from high school to college, how to select a college, and the importance of volunteerism.

The Leadership Program at Buena Vista has not only positively affected the lives of students, both in the classroom and in their various leadership roles, it also has strengthened the relationship between the university and the local and regional communities.

CALIFORNIA STATE UNIVERSITY–FULLERTON

FULLERTON, CA 92834-9480
714.278.2011
http://www.fullerton.edu/

UNDERGRADUATES: 21,000

For program information, please contact:
REBECCA CHAVEZ
rchavez@fullerton.edu

"I gained valuable knowledge and experience on how to be a successful leader. I developed confidence and a better understanding of my surroundings and myself."

—A RECENT FULLERTON GRADUATE

At California State University–Fullerton, a public institution, "students serving students" is key to the success of the student leadership program. Student organizers plan and assist in the overall and day-to-day operations of the University's Student Leadership Institute (SLI) and serve as key role models to participants. The format of the Institute allows for much interaction and reflective thought, which in many cases turns into action via community service. Students may choose to participate in workshops, complete a certificate, introduce a facilitator, lead a workshop, or coordinate an entire educational program. They determine their level of involvement based on their interests and time available. Learning to make these choices and commitments is integral to the success of the SLI program.

Components of the Student Leadership Institute include:

✦ E.M.B.R.A.C.E. (Educating Myself for Better Racial Awareness, Compassion and Education). Students increase and use their knowledge in cross-cultural communication and diversity issues.

✦ PEER EDUCATION. Peer educators expand their knowledge of current social, emotional, and health issues affecting college communities. Students in the Peer Education track apply information they learned in their workshops to various positions on campus, such as in the Student Academic Services Peer Mentor Program and Fullerton First-Year Peer Mentors.

✦ LEADERSHIP FOR PUBLIC SERVICE. Students develop skills related to political and community leadership.

Because 85% of Fullerton graduates reside within a 75-mile radius of the campus, the Student Leadership Institute undoubtedly contributes greatly to the local community. And because it connects classroom learning with leadership training, knowledge, and experiential opportunities, the education that students gain is truly unique.

College of Saint Benedict and Saint John's University

ST. JOSEPH, MN 56374
320.363.5011
COLLEGEVILLE, MN 56321
320.363.2011
http://www.csbsju.edu/

UNDERGRADUATES: 3,700

For program information, please contact:
GAR KELLOM
gkellom@csbsju.edu

"Socially responsible leadership is the most exhilarating thing anyone can realize. If you have the passion within you, the ability to lead for what you believe in will follow close behind."

—A SAINT JOHN'S FOURTH-YEAR STUDENT

The College of Saint Benedict and Saint John's University are private, interconnected liberal arts colleges promoting integrated learning, exceptional leadership for change, and wisdom for a lifetime. The goal of their Leadership Initiative is to nurture the development of individuals who will practice ethical leadership. More than 85% of the student body participate in cocurricular programs including National Global Leadership Week and fireside chats on leadership. Leadership Initiative accomplishes its goals in a variety of ways:

✦ Intentionally linking leadership development with service-learning activities heightens the integration of moral reasoning and ethical behavior.

✦ Embedding leadership education into both the residential life experience and the student employment experiences fosters a broader understanding and commitment to the common good.

✦ Using gender as a category of analysis increases understanding and development of service and leadership in both men and women.

The W. K. Kellogg Foundation has recognized the Leadership Initiative as one of eight exemplary leadership programs in the country, and the Initiative has inspired dozens of programs and activities, such as a "peers teaching peers" program that involves students in shaping the student culture. The College of Saint Benedict and Saint John's University expect and challenge students to practice leadership that promotes peace, justice, and the common good—and through the Leadership Initiative, they prepare students to do just that.

DePaul University

1 EAST JACKSON BOULEVARD
CHICAGO, IL 60604-2287
312.362.8000
http://www.depaul.edu/

UNDERGRADUATES: 11,200

For program information, please contact:
JOHN J. LANE
valuectr@condoe.depaul.edu

"The richness of this program lies in the diversity of the speakers, each of which emphasizes a particular aspect of leadership. The concept of leadership and the principles taught are applicable to daily living."

—A DEPAUL FOURTH-YEAR STUDENT

DePaul University, the largest Catholic university in the country, is endowed with a distinctive spirit to foster in higher education a deep respect for the God-given dignity of all persons. DePaul's Student Leadership Institute fosters social responsibility through a series of workshops and service-learning opportunities that develop personal leadership and relational and managerial skills. Components of DePaul's competency-based leadership program include:

✦ **STANDARDIZED TESTING.** Every participant begins the leadership program by taking the Myers-Briggs Type Indicator and attending a debriefing with an MBTI counselor. The University uses other instruments to help students understand their leadership potential, as well as their communication, learning, and conflict-resolution styles.

✦ **STUDENT LEADERSHIP DEVELOPMENT CERTIFICATE.** Students may earn a certificate in leadership development through the Institute. The core academic requirements include "Leadership Assessment," "Leadership Concepts and Practices," "Servant Leadership in the Vincentian Tradition," and "Reflective Practice."

✦ **LEADERSHIP OPPORTUNITIES.** The Institute serves as a source of team leaders, facilitators, and coordinators for the University's many good works. For example, as many as 40 student leaders help coordinate the annual Service Day efforts of hundreds of DePaul students, faculty, and staff.

The Student Leadership Institute serves as an essential component to the holistic educational experience at DePaul. Certification in Student Leadership Development, mentoring opportunities, portfolio development, and collaboration with Service Learning Offices, along with workshops conducted by dedicated, experienced interdisciplinary faculty and professional staff, result in student leaders who are highly motivated to serve the larger community.

DRURY COLLEGE

900 NORTH BENTON AVENUE
SPRINGFIELD, MO 65802
417.873.7879
http://www.drury.edu/

UNDERGRADUATES: 3,500

For program information, please contact:
ANNE NELMS
anelms@lib.drury.edu

"Leadership Drury has given me the opportunity to see and explore unique ideas, the various people who surround me, and, most of all, myself."

—A DRURY FOURTH-YEAR STUDENT

Drury College, a liberal arts institution with a religious orientation, integrates Leadership Drury, a comprehensive four-year leadership development program, into its core curriculum. As students take classes, Leadership Drury develops and enhances self-understanding, improves their ability to work effectively as group members and leaders, establishes a tradition of community service, and prepares them to make a contribution to their chosen profession and community. Activites include:

✦ **BRIDGES.** First-year students focus on self-development. Activities are designed to help students examine values, build the skills necessary for college success, and learn to build and maintain good relationships with peers and adults.

✦ **CONNECTIONS.** Second-year students strive to improve their ability to work as group members and leaders. Topics include communication, decision-making, collaboration, conflict resolution, diversity, and addressing controversy with civility. Students learn about a variety of leadership theories and develop an understanding of their own leadership style, including strengths and areas that need improvement.

✦ **DIRECTIONS.** Third-year students participate in an in-depth volunteer service experience. Students dedicate several hours each week to working with neighborhood children. Service opportunities include tutoring, working in a classroom, health education, and acting as a Big Brother/Big Sister.

✦ **GATEWAYS.** Fourth-year students network with community leaders and alumni mentors and share their well-developed skills with the college community. In Gateways, they develop a personal mission statement, reflect on the college experience, and direct the activities for other leadership levels.

Community service and the development of a leadership ethic in students are the primary goals of Leadership Drury.

DUKE UNIVERSITY

207 ALLEN BUILDING
DURHAM, NC 27708
919.684.8111
http://www.duke.edu/

UNDERGRADUATES: 6,400

For program information, please contact:
ROBERT KORSTAD, Ph.D.
korstad@duke.edu

"The Hart Leadership Program has completely shattered the notion that leadership cannot be taught or learned inside the classroom."

—A DUKE GRADUATE

Duke University, a private, comprehensive institution, prides itself on a commitment to intellectual and personal growth, and its pervasive sense of enthusiasm. The University's Hart Leadership Program (HLP) combines rigorous academic courses with structured opportunities for students to practice skills and apply knowledge outside of the classroom. The HLP offers thirteen academic courses with experiential learning opportunities, as well as a semester of courses in New York City under Leadership in the Arts. As a result of participation in the program:

✦ Students come to understand that through their background, economic status, and education they have power, and that the most effective thing they can do is to teach others to have power of their own.

✦ Students see leadership through an asset-based viewpoint where people must be involved as part of the solutions to their problems, not simply clients of provided services.

✦ Students learn what it is to live in a democratic society and the responsibilities that go with citizenship.

✦ Students learn they must face community issues with open minds and ears, discovering values, concerns, and the political landscape of the community to effect change.

New program initiatives include mainstreaming leadership studies throughout the University and increasing the number of Hart Fellows-graduate students working with humanitarian organizations throughout the world. Experiences in the Hart Leadership Program often lead students to reevaluate their aspirations and to increase their knowledge of ways to make a difference in the world through active community involvement.

EMORY UNIVERSITY

1380 OXFORD ROAD, NE
ATLANTA, GA 30322
404.727.6123
http://www.emory.edu/

UNDERGRADUATES: 6,000

For program information, please contact:
STACIA BROWN
sbrown06@emory.edu

The Leadership and Life-Work Program of the Center for Ethics at Emory University, a private, comprehensive institution, is dedicated to igniting the moral imagination of 21st-century leaders. The program offers a variety of curricular and extracurricular programs designed to enrich ways of thinking about ethics in leadership, vocation, and life-work. Students may also participate in a variety of programs and courses on the social responsibilities of the professions.

Emory's Center for Ethics sponsors activities in key areas designed for undergraduates, including:

✦ **FRESHMAN SEMINAR.** The Center presents an interactive workshop, "Creating an Awesome Life...In an Ethical Sort of Way," as part of orientation.

✦ **CAMPUS LIFE INITIATIVES.** Planning and training sessions are offered for campus professionals and student leaders. Geared toward building a more ethically oriented campus community, this program fosters a deeper sense of shared identity and purpose for Residence Life.

✦ **LEADERSHIP EMORY.** The Leadership Emory project provides ethics-based leadership training for undergraduate students in a progressive, four-year program.

✦ **RESIDENCE HALL FELLOWS PROGRAM.** This program fosters new patterns of meaningful, engaging, ethically grounded interactions among undergraduates, faculty, alumni, and graduate students.

Through innovative, interactive programs, the Leadership and Life-Work Program helps Emory students grow in their commitment and capacity to shape their lives in ways that serve the common good, educating them to find life-giving vocations and to revitalize and transform existing institutions, creating new models of ethical organizational life.

FORT HAYS STATE UNIVERSITY

600 PARK STREET
HAYS, KS 67601-4099
913.628.4000
http://www.fhsu.edu/

UNDERGRADUATES: 4,500

For program information, please contact:
CURT BRUNGARDT, Ph.D.
cbrungar@fhsu.edu

Fort Hays State University, a public, comprehensive institution, is committed to the preparation of students for positions of leadership as an essential component of the educational mission. The mission of the University's leadership program is to nurture leaders who will be able to cope with the complex problems of a changing world. The program's three themes—creating change, collaboration, and civic leadership—provide the foundation for all leadership development activities. Students are able to make their own decisions on how involved they want to be in leadership education by choosing among three programs. They first can participate in an introductory Leadership Certificate Program. After successful completion of this component, participants have the option of pursuing a Leadership Studies Field of Emphasis that can be attached to any academic major. Finally, for those students who are interested in a degree program focusing on leadership, the Bachelor of General Studies—Organizational Leadership Concentration degree is available.

Leadership Studies Program graduates are characterized as being:

✦ **KNOWLEDGEABLE.** Able to understand leadership, self-reflect, think critically, and have a holistic perspective;

✦ **CIVIC-MINDED.** Possess a sense of community and a commitment to civic responsibility and action;

✦ **COOPERATIVE.** Successful in interpersonal relationships and group interaction;

✦ **CREATIVE/INNOVATIVE.** Able to problem solve and establish a vision for the future;

✦ **CREDIBILITY/TRUSTWORTHY.** Aware that honesty serves as the heart of integrity.

Graduates of the Fort Hays Leadership Studies Program serve as architects and catalysts for change, challenging the status quo and initiating and sustaining transformational change for the common good.

KENTUCKY WESLEYAN COLLEGE

3000 FREDERICA STREET
OWENSBORO, KY 42302-1039
502.926.3111
http://www.kwc.edu/

UNDERGRADUATES: 800

For program information, please contact:
MIKE FAGAN, Ph.D.
mikefa@kwc.edu

Kentucky Wesleyan College, a church-affiliated, liberal arts institution, has created Leadership KWC, a constellation of academic courses, public lectures, workshops, and other experiences to enhance leadership development among its students. Leadership KWC bridges the gap between classes and cocurricular life, enabling students to learn leadership concepts in the classroom and then participate in activities outside the classroom that complement their academic experience.

Components of Leadership KWC include:

✦ **LEADERSHIP XXI.** A comprehensive, four-year program in which participants are required to: maintain at least a 2.25 GPA, take "Profiles in Leadership" in their first year and in subsequent years take two other leadership courses, participate in the EMERGE and SUCCEED workshop series offered by the Student Life Office, and apply the principles of leadership by participating for at least three years in one (or more) campus organization(s), including serving in a leadership role for at least one year, or by performing at least 30 hours of community service per year.

✦ **LEADERSHIP SPEAKER SERIES.** A lecture series that brings leaders in various fields to campus for presentations that are also open to the local community. Past presenters have included: Maya Angelou, author and civil rights activist; Doris Kearns Goodwin, author and historian; Leon Lederman, Nobel Prize winner in physics; and Alan C. Page, pro football Hall of Famer and Minnesota Supreme Court Justice.

✦ **LEADERSHIP SYMPOSIUM.** An all-day student conference that includes plenary sessions led by nationally known speakers and more than a dozen concurrent sessions conducted by local leaders, usually alumni.

Through leadership courses that offer students the opportunity to explore the lives and ideas of world leaders past and present, as well as cocurricular leadership activities, Kentucky Wesleyan students are well prepared to serve as vital leaders in the broader community.

MARIETTA COLLEGE

215 NORTH FIFTH STREET
MARIETTA, OH 45750
740.376.4760
http://www.marietta.edu/

UNDERGRADUATES: 1,100

For program information, please contact:
STEPHEN W. SCHWARTZ, Ph.D.
schwarts@marietta.edu

"People commonly ask the question, 'Why should I serve the community? What has it done for me?' As a result of my participation in the McDonough Leadership Program, I now choose to ask, 'How can I do more?'"

—A MARIETTA FOURTH-YEAR STUDENT

In a country described as "a nation of spectators," the McDonough Center for Leadership and Business at Marietta College, a small liberal arts institution, helps students see themselves as citizen-leaders and provides the means by which they can fulfill that role. Students are introduced to the principles of responsible citizenship in a pluralistic democracy and learn to recognize the need to consider multiple perspectives in forging consensus. The role of followers is also studied and considered important in its own right. The program emphasizes effective and respectful communication, problem identification, team membership, valuing diversity, interpersonal adeptness, group facilitation, taking initiative, and acting with a sense of urgency. Community service and simulations create the "lab" in which leadership skills are practiced.

The McDonough Center for Leadership and Business:

✦ Insists that citizen-leaders accept responsibility for their democracy;

✦ Encourages ethical participation in the community;

✦ Stresses service to others as a way of life;

✦ Promotes the recognition and consideration of multiple perspectives;

✦ Recognizes the need for leaders and followers to continually assess themselves and their behaviors.

Central to the practice of leadership is the belief that leadership—as distinct from power wielding—involves action on behalf of others. Special projects organized by the students themselves, such as participation in F.I.R.S.T. (Foundation for Individual Responsibility and Social Trust) and the Annual Free Book Give-Away, put students into positions of power, allowing them to propose, decide, debate, consider logistics, and create programs that affect the common good. The overriding goal of the McDonough Center for Leadership and Business is to educate citizen-leaders who are accustomed to taking thoughtful action.

MARY BALDWIN COLLEGE

STAUNTON, VA 24401
540.887.7000
http://www.mbc.edu/

UNDERGRADUATES: 1,300

For program information, please contact:
BRENDA BRYANT, Ph.D.
vwil@mbc.edu

Mary Baldwin College created the Virginia Women's Institute for Leadership (VWIL) with the challenges of the 21st century in mind, integrating academics and cocurricular activities in a whole new way. The traditional strengths and creativity of MBC, a church-affiliated, liberal arts college for women, are a launching pad for VWIL's intense and all-encompassing leadership development. In addition to taking courses in their major field of study and other program-required courses, VWIL students minor in Leadership Studies. Other components of the curriculum include community-service projects, leadership challenge programs, military leadership training, and physical training. VWIL cadets take a great deal of responsibility for implementation and administration of the program.

Unique aspects of Virginia Women's Institute for Leadership include:

✦ VWIL is the only college program for women that combines leadership education, military training, physical training, and character development in a comprehensive curriculum.

✦ VWIL is the only program in existence with a major military component that is designed and directed by and for women. By participating in an ROTC program with students from other colleges, VWIL cadets experience coeducational training while maintaining the single-sex setting in their own programs.

✦ VWIL brings women into the leadership mainstream. Students explore gender issues, examine the historic contributions of women leaders, and prepare for a future in which the preferred styles of women are the styles of choice for organizations that will thrive in the coming millennium.

By challenging the imagination, the intellect, and the body, VWIL prepares women for positions of responsibility and influence in the private and public sectors, including the military, inspiring them to set high goals and giving them the skills and self-discipline to accomplish them.

MIAMI UNIVERSITY

OXFORD, OH 45056
513.529.1809
http://www.muohio.edu/

UNDERGRADUATES: 21,000

For program information, please contact:
DENNIS C. ROBERTS, Ph.D.
robertd2@muohio.edu

"I have been encouraged to explore my purpose and convictions. This reflection has given me the confidence to engage with others so that we all are able to make a difference in the world in which we live."
—A MIAMI FOURTH-YEAR STUDENT

"Miami's Leadership Commitment" is a commitment to develop the leadership potential in all students. Twenty-four annual programs and services are available to students at Miami University, a public institution in Ohio, as they pursue learning about leadership and service. The comprehensive programs are unified around a framework of nine values that define leadership—values that include seeing potential within self and in others, communicating directly and honestly, being flexible and open to change, and taking appropriate risks.

Components of the program include:

✦ **PEER EDUCATION.** Students have the opportunity to express passion about issues while developing leadership skills that will help them to be heard. Peer educators receive training in presenting workshops and organizing campus events.

✦ **ANNUAL STUDENT LEADERSHIP CONFERENCE.** Nationally prominent speakers deliver keynote addresses, and faculty, staff, and student leaders guide a variety of interest sessions.

✦ **LIVING-LEARNING PROGRAMS.** Every residence hall has positions for students that provide leadership development opportunities throughout the year. Several residence halls are assigned themes that provide an even more intense focus on leadership issues.

✦ **LEADERSHAPE.** This intensive six-day program of interactive learning helps students clarify personal values and standards, respect the values of other individuals, and practice decision-making for ethical dilemmas.

As the first comprehensive leadership development program in the nation to use the *CAS Standards for Student Leadership Programs,* Miami's Leadership Commitment is being studied by other institutions for implementation in various campus cultural contexts. Such interest increases the likelihood that even more students will explore the value and character issues that will shape their perspectives for a lifetime of service.

Mount Saint Mary's College

12001 CHALON ROAD
LOS ANGELES, CA 90049
310.954.4000
http://www.msmc.la.edu/

UNDERGRADUATES: 1,700

For program information, please contact:
CHERYL MABEY, Ph.D.
adelucca@msmc.la.edu

"I feel I am a more confident, determined, and prepared woman because of the Leadership Program, which has enriched my education in so many ways."

—A MOUNT SAINT MARY'S FOURTH-YEAR STUDENT

Leadership education at Mount Saint Mary's College, the only Catholic women's college west of the Mississippi, is dedicated to engendering a sense of civic responsibility and personal integrity while empowering young women to make a difference. Students take advantage of a Leadership minor, annual fall and spring leadership conferences, and a number of leadership training activities on and off campus.

Highlights of the Women's Leadership Program include:

✦ Through reflective writing, all entering students develop a Leadership Portfolio with initial views on values, definition of leadership, and personal mission statements. The portfolio continues to document service to the school and community, skill mastery, and personal reflections throughout college.

✦ The Fall Leadership Conference includes an educational emphasis on trust, group interaction, and risk taking.

✦ The Women's Internship Network provides a spring break experience in which students shadow women of influence throughout southern California.

✦ In the introduction seminar, students explore the theories of leadership, studying the richness of collaborative leadership models and the collective nature of leadership.

✦ Students participate in the Public Leadership Education Network (PLEN), a consortium of women's colleges dedicated to preparing young women to lead. Based in Washington, D.C., PLEN seminars and internships explore the juxtaposition of power, responsibility, gender, and leadership.

Mount Saint Mary's expands its leadership programs by assessing the needs of students through the individual Leadership Portfolios, evaluating the growth in distinct skills and competencies. Through community service and mentorship opportunities, students build an invaluable sense of self-esteem, civic responsibility, and public engagement.

North Georgia College & State University

DAHLONEGA, GA 30597
706.864.1800
http://www.ngc.peachnet.edu/

UNDERGRADUATES: 3,400

For program information, please contact:
MELANIE CLARK
mclark@nugget.ngc.peachnet.edu

North Georgia College & State University, founded in 1873, is a public institution. The mission of the University's Corps of Cadets is to infuse the nation and the armed forces with college graduates who understand the dynamics of leadership and who already have leadership experience. In the Corps, students progress from recruit to squad leader, to senior non-commissioned officer, to officer.

Components of North Georgia's Corps of Cadets program are:

✦ Leadership development begins the first year with emphasis on followership and peer leadership.

✦ Second-year students may attend the Non-Commissioned Officers Academy (NCOA). Following completion of the academy, cadets are selected to become section or squad leaders, responsible for the discipline, morale, training, and welfare of four to nine cadets.

✦ During the third year, successful entry-level supervisors are selected for platoon, company, and staff assignments, in which they are responsible for the planning, execution, and control of activities involving up to 75 cadets and nine entry-level managers. Intensive leadership workshops develop physical fitness, improve problem-solving skills, and refine leadership development through role-playing situations.

✦ In the final year, cadets move into positions that include command of a company (50–70 cadets). Classroom instruction explores theories of leadership, while daily life in the Corps provides ample opportunity for putting theory into practice.

While the Corps of Cadets has an impact on the entire campus community, the most positive impact is on the members themselves. In the Leadership Evaluation Category in the Army's 1998 Advanced Camp, for instance, cadets from this Corps earned scores higher than any of the other five military colleges in the nation—clear evidence of the program's effectiveness.

Northern Michigan University

1401 PRESQUE ISLE AVENUE
MARQUETTE, MI 49855
906.227.1000
http://www.nmu.edu/

UNDERGRADUATES: 6,600

For program information, please contact:
RACHEL HARRIS
raharris@nmu.edu

"It's the smiles on the faces of those who realize they have the courage to go for it. It's the laughter of children who enjoy your assisting presence. That's community leadership. That what SLFP showed me."

—A NORTHERN MICHIGAN GRADUATE

Northern Michigan University joined forces with the W. K. Kellogg Foundation in 1991 to launch the Student Leader Fellowship Program (SLFP). Built on the premises that everyone is capable of being a leader and that the local community provides hundreds of opportunities for high-impact leadership, SLFP is committed to developing competent, ethical, and community-centered leaders. Components include an annual overnight Fall Retreat for all 100 Student Fellows, a two-credit "Leadership Theory and Practice" course, a yearlong mentoring relationship with a community leader, a series of Skill Builder! workshops, and a yearlong community-service internship that Student Fellows plan, organize, and implement. During their two years in SLFP:

✦ Student Fellows learn theories and approaches to leadership, assess their own styles and skills, and create an "action plan" for their own leadership development.

✦ Through their mentors and during their community-service internships, Student Fellows come to appreciate what a community is and how they can have an impact on it, and they discover that when they perform community service, they usually receive much more than they give.

✦ Through weekly journal assignments, small-group discussions, monthly reflection meetings during their community-service internships, one-on-one meetings with SLFP staff, and a final reflection paper, Student Fellows are constantly assessing what they have done and learned and where they are headed.

Information on the Student Leader Fellowship Program has been shared at three national conferences and has been sent to more than 200 colleges and universities. Most important, three outside evaluations have confirmed the impact that the Student Leader Fellowship Program has had on the growth and development of Student Fellows as leaders and as involved, concerned citizens in their communities.

Ohio University

CHUBB HALL 120
ATHENS, OH 45701
740.593.4100
http://www.ohiou.edu/

UNDERGRADUATES: 24,000

For program information, please contact:
BECKY BUSHEY-MILLER
millerb3@oak.cats.ohiou.edu

Leadership classes and programs at Ohio University prepare students for lives of personal and civic responsibility. Students also enjoy leadership opportunities through innovative programming by the Division of Student Affairs. In the Emerging Leader Program, students explore personal awareness and development issues related to leadership, study leadership theory, and practice, becoming effective leaders through participation in a community-service project. The program offers students the opportunity to network with Peer Leadership Consultants, a group of accomplished student leaders who serve as facilitators for the Emerging Leader Program.

Additional leadership opportunities include:

✦ **THE CUTLER SCHOLARS PROGRAM.** Student scholars can enroll in any degree program. They receive annual stipends to support four years of study, including summer programs, which are designed to enrich the scholars' understanding of themselves, to provide insight into civic responsibility and into the free-enterprise system, and to offer meaningful exposure to another culture.

✦ **CORPORATE LEADERSHIP PROGRAM.** This program is designed to provide top College of Business students with the opportunity to interact with corporate executives. Those selected participate in an internship and roundtable discussions with top executives, and they represent the College of Business while visiting corporations off campus.

✦ **CLASSROOMS OF INTEGRITY.** Professors and students work together to create climates of integrity, ensuring that each course, regardless of purpose or discipline, has a character-building component.

Students who serve others build character and become leaders, thereby participating in an illustrious tradition of leadership at Ohio University and proving, as President Robert Glidden observes, "that one person who is both articulate and committed can make a difference."

RENSSELAER POLYTECHNIC INSTITUTE

110 8TH STREET
TROY, NY 12180-3590
518.276.6000
http://www.rpi.edu/

UNDERGRADUATES: 4,500

For program information, please contact:
LINDA MCCLOSKEY
teitel@rpi.edu

"The Archer Center is a great opportunity for us to develop our leadership potential."

—A RENSSELAER FOURTH-YEAR STUDENT

Dedicated to creating leaders for the 21st century, the Archer Center for Student Leadership Development at Rensselaer Polytechnic Institute, a private, technical institution, provides students with diverse opportunities to develop their leadership potential and personal character. To complement Rensselaer's rigorous technology-oriented curricula, staff members offer classes, conferences, and workshops that explore such topics as communication skills, conflict management, teamwork, multiculturalism and diversity, values and ethics, and self-awareness. Leadership concepts are taught via small-group discussions and hands-on exercises.

Activities of the Archer Center for Student Leadership Development include:

✦ LIFESKILLS LEADERSHIP PROGRAM. This one-semester class focuses on personal development relative to leadership.

✦ KEY EXECUTIVE LEADERSHIP PROGRAM. One hundred students join Rensselaer Key Executives to discuss issues of values, ethics, and teamwork.

✦ PROFESSIONAL LEADERSHIP PROGRAM. This renowned yearlong program, open to selected third-year students, focuses on personal development and on maximizing individual strengths. Its emphasis is on business and career development.

In recognition of the need for students to behave as leaders and good citizens, the Schools of Management and Engineering have incorporated leadership courses into their required curricula. Rensselaer is committed to producing assertive, well-rounded individuals who espouse principle-centered leadership. The Archer Center is evidence of this commitment—improving the world not just through technological advancement, but by creating the leaders of tomorrow.

SAINT LOUIS UNIVERSITY

221 NORTH GRAND BOULEVARD
ST. LOUIS, MO 63103
314.977.2222
http://www.slu.edu/

UNDERGRADUATES: 6,500

For program information, please contact:
DONNA CHAPA
chapad@slu.edu

"The Service Leadership Program has been a great opportunity for me to strengthen my leadership skills while helping the community through service."

—AN SLU FOURTH-YEAR STUDENT

Saint Louis University, a private, church-affiliated institution, strives to develop leaders who demonstrate competence, conscience, compassion, and commitment to community. Reflecting the Jesuit tradition of true leadership, one that is learned and demonstrated through service to others, the University's School of Business and Administration offers an undergraduate certificate in Service Leadership. The program provides students with opportunities to learn leadership skills, apply knowledge acquired in the classroom to real community issues, and develop the habit of incorporating service to others into their personal and professional lives. The Service Leadership Certificate includes three components:

✦ 15 CREDIT HOURS OF COURSE WORK. This requirement can be fulfilled through the normal business degree requirements. Courses may be selected from an array of offerings in various disciplines emphasizing service or leadership constructs.

✦ 300 HOURS OF COMMUNITY SERVICE. In cooperation with local not-for-profit agencies and the University's Community Outreach Center, students select one or more agencies to serve the poor and marginalized of society.

✦ LEADER DEVELOPMENT. Students attend six leader development workshops. The topics covered include theories of leadership, interpersonal communication, diversity in leadership, and a service field trip.

Components of SLU's Service Leadership Certificate program—service to the community, leader development workshops, service learning, reflection retreats, mentoring, and personal interaction between students and community members—create a synergistic experience for students by bridging Ignatian philosophy with academic learning and personal experience. Such components encompass a new vision of true leadership—one that is learned and demonstrated through service to others.

St. Norbert College

100 GRANT STREET
DEPERE, WI 54115
920.403.3020
http://www.snc.edu/

UNDERGRADUATES: 1,900

For program information, please contact:
EMILY LANGDON, Ph.D.
langea@mail.snc.edu

"St. Norbert provides many opportunities for students to develop passions in life that lead them to successful, fulfilling futures."

—A SAINT NORBERT FOURTH-YEAR STUDENT

At St. Norbert College, a private, church-affiliated, liberal arts institution, the Department of Leadership, Service, and Involvement (LSI) assists students in their personal, intellectual, and spiritual growth through leadership development, community-service programming, and college community–involvement opportunities. LSI offers a wide range of cocurricular programs and services emphasizing experiential learning, academic and community partnerships, and advocacy. Components of the leadership program include:

✦ LEADERSHIP STUDIES ACADEMIC MINOR. A multidisciplinary academic program that has as its central concerns the ethical dimensions of leadership and the global common good.

✦ OUTDOOR LEADERSHIP CENTER. A service for students, faculty, and staff seeking to develop personal and team leadership skills. The Center, located on campus, consists of a low- and high-ropes course. In addition, LSI offers seven adventure-based trips at a low cost for students throughout the year.

✦ LEADERSHIP RESOURCE LIBRARY. Contains more than 400 books/resources on leadership, organizational and human development, organizational management, and service. Numerous audiotapes, videotapes, and volumes of training, development, and evaluation materials are also available.

✦ ALL CAMPUS LEADERSHIP EXPERIENCE. An annual program that focuses on a leadership topic of interest to the campus community. The conference is planned by students and staff under the leadership of LSI.

LSI serves students as the primary connection to a variety of leadership programs and services on campus. As a result, St. Norbert students develop extensive leadership skills in both a theoretical and practical realm.

Santa Clara University

500 EL CAMINO REAL
SANTA CLARA, CA 95053-1019
408.554.4000
http://www.scu.edu/

UNDERGRADUATES: 4,200

For program information, please contact:
JEANNE ROSENBERGER
jrosenberger@scu.edu

"The Center for Student Leadership has enhanced my leadership skills while opening doors to endless leadership opportunities on campus."

—A SANTA CLARA SECOND-YEAR STUDENT

The Jesuit tradition of excellence and service is at the core of the Center for Student Leadership at Santa Clara University, a private, comprehensive Catholic institution. Since 1993, with participation from the Markkula Center for Applied Ethics and the Leavey School of Business, CSL has prepared students to lead through innovative programs:

✦ EMERGING LEADERS. This first-year academic course uses the values-based Scale Change Model of Leadership Development to help Santa Clara students learn leadership as a process through the benefits of collective action, shared power, and commitment to justice, equality, and service.

✦ STUDENT REFLECTION LEADERS. Since 1996, this program, which includes the Markkula Center's Ethical Decision Making Framework, has integrated "rigorous inquiry, creative imagination, reflective engagement with society, and a commitment to fashioning a more just and humane world."

✦ PRISM (Presenting Real Issues Surrounding Multiculturalism). Through this program, students are exposed to diversity issues and learn to design workshops for the community.

✦ THE RIORDAN STUDENT LEADERSHIP INSTITUTE. A nine-course track in Leadership Skills Development provides skill-builders such as Conflict Resolution, Building Community, Seeing Yourself as a Leader, and Mentoring Others.

✦ LEADERSHIP EDUCATION. The Leadership Practicum enables Chartered Student Organizations and Residence Hall Association officers to explore the connection between leadership and management. The experimental Leadership Studies Certificate Program integrates course work with active learning to give Santa Clara students real leadership experience.

Students leave college well prepared to serve others and live ethical lives as a result of Santa Clara University's skillful leadership development programming.

Seattle Pacific University

3307 THIRD AVENUE WEST
SEATTLE, WA 98119
206.281.2000
http://www.spu.edu/
UNDERGRADUATES: 2,600

For program information, please contact:
GWEN SPENCER, Ph.D.
gspencer@spu.edu

"I've learned that leadership is much more than simply holding a position—it's an act of service. This practical lesson has not only helped prepare me for a career, but for life."

—A SEATTLE PACIFIC GRADUATE

Character, competence, and commitment are all hallmarks of the student leader at Seattle Pacific University, a private, church-affiliated, comprehensive institution. At Seattle Pacific, leadership is a form of service. Leadership classes, quarterly events, and a diversity of leadership activities provide a platform for outreach and connection to others. Cooperation between faculty, students, and Student Life staff has resulted in a comprehensive student leadership program that incorporates innovative educational ideas such as:

✦ Collaboration among student leaders from residence halls, student government, campus ministries, clubs, publications, and University organizations to create a supportive, service-focused educational community;

✦ Integration of values and Christian faith into the challenges of leadership and constructive use of political power;

✦ Understanding of "everyday people" who have brought courageous leadership to particularly difficult challenges;

✦ Introduction of leadership theory and skills.

Civic responsibility and service to others are strongly articulated at Seattle Pacific. For example, within days of arriving on campus, new students go on CityQuest, a one-day introduction to the urban outreach ministries and services of Seattle. Many students opt to take an "Urban Plunge," where for four to five days they live in downtown Seattle as best they can, using the same urban services that the destitute must use to survive. Seattle Pacific faculty members embrace student leadership programs with great enthusiasm. They speak at leadership classes and events, work alongside students at CityQuest, accompany students on international ministry opportunities, and model the idea of servant leadership.

From Hurricane Mitch relief to the Kosovo crisis, Seattle Pacific University students step up to the responsibility of leading others by first serving them.

Southwestern College

100 COLLEGE STREET
WINFIELD KS 67156-2499
316.221.8236
http://www.sckans.edu/
UNDERGRADUATES: 1,000

For program information, please contact:
CHERYL L. RUDE
clrude@jinx.sckans.edu

"A good leader accomplishes, but an excellent leader also influences."

—A SOUTHWESTERN THIRD-YEAR STUDENT

Leadership through service in a world without boundaries is central to the vision of Southwestern College. Established in 1885, Southwestern is a private, four-year liberal arts college affiliated with the United Methodist Church. The leadership program, Leadership Southwestern, includes academic course work, projects on campus and in the community, and travel. The bedrock of Leadership Southwestern is an ethic of service from which leadership builds.

Highlights of Leadership Southwestern include:

✦ Academic challenges to help students think of leadership beyond a position;

✦ Projects that benefit others and provide an active learning experience;

✦ Travel that includes service to others and an opportunity for students to expand their worldview;

✦ Acceptance of the responsibility to serve and the responsibility to influence others to serve.

First-year Southwestern students engage in group projects that build their collegiate network and introduce them to leadership and service as a hand-in-hand concept. Second-year students organize leadership development activities for students in grades K-12. Third-year students operate as an executive administrative group to facilitate the goals of the team. Fourth-year students engage in leadership projects of their own design that follow a personal passion and are a new venture.

Cheryl L. Rude, the director of Leadership Southwestern, hopes that in the four-year experience "students will understand themselves, gain confidence, learn about how people relate to one another, try a new idea or two, experience the thrill of helping to make changes, and deepen their character through service."

Spalding University

851 SOUTH FOURTH STREET
LOUISVILLE, KY 40203
502.585.9911
http://www.spalding.edu/

UNDERGRADUATES: 1,100

For program information, please contact:
LAURA NAFF
lnaff@spalding.edu

"I have a better understanding of what it means to lead by example and I now know that the most effective leaders are true servants."

—A SPALDING THIRD-YEAR STUDENT

Leadership, service, and academic excellence are essential to success at Spalding University, a private, liberal arts institution rooted in the Catholic tradition. The University's Leadership Medallion Program provides opportunities for students to increase personal development skills, begin career development activities, and serve others in the community.

Specific components related to character development at Spalding include:

✦ Values-based problem-solving is shaped through the Leadership Medallion Program. This component seeks to assist students with critical thinking about complex decisions in terms of values and an overall sense of justice.

✦ The program includes workshops on such areas as time management, etiquette, leadership styles, self-image, drug/alcohol education, and spiritual development.

✦ Forty hours of community service, journaling, and reflecting are also important pieces of the program. People of character regard the needs of others and respond thoughtfully to those needs.

✦ Each student develops his or her own personal mission statement upon completion of the Leadership Medallion Program. This requires students to reflect on their values and to set goals.

Spalding's Leadership Medallion Program offers students a challenging curriculum and has proven to be very rewarding and beneficial during a time of significant character development at the institution. Through their participation in the program, students gain the skills they need to become effective leaders and citizens of character.

United States Air Force Academy

USAF ACADEMY, CO 80840-5025
719.333.4904
http://www.usafa.af.mil/wing/

UNDERGRADUATES: 4,100

For program information, please contact:
DANIEL W. JORDAN, Ph.D.
jordand.34trg@usafa.af.mil

"The challenge of commanding 4,000 peers developed an inner character that will always be part of me."

—A USAF ACADEMY FIRST-CLASS CADET

Leadership experience is not just an opportunity, but a requirement at the United States Air Force Academy. In the Academy Leadership Development Program (ALDP), cadets learn, understand, and practice the virtues of good leadership. Components of the ALDP include:

✦ CORE COMPETENCIES. The ALDP has four outcome goals:

Fourth Class (first year): Demonstrate assertive followership skills in support of unit mission objectives;

Third Class (second year): Demonstrate effective instruction skills in support of unit mission objectives while preparing to be supervisors in the cadet wing;

Second Class (third year): Demonstrate effective supervisory skills in support of unit mission objectives while preparing to be cadet officer-leaders of the cadet wing and exemplifying assertive followership skills;

First Class (fourth year): Demonstrate effective leadership skills in support of unit mission objectives while preparing to be commissioned officers.

✦ LDM (Leadership Development Manual). Through each progressive year, cadets are expected to "Be" by possessing certain attributes of a leader, including strong and honorable character, "Know" certain principles such as core values, and "Do" certain actions, such as doing the right thing, serving others before self, and striving for excellence.

✦ ASSESSMENT. Surveys of supervisors of Academy graduates indicate that graduates exhibit excellent leadership and character. Surveys also indicate that graduates believe they are prepared and inspired to lead.

By placing cadets in real leadership positions, the United States Air Force Academy proves its commitment to forming leaders with essential knowledge and impeccable character, who are prepared to lead our Air Force and the nation.

United States Coast Guard Academy

15 MOHEGAN AVENUE
NEW LONDON, CT 06320-4195
860.444.8444
http://www.cga.edu/uscga.html/

UNDERGRADUATES: 800

For program information, please contact:
THOMAS J. HAAS, Ph.D.
thaas@cga.uscg.mil

"The Academy develops leaders who can not only pilot a ship, but command a crew and inspire confidence."

—A USCGA FIRST-CLASS CADET

The United States Coast Guard Academy is the public service academy of the U.S. maritime service. Its faculty and curriculum are dedicated to its institutional mission: "To educate, develop, and train leaders who are ethically, intellectually, professionally, and physically prepared to serve the nation and humanity by carrying out the Service's missions."

The Academy has adopted these guiding principles:

✦ Everyone connected with the Academy is a member of a diverse community of learners, committed to service.

✦ The Academy actively challenges and inspires learners to become leaders of character who epitomize Coast Guard core values of honor, respect, and devotion to duty.

✦ The Academy actively practices individual responsibility and accountability, teamwork, and continuous improvement in support of its shared learning outcomes.

✦ The Academy's environment is enlightened and constantly enriched by evolving knowledge, emerging technologies, innovation, and best practices.

✦ Academy graduates, military and civilian, represent the institution's contribution to the nation and to sharing this strength with the global community.

The Academy's four-year undergraduate Cadet Program's mission is to graduate young men and women who are worthy of the traditions of commissioned officers in the Coast Guard. The Leadership Development Center consists of seven schools that offer advanced training to those who have already served some time in the Coast Guard. In keeping with the Commandant's statement that the Academy is "the home for leadership and excellence in the entire Coast Guard," USCGA prepares its cadets for lives of dedication and service to their country and to humanity.

United States Military Academy

606 THAYER ROAD
WEST POINT, NY 10996
914.938.4041
http://www.usma.edu/

UNDERGRADUATES: 4,000

For program information, please contact:
JEFFREY M. WEART
sj6118@exmail.usma.army.mil

The mission of the United States Military Academy, the nation's oldest service academy, is to develop commissioned leaders of character committed to the values of duty, honor, country, and professional growth throughout a career as an Army officer and a lifetime of service to the nation. West Point takes a holistic approach to leader development that spans all three developmental programs—Academic, Military, and Physical. This comprehensive approach to leader development at West Point dates back to the first half of the nineteenth century. Recognized worldwide for its integrated approach to leadership and character development, the Academy has hosted conferences such as the National Conference on Ethics in America, the Robert T. Steven's Service Academies Leaders Conference, and the Cadet Leader Development Conference, which brings together students to discuss character and leader development on college campuses.

Components of West Point's leadership program include:

✦ **CADET LEADER DEVELOPMENT SYSTEM.** Cadets and faculty are expected to be leaders as well as leader developers. The System encompasses all aspects of the cadet life, whether in the classroom, on the athletic field, in the cadet barracks, or away from West Point.

✦ **THE MILITARY PROGRAM.** Courses within the Military Program's curriculum are explicitly designed to address leader and character development. All cadets participate in the four components of the Military Program: Military Training, Military Science, Cadet Professional Development, and Cadet Environment. The program provides each cadet with leadership opportunities that are increasingly more demanding and with the motivation to seek even greater leadership opportunities through a sequential and progressive 47-month process of education, training, and performance evaluation.

In every way possible, the Academy strives to ensure that cadets are provided with the tools needed to be leaders of character at West Point, in the Army, and for the nation.

UNITED STATES NAVAL ACADEMY

121 BLAKE ROAD
ANNAPOLIS, MD 21302
410.293.1000
http://www.USNA.edu/

UNDERGRADUATES: 4,000

For program information, please contact:
LIZ STERNAMAN
sternama@nadn.navy.mil

"The Academy is more than a four-year college, it's a four-year leadership academy. I am confident I have the ability to succeed as a leader anywhere."
—A USNA FOURTH-YEAR STUDENT

The U.S. Naval Academy's mission is to produce graduates who have the potential to assume the highest responsibilities of command, citizenship, and government. Naval Academy alumni have excelled as leaders in the military, in the space program, in business, and throughout government, including the White House.

Components of the Naval Academy's leadership program include:

✦ **BRIGADE STRUCTURE.** First-year students are immersed in the "leadership laboratory" that begins the four-year experience of the Brigade of Midshipmen. Incoming students work within an established hierarchical structure that reinforces the standards of accountability and responsibility for the unit. Midshipmen are steadily promoted throughout their four years to positions of increased responsibility.

✦ **ACADEMIC STUDY.** Four core leadership courses and six electives are devoted to the different aspects of leadership. The core courses also examine the importance of sound ethical reasoning in the profession of arms.

✦ **SUMMER CRUISE.** Midshipmen spend summers assigned to Navy ships, aircraft squadrons, and Fleet Marine Force units. Exposure to the professionalism of the troops that they will someday lead and the example of the officers already in charge galvanize the midshipmen in their studies.

The United States Naval Academy exists solely to produce leaders for the Navy and Marine Corps. The integrated four-year leadership experience at the Academy prepares young men and women to be leaders in all aspects of their life: military, community, and as American citizens.

UNIVERSITY OF CALIFORNIA, LOS ANGELES

405 HILGARD AVENUE
LOS ANGELES, CA 90095-1436
310.825.4321
http://www.ucla.edu/

UNDERGRADUATES: 24,100

For program information, please contact:
CHARLES OUTCALT
blp@saonet.ucla.edu

"I have learned that for successful group work, incorporation of all opinions provides the best path."
—A UCLA FIRST-YEAR STUDENT

An integral component of leadership development at the University of California, Los Angeles, an urban, public research institution, the Bruin Leaders Project uses the Social Change Model of Leadership to develop students' leadership skills, including their commitment to community service for social change, their ability to work collaboratively, and their appreciation for diversity. Project students have explored the advantages of nonhierarchical leadership and have presented their findings at regional and national conferences. Program staff are currently editing a book on nonhierarchical leadership development that will include the work of leaders in this field.

The Bruin Leaders Project has two major components:

✦ **SEMINAR SERIES.** Students attend seminars on topics related to leadership and service, including public speaking, diversity awareness, volunteer recruitment, collaborative leadership practice, conflict resolution, and identity development.

✦ **COMMUNITY SERVICE.** Students provide service to local organizations dedicated to disadvantaged children, domestic-violence awareness and prevention, literacy efforts, and environmental cleanup.

Students who complete the seminar series and provide community service are awarded a leadership certificate at an awards ceremony held each year in June.

Through participatory, thought-provoking seminars and community-service projects that are both significant and enjoyable, UCLA's Bruin Leaders Project assists students in creating links between their personal values and the necessity of working toward social change. As a unifying force on a large, decentralized, and diverse campus, the Project provides an environment in which both current and emerging leaders from all segments of campus can meet, develop skills, and form community.

University of Central Florida

4000 CENTRAL FLORIDA BOULEVARD
ORLANDO, FL 32816
407.823.2000
http://www.ucf.edu/

UNDERGRADUATES: 23,800

For program information, please contact:
JAN LLOYD
jlloyd@mail.ucf.edu

The Leadership Enrichment and Academic Development (LEAD) Scholars Program at the University of Central Florida was created to provide an avenue of expression and development for academically talented student leaders. The original vision of the program was to provide an academic foundation of leadership development enhanced by opportunities for community service, social connection, and mentoring relationships. That vision has matured to make leadership the focus and driving rationale for the program.

Components of the LEAD Scholars Program include:

✦ **ACADEMIC COURSE WORK.** Students in the two-year LEAD program take a "Foundations of Leadership" course each semester. Specific subjects range from ethics and moral development to communication and teamwork.

✦ **COMMUNITY SERVICE.** Students are required to provide ten hours of community service that involves reflective learning.

✦ **LEAD SCHOLARS ASSOCIATION (LSA).** All first-year students and many second-year students participate with one of ten LSA teams: Service, Newsletters, Athletic Activities, Promotions, Alumni, Speakers, Video, Leadership Week, Technology, and Social Activities.

✦ **MENTORING.** The assistantship program matches students with faculty and staff for the purpose of mentoring, informal teaching, and experiential learning. An external mentoring program with local community and business leaders is also in place.

The LEAD Scholars Program is instrumental in coordinating Leadership Week, a collaborative effort to celebrate leadership on campus, during which campus members have the opportunity to attend workshops and sessions on leadership and related topics. At the close of the week, faculty, staff, students, and student organizations are recognized for outstanding leadership through a variety of awards.

University of Colorado at Boulder

CAMPUS BOX 17
BOULDER, CO 80309
303.492.8908
http://www.colorado.edu/

UNDERGRADUATES: 25,000

For program information, please contact:
ADAM GOODWIN
adam.goodwin@colorado.edu

The Presidents Leadership Class (PLC) at the University of Colorado at Boulder fosters an extensive understanding of leadership and its responsible application. Based on the premise that leadership involves inspiring a shared vision, empowering others, maintaining open-mindedness, balancing reason and intuition, and being compassionate, ethical, and congruent, the program promotes the development of these abilities in talented undergraduate students in a number of ways:

✦ Once identified through a rigorous selection process, students are enrolled in a special two-year curriculum that combines academic and experiential education, enabling them to learn and practice leadership and community service.

✦ Through an integrated academic curriculum, PLC students study ethics and leadership, as well as community and global issues in leadership.

✦ In addition to the academic component, PLC scholars participate in a variety of programs—lectures by private- and public-sector leaders, community-service projects developed and implemented by the scholars, and on-site seminars at government agencies, nonprofit organizations, and businesses.

✦ The program culminates in a "Walkabout," a semester-long internship for each student.

On campus, PLC members hold positions in student government, minority focus groups, honors societies, and service-learning programs; PLC students and faculty serve as resources for University faculty in experiential and leadership education. In the community, students participate in projects with food banks, correctional facilities, battered women's shelters, and child advocacy programs. Additionally, each year, 60 PLC students design and participate in individual internships with local businesses and community organizations. In all these ways, PLC students acquire core competencies in leadership, allowing them to have a positive impact on others both now and in the future.

UNIVERSITY OF DETROIT MERCY

4001 WEST MCNICHOLS ROAD
DETROIT, MI 48221
313.993.1000
http://www.udmercy.edu/

UNDERGRADUATES: 4,600

For program information, please contact:
COLLEEN KAMINSKI
kaminscm@udmercy.edu

"My time at the Leadership Development Institute changed my perception of leadership. Rather than being in command, I learned how I can lead through service."
—A DETROIT MERCY GRADUATE

The University of Detroit Mercy, a church-affiliated institution, established the Leadership Development Institute (LDI) in 1995. Components of LDI include:

✦ ACADEMICS. Courses throughout the curriculum incorporate a leadership focus or community-service component; select courses offer the option of engaging in community service as part of the course requirements.

✦ LEADERSHIP WORKSHOPS. Skill-building workshops are offered bimonthly. University and community experts present interactive sessions on topics that include servant leadership, personal motivation, cross-cultural awareness, goal setting, spirituality, ethics and leadership, and conflict resolution.

✦ COMMUNITY SERVICE. Opportunities for service in the local community are endless. LDI places students in programs that address issues such as homelessness, domestic abuse, poverty, and hunger.

✦ LEADERSHIP IN SERVICE PROGRAM. Focused on building leadership potential, increasing awareness of urban conditions, and providing skills to address problems and effect change, this program provides an array of activities that complement classroom learning and give students the competitive edge to enter the workforce as servant leaders.

✦ LEADERS EMPOWERED TO SERVE (LETS). LETS encourages the University community to participate in projects that foster compassionate service to others and the promotion of justice. Participants are responsible for coordinating a community-service project during the academic term.

The Leadership Development Institute provides opportunities for students to prepare themselves not only to respond to change, but also to effect change. In this way, they can profoundly influence the future of their communities.

THE UNIVERSITY OF MEMPHIS

MEMPHIS, TN 38152
901.678.2000
http://www.memphis.edu/

UNDERGRADUATES: 14,800

For program information, please contact:
WARREN "BUD" RICHEY
wrichey@memphis.edu

"This program, paired with outstanding service opportunities, gives us the wisdom, confidence, and values needed in our future endeavors."
—A MEMPHIS GRADUATE

The University of Memphis, a comprehensive, public university, has implemented a four-year, cocurricular leadership experience for students, enabling them to serve as leaders of student organizations while completing their undergraduate work. The Emerging Leaders Program, which blends theoretical and practical experiences, also helps students prepare themselves for service as leaders in their communities upon graduation.
Components of the Emerging Leaders Program include:

✦ COURSE WORK. During their first two academic years, students are enrolled in classes that provide the opportunity to learn, explore, and process leadership experiences. Units in each of the two fall courses focus on the responsibilities of leaders to lead by example and the ethics of leadership.

✦ COMMUNITY SERVICE. During each semester, students participate in service-learning activities in the local community. Facilitated discussions help students make sense of what they are doing and the importance of their work.

✦ YEARLONG PROJECTS. During their third and fourth academic years, students engage in yearlong projects that focus on doing things for the betterment of others.

✦ CORE SPEAKERS. All Emerging Leaders must attend the annual presentation by a core speaker, who addresses issues of character, ethical decision-making, or a related topic.

Taken together, these components help students develop a personal philosophy of leadership that includes the values of personal responsibility and responsibility to others. As evidence of The University of Memphis' commitment to offering superior leadership and educational experiences, it provides scholarships to Emerging Leaders and awards academic credit for leadership courses. Such a commitment instills in students pride not only in their participation in the Emerging Leaders Program but also in serving the campus and local community.

University of Northern Iowa

1222 WEST 27TH STREET
CEDAR FALLS, IA 50614-0033
319.273.2311
http://www.uni.edu/

UNDERGRADUATES: 11,000

For program information, please contact:
GERRI PERREAULT, Ph.D.
geraldine.perreault@uni.edu

"Do what you think is right or best and choose integrity over glory. That is what I have learned at UNI."

—A NORTHERN IOWA GRADUATE

Educating students for ethical leadership in a democratic society is the emphasis of the interdisciplinary Leadership Studies Program (LSP) at the University of Northern Iowa, a public, comprehensive institution. At Northern Iowa, the subject of leadership is inextricably intertwined with issues of ethics—ethics is treated as fundamental to leadership, not as a separate topic. For that reason, consideration of ethics is included in almost all LSP activities:

✦ Ethical perspectives and questions are raised in nearly every class sessions, for instance, "What does it mean to lead?" "Can one be an 'effective' leader without being an ethical leader?" "Can a tyrant be considered a leader?" "Was Hitler a leader?"

✦ In the discussion of the relationship of leaders and followers, students are asked to consider the extent to which the responsibility of a leader (for the impact of one's actions) extends beyond one's own group to the wider community, even to include one's enemies.

✦ A specific class session on ethics uses cases to ask students to identify ethical issues, the factors that would influence a decision, and strategies that would help them make the ethical decision.

✦ Students are provided with multiple examples of individual and organizational integrity.

✦ Leadership skills such as delegation are taught as abilities that involve inherently ethical issues; skills are not viewed as value-neutral.

Northern Iowa offers students a minor in Leadership Studies, and sponsors an annual leadership essay contest. The University seeks to challenge students to live with integrity, and the LSP program works to assist them in their development as caring people who can help in shaping a more humane future for all.

Wake Forest University

1834 WAKE FOREST ROAD
WINSTON-SALEM, NC 27106
336.758.5255
http://www.wfu.edu/

UNDERGRADUATES: 3,900

For program information, please contact:
MIKE FORD
fordmg@wfu.edu

"Wake Forest is all about developing leaders for the 21st century. Students are encouraged to pursue their dreams and make a difference for the betterment of the campus, local community, and society."

—A WAKE FOREST FOURTH-YEAR STUDENT

Wake Forest University, a private, comprehensive institution, seeks to develop students to be principled and responsible leaders. To that end, the Leadership Program Initiative consists of an annual Leadership Academy, retreats and conferences for special populations such as fraternity and sorority members, an emerging leaders' program, a speakers' series, academic courses, a leadership newsletter, and a resource center.

Each year the President's Leadership Conference selects a focus for group discussion and action. Recent themes and outcomes have included:

✦ ETHICS AND HONOR. The conference set the stage for renewal of the campus community's commitment to the honor system and a major reform in the campus judicial system.

✦ MULTICULTURALISM AND DIVERSITY. The conference addressed the problems of stereotypes and insensitivity and set in motion programming initiatives to improve race relations.

✦ ACTIVISM AND SERVICE. The conference, which focused on "creating a better society," resulted in a greater institutional commitment to volunteer programs.

✦ SOCIAL AND PERSONAL RESPONSIBILITY. The conference addressed the issues of alcohol use and abuse and gender concerns. The discussions laid the groundwork for new health prevention and education initiatives as well as the strengthening of University social policies, and it helped galvanize students to lobby the State Assembly for stricter DWI legislation.

At the heart of the Leadership Program are the moral questions: "How shall we live and lead?" "What does it mean to be a servant leader?" "What are the ethical underpinnings that should guide our leadership practices?" By pursuing the answers, Wake Forest students are better prepared to serve as leaders in society.

William Penn College

201 TRUEBLOOD AVENUE
OSKALOOSA, IA 52577
515.673.1001
http://www.wmpenn.edu/

UNDERGRADUATES: 1,200

For program information, please contact:
TERRANCE S. WEBB, Ph.D.
webbt@wmpenn.edu

"At Penn I learned and benefited from community service by working with young mothers and their children in our community through MOPS (Mothers of PreSchoolers)."

—A WILLIAM PENN THIRD-YEAR STUDENT

William Penn College is a church-affiliated institution dedicated to providing students with an education grounded in leadership development. William Penn's general education curriculum, the Leadership Core Program, is designed to give students a solid intellectual foundation for future service, a lifetime of learning, enlightened leadership, and ethical practice. The program, the framework for all academic programming at William Penn, consists of an integrated sequence of 17 required courses addressing the skills of effective leadership —critical thinking, communication, and decision-making. Interdisciplinary courses and service-learning programs complement every major. Components include:

✦ **SERVICE REQUIREMENT.** A service requirement exists in several program courses. Students choose to become involved in projects such as building and repairing homes with Habitat for Humanity, volunteering at local daycare centers, visiting shut-ins, assisting elementary and junior high–school athletic teams, tutoring homeless or at-risk children and their families, and sprucing up the town square.

✦ **STUDENT LEADERSHIP.** All student activities center on the leadership theme. The Student Government Association (SGA) nurtures community among students and serves as a liaison between the student body and the rest of the college community. Acting as role models for other student leaders, SGA leaders are expected to respond to the highest level of accountability. Student leadership of students is a consistent theme of campus life at William Penn.

The traditional liberal arts with a leadership focus are the core of William Penn's educational program, as the College believes that liberally educated women and men have the skills and confidence to face whatever the future holds. The practice of leadership teaches students to be leaders. The experience of leadership encourages such virtues as self-control, ethical decision-making, and civic responsibility.

Wilmington College

251 LUDOVIC STREET
WILMINGTON, OH 45177
937.382.9318
http://www.wilmington.edu/

UNDERGRADUATES: 1,100

For program information, please contact:
KEN PERESS, Ph.D.
ken_peress@wilmington.edu

"The leadership program at Wilmington is a great opportunity to acquire the skills that we need to have a strong family life, a successful career, and a spiritual life."

—A WILMINGTON FOURTH-YEAR STUDENT

Leadership for Effective Citizenship (LEC) embodies Wilmington College's Quaker commitment to peace-making, social justice, service, and respect for all persons. The LEC program presents an environment in which students learn theory, practice skills, and explore leadership opportunities. LEC educates, trains, and develops nascent leaders over a four-year period. Students may apply in the fall of their first, second, or third year of enrollment. After a three-credit course, students participate in and lead service activities and campus organizations. As students grow increasingly more competent, they mentor new students entering the LEC program.

Key elements of Wilmington's Leadership for Effective Citizenship program include:

✦ Studying ethical and moral practices in leadership;

✦ Exploring cultural and gender influences on leadership;

✦ Addressing risk-taking and creativity;

✦ Understanding the process of consensus seeking, enhancing collaborative efforts, and managing conflict;

✦ Developing motivational skills and mentoring abilities.

As part of LEC, students participate in annual events such as the Westheimer Peace Symposium, the Quake, and Community Day. A ceremonial distribution of leadership pins designates the number of years a student has participated in the program, and membership in an honorary society is possible.

Each year the LEC program focuses on different aspects of leadership: academic foundations, personal skills, organizational elements, and finally community issues. As a result, students participating in Wilmington's Leadership for Effective Citizenship program gain the skills they need to be effective leaders on campus and in the broader community.

SPIRITUAL GROWTH PROGRAMS

Students searching for meaning, connectedness, and significance present both a challenge and an opportunity for colleges and universities. Programs that foster spiritual growth provide a means to develop a vision of moral integrity that coheres and connects belief to behavior. Exemplary programs affirm the integral role that spirituality and religion often play in shaping character. Clearly, a college does not have to be a faith-centered or church-related institution to encourage spiritual growth.

ALLEGHENY COLLEGE

520 N. MAIN STREET
MEADVILLE, PA 16335
814.332.3100
http://www.alleg.edu/

UNDERGRADUATES: 1,900

For program information, please contact:
JOHN PATRICK COLATCH
jcolatch@alleg.edu

"The most life-changing aspect of this program was experiencing how through my service to others I was serving God."

—AN ALLEGHENY GRADUATE

Allegheny College, a church-affiliated, liberal arts institution, fosters solid personal faith through three very active Christian groups, a wonderfully ecumenically spirited Hillel, as well as through regular worship and small-group discussions and studies. Each of the groups also considers community service and outreach as essential components of the total spiritual life experience. Two of the groups, Allegheny Christian Outreach and Sojourners Christian Fellowship, have recently received the college's annual Outstanding Organization Leadership Award. Additionally, increasingly large numbers of students choose mission work or the ministry as the next step in their professional lives after leaving Allegheny.

Highlights of Allegheny's religious life program include:

✦ **HOSPITALITY.** Students become involved in the program because of the hospitality that is offered in the way of picnics, ecumenical celebrations, and fellowship opportunities. Students remain involved because they see that they can make a difference on campus and in the larger community.

✦ **WORK TOURS AND MISSION TRIPS.** Several trips go out from campus each year, supplementing a model program of community service that already exists at the college.

✦ **ECUMENICAL LUNCHEONS.** During the year, ecumenical luncheon discussion meetings are held on a variety of topics. Students learn about others' religious traditions and the places where divergent religious viewpoints may intersect.

Students at Allegheny College have the opportunity to learn much about the root beliefs of their own religious traditions. In turn, they are encouraged to think creatively about ways in which their self-understanding can make them better community and world citizens. At Allegheny, religious faith is understood as a dynamic, life-changing influence that should be felt far beyond the campus boundaries.

BELHAVEN COLLEGE

1500 PEACHTREE STREET
JACKSON, MS 39202-1789
601.968.5940
http://www.belhaven.edu/

UNDERGRADUATES: 1,400

For program information, please contact:
WYNN KENYON, Ph.D.
wkenyon@belhaven.edu

"I am beginning to see the big picture of life and how all areas come together in so many united ways. My own fragmented ideas are forming a cohesive whole."

—A BELHAVEN SECOND-YEAR STUDENT

The Honors Program at Belhaven College, a liberal arts college, is structured to encourage in students a cognitive, rational, inductive approach to developing a Christian world view that manifests itself in positive moral and social action. Belhaven professors conduct interactive seminars employing an interdisciplinary methodology—students, for example, simultaneously see art and hear music from a particular era as a means to understanding its underlying philosophy. With this type of preparation, students then attend cultural events, critique them, and form appropriate Christian responses. Christian leaders regularly engage Belhaven students in critical-thinking dialog, encouraging them not to withdraw from their culture, but rather to be compelled to "holy, spirited, creative, compassionate engagement for God's glory."

The Honors Program influences spiritual growth by:

✦ Promoting Christian discernment in the formation of beliefs and in the consequent responses regarding behavior and service to God and humankind.

✦ Promoting both personal and civic responsibility through the examination of current culture, especially pop culture, so that students will not respond to it in an unthinking manner.

Through the interdisciplinary curriculum and a variety of media, speakers, and projects, students analyze culture from a historical perspective, which enables them to better understand their own culture and to effect a thoughtful, positive response to it. The Honors Program at Belhaven helps students develop a Christian world view, proactively engage their culture, and respond in a personally responsible way that exemplifies Belhaven's motto, "to serve, not to be served."

BELMONT UNIVERSITY

1900 BELMONT BOULEVARD
NASHVILLE, TN 37212-3757
615.460.6000
http://www.belmont.edu/

UNDERGRADUATES: 2,500

For program information, please contact:
DANE C. ANTHONY
anthonyd@mail.belmont.edu

Belmont University, a church-affiliated institution, believes that there is more to a good education than just going to class. All Belmont students must complete 60 hours of out-of-class requirements—the Convocation requirements—in order to graduate. Through the Convocation program, the University seeks to integrate its faith heritage with a dynamic liberal arts teaching commitment. The program consists of several components designed to foster deeper understanding and facilitation of learning and practice, creating a "common Belmont experience" for all undergraduate students.

The Convocation program is carefully structured:

✦ Activities are scheduled at various times to accommodate students' busy schedules.

✦ Students entering Belmont as first-year students are required to complete the Convocation requirements within the following categories: faith development, cultural arts, academic lectures, personal/professional growth, and community spirit.

✦ Students who transfer into Belmont have the requirements pro-rated, based on the number of academic hours transferred.

✦ Students accumulate thousands of community-service hours each academic year, many leading them to further service after Convocation requirements have been met.

Through faith-development seminars, academic lectures, cultural-arts events, and community-service work, students enjoy multiple opportunities to interact with their peers and faculty/staff. These events are designed to engage all members of the University community in cocurricular learning and practice. As a variety of cultural, social, and spiritual experiences, the Convocation requirements enable Belmont graduates to develop a well-rounded perspective on life and to learn first-hand that "education" is not confined to the classroom— that learning can and should be a lifestyle.

BROWN UNIVERSITY

45 PROSPECT STREET
PROVIDENCE, RI 02912
401.863.2234
http://www.brown.edu/

UNDERGRADUATES: 6,000

For program information, please contact:
CATHERINE PASTILLE
catherine_pastille@brown.edu

Brown University, a private, Ivy League, liberal arts institution, is home to the Brown/Rhode Island School of Design Catholic Community. The community, guided by student leadership with the support of the Catholic chaplain and campus minister, provides opportunities for the students, staff, faculty, and alumni to celebrate their Catholic faith, expand their knowledge of that faith, and deepen their spiritual lives. The Pastoral Council, which is composed of nine students who commit themselves to living out the Gospel through service to others, coordinates the community's varied activities:

✦ **LITURGY.** Community members participate in choirs, function as eucharistic ministers, sacristans, lectors, and altar servers, and provide hospitality where needed.

✦ **EVENTS.** Members enjoy parties, barbecues, and other social activities, benefit from educational events (speakers, forums, and workshops), and participate in special orientation and commencement functions.

✦ **FELLOWSHIP.** Retreats, Bible studies, RISD fellowship, Emmaus, the Women's Group, and the Men's Group all foster interaction among the members.

✦ **OUTREACH.** Members reach out to others through community service, interfaith dinners, and intercollegiate collaboration.

✦ **COMMUNICATIONS.** The group conveys its mission through publicity pieces, a weekly publication called *The Cenacle,* and the Internet.

The Brown/RISD Catholic Community seeks to bring a belief in the message of the Gospel to their educational communities, which, when expressed in classroom discourse, artistic projects, and discussions of institutional concerns, substantially enriches academic life. The Brown/RISD Catholic Community is constantly finding ways to demonstrate that for the religious believer, faith and intellect are not competing loyalties but rather integral parts of the whole person.

CALIFORNIA LUTHERAN UNIVERSITY

60 WEST OLSEN ROAD
THOUSAND OAKS, CA 91360-2787
805.492.2411
http://www.clunet.edu/

UNDERGRADUATES: 1,700

For program information, please contact:
MARK KNUTSON
mknutson@clunet.edu

"Centered in the Lutheran faith, the Campus Ministry Program at CLU provides a variety of programs to facilitate the spiritual needs of our diverse campus."

—A CLU GRADUATE

California Lutheran University, a liberal arts school, encourages critical inquiry into matters of both faith and reason. CLU's Campus Ministry program provides opportunities for worship and encourages the spiritual growth of students, faculty, and staff. In keeping with the University's philosophy that students need to develop independently, all involvement in religious programming is strictly voluntary.

Facets of the program include:

✦ LORD OF LIFE. The central focus of Campus Ministry is the student congregation. With a governing body composed of students who are elected to fulfill the various functions of the congregation, Lord of Life is an effective training ground for lay leaders in the church.

✦ WORSHIP AND MUSIC. Each Wednesday morning, classes are suspended and offices can choose to close as the community voluntarily gathers for a chapel service. On Wednesday evenings, students gather for an informal communion service, and on Thursday evenings, students gather informally for singing and fellowship.

✦ SOCIAL ACTIVITIES. A retreat is held each semester with an emphasis on community building; Campus Ministry sponsors a variety of alcohol-free social activities.

✦ EDUCATION. Bible studies are offered regularly. A program entitled "Faculty Faith Stories" invites faculty members of different religious backgrounds to share their own faith journeys. Discussion groups are held frequently, focusing on issues such as sexuality, substance abuse, and eating disorders.

Through the Campus Ministry program, CLU furthers its mission to educate leaders for a global society who are strong in character and judgment, confident in their identity and vocation, and committed to service and justice.

CENTRAL METHODIST COLLEGE

411 CENTRAL METHODIST SQUARE
FAYETTE, MO 65248
660.248.3391
http://www.cmc.edu/

UNDERGRADUATES: 1,200

For program information, please contact:
SARA J. CHANEY
schaney@cmc.edu

"It is a good feeling to be able to worship God with teachers and other students. I am strengthened and able to face any obstacle that I might encounter."

—A CMC FIRST-YEAR STUDENT

Spiritual growth at Central Methodist College, a church-affiliated institution of liberal arts and vocational education, involves both curricular and cocurricular dimensions so that students develop a mature and responsible understanding of the integration of beliefs and actions, values and career choices.

Components of CMC's spiritual growth program include:

✦ CURRICULUM. The curriculum opens with the first-year seminar, the CMC Experience, which focuses on the values of the American democratic and Christian traditions. The senior capstone, Humanities 409, integrates the skills of critical thought, writing, speaking, a broad expanse of knowledge, and the application of values and ethics. Students work in teams, often providing service to the larger community. Courses in religion and philosophy are also required, and another core course, Wellness for Life, addresses students' physical, mental, and spiritual well-being.

✦ WORSHIP. Weekly chapel, organized by students who are mentored by the Director of the Wesley Foundation, offers a community worship experience. Students provide leadership in local churches as choir directors, student pastors, liturgists, and teachers. Student-led Bible studies, prayer, and covenant groups round out each week's activities.

✦ SPECIAL EVENTS. The annual Christian Perspectives Week highlights the spiritual dimension of character development through a variety of events, for instance a dramatic interpretation of Bonhoeffer or a powerful message delivered by Mayor Emanuel Cleaver of Kansas City, describing his spiritual motivation for civic responsibility.

Led by the president, faculty and staff are involved in every level of the spiritual growth program. Manifested in course work, service projects, and formal and informal worship, spiritual growth is an essential dimension of the character of Central Methodist College.

CHAPMAN UNIVERSITY

333 NORTH GLASSELL STREET
ORANGE, CA 92866
714.997.6815
http://www.chapman.edu/

UNDERGRADUATES: 2,600

For program information, please contact:
RONALD L. FARMER, Ph.D.
rfarmer@chapman.edu

The mission of Chapman University, a comprehensive, private institution, is to provide students with a personalized education of distinction that will lead them to ethical and productive lives as global citizens. The Ray and Pauline Wallace All Faiths Chapel plays a significant role in helping Chapman fulfill this mission. The chapel provides sacred space and stimulating programming to encourage people:

✦ To explore, discover, and deepen their spirituality;

✦ To develop an appreciation of spiritual diversity with a view to mutual enrichment;

✦ To integrate the spiritual and intellectual dimensions of life;

✦ To engage in ethical reflection and the discussion and development of values;

✦ To construct a vision of what they can contribute to the common good.

Periodically, the chapel brings to campus nationally known speakers from a variety of religious traditions and professions to give special, formal lectures. The chapel regularly draws upon the vast interdisciplinary resources of Chapman and the surrounding community to facilitate lectures, seminars, study groups, and discussion forums on spiritual and ethical topics. The chapel also assists students in becoming actively involved in the ethical issues of today by linking them with service opportunities on campus and in the wider community, especially in the areas of social justice and the environment.

A unique aspect of the program is the Interfaith Communications Team. Chaired by the Associated Students Director of Spiritual Programming and composed of representatives of the various campus religious organizations, this team meets regularly with the chapel staff to plan campus-wide events, coordinate schedules, and assess campus needs. Serving on this team is one of the many ways Chapman students are able to develop leadership and administrative skills while rendering a valuable service to the campus community.

COLLEGE OF THE SOUTHWEST

6610 LOVINGTON HIGHWAY
HOBBS, NM 88240
505.392.6561
http://www.csw.edu/

UNDERGRADUATES: 600

For program information, please contact:
SEAN PATTY
spatty@leaco.net

"The spiritual program at CSW has been a blessing to me. The L.I.F.E. program helps me to get through each week."

—A CSW FOURTH-YEAR STUDENT

The College of the Southwest, founded in 1962, is a private college with a religious affiliation. CSW provides students with encouragement and fellowship in a spiritually stimulating setting through its L.I.F.E. (Life's Insights For Excellence) program. L.I.F.E. is a one-hour credit or non-credit class that meets once each week. The class may be taken three times in place of one three-hour religious requirement. The program is open to all CSW students, staff, and faculty.

The L.I.F.E. program promotes spiritual development in a number of ways:

✦ Each L.I.F.E. class is opened with prayer requests for students, friends, struggles, thanksgivings, faculty members, and world events.

✦ By the very nature of the L.I.F.E. program, students are encouraged to seek the word of God for answers to everyday problems and opportunities. Approximately 15 speakers a semester from a variety of denominations deliver short lessons that address issues related to young people. Students take notes of each speaker and write a one-page reaction paper expressing their thoughts about the presentation. These papers often become expressions of the spiritual journeys many students engage in throughout the semester.

✦ Each week, CSW faculty and staff join L.I.F.E. students simply for their own edification. In addition, each semester two faculty or administration members speak to students on spiritual issues.

In just the past two years, the L.I.F.E. program has grown from forty to sixty participants, including traditional and non-traditional students and representatives from each academic-year class who are all deepening their spiritual lives as part of their total educational experience at the College of the Southwest.

COLUMBIA COLLEGE

1301 COLUMBIA COLLEGE DRIVE
COLUMBIA, SC 29203
800.277.1301
http://www.colacoll.edu/

UNDERGRADUATES: 1,200

For program information, please contact:
CATHY JAMIESON-OGG
cjamiesonogg@colacoll.edu

"Columbia's spiritual growth program has encouraged me to develop into a leader, helping me learn to share God's love with surrounding communities."

—A COLUMBIA FOURTH-YEAR STUDENT

Columbia College, a women's college affiliated with the United Methodist Church, provides a liberal arts education in which spiritual and ethical values are integrated with leadership development. Beginning with new-student orientation, faculty and staff clarify expectations for personal responsibility and integrity. In class, faculty emphasize moral, ethical, and religious values, a designated goal of the General Education curriculum, and the chaplain and Student Affairs staff integrate values into extracurricular activities. Examples of other specific programs include:

✦ **HESED HOUSE.** An endowed program that promotes peace and human rights through Holocaust studies, workshops on discrimination, lectures, and cultural events.

✦ **DEVOTION GUIDE.** Faculty, staff, and students contribute to a Devotion Guide, which applies faith to everyday life.

✦ **SOUL FOOD.** A faculty member leads a morning devotion and discussion of a biblical text.

✦ **CITY AS TEXT.** An orientation program for honors students introduces them to the community; students take a religious diversity tour, visiting a Jewish synagogue, a Hindu temple, and a selection of Christian churches.

✦ **CLUBHOUSE GANG.** Students run an after-school ministry for needy children, providing spiritual, academic, and personal development.

✦ **CHAPEL.** Students take active roles in the weekly worship service, leading with music, drama, and liturgy. A Student Preachers Series allows students to plan a service and preach a sermon, providing positive peer role models for fellow students.

Through this comprehensive approach, Columbia College develops faith-centered leaders who pursue a lifelong journey of responsible citizenship.

CULVER–STOCKTON COLLEGE

ONE COLLEGE HILL
CANTON, MO 63435
217.231.6000
http://www.culver.edu/

UNDERGRADUATES: 900

For program information, please contact:
STEVEN MONHOLLEN, Ph.D.
smonhollen@culver.edu

At Culver–Stockton College, a church-affiliated, liberal arts institution, the spiritual growth program provides the traditional elements of ministry (welcome, worship, solitude, study, service, counseling, and fellowship) as well as the integration of spiritual development into the core curriculum.

Spiritual growth at Culver–Stockton is nurtured through a variety of means:

✦ Students expand their understanding of the world and dispel stereotypes through service trips during which they encounter people of other races and socioeconomic classes.

✦ Students explore their civic responsibilities by connecting their studies to society's needs. One student, for instance, shaped her Senior Honors project to examine U.S. immigration policy after working with the children of illegal immigrants.

✦ Students learn empathy through exposure to other cultures, religions, and races. One example is the annual Interfaith Thanksgiving Assembly, in which college and community representatives of various religions express thankfulness in their own traditions.

✦ The Character and Values Education Series prompts discussion of today's moral issues.

✦ Spiritual issues are incorporated into the core curriculum. A popular ethics course in general education, for example, poses the question for the first response paper: "Who am I and what is my obligation to the world?"

Mentoring faculty, compassionate staff, the counselor, the student development team, the chaplain's office, and caring students all collaborate to create an environment at Culver–Stockton that nurtures students' spiritual growth and embodies the founders' legacy of learning through dialog as a means of meeting the broader world.

DALLAS BAPTIST UNIVERSITY

3000 MOUNTAIN CREEK PARKWAY
DALLAS, TX 75211
800.460.1DBU
http://www.dbu.edu/

UNDERGRADUATES: 2,900

For program information, please contact:
JOHN PLOTTS, Ph.D.
plotts@dbu.edu

Developing committed servant leaders is the fundamental focus of the education programs at Dallas Baptist University, a private, liberal arts institution. Part of the spiritual growth program at DBU includes a very special Spiritual Rush Weekend. The purpose of the weekend's activities is to integrate new DBU students into the life and culture of the University, cultivating a sense of community among faculty, staff, and students. Each year, Spiritual Rush Weekend has a theme related to personal virtue. Past themes have included integrity, spiritual gifts, fruits of the spirit, servant leadership, and truth. After an evening and morning of content discussion, Saturday afternoon is spent practicing the virtue(s) discussed early in the weekend through "random acts of kindness" conducted in the neighborhoods of the faculty and/or staff-member homes where the students are spending the weekend.

During Spiritual Rush Weekend, students learn:

✦ To decompartmentalize their lives by integrating academic learning and service action;

✦ To build a purposeful foundation for altruistic activity;

✦ To understand faculty and staff to be colaborers in the academic and civic community;

✦ To develop an appreciation for the significance of their roles in helping others.

Spiritual Rush Weekend provides a living introduction to the purpose and mission of DBU. The weekend highlights the Christian faith and explains the core of human purpose in this world. In addition, it offers students an opportunity to respond to the Scripture, "Faith without works is dead" (James 3:17), by expressing their faith through works in ways that mesh totally with the development of civic and personal responsibility.

DARTMOUTH COLLEGE

6001 PARKHURST HALL
HANOVER, NH 03755
603.646.1110
http://www.dartmouth.edu/

UNDERGRADUATES: 4,300

For program information, please contact:
GWENDOLYN KING
Gwendolyn.King@mac.dartmouth.edu

Spiritual exploration, guidance, and expression at Dartmouth College, a private, Ivy League institution, are largely coordinated through The Tucker Foundation, which was charged in 1951 to promote the "moral and spiritual work and influence of the College." The Tucker Foundation supports the Dartmouth Chaplaincy, which facilitates the activities of 19 student religious organizations representing a broad spectrum of faith perspectives.

Programs supported through the Dartmouth College Chaplaincy include:

✦ **ROLLINS CHAPEL.** The chapel serves as a locus for ecumenical, interdenominational, interfaith, and interreligious worship and for celebrations and community gatherings. The Chaplaincy collaborates with the Tucker Foundation and with other departments on campus to sponsor concerts, lectures, film discussions, workshops, retreats, and other events.

✦ **ROTH CENTER FOR JEWISH LIFE.** Partly through the college's facilitation, the Upper Valley Jewish Community has become large enough and integrated enough with campus life to inspire the building of the new center, which serves both the college and the surrounding community with a rich program of observance, study, speakers, and student and community special projects.

✦ **THE AQUINAS HOUSE** (AQ) at Dartmouth College, which includes a community center and chapel, has served Catholic students at Dartmouth since 1961 and offers an extensive program of worship, community service, and speakers. The local Lutheran, Episcopal, and United Church of Christ churches also have student centers that provide comfortable spaces for discussion, worship, and fellowship.

In addition to providing pastoral care for all students in need of comfort or who seek spiritual meaning, the Dartmouth Chaplaincy holds up the peaceful coexistence of the school's rich diversity of religious traditions as a much-needed model to the larger world.

Franciscan University of Steubenville

1235 UNIVERSITY BOULEVARD
STEUBENVILLE, OH 43952
740.283.3771
http://www.franuniv.edu/

UNDERGRADUATES: 1,600

For program information, please contact:
CATHY HECK
check@franuniv.edu

At Franciscan University of Steubenville, a church-affiliated, liberal arts institution, two programs—Households and Chapel Ministry—form the nucleus of campus life and have become catalysts for spiritual growth. Twenty-five years ago, scores of students told incoming President Father Michael Scanlan that they had few friends on campus, and he saw that the isolation of college life led many to resort to promiscuity, alcohol and drug abuse, and other destructive behavior. In response, he established faith households, and a chapel ministry was begun.

✦ Households are patterned after the early Christian communities. Small groups of 5 to 25 students support and pray with one another. The members draw up a covenant stating their spiritual goals and moral code. They gather for weekly Lord's Day Celebrations to recall and thank God for the blessings of the prior week; they take part in retreats, sports, social events, and volunteer work. When household members falter in faith or conduct, other members call them into accountability with supportive and compassionate peer pressure. Currently, more than 600 students (42% of undergraduates) belong to 45 households, which adopt names such as Fire of Love, Bride of Christ, Living Stones, and Little Flowers.

✦ Chapel Ministry likewise infuses Franciscan University with a vigorous spiritual life. The numbers tell much of the story: In 1998, more than 700 students attended daily Mass, 300 signed up for a weekly time slot for eucharistic adoration, and more than 350 served as lectors, musicians, and ushers.

Households and Chapel Ministry are two highly effective ways that Franciscan University fulfills its mission of nurturing the moral, spiritual, and religious values of the students, generations of whom have hailed the programs as "life transforming."

Gordon College

255 GRAPEVINE ROAD
WENHAM, MA 01984
978.927.2300
http://www.gordon.edu/

UNDERGRADUATES: 1,500

For program information, please contact:
RICK SWEENEY
rsweeney@hope.gordon.edu

"Through La Vida I've learned that what's around me every day in my life is not necessarily what I need. When all the fluff is eliminated, you confront your character."
—A GORDON FOURTH-YEAR STUDENT

Dangling from a cliff 40 feet off the ground might not be a typical concept of spiritual growth, but the premise of the La Vida program at Gordon College, a Christian liberal arts school, is that a structured wilderness adventure is the perfect crucible for fostering integrity. Throughout history, God has used the wilderness to reveal Himself to men and women and as a means for them to develop their gifts, character, and leadership skills and to prepare for future service.

Phases of the La Vida program are:

✦ TRAINING. The program begins with group initiative/team-building games and an extensive ropes course. Each expedition also includes training in minimum-impact camping skills, rock climbing, rappelling, and backpacking or canoeing.

✦ GROUP EXPEDITION. Each patrol plans and executes a short expedition apart from their La Vida instructor. During this phase, students test their leadership skills, discover the importance of working together, and enjoy the satisfaction of completing a rewarding group challenge.

✦ SOLO. Each group member is assigned a small plot of land along a stream on which to build an individual shelter for the solo experience. During this two-day period, students have a chance to think, pray, read the Bible, write in a journal, and plan future goals.

✦ CELEBRATION AND DEBRIEFING. Students are presented additional challenges and surprises and are then given the opportunity to think over their La Vida experiences and to reflect on and share their personal growth.

Through all four phases of the La Vida program, students translate beliefs into action, plumb the depths of character, and unlock their physical, mental, and spiritual potential. For many students, La Vida becomes the highlight of their Gordon College experience.

GUILFORD COLLEGE

5800 W. FRIENDLY AVENUE
GREENSBORO, NC 27410
336.316.2000
http://www.guilford.edu/

UNDERGRADUATES: 1,100

For program information, please contact:
DEBORAH L. SHAW
dshaw@guilford.edu

"What a divine experience to be connected with this group for four years! I praise God for the immense love in the Quaker Leadership Scholars Program."

—A GUILFORD FOURTH-YEAR STUDENT

Guilford College is an independent liberal arts college founded in 1837 by the Religious Society of Friends—Quakers. Its approach to education is shaped by the values espoused by its founders, including respect for individuals, the centrality of community, the importance of work that benefits society in tangible ways, and governance by consensus. The Quaker Leadership Scholars Program (QLSP), a selective scholarship program developed by Max L. Carter, Director of Friends Center at Guilford College, is dedicated to enriching the educational experience of committed Quaker students and fellow travelers by providing opportunities for spiritual growth and social activism. Within the program, students are encouraged:

✦ To develop leadership skills through practice;

✦ To engage in intense spiritual growth and exploration;

✦ To intensify their commitment to social awareness and social change.

Through academic courses, small-group discussions, worship, mentoring, internships, conferences, retreats, work trips, travel, and exposure to Quaker visitors to campus, participants in QLSP have the opportunity to develop their own spiritual lives while preparing to be of service to Friends and society at large. Most of the resources and opportunities of QLSP are available campus-wide.

Active involvement in Guilford College's Quaker Leadership Scholars Program not only fosters individual spiritual growth but also prepares students for significant contributions in work for peace, advocacy, and service agencies. As graduates enter the work force and apply Quaker principles in the field of business, industry, education, and other professions, the lasting effects of the program are felt far beyond the campus.

HOPE COLLEGE

PO BOX 9000
HOLLAND, MI 49422-9000
616.395.7000
http://www.hope.edu/

UNDERGRADUATES: 2,900

For program information, please contact:
BEN PATTERSON
Patterson@hope.edu

Hope College, founded in 1862, is a church-affiliated, liberal arts institution. The purpose of the College's Chapel program is to draw students, faculty, and staff to public worship, to present the Gospel in a compelling manner, to encourage a sincere profession of faith, to promote biblical and doctrinal literacy, and to further equip professing Christians to live faithful lives.

Highlights of Hope College's Chapel program include:

✦ **STUDENT WORSHIP.** Through worship services, students establish a foundation for their faith. Small-group Bible studies led by peers help students to build friendships based on Christ and learn to live out their convictions in everyday life.

✦ **GOSPEL CHOIR.** The choir currently has more than 150 students involved, worshipping God in chapel as well as in churches throughout the community.

✦ **VOLUNTEER SERVICE.** In mission trips during spring break, students express their faith in tangible ways by helping the needy throughout the United States and abroad. In the local community, students have committed to service in 20 different agencies/ministries.

✦ **LEADERSHIP TRAINING.** The Chapel program offers a course called "Perspectives" for students who are interested in pursuing missions as a career.

✦ **SUMMER OF SERVICE.** Every summer, students can enroll in Summer of Service, an eight-week intensive discipleship training program. Students learn how to study the Bible; they develop biblical convictions through formal teaching each morning and offer service to various community agencies every afternoon. On weekends, they lead worship in local churches through music, drama, testimonies, and sacred dance.

Through worship, small-group Bible studies, service opportunities, and leadership development, Hope College's Chapel program prepares students to grapple with real issues of faith and to embrace a lifelong pursuit of faithful Christian living.

Lincoln Christian College

100 CAMPUS VIEW DRIVE
LINCOLN, IL 62656-2111
http://www.lccs.edu/

UNDERGRADUATES: 500

For program information, please contact:
J.K. JONES, JR.
jkjones@lccs.edu

Lincoln Christian College, a private institution with a religious affiliation, is deeply committed to producing leaders for the 21st century. Civic and personal responsibility are at the very core of the school's mentoring-based education. Accordingly, LCC's approaches to education include formal mentoring in the classroom, a required 12-hour internship, various Christian service projects, and an intentional, required Spiritual Formation Program.

Highlights of the Spiritual Formation Program:

✦ LCC has committed its entire faculty, a significant portion of its staff, and has recruited several community leaders to assist in mentoring students toward Christian leadership around the world.

✦ During a typical semester, approximately 70 groups of five to eight members meet weekly for an hour seeking to create a place of accountability, confidentiality, thankfulness, and stimulation. Each group serves as an extra set of ears and eyes in order to help and encourage love of God and love of neighbor.

✦ Special emphasis is placed on helping first-year students understand and experience the urgency of maturing as leaders.

✦ A selected group of 25 to 30 upperclassmen assist in mentoring the first-year spiritual formation groups.

Spontaneous prayer and accountability groups have sprung up alongside this required program with a focus toward more involvement in the broader Lincoln community. Through its Spiritual Formation Program, LCC has intentionally sought to create a positive environment in which students can learn to balance personal integrity with responsibility for community charity.

Mary Baldwin College

PO BOX 1500
STAUNTON, VA 24401
540.887.7000
http://www.mbc.edu/

UNDERGRADUATES: 1,300

For program information, please contact:
PAT HUNT
phunt@mbc.edu

Many religious traditions, including Presbyterian, Roman Catholic, Baptist, Jewish, Muslim, and Buddhist, are represented at Mary Baldwin College, a church-affiliated, liberal arts college for women. The unique Quest program, begun in 1996 to help students integrate religious commitment, intellectual development, and service, deliberately honors each student's religious experience, faith tradition, and personal values. Concurrent with the college's regular baccalaureate program, Quest entails two years of spiritual direction, academics, and enrichment activities that support students' efforts to make sense of life, learning, and faith. Students have lively discussions that prompt new insights into others' backgrounds and points of view, giving them the opportunity to deepen and explore their own faith.

Quest students are required to:

✦ Complete the course "Faith, Life, and Service," plus three other listed elective courses;

✦ Complete 100 hours of supervised community service;

✦ Work with a mentor who fosters spiritual development;

✦ Participate in a worshipping community of their choice;

✦ Attend two meetings each month, one of which features a guest speaker who discusses issues and life choices;

✦ Meet individually with the program director.

After successfully completing the requirements, Quest students are inducted into the Carpenter Society, an advisory board to the program that also provides mentors for other students.

Quest provides opportunities for Mary Baldwin students to explore their personal beliefs and the beliefs of others by combining spiritual exploration and scholarly insight. Quest students are learning to understand themselves as well as others. They are not changing the whole world, but they are changing their corner of the world—a very important beginning.

MOUNT MARY COLLEGE

2900 NORTH MENOMONEE RIVER PARKWAY
MILWAUKEE, WI 53222
414.258.4810
http://www.mtmary.edu/

UNDERGRADUATES: 1,200

For program information, please contact:
JOAN PENZENSTADLER, Ph.D.
penzenj@mtmary.edu

"Mount Mary is deeply committed to spiritual development. Mind and spirit are both challenged to grow; virtue and intelligence equally sought."

—A MOUNT MARY GRADUATE

Mount Mary College is a Catholic women's college sponsored by the School Sisters of Notre Dame. Instituted nearly 30 years ago, the core curriculum at Mount Mary seeks to equip all students with the knowledge, skills, and values necessary to conduct a personal, ongoing search for meaning. Within this core is the "Synoptics Realm," interdisciplinary courses taught by the Department of Theology and Philosophy in which students explore major questions of human existence and potential. Within this Realm, the Search for Meaning program is offered—the only course required of every Mount Mary graduate.

Team-taught by a philosopher and a theologian, the Search for Meaning program:

✦ Extends from classical to contemporary texts;

✦ Empowers students to reflect personally on such issues as the sources of human happiness, the role of conscience in personal integrity, the meaning of suffering and death, and the transcendent dimension of reality;

✦ Incorporates small-group discussions and analyses of the lives and writings of moral heroes and heroines, including Socrates, Thomas More, Dorothy Day, and Viktor Frankl.

Several years ago, the college invited Viktor Frankl to be honored with a Doctor of Humane Letters degree and to speak to its student body. Frankl accepted the invitation, pleased that the college's curriculum seeks to address the same fundamental question as his seminal work, *Man's Search for Meaning.* Internal, institutional recognition of the importance of the Search for Meaning program is consistent with the endorsement it receives from the external community. Mount Mary students realize that they are being given resources to contend with an issue that will surface again and again in their lives.

MUHLENBERG COLLEGE

2400 CHEW STREET
ALLENTOWN, PA 18104-5586
610.821.3125
http://www.muhlenberg.edu/

UNDERGRADUATES: 1,900

For program information, please contact:
PETER PETTIT, Ph.D.
pepettit@muhlenberg.edu

Muhlenberg College, a private, church-affiliated, liberal arts institution, established the Institute for Jewish-Christian Understanding to foster research and dialog to build bridges of understanding between the two faith traditions. The term "understanding" as used in the name of the Institute includes both interpersonal and intellectual dimensions.

The Institute fosters understanding in a variety of ways:

✦ Chartered to work both on campus and in the community, the Institute provides programs for Muhlenberg students, as well as local high- and middle-school students, to learn about and discuss issues related to the Holocaust, anti-Semitism, and racism.

✦ Programs sponsored by the Institute provide an opportunity for students to meet with Holocaust survivors and to consider how issues related to the Holocaust can shed light on the moral decisions that must be made in today's world.

✦ A student advisory committee to the Institute helps plan events aimed at college students, such as a recent program entitled, "Why do Jews and Christians do what they do?"

✦ The Institute works closely with Muhlenberg's Campus Ministry, which includes Jewish, Protestant, and Roman Catholic student organizations.

✦ The Institute sponsors small discussion groups called "Living Room Dialogues" to allow for informal discussions among Jewish and Christian students.

The Institute for Jewish-Christian Understanding provides Muhlenberg and the community with a wide range of programs; for many students, this is the first opportunity they have had to talk with people from other faith traditions. The programs provide a forum in which difficult questions can be asked and age-old problems can be examined in a safe environment, allowing the students to mature in their understanding of others and in their readiness to be world citizens.

OHIO WESLEYAN UNIVERSITY

61 SOUTH SANDUSKY STREET
DELAWARE, OH 43015
740.368.2000
http://www.owu.edu/

UNDERGRADUATES: 1,900

For program information, please contact:
JON R. POWERS
jrpowers@cc.owu.edu

Ohio Wesleyan University, a private, United Methodist–related, liberal arts institution, has been nationally recognized for the depth and diversity of its spiritual growth program, which consists of 60 groups and projects. Curricular and cocurricular, most of the groups and projects are integrated with community service learning, in which 85% of the students participate voluntarily.

Highlights of Ohio Wesleyan's program include:

✦ **COMMON TEXTS.** Jewish, Christian, and Muslim students study together to learn about one another's faith practices, theological concepts, and ethics.

✦ **SOUL MATTERS.** This interfaith news journal sparks thoughtful dialog between liberal and conservative faith communities on campus, providing a means for building religious tolerance.

✦ **SPRING BREAK MISSION WEEK.** Yearlong interdisciplinary seminars on cross-cultural awareness, service ethics, and practical skills prepare students and faculty for spring break workcamp assignments in North and Central America.

✦ **BACCALAUREATE.** A senior-year capstone seminar culminates in an interfaith worship service celebrating the spiritual journey and growth of the graduates.

✦ **INSTITUTIONAL HONORS.** Trustee-sponsored awards recognize students who promote peace and justice, interfaith and intercultural awareness, humanitarian efforts, and Christian mission.

Through early morning nature walks and prayer chapels, midday leadership lunches, afternoon community service projects, and late-night concerts, lectures, or Bible studies, Ohio Wesleyan promotes spiritual growth through an intentional cross-weaving of the classroom with community and culture. As University Chaplain Jon Powers writes, "Students do not park their faith at the classroom door, nor do they park their minds at the Chapel door. Here, indeed, is a place where knowledge and piety are wed."

ST. OLAF COLLEGE

1520 ST. OLAF AVENUE
NORTHFIELD, MN 55057
507.646.2222
http://www.stolaf.edu/

UNDERGRADUATES: 2,900

For program information, please contact:
BRUCE BENSON
bensonb@stolaf.edu

"Those who are part of the Student Congregation know the peace inherent in communal song and the Lord's Supper."

—A ST. OLAF THIRD-YEAR STUDENT

St. Olaf College, a private, liberal arts institution affiliated with the Evangelical Lutheran Church of America (ELCA), is home to a church congregation fully recognized by the ELCA and run entirely by the students. The St. Olaf College Student Congregation functions like any other congregation, with a church council, various committees, a vital worship life, and outreach efforts. Students plan and organize all of the Congregation's work and its community emphases.

Examples of programs supported by the Student Congregation include:

✦ Every weekday and Sunday morning, Scripture readings by students call the community to mercy, justice, and forgiveness. Students also lead in prayer and in the singing of hymns.

✦ The Congregation Council promises 90% of its budget to be given for charitable work. Recently, the Congregation has supported schools, churches, missions, and disaster-response groups in such locales as Bosnia, Asia, and Nicaragua. It also donates funds to support the work of other St. Olaf College student organizations.

✦ The Student Congregation promotes personal responsibility and health through its Care Ministry program, a peer counseling resource available to all students.

These few examples represent the larger emphasis of the St. Olaf College Student Congregation: that learning, working, and general living is done not alone but in the context of a community created and given by God. The St. Olaf College Student Congregation helps students hear Christ's call to faith and justice for their own lives and for the relationships they encounter as they live in the world.

SEATTLE PACIFIC UNIVERSITY

3307 THIRD AVENUE WEST
SEATTLE, WA 98119
206.281.2000
http://www.spu.edu/

UNDERGRADUATES: 2,600

For program information, please contact:
TIM DEARBORN, Ph.D.
tdearborn@spu.edu

Spiritual growth is integral to the mission of Seattle Pacific University, a private, church-affiliated institution. In keeping with its Wesleyan tradition, SPU aspires to encourage "faithful learning," as well as disciplinary rigor. Students are taught by professors who are experts in their fields *and* committed Christians.

The hallmarks of spiritual formation at SPU are rich and varied:

✦ Regular, student-led chapels and community religious events target the developmental levels of different groups of students.

✦ Student ministry coordinators provide frequent opportunities in residence halls for spiritual discussion and practice.

✦ The presence of a Department of Religion, dean of the chapel, and required courses in spiritual formation and biblical studies establish the preeminence of faith in building lives of character.

✦ Students are challenged by expectations of personal conduct that call them to a higher standard.

✦ SPU's general education core, called the Common Curriculum, is built around themes of love of God, love of neighbor, and love of the world.

The manifestations of spiritual development on the SPU campus are many. Participation in corporate worship, biblical study, and service leadership is high. SPU students volunteer more than 21,000 hours per year to help social service, Christian missions, and community agencies throughout Seattle. Ongoing student-led mission teams travel to impoverished areas of the U.S. and the world to bring spiritual hope and physical relief. SPU's efforts in spiritual formation are many, and they remain at the heart of the University's century-long educational heritage.

SOUTHWESTERN COLLEGE

100 COLLEGE STREET
WINFIELD, KS 67156-2499
316.221.8236
http://www.sckans.edu/

UNDERGRADUATES: 1,000

For program information, please contact:
STEVE RANKIN, Ph.D.
srankin@jinx.sckans.edu

"Our Bible study has taught me a lot about how to be a Christian leader. Through our team experiences, I've started to see how big God is."
—A SOUTHWESTERN FIRST-YEAR STUDENT

Southwestern College in Kansas, a private, church-affiliated institution, offers students the challenge of integrating their Christian faith and their career plans through its Discipleship Southwestern program. Students commit themselves to the spiritual disciplines of Bible reading, prayer, and worship. They gain a vision of the world through the presence of international students and by taking at least one service/education trip outside the United States. Every student in the program also serves in a volunteer capacity, either in a local church or on campus. These experiences are capped in their senior year in a service or ministry project that they design and implement.

Components of Discipleship Southwestern are:

✦ YEAR ONE. DISCIPLE I: Local church participation, weekly service activity, health and fitness plan.

✦ YEAR TWO. DISCIPLE II: Leadership class, local church participation, weekly service activity, health and fitness plan.

✦ SUMMER FOLLOWING YEAR TWO: Students receive assistance in setting up summer ministry.

✦ YEAR THREE. DISCIPLE III: Community-service class, community-service project, mission trip, local church participation, leadership role in the Campus Council on Ministry or in a local church, health and fitness plan.

✦ SUMMER FOLLOWING YEAR THREE: Cross-cultural ministry/service experience.

✦ YEAR FOUR. DISCIPLE IV: Senior internship (students choose the location and kind of experience), local church participation, health and fitness plan.

Discipleship Southwestern is aimed primarily at helping participants gain a sense of vocation about their adult lives—lives given in service to God and to neighbor.

STERLING COLLEGE

125 WEST COOPER
PO BOX 98
STERLING, KS 67579
316.278.2173
http://web.stercolks.edu/

UNDERGRADUATES: 500

For program information, please contact:
STEVEN M. MARSH, Ph.D.
smarsh@acc.stercolks.edu

Sterling College is a private, liberal arts institution whose mission is to develop creative and thoughtful leaders with a maturing Christian faith. To that end, education at Sterling is about spiritual formation, a formation of mind, heart, and spirit.

Spiritual formation programs at Sterling include different facets of spiritual growth:

✦ Chapel Ministry is focused on the process of spiritual formation and the desire to initiate and feed a life of discipleship with Jesus Christ. Three weekly chapel services are available, on Tuesday and Wednesday morning and on Sunday evening, which allow the entire campus community to participate in a variety of worship experiences.

✦ Outreach by student-organized mission teams is encouraged. Faculty and staff members aid interested students in preparing to present the Gospel of Jesus Christ in a variety of ways both within and outside the campus setting.

✦ Student Ministry Teams offer various opportunities for involvement and personal growth. Believing that students need to be challenged to think about and act upon their faith, these five student-led teams encourage spiritual growth and maturity. Their goal is discipleship, motivated by a desire to become mature men and women of God.

Weekly Chapel opportunities, residence-hall discussions, campus forums, ministry training sessions, Convocation lectures, the Good Samaritan Counseling Center, and a special orientation for first-year students all work to foster students' spiritual formation. It is the goal of the Department of Chapel and Spiritual Formation at Sterling College that every graduate understand the character of Jesus Christ and aspire to it in every aspect of life.

STONEHILL COLLEGE

320 WASHINGTON STREET
EASTON, MA 02357
508.565.1000
http://www.stonehill.edu/

UNDERGRADUATES: 2,700

For program information, please contact:
DANIEL J. ISSING
dissing@stonehill.edu

Campus Ministry at Stonehill College, a church-affiliated institution, supports the discovery of a student's deepest longing and educates about the ways of fidelity, justice, and compassion. The fundamental task of Campus Ministry is "to provide an experience of church that enables members of the college community to grasp anew the Gospel of Jesus Christ and to gain a religious and moral competence to live as women and men of peace in a global community, with the personal courage to confront injustice, violence, and inequity, wherever it exists." This mission is accomplished through:

✦ An active chapel program that includes daily Mass and involves about 120 students in various liturgical ministries.

✦ An extensive retreat program that includes three different kinds of experiences and involves about 200 students each year.

✦ A developing community-service leadership program that works toward the betterment of the neighborhood.

✦ An exciting alternative spring break experience that includes four separate sites and involves nearly 80 students.

✦ A college-wide orientation for first-year students that includes full participation in service projects, with faculty, on the day before classes begin, and a presentation on the meaning of the college's mission, "light and hope," in student life.

✦ A residence-hall chaplains program that facilitates spiritual development in each residence area. This includes regular meetings with hall staff and the Campus Ministry team.

Stonehill's Campus Ministry department is committed to working side by side with students in the planning, preparation, and implementation of each program. Campus Ministry educates in the Holy Cross tradition and summons students to live from a deep place within, to speak for what they know to be true in their hearts, and to respond generously to the needs they see around them.

Taylor University

236 WEST READE AVENUE
UPLAND, IN 46989
765.998.5201
http://www.tayloru.edu/

UNDERGRADUATES: 2,200

For program information, please contact:
MARY RAYBURN
mrrayburn@tayloru.edu

Taylor University is an interdenominational evangelical Christian institution educating men and women for lifelong learning and for ministering the redemptive love of Jesus Christ to a world in need. The discipleship program at Taylor is one means of challenging students to fulfill this mission. The student discipleship coordinator selected on each residence wing encourages and guides small groups committed to Bible study, burden-bearing/sharing fellowship, mutual prayer, and outreach projects. Students are encouraged to take individual responsibility for the support and well-being of fellow group members and are challenged to respond to the needs of the world around them.

In addition to small-group ministry, discipleship coordinators also provide other ways for students to deepen their spiritual lives:

✦ Wing spiritual retreats contribute to the development of community within the living unit, demonstrating the importance of intentional, transparent relationships.

✦ Prayer meetings for specifically identified missionaries and countries reinforce each individual's responsibility for involvement with global issues.

✦ Fund drives in response to individual student needs, such as financial inability to cover medical costs, or in response to global tragedies and natural disasters, remind students of their ability to have an impact on a life, a family, or even a country.

The discipleship program works in tandem with the chapel, which meets each Monday, Wednesday, and Friday, and sponsors a spring and a fall spiritual emphasis week, a cross-cultural missions emphasis week, and a relational enrichment week. In addition, faculty mentoring relationships, leadership development classes, and the residence-life program lend themselves to the development of Christian character at Taylor—a function not only of the discipleship and chapel programs but of the entire institution.

Texas Christian University

2800 SOUTH UNIVERSITY DRIVE
FORT WORTH, TX 76129
817.257.7000
http://www.tcu.edu/

UNDERGRADUATES: 7,200

For program information, please contact:
JOHN BUTLER
j.butler@tcu.edu

"From the time I became a TCU student, I have had countless experiences that have enriched my faith and broadened my horizons."

—A TCU FOURTH-YEAR STUDENT

Programs and experiences with a spiritual dimension are found throughout the life of Texas Christian University, a private, church-affiliated institution. TCU programs with a primary spiritual focus include:

✦ UNITING CAMPUS MINISTRIES. This student-led organization is made up of representatives from denominations committed to ecumenism. Task forces focus on the areas of worship, faith education, social justice, and witness.

✦ DENOMINATIONAL FELLOWSHIPS. A dozen different weekly fellowships emphasize student leadership and personal responsibility.

✦ JEWISH AND MUSLIM ASSOCIATIONS. These associations provide opportunities for Jewish and Muslim students to continue the expression of their faith while at TCU.

✦ WORDWISE BIBLE STUDY. This student-led Bible study series is built upon an appreciation for biblical scholarship and respect for the faith commitments of all participants

✦ CHRISTIAN HEALTH DELIVERY ORGANIZATION. Student-led, this organization addresses matters of faith for students preparing for careers in nursing, medicine, and dentistry.

✦ CHRISTIAN FRATERNITY AND SORORITY. Beta Upsilon Chi and Eta Iota Sigma provide a Christian context for social interactions for more than 200 men and women of faith.

✦ COLLABORATIVE ADVISORY BOARD. Residence assistants develop programs in residence halls on the wellness of the mind, body, and spirit. The leadership program in Student Development Services and in Fraternity and Sorority Affairs also develop programs with a spiritual dimension.

TCU students involved in many segments of the campus find they are repeatedly challenged to recognize the faith and values that form an individual and community identity.

UNION UNIVERSITY

1050 UNION UNIVERSITY DRIVE
JACKSON, TN 38305
901.668.1818
http://www.uu.edu/

UNDERGRADUATES: 2,100

For program information, please contact:
TODD BRADY
tbrady@uu.edu

"LIFE Groups afforded me the opportunity to examine my personal relationship with God."

—A UNION GRADUATE

The LIFE Group program at Union University, a private, church-affiliated institution, offers a place for all new students to belong and feel accepted, regardless of where they stand in their spiritual journey. While many who come to Union profess a faith commitment, some do not. The LIFE Group, which fosters "life-sharing," character building, and sincerity, is a place to be honest about the Christian life.

Common understandings that shape Union University's LIFE Group program include:

✦ Adjustment to college is sometimes difficult. To walk through this transition with others who are at the same point in the journey makes the process much easier.

✦ College students want someone with whom they can be genuine—no facades or false pretenses. The LIFE Group is a place where students can be real with themselves, real with others, and real with God.

✦ Spiritual disciplines are necessary to spiritual growth. LIFE Groups offer encouragement, motivation, and needed accountability in the areas of personal spiritual growth. Relationships within the group are strengthened as students work together to make a difference in the local community.

Upperclassmen serve as LIFE leaders who guide their groups through a 10-week study based on the book *Who You Are When No One's Looking,* by Bill Hybels. Groups participate in biblically based conversations about character, courage, discipline, vision, endurance, love, and the character of Christ; they are challenged to integrate these characteristics into every aspect of their lives. Students come to understand that these character traits are fundamental to their spiritual growth and essential to their personal success.

UNITED STATES AIR FORCE ACADEMY

2348 SIJAN DRIVE, SUITE 100
USAF ACADEMY, CO 80840-8280
719.333.4904
http://www.usafa.af.mil/

UNDERGRADUATES: 4,100

For program information, please contact:
HENRY B. WILBOURNE
wilbournehb.hc@usafa.af.mil

"The person I have become at the Academy can be directly attributed to the wonderful opportunities that the Chapel Program has provided me."

—A USAFA FIRST-YEAR CADET

Those who succeed in the Air Force are those who have faced who they are and the causes to which they are committed—possibly to the point of sacrificing their lives. Accordingly, the United States Air Force Academy offers its future officers many opportunities for personal growth and development. The Cadet Chapel supports the Center for Character Development through various initiatives:

✦ CORE VALUES AND COMBAT-SURVIVAL TRAINING. During Basic Cadet Training, cadets attend sessions on core values, such as: "Integrity First," "Service Before Self," and "Excellence in All We Do." Learning is not about just which values to embrace but how to personally integrate them. Second-year training builds on these values to increase the will to survive through spiritual, personal, and group resources.

✦ SPIRE (Special Programs in Religious Education). Voluntary sessions involving cadets, mentors, and leaders develop spirituality with help from para-church ministries and faith groups.

✦ ACES (Academy Character Enrichment Seminars). All staff and faculty participate in this seminar, which contains a section on spirituality and religion.

✦ CADET SUPPORT. Other Chapel-sponsored programs include opportunities for faith-specific and ecumenical worship, fellowship, religious education, prayer groups, retreats, choirs, seminars, study groups, counseling, and support groups. The new Cadet Chapel Student Center is available for reflection, dialog, and study.

USAFA is committed to forming leaders who inspire—perhaps their most critical attribute—and works diligently to ensure that all cadets have the resources they need to develop spiritually as they pursue their military careers.

UNIVERSITY OF PORTLAND

5000 NORTH WILLAMETTE BOULEVARD
PORTLAND, OR 97203-5798
503.283.7202
http://www.uofport.edu/

UNDERGRADUATES: 2,200

For program information, please contact:
BRIAN DOYLE
bdoyle@up.edu

Since its inception in 1901, the University of Portland has been convinced that personal spiritual exploration and growth are essential aspects of a true education. Catholic from its founding, the university seeks out students of all faiths in order to provide learning opportunities that might stimulate students to pursue their own spiritual education. Thus the University houses not only seven Catholic chapels but also an Islamic prayer room; counts among its administrative and faculty leaders Muslims, Jews, Quakers, Baptists, Methodists, Congregationalists, and Lutherans; sponsors numerous programs in spiritual education and retreat; and hosts regular visits from and presentations by speakers and scholars from a wide variety of religious traditions.

Spiritual growth programming at Portland includes:

✦ OFFICE OF CAMPUS MINISTRY. Sponsors retreats, speakers, scholars, seminars, symposia, Masses, sacraments, prayer services, concerts of sacred and religious music, and publications.

✦ THE DIVISION OF STUDENT SERVICES. Sponsors scholars, speakers, symposia, counseling.

✦ PORTLAND MAGAZINE. Publishes essays and articles regarding spiritual education.

✦ UNIVERSITY'S HOLY CROSS COMMUNITY. Offers spiritual and pastoral advice and counseling to all students, faculty, staff, and alumni.

✦ THE BEACON. Student newspaper providing coverage of spiritual and religious events on campus.

The three theology courses required of all graduates, the presence of pastoral residents in the residence halls, the common sight of priests and nuns among the faculty, the staff and faculty's research and scholarship in spiritual matters—all these make very evident Portland's dedication to spiritual growth and to the task of producing graduates who are educated in spiritual matters, religious history, and spiritual exploration.

UNIVERSITY OF SOUTHERN CALIFORNIA

UNIVERSITY PARK
LOS ANGELES, CA 90089-0911
213.740.2311
http://www.usc.edu/

UNDERGRADUATES: 14,800

For program information, please contact:
SUSAN LAEMMLE, Ph.D.
laemmle@usc.edu

"Through several service programs I have developed a deep understanding of the vital connection that exists between helping others and my own spiritual growth."
—A USC GRADUATE

The University of Southern California, the oldest and largest private research university in the American West, offers its students a special program, Alternative Spring Break (ASB)–Monterey: Homelessness with a Spiritual Bent, that exemplifies its strong focus on community service and spiritual growth. Sponsored by the University's Volunteer Center, ASB–Monterey enables students to do service work in an off-campus setting. What sets the Monterey trip apart from the other trips sponsored by the University's Volunteer Center is its spiritual component, which encourages participants to reflect on the implications and meaning of their experience. Lasting five and a half days and limited to 20 students, along with several USC faculty/staff, ASB–Monterey creates an atmosphere in which people of diverse religious backgrounds feel comfortable sharing their spiritual questions.

The centerpiece of ASB–Monterey is a four-day stay at Dorothy's Place, a homeless day shelter in Salinas, where students:

✦ Help prepare and serve a midday meal for two hundred people;

✦ Socialize with the guests when the day room is open;

✦ Help accomplish much-needed repairs and chores;

✦ Make trips to satellite sites connected to Monterey County's effort to eradicate hunger and homelessness;

✦ Participate in evening programs that provide open time to air "thorns and roses" encountered during the day, as well as to share spiritual perspectives on the day's events.

Because of the trip's intensity and its spiritual undercurrent, students emerge from Alternative Spring Break–Monterey with a greatly strengthened sense of social and personal responsibility.

VALPARAISO UNIVERSITY

VALPARAISO, IN 46383-6493
888.GO.VALPO
http://www.valpo.edu/

UNDERGRADUATES: 3,000

For program information, please contact:
MARK R. SCHWEHN, Ph.D.
mark.schwehn@valpo.edu

"Probing diverse texts and participating in intimate discussions encouraged me to identify and explore core questions concerning my spirituality."

—A VALPARAISO GRADUATE

Christ College, the interdisciplinary Honors College of Valparaiso University, a church-affiliated institution, "engenders not only intellectual resourcefulness, but a spiritual maturity that enables students to endure difficult changes in their lives with faith, hope, and charity," states Dean Mark R. Schwehn. Spiritual questions are part of the academic conversation in all Christ College courses. Several courses directly address religious and theological issues:

✦ FIRST-YEAR STUDENTS take a two-semester sequence of courses based on selected great texts, including religious classics.

✦ SECOND-YEAR STUDENTS study the Christian intellectual tradition, explore their own beliefs, and write an academic research paper on a particular religious or ethical issue.

✦ THIRD-YEAR STUDENTS strengthen students' critical-thinking and writing skills and allow them to explore their own religious and ethical convictions.

✦ FOURTH-YEAR COLLOQUIUM provides a capstone experience in which students explore the relationship between faith and contemporary culture and refine their own sense of vocation. Students are led through a process of reflection and of writing a spiritual autobiography.

Weekly symposia feature distinguished speakers, such as internationally known theologians Jürgen Moltmann and David Tracy. The annual All-College Reading and author's lectures have included Rabbi Marc Gellman's *Does God Have a Big Toe?*, Jean Bethke Elshtain's *Democracy on Trial*, Walter Wangerin, Jr.'s *The Book of the Dun Cow*, and Roberta Bondi's *Memories of God*. At Christ College, both the curriculum and the cocurriculum are rich in programs that encourage students to examine their own convictions, thereby fostering a spiritual maturity that will be a great value to them through all of their lives.

VIRGINIA WESLEYAN COLLEGE

1584 WESLEYAN DRIVE
NORFOLK/VIRGINIA BEACH, VA 23502
757.455.3200
http://www.vwc.edu/

UNDERGRADUATES: 1,500

For program information, please contact:
ROBERT M. CHAPMAN
rchapman@vwc.edu

"Religious Life organizations on campus are extraordinarily accepting and very diverse."

—A VIRGINIA WESLEYAN THIRD-YEAR STUDENT

A United Methodist–related institution, Virginia Wesleyan College provides numerous opportunities for spiritual reflection, personal growth, and faith development for all students regardless of their religious backgrounds. The chaplain of the college serves as an ecumenical pastor to students of diverse faith traditions. Religious clubs offered through the Chaplain's Office are wide-ranging in purpose:

✦ CATHOLIC CAMPUS MINISTRY provides an organization for Catholic students on campus. Members learn about the Catholic Church, share ideas, attend Mass together, and minister to the homeless.

✦ CHRISTIAN FELLOWSHIP is an energetic group of students, that encourages new friendships, support for others, and creative spiritual development.

✦ HABITAT FOR HUMANITY builds houses in partnership with the working poor. Motivated by the vision of "a decent house in a decent community for God's people in need," students work at local sites.

✦ RELIGIOUS LIFE COUNCIL is the umbrella organization that supports and coordinates activities with religious life groups on campus.

✦ SHALOM promotes interest and understanding of Judaism in the past, present, and future.

✦ FELLOWSHIP OF CHRISTIAN ATHLETES presents to athletes and coaches and all whom they influence the challenge and adventure of receiving Jesus Christ as Savior and Lord.

The vision of the religious-life program at Virginia Wesleyan can be defined in the theme, "Sharing the Journey." Recognizing that everyone in the college community is on a spiritual pilgrimage, the program seeks to reach all students in its attempts to promote integrity, inclusiveness, understanding, and service.

WELLESLEY COLLEGE

106 CENTRAL STREET
WELLESLEY, MA 02481
781.283.1000
http://www.wellesley.edu/

UNDERGRADUATES: 2,200

For program information, please contact:
VICTOR H. KAZANJIAN, JR.
vkazanjian@wellesley.edu

 In 1993, Wellesley College, a private, liberal arts school for women, realized its historic vision of whole-person education when it installed the Reverend Victor H. Kazanjian, Jr. as dean of the Religious and Spiritual Life Program. By recognizing the moral, ethical, and spiritual issues shared by people of many different religious traditions, Wellesley has become a place of celebration of the spirit. The multi-faith program enables students to gain a deeper understanding of themselves and of their role as global citizens.

The core interreligious programs at Wellesley are:

✦ **MULTI-FAITH RELIGIOUS LIFE TEAM.** Chaplains and advisors of all religious traditions meet weekly at Wellesley for discussion, study, prayer, and program planning and are available to all college and community members.

✦ **MULTI-FAITH COUNCIL.** Two students from each religious tradition form this committee, which discusses spiritual issues, plans joint worship services and educational programs, and advises the dean on Wellesley's religious life.

✦ **BEYOND TOLERANCE.** Speakers and presentations at Wellesley make up this educational program, which explores the complex ethical and moral dilemmas facing the world today.

✦ **MULTI-FAITH COMMUNITY CELEBRATION.** A series of community-wide celebrations enables Wellesley community members to experience unique perspectives on common spiritual themes.

The Office of Religious and Spiritual Life also houses the Education as Transformation Project, through which colleges and universities across the country address issues of religious pluralism and spirituality in higher education. Wellesley's evolving Spirituality and Education Program incorporates collaborative workshops and educational initiatives on the spiritual aspects of health and wholeness, leadership, and learning for students, faculty, and staff. Wellesley students receive help for the journey, no matter what spiritual path they may travel.

WILSON COLLEGE

1015 PHILADELPHIA AVENUE
CHAMBERSBURG, PA 17201-1285
717.264.4141
http://www.wilson.edu/

UNDERGRADUATES: 300

For program information, please contact:
JENNIFER NACHAMKIN
jnachamkin@wilson.edu

"Wilson services have touched on everyone's lives; issues range from homelessness, violence, and cancer to our annual Blessing of the Animals."

—A WILSON GRADUATE

The seal of Wilson College, a church-affiliated college for women, includes three items, *"ars, scientia, religio,"* and the school remains committed to the study of the liberal arts and sciences in a value-rich atmosphere. The purpose of the religious life program at Wilson College is to continually engage the entire college community in the search for truth, goodness, beauty, and faith. Housed in the Office of the Chaplain, the program consists of:

✦ **WORSHIP.** Weekly, optional worship services are held at a time that is set aside for chapel alone.

✦ **STUDY.** Bible study is held in small groups for students and the children of students.

✦ **PASTORAL CARE.** The full-time chaplain lives on campus in order to facilitate pastoral care.

✦ **SOCIAL JUSTICE WORK.** Volunteer opportunities at Wilson abound, including: Alternative Spring Breaks, during which students concentrate their community-service efforts into one week; Sam's Club at the Chambersburg YMCA, at which students assist in providing weekly programming for needy children; and the Big Sisters program, which pairs Wilson women with younger girls for fun and friendship.

Wilson has a significant new program, "Women with Children," which facilitates college attendance for single mothers. These students live in modified dormitory space with their children. Children come to weekly chapel services, and the college has a special "Bible Buddies" club for preschool and primary-grade children living on campus.

The Office of the Chaplain is the center of service and faith on campus. The result is a lively campus dynamic where the question of justice, compassion, fairness, and truth are debated both in terms of politics and religious thought.

WORCESTER POLYTECHNIC INSTITUTE

100 INSTITUTE ROAD
WORCESTER, MA 01609
508.831.5000
http://www.wpi.edu/

UNDERGRADUATES: 2,700

For program information, please contact:
THOMAS J. BALISTRIERI
balisttj@wpi.edu

"Passage helped me to identify what was important in my life and opened my mind to truly appreciate the value of diversity."

—A WPI FOURTH-YEAR STUDENT

The mission of Worcester Polytechnic Institute, a nationally recognized engineering school, is the holistic development of young people. WPI's Student Development and Counseling Center has developed a philosophy called Passage. Not simply a program but rather a holistic, dimensionally based, multi-faceted process, Passage is designed to assist students through their journey into adulthood. Through the voluntary, yearlong Passage process, students learn about themselves, developing a sense of self and self-esteem. They participate in discussions about values, goals, and roles and deliberate about topics such as manhood, womanhood, and marriage. Passage teaches students how to cook, how to show compassion for others, and how to walk carefully in nature and feel comfortable in the wilderness.

Passage is different every year, but its essence remains the same: To connect young people to themselves, to others, to nature, and to God. Passage is intended to assist students in becoming wiser and more effective, balanced adults. It provides them with tools, experiences, behaviors, feelings, and memories they will never forget.

XAVIER UNIVERSITY

3800 VICTORY PARKWAY
CINCINNATI, OH 45207
513.745.3000
http://www.xu.edu/

UNDERGRADUATES: 3,900

For program information, please contact:
THOMAS SHEIBLEY
Sheibley@xavier.xu.edu

"In my four years at Xavier I've come to value reflection, appreciate the importance of community, and put my passionate concern for others into action."

—A XAVIER GRADUATE

Xavier University, a church-affiliated, liberal arts institution, seeks to prepare its students intellectually, morally, and spiritually. Retreats offered by Campus Ministry give Xavier students an opportunity to step away from their daily routines and gain a clearer perspective on their lives. Specific opportunities available through Xavier's retreat program include:

✦ KOINONIA. A program that consists of weekly, small faith-sharing groups, monthly large-group gatherings, social activities, and the four-day Koinonia Retreat that takes place during the fall break, offering students the chance to relax, build friendships, and grow in faith.

✦ "JOURNEY," "APPROACH," "ENCOUNTER," and "PERSPECTIVE." A progression of programs that use peer presentations, quiet reflection, and small-group discussions to encourage a fresh look at relationships, God's presence, and how to live a life of compassion.

✦ REFLECTIVE RETREAT. Allows students to take time to quietly reflect on their image of God and how God may be speaking to them in their own life experiences. A team of both students and staff provides opportunities for private reflection, prayer, small-group sharing, and one-on-one conversations with an adult retreat director.

✦ SENIOR RETREAT. An opportunity to find support and God's presence in a time of transition. Seniors are invited to begin their "Senior Week" by joining classmates for a couple days of reminiscing and celebrating accomplishments. Reflecting on past experiences and looking to the future, seniors find support in an atmosphere of prayer and relaxation.

More than 400 students participate annually in retreats, recognizing their personal strengths, confronting their own struggles, and growing in integrity, respect for others, and awareness of God's presence in their everyday lives.

YALE UNIVERSITY

PO BOX 208234
NEW HAVEN, CT 06520
203.432.9300
http://www.yale.edu/

UNDERGRADUATES: 5,400

For program information, please contact:
KATHERINE BURDICK
dwighthall@yale.edu

"The Magee Fellowship has been instrumental in bringing together the seemingly disparate 'activist' and 'religious' segments of the Yale population. An absolutely wonderful program!"

—A YALE GRADUATE

The John G. Magee Fellowship at Dwight Hall, the Center for Public Service and Social Justice at Yale University, fulfills Dwight Hall's mission to "inspire and enable students to engage in present and future action" for positive social change. Founded by undergraduates in 1886 as the Yale University Christian Association, Dwight Hall is now an independent, nonprofit umbrella organization for more than seventy student-led programs. Although it is no longer a specifically Christian organization, it is still committed to exploring the religious, spiritual, and moral dimensions of direct service and social action.

Every year, one recent Yale graduate or Yale divinity student serves on the Dwight Hall staff as the Magee Fellow. Each Magee Fellow implements programs that demonstrate the praxis of faith and action, provides moral and religious guidance to "Dwight Hallers," and acts as a liaison between the Chaplain's Office, Religious Ministries, and Dwight Hall. Specific duties of Dwight Hall's Magee Fellow include:

✦ Facilitates reflection, text study, and discussion groups;

✦ Coordinates training series on the principles of nonviolence, community organizing, and other topics;

✦ Maintains a library of resources;

✦ Helps students plan vigils and other events;

✦ Provides lay pastoral counseling to students.

Although the Magee Fellow's primary audience is the students of Dwight Hall and Religious Ministries, most Fellowship events are open to the public, and the Magee Fellow is a resource person to people and organizations throughout Yale and New Haven. In myriad ways, the Magee Fellowship encourages and enables spiritual growth and dialog at Yale and beyond.

YORK COLLEGE OF PENNSYLVANIA

COUNTRY CLUB ROAD
YORK, PA 17403-3426
717.846.7788
http://www.ycp.edu/

UNDERGRADUATES: 3,400

For program information, please contact:
ANNE HOPKINS GROSS
ahgross@ycp.edu

"Exploring spirituality at York leads to much personal growth and success in the future."

—A YORK GRADUATE

York College of Pennsylvania, a private, nondenominational, liberal arts college, has developed a strong spiritual dimension for all members of its campus. The hallmark program is the Spiritual Life Week that occurs early in the spring semester. This event is developed and implemented by the Council on Religious Activities, which is composed of students, faculty, and staff. The students on the Council are representatives from various student groups such as Hillel, Inter-Varsity Christian Fellowship, the Newman Club, Habitat for Humanity, and the Black Student Union. The Council's purpose is to foster an atmosphere that will enhance the campus community's awareness of the spiritual dimension of life.

The Council on Religious Activities:

✦ Works to promote spiritual awareness and development;

✦ Fosters dialog and sharing with the different religious groups on campus;

✦ Offers the campus community diverse spiritual programs outside the mainstream religious philosophies;

✦ Encourages student religious organizations to participate in community-service projects;

✦ Promotes awareness and understanding of different spiritual/religious viewpoints.

Programs beyond Spiritual Life Week include performers and musicians, community-service projects, interfaith gatherings and dialogs, open houses, mediation, and weekly religious services. The college's main worship area, the Brougher Chapel, provides a place for religious activities, meditation, counseling, and special events. York's religious-activities program continues to develop and grow based on the needs and expectations of the college community, working on the premise that it is not necessary for an institution to have a religious affiliation in order to be spiritually sound.

CIVIC EDUCATION PROGRAMS

Civic education focuses on the skills and habits of mind necessary for students to become active, well-informed, responsible citizens in our democratic society. By integrating rigorous academic work with public service experiences, effective civic education programs strive to provide opportunities for students to practice the virtues of trust, respect for others, and application of knowledge to promote the common good. When colleges and universities take on this responsibility, they become indispensable in sustaining and strengthening our democratic culture.

ABILENE CHRISTIAN UNIVERSITY

BOX 29100
ABILENE, TX 79699
915.674.2000
http://www.acu.edu/

UNDERGRADUATES: 3,900

For program information, please contact:
MEL HAILEY, Ph.D.
hailey@pols.acu.edu

"As we embark on the 21st century, the need for Christian civil servants is paramount. The Jack Pope Fellows program is committed to educating young people who can shape our society."

—AN ABILENE CHRISTIAN FOURTH-YEAR STUDENT

The mission of this private, comprehensive, church-affiliated university is "to prepare students for Christian service and leadership throughout the world." Inherent in this mission is building strong and active citizens through two programs:

✦ THE JACK POPE FELLOWS PROGRAM offers students scholarships, seminars with public officials, and public-sector internships. Students also take courses in national government, Christian ethics, public service, public policy, and public administration management.

✦ THE CENTER FOR ADVANCEMENT OF COMMUNITY exists "to propose solutions to the crises of community that exist at all levels of society." Although participation is open to all students in most areas, 25 students are selected annually for the following programs:

> Interdisciplinary citizenship, leadership, and service programs on ethics, public and social welfare policy and change, conflict management, and international issues, in addition to volunteer work; short courses and seminars "addressing the community needs and potential in the church, school, workplace, and government"; research and reports on themes related to "renewal and revitalization in spiritual, civic, and corporate contexts"; promotion of "the spirit of public service and volunteerism by encouraging students . . . to put their knowledge into action."

Through the Jack Pope Fellows program and the Center for the Advancement of Community, ACU students have the opportunity to pursue their civic education, thus preparing them to become strong servants in their communities.

ALLEGHENY COLLEGE

520 NORTH MAIN STREET
MEADVILLE, PA 16335
814.332.3100
http://www.alleg.edu/

UNDERGRADUATES: 1,900

For program information, please contact:
ERIC PALLANT, Ph.D.
epallant@alleg.edu

Allegheny College, a church-affiliated, liberal arts college, serves as home to the Center for Economic and Environmental Development (CEED), which connects students, faculty, and community members through projects that promote economic and environmental development within the neighboring French Creek watershed comprising 1,270 square miles and 250,000 people. CEED has created a national model for collaboration between students and faculty at Allegheny and the farmers, planners, industrialists, government officials, bankers, and nongovernmental workers in the French Creek watershed.

Recent CEED projects include:

✦ THE FRENCH CREEK ENVIRONMENTAL EDUCATION PROJECT (FCEEP), which has joined Allegheny faculty and students with regional K-12 schools and local environmental groups to turn the French Creek watershed and waterways in the Pittsburgh metropolitan area into outdoor environmental laboratories. Emphasizing investigation of water quality and biodiversity, this project involves 27 teachers in a hands-on, natural science education for students from 21 schools.

✦ THE MEADVILLE COMMUNITY ENERGY PROJECT, which reduces local energy consumption, thereby stimulating the regional economy, improving social equity, and benefiting the environment.

✦ STRATEGIC ENVIRONMENTAL MANAGEMENT, which conserves and safeguards natural resources and is compatible with sustainable development: meeting today's needs while preserving our descendants' ability to meet the needs of the future.

Allegheny's CEED program encourages students and faculty to participate in community development as the communities around the college begin to reap the benefits. Through CEED, Allegheny trains hundreds of civic leaders for the 21st century who have experienced the responsibilities and benefits of civic action.

ALVERNO COLLEGE

3401 SOUTH 39TH STREET
MILWAUKEE, WI 53234
414.382.6000
http://www.alverno.edu/

UNDERGRADUATES: 2,200

For program information, please contact:
JUDEEN SCHULTE, Ph.D.
Judeen.Schulte@alverno.edu

Alverno College, founded in 1887, is a church-affiliated, liberal arts college for women. Since the early 1970s, Alverno faculty members have developed and implemented ability-based undergraduate education that emphasizes the competencies needed for work, the family, and the community.

The abilities central to Alverno's approach to education are communication, analysis, problem-solving, values in decision-making, social interaction, global perspectives, effective citizenship, and aesthetic responsiveness. An Alverno student develops into an educated, mature adult with such personal characteristics as:

✦ A sense of responsibility for her own learning and the ability and desire to continue learning independently;

✦ Self-knowledge and the ability to assess her own performance critically and accurately; and

✦ An understanding of how to apply her knowledge and abilities in many different contexts.

As a student integrates these abilities, she expands her capacity for personal, professional, and civic responsibility. In various contexts, students identify their values and explore what it means to be an "ethically responsible self" so that they think about and plan for success in their fields and the contribution they can make to those fields, as well as to the broader community.

Encounters with complex ideas should help develop students' ability to reason and question, as well as help them to think and act effectively. By making such expectations explicit and by clarifying the steps students can take to develop cognitive and effective habits, Alverno helps students learn how to learn and how to apply what they have learned in their personal and professional lives.

ANTIOCH COLLEGE

795 LIVERMORE STREET
YELLOW SPRINGS, OH 45387
937.767.7331
http://www.antioch-college.edu/

UNDERGRADUATES: 600

For program information, please contact:
SHOSHANNA SPECTOR
spector@antioch-college.edu

Meeting community needs through education and practical application inspires the College Community Government program at Antioch College, a private, liberal arts school. Through this program, faculty, staff, and students meet weekly in a system of shared governance in which civic awareness and duties converge to empower students in transforming their community. Decision-making opportunities include faculty hiring, faculty review, and budget decisions. Numerous committees handle Affirmative Action policies, sexual harassment, and alcohol and drug policies. A Community Standards Board oversees the fair outcome of unresolved questions and events that require deliberative responses.

More than 100 students attend these weekly meetings, which follow a standard agenda:

✦ Elected student managers lead and maintain a civil discourse throughout the meeting.

✦ Particular problems or issues are showcased and discussed.

✦ Proposals are studied, such as how to best allocate the $230,000 budget.

✦ The "Community Pulse" segment, in which citizens share their concerns, ends the meeting.

This shared governance program enhances cooperative education at Antioch, and local and global civic opportunities abound: students volunteer in rural soup kitchens, assist in elementary schools, work in corporate environments, or travel to foreign countries to work in local businesses. Outstanding U.S. citizens who have benefited from Antioch's classroom, co-op, and community-based curriculum include Coretta Scott King and the noted African-American jurist Leon Higginbotham (deceased).

Antioch students pursue and demonstrate democratic ideals as they work to invigorate their civic involvement both on campus and in the surrounding community.

BOISE STATE UNIVERSITY

1910 UNIVERSITY DRIVE
BOISE, ID 83725
208.385.1011
http://www.idbsu.edu/

UNDERGRADUATES: 13,300

For program information, please contact:
LARRY BURKE
lburke@boisestate.edu

It seems incongruous that Idaho, a state with a sparse minority population and an Aryan Nation band living in the north, would be the setting for a successful Human Rights Celebration during the week of the Martin Luther King Jr. holiday. But such is the case at Boise State University, where students annually organize a week filled with activities that involve both the campus and the community.

During the University's Human Rights Celebration week, students organize an array of activities to celebrate the life and principles of Martin Luther King, Jr. Rather than be confined to a single event, students use the week to stage a major educational program that is as diverse as the culture it honors. Typical celebrations are filled with speakers, art exhibits, films, concerts, panel discussions, an essay contest for elementary students, educational workshops, musical performances, and volunteer opportunities, as well as a march to the state capitol.

Goals of the Human Rights Celebration include:

✦ Addressing the problems of racism today;

✦ Celebrating cultural diversity in Idaho;

✦ Conducting antibias workshops

✦ Understanding hate groups and adopting strategies for their prevention;

✦ Discussing human rights issues throughout the University; and

✦ Integrating public school and community activities.

Through the Human Rights Celebration, Boise State students have taken a bold step to increase the community's awareness and understanding of the diversity that surrounds the University. Through their own initiative, students have funded and staged a celebration that is as educational as anything they experience in the classroom. They have reached out to the community and University to demonstrate how important it is that individuals learn how to live with each other— a powerful and hopeful statement from the next generation of leaders in Idaho.

BRANDEIS UNIVERSITY

415 SOUTH STREET
WALTHAM, MA 02454-9110
781.736.2000
http://www.brandeis.edu/

UNDERGRADUATES: 3,000

For program information, please contact:
MARCI MCPHEE
mcphee@brandeis.edu

"We can never reach a real peace between ourselves and the other parties in a conflict as long as we humiliate other people and disregard their humanity."

—A BRANDEIS THIRD-YEAR STUDENT

The two-year-old International Center for Ethics, Justice, and Public Life Student Fellowship offers undergraduates at Brandeis University the opportunity to study and experience complex questions of social justice and ethics at this private, liberal arts institution. The current theme of the center's work, "Coexistence," goes beyond "peaceful coexistence" between superpowers to cooperation among historically divided, diverse societies. In 1999, six Brandeis second- and third-year students were selected for the fellowship, which takes a seasonal approach to involving students with cultures at home and abroad:

✦ In the spring, fellows participate in course work that explores the underlying theories of coexistence (conflict resolution, reconciliation, and multiculturalism) and approaches to achieving it; identifies and analyzes moral and ethical dilemmas; explores issues through case histories; and develops a method of inquiry for students preparing for coexistence work.

✦ In the summer, fellows work in a grassroots coexistence organization, from participation in racial dialog groups in Baltimore to establishing a multicultural museum in the Amazon jungle or documenting human rights violations on the West Bank.

✦ In the fall, fellows integrate their experiences through an independent analysis course. They also present what they've learned through "Brown Bag Lunches," expositions, conferences, roundtable discussions, and publications.

By integrating experience with course work, fellows resolve ethical dilemmas intellectually and personally. Through sharing their experiences with peers and faculty, fellows enable the campus community to explore issues of coexistence and justice. The fellowship program helps develop strong leaders who not only enrich the Brandeis community but also strengthen our global society.

CALVIN COLLEGE

3201 BURTON STREET, SE
GRAND RAPIDS, MI 49546
616.957.6142
http://www.calvin.edu/
UNDERGRADUATES: 3,900

For program information, please contact:
JAMES PENNING, Ph.D.
penn@calvin.edu

"In many ways, including classroom discussions, college programs, and community service opportunities, Calvin has challenged me to examine political issues and turn my thought into action."

—A CALVIN THIRD-YEAR STUDENT

Calvin College, a private, liberal arts institution affiliated with the Christian Reformed Church, emphasizes the development of moral character in its students and considers civic education to be a way in which to accomplish that objective. In 1997 Calvin established the Paul B. Henry Institute for the Study of Christianity and Politics. Named after the late Calvin political science professor and congressman Paul Henry, the Institute promotes research and action in the area of faith and politics by sponsoring:

✦ Regular national conferences on critical topics;

✦ Collaborative research projects dealing with faith and political issues;

✦ Graduate and undergraduate courses and seminars on religion and public life;

✦ Summer research opportunities and fellowships;

✦ A research and data center serving as a resource for students and scholars;

✦ Internships and research opportunities in Washington, DC; and

✦ The annual Paul B. Henry lecture, featuring a Christian who has served or is serving in public life.

Calvin promotes civic education in diverse ways. Particularly important is Calvin's annual January Series, which brings prominent civic leaders, politicians, and the like to campus. In addition, about 40% of Calvin students take political science as part of the College's core requirements. Many political science courses focus on civic participation and often include internships in local, state, and national government.

In response to the biblical admonition to "do justice, love mercy, and walk humbly with [our] God," Calvin students seek to be civic-minded citizens in all that they do.

CENTRAL COLLEGE

812 UNIVERSITY
PELLA, IA 50219
515.628.9000
http://www.central.edu/
UNDERGRADUATES: 1,300

For program information, please contact:
CHERI DOANE
doanec@central.edu

Central College is a private, four-year, liberal arts college affiliated with the Reformed Church in America. One of the College's goals is for students to experience the diversity of cultures in the United States and the world. Central has a tradition of international study programs, and 40% of the College's students participate in the study abroad program. For students who are unable to travel abroad, Central instituted PLACES, which provides students with opportunites to experience the cultural diversity within the U.S. Students tutor and serve as mentors to inner-city youth, assist with English-as-a-second-language classes, and help refugees to resettle in Iowa. Programs have also been developed outside of Iowa, including in Grand Isle, Louisiana, and Santa Fe, Mexico.

As part of Central's civic education initiatives:

✦ All students are required to complete a cultural awareness experiential component, including 15 to 30 hours of direct contact.

✦ Students receive credit for their activities as part of a course, an internship in their major, or an independent project.

✦ Students, faculty, and PLACES staff select a culture and develop a proposal and readings appropriate to the experience.

✦ Throughout the experience, students use reflection and discussion to integrate their experience and their academic program.

By requiring students to interact with people from cultural backgrounds different from their own, Central teaches students the values and skills they need to live responsibly in the multicultural world of the 21st century.

Colgate University

13 OAK DRIVE
HAMILTON, NY 13346
315.228.1000
http://www.colgate.edu/
UNDERGRADUATES: 2,900

For program information, please contact:
DONNA SWARTWOUT, Ph.D.
dswartwout@mail.colgate.edu

"Skin Deep was a profound experience, and I am sure it will continue to affect how I view relationships with others throughout my life."

—A Colgate third-year student

Colgate, founded in 1819, is a private, liberal arts university. During the Skin Deep weekend retreats, the University invites a diverse group of students to participate in a forum to examine their attitudes about race and explore the barriers that stand in the way of building a society that truly respects all races.

Skin Deep is designed to provide a safe and structured environment in which students are able to talk about themselves, how they perceive others, and how others perceive them. Faculty, staff, and students participate on the same level, and the program is free of cost to all participants.

Discussion topics include:

✦ Race privilege

✦ Racial identity development

✦ Race at Colgate

✦ Stereotypes

✦ Self-exploration

✦ Action planning

In recent years, Skin Deep participants have left the weekend retreat and created new campus programs to address issues of racial difference. For example, the Dream Team, students who develop educational programs dealing with issues of race, created a "Solidarity Line" around the campus quad to promote racial unity.

Without a sound understanding and awareness of issues such as racism, oppression, prejudices, and stereotypes, future leaders will not be able to serve or represent all of America. Skin Deep allows Colgate students to grapple with these issues in a safe, supportive, yet challenging environment. Colgate students leave a Skin Deep weekend empowered to make a difference, ready to take a stand, and with a better understanding of themselves as individuals and as members of society.

College of the Atlantic

105 EDEN STREET
BAR HARBOR, ME 04609
207.288.5015
http://www.coa.edu/
UNDERGRADUATES: 250

For program information, please contact:
DAVID MAHONEY
dmm@ecology.coa.edu

"You do a lot of talking at COA. While people respect your right to contribute, they also never hesitate to challenge what you say. It takes some getting used to, but by the end you are articulate, confident, and brave."

—A College of the Atlantic fourth-year student

Founders of the College of the Atlantic created in 1969 a private institution that offers a single degree program in human ecology. The institution is dedicated to the interdisciplinary study of human ecology, in which students integrate knowledge across traditional academic lines.

In keeping with the central ideas of community and responsibility, the College governs itself through a combination of participatory and representative democracy.

✦ Students serve on all college committees, with full voting rights.

✦ At the All-College Meeting, held every third week and moderated by a student, the community reviews the work of the committees.

✦ Students create individualized courses of study as they work with faculty to expand their academic horizons and develop their sense of responsibility.

✦ Professors challenge their students to think for themselves, to question the status quo, and to push their inquiries into unexplored areas.

Students attend College of the Atlantic because they are concerned with values. Through human ecology they address value questions, as reflected in the college's vision statement: "The faculty, students, trustees, staff and alumni of College of the Atlantic envision a world where people value creativity, intellectual achievement, and the diversity of nature and human cultures. With respect and compassion, individuals will construct meaningful lives for themselves, gain appreciation for the relationships among all forms of life, and safeguard the heritage of future generations." Students at the College of the Atlantic build their competence and confidence for life-long learning and prepare themselves to be effective citizens and leaders.

COLLEGE OF THE OZARKS

POINT LOOKOUT, MO 65726
417.334.6411
http://www.cofo.edu/

UNDERGRADUATES: 1,500

For program information, please contact:
LARRY L. COCKRUM
cockrum@cofo.edu

The College of the Ozarks, founded in 1906, is a church-affiliated, liberal arts institution. A fivefold mission stresses not only civic responsibility but also academic, vocational, cultural, and spiritual growth. Rigorous academics and high expectations in the classroom prepare students to be lifelong learners as well as men and women of maturity and responsibility. The College believes that character is best developed from an education that includes the head, the heart, and the hands.

Civic education initiatives sponsored by the College of the Ozarks include:

✦ THE KEETER CENTER, which provides programs and activities that enhance the development of character and good citizenship;

✦ CITIZENSHIP AND HEALTHY LIFESTYLES, a two-semester course that promotes patriotic growth, citizenship, and the development of leadership skills;

✦ CHARACTER CAMP, a two-week orientation that encourages new students to think about what is important to them and how their ideals can make them contributing members of the democracy in which they live.

Publications such as *U.S. News & World Report* and *Money* repeatedly recognize the college for its overall excellence and for its status as one of the "Best Buys" in the U.S. Through a no-tuition, work/study program the college has provided an opportunity for thousands of young people who would not otherwise have received a college education. Even more noteworthy is that College of the Ozarks—a tiny school by many standards—is recognized nationally for preparing its students for their future roles as active citizens and leaders.

CONNECTICUT COLLEGE

270 MOHEGAN AVENUE
NEW LONDON, CT 06320-4196
860.447.1911
http://www.camel.conncoll.edu/

UNDERGRADUATES: 1,600

For program information, please contact:
TRACEE REISER
tlrei@conncoll.edu

Connecticut College, a private, liberal arts institution, is home to the Center for Community Challenges, a multidisciplinary, academic center that is dedicated to teaching, research, and community collaborations that foster active citizenship and community leadership in a multicultural, democratic society. Directed by an advisory board composed of College and community representatives, the Center oversees three major areas: the institution's Program in Community Action, service-learning course development, and college-community partnerships.

Civic education initiatives at Connecticut College include:

✦ THE CENTER FOR COMMUNITY CHALLENGES, which offers a gateway course each spring semester, either "The Good Society" or "The Citizen and Community: Leadership and Participation," in which students study issues of community, civic responsibility, justice, and compassion;

✦ SERVICE-LEARNING COURSES, which connect the course content to community challenges, with student participants completing four to ten hours of service work in community settings;

✦ THE OFFICE OF VOLUNTEERS FOR COMMUNITY SERVICE, which trains and places students in community projects connected to issues of poverty, education, health, legal rights, and housing.

Students describe the impact civic education and service-learning opportunities have had on their development, how they experienced ethnic and cultural diversity, and how civic education strengthened their commitment and sense of collective and personal responsibility and enhanced their leadership and citizenship skills. At Connecticut College, students integrate civic education and service learning into their academic life and receive skills that will help them to become engaged and productive citizens.

DARTMOUTH COLLEGE

6001 PARKHURST HALL
HANOVER, NH 03755
603.646.1110
http://www.dartmouth.edu/

UNDERGRADUATES: 4,300

For program information, please contact:
JAN TARJAN
jan-roberta.tarjan@dartmouth.edu

Dartmouth, founded in 1769, is a private, Ivy League college that serves as home to the Tucker Foundation, named in honor of William Jewett Tucker, the ninth president of the institution. Created in 1951, the Tucker Foundation meets the developmental needs of students through more than 40 ongoing programs. Tucker Foundation programs addressing civic education issues include:

✦ **AMNESTY INTERNATIONAL,** which advocates fair and prompt trials, opposes death sentences and torture, and seeks the release of prisoners of conscience. The Amnesty International Student Group promotes human rights education in the community and thus creates awareness of human rights violations around the world.

✦ **THE DARTMOUTH COMMUNITY MEDIATION CENTER** (DCMC) promotes understanding of mediation, trains students and administrators in mediation skills, provides a forum for resolving disputes, and serves as a resource for individuals who may find it necessary to use conflict resolution techniques in other than a DCMC setting.

✦ **THE INTERRACIAL CONCERNS COMMITTEE** raises personal and collective awareness and understanding of racial, ethnic, and cultural issues on campus.

Personal and civic responsibility is at the heart of the Tucker Foundation, which teaches students that intellectual exploration and vocational competence must be complemented and informed by engagement with others in need, by reflection upon the larger systems of meaning and belief, and by striving to understand those who are different from ourselves. Through its relationships with students and the outside community of schools, social-service agencies and religious organizations, the Tucker Foundation strives to exemplify the engaged campus, thus benefiting not only students but also members of the campus, local, and world communities.

THE DEFIANCE COLLEGE

701 NORTH CLINTON STREET
DEFIANCE, OH 43512
800.520.4632
http://www.defiance.edu/

UNDERGRADUATES: 800

For program information, please contact:
BRUCE BUSBY, Ph.D.
Bbusby@defiance.edu

"The Program for Responsible Citizenship has given me a different perspective of the world and how I connect with it."

—A DEFIANCE FOURTH-YEAR STUDENT

The Defiance College, founded in 1850, is a church-affiliated, liberal arts institution serving as home to the Program for Responsible Citizenship (PRC). The Program enables students to understand and practice the virtues of personal responsibility through the following five initiatives:

✦ **THE ANNUAL THEME FOR GENERAL EDUCATION.** The development of an annual theme establishes a basis for relating speakers, films, concerts, art shows, and other performances to key courses in the curriculum, which incorporates civic education.

✦ **THE RANDALL L. BUCHMAN SYMPOSIUM SERIES.** Current regional, national, and world issues are addressed within the context of responsible citizenship through the use of notable guest authorities.

✦ **THE DEFIANCE COLLEGE HUMANITARIAN AWARD.** Beginning in 1999, this honor will be awarded to an outstanding figure in civic leadership.

✦ **THE CAROLYN M. SMALL HONORS PROGRAM.** This program presents the opportunity for all Defiance College students to participate in an honors curriculum based in the study of the arts and humanities.

✦ **THE HERMANN WIEBE FACULTY DEVELOPMENT FUND.** This fund provides annual support for college-wide faculty development with priority given to activities addressing the objectives of the PRC.

The Defiance College Program for Responsible Citizenship seeks to instill in Defiance students a sense of civic responsibility to lead and serve in their community and the world. It is based upon a study of our Western heritage within the tradition of the liberal arts.

EASTERN MENNONITE UNIVERSITY

1200 PARK ROAD
HARRISONBURG, VA 22802-2462
540.432.4000
http://www.emu.edu/

UNDERGRADUATES: 1,000

For program information, please contact:
ORVAL GINGERICH, Ph.D.
gingerio@emu.edu

Eastern Mennonite, founded in 1917, is a church-affiliated, liberal arts university offering a cross-cultural program designed to develop students' global awareness through an experience of living and learning in a different culture. The focus of the program is for students to learn *from* and *with* others, which goes beyond and is more interactive than learning *about* others.

Eastern Mennonite University (EMU) sets four goals for cross-cultural learning: cross-cultural understanding, cultural self-awareness, global awareness, and understanding religious values and institutions.

All Eastern Mennonite graduates are required to have nine semester hours of cross-cultural credits. To receive credit, students choose from the following options: semester cross-cultural programs; summer cross-cultural programs; the Washington Study-Service Year; service-learning programs; and student-selected cross-cultural experiences such as study abroad or directed studies.

EMU's general education program is called the Global Village Curriculum, which is divided into four areas: Learning for Life from the Humanities; Learning for Life Through Faith; Learning for Life in the Village; and Learning for Life in the World. The cross-cultural program fits into the last area.

Eastern Mennonite University's cross-cultural seminar enables students to become more independent and responsible. Leaving one's comfort zone and encountering both new freedoms and new constraints force students to make lifestyle choices. Required journal-keeping leads students to new levels of introspection and encourages them to examine their own lives in relation to their experiences in a different culture. These experiences promote greater self-confidence in students and results in civic-minded graduates.

EDGEWOOD COLLEGE

855 WOODROW STREET
MADISON, WI 53711
608.257.4861
http://www.edgewood.edu/

UNDERGRADUATES: 1,500

For program information, please contact:
LAWRENCE J. ENGEL, PH.D.
engel@edgewood.edu

Traditionally understood, a liberal arts education explores the arts and skills of a free society, and Edgewood College offers a curriculum that seeks to enact that tradition. Unique to Edgewood, however, is its graduation requirement called Human Issues, a comprehensive student study that includes personal service, interdisciplinary study, and reflection upon values.

Students may fulfill the Human Issues requirements through either independent study or participation in a year-long seminar. Whatever form is chosen, the following elements characterize Human Issues study:

✦ INTERDISCIPLINARY INQUIRY, which demonstrates the student's familiarity with sources and/or methodologies from several disciplines, as well as the student's ability to integrate, apply, and make critical judgments on the basis of them;

✦ VALUES, a project that involves articulation of the student's values and the application of values to the development of a just and humane society;

✦ PERSONAL EXPERIENCE/SERVICE, a project that involves experience or personal commitment on the part of the student;

✦ INTELLECTUAL AND ETHICAL MATURATION, a project that includes reflection on the values involved in an issue.

Edgewood College's Human Issues program draws its faculty from the College and from the broader Madison community. The Human Issues program includes consideration of issues in relationship to the student's role as a responsible member of society. The program often may reveal a transformation of a student's values and a deepened understanding of the relationship among actions, values, and intellectual life.

GARDNER-WEBB UNIVERSITY

BOILING SPRINGS, NC 28017-9980
704.434.2361
http://www.gardner-webb.edu/

UNDERGRADUATES: 3,000

For program information, please contact:
MARK TEMPLEMAN, Ph.D.
mtempleman@gardner-webb.edu

"My Gardner-Webb journey has allowed me to experience leadership training for a lifetime!"

—A GARDNER-WEBB SECOND-YEAR STUDENT

Gardner-Webb University is a private, church-related, liberal arts university. The mission of the University's Leadership Through Civic Responsibility certificate program is to ensure the continuing viability of American democracy by cultivating good citizens, and men and women of sturdy character. Through academic instruction, work experience, and professional relationships, students are introduced to leadership theory and practice, participate in volunteer service, and experience Christian service through servant leadership.

As part of its Leadership Through Civic Responsibility certificate program, Gardner-Webb University currently offers two paths of specialization:

✦ LEADERSHIP THROUGH PUBLIC SERVICE participants receive a hands-on education through involvement in governmental and political activities, internships, and opportunities to meet and work with notable public servants.

✦ LEADERSHIP THROUGH COMMUNITY SERVICE participants volunteer many hours of service to needy individuals and families and directly assist leaders of a variety of community-service programs.

Additionally, all students in the certificate program are involved in campus leadership and service organizations; attend educational workshops, retreats, and conferences; interact with guest lecturers and speakers; and travel through program-sponsored field trips.

Gardner-Webb University's Leadership Through Civic Responsibility certificate program was created as an opportunity for instruction, experience, and mentor relationships by which students could apprentice in civic stewardship. Governed by the faith that the vitality of a democracy is beholden to the vigor of its citizenry, the program serves the University in its enduring obligation to cultivate good citizens, enlightened leaders, and men and women of sturdy character.

HAVERFORD COLLEGE

370 LANCASTER AVENUE
HAVERFORD, PA 19041
610.896.1000
http://www.haverford.edu/

UNDERGRADUATES: 1,100

For program information, please contact:
MARY LOUISE ALLEN
mlallen@haverford.edu

The 8th Dimension program at Haverford, a Quaker-affiliated college of the liberal arts and sciences, enables student participants to broaden their civic education and service-learning experience as a prelude to using such knowledge to serve society.

The concept of an eighth dimension was developed more than 20 years ago by a group of Haverford students who believed service to the community should be included as one of the College's academic dimensions of a liberal arts education (natural science; quantitative analysis; history; social and behavioral science; literature; laboratory; and field or artistic experience).

Activities of Haverford College's 8th Dimension program include:

✦ AIDS SERVICE NETWORK. Students organize a campus awareness program, provide companionship to people with AIDS in hospitals and hospices, and work with local AIDS service agencies.

✦ STREET OUTREACH. Students bring food and other supplies to homeless people living in Philadelphia.

✦ ELDERLY OUTREACH. Students meet and develop friendships with local elderly citizens.

✦ HOUSING IMPROVEMENT PROJECT. Students work with local agencies to renovate housing in low-income communities.

8th Dimension assists the efforts of local human-service agencies, schools, homeless shelters, and other organizations by providing them with student volunteers. Haverford's 8th Dimension meets the needs of students who want to expand their educational experience to include meaningful contact with those in need through community service. The program provides a successful model for active student commitment to service and continues to forge a tangible link between academic studies and the world of work and service.

Hillsdale College

33 EAST COLLEGE STREET
HILLSDALE, MI 49242
517.437.7341
http://www.hillsdale.edu/

UNDERGRADUATES: 1,200

For program information, please contact:
JON COROMBOS
jon.corombos@ac.hillsdale.edu

"The Center for Constructive Alternatives shows students the importance of integration of virtue and character in every aspect of life."
—A HILLSDALE FOURTH-YEAR STUDENT

Hillsdale College is an independent, nonsectarian, four-year liberal arts college. As the first college in the nation with a written charter prohibiting discrimination on the basis of race, ethnicity, or sex, and as one of a very few colleges and universities to refuse all federal funding voluntarily—even for student financial aid—Hillsdale is committed to institutional independence. The principles of individual dignity, responsibility, and self-reliance inform every aspect of life at Hillsdale, especially the seminars sponsored by the Center for Constructive Alternatives (CCA) and the Shavano Institute for National Leadership:

✦ At each of four annual weeklong CCA seminars, approximately 12 leaders lecture on an interdisciplinary topic that requires students to integrate the concepts of virtue, prudence, and good citizenship taught in Hillsdale's traditional core curriculum.

✦ Integration of the CCA into the mandatory core curriculum ensures that all students enroll in at least two CCA seminars for academic credit and complete final exams demonstrating their intellectual mastery of and personal reflections on the material presented.

✦ Select student leaders are rewarded for their demonstrations of mature citizenship by being invited to attend a two-day Shavano Institute seminar held in a major metropolitan area for business and community leaders.

Hillsdale's outreach programs have won praise from many quarters, but the most telling measure of the seminars' success is their student enrollment. Fully one-third of students who enroll in CCA seminars for academic credit do so voluntarily, having already fulfilled the minimum requirement. These voluntary enrollees are disproportionately upperclassmen, who have learned by experience the important and challenging perspectives offered by CCA lecturers.

Indiana University Bloomington

300 NORTH JORDAN AVENUE
BLOOMINGTON, IN 47405
812.855.4848
http://www.indiana.edu/

UNDERGRADUATES: 27,000

For program information, please contact:
HELEN INGERSOLL
hingerso@indiana.edu

Indiana University Bloomington, founded in 1820, is a public, comprehensive institution. Civic Leadership Development (CLD) is a cocurricular program that provides opportunities for Indiana's Kelley School of Business undergraduate students to participate in community service, to learn the value of community involvement, and to develop practices of good citizenship and leadership.

The CLD program involves students in voluntary service with local nonprofit agencies. Students commit to a minimum of four hours of service per week for ten weeks, and because their work involves them with a variety of social justice issues, they learn a great deal about themselves and others. Students also come to understand the importance of nonprofit agencies and the role they play in the community.

Indiana University's Civic Leadership Development program holds monthly meetings that provide time for reflection and education. Students are also made aware of campus and community presentations and events that support CLD program goals.

One CLD program that deserves special mention is their partnership with Junior Achievement (JA) of Central Indiana. Since 1991, CLD has worked closely with JA. Each spring student volunteers teach the outstanding national JA elementary curriculum in the local school system. In 1991, Kelley School of Business students taught in 15 classrooms. Today, CLD students staff more than 100 classrooms. Since JA serves as a link between business and education, this partnership provides excellent education and experience for those who serve and those who are served.

MANCHESTER COLLEGE

604 EAST COLLEGE AVENUE
NORTH MANCHESTER, IN 46962
219.982.5000
http://www.manchester.edu/

UNDERGRADUATES: 1,000

For program information, please contact:
JO YOUNG SWITZER, Ph.D.
jys@manchester.edu

Educating students of ability and conviction is at the heart of Manchester's mission. An independent, liberal arts college of the Church of the Brethren, Manchester has been training graduates skilled at resolving conflict since 1948, when the nation's first peace studies major was created. While it has only recently been embraced in the workplace, schools, and communities, educating for constructive conflict resolution has been a tradition at Manchester for more than half a century.

Manchester's educating for conflict resolution includes:

✦ An interdisciplinary peace studies major. Students choose concentrations in international and global studies, interpersonal conflict studies, religious/philosophical bases of peace studies, or an individualized concentration.

✦ Interdepartmental courses, through which students study and practice mediation and conciliation skills.

✦ Peace Studies Institute, which plans conferences, debates, and workshops and provides occasional evening and summer classes and colloquies.

✦ Internships in the Fort Wayne School District mediation program, the Center for Nonviolence, On Earth Peace Assembly, and Education for Conflict Resolution.

✦ Manchester College Reconciliation Service, a student-staffed conflict-resolution resource available to anyone on campus.

The ethos of the College's emphasis on conflict resolution is woven into the experience of each student at Manchester. Gladdys Muir, founder of the peace studies program, described its desired outcomes: "If we do our job well, there will be many whose names the world will never hear, but who will be working quietly and patiently in school rooms, in churches, and in many other types of community service, laying the foundations of peace in many needy places."

MARIST COLLEGE

290 NORTH ROAD
POUGHKEEPSIE, NY 12601
914.575.3000
http://www.marist.edu/

UNDERGRADUATES: 4,100

For program information, please contact:
REGINETTA HABOUCHA, Ph.D.
914.575.3295

"My global outreach experiences pulled everything together for me, giving a fuller dimension to my education."

—A MARIST COLLEGE GRADUATING STUDENT

The Public Praxis Project embodies the highest ideals of Marist College, a private, liberal arts institution. These ideals, articulated in the College's mission statement, include a legacy of commitment to "excellence in education, a pursuit of higher human values, and dedication to the principle of service."

In 1995, as an academic response to the social disintegration characterizing much of present public life, the College's Department of Philosophy and Religious Studies established an interdisciplinary minor in Public Praxis, which became part of the Humanities curriculum. The interdisciplinary minor in Public Praxis is the foundation of the program organized around course work in human rights, human values and choice, affluence and poverty, and public praxis.

Courses in these areas also support the mission of the College in fulfilling college-wide requirements in philosophy, religious studies, history, and the social sciences, among other areas. Faculty and students work together to realize this purpose by combining social research, hands-on experience, and critical reflection at widely varied community sites. Students meet weekly for roundtable discussion. Seminar discussion groups engage shared readings and relevant media, critically analyze social situations, and inquire into values, experiential modes, and attitudes.

The praxis program at Marist College promotes the ethic and practice that personal and civic responsibility are inherently linked. Enlightened self-interest requires recognition that one's own ethical and material well-being is wed to the well-being of others, that is, that the good of each is contingent upon the good of all.

MOLLOY COLLEGE

1000 HEMPSTEAD AVENUE
ROCKVILLE CENTRE, NY 11571
516.678.5000
http://www.molloy.edu/

UNDERGRADUATES: 2,200

For program information, please contact:
STEPHAN MAYO, Ph.D.
smayo@molloy.edu

"Minoring in Public and Community Service has given me the opportunity to work with people of all ages and races in my community, an opportunity for which I am truly grateful."

—A MOLLOY SECOND-YEAR STUDENT

The Social Concerns Programs offered by Molloy College, a four-year liberal arts institution in the Dominican tradition, are dedicated to producing civically responsible graduates prepared to reciprocate in terms of time, talent, and resources for that which they have abundantly received from the community. The three academic programs sponsored by the Molloy College Center for Social and Ethical Concerns are the major in International Peace and Justice, the minor in Public and Community Service, and the minor in Applied Ethics.

Among the ways that each of these programs promotes the civic development of the student are the following:

✦ Each program includes a service-learning component in which students volunteer with an at-risk population in one of 50 service sites throughout the Long Island area.

✦ Foundational and capstone courses are used to integrate the students' community-service experience with a theory of community life and citizenship.

✦ Opportunities are available for students to go on for graduate work overseas through an affiliation with the Catholic University of Leuven, Belgium.

Molloy offers each student participating in its social concerns programs an individualized program of study. Students work with an academic advisor from the Center who guides them through their internship and their academic research. During their senior year all program participants are obligated to write a thesis, which is publicly defended before a board of three service-learning faculty members from various disciplines. Unlike most other academic programs, the aim of the Center's social concerns programs is not simply to acquire information about a certain field of study or even necessarily to prepare students for some future vocation. The aim of each of these programs is to transform students into socially responsible, ethically conscious members of their communities.

NICHOLLS STATE UNIVERSITY

LA HIGHWAY 1
PO BOX 2004
THIBODAUX, LA 70310
504.446.8111
http://www.server.nich.edu/

UNDERGRADUATES: 6,400

For program information, please contact:
JOANNE C. FERRIOT, Ph.D.
Vpsa-jcf@nich-nsuet.nich.edu

Nicholls State, founded in 1948, is a public, comprehensive university. In 1993 the University adopted its current statement of mission which "requires that the University maintain and improve programs which develop the character of its students and encourage responsible citizenship."

Several aspects of Nicholls State University's character-development efforts attempt to inculcate the institution's stated virtues, including:

✦ THE LEADERSHIP PROGRAM. Focused on ethical leadership, this program stresses the concept of leadership through negotiation, considering and weighing the ideas of others, valuing the efforts of others, and having the courage to express and uphold community-wide values.

✦ STUDENT ORGANIZATIONS. Organizations such as Peer Assistance, the Residence Hall Association, and various religious groups have training and discussion opportunities on issues such as compassion, cultural understanding, and civic virtues.

✦ STUDENT PROGRAMMING. Student Affairs departments, such as the Office of Student Life, impress upon students respect for the laws, the value of civility, and relating to others as equal participants in a just society.

✦ THE NICHOLLS CREED: WHAT I BELIEVE. The Office of Student Affairs has initiated and promoted this student-designed and student-run project, which consists of a statement of principles that are, or should be, common to the Nicholls community.

The Nicholls Creed reads: "As a Nicholls State student, above all, I am RESPONSIBLE for my fellow students, and for my environment. Because of this, I believe in and am committed to these principles: Respect, Equality, Success, Perseverance, Open-mindedness, Non-violence, Safety for self and others, Integrity, Benevolence, Loyalty, and Excellence."

OKLAHOMA CHRISTIAN UNIVERSITY OF SCIENCE AND ARTS

2501 EAST MEMORIAL ROAD
OKLAHOMA CITY, OK 73136
800.877.5010
http://www.oc.edu/

UNDERGRADUATES: 2,000

For program information, please contact:
JACK SKAGGS, Ph.D.
jack.skaggs@oc.edu

Oklahoma Christian University of Science and Arts is a four-year, liberal arts institution whose mission is to create lives of leadership and purpose. Part of accomplishing this mission is to provide students with the tools to become active, well-informed, and responsible citizens. This applies not only to the students of Oklahoma Christian, but also to young people of all ages that the University reaches through the American Citizenship Center and Enterprise, USA, which are both housed on campus.

Specific activities of these initiatives include:

✦ **AMERICAN POLITICAL ECONOMY.** Each undergraduate student at Oklahoma Christian is required to take this core curriculum class, which examines the interconnection between the fundamentals of the American government and the basic principles of economy.

✦ **STUDENTS IN FREE ENTERPRISE (SIFE).** By putting students in the role of teaching others, they get a first-hand understanding of economics, management, marketing, and education. Through their outreach programs, SIFE teams teach basic economic concepts to all ages.

✦ **THE AMERICAN CITIZENSHIP CENTER.** Dedicated to building an understanding of America, the center was founded on the principle that the American heritage set forth by our forefathers must be sustained. Through experiential education aimed directly at youth, the founding principles of individual liberty—personal responsibility, free enterprise, and strong moral standards—are brought to the forefront.

✦ **ENTERPRISE SQUARE, USA.** Interactive exhibits are designed to teach about the American free-enterprise system in an entertaining and informational way.

In 1998, the American Citizen Center reached an estimated 25,000 young people through its many programs, and Enterprise Square, USA attracted 15,000 visitors—evidence that Oklahoma Christian University educates not only their own students but also others to be civic-minded citizens.

REGIS UNIVERSITY

3333 REGIS BOULEVARD
DENVER, CO 80221
303.458.4100
http://www.regis.edu/

UNDERGRADUATES: 7,600

For program information, please contact:
RICHARD W. DUNPHY
rdunphy@regis.edu

"While I give my family and hometown credit for my quality of character, Regis has helped me refine it and give it direction."

—A REGIS THIRD-YEAR STUDENT

Regis is a church-affiliated, liberal arts university. Inspired by the on-campus meeting of Pope John Paul II and President Bill Clinton, University President Reverend Michael J. Sheeran, SJ, announced the establishment of the Regis University Institute on the Common Good in October 1998. On the weekend of November 14–15, 1998, the Institute was officially inaugurated with the visit of Nobel Peace Prize Laureate Archbishop Desmond Tutu.

The Institute facilitates dialog aimed at developing strategies to resolve significant social issues. Rooted in the tradition of Roman Catholic social teaching, the Institute asserts the dignity and social nature of the human person. Neither liberal nor conservative in its posture, the Institute operates on the belief that a healthy society is committed to the welfare of all its members, especially those without a voice.

Through its public forums, featuring major speakers, panels, open discussions, and debates, the Institute provides opportunities for its students to participate in dialog that seeks to find common ground about important community issues. Contact with world and community leaders who represent a wide range of viewpoints allows students to experience how significant social issues can be addressed in an atmosphere of mutual respect. The University intends to integrate the yearly theme of the Institute into the curriculum of its various schools; the Institute contributes to the internal transformation of the University by providing greater understanding of its mission, especially with respect to the promotion of social justice, and by educating Regis students to be leaders in the service of others.

SAMFORD UNIVERSITY

800 LAKESHORE DRIVE
BIRMINGHAM, AL 35229
205.870.2011
http://www.samford.edu/

UNDERGRADUATES: 3,000

For program information, please contact:
RICHARD H. FRANKLIN, Ed.D.
rhfrankl@samford.edu

Samford, a private, church-affiliated university, emphasizes character development, academic integrity, spiritual growth, and responsible citizenship. Samford's program is founded on a code of values for which the Christian faith is a primary source. The code of values supports the campus community's standards for conduct and serves as a cornerstone for the discipline system, counseling, and programming for character development, civic and personal responsibility, leadership, and healthy lifestyle choices. All who work, study, and learn at Samford do so voluntarily. As is the case with all communities, reasonable expectations contribute to the common good.

The following sampling of Samford's Code of Values communicates the values, expectations, rights, and responsibilities of students:

✦ WORTH OF THE INDIVIDUAL. We value the intrinsic worth of every individual in the community. Our respect for other individuals includes an appreciation of cultural backgrounds different from our own, an understanding of different attitudes and opinions, and an awareness of the consequences of our actions on the broader community.

✦ RESPECT FOR COMMUNITY AUTHORITY. We value our privileges and responsibilities as members of the University community and as citizens of the community beyond the campus. We value the community standards of conduct expressed in our system of laws and value the fair administration of those laws, including University, municipal, state, or federal laws.

Samford's civic education program enables students to examine their behaviors and values within the context of the values system and goes beyond punishment for breaking rules by illustrating to students how their behavior impacts the larger community.

STATE UNIVERSITY OF NEW YORK COLLEGE AT BROCKPORT

350 NEW CAMPUS DRIVE
BROCKPORT, NY 14420-2915
800.382.8447
http://www.brockport.edu/

UNDERGRADUATES: 5,400

For program information, please contact:
KAREN A. CLINTON-PHELPS
KCPhelps@po.brockport.edu

"I believe the Passport to Leadership Program encompasses many aspects necessary for personal growth and future professional success."

—A BROCKPORT FOURTH-YEAR STUDENT

SUNY College at Brockport, founded in 1835, is a public, liberal arts institution. The College's People Advocating Community Education (PACE) educational series is comprised of SUNY Brockport faculty, staff, and students who are committed to addressing discriminatory or bias-related behavior in the campus and community. PACE addresses these problems through educational workshops, prevention programs, and institutional action.

In conjunction with academic departments and administrative units, PACE provides opportunities for the campus community to interact with and learn from those of different ethnicities and cultures. In support of their mission to supplement in-class learning process by providing cocurricular, educational programs, PACE sponsors workshops on such topics as racism versus prejudice, homophobia, mediation and conflict resolution, establishing better communities, multicultural communications, and ethnoviolence. The workshops are interactive, providing attendees the opportunity to fully participate in the discussion.

The uniqueness of SUNY Brockport's PACE Educational Series is that it cannot successfully function without the support of the University's faculty members and those of neighboring institutions, the University of Rochester and the Rochester Institute of Technology. Moreover, many faculty members not only encourage students to attend those workshops relating to course curricula but have brought entire classes to them in place of academic classes. Recently, the PACE educational series merged with the SUNY Brockport's leadership series, making it a required component of the leadership certificate program.

Through educational initiatives such as the PACE educational series, SUNY College at Brockport plays an important role in ensuring its graduates are civic-minded, responsible citizens who possess the intellectual and practical tools to better their communities.

Swarthmore College

500 COLLEGE AVENUE
SWARTHMORE, PA 19081
610.328.8000
http://www.swarthmore.edu/

UNDERGRADUATES: 1,300

For program information, please contact:
PAT JAMES
pjames1@swarthmore.edu

"Through a biology seminar, I got very interested in stopping the outbreak of Hepatitis A among Native American children. This summer I am on a reservation implementing a prevention program."

—A SWARTHMORE THIRD-YEAR STUDENT

Swarthmore students each year work closely with disadvantaged communities in nearby Chester and Philadelphia through public-service internships that address questions of community empowerment and advocacy. Organized through the Office of Community Service Learning Programs, cornerstone activities include:

✦ COMMUNITY POLITICS/INTERNSHIP SEMINAR. This political science course explores the practice of democratic and multicultural politics through internships, dialog with local activists, reading assignments, and field trips. The course challenges students to integrate reflection with experience and theory with practice to better understand the roles and responsibilities of community activists.

✦ COMMUNITY-BASED LEARNING. The College maintains a clearinghouse of nearly 500 internship and volunteer opportunities congruent with students' interests, skills, personal and academic goals.

✦ CIVIC. The college supports CIVIC (Cooperative Involvement of Volunteers in Communities), a coalition of student-led organizations that address issues of environmental racism, tutor adult immigrants, and take part in other social action initiatives.

True to its Quaker heritage, many Swarthmore faculty offer courses that explore the concept of social change within the context of our democratic traditions and practices. These courses and experiences provide students with a deeper understanding of how struggling communities both respond to challenges and celebrate their achievements.

Tufts University

BALLOU HALL
MEDFORD, MA 02155
617.628.5000
http://www.tufts.edu/

UNDERGRADUATES: 4,500

For program information, please contact:
BADI FOSTER, Ph.D.
bfoste01@emerald.tufts.edu

"The concept of a College of Citizenship and Public Service made sense to me immediately. The linkage between service and learning helps students understand the power of active citizenship and service to society."

—A TUFTS UNIVERSITY FOURTH-YEAR STUDENT

Committed to making values and skills of active citizenship a hallmark of Tufts University degrees, the University College of Citizenship and Public Service (UCCPS) aims to orient and prepare graduates for a lifetime commitment to service to society both domestically and abroad. UCCPS encourages students to integrate their academic interests with issues affecting society. Taking an "across the curriculum" approach, the initiative supports and elevates programs throughout Tufts.

✦ UCCPS. This program offers students service-learning courses that promote values and skills of active citizenship. UCCPS assists faculty members to connect community learning opportunities and traditional academic work in each department. Faculty mentor students interested in linking their course work to community issues. The University College continues to build relationships with community organizations, schools, and individual leaders. Community resources are utilized for volunteer work, internship opportunities, research topics, and service-learning courses.

✦ THE LINCOLN FILENE CENTER FOR CITIZENSHIP AND PUBLIC AFFAIRS (LFC) is an institutional resource coordinating the administrative aspect of the University College of Public Service. The mission of LFC is to increase the will and the capacity of individuals and organizations to build healthy communities through active citizenship and public service.

Utilizing resources such as the Lincoln Filene Center for Citizenship and Public Affairs, UCCPS reinforces existing programs and activities at Tufts University. It enhances education for citizenship by strengthening course work and providing additional opportunities for community service learning within academic courses. UCCPS accomplishes lasting improvements in selected areas of curriculum and extracurricular programming.

University of Cincinnati

CINCINNATI, OH 45221-0091
513.556.6000
http://www.uc.edu/

UNDERGRADUATES: 21,000

For program information, please contact:
MITCHEL LIVINGSTON, PH.D.
mitchel.livingston@uc.edu

The University of Cincinnati, a comprehensive, public institution, encompasses diverse groups of people in the process of conducting their academic, professional, and social lives. All too often, however, such activities and interaction are segregated along a variety of lines, including race, sex, or college affiliation. The University's Just Community Initiative is intended to help coalesce the members of the University's diverse population around a unifying set of principles in order to build community and enhance individuals' experiences at the institution.

In an effort to better address the needs and enterprises of all its constituents, the Just Community program promotes:

✦ Civil, frank discourse;

✦ Respect for self and others;

✦ A heightened understanding of self and others;

✦ An equal opportunity to achieve and flourish; and

✦ Social action among community members.

As the Just Community Initiative becomes more integrated into the University, so have programs designed to increase leadership and involvement. For example, an academic scholarship competition, Cincinnatus, requires all scholarship winners to contribute 20 hours a year to community service on or off campus for each year they receive scholarship support. Efforts are also underway to increase the numbers of students participating in off-campus service to the broader community. In addition, all first-year students are encouraged to read a series of articles, short stories, and poetry entitled the Just Community Readings before they begin their careers at the University. The Just Community Initiative encourages all members of the community to contribute their time and energies to making the University a better place.

University of Mary Hardin-Baylor

900 COLLEGE STREET
BELTON, TX 76513
254.295.8642
http://www.umhb.edu/

UNDERGRADUATES: 2,600

For program information, please contact:
CAROL WOODWARD
cwoodwar@umhb.edu

Strong moral character development and civically responsible behavior are an integral part of innovative holistic education at the University of Mary Hardin-Baylor, a private, faith-based liberal arts institution. The University's Social Work Club, an integral part of the Social Work department, affords opportunities for social work majors and other interested students to expand their academic knowledge and experience in areas that promote character development and active, well-informed, responsible citizenship.

Activities of the Social Work Club include:

✦ Student Day at the Legislature gives students the opportunity to focus on current social problems and advocate for those groups who are the most needy.

✦ Social Work Advisory Board and National Association of Social Workers/Texas Central Counties Steering Committee help students to develop task group and professional networking skills.

✦ Community-service projects give students the opportunity to help others by volunteering at social-service agencies.

Through the Social Work Club, students are provided with opportunities to participate in community-service projects, legislative advocacy for the disadvantaged, leadership development activities, and competitions that promote personal growth and sharing—activities that help Mary Hardin-Baylor students evolve into well-rounded, active, and involved citizens and future leaders in American communities.

UNIVERSITY OF PENNSYLVANIA

PHILADELPHIA, PA 19104
215.898.5000
http://www.upenn.edu/

UNDERGRADUATES: 11,400

For program information, please contact:
IRA HARKAVY, Ph.D.
harkavy@pobox.upenn.edu

At the heart of civic responsibility is the concept of neighborliness—caring about and assisting those living in proximity. As an institution, a university's actions express morality; a university's civic engagement teaches lessons to its students and to society. The University of Pennsylvania, a private research university, has sought to develop mutually beneficial partnerships with its West Philadelphia community. Penn's approach, a nationally recognized model for higher education, has been to advance academically based community service rooted in and intrinsically tied to teaching and research.

Program highlights include:

✦ THE PUBLIC SERVICE SUMMER INTERNSHIP supports more than 20 Penn undergraduates in an intensive 12-week action research seminar connected to their work on a pressing moral issue in American society. The interns also assist with development and teaching of a community-focused, problem-solving curriculum at West Philadelphia middle schools.

✦ THE CENTER FOR COMMUNITY PARTNERSHIPS coordinates more than 80 undergraduate and graduate courses to link Penn faculty and students to work in public schools, helping to create University-assisted community schools that address the educational, recreational, and social service needs of the community.

✦ CIVIC HOUSE, a student volunteer center, coordinates student service activities citywide and provides training and opportunities for reflection on the service experience.

The University of Pennsylvania's work reflects a deep commitment to collaborative partnerships with its community—partnerships that teach students the ethic of service, as well as engage them in projects that can, over time, bring about structural, enduring community improvements such as effective public schools, neighborhood economic development, and vital community organizations. Penn students are learning not only to care but also to be effective contributors.

UNIVERSITY OF SAN FRANCISCO

2130 FULTON STREET
SAN FRANCISCO, CA 94117
415.422.6136
http://www.usfca.edu/

UNDERGRADUATES: 4,700

For program information, please contact:
KUNI HAY, Ph.D.
hayk@usfca.edu
ROBERTA JOHNSON, Ph.D.
johnson@usfca.edu

"Being a part of PMC was a life-changing experience. It taught me how to live a life congruent with my values."
—A SAN FRANCISCO SECOND-YEAR STUDENT

The University of San Francisco (USF) is a private, church-affiliated university that serves as home to the Phelan Multicultural Community (PMC). The program provides a living-learning experience for 24 self-selected students to explore their process of socialization in relation to one another. In addition, the USF Public Service Program (PSP) offers students the opportunity to explore their own ideas regarding serving the public.

Components of the Phelan Multicultural Community include: a three-unit course each semester that helps students to recognize, explore, and celebrate traditions and heritages that contribute to the development of individual identity; weekly discussion sessions that explore examples of intercultural influences in students' daily lives through selected readings, videos, and guest lecturers; and special events in which residents contribute their unique worldviews to create a model for harmonious living.

By combining learning with participation, USF's Public Service Program challenges students to think about their values as they relate to their role in society and enables them to expand their education beyond the classroom. PSP students participate in a public service placement for at least one semester or summer. Students can feed the poor, assist grassroots and community-based organizations, or volunteer through the University's Campus Ministry. Students may also receive academic credit by integrating their volunteer experiences with corresponding course work.

USF's Public Service Program allows students to experience public service from the point of view of the bureaucracy and from the point of view of the person in need. By offering students two unique perspectives, PSP better prepares them to be civic-minded, concerned citizens.

The University of South Dakota

414 EAST CLARK STREET
VERMILLION, SD 57069
605.677.5011
http://www.usd.edu/

UNDERGRADUATES: 4,900

For program information, please contact:
WILLIAM RICHARDSON, Ph.D.
wrichard@usd.edu

The University of South Dakota, founded in 1862, is a public, comprehensive institution that serves as home to the W. O. Farber Center for Civic Leadership. The W. O. Farber Center has a threefold mission to provide academic courses, enrichment through conferences and forums, and community outreach through internships and workshops.

Approximately 20 students from each first-year class are chosen each year for participation in the Civic Leadership Studies Program. Students are selected based upon their high-school academic performance, academic potential, and record of leadership in school or community activities. All students, regardless of academic major, are eligible for consideration for one of ten scholarships.

The Civic Leadership Studies program was designed as a minor so that it could be readily incorporated into any of the existing majors on campus. The proposal establishing the program envisions a graduate concentration in leadership studies within the existing political science programs.

Although it is less than two years old, the University of South Dakota's W. O. Farber Center program has seen its first class of 13 students enter the academic program. It has hosted one major conference on civic responsibility in which Colin Powell was the featured speaker, three "Farber Forums" about significant political/cultural issues, and a major conference entitled, "Citizenship, Leadership, and Character: The WWII Generation and the Baby Boomers," which featured panels that included WWII veterans, Vietnam veterans, scholars, WWII-era elected officials, citizens, and student leaders. Such activities benefit not only student participants affiliated with the Farber Center but also the broader campus community.

University of Wisconsin– Oshkosh

800 ALGOMA BOULEVARD
OSHKOSH, WI 54901
920.424.1234
http://www.uwosh.edu/

UNDERGRADUATES: 9,300

For program information, please contact:
AARON WINOWISKI
winowa20@homer.mio.uwosh.edu

The University of Wisconsin–Oshkosh is a public, comprehensive institution. Nearly one-third of the 11,000 students who attend the University live in one of the institution's 11 residence halls. Therefore, it is natural that citizenship and service learning should be incorporated into students' living environment. Each year the University's Department of Residence Life sponsors a Citizenship Program to encourage students to become involved in community-service activities. Through the selection of an annual theme and a monthly poster series, students are made aware of their responsibilities as citizens. Unique and creative events and programs have been organized, including Halloween parties for local children, food and clothing drives, a holiday party for unmatched children from the Big Brothers/Big Sisters program, and safety and security programs.

In addition to the theme and poster series, components of the University of Wisconsin's Citizenship Program include:

✦ A panel of faculty, staff, community leaders, and students chooses the top three residence halls that exemplify good citizenship. Individual people and programs are also recognized.

✦ Students learn about specific needs they can meet in a variety of organizations in Oshkosh.

The University of Wisconsin—Oshkosh's Citizenship Program has been in existence since 1986. Next to social programming, citizenship programming is the most popular type of programming that occurs in the University's residence halls. UW students want to do well by others and will become involved in community events if they know that they can assist another human being.

Washington and Lee University

LEXINGTON, VA 24450
540.463.8400
http://www.wlu.edu/

UNDERGRADUATES: 1,700

For program information, please contact:
HARLAN BECKLEY
beckleyh@wlu.edu

"The Shepherd Poverty Program awakened an interest in serving others."

—A WASHINGTON AND LEE UNIVERSITY FOURTH-YEAR STUDENT

Washington and Lee is a private university that serves as home to the Shepherd Poverty Program, which involves students, faculty, and alumni to address poverty as a persistent obstacle to individual and community development.

Characteristics of Washington and Lee University's Shepherd Poverty Program include:

✦ An introductory, interdisciplinary study of poverty, after which undergraduates may apply for an eight-week service-learning project during the summer. Law students are also eligible for these service-learning opportunities, which are arranged through agencies in rural and urban areas in the U.S., as well as in other parts of the world.

✦ The summer program, conducted in cooperation with Spelman College in Atlanta and Berea College in Kentucky. These students meet prior to undertaking their service and reconvene to share, interpret, and evaluate their eight-week work experience.

✦ An advanced seminar, for which students apply after completely their summer service work. This seminar culminates with a term paper focusing on a particular area of poverty studies from the perspective of legal studies or a specific undergraduate major. Research and writing takes place under the supervision of the director of the program, and work on these papers is guided by advisers in the student's major area of study.

Washington and Lee University's Shepherd Poverty Program helps to prepare students for vocations in education, health care, law, social services, public policy, and religious ministry. Through this special study and volunteer service, the University promotes two vital aspects of its mission: to cultivate in students "the responsibility to serve society through the productive use of talent and training" and a capacity "for self-sacrifice in behalf of their fellow citizens."

Winthrop University

701 OAKLAND AVENUE
ROCK HILL, SC 29733
803.323.2211
http://www.winthrop.edu/

UNDERGRADUATES: 4,300

For program information, please contact:
RODNEY BENNETT, Ph. D.
bennettr@winthrop.edu

"At Winthrop University, your experience inside the classroom is as important as the one outside."

—A WINTHROP FIFTH-YEAR STUDENT

As a public, four-year residential institution, Winthrop University is committed to providing students with a distinctive education. To this end, the Student Government Association adopted the Dedication for Excellence in April 1994. The six fundamental components of the Dedication for Excellence are:

✦ FREEDOM OF SPEECH. Each person brings a set of different experiences and beliefs to the campus community, and all expressions of thought will be received in a manner that supports the teaching/learning experience at Winthrop.

✦ ACADEMIC INTEGRITY. Students will dedicate themselves to the pursuit of knowledge and truth.

✦ A DIVERSE CULTURAL ENVIRONMENT. Students will respect the integrity of each person and value individuals for their creations, achievements, and contributions.

✦ PERSONAL RESPONSIBILITY. Students will assume full responsibility for their actions, thoughts, personal growth, and development.

✦ SOCIAL RESPONSIBILITY. Students will contribute to the university community and leave Winthrop a better place for their having been here.

✦ CONSIDERATION OF OTHERS. Students will demonstrate a concern for the welfare and rights of others and will respect the dignity of all people.

Each year at fall convocation all faculty, staff, and students pledge their commitment to the Dedication for Excellence. The Dedication for Excellence is integrated into campus life through new student orientation initiatives, appears in faculty course syllabi, and serves as a programming model for the University's Department of Residence Life. Additionally, the document provides the groundwork for partnerships between Greek and multicultural student life, as well as student activities with its programming boards and committees.

Wofford College

429 NORTH CHURCH STREET
SPARTANBURG, SC 29303-3663
864.597.4000
http://www.wofford.edu/

UNDERGRADUATES: 1,100

For program information, please contact:
DOYLE BOGGS, Ph.D.
boggsdw@wofford.edu

Wofford is a church-affiliated, liberal arts college whose commitment to civic education is exemplified by its vision statement: "The leaders of the 21st century must be persons of intelligence, of cultural breadth, of moral vision and civic conscience. . . ."

Civic Education activities at Wofford College that support that vision include:

✦ THE BONNER SCHOLARS PROGRAM offers a small group of students substantial scholarship help, additional financial support, and enrichment activities while attending college.

✦ THE TWIN TOWERS program fosters a sense of community between the Wofford College family and the citizens of Spartanburg, and instills in Wofford students the importance of giving something back.

✦ ETHOS COUNCIL, composed of faculty, staff, and students who meet monthly to discuss civic education issues and sponsor campus-wide forums on ethical and leadership issues.

✦ JANUARY INTERIM, a four-week, one-project experience, offers structured and independent civic leadership efforts such as internships in Washington, DC.

Wofford is located in the downtown area of a medium-sized Southern city that has become a center of international investment and a rapidly expanding 21st-century economy. However, the immediate vicinity of the campus has a number of less affluent neighborhoods with typical urban problems. Wofford has developed partnerships with many human-service agencies in Spartanburg, such as Habitat for Humanity; the Bethlehem Center, a church-related community center; Cleveland Elementary School, where there are extensive after-school tutoring programs; and a student-athletes' speaker's bureau that carries the message, "Stay off drugs, stay in school" to classrooms across the county. Such partnerships benefit not only those in need but also members of the Wofford community who participate.

Youngstown State University

ONE UNIVERSITY PLAZA
YOUNGSTOWN OH 44555
330.742.2000
http://www.ysu.edu/

UNDERGRADUATES: 12,500

For program information, please contact:
NATHAN P. RITCHEY, Ph.D.
nate@math.ysu.edu

"Not only does the University Scholars Program provide an outstanding undergraduate education, but it motivates me toward continued involvement in my community."

—A YOUNGSTOWN STATE FOURTH-YEAR STUDENT

The University Scholars Program at Youngstown State University, a public institution, is based on the premise that academic excellence deserves to be recognized on a par with achievement in the highest areas of human activity. This recognition takes the form of an award of full tuition and room and board for four years for those able to maintain their high level of excellence. The program provides a balanced education for each of the 200 University Scholars by providing rigorous academic challenges, opportunities to participate in community service and cultural events, and a living/learning center where students enhance their college experience and prepare for the responsibilities of life.

Program highlights include:

✦ Each University Scholar completes a minimum of 60 hours of community service annually. The program views community service as an opportunity for students to learn about themselves, each other, and the community.

✦ University Scholars participate in weekend honors seminars designed to investigate social, political, historical, and scientific issues and their effect on society.

✦ Each University Scholar attends cultural events that nurture an appreciation for the fine and performing arts.

✦ All University Scholars live in Cafaro House, a living/learning honors residence hall that provides an educational and social climate that enhances the students' communication skills and fosters an environment of scholarship.

All of these components, when combined with discipline-specific education, impart values of leadership, integrity, and civic commitment. Since its inception in 1992, the University Scholars Program has had a significant impact on the University and the surrounding communities, and it promises to be a vital component of the University's mission in the future.

CHARACTER AND SEXUALITY PROGRAMS

There is a growing awareness in higher education that matters of personal character and responsibility must be applied to sexual behavior. In addition to providing students with information about STDs or sex-related problems such as date rape and sexual harassment, a growing number of campus-based programs encourage students to reflect on the emotional, psychological, and moral aspects of sexuality. Students learn to appreciate and apply the core virtues of self-control, respect, responsibility, and integrity in their relationships with others. In short, these exemplary programs emphasize the dimension of character development.

ANTIOCH COLLEGE

795 LIVERMORE STREET
YELLOW SPRINGS, OH 45387
937.767.7331
http://www.antioch-college.edu/

UNDERGRADUATES: 600

For program information, please contact:
CHRISTINA CAPPELLETTI
cappelle@antioch-college.edu

"The program allowed me to look at myself and return to strength and self-respect in my relationships."

—AN ANTIOCH FOURTH-YEAR STUDENT

Focusing on consent and communication, students at Antioch College, a private, liberal arts school, have initiated several programs aimed at preventing sexual offense. The SOPP (Sexual Offense Prevention Policy) and SOP/SAP (Sexual Offense Prevention and Survivors' Advocacy Program) provide on-campus guidelines for consent and sexual behavior. The "Ask First" prevention policy specifies what steps should be taken to ensure clear communication of consent and respectful sexual behavior. The policy educates the Antioch community not only by identifying the parameters of sexual offense but by affirming the safety and livelihood of each person. The SOPP has garnered national and international esteem as a model policy and program for sexual violence prevention.

The SOPP states that any person (any gender) initiating sexual behavior must:

✦ Request consent at each stage of interaction;

✦ Receive verbal consent;

✦ Not proceed if there is silence, a denial or withdrawal of consent, or consent given while inebriated.

Through SOP/SAP, students organize community events to further advance the cause of sexual offense prevention. Events such as forums, dances, expositions, marches, community art projects, and performances are all designed to discourage violence and celebrate visions of consensual intimacy and community building. One group of Antioch students took the initiative to further communicate the SOPP message by forming "BRIDGES," a performance troupe that travels regionally, providing educational outreach on a range of issues related to prevention of sexual offenses.

Antioch students who are involved in the programs help create a community where everyone can safely and creatively experience profound human communication that will endure throughout their years at Antioch and beyond.

CALVIN COLLEGE

3201 BURTON STREET SE
GRAND RAPIDS, MI 49546
616.957.6000
http://www.calvin.edu/

UNDERGRADUATES: 3,900

For program information, please contact:
DALE COOPER
coop@calvin.edu

"Calvin encourages a personal, spiritual, emotional, and physical integrity through responsible decision-making and expects moral Christian living within the context of a larger secular world."

—A CALVIN FOURTH-YEAR STUDENT

Christian faith and identity are at the center of character development and sexual awareness at Calvin College, a liberal arts institution affiliated with the Christian Reformed Church. Calvin's multifaceted program offers specific courses, panels, seminars, and presentations held outside the classroom—all designed to connect one's Christian faith to responsible decision-making. "We want students to develop a balance between responsibility and freedom," says program director and Calvin chaplain Dale Cooper. "Appropriate actions flow out of hearts that are prompted and shaped toward obedience, and we strive to give our students the spiritual and moral shaping to help them concretely express these principles in their own lives." Calvin's distinct approach to guiding students on sexuality issues includes the following:

✦ GOOD SEX, GOOD PEOPLE: A CALL TO PURITY. This weeklong series "encourages campus-wide conversation about the holy mystery of being male and female." Topics include "Sexuality and Singleness," "Sexuality in the Media," and "Sexual Intimacy: How Far?"

✦ PSYCHOLOGY COURSE. A faculty member teaches "Christian Issues in Gender and Sexuality."

✦ PASTORAL GUIDANCE. The chaplain's office and the Counseling Center advise students on sexual issues.

✦ MARRIAGE. The "Engaged Encounter" weekend is for couples considering marriage.

The Calvin program has campus-wide support. Faculty members teach six classes throughout the academic year that incorporate character and sexuality issues. Each semester, students quickly fill such popular courses as "Birth, Sex, and Death in the Biblical World" and "The Nature of Sex." Comprehensive and faith-centered, Calvin's character and sexuality program is helping students create lives of responsibility and balance.

CHARLESTON SOUTHERN UNIVERSITY

9200 UNIVERSITY BOULEVARD
CHARLESTON, SC 29423-8087
843.863.7000
http://www.csuniv.edu/

UNDERGRADUATES: 2,400

For program information, please contact:
SUSAN STYLES, Ph.D.
sstyles@csuniv.edu

Abstinence is the goal of the sexual education effort at Charleston Southern University (CSU), a private, liberal arts institution. Realizing that the world sometimes views a "life of personal responsibility and self-control as counter cultural," CSU officials and Heritage Community Services, an educational services agency, have jointly developed a character and risk-reduction program. The CSU/Heritage program empowers students to reach their goals through making value-based decisions. The nationally acclaimed Heritage Method© Sexual Abstinence Program is based on psychological theory that incorporates the affective, behavioral, and cognitive dimensions of decision-making.

The program addresses sexuality education through several campus initiatives:

✦ **FRESHMAN ORIENTATION.** This interactive seminar emphasizes the benefits of abstaining from sex outside of marriage and examines sexual decision-making, featuring a peer panel of virgins and secondary virgins.

✦ **CONTINUOUS LEARNING OPPORTUNITIES.** The Heritage Keepers Club©, peer mentor training, and programs for student athletes promote self-control, character development, leadership, and community service through ongoing programs.

✦ **GRADUATE STUDIES.** A sexual education course is offered to master's-level education students, sex education instructors, and public/private community agency participants.

The CSU/Heritage program will continue to have a sustained influence in the classroom, as the University's Curriculum Committee and Heritage jointly develop a plan to incorporate CSU's Five Life Preparation Concepts: values, ethics, communication, leadership, and service. This project will challenge the faculty to address character development and professional ethics implications through each academic discipline. Comprehensive and collaborative, the CSU/Heritage program is helping students learn to "go against the grain" to pursue lives of sexual responsibility and abstinence.

COLLEGE OF THE HOLY CROSS

1 COLLEGE STREET
WORCESTER, MA 01610
508.793.2011
http://www.holycross.edu/

UNDERGRADUATES: 2,800

For program information, please contact:
MATTHEW R. ELIOTT, Ph.D.
meliott@holycross.edu

One of the most sought-after volunteer opportunities for students at College of the Holy Cross, a private, Jesuit, liberal arts institution, is the Relationship Peer Education program. Students who become Relationship Peer Educators (RPEs) teach and encourage program participants to examine important issues surrounding intimate relationships, sexual responsibility, the differences and similarities among men and women, attitudes and beliefs as they are related to sociocultural expectations, the development of healthy and unhealthy relationships, and the factors surrounding sexual assault and its prevention. Program coordinators help shape the program using the principle of "primary prevention," which they define as the promotion of healthy behaviors and attitudes and/or reduction of the likelihood of new problems.

RPE programs incorporate a wide range of initiatives related to character development and sexuality, including:

✦ **SEXUAL ASSAULT.** RPEs are trained to facilitate programs that address issues of sexual consent and decision-making.

✦ **UNHEALTHY RELATIONSHIPS.** Student educators help students spot warning signs of unhealthy relationships and guide them through strategies for developing healthy relationships.

✦ **EDUCATIONAL THEATER.** RPEs have scripted and staged a dramatic production of an acquaintance rape as it might occur at Holy Cross. Actors remain in character after the performance as they answer audience questions.

Over the past five years, RPEs have produced approximately 175 programs, attracting several thousand student participants. The program, which enjoys a 95% approval rate from participants, has received recognition and reward for its efforts through two recent grants. Faculty members who teach the First Year Program, Women's Studies, English, Psychology, and Religious Studies use elements of the program. Relationship Peer Educators work to make *all* Holy Cross students more sexually responsible, helping to create a new generation that understands how to build healthy relationships.

CREIGHTON UNIVERSITY

2500 CALIFORNIA PLAZA
OMAHA, NE 68178
402.280.2700
http://www.creighton.edu/

UNDERGRADUATES: 4,000

For program information, please contact:
MICHELE MILLARD
mmillard@creighton.edu

Creighton University, a private Jesuit institution, has initiated a comprehensive peer education program that helps students view sexuality in the context of their whole selves, taking into account social, spiritual, physical, intellectual, and emotional development. The PROP Program (People Reaching Out to People) provides "psycho-educational" opportunities for students to examine their values and choices and helps students unite their behavior with personal beliefs and a knowledge of the consequences of their decisions. Students who choose to volunteer as peer educators receive their training in "Introduction to Peer Education," a three-credit class that covers character development and life-choice issues. Upon completion of the course, students begin creating interactive educational programs that weave sexuality issues throughout:

✦ **THE DATING GAME.** This popular program, in a game format, allows men and women to explore components of healthy relationships and dialog between genders.

✦ **ALCOHOL.** This series of programs focuses on alcohol use and how it affects sexual activity. Topics covered include lowered inhibitions, unprotected sex, and "regretted" sex.

✦ **DATE RAPE.** In this program, students explore issues of gender communication, alcohol use, and ways to protect themselves and others in a variety of situations.

✦ **STRESS MANAGEMENT.** This program explores ways that good relationships can help students cope with stress.

Other PROP programs that enrich student understanding of character development and sexuality issues include a self-esteem course, a holistic health fair, and a mock trial. The peer education program widens its reach by collaborating with departments across the Creighton campus, reaching nearly 1,700 students per year in Freshman Seminars, Greek organizations, ROTC, athletic organizations, and residence halls. This program creates trained students who can help others understand themselves better, creating positive change in their lives and in the campus culture.

DUQUESNE UNIVERSITY

600 FORBES AVENUE
PITTSBURGH, PA 15282
412.396.6000
http://www.duq.edu/

UNDERGRADUATES: 5,500

For program information, please contact:
ELLEN CROSSEY
crossey@duq2.cc.duq.edu

"I really liked the interaction and relevance of this program. Sometimes I get discouraged and it helps to hear what my peers are thinking. The program reinforces my values."

—A DUQUESNE FOURTH-YEAR STUDENT

Duquesne University, a Catholic private school, offers a nationally recognized program that has helped students understand sexuality as a natural component of life and wellness. The SHR Program (Supporting Healthy Relationships) provides students with the information and skills they need to help them make responsible decisions about sexuality that incorporate their own moral and ethical beliefs. Sponsored by the University's Student Health Service, SHR addresses several key issues related to character development and sexuality:

✦ **PRESSURES OF YOUTH.** Young adults face a variety of pressures and often feel their only choice is to become sexually active. Students learn that the consequences of their actions can compromise their personal values, sense of self, relationships, and health.

✦ **DECISION MAKING.** Students learn that they must empower themselves to make decisions that will create a positive balance in physical, emotional, social, spiritual, intellectual, and occupational areas of wellness.

✦ **COMMUNICATION SKILLS AND SELF ESTEEM.** Students learn how to communicate clearly and effectively through their decisions to apply the virtues of self-control and respect.

SHR has a wide reach on the Duquesne campus, involving institutional leaders, faculty members, staff, and students. First-year courses and part of the School of Education curriculum include elements of the SHR program. The program consistently receives positive student and professional peer evaluations and is recognized by the Mid-Atlantic College Health Association Conference and other national organizations. Closely aligned with Duquesne's mission to "seek truth and to disseminate knowledge within a moral and spiritual framework," it is no surprise that 70% of students who complete the program say their future behavior will change for the better.

JOHN BROWN UNIVERSITY

2000 WEST UNIVERSITY STREET
SILOAM SPRINGS, AR 72761
501.524.9500
http://www.jbu.edu/

UNDERGRADUATES: 1,400

For program information, please contact:
MEL FRATZKE, Ph.D.
mfratzke@acc.jbu.edu

Developing healthy relationships is a core goal of the Character and Sexuality program at John Brown University (JBU), a Christian liberal arts college. The program's conceptual framework is based on the belief that sound character, good values, and exemplary behavior emerge as one develops more healthy relationships and a better knowledge of character and sexuality issues. JBU employs multiple strategies and resources to promote its program, including two required courses, "Introduction to Higher Education" and "Foundation of Wellness," and special events such as Human Sexuality Week and Marriage and Family Week. Under the direction of Dr. Gary Oliver, the Center for Marriage and Family Studies offers seminars and programs on relationships, marriage, and families. The offices of Student Development and Campus Ministry also schedule retreats, workshops, and special chapels relating to character and sexuality.

There are several overlapping character development objectives to the JBU program:

✦ Students acquire skills and knowledge that will help them develop successful and healthy relationships.

✦ With the goal of empowerment, students analyze relational issues that stem from family experiences.

✦ The roles of men and women are discussed to help students come to a better understanding of themselves and the opposite sex.

Students at JBU participate in a program that draws from Bible concepts to provide them with the understanding and experience necessary to develop personal integrity and productive relationships. Their experience at JBU helps make them more stable, focused, and healthy members of society.

LYCOMING COLLEGE

700 COLLEGE PLACE
WILLIAMSPORT, PA 17701
570.321.4000
http://www.lycoming.edu/

UNDERGRADUATES: 1,500

For program information, please contact:
MARK BRITTEN
britten@lycoming.edu

"Relationships Month and its many programs really help us think about how we treat others and how we want to be treated."

—A LYCOMING FOURTH-YEAR STUDENT

Every October during Relationships Month, students at Lycoming College, a private, liberal arts, church-affiliated institution, plan, sponsor, and present events that help them to reflect on their relationships. Programs include:

✦ THE CAMPUS CLOTHESLINE PROJECT. More than 300 students have created and displayed T-shirts protesting sexual assault and violence in relationships. The shirts are then hung on a clothesline for everyone on campus to read.

✦ THE "TAKE BACK THE NIGHT" MARCH. Students, faculty, and staff unite in a march and candlelight vigil calling for an end to sexual assault and violence in relationships.

✦ THE NAMES PROJECT AIDS MEMORIAL QUILT. In 1998, the NAMES Project, which manages the more than 45,000 panels that comprise The Quilt, sent 743 panels for display at Lycoming. During the display, students spent more than 500 hours in volunteer service checking in panels, greeting visitors, and providing information and emotional support. A Lycoming sorority made a panel commemorating a local man who died of AIDS-related diseases, which was incorporated into The Quilt while it was displayed on campus.

Programs during Relationships Month range from large presentations to small-group and classroom discussions with faculty giving course credit for class projects related to the programs. Relationships Month "enables Lycoming students to consider, discuss, and make healthy decisions about the many different relationships in their lives," says Mark Britten, Director of Counseling Services. "I follow the adage 'Involve me, and I'll understand and make use of my knowledge.'"

Ohio University

ATHENS, OH 45701
740.593.1000
http://www.ohiou.edu/

UNDERGRADUATES: 24,000

For program information, please contact:
CHARLENE KOPCHICK
kopchicc@oak.cats.ohiou.edu

"There are many programs on gender and health issues coming from all the organizations on campus and the diverse interests of students. There are many support groups and events that raise awareness of these important issues."

—AN OHIO SECOND-YEAR STUDENT

Ohio University's wellness program has been so successful that it has had a positive ripple effect across the student body and into the local community. POWER (Promoting Ohio University Wellness, Education, and Responsibility) begins in the classroom, with an innovative course that trains POWER members to be peer health educators. The course covers critical health and wellness issues that college students face, such as sexual responsibility, sexual assault, low-risk alcohol use, eating behavior, and spirituality. POWER members learn to be excellent communicators as they pass along the message of personal responsibility and respect to students in OU classes and student organizations, and to provide outreach to students in local middle and high schools.

Several aspects of the POWER program at this public, comprehensive institution reflect its continuing effectiveness:

✦ Students learn to understand and practice the virtues of personal responsibility.

✦ Students learn that to be effective peer health educators, they also must be positive role models.

✦ POWER concepts are integrated into other OU curricula, including classes taught in the Department of Health and Women's Studies.

With a motto of "Respect yourself, respect others, protect yourself and others," POWER was selected to be featured at a regional BACCHUS (Boosting Alcohol Consciousness Concerning the Health of University Students) conference. Through their personal actions and interactions with others, POWER members send a powerful and far-reaching message of personal responsibility and respect for others.

Pace University

ONE PACE PLAZA
NEW YORK, NY 10038
212.346.1200
http://www.pace.edu/

UNDERGRADUATES: 9,000

For program information, please contact:
FRANKLIN M. RICARTE
fricarte@pace.edu

"The group activities and scenarios allowed me to be more comfortable and open to talking about sex with other people."

—A PACE FIRST-YEAR STUDENT

From the very outset of their college careers at Pace University, a private, comprehensive institution, students are encouraged to participate in a series of programs and open discussions about sexuality. Pace requires all first-year students to take University 101, a introductory one-credit student-life course overseen by the Office of Newly Enrolled Undergraduate Students. Among the menu of interactive workshops offered through the course are three that focus on character development and sexuality. Geared toward entering students but offered to the entire Pace community, these workshops are cosponsored by the Office of Student Life and the Counseling Center:

✦ **LOVE ON THE ROCKS.** This popular workshop, modeled after a similar one at New York University, focuses on issues that spring from mixing alcohol use and sex. After an opening group discussion, facilitated by staff members, students volunteer to participate in a series of role-playing exercises involving two hypothetical couples.

✦ **LET'S TALK ABOUT SEX.** Through a combination of group discussion and role-playing exercises, students talk about such topics as sexual assault and gender differences in attitudes about sex.

✦ **SEX MATTERS.** This workshop provides an opportunity to increase understanding of communication within relationships. Facilitated by a health educator, students discuss how to communicate clearly about difficult topics such as contraception.

The Pace program has received positive feedback from students, who attend in large numbers and are often so involved in the activities and discussions that the workshops run longer than expected. Pace students who participate develop strong communication and decision-making skills that will promote better relationships throughout their lives.

PALM BEACH ATLANTIC COLLEGE

901 SOUTH FLAGLER DRIVE
W. PALM BEACH, FL 33416
561.803.2100
http://www.pbac.edu/

UNDERGRADUATES: 2,000

For program information, please contact:
CARL SMITH
smithcb@pbac.edu

"The series offers practical, relevant teaching for college students that encourages and deepens Christian values in daily living."

—A PALM BEACH ATLANTIC THIRD-YEAR STUDENT

Palm Beach Atlantic College, a liberal arts college in the Christian tradition, has developed a series of programs designed to help students grow and achieve success in every area of life. Through Campus Ministries, Palm Beach Atlantic offers several seminars that engage students both inside and outside the classroom, focusing on academic, social, and spiritual issues. Of these series of seminars, two focus on character development and sexuality:

✦ LOOKING FOR LOVE. This spring-semester series comprehensively examines relationships and sexual behavior. Students have the opportunity to take seminars on Sexual Abuse, Love Addictions, Foundations for a Healthy Self-Esteem, Lust, Being Secure in Your Singleness, and AIDS Awareness.

✦ REAL LIFE/REAL FAITH. Also offered in the spring, this series covers a broader range of social issues but includes such topics as Abortion and Homosexuality in the Church.

These seminars, and other programs at Palm Beach Atlantic, such as chapel and discussions on diversity, provide students with opportunities to reflect and be challenged through discussions on important issues. Through such programs, small-group sessions, and one-on-one interactions, students at Palm Beach Atlantic live in an environment that nurtures their holistic development into individuals who have effective relationships, strong character, and lifestyles based on Christian teachings.

SEATTLE PACIFIC UNIVERSITY

3307 THIRD AVENUE WEST
SEATTLE, WA 98119
206.281.2000
http://www.spu.edu/

UNDERGRADUATES: 2,600

For program information, please contact:
LES PARROTT, Ph.D.
lpiii@spu.edu

The Center for Relationship Development (CRD) on the campus of Seattle Pacific University, a church-affiliated institution, is a groundbreaking program dedicated to solving relationship problems before they begin. The central goal of CRD is to help students foster positive relationships with classmates, roomates, parents, teammates, siblings, supervisors, or potential marriage partners. Founded and directed by the husband-and-wife team of Drs. Les and Leslie Parrott, the CRD program is taught through Seattle Pacific courses and seminars attended by 800 students annually and in CRD-sponsored chapels, which attract 1,500 individuals annually. Character development aspects of CRD include:

✦ DIVERSE COURSE TOPICS. The CRD curriculum includes classes such as "Sex, Lies, and the Great Escape," "Keeping Family Ties from Pulling Strings," and "Falling in Love Without Losing Your Mind."

✦ COUPLE-TO-COUPLE MENTORING. Seasoned married couples, often Seattle Pacific faculty and staff members, work directly with soon-to-be-married couples, acting as guides and role models.

✦ RELATIONSHIP EMPHASIS WEEK. This special program expands the CRD scope by bringing in nationally recognized speakers such as Stephen Arterburn, author of *Addicted to Love;* Lewis Smedes, *Caring and Commitment;* and John Trent, *Love Is a Decision.*

There is also a community outreach component to CRD, which brings the programs to church communities locally, regionally, and nationally. In the fall of 1998, more than 400 pastors came to Seattle Pacific for a half-day seminar on how to implement "Saving Your Marriage Before it Starts," a CRD program that has been featured in national print and broadcast media. Character formation and commitment do not happen by accident, and at Seattle Pacific's Center for Relationship Development, they mark the beginning of a successful, long-term strategy of developing whole individuals.

SOUTHERN METHODIST UNIVERSITY

6425 BOAZ STREET
DALLAS, TX 75275
214.768.3000
http://www.smu.edu/

UNDERGRADUATES: 5,600

For program information, please contact:
CATHEY SOUTTER, Ph.D.
csoutter@mail.smu.edu

An innovative series of programs offered by Southern Methodist University (SMU), a private, liberal arts institution, is helping students tackle relationship issues between women and men. Seminars, academic classes, and interactive dramatic presentations help provide a supportive environment for young men and women who are working to better understand themselves and the patterns they exhibit in relationships. The Office of Psychological Services for Women and Gender Issues launched this effort with three central goals: to raise awareness of cultural attitudes and values that foster unhealthy views of self and others; to advocate the importance of wise decision-making in relationships; and to promote attitudes toward a healthy expression of sexuality. The SMU approach to building character as it relates to sexuality includes:

✦ **PRIMARY PREVENTION.** Sexuality-related educational programming is developed for classes, residence halls, Greek organizations, and other student groups. Topics include "Healthy Relationships," "Violence Against Women," and "What Men (and Women) Wish They Knew About Women (and Men)."

✦ **DATE RAPE MOCK TRIAL.** Audience members participate as jurors, the Dallas County Criminal Court judge presides over the proceedings, and students from SMU's law school serve as prosecution and defense.

✦ **THE GREAT SEX DEBATES.** Set in an informal and non-threatening environment, these debates give students the opportunity to discuss intimate relationships and sexuality.

✦ **FIRST-YEAR STUDENTS.** The program director instructs new students on wellness in a program focused on topics ranging from sexuality to eating disorders.

Program director Cathey Soutter and guest speakers incorporate aspects of the sexuality program into classroom lectures comprising "Psychology of Women," an SMU course offered annually. Students who participate in these programs develop a stronger knowledge of self and a fuller understanding on achieving better relationships throughout their lives.

STONEHILL COLLEGE

320 WASHINGTON STREET
EASTON, MA 02357
508.565.1000
http://www.stonehill.edu/

UNDERGRADUATES: 2,700

For program information, please contact:
NEAL I. PRICE, Ph.D.
nprice@stonehill.edu

Respect for others, highly valued at Stonehill College, an independent, church-related institution, is the focus of a unique program for first-year students that combines group discussions and theater to increase awareness of the importance of respect and communication in "partner relationships." While programs focusing on character and sexuality are offered to all Stonehill students, it is the Relationship/Respect program offered during orientation that sets the tone for on-campus relationship behavior. The five-year-old program, which evolves each year, consists of several elements:

✦ **"THE MORNING AFTER."** This original true-to-life drama, written by two Stonehill resident directors, depicts a sexual assault on campus. The presentation delves into the nuances of communication and the value of respect and character in a sexual relationship. Always prompting a thoughtful conversation about relationship dynamics, "The Morning After" has become the focus of the Relationship/Respect program.

✦ **COMMUNICATION AND CONVICTIONS.** Men and women students talk about the importance of verbal and nonverbal communication and discuss beliefs that help clarify convictions and expectations in relationships.

Every year, a variety of campus organizations offers programs that address issues of character and sexuality. In addition, the Office of Campus Ministry offers "Theology of Human Sexuality," an elective, three-credit course that addresses "embodiment and sexuality in the college environment." SAVE (Stonehill Against Violence Everywhere) is a new student group that develops educational programs on sexual and gender relations. SAVE's mission statement states that "awareness of healthy relationships is the responsibility of higher education institutions." Stonehill's programs have proven that promoting respect in relationships has positive and lasting effects on students.

THE UNIVERSITY OF ALABAMA

TUSCALOOSA, AL 35487-0132
205.348.6010
http://www.ua.edu/

UNDERGRADUATES: 12,900

For program information, please contact:
WHITNEY BURKE
wburke5858@aol.com

"Wasted Times" is a thought-provoking traveling theater troupe at The University of Alabama that helps audiences come to grips with the difficult decisions and issues that young adults face these days. Created in 1996 at this public, liberal arts institution, "Wasted Times" brings to life the feelings, beliefs, and behaviors common to students confronted with choices and temptations stemming from seduction, substance abuse, and social pressure.

The eight-student "Wasted Times" cast uses an original script and an improvisational approach to create scenarios addressing dating violence, substance abuse, sexuality, sexually transmitted diseases, and acquaintance rape. Each performance tackles character and sexuality by exploring myths and facts about sexuality, helping students minimize risk behaviors. The program emphasizes the development of healthy decision-making skills.

The fifty-minute performance is followed by a facilitated discussion and question-and-answer session with the cast members. Sponsored by The University of Alabama Women's Center, "Wasted Times" has performed for campus organizations, church youth groups, conferences, and high schools across Alabama, reaching more than 1,200 people in three years. A consultant hired when the program was founded wrote the original script, directed the production for its first two years, and continues to act as advisor to the current director and cast. Revisions are made to the script each year based on input from audience evaluations, which consistently give high ratings to the quality of the production and the content. This performing troupe is changing the way University of Alabama students and others think about sexual issues and helps make the college years something students will always look back on as good times and not "wasted times."

UNIVERSITY OF NEBRASKA–LINCOLN

14TH AND R STREETS
LINCOLN, NE 68588-0417
402.472.7211
http://www.unl.edu/

UNDERGRADUATES: 22,400

For program information, please contact:
PAT TETREAULT, Ph.D.
ptetreault1@unl.edu

"Not all students are educated about sexuality issues and sexual health. We educate to encourage informed, responsible attitudes and behaviors regarding sexuality."
—A NEBRASKA FOURTH-YEAR STUDENT

The University of Nebraska–Lincoln (UNL), a public, liberal arts institution, has created a comprehensive peer education program that helps promote an environment of responsible sexuality and encourages students to develop a greater sense of personal responsibility in relationships. The network of students that comprise PERSUNL (Peers Encouraging Responsible Sexuality at the University of Nebraska–Lincoln) offers comprehensive programming and instruction about sexuality and sexual health that has promoted greater student awareness of these issues. The coordinator of the peer program provides presentations, educational resources, training, and supervision for Peer Sexuality Educators. PERSUNL promotes character and sexual health by advocating a core set of sexual health messages:

✦ **COMMUNICATION.** Successful relationships rely on open, honest, and direct communication.

✦ **DIVERSITY AWARENESS.** Health education must be inclusive and promote awareness of stereotypes, attitudes, and language usage.

✦ **CONSENT.** All individuals have the right to make informed and noncoerced choices about their sexuality and behavior.

✦ **RESPECT AND SELF-RESPECT.** Everyone has the right to protect him- or herself and the responsibility to respect the rights of others.

The PERSUNL program has also led to collaborations with off-campus groups, including both the state and county Health Departments, and received the Community HIV/AIDS Education Award in 1997. Through PERSUNL's comprehensive and inclusive peer education initiatives, UNL students are becoming better informed and better communicators on the topics of sexuality and sexual health.

UNIVERSITY OF REDLANDS

1200 EAST COLTON AVENUE
REDLANDS, CA 92373
909.793.2121
http://www.redlands.edu/

UNDERGRADUATES: 1,600

For program information, please contact:
CHARLOTTE G. BURGESS
burgess@uor.edu

A student-managed organization has reformed sexual attitudes and behavior at University of Redlands, a private, liberal arts institution near Los Angeles. PRIDE (Promoting Responsible and Informed Decisions through Education), a peer education network, provides information, guidance, and resources to help members of the Redlands community make better decisions about key issues, including sexuality, in their lives. Formed in 1993, PRIDE is composed of several peer education groups and offers a series of programs and presentations throughout the school year:

✦ **PEER THEATER.** Students present more than 15 "playlets," each addressing a unique topic to promote character development and mature decision-making.

✦ **STRAIGHT TALK.** Appearing both on campus and in public schools, Straight Talk features a panel of Redlands students talking about their own lives and experiences and how they have dealt with various issues and challenges involving character and college life.

✦ **NEW STUDENT CHARACTER AND SEXUALITY PROGRAM.** New students learn about issues relating to sexual assault during this multifaceted program featuring guest speakers, a Peer Theater performance of "Unspeakable Acts," and a panel discussion.

✦ **SEX IN THE LOBBY.** Educators at the University's Health Center and student leaders jointly prepare a "menu" of topics in a residence-hall program that allows attendees to choose subjects for discussion.

At the close of each academic year, members of PRIDE assess their work and prepare for future projects by evaluating program response forms and revising program manuals. Involving students as well as several offices across the Redlands campus, PRIDE is helping students develop character in making sexual decisions by encouraging them to confront difficult issues honestly and cooperatively.

UNIVERSITY OF RICHMOND

28 WESTHAMPTON WAY
RICHMOND, VA 23173-1903
804.289.8000
http://www.urich.edu/

UNDERGRADUATES: 4,400

For program information, please contact:
CAROL JOHNSON
cjohso2@richmond.edu

"The Wellness course at Richmond encompasses sensitive topics that require students to learn to face issues that make them question their values and opinions."

—A RICHMOND SECOND-YEAR STUDENT

The University of Richmond's commitment to educating students about the link between character and sexuality is comprehensive and creative. Cornerstone strategies at this private, comprehensive institution include:

✦ **DIMENSIONS OF WELLNESS COURSE.** This required, two-credit course strives to do more than simply transmit information about sexual health or to prevent sexual assault. It challenges students to examine the values and virtues that underpin a mature, respectful relationship. A series of classes examines the relationship between alcohol and sex. Overall, the course combines academic assignments with thoughtful and effective character development activities.

✦ **IMAGE SUPPORT NETWORK.** This campus-wide network focuses on preventing and treating eating disorders. Workshops examine the connections between body image, sexuality, and healthy relationships. The network educates students about the character dimension of image and sexuality.

✦ **INTIMACY WITHOUT INTERCOURSE WORKSHOP.** This popular workshop—open to all students—provides information about sexual abstinence. Facilitated by Carol Johnson, the University's Director of Wellness Programs, the workshop provides an opportunity for students to talk openly about the values and belief systems that inspire them to abstain from sexual intimacy. The workshop sends a strong signal to Richmond students that their peers are choosing the safest alternative to promiscuous sex.

Students who complete this program have a greater respect for themselves and are better able to pursue healthy relationships with others.

University of Tulsa

600 SO. COLLEGE
TULSA, OK 74104
918.631.2000
http://www.utulsa.edu/

UNDERGRADUATES: 2,900

For program information, please contact:
MARY SMITH, R.N.
mary-smith@utulsa.edu

Students teach students about character and sexuality in the University of Tulsa's innovative Peer Education Program (PEP). A student organization whose members' formal training begins in classrooms at this public university, PEP focuses on personal responsibility to help students make wise health decisions about sexual behavior, substance use, sexual assault, and other health concerns. PEP promotes character and sexual health through various campus awareness weeks, individual presentations, first-year orientation and experience classes, and one-on-one peer classes. Students who serve as Peer Educators provide an interactive learning experience in an environment that is informal, nonthreatening, and nonjudgmental.

The following major events are among those led by Peer Educators:

✦ **Sexuality Responsibility Week.** Programs cover abstinence, sexual postponement, relationship and communication issues, and the importance of sexually transmitted disease (STD) prevention methods.

✦ **White Ribbon Campaign.** The campaign focuses on men stopping men's violence against women and holds sexual assault prevention workshops.

✦ **World AIDS Day.** Numerous educational activities are offered on campus to educate students about HIV and AIDS. This program is also open to students from local public high schools.

Students working to become Peer Educators enroll in a full-semester course, "Strategies for Healthy Living," with a lab practicum in peer education. The program is overseen by the University's Health Center, Counseling and Psychological Services, Office of Student Affairs, and Student Association. The Tulsa student body has identified PEP as a vital campus resource, and the end result is a community of students who help each other make better informed decisions about sexuality.

Wheeling Jesuit University

316 WASHINGTON AVENUE
WHEELING, WV 26003
304.243.2000
http://www.wju.edu/

UNDERGRADUATES: 1,200

For program information, please contact:
JEANNE KIGERL
jeanne@wju.edu

"I found the program helpful. It helped bridge the gender gap—students could be honest with each other across gender lines. It made me think about my values and how I communicate with and relate to women."

—A Wheeling first-year student

Through "Sex and Communication," an interactive program for first-year students at Wheeling Jesuit University, a private, liberal arts institution, students have the opportunity to clarify their values about sexual behavior. Focusing on discussions about sexual values and how those values are communicated, the program is part of the University's First-Year Program. This cooperative effort between Academic Affairs and Student Development involves all first-year students and fulfills a required wellness credit through the University's Wellness Program. Coordinated by the Counseling Center, various staff initiate candid discussions between young men and women that concentrate on exploring one's own sexual values, communicating those values to others, especially in dating relationships, and hearing and respecting the values of others.

"Sex and Communication" engages students facing troublesome sexual situations with directness and cross-gender discussion. The program opens with a discussion of verbal versus nonverbal communication in expressing sexual values and interest. After viewing a video that depicts two college students on a date that turns into a rape, students divide into groups to explore themes such as the role of alcohol, stereotypical gender roles, attitudes and expectations about dating and relationships, and the kinds of communication that led to the incident. They consider other, clearer ways the couple could have communicated. Faculty members ask students to write a journal entry about the program as a follow-up activity. Attendance at the program is a component of the course grade.

Wheeling students have responded positively to the program. In annual course evaluations, first-year students have agreed that what they have learned will remain a part of their lives.

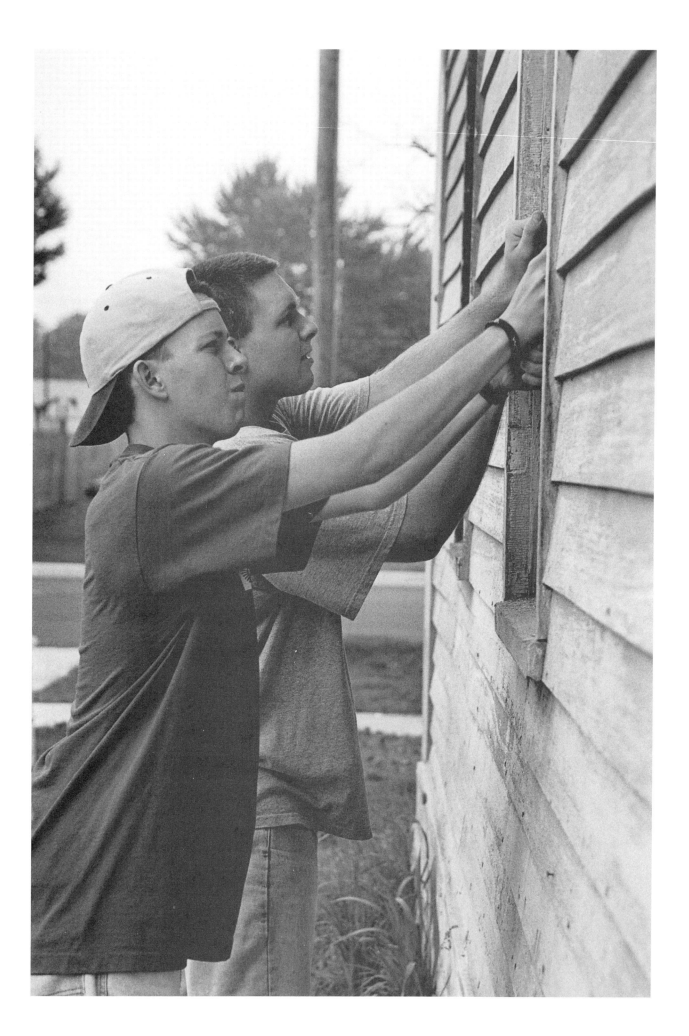

SENIOR-YEAR PROGRAMS

Whether through a capstone course or a series of
experiences, the focus of senior-year programs is to
help seniors reflect on, connect, and attach meaning
to their diverse undergraduate experiences. Although
some senior-year programs foster integration within
an academic major or connect academic work and
career experiences, other programs develop skills
and perspectives that encourage personal and civic
responsibility beyond the college years. These programs
offer seniors a challenging seminar or experience
that addresses the fundamental question:
What sort of life do I want to live?

Abilene Christian University

BOX 29100
ABILENE, TX 79699
915.674.2000
http://www.acu.edu/

UNDERGRADUATES: 3,900

For program information, please contact:
DWAYNE VAN RHEENEN, Ph.D.
Dwaynevr@nicanor.acu.edu

"I appreciate this opportunity very much. . . . It was a wonderful time to think about our lives and what our priorities are."

—AN ACU FOURTH-YEAR STUDENT

The mission of Abilene Christian University (ACU) is to educate students for global service and leadership. ACU, a religiously affiliated liberal arts university, demonstrates its commitment to this mission by providing opportunities for seniors to explore issues of faith and character in a variety of settings. As seniors prepare to enter the workforce, ACU strongly believes in the necessity of character and moral development. As a result, two programs exist at ACU that are instrumental in that process of student development.

The Department of Biology and College of Business Administration (COBA) initiated courses that addressed the need of student/faith interactive experiences and workforce preparation. The Department of Biology offers students the opportunity to participate in readings and discussions that focus upon worldviews, the role of values on hypothesis, data collection, and interpretation. The class meets weekly throughout the semester. COBA coordinates a one-day retreat, Senior Blessing, for all of their graduating seniors. Issues addressed include workforce preparation, family life foundations, and moral-based decision-making strategies. "We desire to communicate that great success in the business world is not measured in fame or wealth. Rather, it is measured by the depth of one's faith and character," says Dr. Rick Lytle.

Student evaluations indicate positive growth in the following areas:

✦ Following Christian principles for a successful life;

✦ Developing spiritual disciplines;

✦ Actualizing ethical and moral decision-making practices.

The belief that capstone experiences will contribute to the preparation of motivated students is the guiding force behind the implementation of reflective and thought-provoking topical seminars. ACU does its best to graduate students of integrity and value.

Beaver College

450 SOUTH EASTON ROAD
GLENSIDE, PA 19038-3295
215.572.2900
http://www.beaver.edu/

UNDERGRADUATES: 1,600

For program information, please contact:
MICHAEL L. BERGER, Ph.D.
Berger@beaver.edu

The capacity to communicate and act effectively upon one's knowledge is an expectation of all Beaver College's graduates. As a small, Presbyterian liberal arts college, Beaver also demands integrity in all things. As a result, seniors participate in Beaver's Senior Seminar experience, highlighted by a Senior Project. The project is described as an intellectual activity that "includes substantial written work and the opportunity to integrate what has been learned." Generally part of one or more required major courses, the Senior Project is student-directed—by topic, by understanding, and by presentation. Students demonstrate their knowledge of their chosen field while focusing on a specific issue.

Students develop lifelong skills during their Senior Seminar and Project experience, including:

✦ Collaborative and team-building skills;

✦ Celebrating team effort as opposed to individualism;

✦ Ethical decision-making abilities;

✦ Developing an acute sense of self and how others perceive their person.

More than 70 full-time faculty members participate in the Senior Project program. Serving as readers, consultants, or mentors, faculty are able to observe the fruits of their labors. Presentations and papers are commemorated during Senior Thesis Week. In 1998, Senior Projects were recognized at the 34th Annual International Collegiate Business Policy Competition, World Intercollegiate Business Game, and Student Design Competition of Greater Philadelphia. Having recently celebrated its 30th anniversary, the Senior Project program has established itself in the undergraduate academic life of Beaver. Through self-driven projects, group interactions, and faculty participation, Beaver graduates have the best of all worlds. They are given the tools to succeed—academically, socially, and spiritually.

BETHANY COLLEGE

BETHANY, WV 26032
304.829.7000
http://www.bethanywv.edu/
UNDERGRADUATES: 800

For program information, please contact:
ANTHONY L. MITCH
amitch@mail.bethanywv.edu

Providing an opportunity for students to demonstrate their ability to use, evaluate, and apply their academic degree and knowledge is the primary objective behind Bethany College's senior-year comprehensive examination and project. Since 1934, Bethany College, a small, religiously affiliated liberal arts institution, has required all students to undertake and pass a comprehensive senior exam; however, in 1972, the program was revised and the senior project was added. The comprehensive exam is focused in the student's major and developed by various faculty members. It includes a written and an oral section; the oral section mirrors the doctoral defense experience.

The senior project is an independent effort deriving from each student's studies in the major. A senior project may take any form deemed appropriate by the faculty of the academic department of the student's major, such as traditional library, laboratory, or field research; the application of a perspective, theory, or technique to a practical or hypothetical situation; or a creative or interpretive endeavor. The completed project is evaluated by a minimum of two faculty members, generally those who have served as the student's project mentors.

For the senior project, students must develop a proposal, identify specific tasks, organize their work, and plan and develop their presentations. Although faculty mentors are readily available to provide assistance, discuss ideas and interpretations, or examine work in progress, students assume responsibility for determining when to consult their mentors and how their mentors can productively assist them. Sometimes academic departments and/or mentors develop deadlines for the completion of project phases; but day-to-day scheduling is the responsibility of the student. Upon examination and project completion, students have learned the value of their liberal arts education, are able to articulate its global application, and have developed an appreciation for academic collaboration.

BETHEL COLLEGE

300 EAST 27TH STREET
NORTH NEWTON, KS 67117-0531
316.283.2500
http://www.bethelks.edu/
UNDERGRADUATES: 500

For program information, please contact:
DUANE K. FRIESEN, Ph.D.
Dfriesen@bethelks.edu

Seeking to be a diverse community of learners committed to the search for authentic faith and empirical understanding, Bethel College strives to develop three sets of fundamental capacities in its students. A small, Mennonite, liberal arts college, Bethel seeks to develop basic academic skills, understandings of academic disciplines and global issues, and integrative abilities. By enrolling in Basic Issues of Faith and Life, the Bethel senior capstone course, students are provided the venue in which those capacities are strengthened.

Basic Issues of Faith and Life is informed by four central values, including:

✦ An ethic of discipleship that recognizes Christ as the model for Christian life;

✦ An ethic of scholarship that believes academic achievement to be an outcome of intellectual stewardship;

✦ An ethic of services that stresses action and peacemaking; and

✦ An ethic of integrity that celebrates the fundamental connections among spirit, faith, mind, and learning.

Characterized by interdisciplinary faculty participation, interactive classroom experiences, and thoughtful verbal and written reflections, Bethel's Basic Issues course assists students in the integration of faith and learning. Using great literary works and community classroom seminars, students and faculty discuss basic concerns of faith and fundamental value questions. This combination graduates students who are well versed in the intellectual, cultural, and spiritual disciplines, engendering a well-rounded student body that will contribute to the good of their community and their world.

BLUFFTON COLLEGE

280 WEST COLLEGE AVENUE
BLUFFTON, OH 45817
419.358.3000
http://www.bluffton.edu/

UNDERGRADUATES: 1,000

For program information, please contact:
SALLY WEAVER SOMMER
sommers@bluffton.edu

"I learned that just because something doesn't affect me directly or right now, it doesn't mean that it won't in the future. I now care about what's going on everywhere."

—A BLUFFTON FOURTH-YEAR STUDENT

At Bluffton College, a small, Mennonite-affiliated, liberal arts school, the senior capstone course for the general education curriculum provides an interdisciplinary forum for examining ethics, community, and the environment. Using a seminar format, its aim is to help students develop a framework for practicing global citizenship in the peace church tradition. This reflective course asks students to bring their liberal arts and religious studies, cross-cultural experiences, and disciplinary perspectives together. Working with their peers, Bluffton students integrate their learning and construct ethical responses to community problems.

Program components and objectives include:

◆ An interdisciplinary values orientation focused on specific problems;

◆ Weekly journals focused on a sequential series of questions that guide the student in forming values;

◆ Developing a definition of "humane community" and defining the student's contribution to the "shalom" of the larger society; and

◆ Exploring a community issue and collectively developing a values-based, ethical response based on their Bluffton experience.

When they enter college, students ask, Who am I? How did I get to be who I am? As they prepare to enter the world, their inquiries shift to lifetime perspectives and their commitment to understanding their place in the human and global communities. In this context, students' reactions to penetrating questions form the basis not only for classroom encounters but also for life. Graduates leave Bluffton prepared to create and contribute to human community wherever they travel, live, and work.

CALIFORNIA STATE UNIVERSITY— SAN MARCOS

SAN MARCOS, CA 92096-0001
760.750.4000
http://www.csusm.edu/

UNDERGRADUATES: 3,000

For program information, please contact:
ALAN OMENS, Ph.D.
aomens@mailhost1.csusm.edu

"The Senior Experience is more than the pinnacle of my undergraduate studies. Successful completion of this program validated all my academic knowledge, work experiences, and diligence."

—A CSUSM RECENT GRADUATE

Conceptualized as an opportunity for students to make the transition from the university to the workplace, California State University San Marcos' (CSUSM) Senior Experience program has challenged students to develop personal and civic responsibility. CSUSM, a four-year liberal arts university, developed this program in 1992. Housed in the College of Business Administration, the Senior Experience is a two-semester program. By working with significant organizations and conducting rigorous projects, students are impacted in various settings and ways.

CSUSM student-teams select consulting projects submitted by local businesses, government, and nonprofit agencies. Faculty supervisors, who act as advisors, are assigned to each team. Teams often face challenging ethical situations and team-process issues. Students are encouraged to give and receive interpersonal feedback with others and, through this process, develop their personal integrity as contributing team members. By interacting with the organizations, they learn about the culture of various organizations. The final task for the students is to write individual self-reflection reports in which they discuss the process of the projects, the team dynamics, and the relevance of the Senior Experience to their future careers. Through collaborative faculty-student efforts, team-building experiences, and observations of organizational culture, graduates are inculcated with a sense of civic, personal, and professional responsibility. Integrity, personal ethical development, and commitment to a team effort are natural byproducts of CSUSM's Senior Experience.

CENTRAL METHODIST COLLEGE

411 CENTRAL METHODIST SQUARE
FAYETTE, MO 65248
660.248.3391
http://www.cmc.edu/

UNDERGRADUATES: 1,200

For program information, please contact:
DAVID HERINGER
dhering@cmc.edu

Character building among individuals and within communities is the primary focus at Central Methodist College (CMC), a church-related liberal arts college. The Senior Capstone course addresses the need for reflection and analysis of character, integrated with the development of skills to apply personal values and strengths toward creative problem-solving and service within communities.

The Senior Capstone course emphasizes individual character development by thorough self-examination.

During the Senior Capstone experience:

✦ Students learn to assess their abilities in the context of their values and in relationship to their own aspirations. They design portfolios and develop interview skills that reflect who they are in professional, technological, and personal terms.

✦ Students relate these experiences to the values and goals of their prospective profession and communities of which they are to become a part.

✦ Students discuss societal issues in terms of ethics and responsibilities.

✦ Students learn to apply personal strengths within interdisciplinary teams to solve problems creatively and implement change within local or extended communities.

The CMC senior-year program culminates with the Capstone project. Students are able to make the connection between academic and professional preparation. In addition, they are able to practically apply their skills toward doing good and making a positive difference in the world. In designing, researching, actively implementing, and formally presenting their projects, students gain life-changing perspectives, learn invaluable organizational and leadership skills, and experience the rewards of helping others through their creative efforts.

COLLEGE OF THE SOUTHWEST

6610 LOVINGTON HIGHWAY
HOBBS, NM 88240
505.392.6561
http://www.csw.edu/

UNDERGRADUATES: 600

For program information, please contact:
TOM SCHWARTZ
stpaul@leaco.net

Building personal and vocational effectiveness through the teaching of timeless principles and practices related to human character is the guiding purpose of College of the Southwest's (CSW) Senior Seminar in Leadership and Ethics. A small, private, liberal arts college, CSW provides its seniors with classroom instruction and guest lectures on various topics. Community and business leaders share their perspectives on ethics, character development, and practices that will engender long-term success both professionally and personally. The seminar also provides a forum for developing skills such as business etiquette, time management, and project administration.

Special Seminar Offerings include:

✦ Mock interview programs;

✦ Employer panels;

✦ Interaction with the president and other key faculty.

The foundational text, *Seven Habits of Highly Effective People* by Steven Covey, provides students with foundational guidelines and principles for everyday experiences. Students are required to outline each chapter and submit a personal reflection paper. In addition, peer instruction is used to encourage student involvement and development. The Senior Seminar in Leadership and Ethics has received extensive endorsement by the surrounding business and educational community as being a cutting-edge tool for personal character development.

According to Tom Schwartz, seminar instructor, students consistently rank the seminar as "one of the best classes of my college career." In addition, the College notes an increase in postgraduate professional employment. The College of Education enjoys a 95% placement rate. Personal reflection, professional maturation, and ethical development combine to make CSW's Senior Seminar an effective and useful capstone experience.

Columbia College

600 SOUTH MICHIGAN AVENUE
CHICAGO, IL 60605
312.663.1600
http://www.colum.edu/

UNDERGRADUATES: 7,500

For program information, please contact:
WILLIAM HAYASHI
Whayashi@popmail.colum.edu

"It was eye-opening to sit down and figure out what my values really are, as well as to be capable of justifying them to other students' questions."

—A COLUMBIA FOURTH-YEAR STUDENT

"Character is higher than intellect," says Ralph Waldo Emerson. Columbia College, a private, arts-related college, wholeheartedly ascribes to this statement. Students who participate in Senior Seminar: Voice, Values, and Vision complete their Columbia experience by immersing themselves in intellectual, moral, and social dialogs. The aim of this seminar is "to educate the whole person toward emotional, moral, and cognitive intelligence." The function of this course is to provide readings, assignments and a supportive environment for students to discover the link between belief and behavior. Throughout the course, emphasis is placed on "values in action."

In a small classroom environment, students assume responsibility for their learning community. Encouraged by carefully selected instructors, students express themselves freely and openly. Such activities include:

✦ Generation of a peer community value list;

✦ Monitoring the absences and tardiness of classmates;

✦ Preparing and presenting in dynamic student teams;

✦ Producing the midterm essay, "What I Believe."

Self-discovery and value clarification lie at the heart of every seminar. By integrating readings with their experiences, through journal writing and interactive discussions, students identify their core work, relationship, family, and community values. They move from text to life, constantly evaluating and understanding. In the second half of the semester, students participate in community service, reflect on future professional goals, and begin their workforce preparation. The course culminates in a final project that expresses each student's personal vision of a future "good life." This concluding life chapter will form a bridge into universal meaning that can touch, inspire, and transform Columbia graduates for years to come.

The Defiance College

701 NORTH CLINTON STREET
DEFIANCE, OH 43512
800.520.4632
http://www.defiance.edu/

UNDERGRADUATES: 800

For program information, please contact:
MARK A. MINGLIN
mminglin@defiance.edu

The mission statement of The Defiance College, a small, independent, Church of Christ–affiliated school, states, "We seek to inspire within our students a search for truth, a sensitivity to our world and the diverse cultures within it, the ability to lead in their chosen professions, and a spirit of service." Accordingly, Defiance has developed the Service Leaders program, headed by Mark A. Minglin, Director of Service Learning, that acts to promote the concept of service. Participating students apply classroom knowledge, explore careers or majors, develop civic and cultural literacy, and enhance personal growth and self-image. The program structure is as follows:

✦ Each year, 10 to 15 students are selected as Service Leaders and receive a $7,500 scholarship. These students coordinate and promote volunteer service projects for the Office of Service Learning and are expected to volunteer at least one hour per week in an agency of their choice, coordinate a one-time project in their community that addresses a specific need, attend a weekly Service Leader organizational meeting, meet monthly with the Director of Service Learning, and participate in the end-of-the-year service project.

✦ As a capstone to their experiences, students can participate in an international service trip in their senior year in which they are immersed in a new culture and work with residents to improve the community. Students are encouraged to remove themselves from their comfort zone and try to understand and work with people within the context of their native environment.

Throughout the program, students participate in reflection sessions that enable them to process their experiences. Students are able to express freely their accomplishments and challenges. They emerge from this program with a greater sense of self and responsibility to give back to society in a much larger context than is possible in just their home communities.

Drury College

900 NORTH BENTON AVENUE
SPRINGFIELD, MO 65802
417.873.7879
http://www.drury.edu/

UNDERGRADUATES: 3,500

For program information, please contact:
BECKY BOYD
bboyd@lib.drury.edu

Preparing students for professional and personal life experiences is the foundational goal of Drury College's (DC) "Leadership Drury" program. A small, private, liberal arts institution, DC offers students the opportunity to learn more about themselves, their peer group, their community, and society. Specifically, the senior-year component (Leadership Drury IV) is designed to facilitate the development and understanding of skills that will serve students in their career and community. The program includes retreats, guest speakers, class projects, and "Senior Success Groups." Administered through the Student Development Office, Leadership Drury IV may be a for-credit experience.

Leadership Drury IV encourages the student's personal and professional development through various means:

✦ Interaction with community and alumni leaders;

✦ Participation in "Alumni Connections," a mentoring and networking program;

✦ Taking part in a community-service project.

Led by the Dean of Students, Career Center Director, and Associate Director, Leadership Drury IV has an enrollment of 26 students—from a senior class of 240. Becky Boyd, Career Center Director, says students who participate in the program "are sought after for planning groups, task groups, and community-service projects." The program has been in existence for five years and has consistently received high ratings from its participants. Through peer interaction, exposure to community leadership, and professional development opportunities, Leadership Drury IV provides students with a solid foundation for their future, a future in which they will reflect the values and experiences learned at DC.

Duquesne University

600 FORBES AVENUE
PITTSBURGH, PA 15282
412.396.6000
http://www.duq.edu/

UNDERGRADUATES: 5,500

For program information, please contact:
TIM LEWIS
lewis@duq2.cc.duq.edu

Offering a series of events for seniors to reflect upon, connect with, and attach meaning to their diverse undergraduate experiences, Duquesne University's "Senior Celebration" allows graduating seniors to address life's core question: What sort of life do I want to live? At Duquesne, a private Catholic university, Senior Celebration includes a religious service, University-wide reception, and dinner annually attended by more than 700 individuals. Addressed by a prominent guest speaker, the dinner guests are encouraged to reflect upon their personal and professional values, leadership skills and abilities, and a self-driven definition of ethical leadership.

In addition, the University awards its graduates for various academic and leadership honors. This series of events was inspired by a challenge from Rev. Sean Hogan, Executive Vice President for Student Life. He encouraged various core groups of student leaders to inaugurate an event that would celebrate the senior experience. In sum, seniors are once again reminded of the importance of moral and ethical leadership as they take their positions as members of their global communities.

ELON COLLEGE

2700 CAMPUS BOX
ELON COLLEGE, NC 27244
336.584.9711
http://www.elon.edu/

UNDERGRADUATES: 3,600

For program information, please contact:
BOB ORNDORFF
Orndorff@elon.edu

Believing that the transition from college into the workplace is a significant one, Elon College, a small, church-affiliated, liberal arts college, arms its seniors with "Transition Tactics" (TT). TT is a three-day career-development conference sponsored by Elon's Career Services Center. Designed to give seniors a jump-start on their job search, TT offers a unique workshadowing experience complemented by employability skills workshops. Students spend two days at their chosen work site, gaining valuable insights and perspectives on their profession of interest.

Workshop seminars include:

✦ Job searching strategies;

✦ Professional etiquette;

✦ Networking techniques;

✦ Résumé and interviewing skills.

A unique facet of TT is the mentoring component. While participating in the workshadowing experience, students are assigned an on-site mentor. In many cases, these contacts lead the student to additional employment opportunities. The relationship develops into a mutually informative and enjoyable one. As experiential learning goes, TT is one of the students' most valuable opportunities.

Overall, Elon is proving itself to be a trailblazer in the experiential learning arena, and the college's mission reflects those efforts. Providing an innovative professional experience at the opening of the senior year allows Elon students to get a jump-start on the professional development process while enhancing their personal abilities.

GREENSBORO COLLEGE

815 WEST MARKET STREET
GREENSBORO, NC 27401
336.272.7102
http://www.gborocollege.edu/

UNDERGRADUATES: 1,100

For program information, please contact:
TIFFANY MCKILLIP FRANKS
Frankst@gborocollege.edu

At the heart of Greensboro's Senior-Year Program is the desire to create a set of meaningful experiences for juniors and seniors that would intentionally prepare them for a successful transition into life beyond college. Greensboro College, a small, Methodist, liberal arts college, provides an innovative event for students—the Reality Check Conference. Through seminars, speakers, and small group discussions, this two-day "Reality Check" provides opportunities for students to explore topics ranging from ethical issues in the workplace to developing a lifestyle that integrates one's personal and professional values. Other conference activities include planning a personal budget, avoiding credit-card debt, and workplace and social etiquette.

Seniors leave the conference with a clearer life plan that integrates their personal, professional, and vocational goals and values. The conference is funded by a gift to the endowment from Ruth C. and Jack H. Campbell (Ruth graduated from Greensboro in 1943). Although the conference is organized by the Student Development staff, the President of the College is closely involved in all aspects of the college, as are many faculty members. Indeed, the President hosts a formal dinner at a local country club where students learn appropriate etiquette, wardrobe, and presentation skills.

The overriding goal of the Reality Check Conference is to help students better understand and practice the virtues of personal responsibility once they graduate from the College. The College encourages students to be successful not only in their chosen careers, but also in their families and communities.

Hope College

PO BOX 9000
HOLLAND, MI 49422-9000
616.395.7000
http://www.hope.edu/

UNDERGRADUATES: 2,900

For program information, please contact:
JOHN D. COX
cox@hope.edu

"The Senior Seminar provided a forum for reflecting on my experiences to date, an opportunity for synthesizing and defining life values to carry with me into the world, and a special way of bringing closure to my college years."
—A HOPE GRADUATE

Confronting questions of value and belief and clarifying how the Christian faith informs a philosophy for living is the vision of Senior Seminars at Hope College. A small, Christian institution, Hope offers students an opportunity to face questions of value in a sustained and critical manner. Teachers of the Senior Seminars challenge students to consider their own value commitments in light of the Christian faith. Common seminar elements include a pedagogical emphasis on instructional discussion, a "life-view" paper, and meaningful teacher/student dialogue.

Senior Seminar topics take various forms. Some examples include "Virtue and Vice in Everyday Life" and "Medicine and Morals." Dr. Cox, the director, states "The open expression of widely differing viewpoints on issues of fundamental value . . . requires restraint, empathy, civility, and patience on the part of everyone, including the instructor, if it is to succeed." Senior Seminars strive to model civility in the classroom community, allowing full and free expression while privileging none without reason.

Since the seminar's inception in 1970, more than $200,000 in grant monies has been awarded in support of the Seminars. In 1997, Professor Timothy Pennings' description of his Senior Seminar, "Infinity and the Absolute," was awarded a $10,000 prize by the John Templeton Foundation as the winner in its "Science and Religion Course Competition."

Senior Seminars are not simply discussion and discourse. In 1992, a group initiated an outreach to a local, ethnically diverse elementary school. A wellness clinic, student-to-student tutoring program, mentoring program, and a music enhancement program are among the fruits of the group's efforts. Through dialogue and reflection in a civil and charitable environment, Hope's students exemplify the College's definition as "an institution where life is regarded as God's trust to humankind."

John Brown University

2000 WEST UNIVERSITY STREET
SILOAM SPRINGS, AR 72761
501.524.9500
http://www.jbu.edu/

UNDERGRADUATES: 1,400

For program information, please contact:
DOYLE BUTTS, Ph.D.
dbutts@acc.jbu.edu

Providing maximum academic benefits and opportunities for Christian character development is the underlying purpose of John Brown University's (JBU) General Education Capstone Program. At JBU, capstone courses are common in most major fields; however, six senior-level courses (three traditional-style and three honors) constitute the capstone experience. Courses such as "Christian Life," "American Studies," and "Masterpieces in World Literature" give students the opportunity to reflect on their undergraduate experience and integrate those experiences into a relevant worldview.

Students develop their understanding of personal and civic responsibility by:

✦ Examining issues of personal freedom;

✦ Addressing the relationship between Christian faith and civic duty;

✦ Organizing and participating in community-service experiences; and

✦ Exploring their relationship to the arts and humanities.

The Capstone Program was established in 1987. As a part of JBU's core curriculum, the Capstone Program receives support through undergraduate studies, the University provost, and participating faculty members. Recently, JBU's course was featured at the National Collegiate Honors Council and was included in *Peterson's Honors Programs*.

Given that JBU currently serves students from 44 states and 38 countries, the impact of the Capstone Program is widespread. Through emphasis on relationship to others, community, global society, and faith, the JBU Capstone Program provides students with a firm foundation and the resources necessary to make a profound contribution to their world.

MICHIGAN STATE UNIVERSITY

EAST LANSING, MI 48824-0590
517.355.1855
http://www.msu.edu/

UNDERGRADUATES: 33,300

For program information, please contact:
FRANK FEAR
fear@pilot.msu.edu

It's nearly 6 p.m. on a snowy Tuesday evening. Students and faculty hurry from all parts of campus and from all sorts of activities—classes, labs, meetings, presentations, and dinner—to come to Wills House. Located on the campus of Michigan State University (MSU), the Wills House is home to the Liberty Hyde Bailey Scholars Program. At MSU, a large, public, land-grant university, the Bailey Scholars Program seeks to be a community of scholars dedicated to lifelong learning.

Bailey Scholars Program opportunities and activities include:

✦ **WEEKLY LUNCHTIME CONVERSATION.** Bailey community members gather for homemade meals and converse about issues facing the Bailey community, and reflect on recent learning experiences.

✦ **WEEKLY READING CIRCLE.** Participants identify books and articles of interest and gather to share interpretations and learn from each other.

✦ **MONOGRAPH SERIES.** A publication opportunity designed to stimulate the preparation of scholarly manuscripts about learning.

✦ **CAMPUS PRESENTATIONS.** Bailey students and faculty coordinate learning experiences for the MSU community. Examples include the MSU Student Leadership Conference for students and MSU Lilly Fellows program for faculty.

Launched in January 1998, the Bailey Scholars Program is supported by the Provost's office. Faculty and institutional leaders are the driving forces behind Bailey's learning innovations; thus, MSU's program has gained respect in academic circles. For example, the National Association of State Universities and Land Grant Colleges has recognized the program as a "best practice." Collaborative learning experiences, faculty-student initiatives, and innovative educational approaches are the hallmarks of the Bailey Scholars Program. Such experiences will be imprinted on the mind, heart, and soul of all those who participate.

MILLSAPS COLLEGE

1701 NORTH STATE STREET
JACKSON, MS 39210
601.974.1000
http://www.millsaps.edu/

UNDERGRADUATES: 1,200

For program information, please contact:
KEVIN RUSSELL
russeka@millsaps.edu

"My senior year pulled together three years of education for me. As I graduate from Millsaps, I have clear goals and expectations for my future development."

—A MILLSAPS FOURTH-YEAR STUDENT

The senior year of college is one of great anticipation. Millsaps College, a private, church-affiliated, liberal arts institution has developed several programs that facilitate a smooth transition from "backpack to briefcase." Whether a student's destination is graduate/professional school or the workforce, the Millsaps senior year is one of reflection and encouragement that affirms the beliefs and crystallizes the options of the new graduate.

Components of Millsaps College's senior year include:

✦ Mandatory enrollment in "Senior Seminar," a capstone class that encourages past reflection and future projection;

✦ Participation in LEAD, a program that focuses on leadership skills development;

✦ Oral and written comprehensive exams that demonstrate students' accumulation of knowledge throughout their Millsaps experience.

In addition, a key experience during the final year at Millsaps is the Senior Institute. Launched in 1998, the Institute was developed and implemented in response to student needs. A campus-wide survey indicated the desire for career planning, development, and direction. Under the direction of the Career Center, the Institute was designed to encourage students to implement a career planning strategy and to involve themselves in their personal and professional futures. By exploring various educational and professional opportunities, students take responsibility for their postgraduation plans and aspirations. Through reflecting on the past and planning for the future, Millsaps graduates utilize today to make a better tomorrow. The senior year at Millsaps is like no other.

MOUNT VERNON NAZARENE COLLEGE

800 MARTINSBURG ROAD
MOUNT VERNON, OH 43050
800.782.2435
http://www.mvnc.edu/

UNDERGRADUATES: 1,900

For program information, please contact:
RANDIE L. TIMPE, Ph.D.
Randie.Timpe@mvnc.edu

Mount Vernon Nazarene College (MVNC), a small, church-related, liberal arts college, seeks to enhance the holistic development of all its learners via its curricular and cocurricular programs. Designed to provide closure to the undergraduate career, the Senior Colloquium is the culmination of four years of interdisciplinary studies. Required of every senior, the Senior Colloquium focuses on contemporary issues that students will face as they function as professionals, citizens, and Christians in society.

Senior Colloquium contains four basic elements of the core curriculum, which include:

✦ Writing;

✦ Reflecting and articulating one's worldview;

✦ Developing critical thinking skills;

✦ Enhancing oral presentation abilities through use of various media and public-speaking techniques.

At Mount Vernon, Senior Colloquium serves as the final course in a "writing-across-the-curriculum" organization spanning departmental and core curricula. In addition, many departmental units augment the colloquium experience with internship and practicum experiences.

Functioning as learning facilitators, instructors are encouraged to use traditional and nontraditional learning methods. The use of service-learning projects and classroom debates adds to the energy of the colloquium. Full-time transdisciplinary faculty, holding a minimum rank of associate professor, teach the Senior Colloquium. While students' majors equip them to be competent professionals, the general education program directs student development toward virtuous living and civic responsibility. By combining classroom learning and "real world" experiences, Mount Vernon Nazarene College's Senior Colloquium combines the best of both worlds—to produce a well-rounded citizenry who will impact society.

OLIVET COLLEGE

320 SOUTH MAIN STREET
OLIVET, MI 49076
616.749.7000
http://www.olivetnet.edu/

UNDERGRADUATES: 900

For program information, please contact:
ROBERT PETRULIS, Ph.D.
rpetrulis@olivetnet.edu

"Olivet's emphasis on education for individual and social responsibility has had a profound effect on the direction of my life."

—AN OLIVET FOURTH-YEAR STUDENT

Olivet College, a small, church-affiliated, multipurpose college, has renewed its commitment to its founding vision and established the Olivet Plan. A key component of the plan is the Senior Year Experience program, implemented in fall 1998. Students participate in a yearlong capstone course and complete a personal/professional portfolio.

Under the theme of "Education for Individual and Social Responsibility," Olivet seniors examine issues of diversity, community, and personal involvement. To enhance those discussions, students may participate in Olivet Symposiums, cocurricular activities, and community-service projects. The student portfolio is the culmination of four years of knowledge gathering and experiences, demonstrating students' ability to synthesize and summarize their undergraduate careers.

Notably, the Kellogg Foundation has recognized the College as one of five institutions it has supported for their work in comprehensive institutional transformation. By reaffirming their institutional commitment to "doing good to/for their students," Olivet has blazed a new trail for other institutions to follow. Olivet College allows students to reflect upon and integrate their undergraduate experiences into the real world. Such reflections will affect the course of their lives, enhancing their personal and global communities.

OTTERBEIN COLLEGE

102 WEST COLLEGE
WESTERVILLE, OH 43081
614.890.3000
http://www.otterbein.edu/

UNDERGRADUATES: 2,500

For program information, please contact:
CHRISTINA REYNOLDS
creynolds@otterbein.edu

"The reflective process of the Senior Year Experience helped me to view my four years as a whole learning experience for life."

—A RECENT OTTERBEIN GRADUATE

The Senior Year Experience program at Otterbein College emerged from discussions by faculty, alumni, and administrators concerned with providing seniors an opportunity to reflect on the meaning and purpose of their liberal arts education. All students seeking an undergraduate degree at this private, liberal arts school founded in 1847 and affiliated with the United Methodist Church must complete the SYE. The courses are designed to prompt students to recognize that their choices affect society, that they are accountable for their decisions and actions, and that learning is lifelong. All SYE options are expected to meet the following criteria:

◆ Analyze and synthesize contemporary issues;

◆ Connect learning in the student's major with the liberal arts core curriculum;

◆ Articulate beliefs and values based on an ethical stance;

◆ Reflect critically on the strengths and limits of different disciplines; and

◆ Provide service beyond the college to the wider community.

The SYE has also proven to be an exciting faculty development tool. The courses require educational staff to develop pedagogies that connect academic knowledge and significant contemporary issues. All options have an interdisciplinary, team-teaching approach, involving to date more than 27% of the faculty. Instructors immerse themselves in disciplines outside of their own and are energized by the experience of sharing, debating, and reflecting in new ways.

In part because of its SYE program, Otterbein has received national recognition and support for its efforts to integrate mission and curricula. Students leave college prepared to live according to the deep understanding of life issues that they gain through Otterbein's approach to helping them to synthesize their undergraduate experience.

PORTLAND STATE UNIVERSITY

PO BOX 751
PORTLAND, OR 97207
503.725.3000
http://www.pdx.edu/

UNDERGRADUATES: 14,000

For program information, please contact:
JUDITH PATTON, Ph.D.
pattonj@irn.pdx.edu

"The Capstone was a perfect expression of my personal and academic growth. It strengthened my connection to the community that I began as a freshman."

—A PSU FIFTH-YEAR STUDENT

Assisting students in making the critical transition from being fact receptors to lifelong learners is the central tenet of Portland State University's (PSU) newly reformed general education program. The Senior Capstone is the culminating experience at PSU, a medium-sized, liberal arts university. Senior Capstone students are required to engage in purposeful community-based learning, develop morally based critical-thinking skills, and to engender long-term dialog about social, cultural, and environmental issues facing today's society.

The focal thrusts of PSU's Senior Capstone are:

◆ To build cooperative and collaborative learning communities;

◆ To enhance student self-efficacy;

◆ To advance student abilities and skills while educating students in their moral and civic lives.

Senior Capstone was created in part by a half-million-dollar anonymous donation. A six-credit-hour course, Senior Capstone is a requirement of all PSU students. The program is housed in the College of Liberal Arts and Sciences and is supported by numerous faculty, staff, and administrative staff members. PSU has received several significant recognitions for its self-generated educational reform and Senior Capstone course. Throughout their undergraduate experience, PSU students are engaged in meaningful action, learning, and dialogue. Students leave PSU with a sense of accomplishment and an awareness of what they have learned and its importance in their future personal and professional lives.

PRESBYTERIAN COLLEGE

503 SOUTH BROAD STREET
CLINTON, SC 29325
864.833.2820
http://www.presby.edu/

UNDERGRADUATES: 1,100

For program information, please contact:
ANDREA LONG
aalong@cs1.presby.edu

Preparing students to make a life as opposed to simply making a living is the Presbyterian College creed. At Presbyterian College, a small, faith-related, liberal arts college, the focus is on developing the whole capable person. Presbyterian enables students to mature in intellectual, spiritual, aesthetic, and professional dimensions. In 1996, the Office of Career Planning and Placement designed and implemented Strategies for Seniors, a 10-week mini-course designed to offer seniors support and guidance as they transition into the next phase of their lives.

Through the use of the Myers-Briggs Personality Type Indicator and Strong Interest Inventory, students assess vocational interests, personalities, and skills, as well as develop an appreciation of personal strengths and weaknesses. Weekly topics of the sessions include decision-making, preparing for graduate school, résumé preparation and interviewing, financial planning, developing healthy lifestyles, the benefits of a liberal arts education, and life as an alumni.

In Strategies for Seniors sessions, students learn to identify and appreciate their God-given talents, understand that their life's work is a ministry to others and a reflection of their faith and values, and educate themselves on the lifestyle of their chosen profession.

In the last three years, 25% of the senior class participated in Strategies for Seniors, though it is not required and carries no academic credit. In addition, Presbyterian's annual placement report indicates that more than 98% of the senior class has a permanent job offer or was enrolled in a graduate program within six months after graduation. Through self-assessment and career planning, Presbyterian College's Strategies for Seniors assists soon-to-be graduates in taking a significant step across the threshold from college student to responsible global-community member.

SOUTHWEST MISSOURI STATE UNIVERSITY

901 SOUTH NATIONAL
SPRINGFIELD, MO 65804
417.836.5000
http://www.smsu.edu/

UNDERGRADUATES: 14,000

For program information, please contact:
JOHN CATAU, Ph.D.
jcc351f@mail.smsu.edu

"This class has affected my view toward being a responsible citizen. I realized that I don't have to do great things to protect the environment. I should do what I can."

—A SMSU FOURTH-YEAR STUDENT

Improving one's ability to make important choices involves attention to intellectual abilities, knowledge, and understanding, which help to guide one's significant choices. Driven by this belief, Southwest Missouri State University (SMSU), a small, public, comprehensive university, has initiated a new general education program that culminates in a series of thought-provoking capstone courses. Under the direction of Dr. John Catau, SMSU's faculty have developed and implemented a series of interdisciplinary capstone courses that tackle societal and cultural issues. In most cases, these courses are team-taught with a cross-disciplinary perspective.

Capstone course issues include:

✦ Business and Society in Modern America

✦ Biological Perspectives for Our Environmental Future

✦ Democratic Ideals and Principles: Theories and Designs for the 21st Century

✦ Exploring Community Well-Being Through Performance

✦ Religion, Public Virtues, and the Citizen

At SMSU, the general education program and the capstone courses challenge the student to develop self-knowledge, cultural understanding, and a global perspective. SMSU recognizes the student as a whole person and seeks to educate the *whole*. Interdisciplinary courses, cross-disciplinary faculty, and contextual perspectives encourage SMSU students to tackle societal issues from diverse standpoints. This combination results in an enlightened University community, and more significantly, an informed citizenry.

SPALDING UNIVERSITY

851 SOUTH FOURTH STREET
SPALDING, KY 40203
502.585.9911
http://www.spalding.edu/

UNDERGRADUATES: 1,100

For program information, please contact:
THOMAS G. TITUS, Ph.D.
tituspp@ibm.net

"The undergraduate psychology practicum experience has affirmed without a doubt that I have chosen a satisfying and rewarding field to work in."

—A SPALDING FOURTH-YEAR STUDENT

Spalding University, a small, private, Roman Catholic institution, recently revised its undergraduate program goals, committing itself and its students to rigorous intellectual and community-building lives. In response, Spalding's Psychology Department has highlighted its undergraduate practicum as the major's capstone experience. Each senior Psychology major spends 100 hours in a clinical agency setting, gaining hands-on experience and life-changing insights.

In addition, student participants are required to reflect on their experiences in a variety of ways. Through an all-encompassing integrative paper, supervisory sessions with a respected psychology faculty member, and empowering service encounters with clients, students strive to reach their fullest potential. Furthermore, faculty members indicate that the practicum is a useful tool in determining commitment to a professional career in psychology.

Examples of practicum settings include:

◆ Crisis counseling centers;

◆ Emergency psychiatry services;

◆ Local youth service agencies;

◆ Centers for women and families.

Such experiences "touch the hearts" of the students, says Dr. Thomas Titus, the practicum supervisor. In addition, students learn that they have a responsibility to use their education, gifts, and talents to assist those less fortunate. They respond with compassion in all interactions and place value on each individual and situation. Most important, students gain a true understanding of the powerful difference their chosen profession will make in the lives of others. Reaching out to a hurting world is the greatest gift that Spalding seniors have to offer. Indeed, theirs is a gift that will be gratefully accepted.

STONEHILL COLLEGE

320 WASHINGTON STREET
EASTON, MA 02357
562.907.4200
http://www.stonehill.edu/

UNDERGRADUATES: 1,300

For program information, please contact:
JOHN J. KING
King@Stonehill.edu

Stonehill College offers its seniors a unique seminar experience. Through the Senior Transitions Conference, instructors hope to impress upon its participants the intrinsic value of each individual and dignity of all. One of the Conference objectives is to challenge graduating seniors to think of their future living community as an environment in which the campus values they lived and witnessed are daily practices. A collaborative effort among Alumni Affairs, Career Services, and Residence Life, the conference offers students access to informative workshops, alumni panels, and relevant keynote speakers.

The Senior Transition Conference objectives include:

◆ Assisting graduating students in making the transition to worlds of work, service, and alumni status.

◆ Supporting the culmination of Stonehill's four-year Career Planning Program.

◆ Intentionally providing opportunities for students to reflect on their undergraduate past, their current situation, and their professional and personal future lives.

Thirty-five percent of Stonehill's graduates have participated in the conference, which was inaugurated in January 1997. Senior Transitions has been recognized by the National Association of Student Personnel Administrators (NASPA)—Region 1 as the 1997 Regional Program of the Year. In addition, a program profile was included in NASPA's "Bridges to Student Success—Exemplary Programs 1998." Through interactive workshops, alumni insights, and faculty interaction, Stonehill graduates are given valuable tools for life after college. Such experiences will benefit them long after the graduation processional.

University of Arkansas at Little Rock

2801 SOUTH UNIVERSITY AVENUE
LITTLE ROCK, AR 72204-1099
501.569.3000
http://www.ualr.edu/

UNDERGRADUATES: 8,700

For program information, please contact:
CHERYL CHAPMAN
cachapman@ualr.edu

"The Friday and Sturgis Leadership engaged my heart and mind. I realized the link between leadership and community service and I gained the knowledge and skills to become that link."

—A LITTLE ROCK FOURTH-YEAR STUDENT

Societal change, character development, and community enhancement are the underlying purposes of University of Arkansas at Little Rock's (UALR) Friday and Sturgis Fellows Leadership Program. UALR initiated the Friday and Sturgis Fellows Leadership Program to develop students who are committed to leadership, community understanding, and a lifetime of service. A committee consisting of campus and community representatives selects students based on academic and civic service criteria.

Fellows selected serve both campus and community by:

✦ Attending weekly seminars conducted by civic and community leaders during their junior year;

✦ Contributing a minimum of 125 pre-approved volunteer service hours;

✦ Participating in spring and summer break service opportunities;

✦ Developing and researching an in-depth topic related to their community;

✦ Presenting their research at UALR's Service Learning Symposium.

The Friday and Sturgis Fellows Leadership program is evidence of UALR's efforts to expand service learning across the campus.

Taking their classroom knowledge to the streets, students strive to make their communities better. The combination of hands-on activity and in-depth study of pressing community issues instills a sense of civic and personal responsibility that creates a legacy of meaningful participation in the lives of others.

University of Redlands

1200 EAST COLTON AVENUE
REDLANDS, CA 92373
909.793.2121
http://www.redlands.edu/

UNDERGRADUATES: 1,000

For program information, please contact:
NEAL K. PAHIA
slnpahia@uor.edu

At University of Redlands, a small, private, liberal arts university, graduating seniors have the opportunity to participate in "Real World 101: Life After College." "Real World" provides students with practical information on useful topics such as buying/leasing a car, retirement/investment options, and maintaining a positive credit record. Offered in the January interim semester, the "Real World" text is an alumni-driven publication, "Lessons Learned: A Survival Guide for Young Alums." Redlands alumni contribute insight and guidance on personal finances, professional lives, and civic responsibility.

Other significant issues addressed by "Lessons Learned" include:

✦ Personal integrity;

✦ Professional ethics and lifestyle choices;

✦ Interpersonal relationships;

✦ Health, nutrition, and wellness.

Facilitated by Redlands' Student Life administrators, students benefit from alumni panels, employability workshops, and informative seminars. "Real World's" purpose is to give students a valuable packet of information, useful in making their life transition as painless as possible. Dr. Neal Pahia, Associate Dean of Student Life, says, "the intention of this course is to sow the seeds of responsible behavior" in student lifestyles. By integrating practical life information with alumni real-world experiences, graduating seniors gain confidence in their abilities to thrive and survive in a fast-paced world.

Valparaiso University

KRETZMANN HALL
VALPARAISO, IN 46383-6493
800.GO.VALPO
http://www.valpo.edu/

UNDERGRADUATES: 3,000

For program information, please contact:
MARGARET FRANSON
margaret.franson@valpo.edu

Inspiring a love of learning, enriching moral and intellectual life through purposeful thought and inquiry, and developing an interactive community of scholars is the mission of Valparaiso University's Christ College Honors Program. Valparaiso, a small, liberal arts, Lutheran university, invites all upper-level students to engage in integrative scholarship. Seniors who complete the Christ College (CC) requirements are required to write an honors thesis, focused on weaving together their undergraduate experiences and academic pursuits. CC scholars and those students completing a major or minor in the humanities field are required to participate in the capstone Senior Colloquium.

Through class conversations, panel presentations, outside readings, and written work, students are led to give shape to the substance of their lives through an autobiographical narrative. This narrative also encourages the writers to reflect upon the meaning of their future work, to give attention to the transition from college, and to draft thoughtful recollections of their undergraduate experiences. Students must develop a portfolio that includes a résumé, vita, academic transcripts, and cocurricular activities.

Examples of interdisciplinary seminars include:

◆ **Becoming Individual**

◆ **Children, Family, and Faith**

◆ **Capitalism and the Human Spirit**

◆ **Ethical Reflection and Modern Literature**

Valparaiso has been recognized as a "Model of Christian Higher Education" and has enjoyed significant philanthropic support for its endeavors. Through a flexible and interdisciplinary approach and its emphasis on service to others, Valparaiso graduates have much to offer the world. Such experiences produce scholars with an appreciation for diversity, a thirst for spiritual excellence, and a desire for lifelong learning.

Whittier College

13406 EAST PHILADELPHIA STREET
WHITTIER, CA 90608
562.907.4200
http://www.whittier.edu/

UNDERGRADUATES: 1,300

For program information, please contact:
JOYCE P. KAUFMAN, Ph.D.
jkaufman@whittier.edu

"The Senior Project experience allowed me to take ownership of and to implement an original idea. I grew intellectually and emotionally throughout the entire process."

—A Whittier fourth-year student

Offering motivated and independent students the opportunity to take responsibility for their own education is the underlying purpose of the Whittier Scholars Program (WSP). At Whittier, a small, private, liberal arts college, the WSP culminates with the Senior Project, Senior Seminar and Senior Symposium experiences. In their third year, WSP students must defend their Senior Project proposal. Thus, as a senior, the students are required to present the results of their own work to the symposium community. The WSP program was established in 1977, improving Whittier's student retention and overall student satisfaction rates.

As senior participants, students are immersed in a unique learning community characterized by:

◆ Intellectual honesty;

◆ Pursuit of varied and diverse perspectives;

◆ Respect for the ideas of others;

◆ Meaningful and challenging dialog with peers and faculty.

Through a combination of independent work (Senior Project), formal course work (Senior Seminar), and interaction with the community (Senior Symposium), WSP seniors learn what it truly means to be a member of a community of scholars. Via such experiences, they learn to take responsibility for their academic and professional lives. In addition, they gain team-building and group-interaction skills that will benefit them long after the graduation processional. Most significantly, WSP graduates establish a firm foundation based on positive values and academic knowledge. Such a foundation will put them in good stead throughout their lives.

Purpose

The 50 college and university presidents profiled in the Presidential Leadership section of the guidebook demonstrate a personal commitment to a wide variety of character-development activities and issues on their campuses. Although their priorities, strategies, and approaches may differ, all of these college leaders have made it their priority to prepare students for lives of personal and civic responsibility. By recognizing these men and women, we hope that they will become beacons of inspiration for college administrators across the United States who are interested in learning ways to establish character development as an essential aspect of an undergraduate education.

Selection Criteria

◆ Establishes character development as a high priority

◆ Serves as a catalyst for the design and implementation of campus-wide activities that prepare students for lives of personal and civic responsibility

◆ Provides national leadership and sustained commitment in promoting the importance of character development in higher education

◆ Models in professional and personal life those aspects of character and integrity that students should emulate

ROYCE MONEY

PRESIDENT
ABILENE CHRISTIAN UNIVERSITY

BOX 29100
ABILENE, TX 79699–9100

915.674.2000
moneyr@nicanor.acu.edu
http://www.acu.edu/

UNDERGRADUATES: 3,900

"Through his leadership, vision, and personal integrity, Dr. Money has been an outstanding example and powerful influence in my life."

—AN ACU FOURTH-YEAR
STUDENT

Other ACU Profiles :

• Civic Education Program
• Senior-Year Program

PRESIDENT OF ABILENE CHRISTIAN UNIVERSITY SINCE 1991, Royce Money demonstrates exemplary Christian servant-leadership. As the 10th president, his mission for ACU, a private, four-year comprehensive university affiliated with the Churches of Christ, is to transform student character in the likeness of Jesus' character to help them become visionary leaders of integrity. President Money regularly speaks in ACU's daily chapel assembly on spiritual values, becoming more politically involved, serving others in the community, and reducing world hunger. He also speaks to civic organizations, churches, and student groups regarding such issues and values as "True Success," "Persistence," "Celebrating Fatherhood," "Love Is Patient," and "The 12 Attributes of a Committed Family." On mentoring the new president of another Christian college, one of President Money's admonitions was to "build character in your students, give them a foundation for a life—not just a career."

Since 1906, ACU has focused on preparing students to lead meaningful lives that will make a real difference. President Money puts this mission into practice through various character-building initiatives:

✦ **CHARACTER DEVELOPMENT.** He led the development of the Centennial Vision, founded on the belief that ACU community life "is committed to students' emotional and physical health, their spiritual faith, their intellectual development, and their growth as volunteers, leaders, and team members." He meets with ACU faculty, staff, board members, and students to discuss program implementation.

✦ **CIVIC EDUCATION.** Through Centennial Vision, President Money helped establish and actively supports ACU's Student Achievement Team, which focuses on the overall character development of students, and the Center for the Advancement of Community.

✦ **VOLUNTEER SERVICE.** He also helped establish a new Volunteer and Service-Learning Center, where students find opportunities to serve the community— tutoring children in reading, serving meals to shut-ins, and simply cleaning up Abilene.

President Money has promoted character development in higher education at local, state, national and international levels. He has supported Habitat for Humanity; has served on numerous community boards, including campaign chair and chairman of the board for United Way; and is on the board of the Independent Colleges and Universities of Texas. President Money was recently named president of the board for the Council of Christian Colleges and Universities, which believes that personal and civic responsibility are crucial to a complete education. He also serves on the Advisory Council of Dr. James Dobson's Focus on the Family's Institute for Family Studies and, as a certified member of the American Association for Marriage and Family Therapy, has written two books and numerous articles on the family. President Money has also traveled throughout Europe to meet with government officials about education programs, curriculum development, and student/faculty exchanges. His leadership has earned him numerous awards and honors, including an honorary Doctor of Laws degree from Pepperdine University.

Students who attend ACU must be armed with a powerful conviction to serve others in order to follow in the footsteps of this dynamic president.

THE LEADERSHIP STYLE OF THE 14TH PRESIDENT OF ASBURY COLLEGE, a small, liberal arts school with a Christian heritage, infuses campus life with academic excellence and spiritual vitality. David J. Gyertson encourages students to develop "tough minds *and* tender hearts." Currently, 70% of the students participate in community service projects each year—a rate that has more than doubled during President Gyertson's six-year leadership at Asbury.

"We find out who we are and what we can be," writes Dr. Gyertson. "These are life questions. These are religious questions." President Gyertson's administration emphasizes character development through various service-learning programs that encourage Asbury students to "give back to the community they live in." He also draws on his rich community service involvement with United Way, the Salvation Army, Christian Broadcast Associates, and the Christian Holiness Association. From chapel services to sharing meals with students, President Gyertson models a "lifestyle for a lifetime" that tests and strengthens student citizenship and develops an attitude of civility.

Among Asbury's innovative program initiatives supported by President Gyertson are:

✦ **COMMUNITY SERVICE LEARNING.** This active campus-wide program links student resources to community needs. The centerpiece of the program is the Aldersgate Service and Leadership Apartment Complex. Residents of the complex demonstrate civic responsibility by taking on leadership positions in the community.

✦ **OUTREACH COALITION.** Through a relationship forged between the Leadership and Campus Ministry Departments, faculty and staff volunteer to lead students in community-wide events.

✦ **STUDENT LEADERSHIP PROGRAMS.** Sponsored by the office of Student Development, "Lead-on!" implements training workshops for students who wish to pursue civic service and Christian leadership. Students develop a portfolio of outreach and leadership experience.

✦ **INTERNATIONAL OUTREACH.** Service teams of Asbury students reach out beyond the campus to locations such as Honduras, Appalachia, Jamaica, Ecuador, and inner-city St. Louis. The 1996 Atlanta Olympic Broadcasting program provided 170 paid positions for Asbury students who participated as professionals during this international event.

Having delivered more than 1,000 lectures and papers, President Gyertson is a vigorous spokesman for character development among college students on campus and off. Because of the kindness shown to his family during his childhood, he maintains strong ties to the Salvation Army, often speaking to the leadership and youth conferences about the benefit to the community of integrating Christian faith with action.

"The Asbury College experience down through the years has been shaped by a commitment to an education that focuses on both character and competence. *Eruditio et religio* . . . academic excellence and spiritual vitality." Thus notes the service-oriented president of Asbury College.

DAVID J. GYERTSON

PRESIDENT
ASBURY COLLEGE

I MACKLEM DRIVE
WILMORE, KY 40390–1198

606.858.3511
president@asbury.edu
http://www.asbury.edu/

UNDERGRADUATES: 1,300

"President Gyertson leads by example, showing true character and upholding standards of excellence and integrity. Students greatly respect his sincere commitment to them and his willingness to be 'real.'"

—AN ASBURY FOURTH-YEAR
STUDENT

Other Asbury Profiles :

• Honor Roll School
• Student Leadership Program

SR. JEANNE O'LAUGHLIN

PRESIDENT
BARRY UNIVERSITY

11300 NE SECOND AVENUE
MIAMI SHORES, FL 33161–6695

305.899.3000
jolaughlin@mail.barry.edu
http://www.barry.edu/

UNDERGRADUATES: 4,700

"Sister Jeanne brings a sense of community to Barry and to the world around us."

—A BARRY FIRST-YEAR STUDENT

SINCE HER APPOINTMENT IN 1981 as the fifth president of Barry University, Adrian Dominican Sister Jeanne O'Laughlin has been an outstanding leader, stressing a values-based mission. Her commitment to character education and diversity at this coeducational, Catholic, comprehensive university has won national and international recognition from pope and president alike. Her zeal for the less fortunate has been a personal, spiritual mission for Sister Jeanne, who took her vows at age 16. Sister Jeanne continues her passion for ministering to the homeless by heading up the Governor's Commission on the Homeless and directing outstanding volunteer and service-learning programs at Barry. "I realized I truly loved the church with all its problems, and that what really mattered was the ability to minister."

✦ **SERVICE LEARNING AND DIVERSITY.** Through grant funding, Sister Jeanne initiated the Central and South Florida Higher Education Diversity Coalition to help underskilled adults find the training they need for productive citizenship. "I am proud that 11 area colleges and universities are united in their desire to provide this service to our region and to put diversity at the top of everyone's agenda," notes Sister Jeanne, who continually seeks ways to improve race relations.

✦ **COMMUNITY OUTREACH AND VOLUNTEERISM.** Under Sister Jeanne's leadership, Project "Pockets of Pride" creates a safe, productive environment for neighboring communities with funding from a $100,000 grant. Through the office of Mission and Ministry, Sister Jeanne created the Volunteer Center, which promotes student community service.

✦ **MEDICAL MISSION.** Staff members for Primary Care Nursing Centers in seven low-income elementary schools train at Barry's School of Nursing. This hands-on experience is also offered through Barry's Podiatric Medicine program, in which faculty and students perform foot surgery on indigent children in the Yucatan.

✦ **EDUCATION AND SERVICE.** The Adrian Dominican School of Education offers free tutoring to low-income students. This commitment led to Barry's design for a charter school that has set a national standard for middle-school education.

Sister Jeanne models compassionate leadership and proactive citizenship building. She not only chaired the Miami Coalition for a Safe and Drug-Free Community, but also "We Will Rebuild" to repair the destruction caused by Hurricane Andrew. Raising community awareness and involvement infuses Sister Jeanne's many initiatives at Barry. She helped create a doctorate in ministry specifically addressing community needs and served concurrently as chair of the Association of Catholic Colleges and Universities and the Council of Independent Colleges. Following Pope John Paul II's visit to Cuba, Sister Jeanne directed an ecumenical group of religious leaders on a follow-up mission to answer two questions: "Is Cuba ready for a major change?" and "Does religious freedom really exist in Cuba?" Sister Jeanne received the Humanitarian Award from the Metro-Dade Office of Homeless Program in 1994 and has also won awards from women's and other community groups, reflecting her commitment to bettering the lives of others.

Internationally and locally, Sister Jeanne exemplifies for Barry students outstanding awareness of and service to the less fortunate.

In a once economically depressed region of Southern Appalachia, Larry D. Shinn, the eighth president of Berea College, embraces the notion of providing an education to people who could not otherwise afford it. President Shinn, who has been at the helm of this Christian, liberal arts college since 1994, also leads Berea's efforts to put students to work in the surrounding community, both in paying jobs and in volunteer public service positions. Further, by creating a four-part strategy for learning and curriculum, he has created a new sense of purpose among students, faculty, and staff. President Shinn's four primary learning goals are critical thinking and moral reflection; creating sensitivity as the natural and fabricated environments merge; valuing cultural traditions and differences; and thinking independently while working collaboratively.

Numerous initiatives and programs reflect President Shinn's service-oriented approach to higher education:

✦ **Community Outreach.** "Berea Buddies," a program run and staffed by Berea's "Students for Appalachia," matches at-risk elementary school children with Berea students, who become their mentors and friends. "Partners in Education" offers Berea students the opportunity to tutor at-risk middle-school students in math during school hours and on the weekends to help these children attain long-term educational goals. Through "People Who Care," Berea students travel regularly to mental health and geriatric facilities, where they befriend and assist residents.

✦ **The Appalachian Center.** This new initiative will provide programs ranging from leadership training for students heading into public service to a "learning-through-service" center that will merge classroom events with practical community work. The Appalachian Center will also house a regional leadership program that provides instruction and support for community improvement initiatives as it continues well-established programs that preserve traditional Appalachian music and dance.

✦ **Work Colleges Consortium.** President Shinn supports Berea's membership in this collaboration among six leading "work" colleges. The consortium's bottom-line goal is to strengthen students' understanding of work as a tool for experiential learning and serving the community.

✦ **Brushy Fork Institute.** Launched in 1988, this program has continued to flourish during President Shinn's term at Berea. Through the institute, Berea helps communities articulate and achieve their vision and provides leadership development training.

President Shinn is deeply committed to the welfare of his students and invests personally in advancing their goals. He invites students to his home for coffees, ice cream socials, and conversation, and he takes sincere interest in their academic and personal goals. He visits residence halls and participates in student meetings in an effort to learn more about students' lives.

Berea students have an outstanding model of caring civic leadership in President Shinn, who not only dedicates himself and inspires others to give public service, but makes higher education available to so many who might not otherwise ever experience it.

LARRY D. SHINN

PRESIDENT
BEREA COLLEGE

CPO 2344
BEREA, KY 40404

606.986.9341
larry_shinn@berea.edu
http://www.berea.edu/

UNDERGRADUATES: 1,500

"President Shinn is a role model and modern-day hero to me. He fulfills his position with professionalism while also conveying compassion and maintaining integrity."

—A Berea second-year
student

NEAL R. BERTE

PRESIDENT
BIRMINGHAM-SOUTHERN COLLEGE

900 ARKADELPHIA ROAD
BOX # 549002
BIRMINGHAM, AL 35254

205.226.4620
nberte@bsc.edu
http://www.bsc.edu/

UNDERGRADUATES: 1,400

"BSC students consider Dr. Berte a true friend and mentor. His compassion to serve the campus and community, coupled with his dedication to excellence, is unparalleled."

—A BSC FOURTH-YEAR
STUDENT

Other BSC Profiles:

• Honor Roll School
• Student Leadership Program

IN HIS 23 YEARS AS THE 11TH PRESIDENT OF BIRMINGHAM-SOUTHERN COLLEGE, Neal R. Berte has developed and expanded an appropriate role for this church-affiliated, liberal arts school located in the inner city of a large metropolitan area. In the mission of the College and its relationship to both the community and the United Methodist Church, President Berte encourages students to develop values and ethics that will lead to productive, fulfilled lives. He is also at the forefront of an important mission for United Methodists—connecting *faith* with *knowledge*—and he coauthored *Courage in Mission: Presidential Leadership in the Church-Related College* published by CASE Publications (1988).

President Berte strives to provide an educational environment that challenges students to think independently and communicate clearly as part of their commitment to both intellectual and social responsibility. Working closely with members of the Board of Trustees, the Norton Board of Advisors, the President's Advisory Council, the Pastoral Advisory Board, and other on-campus and community groups, he led BSC to a top ranking by *U.S. News & World Report* as the best southern regional liberal arts college. Subsequently, the Carnegie Foundation for the Advancement of Teaching elevated the institution to the National Liberal Arts I category, and BSC now ranks among the top 80 U.S. liberal arts colleges.

President Berte seeks to unite the "in-class" and "out-of-class" educational experiences through responsibility-oriented programs:

✦ LEADERSHIP STUDIES PROGRAM. BSC's interdisciplinary program focuses on the intellectual, ethical, and spiritual development of individual students, helping them realize leadership potential by combining the academic study of leadership with significant community service.

✦ SERVICE-LEARNING PROGRAM. Under the leadership of President Berte, BSC has distinguished itself through local and international community activism, encouraging students to engage in service to others. Believing that service enriches our lives, President Berte exemplified that belief by twice going to Calcutta, India, with students and the College Chaplain to work in the "House of the Dying" during Interim Term.

✦ INTERIM TERM. Birmingham-Southern's month-long Interim Term allows many opportunities for personal growth each January. Most recently, four Interim courses centered on service projects such as building a Habitat for Humanity house, the trip to Calcutta, and rejuvenating a school in Belize. Concomitantly, multiple activities were held on campus to promote the guiding theme, "Diversity."

President Berte has played a vital role in serving both the scholastic and local community, and he has won many awards and types of recognition in serving the church as well as local, state, and educational communities. His most recent accomplishment is cochairing a citizen-driven, region-wide planning process for the central Alabama area, "Region 2020," which is developing a strategic plan for growth based on input from the community. Under President Berte's leadership, goals have been established and implementation plans are in place.

President Berte continues to exemplify for BSC students the role of a powerful community leader who has committed his life to service with spiritual vitality.

ACTIONS LITERALLY HAVE SPOKEN LOUDER THAN WORDS from the beginning of E. Gordon Gee's term as Brown University's 17th president in 1998. Foregoing a ceremonial inauguration so that he could immediately get to work, President Gee donated a portion of the inaugural budget to Brown's libraries and scholarship funds. When he was formally installed as president several months later during Brown's commencement, he offered a new definition of "student": "The true scholar is of service . . . a free thinker with a sense of responsibility." Wasting no time to underscore his convictions, President Gee quickly became involved in community activities on the local and state level, acting on his vision for this liberal arts school as "a private university with a public purpose." The former president of three public universities, he chaired the committee to select the superintendent of Providence public schools, showing his commitment to public education as a critical element of democracy.

While donating his time to the university's surrounding community, Gee also has become a most visible presence on campus, providing an unprecedented level of accessibility for Brown students. His early initiatives extend that accessibility and demonstrate his commitment to the community:

✦ THE PRESIDENTIAL SEMINAR. This new course is part of a university-wide initiative President Gee created to promote discussion of the role and nature of civility and community within the modern university. Open to both undergraduate and graduate students, the seminar is a forum to explore the obligations of the Brown community to the city of Providence, the state of Rhode Island, and the nation. It includes classroom seminars, public lectures by invited speakers, and service-learning projects overseen by the university's Swearer Center for Public Service.

✦ THE CAMPUS COMPACT. One of the nation's primary advocacy organizations for community service for the past 13 years, the Campus Compact, has accepted President Gee's offer of a permanent home as a separate organization within Brown. The Compact is launching a $3.2 million national initiative to promote civic engagement among college students.

✦ WIRING SCHOOLS. President Gee hosted a fundraising event at Brown for a nonprofit Rhode Island organization that wires schools for high-speed connections to the Internet. He enlisted the help of the Brown community to join the volunteer work force installing the equipment.

One of the nation's most outspoken advocates for higher education, President Gee served as chair of the Association of American Universities for the 1997–98 academic year; he also serves on the board of the HELP (Health and Education Leadership for Providence) Coalition. He continues to teach, holding a Brown faculty appointment as professor of education and public policy. Beyond the classroom, President Gee is dedicated to students and to tackling issues such as binge-drinking, campus safety, and responsibility. He says he hopes to host every student at his home before they graduate, sincerely wanting students to think of him as a friend.

A firm believer that institutes of higher education have an obligation to help students develop character, conscience, and civility, President Gee works and lives with conviction of purpose that inspires students to strive toward leaving Brown—and the world—a better place than they found it.

E. GORDON GEE

PRESIDENT
BROWN UNIVERSITY

45 PROSPECT STREET
BOX 1860
PROVIDENCE, RI 02912

401.863.2234
e_gordon_gee@brown.edu
http://www.brown.edu/

UNDERGRADUATES: 6,000

"President Gee has institutionalized the concept of a private university with a public mission through both words and actions."

—A BROWN FOURTH-YEAR STUDENT

Other Brown Profiles :

• Spiritual Growth Program
• Volunteer Service Program

JOHN D. WELTY

PRESIDENT
CALIFORNIA STATE UNIVERSITY–
FRESNO

THOMAS ADMINISTRATION 103
5241 NORTH MAPLE AVENUE
FRESNO, CA 93740–8027

559.278.2324
john_welty@csufresno.edu
http://www.csufresno.edu/

UNDERGRADUATES: 14,800

"President Welty's dedication to community service sets a high standard that students try to emulate. His leadership and support are ever present on our campus."

—A FRESNO FIRST-YEAR STUDENT

Other Fresno Profiles :

• First-Year Program

THE SEVENTH PRESIDENT OF CALIFORNIA STATE UNIVERSITY, FRESNO, John D. Welty, appointed in 1991, has passionately led his students in a values-rich education. His energetic, community-based initiatives have created several nationally recognized programs that demonstrate the service orientation of this large, public, comprehensive institution. Fresno State students are encouraged to complete a community service project to graduate, and multiple volunteer opportunities have increased under President Welty's leadership. The school won its first Institutional Service Award in 1994 from California Campus Compact for "Excellence and Commitment to Service." The core tenet of service to the community drives President Welty's "Vision for the 21st Century: A Plan for Excellence," helping to elevate Fresno State to the stature of a model institution in the Central California Valley.

"Students must be inspired by a larger vision, using the knowledge they have acquired to discern patterns, to form values, and to advance the common good," says President Welty, who implements and supports a multitude of citizenship-building opportunities at Fresno.

✦ STUDENTS FOR COMMUNITY SERVICE. Developed and implemented by President Welty, this program promotes community-improvement partnerships between Fresno State and the surrounding area. More than 800 students have contributed 30,000 hours of service in activities such as blood drives; "Kids Day," a Children's Hospital fundraiser; and outreach to underrepresented students, including recruitment of African-American students in community and campus events. The El Dorado Park Project, or the "Stone Soup" component of this program, serves the needs of low-income families from Southeast Asia, providing medical and dental care, antiviolence programs, community theater, and other social support. The Community Services Opportunity Fair includes 44 nonprofit agencies that encourage volunteerism among the student body. University HOPE engages in building low-income housing. "Fresno READS" encourages reading programs with student mentors in the Central San Joaquin Valley.

✦ COMMUNITY SERVICE SCHOLARSHIP PROGRAM. Through a private endowment of $300,000, students can obtain a $1,000 scholarship and three academic credits in exchange for 100 or more hours of community service. Working with nonprofit agencies in the Fresno County area, these students are involved in education, crime issues, youth programs, public health, and arts promotion.

✦ CROSS-CULTURAL STUDENT LEADERSHIP RETREAT. Every year, students from diverse cultural backgrounds have an opportunity to step outside of their academic routine and develop leadership qualities and global cultural awareness. The program has contributed to Fresno's recognition as one of the top 30 schools in the nation to graduate Hispanic students.

Among his civic leadership activities, President Welty serves as Chair of the New United Way Campaign of Fresno County, Chair of the Central California Blood Center's Annual Giving Campaign, Co-Chair of the National Forum on Elimination of Drug and Alcohol Abuse on College Campuses, and Vice Chair of the Board of BACCHUS (Boosting Alcohol Consciousness Concerning the Health of University Students), an international organization committed to using peer education to promote responsible alcohol consumption. The U.S. Department of Education has published his article "Five Strategies for Eliminating Alcohol Abuse and Other Drug Abuse on Campus." Fresno State students can look to President Welty as a committed, civic-minded administrator and an engaged citizen with a creative vision for the future.

SINCE ARRIVING AS THE 16TH PRESIDENT OF COLLEGE OF THE OZARKS IN 1988, Jerry C. Davis has carried out a labor of love. Dubbed "Hard Work U" by the *Wall Street Journal,* this Christian liberal arts college's mission is to provide an education to "those found worthy but who are without sufficient means" to pay for it. The school charges no tuition, but requires all students to work on campus to earn their room, board, and tuition (the school accepts no federal student loans). President Davis daily reinforces this ethic of responsibility and hard work in his students. He ardently believes that, as educated people and leaders of society, graduates have a responsibility to pursue more than money—they must become models of citizenship. Having attended a work school in Georgia himself and earning his doctorate in biology at Ohio State University, Jerry Davis has been a teacher or administrator in higher education for 30 years. As president of a small college in Kentucky for students from Appalachia, he laid the foundation for his future work at C of O.

President Davis's commitment to helping students thrive as citizens starts with "raising expectations" in all areas of life: improving personal appearance; hiring professors committed to C of O's values; expanding the work-study program to 15 hours of work per week for both commuting and resident students; implementing an honor code; and raising the required GPA level. His commitment of time, personnel, and financial resources has created an institution that demonstrates a high level of loyalty from students, faculty, and staff. President Davis supported initiatives for the following character development programs:

✦ **"CHARACTER" CENTER.** In 1998, President Davis's passion for good citizenship resulted in opening The Keeter Center for Character Education. Based on C of O's mission of academic, vocational, spiritual, patriotic, and cultural growth, the Center increases awareness of these issues within the higher education community; serves as a resource for faculty, staff, parents, and students; develops publications on character building; and serves as a model for similar centers in the US.

✦ **"CHARACTER" SPEAKERS.** After former Iranian hostage Terry Waite spoke at a C of O convocation, President Davis continued to bring well-known speakers to campus to instill concepts of responsibility in students. They include Barbara Bush, Margaret Thatcher, Norman Schwarzkopf, and Elizabeth Dole, who said, "I feel a different spirit on this college campus."

✦ **"CHARACTER" ACADEMICS.** Through a college honors program, those who model lives of character—public school teachers, small business leaders, and representatives from organizations devoted to character—meet with C of O students.

✦ **"CHARACTER" CAMP.** In 1992, President Davis established Camp Lookout at C of O, a free summer camp for children from the Family Services Rolls.

President Davis has been nationally recognized for his work. In 1993, the National Beta Club named him a "Beta Great," and in 1994 he was named an Eisenhower Fellow to Taiwan. In 1997, he was awarded two national honors—the Young America's Foundation presented him with its "Guardian of Freedom Award," and Students in Free Enterprise (SIFE) International named him "Best College Administrator" for that year. He also serves on the Boards of Directors of various educational organizations. President Davis says that C of O is "a uniquely American institution, providing opportunities to deserving young people willing to work for a higher education and better way of life." Students need look no further than the president's office for a living example of a hardworking success story.

JERRY C. DAVIS

PRESIDENT
COLLEGE OF THE OZARKS

POINT LOOKOUT, MO 65726

417.334.6411
pres@cofo.edu
http://www.cofo.edu/

UNDERGRADUATES: 1,500

"The first time I met President Davis, I knew he had a genuine care and concern for students. He remembers names and even where a lot of us come from. He is very down-to-earth and certainly a man of great character."

—A C OF O THIRD-YEAR STUDENT

Other C of O Profiles:

• Honor Roll School
• Academic Honesty Program
• Civic Education Program
• First-Year Program

CLAIRE L. GAUDIANI

PRESIDENT
CONNECTICUT COLLEGE

270 MOHEGAN AVENUE
FANN 201
NEW LONDON, CT 06320–4196

860.447.1911
clgau@conncoll.edu
http://www.camel.conncoll.edu/

UNDERGRADUATES: 1,600

"President Gaudiani exemplifies leadership, treating students as mature, responsible adults. Asking us to govern ourselves through an honor code encourages character development in and beyond the classroom."

—A CONNECTICUT FOURTH-
YEAR STUDENT

Other Connecticut Profiles :

• Academic Honesty Program
• Civil Education Program

SINCE 1988, CLAIRE L. GAUDIANI HAS CHARTED A SOLID COURSE FOR CONNECTICUT COLLEGE, establishing a tradition of global citizenship in this private, liberal arts institution as its eighth—and first alumni—president. Under her leadership, the ethical choices and level of trust among Connecticut students and faculty have flourished, supported by the 80-year-old Honor Code, the involvement of students and faculty in shared governance, and the bold initiatives of volunteerism in numerous local and international programs. President Gaudiani encourages students to achieve their potential through active community service combined with classroom analysis. "It is not just what they come here to do, but who they come here to be."

President Gaudiani has promoted and supported character development through Connecticut's initiatives of intense civic responsibility:

✦ **HONOR CODE.** One of 12 nationally recognized Honor Codes stands as a core tenet of President Gaudiani's commitment to encouraging moral decision-making. Connecticut students demonstrate character awareness through unproctored exams, self-managed dormitories, and advice on tenure decisions.

✦ **CENTER FOR COMMUNITY CHALLENGES.** Center activities cultivate leadership attuned to how communities function and how an appreciation of diversity can help foster civic engagement.

✦ **CERTIFICATE PROGRAM COMMUNITY ACTION.** President Gaudiani supports this four-year program that concentrates on the roles and responsibilities of citizenship in a multicultural democratic society.

✦ **CIVICS IN ACTION.** Over January break, the Dean's Term focuses on skills in negotiating, public speaking, and team building in multicultural settings, complementing traditional academics to foster global leadership.

✦ **OUTREACH PROGRAMS.** The High-School Student Advanced Placement Program brings disadvantaged inner-city high-school students from the Northeast to Connecticut, where students encourage them to aspire to a college education. Through teaching and serving in less technologically advanced areas such as Tanzania, India, and Mexico, Connecticut students in the Toor Cummings Center for International Studies and Liberal Arts are able to experience global citizenship.

President Gaudiani exemplifies scholar-teachers who identify civic virtues in teaching and practice. She accelerates progress through community-centered planning and work. "Our forebears struggled to settle new geographical space. Today, our job is to settle new psychological and social space where men and women of diverse backgrounds can live and work together."

In 1994, President Gaudiani became Chair of Campus Compact, a national coalition of 500 colleges and university presidents who support community service. She led a faculty project to study present and potential ethical systems across cultures. As a representative of the Fulbright Foundation, in 1996 President Gaudiani toured Morocco, discussing global ethics. Connecticut subsequently sponsored the first International Conference on Ethics in Government. President Gaudiani's drive to enrich character consistently merges with her promotion of civic responsibility, providing Connecticut students with an innovative way to seek ethical leadership skills that ultimately strengthens our democracy.

"To know, to lead, to serve, to understand." It isn't sufficient for a school to have a mission statement; someone must model it. James T. Harris, the 16th president of The Defiance College, a liberal arts school affiliated with the United Church of Christ, does just that. After arriving at Defiance in 1994, President Harris initiated a campus-wide initiative requiring all students to complete four years of service-learning courses and a senior capstone course. In addition, he is one of 18 current education professionals helping to design the National Service Leader Schools program, the third part of President Clinton's Corporation for National Service, and will focus on service learning at the secondary school level. Comprehensive traditional coursework combined with rigorous community service have made Defiance a national model.

Drawing on his doctoral work in educational management from Harvard, President Harris has established numerous programs for building student citizens:

✦ CITIZENSHIP. President Harris recently secured a $1.1 million donation for the Program for Responsible Citizenship, an arts and sciences project designed to instill a sense of civic responsibility managed through the Defiance Arts and Humanities Center. Students pursue various opportunities to serve their community and the world. The Center awards 15 fellowships each year to those who demonstrate outstanding personal commitment to volunteerism.

✦ OUTREACH. Each year, President Harris oversees a group of faculty and students on a weeklong service-learning mission renovating homes for the elderly and disadvantaged in Mississippi, tutoring school children in Appalachia, or building a new schoolhouse in Kenya.

✦ VOLUNTEER SERVICE. A major part of life for Defiance students consists of serving the community by tutoring neighborhood children, pursuing work-study options through "DC Connects," or taking advantage of AmeriCorps options that provide educational awards in exchange for service. Such initiatives help dedicated students become involved citizens.

President Harris particularly enjoys "President for a Day," which gives him a chance to be a student while a student takes over his schedule for the day. President Harris also speaks frequently at national conferences and was honored by the Pennsylvania State University's College of Education with its Leadership and Service Award in 1996. Demonstrating that he requires service of himself as well as of his students, President Harris is chairman of the annual campaign of DASH (Defiance Area Society for the Handicapped) and serves on the boards of Olivet College and "Leadership Defiance." He volunteers for the Positive Attitudes for the Homeless Organization and was the honorary chair of the 1995 Defiance Area Crop Walk that raised funds for local food pantries.

"Above all, we must get across the idea that the individual flourishes best in a genuine community to which the individual in turn has an obligation to contribute." Living these words, President Harris hopes to persuade those at Defiance that the purpose of education is the "development of character and citizenship as well as preparation for careers and commerce." Defiance students leave the school knowing—and living—that ideal.

JAMES T. HARRIS

PRESIDENT
THE DEFIANCE COLLEGE

701 N. CLINTON STREET
DEFIANCE, OH 43512

419.784.4010
jharris@defiance.edu
http://www.defiance.edu/

UNDERGRADUATES: 800

"President Harris works side-by-side with students, showing them that leadership is not a skill taught through textbooks, but a lesson learned through life."

—A DEFIANCE FOURTH-YEAR STUDENT

Other Defiance Profiles :

• Honor Roll School
• Civic Education Program
• First-Year Program
• Senior-Year Program
• Volunteer Service

NANNERL O. KEOHANE

PRESIDENT
DUKE UNIVERSITY

207 ALLEN BUILDING
BOX 90001
DURHAM, NC 27708–0001

919.684.8111
president@valkyrie.oit.duke.edu
http://www.duke.edu/

UNDERGRADUATES: 6,400

"President Keohane is an intellectual in the best sense of the word. Her leadership has helped me to understand that a true education is a moral education. It involves constant reflection on two things: the information I am learning and the kind of person I am becoming."

—A DUKE THIRD-YEAR STUDENT

Other Duke Profiles:

• Student Leadership Program

IMPROVING THE WORLD FOR OTHERS by developing an ardent dedication to civic involvement in her students is Nannerl O. Keohane's life work. The eighth president of Duke University since 1993, her efforts on behalf of the moral upbringing of students reflect her connection to her own past, as well as her strong commitment to service-minded education in the young people who attend this private, nonsectarian university with Methodist origins. Perhaps as a result of being the daughter of a Presbyterian minister, President Keohane has vocally supported Duke's religious heritage and divinity school and the notion that moral development is an integral part of the college experience—and beyond. President Keohane has supported critical initiatives that help Duke students pursue the larger goals of a true education, one that attends "not only to their intellectual growth but also to their development as adults committed to high ethical standards and full participation as leaders in their communities":

◆ **KENAN ETHICS PROGRAM.** President Keohane established this program to support "the study and teaching of ethics and promote moral reflection and commitment in personal, professional, community, and civic life." She appointed the well-regarded Dr. Elizabeth Kiss as director and involves senior administrative and faculty members in its activities. President Keohane states, "Our work is guided by the conviction that universities have a responsibility to prepare students for lives of personal integrity and reflective citizenship by nurturing their capacities for critical thinking, compassion, courage, and their concern for justice." Program activities have flowed into both campus organizations and academic areas, such as writing, public policy, environmental studies, and religion.

◆ **COLLABORATIVE PARTNERS.** President Keohane also strongly supports three programs that address, in collaboration with the Kenan Ethics program, civic education, character development, and ethical issues:

1. The Hart Leadership Program is the first endowed undergraduate program of its kind. Service Opportunities in Leadership, a year-long experiential education program, prepares Duke students to become an integral part of their community and to contribute to its betterment.

2. The Community Service Center serves as a clearinghouse for volunteer and community service activities available to students, faculty, and staff.

3. The Durham-Duke Neighborhood Partnership is a university-wide effort to promote civic involvement and community development in Durham. To date, it has garnered more than $3 million in corporate, federal, local, and university support for its work in the areas of housing, health, and education. Hundreds of Duke students work with teachers in the public schools and are involved in neighborhood projects.

A front-page article in the January 19, 1999, issue of the *Christian Science Monitor* described The Center for Academic Integrity, a national consortium of colleges and universities that President Keohane invited to move from Stanford University to Duke. Among her many activities, she often speaks about moral education and responsibility at various conferences organized by the Kenan Ethics Program and actively participates in Campus Compact, the national service-learning organization. In the Duke community as well as in the nation, President Keohane is recognized as a leader who supports education as a means of guiding students to pursue enlightened, active service as they leave Duke to enter the workplace and the wider world.

When Duquesne University's 11th president, John E. Murray, Jr., learned of the need for shoes in Nicaragua, within weeks Duquesne had collected, sorted, and shipped 80,000 pairs to the hurricane-ravaged nation. That swift and decisive action exemplifies President Murray's vision of Duquesne as a "noble enterprise," where his sharply focused leadership meshes with a goal articulated in the university's mission statement: to provide an education for the "mind, heart, and soul." President Murray's community service initiatives, teaching, volunteerism, and personal involvement in university life have reflected his dedication to that mission since he became president of this comprehensive, Catholic university in 1988.

At the core of his work is a commitment to spreading Duquesne's service work to the less fortunate in the Pittsburgh community, the nation, and the world. These efforts were praised in a report written in 1998 by the Commission on Higher Education of the Middle States Association of Colleges and Schools: "[A] culture has been created at Duquesne: individuals and offices work together to promote the common good." President Murray has created programs that set examples for personal and civic responsibility:

✦ **Duquesne University Volunteers (DUV).** President Murray created this program to provide community service and outreach to Pittsburgh and beyond. DUV offers a wide range of options to students, faculty, and staff who wish to volunteer. In the 1997–98 academic year, 4,500 Duquesne students and staff served 575 sites, raising a total of $204,000. By choosing a mix of local and global agencies, the university is able to provide donations and assistance to a diverse cross-section of needy individuals and groups. Some volunteer efforts were sparked directly by students who expressed an interest in helping children, the elderly, the disadvantaged, the sick, and people with physical and mental challenges. The result is comprehensive community service that ranges from after-school tutoring in Pittsburgh's Hill District to promoting peace in Africa. President Murray himself volunteers frequently in DUV efforts.

✦ **The Family Institute.** To help establish Duquesne as a center for family research, President Murray founded the Institute to focus on the family from a multidisciplinary perspective and, in the long run, to play a critical role in strengthening the family unit in the US. Under his leadership, the Institute has brought to campus Dr. William Bennett, director of Empower America, and Dr. Wade Horn, president of the National Fatherhood Initiative, to discuss the current and future state of the American family. One of the Institute's goals is to provide a significant database of family-based articles for its website.

In addition to embedding character development initiatives throughout Duquesne's curriculum and culture, President Murray continues to teach contract law and, occasionally, finds time to play piano in performances with faculty and music students. He also serves on numerous boards and committees that drive local and state community efforts and has received special awards from groups such as the Pennsylvania Commission on Crime and the Jewish National Fund. Perhaps President's Murray's own words, published in a special Tenth Anniversary edition of the *University Record* magazine, make the strongest case for his belief in the value of character for himself and for Duquesne students: "We commit ourselves to the pursuit of a virtuous life, a life of prudence, justice, fortitude, moderation, and a life of faith, hope, and love. This is the virtuous life, the only life worth living."

John E. Murray, Jr.

PRESIDENT
DUQUESNE UNIVERSITY

600 FORBES AVENUE
PITTSBURGH, PA 15282

412.396.6000
murray@duq.edu
http://www.duq.edu/

UNDERGRADUATES: 5,500

"President Murray shows a concern for people that is oftentimes lost in today's fast-paced world. When I look for someone who exemplifies outstanding leadership based on character and moral values, I need look no further than President Murray."

—A Duquesne third-year
student

Other Duquesne Profiles:

• Character & Sexuality Program
• Senior-Year Program

KENT R. HILL

PRESIDENT
EASTERN NAZARENE COLLEGE

23 EAST ELM AVENUE
QUINCY, MA 02170-2999

617.745.3000
hillk@enc.edu
http://www.enc.edu/

UNDERGRADUATES: 1,600

"President Hill has spoken candidly in a number of settings to students about his experience and development as a leader. Students have a deep respect for his integrity and character as a role model."

—AN ENC FOURTH-YEAR
STUDENT

KENT R. HILL is a noted international authority on and advocate for religious freedom and human rights, a Russian studies scholar, and the 11th president of Eastern Nazarene College. President Hill has published books and articles on various topics, testified before United States House and Senate Committees on issues of religious freedom, traveled extensively in defense of religious liberty, lectured in this country and abroad, and taught in both the US and Russia. He currently serves as a member of the Board of Trustees of the Russian American Christian University in Moscow, the first Protestant liberal arts university in the former Soviet Union.

President Hill's varied and rich knowledge and experience clearly contribute to programming and curriculum excellence at Eastern Nazarene College, a private, church-related, interdenominational liberal arts school. He emphasizes the need for all faculty to be committed Christians involved in their local communities and churches and has engaged the campus in an ongoing, academic debate on issues of faith and science. Also dedicated to promoting multicultural responsibility in the Christian educational community, President Hill organized a major conference on the responsibility of Christian educational institutions to work more effectively with the diversity of urban students on college campuses.

The President's deep commitment to character development, academic quality, community service, and promotion of civil and constructive dialog is evident in classrooms, dormitories, faculty and administrative offices, and everyday campus life. Under President Hill's leadership, ENC has initiated or continued the following programs:

♦ **THE ROMANIA PROGRAM.** Designed to provide students a unique opportunity to learn and live in a cross-cultural setting, this program is administered and taught by a full-time faculty member in Romania.

♦ **THE LIVING ISSUES CLASS.** As part of ENC's Cultural Perspectives required sequence of courses, "Living Issues" emphasizes the importance of religious values in character development.

♦ **THE PRESIDENT'S ANNUAL APOLOGETICS LECTURE.** Established by President Hill in 1996, this series brings to campus such renowned scholars as Diogenes Allen of Princeton University and the Reverend Dr. John Polkinghorne, former Queens' College president, Cambridge University, to enhance reasonable and civil discussion about the relationship between Christian and other prominent worldviews.

♦ **NATIONAL CONFERENCE ON MINORITY URBAN LEADERSHIP DEVELOPMENT AND CHRISTIAN COLLEGES.** This major conference, held in Boston, explored ways to better foster character and leadership development among minorities in the US, while significantly expanding multicultural educational opportunities on American Christian college and university campuses.

President Hill has stated many times his belief that a high-quality, complete education involves not just preparing for a profession or vocation, but fostering character development. Without this dimension, knowledge cannot be transformed into wisdom and service. Students at ENC leave the campus as educated people prepared to render greater service to the world in which they live and work.

"IDENTITY CRISIS." This is what David E. Shi faced on becoming Furman University's 10th president in 1994—not a personal dilemma but the challenge of leading a university that was not sure where it was going. After Furman severed its 166-year relationship with the South Carolina Baptist Convention in 1992, many predicted that it would become a "secular institution in a valueless world," unable to evolve into a liberal arts college that maintained its Christian tradition. Reflecting the doomsaying, applications, admissions, and entering SAT scores all fell in 1993, and Furman's loss of financial support from its former constituency led to its first unbalanced budget in 20 years. Undaunted by the formidable task before him, President Shi drew on his personal heritage at Furman (as an alumnus and former vice president), his leadership skills, and his faith to lead the school forward. Emphasizing Furman's motto *Christo et Doctrinae* ("For Christ and Learning"), he helped the school rededicate itself to its mission.

Now a revitalized nonsectarian Christian university—and the largest liberal arts college in South Carolina, Furman is renewing a deep sense of community under President Shi's direction. Increasing financial aid, improving faculty salaries, and constructing six new residence halls (three more are under way) to bring upperclassmen back to the campus as models for freshmen and sophomores are part of the renaissance. As chair of the university's Strategic Planning Committee, President Shi championed a balanced education at Furman:

◆ **VOLUNTEER SERVICE.** High priorities for President Shi include helping to establish endowments for the Collegiate Educational Service Corps, through which more than half of Furman's student body volunteers for Greenville-based projects.

◆ **STUDENT LEADERSHIP.** President Shi has created an ethos of leadership that encourages students to take responsibility for their own learning and pursue moral growth. In addition to a four-year student leadership program, he has advocated for activities such as substance-free halls in dormitories and a "ropes course" for campus and community group building.

◆ **CIVIC EDUCATION.** President Shi has obtained corporate and foundation support for the Center for Engaged Learning to encourage local internships in government and nonprofit agencies, as well as collaborative student-faculty research. He obtained similar support for Furman faculty and students to work with local schools in enhancing curricula and tutoring. He also supports the Religion-in-Life lecture program that stresses community involvement.

A respected historian and author (his textbook *America: A Narrative History* is used in colleges throughout the nation, and *The Simple Life: Plain Living and High Thinking in American Culture* was a History Book Club selection), President Shi expresses his concern for ethics, reflection, and Furman's moral and spiritual ethics in on- and off-campus speeches and articles. He is also a member of numerous educational boards and other community organizations.

President Shi has inspired a community of learners who reflect seriously on their values, care about each other, and assume civic responsibility. Since he took office, President Shi has seen applications, admissions, and SAT scores rise steadily. He is leading the university into the 21st century as a Christian liberal arts college with a mission "not to save souls, but to promote soul-searching."

The short-term results of President Shi's efforts may be in campus growth, but the long-term outcome will be the contributions made by Furman graduates.

DAVID E. SHI

PRESIDENT
FURMAN UNIVERSITY

3300 POINSETT HIGHWAY
GREENVILLE, SC 29613

864.294.2000
david.shi@furman.edu
http://www.furman.edu/

UNDERGRADUATES: 2,600

"As a scholar, leader, orator, and friend, President Shi models for us what it means to be 'educated.' He balances masterfully his love of learning with his love for his students."

—A FURMAN FOURTH-YEAR STUDENT

Other Furman Profiles :

• Honor Roll School
• Volunteer Service Program

H. David Brandt

PRESIDENT
GEORGE FOX UNIVERSITY

414 N. MERIDIAN STREET
NEWBERG, OR 97132–2697

503.538.8383
dbrandt@georgefox.edu
http://www.georgefox.edu/

UNDERGRADUATES: 1,700

*"President Brandt
honestly listens to all
opinions, then boldly
makes wise decisions."*

—A GEORGE FOX
FOURTH-YEAR STUDENT

LEADING THE WAY WITH A MISSION THAT EMBRACES a commitment to responsibility, President H. David Brandt is taking George Fox University into the 21st century with a vision of intellectual and personal growth, and participation in the world's concerns. The 11th president of this private, Friends Church-affiliated liberal arts university for the past year, President Brandt has served higher education as a chief academic officer or college president for 22 years. His extensive experience has provided him with a sensitivity to student needs, a commitment to the highest standards of academics, and an appreciation for the role the university can play in the community.

The programs and initiatives supported by President Brandt all reinforce personal responsibility among students and faculty:

✦ **CIVIC EDUCATION.** Ardently believing in the rights and responsibilities of citizenship, President Brandt has demonstrated the mission of the institution to "make itself a community in which studies and activities are made relevant to life, develop insight into social and political issues confronting humanity, and learn to participate democratically in decision making and policy implementing as responsible citizens." An impassioned and popular speaker both on and off campus, his words consistently reflect the priority of character education in George Fox students. He is firmly committed to the idea that educated individuals need to *choose* to live responsibly, as well as become knowledgeable in their field of academic study to benefit their communities.

✦ **LIFESTYLE AGREEMENT.** Considered a condition of admission to George Fox, this lifestyle commitment excludes gambling, the use or possession of non-medicinal substances and obscene or pornographic materials, and promiscuous behavior.

✦ **PROFESSORS AS MODELS.** As a requirement of their teaching responsibilities, professors actively model service and inspire George Fox students. The school's *Student Handbook* tells students to expect this of their professors: "Not only will you become grounded in the basics of your discipline, you also will be challenged to be humble in spirit as you prepare to serve others with what you have learned."

✦ **STUDENT LEADERSHIP.** Actively encouraging the development of a strong student leadership agenda, President Brandt staunchly supports the student government. He advises student leaders and provides funding to assist in sponsoring ELITE ("Empowering Leaders in Integrity Through Experience") a national conference on student leadership. The purpose of the conference is "to provide an opportunity through which leadership qualities will be refined for lifelong service through awareness, motivation, and direct application from a Christian perspective."

President Brandt has been recognized locally and nationally. Among the awards he has garnered is the 1995 Dean's Award from the National Council of Independent Colleges; he was cited for living his values and being "a steadfast advocate for improved campus community and collegiality."

President Brandt stands behind George Fox's fundamental principle that a university is a place that empowers students to take responsibility for themselves and demonstrate it toward others. This philosophy is woven into every aspect of study and student life at George Fox University.

Other George Fox Profiles:

• Honor Roll School

PRESIDENT R. JUDSON CARLBERG ISN'T JUST A PROPONENT of Gordon College's mission statement; he helped write it. And every word reflects his vision, dedication, and leadership: "Gordon College strives to graduate men and women distinguished by intellectual maturity and Christian character, committed to a lifestyle of servanthood and prepared for leadership roles worldwide." President Carlberg, the 7th president, puts into practice Gordon's commitment to its mission. In addition to his teaching and mentoring activities and leadership roles on campus and in the community, he is active in his church—where he has been Chair of the Elders Board, adult Sunday School teacher, and a guest preacher. He has won numerous awards and honors, including the Council of Independent Colleges Service Award and the National Dean's Award for Leadership. He has said of his responsibility to his students, "We want to graduate men and women who are rooted in substance and committed to significance."

The power and passion of his words are strong, but President Carlberg backs them up with action and personal commitment. Despite the demands of a daunting schedule, he teaches a first-year seminar class every year that serves as an introduction to the heart of a Gordon education, focusing on character development and formation of a Christian worldview. President Carlberg also personally mentors freshman scholarship students.

Some of the programs and initiatives supported by President Carlberg include:

✦ MULTICULTURAL PROGRAM. Gordon's multicultural program promotes awareness and appreciation of various ethnic and cultural backgrounds as represented in North America and other countries through programs, worship services, and cultural awareness experiences.

✦ "LA VIDA." This 12-day outdoor adventure gives students the opportunity to discover their physical, mental, and spiritual potential in an environment that encourages them to set new goals, develop new attitudes, and practice faith in the community. By surmounting physical challenges and experiencing solitude, students are compelled to examine their own character, often discovering new dimensions within themselves.

✦ COMMUNITY OUTREACH MINISTRIES. This program serves the Greater Boston area through service projects such as working with AIDS patients, being active in Amnesty International, working with local children, and singing in the choir to raise funds for the summer internship program.

✦ SHORT-TERM MISSIONS. These short trips at home and abroad offer students the opportunity to learn, witness, and serve in cross-cultural settings.

President Carlberg's commitment to guiding others isn't limited to Gordon students. He has an impact on students across the nation through his mentoring of other college presidents through the Council of Christian Colleges and Universities leadership development program. He also writes and speaks frequently on topics of character and leadership development. He authored an acclaimed editorial in the *Boston Sunday Herald* and ran a workshop called "Learning to Lead Within a Lifestyle of Service" at a Christian convention in Boston. In 1994, President Carlberg was invited by the Russian Ministry of Education to lecture educators in Moscow about the moral development of university students. "At Gordon we strive to . . . mentor [students] and help them mature in character and integrity," President Carlberg writes. Through his leadership, Gordon will indeed graduate men and women who are rooted in substance and committed to significance.

R. JUDSON CARLBERG

PRESIDENT
GORDON COLLEGE

255 GRAPEVINE ROAD
WENHAM, MA 01984

978.927.2300
carlberg@hope.gordon.edu
http://www.gordon.edu/

UNDERGRADUATES: 1,500

"President Carlberg demonstrates that intellectual and character development are necessarily linked. I so respect and admire President Carlberg and count myself extremely blessed to have him as my mentor at Gordon College."

—A GORDON FIRST-YEAR STUDENT

Other Gordon Profiles :
• Honor Roll School
• First-Year Program
• Spiritual Growth Program

AXEL D. STEUER

PRESIDENT
GUSTAVUS ADOLPHUS COLLEGE

800 WEST COLLEGE AVENUE
ST. PETER, MN 56082–1498

507.933.7538
asteuer@gustavus.edu
http://www.gustavus.edu/

UNDERGRADUATES: 2,400

"Over the past four years, President Axel Steuer has successfully created an environment where Gustavus students can develop the skills, dedication, and sense of responsibility that enable us to make positive contributions to our communities."

—A GUSTAVUS FOURTH-YEAR
STUDENT

NOT EVEN A TORNADO CAN DAMPEN THE RESOLVE of the 13th president of Gustavus Adolphus College, a liberal arts college affiliated with the Evangelical Lutheran Church in America. On assuming office in 1991, President Axel D. Steuer established a goal to "develop a strong service-learning component of the curriculum and strengthen community service programs." As a powerful demonstration of this commitment, he amazed the campus and community by reopening the college three weeks after tornadoes severely damaged much of the campus and surrounding St. Peter. The city saw the restorative hand of Dr. Steuer at work as Gustavus staff and students aided in recovery efforts.

In the spirit of Martin Buber ("education worthy of the name is essentially education of character") and backed by his Harvard divinity degree and University of Pennsylvania doctorate in religious thought, President Steuer has long committed himself to "Education for the Common Good." He contributed to successful grant proposals for professorships in "Ethics and the Professions" and "Religion, Politics, and the Political Process." In 1991, President Steuer was honored by Occidental College's Community Service Office for his key role in starting the institution's community service program.

Through the following programs, President Steuer actively promotes civic responsibility at Gustavus:

✦ ADMINISTRATORS IN COMMUNITY SERVICE. He helped organize the Minnesota Campus Compact, a group of 45 college and university presidents committed to community service. By creating the position of Director for Community Service, he enabled Gustavus to assess service opportunities, screen student volunteers, and expand the service-learning curriculum.

✦ PRESIDENTIAL DISCRETIONARY FUND. President Steuer directed funds to support student involvement in national conferences for peer assistants, student government leadership training, and involvement in Habitat for Humanity.

✦ ALPHA PHI OMEGA. As faculty advisor to the college's service fraternity, President Steuer hosts an annual recognition dinner for students who have demonstrated exemplary community service.

✦ SPONBERG CHAIR IN ETHICS. President Steuer strongly supports this new position and encourages an "ethics across the curriculum" integration of moral reflection into the First-Term Seminar and many capstone courses.

In addition to lecturing on moral development and professional ethics, President Steuer has dedicated 20 years to "The Education of Character" in the community through presentations to church and civic groups, service clubs, and student honor organizations. He served six years on the American Academy of Religion board of directors and has continuing professional relationships with the Society for Values in Higher Education. President Steuer also serves on the National Advisory Council of ForCHILDREN, Inc. And internationally, for leadership in strengthening the ties between Sweden and the United States, President Steuer has been awarded the Royal Order of the Polar Star by His Royal Majesty, King Carl XVI Gustaf of Sweden; he also represents Gustavus at the Nobel Prize Award ceremonies in Stockholm.

These diverse activities demonstrate President Steuer's profound conviction about community commitment in his own life, and his example propels Gustavus students into living similar lives of civic action and responsibility.

OUTSTANDING CIVIC RESPONSIBILITY AND GREGORY S. PRINCE, JR., the fourth president of Hampshire College, are almost synonymous in this private, liberal arts school. Since 1989, President Prince has fostered a deep commitment to citizenship education and a passion for social justice that have become an educational focus for Hampshire students. A bold activist who supports affirmative action, President Prince has dramatically expanded Hampshire's vision of community service, establishing memberships with A Better Chance Inc., the Harlem Writers Guild, and the Schomburg Center for Research in Black Cultures of the NY Public Library. He also created a website to promote intercultural dialog.

One of the nationally recognized achievements in higher education consists of a five-college consortium that includes Hampshire, Amherst, Mount Holyoke, Smith, and the University of Massachusetts at Amherst, where students discover a shared base for community development in the region. This program and others demonstrate what President Prince believes about common purpose and civility: "The essential commonality among civic responsibility, the character of the good citizen, and a liberal arts education is the absolute importance of critical undergraduate thinking that is guided by the values of honesty and respect for other individuals."

Programs that support this conviction include:

✦ COMMUNITY CONNECTIONS. This program focuses on public service, with internships and work experience in women's shelters, healthcare agencies, and after-school settings.

✦ SCIENCE, TECHNOLOGY, AND SOCIETY PROGRAM. As part of community outreach, Hampshire and the Institute for Science and Interdisciplinary Studies work together to educate the less fortunate. Citizen-driven cleanup of military nuclear and toxic waste projects and an Amazon Rainforest project are examples of the far-reaching public issues that this program addresses.

✦ EXPERIMENTAL PROGRAM. This program in nontraditional academics and lifestyle prizes community-based learning. Season-extending technologies and practical work at Hampshire Farm exemplify out-of-class experience.

✦ PUBLIC SERVICE AND SOCIAL CHANGES PROGRAM. To encourage students in public and social policy implementation, this program offers paid and volunteer internships, curriculum development, career counseling, and coalition building with community groups.

When UN Secretary General Kofi Annan came to Hampshire, President Prince challenged students to raise a $10,000 contribution to support schools in Africa. Whether forming a partnership with Springfield Public Schools or participating on the Council on Ethnic and Racial Justice of the American Bar Association, President Prince concentrates his energies on creating a just society. He notes, "This interest in educating for citizenship has brought together groups of thinkers with highly diverse points of view, united by their common call for American education to reach beyond rhetoric."

Hampshire College students receive ample and excellent opportunities in civic responsibility, modeled by President Prince's admirable dedication to action.

GREGORY S. PRINCE, JR.

PRESIDENT
HAMPSHIRE COLLEGE

893 WEST STREET
AMHERST, MA 01002

413.549.4600
gprince@hampshire.edu
http://www.hampshire.edu/

UNDERGRADUATES: 1,200

"President Prince believed in and helped students build the Experimental Program in Education and Community from its grass-roots origins."

—A HAMPSHIRE FOURTH-YEAR STUDENT

WILLIAM R. HARVEY

PRESIDENT
HAMPTON UNIVERSITY

HAMPTON, VA 23668

757.727.5000
presidentsoffice@hamptonu.edu
http://www.hamptonu.edu/

UNDERGRADUATES: 5,200

"I have witnessed Dr. Harvey provide visionary leadership in its finest form. Never satisfied with the status quo, our president works tirelessly to ensure that Hampton provides an everlasting education for life."

—A HAMPTON THIRD-YEAR STUDENT

Other Hampton Profiles:

• Honor Roll School

SINCE 1978, 110 YEARS AFTER THIS HISTORICALLY Black, private, liberal arts institution was founded, Hampton University's 12th president has exemplified values, dignity, and respect for self and others. President William R. Harvey advocates self-sufficiency and empowerment for African-American students, having generated growth in student population from 2,700 to over 5,000 and introduced 45 new academic programs. Using his broad experience in higher education and as a personal business owner, he promotes service learning and a responsible work ethic. Since 1992, he has instituted Hampton programs that combat juvenile delinquency, truancy, and illiteracy. To him, future citizenship means character building. "We must return to being unashamed and unapologetic in openly discussing with young people values, character development, and ethics."

As evidence of this unabashed stance toward personal responsibility through higher education, President Harvey has instituted programs such as:

✦ ADULT EDUCATION. Since 1989, President Harvey's ambitious initiative HOPE (Hampton's Opportunity Program for Enhancement) has admitted African-American men to Hampton who do not necessarily meet academic requirements. With a reduced course load and mentoring, these adult students have newly discovered opportunities to succeed—and they do.

✦ EDUCATIONAL COMMUNITY SERVICE AND LEARNING. President Harvey promoted JET (Job Education Training Corps), a program in which students from nearby school districts learn academic skills and gain work experience. Through intense faculty interaction in FDA (Faculty Advisor Program), Hampton students meet academic challenges and face personal issues. This grant-funded program reduced academic probation and includes a new counseling center with peer-interaction workshops.

✦ ACADEMIC HONESTY. Every Hampton student agrees to honor the Code of Conduct, which requires commitment to a comprehensive set of standards from self-respect to a professional work ethic.

✦ ENTREPRENEURIAL OPPORTUNITIES. President Harvey's entrepreneurial development plans include the Hampton Harbor Project, a university-owned shopping center and 246 two-bedroom apartments, which creates jobs, provides services, increases the number of African-American entrepreneurs, and expands the tax base in the City of Hampton. Proceeds go to Hampton scholarships.

President Harvey's conviction that "to be of service" to others ranks as the greatest accomplishment demonstrates his leadership in civic involvement. "Before graduation, every student [should] be required to work one year in a school, community center, or some other community uplift program." He further asserts that wisdom, boldness, and vision can and do effect positive change. Within them lies the difference between "pedestrian performance and extraordinary achievement." For him, the Hampton spirit endows ordinary people with "extraordinary ideas and strength of purpose."

Through his efforts on behalf of an often underserved student population, President Harvey models the strength of a values-based Hampton education.

FOUNDED ON THE YAKIMA INDIAN RESERVATION by Sister Kathleen Ross in 1982, Heritage College has a mission to serve people with limited access to higher education: 95% need substantial financial aid, and 60% are on welfare at some point during their college careers. This private, four-year liberal arts school may be in an impoverished area, but the multicultural undergraduate community— 34.7% Hispanic, 20.5% Native American—is passionate about instilling respect for the dignity of others and for their advancement through education. Heritage has graduated more than 3,000 people—teachers, social workers, business people, environmental scientists, and others, 90% of whom remain in the community as contributing citizens. Sister Kathleen prepares students for lives of personal and civic responsibility through the following programs:

✦ LEADERSHIP DEVELOPMENT. She initiated this program (and taught one of the courses) for leaders of student organizations, designed to teach cooperation, problem solving, developing consensus, and working with people of other cultures. Six leaders selected as Presidential Fellows attend meetings with Sister Kathleen and community leaders, giving them an opportunity to "job shadow." Sister Kathleen recently donated her MacArthur Foundation "Genius Grant" to the college, partly to support this program.

✦ WORK-STUDY PROGRAMS. To ensure that a Heritage education prepares students for life after graduation, Sister Kathleen has redesigned work-study positions so that students have more access to internships in the community, such as reading programs and other outreach activities. A requirement that students be involved in some form of community service as a condition of graduation is being developed. In addition, Sister Kathleen personally tracks students after graduation and is implementing a system to formally monitor student success in both jobs and citizenship.

Sister Kathleen provides national leadership in promoting the importance of character development in higher education. She chaired the NAICU (National Association of Independent Colleges and Universities) commission on financing higher education and has spoken in many national forums, where her message is always the duty of higher education to ensure respect for the dignity of all people. Featured in newspapers such as *USA Today* and *The Chicago Tribune,* Sister Kathleen's humble but determined pursuit of the Heritage mission has received public recognition. She has received honorary degrees from six schools, including the College of New Rochelle, and will be receiving a seventh from the University of Notre Dame. In addition, she has received the Washington State Medal of Honor, the McGraw prize for education, and many other awards. At the request of supporters from across the country, Heritage is sponsoring a national conference ("Gathering 99") to help other education leaders learn how to improve their schools.

Sister Kathleen models a way of life that inspires community leaders and legislators to seek her advice and students, faculty, and staff to emulate her service to others. She started an independent college with small means but with a great mission. She drives an old car, and uses her small allowance to rent a shared house in a high poverty area. Sister Kathleen is a living example of what one person can do without wealth or status to change a community. By her words and actions, she is making a difference in the world every day—and is inspiring Heritage students to change their world as well.

SR. KATHLEEN ROSS

PRESIDENT
HERITAGE COLLEGE

3240 FORT ROAD
TOPPENISH, WA 98948

509.865.8600
ross_k@heritage.edu
http://www.heritage.edu/

UNDERGRADUATES: 650

"Thanks to Sister Kathleen, I am well on my way toward earning a degree and venturing into a new profession. She has been instrumental in motivating me to be a future educator and leader in my community."

—A HERITAGE THIRD-YEAR
STUDENT

CYNTHIA H. TYSON

PRESIDENT
MARY BALDWIN COLLEGE

P.O. BOX 1500
STAUNTON, VA 24401

540.887.7000
chtyson@cit.mbc.edu
http://www.mbc.edu/

UNDERGRADUATES: 1,300

*"President Tyson is
a role model for
all women at Mary
Baldwin. I know when
I graduate from MBC,
one of my fondest
memories will be of
President Tyson."*

—AN MBC FOURTH-YEAR
STUDENT

Other MBC Profiles:

• Honor Roll School
• Spiritual Growth Program
• Student Leadership Program

THE DELICATE BALANCE BETWEEN TRADITIONAL VALUES and visionary thinking is successfully maintained at Mary Baldwin College, due in great part to the leadership of President Cynthia H. Tyson. Serving since 1985 as MBC's eighth president, Dr. Tyson demonstrates both a respect for tradition and heritage and a strong vision for the future of this private, church-affiliated, liberal arts women's college. President Tyson has led MBC to a focused and intentional emphasis on character development, setting a strong example with her own words and actions.

Early in her tenure, President Tyson led the development of 12 characteristics that MBC would work to develop in its students. These "Characteristics of the Well-Educated Person of the Third Millennium," published each year in the school's academic calendar, include social responsibility, recognition of the values and integrity of different cultures, and the ability to take responsibility for one's actions. However, President Tyson wants faculty, administration, and trustees to do more than just pay lip service to the "list." She encourages an annual strategic planning process to ensure that all efforts and activities are directly related to the college mission and supportive of the characteristics.

A native of Britain and now a US citizen, President Tyson brings a unique perspective to her position. Her views on character development and civic responsibility—the ideal being for young women students to take responsibility for their own actions and personal development, with guidance and role modeling from faculty and staff—are simultaneously progressive and steeped in tradition. She has spoken widely on this topic, and her essay on the role of liberal arts colleges in promoting character development appeared in the *Chicago Tribune*.

The following programs and initiatives supported by President Tyson all reinforce social and personal responsibility:

✦ QUEST. A unique program that helps students integrate religious commitment, intellectual development, and service, Quest entails two years of spiritual direction, academic courses, and enrichment activities that support the student's efforts to make sense of life, learning, and faith.

✦ VIRGINIA WOMEN'S INSTITUTE FOR LEADERSHIP. This program trains young women to become ethical and skilled leaders in whatever career field they choose. VWIL offers a holistic approach to leadership development that integrates academic study, mentoring, community service, and extracurricular activities.

✦ ETHOS, CODES, AND COMMUNITY. In February 1997, President Tyson called a day off from classes for students, faculty, and staff to come together to assess the school's honor code and community values. This milestone event continues through the work of task forces formed to improve systems and address challenges caused by changing times.

Through her actions and words, President Tyson continues to encourage a campus community in which mutual respect, concern for others, social commitment, and civic responsibility are the norm. She spends countless hours personally working with MBC students to prepare these young women to take their values into the greater world.

Transforming beliefs into action is the legacy of Sister Eymard Gallagher, RSHM. As the 4th president of Marymount University since 1993, she has joined national efforts to end sweatshop labor in the garment industry, making this one of her top priorities. By involving the colleges and universities in the Consortium of Universities of the Washington Metropolitan Area, a number of Catholic dioceses and archdioceses on the East Coast, Washington-area business leaders, and the public, Sister Eymard has expanded the caring and vigilance that ultimately will improve working conditions for laborers around the world.

The programs and initiatives supported by Sister Eymard all reinforce social responsibility and community involvement:

✦ **Center for Ethical Concerns.** In 1993, one of Sister Eymard's first tasks was to develop the Marymount University Center for Ethical Concerns, a forum for exchanging ideas about ethical issues through lectures, seminars, workshops, conferences, and symposia for students, faculty, and the public. Under Sister Eymard's leadership, the Center and the Fashion Design and Merchandising programs sponsored two annual consumer surveys on the sweatshop issue and an Academic Search for Sweatshop Solutions conference. While endorsing the National Labor Committee's "National Day of Conscience and Holiday Season of Conscience to End Sweatshops," Sister Eymard asked Marymount University vendors to ensure that they are in compliance with the Workplace Code of Conduct and Principles of Monitoring developed by the White House Apparel Industry Partnership. Barnes & Noble, which operates campus bookstores at Marymount and 300 other colleges nationwide, now requires its clothing suppliers to provide evidence of compliance with the Apparel Industry Code of Conduct.

✦ **Survey and Conference.** Currently, Sister Eymard is spearheading a survey of Washington, DC, area business leaders, cosponsored by the Center and Marymount's School of Business Administration, to gauge the level of concern about various ethical issues that arise in the workplace. As a follow-up, Marymount will sponsor a regional business ethics conference for students, faculty, business leaders, and ethicists.

✦ **Community Outreach to Homeless Children.** On Halloween, Marymount hosts "Halloweenfest," a party for homeless children from several area shelters. The whole campus gets involved as students dress in costumes, decorate their rooms, pass out treats, and organize games and craft activities. This annual event is sponsored by Spirit of Service, the volunteer arm of Marymount's Campus Ministry.

✦ **Marymount University Ethics Award.** This annual award honors an individual who has taken an outstanding leadership role in promoting and developing ethical standards and behavior in his or her field of endeavor.

Sister Eymard has been recognized with awards such as the 1998 Person of Vision Award from the Arlington County (Virginia) County Commission on the Status of Women. Marymount's commitment to providing a values-based education is evident in many of its programs, and Sister Eymard's leadership and vision are dedicated to maintaining this standard.

Sr. Eymard Gallagher

PRESIDENT
MARYMOUNT UNIVERSITY

2807 NORTH GLEBE ROAD
ARLINGTON, VA 22207–4299

703.522.5600
egallagh@marymount.edu
http://www.marymount.edu/

UNDERGRADUATES: 2,000

"Sister Eymard's leadership in reviving discussions of ethics in Marymount's classrooms has been invaluable, allowing students to explore ethical issues within a Catholic moral tradition."

—A Marymount fourth-year student

SR. KAREN M. KENNELLY

PRESIDENT
MOUNT ST. MARY'S COLLEGE

12001 CHALON ROAD
LOS ANGELES, CA 90049

310.954.4000
kkennelly@msmc.la.edu
http://www.msmc.la.edu/

UNDERGRADUATES: 1,700

*"We always know
we can count on the
President's support as
we put into practice the
values learned in the
classroom."*

—A MOUNT THIRD-YEAR
STUDENT

Other Mount Profiles:

• Honor Roll School
• First-Year Program
• Student Leadership Program

THE PRIMARY SPOKESPERSON FOR THE MISSION of Mount St. Mary's College—instilling integrity, respect, service, and leadership in students—is the school's 10th president. Sister Karen M. Kennelly, CSJ, has presided over this private, liberal arts college since 1989. Since that time, she has not only spoken but also written widely about these values. Drawing on her expertise as an historian (she holds a doctorate in history from the University of California, Berkeley and is a former chair of the history department and academic dean at the College of St. Catherine), Sister Karen also teaches Latin American history and "Women in the Americas" at the Mount. In addition to assuming her previous academic posts, Sister Karen has traveled to Peru to research the foreign missionary activity of American women religious and was a resident fellow of the Institute for Ecumenical and Cultural Research. Some of her recent publications include "Religious Institutes and Their History" for the Leadership Conference of Women Religious and "Women Religious in American Catholic History: Religious Life for Women in the United States" for *The Encyclopedia of American Catholic History.* She is also a book reviewer and lecturer and was editor of American Catholic Women: Historical Experiences (Macmillan, 1989).

Sister Karen's passionate work has created campus-wide activities that prepare students for lives of personal and civic responsibility and infuse a community-service mindset across the curriculum:

✦ CIVIC EDUCATION. The nationally recognized Urban and Civic Engagement and Urban Partnership Programs have brought the community and students together to address societal issues of low-income jobs, unemployment, and lack of mentors for young people.

✦ VOLUNTEER SERVICE. The Hewlett Service-Learning Program enhances the learning process by enabling students to apply their classroom knowledge to real-world situations. Through participation in organized service projects, students coordinate and implement programs that meet community needs.

✦ STUDENT AMBASSADORS. Mount students receive training and return to the inner-city high schools from which they graduated to serve as counselors, mentors, and role models for students deciding whether or not to pursue a college education.

Sister Karen's leadership extends to national higher education efforts. She led "The President, Catalyst for Change" in connection with a recent leadership award granted to Mount St. Mary's. She spearheaded the college's 1996–2001 strategic plan outlining commitment to goals built on character development. Sister Karen also serves on the boards of college and university organizations. Among Sister Karen's many honors and awards are a Fulbright Scholarship and an American Council for Learned Societies Fellowship for postdoctoral research in Spain. In 1997, she joined the Los Angeles Regional Board of the United States Holocaust Museum.

Sister Karen's life exemplifies those abundant values of character and integrity that students appreciate while at Mount St. Mary's—and take with them when they graduate.

THE NINTH PRESIDENT OF MOUNT UNION COLLEGE SINCE 1986, Harold M. Kolenbrander puts a priority on student values and holistic development. Ironically, this United Methodist Church-affiliated school had no freestanding chapel until President Kolenbrander raised the funds to build one. Soon, students will be able to worship and gather to plan the school's reenergized efforts in volunteerism and community service. President Kolenbrander is as likely to be eating with students in the cafeteria or jumping up and down with cheerleaders after a Mount Union touchdown as he is to be working with a member of the Board of Trustees. His door is always open, and he makes it clear that Mount Union is there to "provide the best education possible for every student." He believes that his school should be a place where students "learn how to learn, learn how to live, and learn how to communicate."

At Mount Union, President Kolenbrander has developed a strategic plan consisting of four key elements: a curriculum for the future; international, minority, and adult education; enrollment; and endowment. An active and well-known member of the higher education community, he volunteers as Chairman of the Board of Directors for the Council of Independent Colleges and works with other organizations to promote high-quality learning. President Kolenbrander is committed to the local community as well. He participates on the Boards of many community programs, from the Buckeye Boy Scouts Council, Alliance Area Chamber of Commerce, and Alliance Community Hospital to the Mayor's Commission on Aging, Rotary International, and Christ United Methodist Church.

President Kolenbrander has established personal growth and civic involvement as high priorities at Mount Union through several programs and initiatives:

✦ CHAPLAIN'S OFFICE. Among President Kolenbrander's first official actions was to appoint Mount Union's first full-time chaplain to ensure that students have a trusted advisor who provides consistent spiritual guidance and encourages community service.

✦ VOLUNTEER SERVICE. Working with the Chaplain's Office, President Kolenbrander has ensured that community service and volunteerism have flourished at Mount Union. Students tutor underprivileged children and help in homeless and domestic violence shelters. Many other students dedicate their spring breaks to take work-related trips across the US or to politically and economically challenged countries. Still others participate in the Dowling Mentor Program that President Kolenbrander helped establish to match at-risk middle school children with mentors.

✦ MORAL REASONING. This required first-year class helps students develop moral reasoning abilities through a variety of critical thinking and group decision-making skills.

With President Kolenbrander's guidance, the faculty wrote this mission statement: "Mount Union College offers a liberal arts education in the Judeo-Christian tradition. The College affirms the importance of reason, open inquiry, living faith, and individual worth. Mount Union's mission is to prepare students for meaningful work, fulfilling lives, and responsible citizenship." President Kolenbrander models all of these attributes for his Mount Union students.

HAROLD M. KOLENBRANDER

PRESIDENT
MOUNT UNION COLLEGE

1972 CLARK AVENUE
ALLIANCE, OH 44601

330.821.5320
kolenbhm@muc.edu
http://www.muc.edu/

UNDERGRADUATES: 2,000

"Students at Mount Union are impressed with the integrity of President Kolenbrander. He is a 'straight shooter' who has an open door as well as an open mind, and he is willing to work with his students both individually and collectively."

—A MOUNT UNION
THIRD-YEAR STUDENT

ARTHUR R. TAYLOR

PRESIDENT
MUHLENBERG COLLEGE

2400 CHEW STREET
ALLENTOWN, PA 18104

610.821.3125
http://www.muhlenberg.edu/

UNDERGRADUATES: 1,900

"As a graduating senior, I am very grateful for my experiences at Muhlenberg, but am also sad to leave my 'home.' President Taylor and his staff have made my college experience wonderful and more than I ever expected."

—A MUHLENBERG
FOURTH-YEAR STUDENT

WHEN HE WAS INAUGURATED AS THE 10TH PRESIDENT of Muhlenberg College in 1992, Arthur R. Taylor called for a "rededication to ethics and values and providing help to those Americans who are in such desperate need as the focal point for commanding national attention." A vigorous program focused on civic involvement is evident on the grounds and in the classrooms at this private, liberal arts college affiliated with the Evangelical Lutheran Church in America. Under President Taylor's leadership, volunteer opportunities for students are at an all-time high—more than 80% participate in community service projects, ranging from Habitat for Humanity to hospice care. Faculty members are also encouraged to be active in the community.

The programs and initiatives supported by President Taylor all reinforce his dedication to others and pursuit of civic responsibility:

✦ VOLUNTEER SERVICE. Service-learning programs enable students to integrate related community service experiences with academic content in a chosen area of interest.

✦ STUDENT LEADERSHIP. The Emerging Leaders program enables 60 first- and second-year students to explore the moral and ethical aspects of leadership in a 10-week seminar. Through the Peer Leadership Consultant program, eight student leaders each year share their experiences with younger students. The Annual Alumni Leadership Conference encourages connections between students and alumni who are ethical leaders in their fields. Adventure-Based Leadership retreats and hikes challenge students physically and emotionally.

✦ FIRST-YEAR PROGRAMS. Components include a four-day orientation, student and faculty advisors, and team-building activities. A first-year seminar, a small, discussion-oriented course, is limited to 15 students who work with a faculty member to explore various topics about college life.

✦ ACADEMIC HONESTY. The Academic Behavior Code establishes academic honesty as a matter of both individual and college responsibility. Each student pledges to adhere to the provisions of the Code every semester.

✦ CIVIC EDUCATION. The Center for Ethics and Leadership, established by President Taylor in 1995, offers opportunities for dialog on issues of meaning, values, and humane responsibilities of living in a free society. The Institute for Jewish-Christian Understanding encourages pluralism and mutual respect among people of all religions.

✦ SUBSTANCE-ABUSE PREVENTION. Initiatives include Alcohol Awareness Week and Choice Weekend to increase awareness of the effects of alcohol abuse and encourage students, faculty, and staff to pledge responsible behavior.

Nationally, President Taylor has served on many commissions devoted to community, including William Bennett's National Commission for Civic Renewal, and he was founding president of the New York Partnership to save the city's economic and social future. Whether working on civic projects, "Family Viewing Hour" responsible programming, or encouraging Christian, Judaic, or Muslim spiritual activities, President Taylor exemplifies leadership and a dedication to the growth and well-being of others.

Other Muhlenberg Profiles:

• Academic Honesty Program
• Spiritual Growth Program

In 1994, during the inauguration of Nancy Schrom Dye as the first woman president of Oberlin College, Frances Fergusson, president of Vassar College, told the school that it had "chosen a paragon." She knew this from personal experience, as Nancy Dye, a former Vassar dean, had served as acting president at Vassar when President Fergusson was on leave. Immediately, the 13th president of the country's first private, coeducational liberal arts college—and one of the first to grant degrees to African-Americans—successfully directed a campus-wide, long-range planning process to identify the principles that would guide Oberlin's future. Today, the college has defined its "broad directions"—a plan for Oberlin's faculty and staff to fulfill the school's mission of academic rigor; artistic excellence—Oberlin has a renowned conservatory of music; undergraduate education based on civic mindedness; and a commitment to education and community involvement for everyone.

A major philosophy at Oberlin is the belief that a liberal education provides the intellectual foundation for teaching students to think and act in ways that are "humane and generous." With these goals in mind, President Dye has established and supported the following Oberlin programs and initiatives:

✦ **Volunteer Service.** President Dye's commitment to service inspired a $3 million gift to Oberlin to establish and endow the Center for Service and Learning, an office that coordinates student volunteerism with the educational experience. The donors stated that they made the gift to "sustain Nancy Dye's vision of the importance of community service to Oberlin College and Lorain County."

✦ **Civic Education.** With foundation support, Oberlin launched "Common Ground: Education for Democracy," a campus-wide, three-year diversity and community-building initiative. The new Adam Joseph Lewis Center for Environmental Studies is an example of responsible architecture. The building itself will teach students about the ecology of architectural design through its state-of-the-art energy systems.

✦ **Student Leadership.** The Shouse Nonprofit Leadership Program teaches students to manage nonprofit organizations through integrated academic classes, internships, and career-skills workshops.

After being awarded a $150,000 grant for Presidential Leadership, President Dye used the money to create a collaboration between the college and the local public schools. Oberlin students tutor children in science and reading and offer mentoring, and the college holds a summer program to help low-income middle- and high-school students improve and advance their education.

President Dye remains personally involved with Oberlin students, teaching a history course, serving as academic advisor, and regularly opening her office doors. Her concern for the well-being of students has enhanced the sense of community on campus. With President Dye's inspiration and example, Oberlin strives to educate its students to become leaders of character and integrity with a fully developed sense of civic responsibility.

NANCY S. DYE

PRESIDENT
OBERLIN COLLEGE

70 NORTH PROFESSOR STREET
OBERLIN, OH 44074–1090

440.775.8121
Nancy.Dye@oberlin.edu
http://www.oberlin.edu/

UNDERGRADUATES: 2,900

"President Dye spends countless hours attending meetings, soothing tempers, and touting Oberlin's values. Administrators and faculty marvel at her stamina. She is passionately committed to creating a caring community."

—an Oberlin fourth-year
student

SR. MARY ANDREW MATESICH

PRESIDENT
OHIO DOMINICAN COLLEGE

1216 SUNBURY ROAD
COLUMBUS, OH 43219

614. 253.2741
matesicm@odc.edu
http://www.odc.edu/

UNDERGRADUATES: 1,900

"At Ohio Dominican, we are taught to think clearly and make well-reasoned decisions. After graduation, I will be well prepared to go out and work for the greater good of the world."

—AN ODC FOURTH-YEAR
STUDENT

NOW IN HER 21ST YEAR AS PRESIDENT OF OHIO DOMINICAN COLLEGE, a Catholic, coeducational liberal arts school, Sister Mary Andrew Matesich, OP, began her career as a member of the Dominican Sisters of St. Mary of the Springs. In 1978, Sister Mary Andrew Matesich became president of Ohio Dominican when few women were college presidents, having earned her undergraduate degree, taught chemistry, and served as Academic Dean and Executive Vice President at the college. She is a national expert on public policy issues affecting education and is often called for speeches, testimony, and articles for publication, as well as for private consultations by governmental agencies, private associations, and congressional leaders. Sister Mary Andrew knows how to overcome obstacles, from the predicted downfall of small colleges without national reputations and large endowments (Ohio Dominican's enrollment more than doubled in her first 10 years, and her successful campaigns have brought in millions of dollars) to a personal battle with cancer in the early 1990s, which renewed her zeal and purpose.

Sister Mary Andrew's vision to revitalize the community takes an education-dominant approach. Her life-changing Ohio Dominican programs include:

✦ **"VILLAGE 219."** In 1994, Sister Mary Andrew began an outreach program to raise the academic achievement of children in local neighborhoods. "Village 219" includes Upward Bound, a program to identify and assist urban high-school students with college potential; Talent Search, for middle- and high-school students; and Village to Child, a middle-school enrichment program. Middle- and high-school students and their families focus on academic achievement, academic enrichment, and neighborhood improvement through community service. In 1995, the US Department of Justice chose "Village 219" as an urban mentoring demonstration site. The Governor of Ohio selected the program for the Volunteer Ohio Award, and in 1998 it was chosen as a Daily Point of Light by the Points of Light Foundation.

✦ **ADULT HIGHER EDUCATION.** Sister Mary Andrew's dedication to service extends to older students who often are denied access to higher education. She created Weekend College to serve such students, often single heads of households and has now added LEAD (Learning Enhanced Adult Degree), an accelerated learning option for adults, and Operation Second Chance, primarily for minority and/or first-generation students who had dropped out of college. The program and Sister Mary Andrew were honored by The Columbus Foundation and the Leo Yassenoff Foundation.

✦ **"PATRIOTS."** Through a Presidential Leadership grant, Sister Mary Andrew established this nationally recognized program in 1991 to provide services and educational support to veterans who have served their country.

Hallmark features of Sister Mary Andrew's tenure as ODC president are innovation and flexibility, combined with her fierce determination to serve the community by helping people help themselves through higher education. The college has earned a national reputation for its forward-looking approaches to education, including the new "Invitation to Tomorrow" program consisting of the latest advances in learning theory and technology. This program prepares students for life and work in the new millennium, removing the barriers of time and space to create a collaborative learning environment for students and faculty. ODC students graduate with an education-rich sense of responsibility as they go out into the world.

O HIO UNIVERSITY, A PUBLIC, COMPREHENSIVE INSTITUTION, prizes character-building education, and President Robert B. Glidden tackles such problems as high-risk drinking by appealing to civic virtue and personal responsibility. On becoming the university's 19th president in 1994, President Glidden predicted that renewed emphasis on values was essential if students were to be equipped for worldwide leadership and problem-solving. Twenty years of experience in higher-education enables President Glidden to identify the ethical standards that shape the numerous civic programs at OU. "Our commitment to address the matter of ethical thinking and behavior has to do with several factors, especially the rate at which knowledge is expanding in many of our disciplines. New technologies abound. . . . If we do not emphasize basic values in an era of transition, we will not be living up to our legacy of excellence in education at Ohio University."

Serving his community proactively, President Glidden is dedicated to the premise that character-building programs such as these "help change the culture . . . before the culture changes us." Some of the programs he has helped to establish include:

✦ **CAREER ETHICS.** The Institute for Applied and Professional Ethics sponsors ethics-related workshops, seminars, student projects, and travel, helping organizations to promote ethical causes in diverse areas such as journalism, business, and philosophy.

✦ **MORAL DECISION-MAKING.** Recognized nationally, the civic virtues program challenges the 27,000 undergraduates to pursue PATH: Personal Accountability, Trust, and Honor, specifically to combat alcohol abuse and generally to confront all academic and off-campus adverse events (http://www.ohiou.edu/~president/PATH.html). President Glidden's social marketing campaign speaks directly to students' decision-making abilities, and the Binge Drinking Prevention Coalition implements small group discussion to encourage PATH values.

✦ **LEADERSHIP IN TECHNOLOGY.** Bringing computers to low-income rural communities is part of the public service mission of the College of Education's Learning Community Link program. President Glidden emphasizes expanding technological expertise with civic responsibility.

✦ **SERVICE LEARNING.** OU students receive hands-on leadership experience through the Institute for Local Government Administration and Rural Development. Applied research and technical skills enable students to participate in state and local governments, practicing citizenship and its valuable lessons.

✦ **COMMUNITY OUTREACH.** Summer enrichment and nutrition are provided through the Kids on Campus program. President Glidden calls this "our most significant kind of regional outreach" and supports this opportunity for OU students to serve their community and work with five school districts.

President Glidden oversees an evolving leadership initiative that promotes academic honesty and integrity. The Ohio University Student Judiciary is currently developing a "classrooms of integrity" program in which leadership skills can be studied, much like those demonstrated by President Glidden. "Success is not only what we make of it, but how we define it," he states, emphasizing personal accountability and academic achievement for all OU students.

ROBERT B. GLIDDEN

PRESIDENT
OHIO UNIVERSITY

CUTLER HALL, ROOM 108
ATHENS, OH 45701–2979

740.593.1000
glidden@oak.cats.ohiou.edu
http://www.ohiou.edu/

UNDERGRADUATES: 24,000

"President Glidden is warm and dedicated— he genuinely cares about the growth and development of each and every single student at Ohio University."

—AN OU FOURTH-YEAR STUDENT

Other OU Profiles:

• Honor Roll School
• Character & Sexuality Program
• Student Leadership Program
• Substance-Abuse Prevention Program
• Volunteer Service Program

GRAHAM B. SPANIER

PRESIDENT
THE PENNSYLVANIA STATE
UNIVERSITY

UNIVERSITY PARK CAMPUS
201 OLD MAIN
UNIVERSITY PARK, PA 16804

814.865.7611
gspanier@psu.edu
http://www.psu.edu/

UNDERGRADUATES: 70,000—
24 CAMPUSES
(35,000 AT UNIVERSITY PARK)

"President Spanier is one of today's leading university presidents. Through his commitment, example, and communication skills, he shows students that they can make a difference."

—A RECENT PENN STATE
GRADUATE

Other Penn State Profiles:

• Substance-Abuse Prevention Program

ONE OF THE FIRST SURPRISES FOR NEW PENN STATE STUDENTS is the sudden appearance of the university's president, hands outstretched to grab their bags as they move into the dorm. Later, during freshman convocation, President Graham B. Spanier gives them a pep talk—not so much about academic achievement and career goals as about extracurricular, community-building activities: "Everyone at the university has a role to play in creating a strong and caring community at Penn State and in the local community we share."

Leading by example, Pennsylvania State University's 16th president pledged a donation to the school of $100,000 on taking his oath of office in 1995. Over the past several years, President Spanier has found many opportunities to promote character development, including the following innovative programs and initiatives:

✦ THE AMERICA READS PROGRAM. A member of the national program's steering committee, President Spanier enlisted hundreds of students from Penn State campuses in work-study programs to teach young people to read.

✦ THE NEWSPAPERS IN THE RESIDENCE HALLS PROGRAM. In a recent nationally syndicated *Chicago Tribune* column, President Spanier stated that reading a newspaper is "the single most important part of being an informed and educated citizen." He proposed this model program—now reproduced at other colleges—to help students understand and participate in their world.

✦ BINGE-DRINKING PREVENTION. President Spanier has declared war on what he believes is a major problem in higher education: alcohol abuse. "If students think they're coming to Penn State to drink, they should go somewhere else." He launched an intervention and educational program with the Pennsylvania Liquor Control Board and has committed significant funds to his anti-alcohol effort. In addition, President Spanier authorized a $30 million renovation of the student union building and expanded its "Late Night" activities to free concerts, films, comedians—and even his own brand of amateur magic, tripling attendance from 7,000 to 22,000 students.

✦ RELIGIOUS LIFE. New Penn State students can count on hearing about President Spanier's commitment to the education of the "whole person," including the Eisenhower Chapel programs in support of all the religions represented on campus, which offer "a wonderful source of friendships, a constructive way to have some fun, and a tremendous avenue of personal growth." In announcing a $5 million donation to Penn State for expansion of the Chapel, President Spanier noted, "The most fundamental challenge facing colleges and universities today is developing conscience, character, citizenship, and social responsibility in their students."

✦ OUTREACH PROGRAMS. President Spanier also places a high value on integrating teaching, research, and outreach. Programs include 4-H Clubs, in which 150,000 children participate statewide; continuing education courses offered through the Penn State Cooperative Extension program; and public television broadcasting by WPSX-TV. President Spanier personally responds to hundreds of emails from Penn State students each month and hosts a monthly local call-in public radio show on WPSU.

A leader who tirelessly and proactively serves his school and community, President Spanier is changing the character of Penn State by instilling the desire to develop character in the students who follow his example.

A MAJOR GUIDING PRINCIPLE OF THE 3RD PRESIDENT of Richard Stockton College of New Jersey has been the development of individual purpose and community responsibility in her students. Since her 1983 inauguration, Vera King Farris has presided over a number of major advancements at this public, liberal arts college named for Richard Stockton, one of the New Jersey signers of the Declaration of Independence. Her accomplishments include a 40% enrollment increase, a 22% rise in entering SAT scores, and a 100% increase in the number of African-American and Hispanic students.

Dedicated to celebrating human diversity, President Farris has created a strong foundation for advancing the character education of all individuals:

✦ "CHEER." She originated the statewide conferences on Civility, Harmony, Education, Environment, and Respect to eliminate prejudice, violence, and bigotry in schools while championing cultural diversity. The award-winning program draws 1,000 students of all ages, teachers, faculty, and law enforcement officials to the college each spring with its hands-on, lighthearted "play" approach to a serious topic. Featuring age-appropriate games and activities to illustrate teamwork, cooperation, and peer-mediation of disputes, the highly successful program is now in its sixth year, having grown from a small seminar of about 200 participants to an event limited only by the capacity of the college's gymnasium. Participants agree that the nonthreatening atmosphere helps them learn to work with others, and many have returned to their home school districts and formed CHEER clubs of their own.

✦ HOLOCAUST RESOURCE CENTER. President Farris has been an ardent promoter of Holocaust education at Stockton, creating one of first resource centers at a public college as well as the nation's first Holocaust and Genocide Studies master's program at this formerly all-undergraduate college.

✦ EDUCATIONAL ACCESS. President Farris chaired the New Jersey Committee on Advancement, Excellence, and Accountability Reporting and organized the nation's first statewide conference to explore the nature of college costs. Her "Key Common Indicators" has served as a model document for other organizations addressing financial aid, cost containment, affordability, and perceptions that college is out of reach for many middle- and lower-income students. President Farris was also selected to the 10-member US delegation to the UNESCO (United Nations Educational, Scientific, and Cultural Organization) World Conference on Higher Education held in Paris in 1998. There, she advocated for wider access to higher education based on merit rather than finances as part of the conference's effort to reform higher education throughout the world.

An innovative educational leader who has earned a national reputation, President Farris was named 1997 Chair of the American Association of State Colleges and Universities, which represents the interests of more than 400 public colleges and universities in North America and US territories. She is an indefatigable leader and role model for the Stockton students who are fortunate enough to have her example to follow.

VERA KING FARRIS

PRESIDENT
RICHARD STOCKTON COLLEGE
OF NEW JERSEY

JIM LEEDS ROAD
P.O. BOX 195
POMONA, NJ 08240

609.652.1776
farrisvk@loki.stockton.edu
http://www.stockton.edu/

UNDERGRADUATES: 6,000

"As someone who was raised in my hometown of Atlantic City, NJ, and achieved national prominence, President Farris is more than a role model—she is an inspiration. She took a personal interest in my future success after college, and as a result, we have formed a close, lasting relationship."

—A RECENT STOCKTON GRADUATE

WILLIAM C. CROTHERS

PRESIDENT
ROBERTS WESLEYAN COLLEGE

2301 WESTSIDE DRIVE
ROCHESTER, NY 14624–1997

716.594.6100
crothersw@roberts.edu
http://www.roberts.edu/

UNDERGRADUATES: 1,200

"President Crothers' commitment to character development is demonstrated through his personal integrity. His decisions regarding the institution are made within the framework of moral standards."

—A ROBERTS FOURTH-YEAR STUDENT

WILLIAM C. CROTHERS SELDOM STANDS STILL. As the 25th president of Roberts Wesleyan College, he has made growth, innovation, and leadership his watchwords. During his 18-year tenure at this Christian liberal arts school, President Crothers has doubled enrollment, launched pace-setting academic programs for working adults, multiplied Roberts' endowment and led campaigns that have provided exceptional campus facilities to meet student and community needs, established a student volunteer program, gained funding to emphasize ethical values in the business program, and built an 87-acre college-sponsored retirement community. After obtaining his doctorate in higher education administration from Michigan State University, President Crothers served as an administrator in that state's university system before being attracted to Roberts traditional academics integrated with Christian learning in 1981. The focus on "Education for Character" reflected President Crothers' own beliefs and is now a strong element of a Roberts education: every applicant must sign a commitment to "Standards for Community Life." Students are further encouraged in every aspect of campus life—from values clarification to responsible sexuality—through numerous programs and initiatives:

✦ CIVIC EDUCATION AND STUDENT LEADERSHIP. Students hear civic leaders speak in classes, chapels, and special programs. About one-third of Roberts' undergraduates are involved in internships, practicums, and cooperative education, and student leaders undergo a weeklong training program and attend monthly meetings on leadership, mentoring, and service.

✦ PERSONAL AND COMMUNITY RESPONSIBILITY. Students must abide by the standards of behavior exemplified by everyone on campus. Education through the resident life program and counseling office includes discussing alcoholism, signs of dependence, and participating in recovery programs, as well as sessions dealing with AIDS awareness and relationships.

✦ VOLUNTEER SERVICE. The Campus Ministries Office connects student interests with community needs. Roberts students are actively involved in inner-city schools, churches, camps, Big Brothers/Big Sisters, Habitat for Humanity, United Way, Open Door Mission, and the Salvation Army.

✦ SPIRITUAL GROWTH. Spirituality is a key component of life at Roberts, including weekly chapel services and religion courses and seminars.

President Crothers encourages faculty to model their Christian faith, values, and lives and urges graduates to be servant-leaders in society. Accordingly, he himself participates in the Council of Independent Colleges and Universities, Council for Christian Colleges and Universities, Boy Scouts of America, and Faith Haven, a home for unwed pregnant teens. He has had a leadership role in Middle States Association of Colleges and Schools and is President of Rochester Area Colleges. In 1986, the Rochester area Chamber of Commerce named him "Citizen of the Year," recognizing his ability to promote progress at Roberts, create interaction with the business community, and effect change without sacrificing principles; in 1997, it gave him its Education award.

President Crothers shows exceptional strengths for creative entrepreneurship, combined with compassion and vision, setting an example for Roberts graduates to follow throughout their lives.

DIVERSITY AND SOCIAL CONSCIOUSNESS ARE MORE THAN JUST WORDS to Robert A. Corrigan, who became the 12th president of San Francisco State University in 1988. He has long maintained a vision of multiculturalism and community service that pervades his life and sets an example for SFSU students. Although President Corrigan ardently encourages intercultural understanding at SFSU, this is not a new passion for him. The former Fulbright scholar established African-American Studies and Women's Studies programs at the University of Iowa, where he taught from 1964 to 1973. He writes, "We are certain—and proud—of our special social role on educating a broadly diverse student population." This commitment is evident in the special programs and unique SFSU curriculum offered through the College of Ethnic Studies, begun in the late 1960s as the only school of ethnic studies in the US.

A visionary by nature, President Corrigan helped establish a Committee on University Strategic Planning to promote a sense of the institution "as it is now and as we wish it to become." His commitment to the future—not just of SFSU but of our country—earned him an appointment by President Clinton to head a national steering committee of college and university presidents participating in the "America Reads" literacy program.

With President Corrigan's strong encouragement and support, SFSU offers programs, courses, and activities that emphasize multicultural understanding, community involvement, and leadership:

✦ DIALOGUE ON RACE. SFSU hosted this program, bringing together community leaders and experts from across the nation to explore the legacies of racism in the US and opportunities for reconciliation.

✦ JUMPSTART. Many students participate in this 20-month AmeriCorps program to help at-risk preschool children prepare for elementary school by building their literacy and learning skills.

✦ COMMUNITY PARTNERSHIPS. SFSU has more than 100 centers, institutes, and other special programs that link the University to the Bay Area community and beyond. Students work side-by-side with school faculty and members of the community on projects that touch lives in many ways. Partnerships include the Ethnic Diversity Training Project, Bay Area School Development Program, and Child Study Center.

✦ CAMPUS OUTREACH COMMUNITY LEAGUE COURSE. This course offers leadership training in the private and public sectors through public speaking and volunteer activities in on- and off-campus organizations. The Leadership Institute gives credit to students assuming leadership roles.

✦ SFSU RECYCLING/RESOURCE CENTER. This center provides the campus with comprehensive, high-quality recycling services and serves as a key resource for teaching environmental issues facing the world today.

"A college education is the gateway to self-discovery, to full development of individual talent, to economic opportunity," states President Corrigan. He talks proudly about his students, often praising those involved in programs and activities such as tutoring children, working with Meals on Wheels, collecting items for survivors of Hurricane Mitch in Honduras and Nicaragua, trying to end the death penalty, or volunteering to work with young offenders. "I cannot imagine better custodians of our future than young people like we have here at San Francisco State University," he says.

ROBERT A. CORRIGAN

PRESIDENT
SAN FRANCISCO STATE UNIVERSITY

1600 HOLLOWAY AVENUE
SAN FRANCISCO, CA 94132

415.338.1381
corrigan@sfsu.edu
http://www.sfsu.edu/

UNDERGRADUATES: 20,700

"President Corrigan has laid the foundation for a community in which the lives of people with either similar or conflicting histories can be enriched through the simple sharing of a classroom."

—A SFSU THIRD-YEAR STUDENT

Other SFSU Profiles:

• Volunteer Service Program

PHILIP W. EATON

PRESIDENT
SEATTLE PACIFIC UNIVERSITY

3307 THIRD AVENUE WEST
SEATTLE, WA 98119–1997

206.281.2000
peaton@spu.edu
http://www.spu.edu/

UNDERGRADUATES: 2,600

"As a student of Seattle Pacific and editor of the student newspaper, it has been my privilege to work with President Eaton. He is a man of true moral and Christian character."

—AN SPU THIRD-YEAR STUDENT

Other SPU Profiles:

• Character & Sexuality Program
• First-Year Program
• Honor Roll School
• Spiritual Growth Program
• Student Leadership Program

THE 9TH PRESIDENT OF SEATTLE PACIFIC, a private Christian university of the liberal arts, sciences, and professions, has a deeply held conviction that character formation is the ultimate purpose of a college education. Over his distinguished eight-year career in business and more than two decades of teaching and administration in Christian higher education, President Phillip W. Eaton has demonstrated a lifelong concern for personal and civic responsibility. At SPU, where he has been president since 1996, President Eaton supports scholarship that is relevant to world issues. "We educate our students to become thinking Christians who are able to speak intelligently about their ideas. It's this process that produces leaders who are people of competence *and* character."

President Eaton has made character development one of the "first things" in an SPU education. He writes that "Character can be learned. It demands training and discipline. It demands commitment and even courage. We must expect our homes, our churches, our schools and our universities to be intentional about character formation." His SPU vision and programs attest to this conviction:

✦ **CORE CHARACTER CURRICULUM.** Under President Eaton's leadership, SPU has initiated the Common Curriculum, a required program in which faculty and students examine such selected works as *The Chosen, The Imitation of Christ,* and the *Narrative of the Life of Frederick Douglass,* texts that demonstrate the life-changing effects of noble character.

✦ **COMMUNITY SERVICE.** Since 1996, SPU students have invested 65,000 hours in service to the community. SPU's emphasis on service as vital to a college education begins with "CityQuest," a program in which new students spend a day volunteering in the inner city.

✦ **"A GRACE-FILLED COMMUNITY."** President Eaton champions a "grace-filled" campus community that shapes students of character and spurs them on to leadership and service in the world. SPU initiatives such as the nationally respected Center for Relationship Development focus on kindness, civility, respect, and collaboration.

✦ **"COMPREHENSIVE PLAN FOR THE 21ST CENTURY."** SPU's strategic "blueprint" for the new millennium is based on President Eaton's vision of engagement between university and community. "Our great hope is to address our culture's crisis of meaning in a way that is helpful and transforming," he says. The formation of character is a cornerstone in SPU's effort to define a "new kind of Christian university," one that will lead to positive change in the world.

President Eaton has served as a director on the board of the Northwest Leadership Foundation, which works to revitalize the inner city, and is a member of the Downtown Seattle Association, which strives to build a strong downtown district that serves the community. Speaking to an SPU-sponsored gathering of 900 Seattle business and community leaders, he stated: "We are dedicating ourselves, in fresh and bold new ways, to be change-agents for good in this city." The meeting's keynote speaker, George Will of the *Washington Post,* said, "SPU is seeding the community with ideas and with graduates who bring with them a coherent world view." Based on President Eaton's work in the present and vision for the future, students and their families know that character is a cornerstone principle at SPU.

FOUNDED THE YEAR THAT CONGRESS RATIFIED THE 13TH AMENDMENT abolishing slavery, Shaw University is the oldest historically Black university in the South. In 1987, with more than 33 years' experience in higher education—including his tenure as Dean of Arts and Sciences at Morgan State University and as Acting Dean of the School of Religion and Chairman of the Department of Ethics and Society at Howard University—Talbert Oscall Shaw became the 12th president of this Baptist, liberal arts institution.

President Shaw, who has a doctorate in ethics and society, has committed himself to the study and practice of ethics, believing that "the ultimate goal of education is the development of character which will enable citizens to function productively and morally in pursuit of the common good." To that end, he has established the following programs and initiatives:

✦ ETHICS AND VALUES CURRICULUM. In 1993, courses in ethics and values became part of the core curriculum. Students are required to take nine credit hours in ethics, and freshmen must enroll in an ethics seminar.

✦ FIRST-YEAR PROGRAM. Freshmen are also required to attend weekly vesper services, as well as all official university functions. They are assigned a mentor, who carries out the program's overall objective to introduce freshmen to university life and provide settings that foster academic, social, and spiritual development.

✦ THE AMERICAN HUMANICS CERTIFICATION IN NONPROFIT MANAGEMENT. This intensive certificate program instills the principles of effective management for the not-for-profit sector. Requirements include 200 hours in volunteer community service and 480 hours of supervised internship.

✦ LECTURES. During "Religious Emphasis Week" and through "The Bessie Boyd Holman Lecture Series on Ethics and Values," lecturers discuss moral and social issues to build and enhance character development. The programs are also a time of spiritual renewal when members of the university community can discuss and reaffirm personal commitments.

✦ SEXUALITY EDUCATION. Shaw students and staff receive annual HIV/AIDS training and certification and recently took their knowledge into local classrooms. As a result, 473 college students, 23 staff, and 21 middle-school students have heard lectures on character and sexuality.

An essay by President Shaw, *Ethics and Values: Shaw University's New Academic Thrust,* outlines the university's character-building initiatives. An article in Raleigh's *The News & Observer* specifically praised the Ethics Program, stating that Shaw has "some of the broadest ethics course requirements in the nation."

President Shaw's dedication to ethics studies and service work have enriched the lives of many Shaw students who conclude that they find the ethics curriculum to be personally beneficial. Many also report that their desire to discuss and participate in problem solving and conflict resolution has increased as a result.

Students leave Shaw with well-honed tools for creating a more ethical, productive society, as well as for pursuing rich and rewarding lives.

TALBERT O. SHAW

PRESIDENT
SHAW UNIVERSITY

118 E. SOUTH STREET
2ND FLOOR, DEBNAM HALL
RALEIGH, NC 27601

919.546.8300
toshaw@shawu.edu
http://www.shawuniversity.edu/

UNDERGRADUATES: 2,500

"President Shaw has exemplified character and leadership by implementing mandatory ethics courses for all students. My outlook on life and perception of others have expanded because of the emphasis he places on character development."

—A SHAW SECOND-YEAR STUDENT

R. GERALD TURNER

PRESIDENT
SOUTHERN METHODIST
UNIVERSITY

P.O. BOX 750100
6425 BOAZ STREET
DALLAS, TX 75275–0100

214.768.3000
mjj@mail.smu.edu
http://www.smu.edu/

UNDERGRADUATES: 5,600

"I cannot imagine a university president more aware of the issues that face students than President Turner. He is always ready to listen to our concerns or offer guidance; more importantly, he shows us the right path to take through strong role modeling."

—AN SMU FOURTH-YEAR
STUDENT

Other SMU Profiles:

• Character & Sexuality Program

SINCE BECOMING THE 10TH PRESIDENT OF SOUTHERN METHODIST UNIVERSITY in 1995, R. Gerald Turner has reaffirmed character development as a high priority of SMU's educational mission. The Strategic Plan he helped develop makes clear the primary objective of his vision: "The encouragement and support of ethical reflection on questions of moral integrity and on issues of the public good throughout the University's programs and curricula." This commitment is manifested in a number of SMU's strong civic-minded programs:

✦ **COMMUNITY SERVICE.** Through the ICE (Inter-Community Experience) Program, students from urban studies classes provide daily tutoring for low-income area children, and some students actually live in the neighborhood to personally serve and learn from the residents. Emphasizing the importance of this program in promoting civic responsibility, President Turner designated ICE as the Center for Inter-Community Experience in SMU's Dedman College of Humanities and Sciences. As part of the "The Campaign for SMU: A Time to Lead," President Turner has earned grant funding for the Center to expand.

✦ **STUDENT LEADERSHIP.** President Turner interacts closely with the Hunt Leadership Scholars Program, which supports 100 students who are active in SMU's leadership and service initiatives while maintaining high academic standards. Both Hunt and President's Scholars are guests at the president's dinners for national and international leaders, where they listen to such distinguished speakers as former President George Bush, Mikhail Gorbachev, and Marian Wright Edelman. Students also participate in SMU governance; one student serves as a voting member of the Board of Trustees, and nine serve on Board committees.

✦ **SERVICE AND VOLUNTEERISM.** Under President Turner's leadership, SMU established Service House, a residence hall for students devoted to community involvement that draws many student volunteers. Hunt and President's Scholars as well as other civic-minded students are active in such programs as Alternative Spring Break, in which they work for one week at homeless shelters and other agencies across the nation.

✦ **CHARACTER AND ETHICS.** The Cary M. Maguire Center for Ethics and Public Responsibility serves as a forum for exploring issues affecting the public good. It sponsors national conferences and faculty lectures, places students in civic internships, and publishes papers on key issues.

✦ **SUBSTANCE-ABUSE PREVENTION.** The Center for Alcohol and Drug Abuse Prevention provides counseling, referrals, and educational programs. SMU now participates in the OCTAA program (On Campus Talking About Alcohol) and is one of the first schools in the nation to form a partnership with the Betty Ford Center. President Turner encourages responsible use of alcohol both on- and off-campus through letters and speeches. President Turner has also called on fraternities to initiate reforms with support from Student Life staff. The time period for Greek rush is being shortened, and more organizations are changing the focus of their rush activities.

President Turner is a member of numerous civic organizations, including the "Dallas Is Diversity" Steering Committee, the Board of Directors of the Dallas Citizens Council, the Board of Dallas United Way, and the Board of the Methodist Hospital Foundation. He instills civic values in students, enabling them to graduate from SMU inspired to lead lives of commitment and purpose.

Southwest Missouri State University, a public comprehensive institution, has been led since 1993 by John H. Keiser, its 8th president. The exemplary public affairs program that President Keiser established and sustains spans the university's three campuses, touching the lives of more than 15,000 undergraduates. His goal at SMSU is "to develop citizens of enhanced character, more sensitive to the needs of community, more competent and committed in their ability to contribute to society, and more civil in their habits of thought, speech, and action." An historian and specialist on the labor movement in America, President Keiser envisions strengthening democracy by integrating SMSU's intensive citizenship education with vocation. In June 1995, Missouri's governor signed into law a statewide public affairs mission initiated by President Keiser.

SMSU demonstrates inspirational civic involvement through the following activities supported by President Keiser:

✦ CIVIC CURRICULUM. The required Freshman Interdisciplinary Studies course concentrates on the role of citizen students in the classroom, in the wider community, and in dialog about the qualities that promote academic achievement. In the Citizenship and Service Learning Program, the community becomes a laboratory, requiring 40 hours of service per semester. Mandatory capstone courses—"Biological Perspectives for Our Environmental Future" and "Corporate Responsibility: The Role of Business as a Corporate Citizen"—integrate civic obligations and individual disciplines, the intersection of public affairs and academics.

✦ CITIZENSHIP AND COMMUNITY SERVICE. Hands-on public service and course work form the basis for this citizenship program. Community service is also promoted through 11 student organizations and the Campus Volunteer Center. The Student Community Action Team devotes weekly time to community agencies. More than 100 nonprofit community agencies benefited from SMSU student service in the last year—nearly 89,000 hours of volunteer service were recorded.

✦ PUBLIC AFFAIRS STRATEGIES. Discussions of character and citizenship are available on *The Common Purpose,* a weekly television program; on the Public Affairs Website; in the annual *SMSU Journal of Public Affairs;* through the Public Affairs Convocation Series; and through programs at the Public Affairs Residence Hall. Also, tangible awards for outstanding achievements in civic life abound for SMSU citizen students through the Pepsi Cola/Public Affairs Scholarships and the Joseph N. Boyce/*Wall Street Journal* Public Affairs Award.

President Keiser also serves as President of Missouri's Council on Public Higher Education and as a member of the Board of Directors for both National Public Radio and the United Way of the Ozarks. Campus-wide discussions such as "Implementing the Public Affairs Theme Through the Existing Curriculum" put his character-building strategy in front of faculty and staff. As President Keiser notes, "The University believes that public works are key to a sense of commonwealth, key to public affairs, and key to becoming an educated person." The new College of Humanities and Public Affairs is one focus of this mission.

President Keiser's outstanding civic leadership provides an excellent model for SMSU students of successful citizenship and meaningful service.

JOHN H. KEISER

PRESIDENT
SOUTHWEST MISSOURI
STATE UNIVERSITY

901 SOUTH NATIONAL AVENUE
SPRINGFIELD, MO 65804

417. 836.5000
president@mail.smsu.edu
http://www.smsu.edu/

UNDERGRADUATES: 14,000

"President Keiser exemplifies the principles of character such as honesty and fairness that he champions at SMSU."

—AN SMSU FOURTH-YEAR STUDENT

Other SMSU Profiles:

• Honor Roll School
• First-Year Program
• Senior-Year Program
• Substance-Abuse Prevention Program
• Volunteer Service Program

JAY L. KESLER

PRESIDENT
TAYLOR UNIVERSITY

236 WEST READE AVENUE
UPLAND, IN 46989–1001

765.998.5201
almiller@tayloru.edu
http://www.tayloru.edu/

UNDERGRADUATES: 2,200

*"President Kesler is
a man of wisdom, able
to exemplify leadership
to its fullest capacity.
His ability to talk with
students of today
inspires us to pursue our
own character growth."*

—A TAYLOR FOURTH-YEAR
STUDENT

Other Taylor Profiles:

• Spiritual Growth Program

WITH AN OPEN-DOOR POLICY THAT PROVIDES EASY ACCESS for freshmen and the chairman of the Board of Trustees alike, Jay L. Kesler, Taylor University's 28th president since 1985, is a leader who promotes civic values and sound relationships as part of an integrated education. At this private, evangelical and interdenominational Christian liberal arts institution, President Kesler prepares young men and women to serve a world in need. He promotes modeling and mentoring as effective ways to develop civic and personal responsibility, believing that by demonstrating high standards leaders challenge students to raise their standards to the same level.

President Kesler's philosophy—based on the assumption that true leaders acknowledge their weaknesses as well as develop their strengths—is summed up simply: "People are afraid of letting others in close because they don't want to share their weaknesses. . . . But young people tend to identify more with people they see as human. There are risks in being vulnerable with students, but the rewards are worth it." He devotes blocks of time away from his busy schedule to work directly and personally with others, particularly students:

✦ FORUM FOR STUDENT LEADERS. Twice a month, President Kesler hosts a forum for student leaders to discuss the roles and responsibilities of Taylor administrators, who model servanthood that student leaders can emulate.

✦ CREATING CAMPUS COMMUNITY. For the past 10 years, President Kesler has spent one evening a week watching films, reading books, and talking about the impact of the media on culture with a small group of young Taylor men. Christmas is another community-building event on campus. For the past 12 years, the Keslers have hosted a "pajama party" at Hodson Dining Commons— the Kesler home being a bit too small to house the hundreds of students who attend.

✦ "COMMUNITY PLUNGE." One day a year for the past six years has been devoted to the town of Upland. More than 600 Taylor students and faculty— including President Kesler—participate in painting, weeding, and raking.

✦ TEACHING SUCCESS. For several years, President Kesler has met with National Merit Scholars to discuss the characteristics of teachers who encourage success, and has written thank-you notes to their teachers.

✦ PRISON FELLOWSHIP MINISTRY. As a founding board member of the prison fellowship committee, President Kesler reaches out to prisoners and their families to share a message of hope.

✦ NATIONAL PRAYER BREAKFAST. President Kesler has been involved with the National Prayer Breakfast for the past 28 years, traveling across the US to speak with mayors and governors to promote strong communities.

The recipient of the Gold Medallion Award for his book *Parents and Teenagers*, President Kesler is a prolific and respected writer. His 23 books offering advice on relationships have been translated into seven languages. In addition to numerous awards that reflect his energetic, religious-oriented civic responsibility, President Kesler's board and committee memberships include work on *Campus Life* magazine and the faculty for Billy Graham Schools of Evangelism. A strong and sincere mentor to students, staff, and faculty, President Kesler is an outstanding leader and a true friend to everyone on the Taylor campus.

THE 18TH PRESIDENT OF TRINITY COLLEGE SINCE 1995, Evan S. Dobelle has demonstrated dynamic community involvement at this private, liberal arts school. For him, a Trinity education includes meaningful public service. "True stewardship requires us to draw our students to a higher ethical and moral plane. It requires us to build on the potential of youthful minds and to inspire an informed awareness of what it is to be a citizen of the world." Personal and civic responsibility infuse President Dobelle's vision for Trinity, which was recognized in the *Time/Princeton Review* as one of the top six US colleges for strengthening community and encouraging access to higher education. In 1998, Trinity received a $5 million grant to support its plans "to build further College-community connections that emphasize civic responsibility and educational innovation."

President Dobelle states, "We have an obligation to invest in building community and rebuilding cities." Accordingly, in a speech at the Brookings Institution's National Issues Forum on Cities in 1998, he called for all American universities and colleges to "exercise their civic responsibility" and "assert their moral authority" by fulfilling their obligations to the cities and towns in which they operate. At Trinity, President Dobelle has initiated comprehensive initiatives that exemplify the importance of community involvement and the exercise of personal and civic responsibility:

✦ THE LEARNING CORRIDOR. President Dobelle called for a $175-million neighborhood revitalization initiative in collaboration with the community and with public, private, and government institutions. The centerpiece of this initiative, The Learning Corridor, will include a new Montessori-style elementary school, a neighborhood middle school, and an interdistrict high-school resource center. By emphasizing education and home ownership, the project is designed to promote personal and civic responsibility by building a community infrastructure. In spearheading this effort, President Dobelle has modeled civic responsibility that Trinity students are emulating: Through this initiative, two-thirds of the student population now engages in community-oriented service.

✦ THE BOYS & GIRLS CLUB. The only such club affiliated with a college or university in the country, the Boys & Girls Club at Trinity inspired more than one-third of the first-year class to volunteer, giving students a meaningful sense of service and civic responsibility. Trinity's efforts to improve Hartford's quality of life received national attention when Retired General Colin Powell named Trinity the first "College of Promise" in 1998 for its commitment to educational innovation and community renewal.

✦ CHARACTER BUILDING THROUGH ACADEMICS. A reconfigured educational plan initiated by President Dobelle in 1997 and adopted in 1998 emphasizes academic and campus-wide initiatives that create a sense of common purpose between the Trinity campus and its neighbors. These initiatives engage students to collaborate with one other, faculty, staff, and neighbors to build a community of mutual respect and responsibility.

President Dobelle models civic engagement locally and nationally, and has received the New Englander of the Year Award, the Civitan Club of Hartford's Citizen of the Year award, and the University of Massachusetts Chancellor's Medal. Through dynamic leadership, he has instituted programs and initiatives that demonstrate the equal importance of education in developing character.

EVAN S. DOBELLE

PRESIDENT
TRINITY COLLEGE

300 SUMMIT STREET
HARTFORD, CT 06016

860.297.2087
evan.dobelle@trincoll.edu
http://www.trincoll.edu/

UNDERGRADUATES: 2,100

"Civic engagement is a strong characteristic of Trinity students. Both on campus and in Hartford, President Dobelle has encouraged us to be active and knowledgeable participants of our community, not just passive members."

—A TRINITY FOURTH-YEAR
STUDENT

Other Trinity Profiles:

• First-Year Program

John DiBiaggio

PRESIDENT
TUFTS UNIVERSITY

BALLOU HALL
MEDFORD/SOMERVILLE CAMPUS
MEDFORD, MA 02155

617.628.5000
president@infonet.tufts.edu
http://www.tufts.edu/

UNDERGRADUATES: 4,500

"President DiBiaggio encourages students and faculty to take an active role within their community and the world. Like all effective leaders, he teaches by example. He is exactly what a university president should be— a model teacher."

—A TUFTS FOURTH-YEAR STUDENT

Other Tufts Profiles:

• Civic Education Program

VIGOROUSLY CHAMPIONING THE PRINCIPLES OF CIVILITY and public service at Tufts University since his appointment as its 11th president in 1992, John DiBiaggio daily inspires everyone at this private, liberal arts institution. Whether he's reading stories to preschool children in the Tufts bookstore, writing in the student newspaper about the importance of decency and compassion, or working to develop a curriculum that will promote public service, President DiBiaggio is actively involved in students' education and their lives. "Schools have a responsibility that extends beyond jobs and future studies. They have an equal responsibility to produce students with characteristics of good citizenship," he said at a Presidents' Symposium in 1998 at Milton Academy.

Through his creative leadership and innovative programs, President DiBiaggio provides many opportunities for Tufts students to improve and revitalize the communities in which they find themselves:

✦ COLLEGE OF PUBLIC SERVICE. With the intention of unifying and strengthening the university's focus on civil responsibility, President DiBiaggio has been developing the concept of the "College of Public Service" since his second year at Tufts. The new program, targeted for a fall 1999 launch, will provide the resources and support required by students and faculty members who wish to pursue public service projects and education. Plans for the new initiative include establishing a resource center, training workshops, curriculum development training, and awards for public service leaders in the Tufts community.

✦ LEONARD CARMICHAEL SOCIETY (LCS). This student organization for volunteerism and community outreach has increased its membership to 700 since President DiBiaggio arrived at Tufts and became a key supporter. With a mission of creating a "more socially sensitive and responsible world," LCS works in surrounding communities on issues of critical importance, such as homelessness, hunger, health, and literacy.

✦ MASTER OF ARTS IN HUMANITARIAN ASSISTANCE. President DiBiaggio teamed up with Tufts' Fletcher School of Law and Diplomacy dean to expand its offerings in 1998 to include this one-year degree for mid-career professionals with field experience in famine, international conflict, and other complex emergencies.

✦ TOWARD A CIVIL SOCIETY. In cooperation with the University Press of New England, President DiBiaggio secured the funding for a new series of books to focus on civility and personal responsibility.

Described by students as an "extremely accessible" leader who returns telephone calls personally, President DiBiaggio is a courageous force for good who demonstrates to all who meet him the value of civility and helping others. Trained in dental medicine, he has labored to further incorporate "societal obligation" into the training of future health professionals studying at Tufts' internationally acclaimed schools of Medicine, Dental Medicine, Veterinary Medicine, School of Nutrition Science, and Policy.

As the provost states, the Tufts community should "praise this man of vision, energy, courage, and moral values." Through the power of his personality and his actions, President DiBiaggio is inspiring Tufts students to make a positive impact in the world, today and in the future.

WHETHER COMMANDING FIGHTER AIRCRAFT SQUADRONS or motivating faculty to inspire character development in their cadets, the superintendent of the United States Air Force Academy, Lieutenant General Tad J. Oelstrom, models distinguished leadership and exemplary civic responsibility. Since his appointment in 1997, the Academy's 14th superintendent has expanded the traditional four-year core course of academics, military training, and athletics to include character development. Personal involvement in USAFA Character Enrichment Seminars and the Character Development Commission demonstrate the investment Lt. Gen. Oelstrom is making in leading faculty, staff, and cadets in living lives of which they and their country can be proud.

A catalyst in promoting character development education, Lt. Gen. Oelstrom has established outstanding programs at a time when staffing and funding requirements required creative handling:

✦ THE HOLLAND H. COORS CHAIR IN CHARACTER DEVELOPMENT. As the first of its kind in the country, this $1.5 million endowed chair resulting from Lt. Gen. Oelstrom's efforts resides in the Center for Character Development. For the period 1996–1998, the Academy was granted the Air Force Excellence Award in part because of such innovative initiatives. In addition, the Cadet Chapel actively supports the character development outcomes identified by the Center.

✦ PRIORITY FUNDING FOR CHARACTER DEVELOPMENT. The skillful reprioritizing of the character development program by Lt. Gen. Oelstrom ensured gift giving of more than $80,000 in the 1989–99 academic year. Not only does this demonstrate a 20-fold increase in gift funding since Lt. Gen. Oelstrom's appointment, but also explains why USAFA ranks as a national leader among higher-education institutions. The first nationwide National Character and Leadership Symposium in 1998 and Senior Leadership Roundtable discussion further testify to the broad appeal of Lt. Gen. Oelstrom's focus on personal initiative and civic responsibility.

✦ VECTOR STRATEGIC PLANNING COMMITTEE. The Core Programs and Capstone of Excellence are part of the strategic planning process and committee known as Vector, designed by Lt. Gen. Oelstrom. The Core Programs include the baseline requirements associated with a bachelor's degree and military officer commissioning, plus additional "Elements of Excellence" in leadership education, airmanship programs, athletic programs, and character development experiences. The Capstone of Excellence includes programs and activities that enrich the students' Core Program experience, including the National Character and Leadership Symposium, the Falcon Heritage Forum, and Academy Character Enrichment Seminars.

✦ STUDENT MENTORING. Both the National Character and Leadership Symposium and the Falcon Heritage Forum provide interactive means for cadets and distinguished veterans to discuss perspectives on military heritage and values.

Lt. Gen. Oelstrom models the Air Force Core Values of Integrity, Service, and Excellence, having achieved a position among the highest ranks of military service. To commission a cadet as an Air Force officer implies a deep understanding of personal and civic duty that Lt. Gen. Oelstrom pursues with extraordinary zeal and success.

LT. GEN. TAD J. OELSTROM

SUPERINTENDENT
UNITED STATES AIR FORCE ACADEMY

2304 CADET DRIVE, SUITE 342
USAF ACADEMY, CO 80840–5001

719.333.4904
oelstromtj.supt@usafa.af.mil
http://www.usafa.af.mil/

UNDERGRADUATES: 4,100

"Lt. Gen. Oelstrom's focus on character development exemplifies the Academy's mission of to producing the best possible leaders for the Air Force."

—A USAFA FOURTH-YEAR STUDENT

Other USAFA Profiles:
• Honor Roll School
• Academic Honesty Program
• Spiritual Growth Program
• Student Leadership Program

RICHARD L. BYYNY

CHANCELLOR
UNIVERSITY OF COLORADO AT
BOULDER

REGENT ADMINISTRATIVE CENTER
301, CAMPUS BOX 17
BOULDER, CO 80309–0017

303.492.8908
chanchat@spot.colorado.edu
http://www.colorado.edu/

UNDERGRADUATES: 25,000

"In my time at CU, I have gotten to know Chancellor Byyny as a man with high expectations and strong values. Dedicated to his students and the campus, he is very approachable—he makes everyone he meets feel important. Chancellor Byyny is an example to us all."

—A CU FOURTH-YEAR
STUDENT

Other CU Profiles:

• Student Leadership Program

SINCE 1997, RICHARD L. BYYNY, M.D. HAS SERVED the University of Colorado at Boulder as chancellor, following 20 years at CU—as Interim Chancellor earlier in 1997 and as a faculty member since 1977. As a physician, Chancellor Byyny has established various medical programs, including organized healthcare delivery, restructuring medical education to provide more generalist physicians, and lobbying for federal support of primary care research in education. His distinguished career as a leader in medicine has endowed him with the depth of experience required of a dynamic leader in education.

Chancellor Byyny's strength as a leader stems from his days in medicine; he guides 25,000 undergraduates with the same concern that he shows his patients and their families. Dedicated to the premise that education requires responsibility and commitment to others, he writes: "The campus mission is to advance and impart knowledge across a comprehensive range of disciplines to benefit the people of Colorado, the nation, and the world by educating undergraduate and graduate students in the accumulated knowledge of humankind, discovering new knowledge through research and creative work, and fostering critical thought, professional competence and responsible citizenship."

The programs and initiatives supported by Chancellor Byyny all reinforce civic responsibility and pride:

✦ THE RESIDENTIAL ACADEMIC LEADERSHIP PROGRAM. Through this program, freshmen take courses that emphasize civic responsibility.

✦ "A MATTER OF DEGREE." Chancellor Byyny has supported and actively participated in initiatives through this program that work to reduce student alcoholism. To support this effort, he banned the sale of alcohol at CU's Folsom Stadium.

✦ OFF-CAMPUS LIFE. Drawing on the resources developed during his medical career, Chancellor Byyny handled off-campus student riots with "consistency, diplomacy, and fortitude in the face of great opposition," as one colleague described it. Working with various constituencies, he helped improve student life off campus by encouraging students to assume an active role in ensuring the safety and well-being of their community and its neighborhoods.

✦ CHARACTER DEVELOPMENT EDUCATION. With the College of Arts and Sciences, Chancellor Byyny is working to establish a CU curriculum that includes examining character development themes in literature, as well as in political and sociological contexts.

"I support a student-centered campus community in which the question, 'What is best for the students?' is always asked," writes Chancellor Byyny. What is best for CU students is a chancellor whose decisions regarding campus life and character development are always focused on their growth as individuals. In turn, students actively promote community enrichment, giving back some of what they've gained under the watchful eye of Chancellor Byyny.

O<small>N HIS RANCH OR BEHIND HIS DESK</small>, the 16th chancellor of the oldest independent institution of higher education in the Rocky Mountain West has promoted volunteerism and philanthropy since 1989—without pay but with much vigor. Chancellor Daniel L. Ritchie has personally donated more than $40 million to the University of Denver, a nondenominational, urban institution with historic ties to the United Methodist Church, modeling philanthropic efforts that distinguish DU and its unique chancellor.

As a business leader (he operates two large ranches and served as president and CEO of Westinghouse Broadcasting Company), Chancellor Ritchie's activism inspires student citizens to engage in civic action at DU: "We are vitally interested in civic education and in engaging our students, faculty, and staff in public work." He oversees numerous service-learning and outreach programs that serve as national models:

✦ I<small>NSTITUTE FOR</small> E<small>THICS AND</small> V<small>ALUES</small>. Chancellor Ritchie's $40-million gift spurred another donor to endow this center to support academics and scholarships and to promote ethics, values, and social responsibility on- and off-campus.

✦ S<small>TUDENT</small> O<small>UTREACH</small>. In 1991, Operation Outreach began implementing educational strategies in greater Denver, resulting in 12 new programs. The Quigg Newton Housing Project helps students to mentor school-age urban children. The Bridge Project, directed by DU's Graduate School of Social Work, targets those seemingly destined for a life of poverty; thus far, 11 students have graduated from DU on full scholarships, turning their cycle of underachievement into successful higher education stories.

✦ C<small>OMMUNITY</small> A<small>CTION</small> P<small>ROGRAM</small>. Coordinating more than 100 schools, community centers, and nursing homes, CAP staff provides DU students with varied service learning experiences to enrich their communities.

✦ P<small>IONEER</small> L<small>EADERSHIP</small> P<small>ROGRAM</small>. This four-year program incorporates academics, service learning, and residence hall communal life to hone leadership skills. The Pioneer Charter School, created to combat illiteracy and poor education, represents the outcome of collaboration among parents, community workers, and DU and Denver public school systems.

✦ V<small>OLUNTEER</small> S<small>ERVICE</small>. Chancellor Ritchie's vision for improving the community includes undergraduate courses such as Service Learning in a Multicultural Democracy, requiring at least 20 volunteer hours to tutor in the public schools, work in local soup kitchens and homeless shelters, help in inner-city housing projects, contribute to environmental research and cleanup efforts, and assist in AIDS-related charities. DU volunteerism has changed not only urban Denver, but foreign nations—DU students work in Mexico, Croatia, and Bosnia to tutor English or create vital youth activities in places filled with despair.

In 1994, Chancellor Ritchie was named "Citizen of the West," a highly coveted honor in the Rocky Mountain region. He also received the Distinguished Service Award from DU alumni for developing students of depth and civic responsibility. Under his leadership, DU intends to lead universities across the country in community service. Whether gaining insight into urban issues, strengthening community ties, or discovering human potential, Chancellor Ritchie's initiatives "change the world one life at a time."

D<small>ANIEL</small> L. R<small>ITCHIE</small>

CHANCELLOR
UNIVERSITY OF DENVER

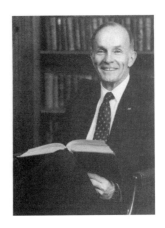

UNIVERSITY PARK
2199 SOUTH UNIVERSITY BLVD
DENVER, CO 80208

303.871.2111
dritchie@du.edu
http://www.du.edu/

UNDERGRADUATES: 3,100

"Chancellor Ritchie's dedication to students is evident in the monumental changes he has made at DU. True leadership and generosity drive his extraordinary vision for the future."

—<small>A</small> DU <small>FOURTH-YEAR</small>
<small>STUDENT</small>

Fr. Edward A. Malloy

PRESIDENT
UNIVERSITY OF NOTRE DAME

130 HAYES-HEALY CENTER
NOTRE DAME, IN 46556

219.631.7505
Malloy.5@nd.edu
http://www.nd.edu/

UNDERGRADUATES: 7,800

"Father Malloy has had a profound impact on my life and the way in which I view the world. I went into his literature seminar expecting to be introduced to a variety of books.... I left with a greater understanding of humanity and my moral responsibilities as a citizen of the world."

—A NOTRE DAME SECOND-
YEAR STUDENT

Other Notre Dame Profiles:

• Honor Roll School
• Academic Honesty Program
• Faculty & Curriculum Program
• Volunteer Service Program

WHEN THE 16TH PRESIDENT OF UNIVERSITY OF NOTRE DAME, Father Edward A. Malloy, CSC, says he "lives" his commitment to his students, he means it—he resides in one of the men's residence halls on campus. It is not unusual to find him holding informal discussions with students in the residence halls, where he also regularly celebrates Mass. Father Malloy touches the lives of Notre Dame students in ways that encourage strong character, community pride, and social responsibility at this Catholic, comprehensive university. Whether teaching the first-year course "The People of the World and Their Cultures" or working at the South Bend Center for the Homeless, a place where people have rediscovered hope and purpose, Father Malloy has shown Notre Dame students the value and effect of moral leadership.

In addition to inspiring a number of campus- and community-based programs, Father Malloy has been active in national efforts to combat substance abuse. He was a member of President Bush's Advisory Council on Drugs; chaired the Commission on Substance Abuse among America's Adolescents and the Commission on Substance Abuse at Colleges and Universities; and currently cochairs the subcommittee on college drinking of the National Institute on Alcohol and Alcoholism. "It is incumbent upon us as college and university presidents to lead the way in fostering an improved campus climate with regard to alcohol use. Much good can be achieved by properly mobilizing our various communities," he wrote, noting that "the first challenge is to have the courage to evaluate the situation on one's own campus."

The programs and initiatives supported by Father Malloy reinforce civic and personal responsibility. His efforts to discourage campus alcohol and drug use exemplify the depth of his commitment and vision, and substance-abuse-prevention initiatives occupy the center of his mission:

✦ SUBSTANCE–ABUSE PREVENTION. Notre Dame's Alcohol and Drug Education Center provides materials and information about drug and alcohol issues to students. The BACCHUS (Boosting Alcohol Consciousness Concerning the Health of University Students) Peer Education Program consists of an on-campus team that uses upbeat discussion to promote healthy attitudes toward substance use—and nonuse. The "Flipside" student club offers and promotes social activities that do not center on alcohol.

✦ KNIGHTS OF COLUMBUS. Among the oldest and largest student groups at Notre Dame, this service organization directs many volunteer projects and raises $35,000 annually for charity.

✦ CENTER FOR SOCIAL CONCERNS. Notre Dame's service-learning center is among the most comprehensive in higher education. It includes programs such as the Summer Institute, which enables students to spend four weeks with others who have similar ideas and values, providing them with an opportunity to learn, reflect, and share.

Father Malloy's visionary leadership is well known and has an impact beyond Notre Dame's campus. Vanderbilt University recently announced the establishment of The Rev. Edward Malloy Chair in Catholic Studies in its school of divinity, a high honor rarely awarded to a living university president. Passionately committed to providing a positive environment for education, learning, personal growth, and character development, Father Malloy shepherds Notre Dame students toward lives of enlightened purpose.

Whether visiting with the Pope or having lunch with Vaclav Havel, Father David T. Tyson, CSC, the 18th president of the University of Portland since 1990, cherishes a community environment that integrates faith and learning. This private, Catholic institution works actively toward character and moral development in and out of the classroom and challenges UP students to minister to those in need. Father Tyson says, "We are called by Christ to serve the people of God in many ways." A member of the Congregation of Holy Cross, which is affiliated with UP and founded the University of Notre Dame, Father Tyson supports active and broad volunteerism among the 2,200 UP undergraduates, who acquire a mature approach to service through UP's community-oriented programs.

Father Tyson's commitment to volunteerism focuses on his belief that community involvement is "prayer in action":

✦ **Character Development Curriculum.** In 1997, Father Tyson introduced this refocused curriculum, which includes environmental ethics, theology, philosophy, and a plan for an endowed chair in ethics. These education strategies and others contribute to UP's top ranking among regional universities in the American West by *U.S. News & World Report*.

✦ **Volunteerism.** The "Christmas in April" program, led by Father Tyson, involves 400 students, faculty, and alumni in renovating lower-income homes in Portland. Also, seven programs that help the homeless, jailed, poor, and elderly, begun in 1991, have blossomed into 32 programs, and as a result Oregon's governor rewarded UP students for extraordinary community service under Father Tyson's leadership. The Pacific Alliance for Catholic Education enables graduate students to earn their master's degrees by teaching for two years in Catholic elementary and high schools in the West and Northwest, demonstrating Portland's commitment to improving education national wide.

✦ **Spirituality.** Father Tyson encourages students in the Catholic tradition by inviting outstanding moral teachers such as Martin Marty and Barry Lopez for campus meetings. He also welcomes those from other faiths—Muslims, Quakers, Mormons, and Protestant denominations—to religious services and spiritual retreats sponsored by the campus ministry office.

Father Tyson has also distinguished himself by helping restructure the NCAA (National Collegiate Athletic Association), specifically in battling corruption among college athletes. He served as director of the American Association of Catholic Colleges and Universities and as trustee of the University of Notre Dame, the Air Force's Air University, and Saint Edward's University in Texas. Father Tyson's record also includes doubling UP's endowment, having two students named as Rhodes Scholar finalists, and overseeing the largest freshman class in UP's history. Award-winning faculty—including 42 priests of the Congregation of Holy Cross who further enrich the intellectual and spiritual life of the campus—participate in UP's intimate learning environment, with a 14:1 student-teacher ratio.

Father Tyson's example blends those heart, mind, and body aspects of education that create spiritual purpose and outstanding civic involvement in every student that attends UP.

Fr. David T. Tyson

PRESIDENT
UNIVERSITY OF PORTLAND

5000 NORTH WILLAMETTE BLVD.
PORTLAND, OR 97203–5798

503.943.7101
tyson@up.edu
http://www.up.edu/

UNDERGRADUATES: 2,200

"Father Tyson's continuous vision has helped to create a university in which the education of the heart is as important as the education of the mind."

—A UP fourth-year student

Other UP Profiles:

• Honor Roll School
• Spiritual Growth Program

John T. Casteen III

PRESIDENT
UNIVERSITY OF VIRGINIA

P.O. BOX 9017
CHARLOTTESVILLE, VA 22906–9011

804.982.3200
jtc@virginia.edu
http://www.virginia.edu/

UNDERGRADUATES: 12,400

"President Casteen has a profound faith in student self-governance, exemplified in his hands-off, students-should-solve-their-own-problems approach."

—A UVA FOURTH-YEAR
STUDENT

Other UVA Profiles:

• Honor Roll School
• Academic Honesty Program
• First-Year Program
• Volunteer Service Program

OUTSTANDING LEADERSHIP, ACADEMIC EXCELLENCE, and moral development of students are the hallmark of the presidency of John T. Casteen III at the University of Virginia. The university's 7th president since 1990, he has contributed to UVA's distinction as a top-ranked public institution for five consecutive years in the *U.S. News & World Report* annual survey. His teaching and scholarly writing in medieval English and his previous tenure in the Virginia Governor's cabinet as secretary of education are only two of the many experiences in higher education he draws on. His goal is to empower the students who walk in the footsteps of Thomas Jefferson, a figure President Casteen deeply admires for defining the values etched in our schools, colleges, and nation. He notes, "For Jefferson, the common good . . . the public good, is the first good. Education in this society, as in all societies, is the one and only guarantor of the existence of human freedom."

President Casteen has led one of the most successful capital campaigns in public universities, raising more than $800 million for UVA. Public service and outreach are among those initiatives that benefit directly from his vision of the role of higher education in the new century:

✦ **STUDENT CITIZENSHIP.** The nation's oldest honor system encourages UVA students to act with honor and civility in and out of the classroom. President Casteen says, "This is our fundamental pledge to one another, a covenant that must govern your actions and inform your relations with all persons with whom you come in contact."

✦ **BINGE-DRINKING PREVENTION.** These bold responses to alcohol and substance abuse have earned UVA national recognition under President Casteen's leadership: modified fraternity and sorority rush activities, a substance-abuse center, an extensive schedule of alcohol-free social programming, classes in alcohol abuse, and an alcohol awareness week.

✦ **VIRGINIA 2020 INITIATIVE.** This long-range, strategic planning initiative will inform the university's decision-making for the early decades of the 21st century. The project focuses on science and technology, the fine and performing arts, public service and outreach, and international programs. Continued improvement in these areas will benefit not only the university's students and faculty, but also the citizens of Virginia and beyond.

Led by the Faculty Senate and President Casteen, a dialog has begun about strengthening the university's intellectual community. Through a revised orientation program, a new Life Skills Workshop, and other means, students have frequent contact with faculty and other mentors who help them achieve their goals, not only academically but also in their personal lives.

President Casteen currently is president of the Southern Association of Colleges and Schools, serves on the board of directors of the Council on Higher Education Accreditation, and is a member of the Association of Governing Boards. In May 1998, UVA's governing board passed a resolution recognizing the tremendous value of his leadership to the institution.

President Casteen focuses on the intellectual and moral development of UVA's students and provides a lesson for life in outstanding citizenship.

Trust has been a principle at the core of Andrew T. Ford's leadership of Wabash College since he became its 14th president in 1993. As president of one of the three remaining liberal arts colleges for men in the United States, President Ford believes that trust leads to strengthened personal responsibility and works hard to see that students are given the chance to develop the skills to be lifelong leaders. He established that trust at Wabash through "The Gentlemen's Rule," which states that a "student will conduct himself, at all times, both on and off the campus, as a gentleman and responsible citizen."

President Ford has placed character development at the center of the Wabash mission through several programs and initiatives:

✦ First-Year Orientation. Wabash's weeklong program for new students establishes the connection between a student's life and his sense of responsibility to others. Freshmen become involved with a community service project their second day on campus, learning the commitment, common purpose, and shared values required for community building.

✦ LIFE (Lilly Initiative for Education). President Ford worked with Wabash alumni to develop this program aimed at increasing the number of Indiana residents with college degrees. LIFE has worked with hundreds of junior-high and high-school students to help young people become the first in their families to attend college. More than 90% of LIFE participants entered college in the fall 1998 term, and the program also offers opportunities for Wabash students to mentor young scholars.

✦ Community Building. Nearly three-fourths of the Wabash student body takes part in ongoing community service projects. Students designed and continue to conduct an after-school mentoring program, working with local children. Other projects include cleaning the banks of Sugar Creek, collecting $12,000 worth of toys for the "Toys-for-Tots" campaign, and canvassing door-to-door for the United Fund.

✦ Culture and Traditions. This 25-year-old course focusing on the diversity of cultures worldwide is required of all Wabash sophomores. President Ford recently taught a 15-student section of the course, emphasizing the course's character and values education components. Two objectives of this course enable students to strive toward self-knowledge by examining values and beliefs and to "widen their horizons" by studying the art, religion, social theories, and other aspects of various cultures.

✦ Spiritual Growth. Working with faculty in the philosophy and religion department at Wabash, President Ford helped to secure $10 million in funding to establish the Wabash Center for Teaching and Learning in Theology and Religion. Each year, the Center attracts top scholars and teachers from leading US undergraduate, graduate, and seminary programs to discuss critical issues for the future of teaching in these important areas.

A man who works tirelessly to facilitate collaboration among students, faculty members, and staff at Wabash, President Ford also works at building relationships among the region's higher-education institutions. As president of the 14-member Great Lakes Colleges Association Presidents Council, he has improved resource sharing and various opportunities at all member schools. President Ford underscores his belief in the importance of civility and openness through a quarterly column in *Wabash Magazine* and has created an environment of trust, candor, and personal responsibility that enables young men to discover for themselves values by which to live meaningful lives.

Andrew T. Ford

PRESIDENT
WABASH COLLEGE

P.O. BOX 352
301 W. WABASH AVENUE
CRAWFORDSVILLE, IN 47933–0352

765.361.6221
forda@wabash.edu
http://www.wabash.edu/

UNDERGRADUATES: 800

"Students truly appreciate President Ford's compassion for the Wabash community. He sets an example that makes us all want to be better gentlemen".

—A Wabash fourth-year student

THOMAS K. HEARN, JR.

PRESIDENT
WAKE FOREST UNIVERSITY

1834 WAKE FOREST ROAD
WINSTON-SALEM, NC 27106

336.758.5211
tkh@wfu.edu
http://www.wfu.edu/

UNDERGRADUATES: 3,800

"As a student leader, I value President Hearn's dedication and service, his integrity, and the vision with which he leads Wake Forest. He is truly an exemplar of leadership and character."

—A WAKE THIRD-YEAR STUDENT

Other Wake Profiles:
- Honor Roll School
- Academic Honesty Program
- Student Leadership Program
- Substance-Abuse Prevention Program

APPOINTED WAKE FOREST UNIVERSITY'S 12TH PRESIDENT IN 1983, Thomas K. Hearn, Jr., has since demonstrated powerful leadership in many public arenas at this private comprehensive institution. In a 1989 lecture he said, "Education for citizenship is one of the foundational ideas of liberal education, an ideal we must restore for ourselves and our society." Accordingly, President Hearn has upheld Wake Forest's *Pro Humanitate* motto, "For the good of humankind." He initiated the ACC (Atlantic Coast Conference) Alcohol Conference in 1996 and was one of the first college presidents to approve parental notification of student drinking. Concerned about AIDS, President Hearn has worked to ensure that the 3,800 Wake Forest students are well-informed about all aspects of the epidemic, and he was the keynote speaker at a recent national AIDS conference. In addition, his commitment to transcendent life combined with the school's historic church ties led to the new Wake Forest Divinity School.

President Hearn has established formidable leadership and citizenship through:

✦ **CURRICULUM.** In addition to teaching a first-year seminar on "Leadership in American Life," he supported the LEAD I/II (Leadership: Excellence, Application, and Development) program that teaches a variety of leadership skills and ethics in freshman and sophomore workshops.

✦ **CONFERENCES AND LEADERSHIP.** With the student government association, President Hearn created the Presidents' Leadership Conference, which gathers 40 students, 20 faculty, and 20 administrators for a campus dialog. He also helped develop the ACC Student Government Conference that brings together student leaders from all nine ACC schools each year.

✦ **COMMUNITY SERVICE.** The Volunteer Service Corps provides Wake students opportunities to tutor local children, create safe Halloween activities, and work in area shelters. President Hearn also established the Leadership Winston-Salem Program in 1984 to bring together 30–50 community leaders for ongoing discussion about improving education, race relations, culture, the arts, and economic development. And through Student Action for Eliminating Reckless Drivers, students pursue "Safe Roads" legislation and drinking awareness training for student drivers.

✦ **CULTURAL STUDY AND WORK.** Under President Hearn's leadership, the City of Joy and Hope Scholars programs send students to India and Honduras to work over semester breaks. He also established the Office of Multicultural Affairs to recruit and support minority students, for whom the Joseph G. Gordon Scholarship was established, quadrupling minority enrollment.

✦ **SCHOLARSHIPS.** Presidential Scholarships are offered for volunteerism and leadership. The Thomas K. Hearn Leadership and Ethics fund promotes ethics, leadership, and civic responsibility. And the Thomas K. Hearn, Jr. Scholarship for Excellence in Leadership and Service was created by Student Government in honor of his 10th anniversary as Wake's president.

President Hearn was elected chairman of the board at the nationally recognized Center for Creative Leadership in Greensboro. But perhaps the greatest testament to his leadership is found in the fall 1998 *Student Body Resolution of Appreciation:* "The student body hereby expresses its continuing appreciation and gratitude of Thomas K. Hearn, Jr., for his exemplary leadership and commitment to upholding the high standards of Wake Forest University, furthering its character, and enriching the integrity of our fine institution."

In 1994, Diana Chapman Walsh began her tenure as Wellesley College's 12th president by boldly supporting the implementation of a new program of religious and spiritual life. Based on principles of religious pluralism, all religious faiths are celebrated and nurtured at Wellesley. This was an unusual step for this leading private, secular liberal arts college for women, and President Walsh has deftly established a nationally recognized model for incorporating spirituality into the educational process. In so doing, she drew on her expertise and tenure in public health policy as the Florence Sprague Norman and Laura Smart Norman Professor at the Harvard School of Public Health, where she also chaired the Department of Health and Social Behavior. As Kellogg National Fellow, she traveled widely in the United States, studying and establishing leadership models that included spiritual dimensions.

President Walsh has consistently called for Wellesley to be "a community that practices truth . . . founded not on false unanimity or illusory value consensus, but on profound mutual respect for the fragile essence of each of us." Her inspiring leadership speaks directly to character development through spiritual endeavors. She envisions a holistic education, including spirituality, to be at the heart of Wellesley's future, and various programs establish an educational context for President Walsh's vision:

✦ **National Leadership in Higher Education.** Teaching values through spirituality in the "Education as Transformation: Religious Pluralism, Spirituality, and Higher Education" project places Wellesley as the national leader among 350 other universities participating in this character education effort. This project not only promotes a national dialogue to study the potential of religious pluralism, but also focuses on spirituality's impact in pedagogy, ethical development, and global citizenship.

✦ **Multi-Faith Programs.** The Religious and Spiritual Life Program, Religious Life Team, Multi-Faith Council, Beyond Tolerance Program, and Multi-Faith Community Celebration provide numerous opportunities for Wellesley students to deepen their spiritual lives and to expand their faith experiences on- and off-campus.

✦ **Holistic student life.** The Spirituality and Education Program integrates Wellesley services offered by the health system, Stone Counseling Center, and the Center for Work and Service to encourage student understanding of health and spiritual issues. Together with Residence Life and The Wellness Program, the Religious and Spiritual Life Program offers daily and weekly meditation and dorm-based programs about balanced-life issues.

President Walsh has written prolifically on the spiritual dimensions of leadership. As a major national voice for incorporating spirituality into a holistic educational process, she states: "Creating a new vision for spirituality in higher education is an essential component of the effort to invent a new educational process that responds fully to the challenges the world presents us now—challenges to our teaching, our learning, our living."

By elevating the spiritual dimension of learning to such a lofty level, President Walsh urges Wellesley students to discover the true meaning of "higher" education.

DIANA CHAPMAN WALSH

PRESIDENT
WELLESLEY COLLEGE

106 CENTRAL STREET
WELLESLEY, MA 02481–8203

781.283.1000
dwalsh@wellesley.edu
http://www.wellesley.edu/

UNDERGRADUATES: 2,200

"Developing the spiritual dimension of my life with women from other traditions has added another level to my education, allowing me to understand what it means to be a whole person."

—A Wellesley third-year
student

Other Wellesley Profiles:

• Spiritual Growth Program

DAVID K. WINTER

PRESIDENT
WESTMONT COLLEGE

955 LA PAZ ROAD
SANTA BARBARA, CA 93108

805.565.6000
winter@westmont.edu
http://www.westmont.edu/

UNDERGRADUATES: 1,400

"Dear President Winter: I admire your dedication and diligence, joyful service, and humility before all. It was a pleasure serving with you last year."

—LETTER FROM WESTMONT
FOURTH-YEAR STUDENT AND
STUDENT BODY PRESIDENT

Other Westmont Profiles:

• Honor Roll School

FOR MORE THAN 20 YEARS, DAVID K. WINTER has led Westmont College in its effort to assist college men and women "toward a balance of rigorous intellectual competence, healthy personal development, and strong Christian commitments." Appointed as the 7th president of this liberal arts college in 1976, President Winter has frequently spoken out both on- and off- campus about the important role that colleges must play in the character development of their students. "What is the number one vocational skill?" President Winter asked in a recent Westmont Chapel service. "It is the ability to work well with others. So our humility, our sensitivity to others, our willingness to learn how to act and relate to people of all ages and cultures are very important."

Under President Winter, Westmont has become known as a community where students are given extraordinary opportunities to explore leadership gifts and to serve others on-campus, in the community, and throughout the world:

✦ **CHRISTIAN CONCERNS.** Westmont's student government sponsors this umbrella student organization, whose more than 30 student projects make up Westmont's core community service efforts. These are just a few examples of outreach missions.

1. Potter's Clay is one of Christian Concerns' largest ministries, bringing 400 students to Ensanada, Mexico, to work among the poor during spring break.

2. Adopt-a-Grandparent places students among the elderly in Santa Barbara through frequent nursing home visits.

3. AIDS C.A.R.E. is a weekly visitation ministry that offers friendship, support, and inspiration to people suffering from this devastating syndrome.

4. Casa Rosa works with chemically dependent new mothers, helping ease their transition into motherhood.

5. Habitat for Humanity strives to eliminate poverty housing by helping to build and improve homes for the needy.

✦ **MENTORS.** Part of Westmont's leadership development efforts, Mentors are faculty, staff, and community members who support, challenge, and help guide students in their personal growth. Mentors serve as friends and models to encourage students in developing the skills, responsibility, and vision necessary for effective leadership.

✦ **WESTMONT IN THE ARTS.** This program is an outgrowth of President Winter's focus on preparing students for productive collaboration with community leaders. One hundred students attended cultural events in the community with faculty members, learning about the content and etiquette of arts performances and interacting with community members and leaders.

President Winter has been very active nationally in many higher-education associations. In each of these settings, he has promoted the importance of character development as a primary goal of higher education. During the summer of 1998, President Winter lost approximately 80% of his eyesight. Students, as well as other members of the college and local community, have expressed their great admiration for the ways in which he has reflected on and remained positive as he adjusts to this life change. President Winter's courageous and enduring leadership has touched the lives of an entire generation of Westmont students, inspiring them to become competent and caring leaders.

Blending his Christian commitment to rigorous academics with a vision of higher education as a major contributor to character formation, the seventh president of Wheaton College, Duane Litfin, is now in his sixth year of service at this private, Evangelical Christian (nondenominational) liberal arts school. After completing his first doctorate at Purdue University in speech communications and rhetoric, he served as a seminary professor of homiletics and practical theology. Then, after completing his second doctorate at Oxford University in New Testament studies, he returned to pastoral ministry, serving one of the largest evangelical congregations in Memphis.

President Litfin has followed through on his church-centered educational vision of service to others through financial and personal support of the following programs and initiatives at Wheaton:

✦ **Curricular Service Learning.** Under President Litfin's leadership, Wheaton has deepened its commitment to service learning through the curriculum. He has strongly supported the Human Needs and Global Resources program that sends 20 to 30 students a year on a six-month development tour of service in developing nations. He has also supported establishment of the semester-long "Wheaton in Chicago" residential program, which fosters student commitment to urban service.

✦ **Cocurricular Service Learning.** Through extensive programs of community service, Wheaton students are challenged to develop a commitment to the world around them. Between one-third and one-half of Wheaton students are involved in meaningful service in diverse areas, including soup kitchens, homeless shelters, AIDS hospices, community clinics, tutoring programs, and prisons.

✦ **CACE (Center for Applied Christian Ethics).** CACE encourages and supports the growth in ethical character of our faculty and students through innovative, interactive programs such as debates, panels, and dialogs, as well as curricular enhancement. President Litfin has invested significant financial resources in expanding and enhancing this program.

✦ **Faculty Faith and Learning Initiative.** Faculty are the agents for student formation at Wheaton. President Litfin has helped establish a $2 million endowment to support programs that deepen faculty appreciation of Wheaton's spiritual and theological traditions, which they are encouraged to combine with their academic work.

One of the few presidents who takes the opportunity to address faculty and students regularly on issues of character formation, President Litfin, speaking at Wheaton's required chapel program, often passionately addresses matters of ethics, character, and integrity. He also speaks about these matters in seminary, university, and church settings.

President Litfin is personally engaged with Wheaton students. Rarely declining an invitation to talk with them, whether at a "forum," Bible study, or an informal event, he shares his passionate desire that all students leaving Wheaton will be persons of moral strength and personal integrity.

DUANE LITFIN

PRESIDENT
WHEATON COLLEGE

501 EAST COLLEGE AVENUE
WHEATON, IL 60187–5593

630.752.5000
d.litfin@wheaton.edu
http://www.wheaton.edu/

UNDERGRADUATES: 2,300

"I would not be who I am without the consistent example of strong character and integrity exhibited throughout every aspect of Dr. Litfin's life."

—A Wheaton fourth-year student

Other Wheaton Profiles:

• Honor Roll School
• Faculty & Curriculum Program

Purpose

In 1989, the John Templeton Foundation established
the Honor Roll for Character-Building Colleges to
recognize biennially those institutions that emphasize
character development as an integral aspect of the undergraduate experience. To date, more than 350 colleges and universities
have been named to one or more Honor Rolls.

Continuing this tradition of affirming excellence,
the Templeton Honor Roll section of the guidebook
profiles 100 colleges and universities. Although particular
practices and emphases may differ, all 100 institutions exhibit
a strong and inspiring campus-wide ethos that articulates the
expectations of personal and civic responsibility in all
dimensions of college life.

Selection Criteria

✦ A clear and compelling vision and mission that
express a commitment to prepare students for lives
of personal and civic responsibility

✦ The significant involvement and participation
of faculty in forming and shaping the ideals
and standards of personal and civic responsibility

✦ Evidence that a wide variety of programs exists to
prepare students for lives of personal and
civic responsibility

✦ The integration of personal and civic responsibility
standards and activities into the core curriculum or
areas of academic study

✦ External recognition or honors

✦ Procedures to assess effectiveness of campus-wide
character-development programs

ALMA COLLEGE

614 WEST SUPERIOR
ALMA, MI 48801-1599

517.463.7111
http://www.alma.edu/

UNDERGRADUATES: 1,400

"Alma has shown me the world. In 1997, I traveled to India as Alma's Global Service Fellow—thousands of miles away and still getting the education of my life. On campus or in India, Alma gave me the best."

—AN ALMA FOURTH-YEAR STUDENT

MORE THAN A CENTURY AGO, in 1886, a group of devoted Presbyterian clergy and laypersons realized their dream of establishing a church-affiliated, liberal arts institution based on the loftiest ideals—unifying the mind and the spirit through knowledge. Today, Alma College faculty and staff continue this tradition of cultivating an ethos of personal and civic responsibility through the following character-building programs:

✦ FACULTY AND CURRICULUM. Alma recently received a "Universities as Citizens" grant to develop a core curriculum that involves a civic literacy component. The college has also been extremely successful in offering more than 30 courses that integrate service-learning activities. Faculty members are among the most ardent supporters of Alma's Service-Learning Program, recognizing community service as an important aspect of faculty and staff development and responsibilities. These service activities are rewarded in annual merit pay increases and through campus-wide recognition, distinctions, honors, and awards.

✦ VOLUNTEER SERVICE. Alma has a highly successful Service-Learning Program. It has remained deeply committed to learning and service opportunities that bring students in contact with public and private economic development, employment, educational, and health agencies. Through Global Service Fellowship, students travel to Kerala, India, to teach at an English-language school. Other international Service-Learning courses take place in Jamaica, Honduras, and on the Texas-Mexico border.

✦ STUDENT LEADERSHIP. Hundreds of Alma students each year are involved in the Student Congress. The student body is actively involved in governing the college—an ideal vehicle through which to develop student leadership skills. Alma's Community Government system brings together faculty, administrators, and students as members of committees to address areas of mutual concern. As members of the Board of Trustees, students are entrusted with full voting privileges and actively participate in the Board's various committees.

✦ CIVIC EDUCATION. Political involvement is encouraged at Alma, especially through the Young Republicans and College Democrats organizations. Several environmental student organizations, including "SUN" ("Students Understanding Nature"), raise awareness regarding ecological issues.

✦ SPIRITUAL GROWTH. Alma champions religious life development, and numerous groups demonstrate growing student awareness and involvement. Chapel, vespers, Bible study groups, the Alma College Christian Association, and the Fellowship of Christian Athletes are an integral part of campus life.

Alma's long-range strategic "Evergreen Plan," which regularly renews itself, reinforces the college's commitment to creating a campus-wide "quality ethos." This ethos articulates a strong set of values, especially those that form the school's core mission: "The liberation of people from ignorance, prejudice, and parochialism." Toward that end, Alma has created a groundbreaking exchange program with Stillman College, an historically Black institution in Tuscaloosa, Alabama, to promote racial, cultural, and geographic diversity. Alma remains at the forefront of exposing students to learning opportunities that are both academically challenging and personally rewarding.

SPONSORED BY THE BERNARDINE SISTERS of the Third Order of Saint Francis, Alvernia College is a Catholic, coeducational liberal arts school established in 1958. The Franciscan core values of service, humility, peacemaking, contemplation, and collegiality serve as the foundation and catalyst for the college's emphasis on character development. Alvernia was one of the first institutions of higher learning in the state of Pennsylvania to require 40 hours of uncompensated service to others as a requirement for a baccalaureate degree.

Other character-development programs of distinction include:

✦ FACULTY AND CURRICULUM. The specific goal of Alvernia's Service Learning Credit Program is to link service with academic work. The program adds a fourth credit to existing academic courses by challenging students to perform a service project related to the course in which they are enrolled.

✦ VOLUNTEER SERVICE. The college's "La Mission De Amistad" is a community service project to a barrio in the Dominican Republic that incorporates courses in both Spanish and social work. Students learn to communicate effectively with the barrio community and have developed the first barrio-based agricultural program in the country. Students also connect barrio residents without birth certificates with representatives from Rotary International's birth certificate program.

✦ SUBSTANCE-ABUSE PREVENTION. Alcohol is prohibited on Alvernia's "dry" campus. Drug and alcohol education programs are held throughout the year to inform the entire college community of the risks and dangers of substance abuse. The college has recently received a grant from the Pennsylvania Liquor Control Board to expand the activities of its Alcohol and Other Drugs Task Force, as well as to form a campus-community coalition to discourage underage drinking on and off campus.

✦ SPIRITUAL GROWTH. Under the guidance of the Assistant to the President for Mission and Ministry, Alvernia recently celebrated its heritage and its Franciscan mission in a unique public 40th-anniversary celebration. Beginning on the morning of Ash Wednesday (1999) and lasting for a continuous 40 hours, Alvernia held its "Forty Hours of Prayer and Service" event. The entire campus community, alumni, and members of the Reading community took part in interdenominational continuous prayer, seminar sessions, and community service. A closing session celebrated the love commandment and the joy of service.

Alvernia's commitment to preparing students for personal achievement, social responsibility, and moral integrity is what draws students to its campus. A significant number of the college's classroom and community-based programs offer students real life experiences designed to foster an ethic of service to others. In short, these character-building experiences develop students' professional skills while providing them with a foundation that will enable them to eventually assume leadership roles in the church and community.

ALVERNIA COLLEGE

400 ST. BERNARDINE STREET
READING, PA 19607-1799

610.796.8200
http://www.alvernia.edu/

UNDERGRADUATES: 1,300

"Alvernia develops well-rounded individuals prepared for the 'real world.' I feel at home on campus because faculty and staff take an active role in each student's education."

—AN ALVERNIA FOURTH-YEAR STUDENT

Other Alvernia Profiles:

• First-Year Program
• Volunteer Service Program

ANDERSON UNIVERSITY

1100 EAST FIFTH STREET
ANDERSON, IN 46012-3495

765.649.9071
http://www.anderson.edu/

UNDERGRADUATES: 2,000

"Empowering students to experience education as freedom, service as pure joy, and faith in God as sustaining hope, Anderson University is a matchless community!"

—AN ANDERSON FOURTH-YEAR STUDENT

THE MISSION OF ANDERSON UNIVERSITY, founded in 1917 as a church-affiliated, liberal arts school, is to educate young people for lives of faith and service in the church and society. Dedicated to graduating men and women with a global perspective who are competent, caring, and people of character, the Anderson faculty and staff have assumed a leadership role in Christian higher education.

The following programs and activities serve as examples of Anderson's commitment to character development:

✦ FACULTY AND CURRICULUM. Anderson has for many years sought to hire faculty who model the standards of Christian servant leadership and are committed to the pursuit of truth from a Christian faith perspective.

✦ FIRST-YEAR PROGRAM. All first-year students are required to take the Liberal Arts Seminar, which focuses on the concept of Christian servanthood and Christian values as an ethical system.

✦ STUDENT LEADERSHIP. More than 50 sophomores and juniors serve as Resident Assistants in the university residence halls every semester. These students are selected by faculty, staff, and peers and are responsible for implementing the university's "living-learning" centers. These student leaders are entrusted with considerable responsibility and serve as role models for first-year students.

✦ SPIRITUAL GROWTH. The Office of Campus Ministries plans and implements a wide range of student worship, leadership, and service opportunities on and off campus. Each fall, the campus commits itself to a three-day "Spiritual Emphasis Week," during which nationally known speakers spend time with students in chapel services and classes. "S.O.U.L." ("Students Offering Unconditional Love") is a student-led university program that provides unwed mothers with a support network. This program was recognized nationally in 1995 by the Points of Light Foundation. Chapel-Convocation is required weekly, and chapel presentations offer student leaders the opportunity to discuss how the university can respond to local, national, or international concerns.

✦ VOLUNTEER SERVICE. Every year, Campus Ministries sponsors an "Impact Your World Week" that emphasizes service to others outside the university community. In addition, nearly 500 students each academic year participate in the university's "Tri-S" ("Study/Serve/Share") program. Organized by university faculty and staff, the program provides learning and service opportunities in Africa, Asia, Europe, and Latin America. Anderson has also served for 15 years as a regional site for the Special Olympics program, and 200 students each year serve as "huggers" to more than 100 Special Olympians.

Over the last 75 years, Anderson has sought to strengthen the body, mind, and spirit of its students and to enable them to experience what it means to love God and neighbor through adopting a life of Christian service in all dimensions of life.

ASBURY COLLEGE, founded in 1890, emphasizes love for God and others and service to all. This Christian, liberal arts college has a tradition of nurturing the mind, body, and spirit toward maturity and wholeness. Because Asbury seeks to promote lifestyles that will last a lifetime, students, faculty, and administrators pledge themselves to standards of self-discipline, integrity, and excellence anchored to biblical principles. Many Asbury elements focus on the responsibilities of personhood learned during the college years:

✦ FIRST-YEAR PROGRAMS. During fall orientation and throughout the fall semester, 42 upperclassmen, known as "TAG" ("Transition and Guidance") Leaders, guide first-year and transfer students through their transition to college life through meetings, activities, and mentoring.

✦ VOLUNTEER SERVICE. Almost three-quarters of the Asbury student body is involved in community service each semester. Many opportunities to serve exist, such as "Reach Out" community service days, international service opportunities, and a servant-leader residential complex that confers more privileges than the other residence halls on campus but requires vigorous participation in community improvement as well as campus leadership.

✦ STUDENT LEADERSHIP. The "LEAD-ON!" program gives students the chance to develop their leadership abilities by working through a prescribed curriculum and attending workshops, seminars, and other special events.

✦ FACULTY AND CURRICULUM. Faculty members integrate mind-broadening study with Christian principles and an emphasis on servant leadership. Professors work side-by-side with students in community service events and host international service travel opportunities. Many faculty members also voluntarily pray before their classes and lead students in short devotionals. Forums for the discussion of moral and ethical behavior are provided in many classes, such as Introduction to Philosophy and Western Civilization.

✦ CIVIC EDUCATION. Most of Asbury's majors encourage—if not require—an internship to enable the student to apply classroom skills in real-world environments. The teacher education program requires students to complete a semester of student teaching before receiving their diplomas. These students must demonstrate 10 standards of excellence that include showing "moral and ethical character." As they did in the 1996 Atlanta Olympics, media communication students will work alongside professionals to broadcast the 2000 Sydney Olympics and the 2002 Salt Lake City Olympics.

✦ SPIRITUAL GROWTH. The spiritual life of students is an important part of their Asbury experience. More than 100 small groups devoted to spiritual growth and accountability meet regularly. Three student chapels, also attended by faculty and staff, are held weekly. By living in an environment that challenges growth through personal relationships and critical thinking, students are better able to define their beliefs and ascertain their responsibilities in the world.

Asbury is devoted to its mission of academic excellence and spiritual vitality to equip men and women for a life of learning, leadership, and service to the professions, society, family, and the church.

ASBURY COLLEGE

1 MACKLEM DRIVE
WILMORE, KY 40390

606.858.3511
http://www.asbury.edu/

UNDERGRADUATES: 1,300

"My experiences at Asbury have cultivated my understanding that to freely give of myself in serving others, I must work to develop within myself the qualities I so deeply desire to share."

—AN ASBURY THIRD-YEAR STUDENT

Other Asbury Profiles:

• Profile of President Gyertson
• Student Leadership Program

AUGUSTANA COLLEGE

2001 SOUTH SUMMIT
SIOUX FALLS, SD 57197-0001

605.336.0770
http://www.augie.edu/

UNDERGRADUATES: 1,600

"When you attend Augie, you can't help but grow in a positive way as a Christian, student, leader, and friend."

—AN AUGUSTANA SECOND-YEAR
STUDENT

AUGUSTANA COLLEGE, founded in 1860, is the largest private college in South Dakota. At this four-year liberal arts school affiliated with the Evangelical Lutheran Church in America, where a liberal arts education means "providing an education of enduring worth," the faculty and staff strive to help students develop skills that are crucial in this changing world.

Augustana's cornerstone character-development programs include:

✦ FIRST-YEAR PROGRAMS. First-year students work together on service projects during orientation and attend monthly residence hall programs on themes such as effective decision-making and leadership. The Dean of Students office provides special academic and social support for first-year students and communicates regularly with parents.

✦ FACULTY AND CURRICULUM. The Core of Liberal Studies requires all students to take courses such as "Faith and Meaning" and "Developing Values, Perspectives, and Commitments." All faculty members are expected to contribute to Augustana's spiritual and religious mission. The college's endowed Chair of Moral Values has the responsibility of ensuring that both curricular and cocurricular activities reflect Augustana's focus on ethics and character development.

✦ SPIRITUAL GROWTH. Two full-time campus pastors lead weekday chapel services and Sunday worship, as well as provide students with individual counseling from a Christian perspective. The campus ministry coordinates a wide range of religious and social action programs, including discipleship groups, Bible study groups, and ministry outreach groups. The Director of Outreach Ministries coordinates Augustana's "SALT" ("Serving and Learning Together") program, which helps students secure off-campus service opportunities. All Augustana students are required to take two religion courses.

✦ SENIOR-YEAR PROGRAMS. Senior capstone courses, required of all students, are taught by interdisciplinary faculty teams and challenge students to wrestle with issues of meaning and moral values. Through exploring a variety of topics, seniors explore the relationship between their college courses and the perennial questions and issues of human purpose.

Augustana students are asked to view their education not as an advantage they can use for their own profit but as a tool they can use to benefit others. The college works hard to nurture students into developing a strong sense of responsibility and commitment. At graduation, the college asks each student to contribute fully to their families, congregations, communities, and country. As one graduating senior put it, "I don't feel any other college could have provided the personal attention, both in and out of the classroom, that Augustana has given me to prepare me to enter the world as a contributor."

In short, Augustana students graduate ready to lead lives that exemplify the college's motto: "Enter to learn; leave to serve."

Azusa Pacific emerged in 1965 as a contemporary institution formed nearly 100 years ago from two independent schools—Los Angeles Pacific College and Azusa College founded in 1899 as the Training School for Christian Workers. The Azusa Pacific mission is to "advance the work of God in the world through academic excellence in liberal arts and professional programs of higher education that encourage students to develop a Christian perspective of truth and life." The cornerstones of this church-affiliated school that gained university status in 1981—Christ, Scholarship, Community, and Service—represent Azusa Pacific University's vision for developing citizenship and Christian character.

Exemplary programs cultivate a dedication to service and a personal faith:

✦ **First-Year Programs.** At APU, a special effort is made to involve first-year students in volunteer activities. Every fall, new students volunteer for one day at a community clean-up project or participate in "Bridges," a program that takes them to San Francisco to serve for a week in homeless shelters and AIDS hospices. Also, several hundred new students recently cleaned up the Azusa Canyon in the Angeles National Forest.

✦ **Faculty and Curriculum.** A Christian moral perspective is explored in all integrative core courses at APU, and students specifically address issues of personal responsibility and moral character in each of the six required religion courses. The Office of Community Service Learning works alongside more than 50 faculty members who require service-learning projects in their courses and coordinates service projects for nearly 700 students each semester.

✦ **Volunteer Service.** Every undergraduate student gives 30 hours of service each year to surrounding communities. The Office of Campus Ministries and the Institute for Outreach Ministries coordinate numerous service/ministry opportunities, such as mentoring local fourth graders; building houses with Habitat for Humanity; staffing a national youth runaway hotline (1-800-HIT-HOME); tutoring prison inmates earning their GED; and working with teenage mothers, disabled adults, or disadvantaged children.

✦ **Spiritual Growth.** APU prizes spiritual formation as a foundational part of education. Required chapel worship occurs three times a week and remains one of the most popular activities on campus. The faculty, staff, and members of the associated student body coordinate a number of discipleship and counseling programs, including the annual "purity pledge" campaign and the university-sponsored Fellowship of Christian Athletes' "Night of Champions" event, at which world-class athletes invite 4,000 youngsters to make moral and ethical commitments to a healthy, safe lifestyle.

✦ **Senior-Year Programs.** A required senior-year seminar prepares students to understand and express a Christian perspective in the contemporary world. Individual seminar sections focus on social ethics and contemporary social problems, the ethical distinctiveness of Christianity, and professional ethics.

APU fosters the development of the whole person within the context of a Christian worldview. The college's commitment to character development is clearly evident in both the classroom and throughout the campus.

AZUSA PACIFIC UNIVERSITY

901 EAST ALOSTA AVENUE
AZUSA, CA 91702-2701

626.969.3434
http://www.apu.edu/

UNDERGRADUATES: 2,500

"The most influencial and life-changing aspect of my experience at APU has been the countless opportunities to get involved and to serve others."

—AN APU FOURTH-YEAR STUDENT

Other APU Profiles:

• Volunteer Service Program

BAYLOR UNIVERSITY

PO BOX 97056
WACO, TX 76798-7056

254.710.1011
http://www.baylor.edu/

UNDERGRADUATES: 11,000

"The Baylor experience encompasses much more than attending class; it is about developing the whole person. I have been encouraged and mentored not only by professors and administrators but by my peers as well."

—A BAYLOR FOURTH-YEAR STUDENT

OFFERING CHALLENGING EXAMINATION of the world in a Christian context, Baylor University integrates faith with academics to provide the best of both. Chartered in 1845 by the Republic of Texas and affiliated with the Baptist General Convention of Texas, Baylor is the state's oldest institution of higher education in continuous operation and the world's largest Baptist university.

Baylor focuses on character development through these faith-based and academically intensive programs:

◆ FIRST-YEAR PROGRAMS. Freshmen and transfer students are encouraged to begin their Baylor careers with "Welcome Week," a time to become acclimated to the campus and provide a foundation for success in all areas of life. Current students work with small groups of newcomers to introduce the educational ideal of a balanced development of the whole person—spiritual, intellectual, social, and physical—in the university's Christian environment.

◆ FACULTY AND CURRICULUM. While the Baylor Interdisciplinary Core and Honors and University Scholars programs underscore the academic challenges to be found at the university, students select Civic Education and Community Service courses that combine service with academic components.

◆ VOLUNTEER SERVICE. More than 250 university-recognized social, honor, and service organizations give students opportunities to develop personal skills and to engage in community outreach throughout the year. Also, the university's award-winning "Steppin' Out" program establishes a day each semester dedicated for students, faculty, and staff to give back to the community—from painting homes for senior citizens and repairing neighborhood parks to tutoring at-risk children in local schools.

◆ SPIRITUAL GROWTH. Building on its heritage, Baylor recently created the Institute for Faith and Learning to enhance the university's distinctive educational environment. The Institute exists to exemplify, sustain, and deepen faith commitments in academically responsible ways to cultivate a continuing conversation among faculty, staff, and students about religious identity and its place at the university.

The university's mission statement articulates a commitment to "provide an environment that fosters spiritual maturity, strength of character, and moral virtue." Of the more than 80,000 living Baylor alumni, graduates take on leadership roles in their communities, and pursue careers that lead them to service as ministers and judges, doctors and teachers, artists and business leaders.

L<small>EARNING AND FAITH</small> go hand-in-hand at Bethel College, where faculty begin their classes with prayer and chapel shapes the core of campus life. This private college is part of the Missionary Church, an evangelical denomination with roots in both the Mennonite and Methodist traditions. Bethel's character-building programs include:

✦ F<small>IRST-YEAR</small> P<small>ROGRAMS</small>. The "Freshman Year Experience" is a sequence of courses that introduces students to biblical principles and instills the value of community service. Students learn the joy of giving by serving at Hannah's House, a home for unwed mothers founded jointly by the college and other regional organizations; at Hope Rescue Mission; and through various initiatives, including volunteer tutoring.

✦ V<small>OLUNTEER</small> S<small>ERVICE</small>. In the fall semester, all students spend one day working throughout the community washing windows, raking leaves, and cleaning up. Bethel nursing students volunteer in inner-city clinics, and other students work on Habitat for Humanity projects and the Shelter for the Homeless. In 1998, Bethel students recorded more than 28,000 hours of community service, and Bethel received the Chairman's "Top Hat" Award from the South Bend Chamber of Commerce for its community efforts.

✦ S<small>TUDENT</small> L<small>EADERSHIP</small>. Students are elected as full members of all standing college committees at Bethel, giving them practical opportunities to understand how to run an institution, translate moral and ethical precepts into administrative processes, and manage people. For example, by participating in the interview process for new faculty, students gain the opportunity to observe how character and faith can be professional criteria.

✦ S<small>PIRITUAL</small> G<small>ROWTH</small>. Discipleship houses and chapels promote spiritual growth. In the "Houses of Higher Learning," cross-cultural living and sharing are the main focus of the living experience. Anglo–African–American houses have been the most common, but Asian, Latino, Hawaiian, and American Sign Language students have also participated.

✦ C<small>IVIC</small> E<small>DUCATION</small>. The Task Force Program enables students to participate in short-term missions and work teams throughout the world. To date, more than 900 students and staff have taken more than 40 overseas trips. The program exposes students to living conditions that expand their understanding of the scope and depth of their privileges and responsibilities as Americans. In the summer of 1998, seven Bethel students traveled to an Eskimo village in the Arctic Circle and eight traveled to a Yanomamo village in southern Venezuela.

✦ S<small>ENIOR-YEAR</small> P<small>ROGRAMS</small>. "The Senior Experience" capstone course reinforces the ethical and moral values that have been taught to and modeled for Bethel students since their freshman year. The students write a thesis in which they assess their goals and values as well as the effects of their actions in the world.

In the words of President Norman Bridges, Bethel's purpose is "to teach students to love wisdom and justice, to love fairness and right dealing, and to care deeply for the world around them." Students leave Bethel with a strong commitment to Christian values and service to others.

B<small>ETHEL</small> C<small>OLLEGE</small>

1001 WEST MCKINLEY AVENUE
MISHAWAKA, IN 46545

219.259.8511
http://www.bethel-in.edu/

UNDERGRADUATES: 1,500

"Through a dedicated faculty, a variety of opportunities, and a vital faith, Bethel encourages its students to discover their passions and strengths."

—A B<small>ETHEL</small> <small>SECOND-YEAR</small>
<small>STUDENT</small>

BIRMINGHAM-SOUTHERN COLLEGE

900 ARKADELPHIA ROAD
BIRMINGHAM, AL 35254

205.226.4600
http://www.bsc.edu/

UNDERGRADUATES: 1,400

*"A BSC education
is not limited to the
facts of the textbook
or the material of the
syllabus. I have learned
that practical, real-
world experience is
necessary for us to be
better citizens of our
communities."*

—A BSC FOURTH-YEAR
STUDENT

Since its founding in 1856, Birmingham-Southern College has encouraged academic and moral distinction in its students. The stated mission of this liberal arts college affiliated with the United Methodist Church is "to provide a liberal arts education of distinctive quality that challenges students to think independently and communicate clearly, to examine the arts and sciences aesthetically and critically, and to be committed to intellectual and social responsibility." BSC's contributions to character education include:

✦ ACADEMIC HONESTY. BSC conveys the importance of developing personal responsibility and integrity by its Honor Code. Students pledge that they will abide by the Code, neither giving nor receiving aid on academic work. A student-run Honor Council handles violations of the Code. Through this system of self-governance, students play an integral role in providing a campus atmosphere in which to develop intellectually, morally, and socially with maturity and self-esteem.

✦ FACULTY AND CURRICULUM. BSC recently revised its general education curriculum. Entitled the "Expanded Paradigm of General Education," this initiative has eight areas, such as "Moral and Civic Imagination," which BSC considers to be critical areas of learning for all students.

✦ STUDENT LEADERSHIP. BSC has been nationally recognized by the Center of Creative Leadership. This interdisciplinary program helps students realize leadership potential by combining academic studies with significant community service.

✦ VOLUNTEER SERVICE. In 1999, the Leadership Studies and Service Learning Programs were combined to form the Hess Center for Leadership and Service Learning. Service Learning is an approach to local and international community involvement that encourages students to engage in service to others and reflect on their experience. The Service Learning office operates 11 student-run, ongoing community service projects and coordinates international trips to such places as Calcutta, India, working with Mother Teresa's Missionaries of Charity, as well as domestic service-learning projects during the year.

✦ CIVIC EDUCATION. Every year BSC offers programs for high-school students on the topic of ethics and values. Also, BSC has hosted speakers such as nationally recognized ethicist Michael Josephson.

✦ SPIRITUAL GROWTH. As a faith-centered, church-related institution, BSC intentionally promotes spiritual growth and moral values. The school operates under the auspices of the United Methodist Church and is mindful of the ecumenical spirit of Methodism. As a part of that atmosphere, BSC supports students seeking spiritual meaning in their lives by offering six weekly chapel services and opportunities for Bible study.

Grounded in a commitment to liberal arts and community-oriented education, BSC focuses on helping students grow intellectually, spiritually, and morally to help them commit themselves to life-long learning and social responsibility.

Other BSC Profiles:

• Profile of President Berte
• Student Leadership Program

Since 1899, Bluffton College has preserved its Mennonite "peace church" tradition, which emphasizes a commitment to truth and nonviolence. At the heart of a Bluffton education is its motto: "The Truth Makes Free." In addition to maintaining the academic standards required for a high-quality liberal arts education, Bluffton encourages its faculty, staff, and students to commit themselves to the Christian faith and life. This mission is evident in Bluffton's various objectives and programs:

✦ First-Year Program. One of Bluffton's goals is to develop in its students a global perspective and instill in them the responsibility to create a more humane community. The general education curriculum begins and ends with courses that develop that moral foundation. The interdisciplinary "Seminar in Identity" challenges first-year students with questions of how we come to be who we are.

✦ Academic Honesty. A "community of respect" statement, which is used extensively in new student orientation, reminds students that building trust and fairness into academic life is a shared responsibility. A distinctive honor system requires and respects students' pledges to academic honesty and good citizenship. Students observe this honor system in taking examinations and writing research papers.

✦ Faculty and Curriculum. Faculty members pursue intellectual excellence and maintain a commitment to lives of integrity, service, justice, peace, and community. Lectures and presentations cover topics that challenge students personally and spiritually.

✦ Volunteer Service. Service is a core value at Bluffton. A required cross-cultural and service-learning experience helps students develop compassion, justice, and peacemaking. Local service projects for new students, student organizational trips, and participation in the campus chapter of Habitat for Humanity provide positive ways to counter the self-centeredness of today's popular culture.

✦ Substance-Abuse Prevention. "BChamps," a program for student athletes, and "PALS" (Peer Awareness Leaders), a student peer education organization, emphasize values clarification, avoiding addictive behaviors, sexual responsibility, diversity appreciation, community building, and positive self-esteem. Last year, PALS was one of 12 nationwide chapters to receive an Outstanding Affiliate Award.

✦ Spiritual Growth. Students explore the spiritual dimension of community life through structured and informal activities. A campus pastor and assistant provide leadership for formal religious life; residence hall chaplains serve as peer spiritual resources; and Brothers and Sisters in Christ integrates Bible study and values development.

✦ Senior-Year Program. The senior capstone course, "Christian Values in Global Community," examines ethics, community, and the environment.

Bluffton equips its students with the skills and values for lifelong learning, a strong service ethic, and an understanding of their role as world citizens. The pursuit of truth at Bluffton encourages students to become critical thinkers shaped by a commitment to moral values and spiritual wholeness.

BLUFFTON COLLEGE

280 WEST COLLEGE AVENUE
BLUFFTON, OH 45817

419.358.3000
http://www.bluffton.edu/

UNDERGRADUATES: 1,000

"The classes, programs, and activities at Bluffton have strengthened my beliefs and skills. I have been challenged to develop a value system that can stand up to criticism but that is also open to the opinions and ideas of others."

—A Bluffton fourth-year student

Other Bluffton Profiles:

• Academic Honesty Program
• First-Year Program
• Senior-Year Program

BRIGHAM YOUNG UNIVERSITY

PROVO, UT 84602-0002

801.378.1211
http://www.byu.edu/

UNDERGRADUATES: 27,000

"My education at BYU has enabled me to learn that character is much more than just personal integrity; it becomes a matter of love for humanity. My education is not solely for my own benefit—it is a gift to the world."

—A BYU FOURTH-YEAR STUDENT

"EDUCATION is the power to think clearly, the power to act well in the world's work, and the power to appreciate life." So stated Brigham Young early in the century about the private, church-affiliated, liberal arts institution erected in his name in 1875. An undergraduate education at Brigham Young University—founded, supported, and guided by The Church of Jesus Christ of Latter-day Saints—brings together academic scholarship and a commitment to spiritual integrity. A rich offering of religion classes and devotionals contribute to the spiritual strength of BYU students.

BYU's numerous programs demonstrate faculty, staff, and student commitment to establishing responsible citizenship and strengthening spiritual faith:

✦ FIRST-YEAR PROGRAMS. Each new BYU student is welcomed to the university by a trained upperclass advisor, who assists the new student in his or her adjustment to campus life. New students can also participate in the Freshman Academy program, which seeks to help first-year students succeed socially and academically by enrolling groups of students together in classes. These groups of students eat, live, and study together.

✦ ACADEMIC HONESTY. As a matter of personal commitment, BYU students, staff, and faculty are asked to demonstrate in daily living those moral virtues encompassed in the Gospel. Honesty, virtue, obedience to the law, clean language, respect for others, and abstinence are ingredients of the campus Honor Code, and the Student Honor Association works to inspire individual students to meet and strengthen their personal commitments.

✦ FACULTY AND CURRICULUM. BYU aims not merely to teach students a code of ethics but to help them develop character traits that flow from the long-term application of Gospel teachings to their lives. Moral choices are carefully examined in classroom discussions, leadership conferences, forums, and seminars. A rigorous general education requirement exposes all undergraduates to the philosophies and critical reasoning of humanity's significant philosophers and leaders.

✦ VOLUNTEER SERVICE. Along with developing young people of faith, intellect, and character, BYU prepares students for a lifetime of learning and service. A service ethic permeates every part of BYU activities, from the admissions process through classroom and cocurricular activities. Each year, the university publicly honors students who have made significant contributions of service to others.

✦ SUBSTANCE-ABUSE PREVENTION. Every student enrolled at the university agrees in writing to abstain completely from any illegal drug use, as well as to abstain from the abuse of legal drugs. The university has a "zero-tolerance" policy for illegal drug use, and those involved in such use are asked to leave the university. Student leaders and athletes regularly meet with local high-school students in an effort to decrease drug use in the Provo community.

BYU's founders believed that the university's commitment to character development was essential to its mission and purpose. Today, faculty and staff remain focused on providing students with a challenging learning environment that connects scholarship with a rich and inspiring religious tradition.

Iɴ ᴀ sᴍᴀʟʟ ᴍᴏᴜɴᴛᴀɪɴ ᴠɪʟʟᴀɢᴇ in Ecuador, clean drinking water is available where there had been only a polluted stream. In 1994, a team of Calvin College engineering students designed and installed a water collection and distribution system in Calohousi Grande, but "learning to serve" is not unique to the engineering department.

Founded in 1876, this Christian, liberal arts college is not for everyone. Calvin couples rigorous academic demands with a worldview that requires engagement in community issues. Faculty and students live Calvin's mission statement: "Through our learning, we seek to be agents of renewal in the academy, church, and society... offering our hearts and lives to do God's work in God's world." And every part of the world is open to study, with the goal of teaching students to commit themselves to an intentional way of life through numerous programs and requirements:

3201 BURTON STREET SE
GRAND RAPIDS, MI 49546

616.957.6000
http://www.calvin.edu/

UNDERGRADUATES: 3,900

✦ Vᴏʟᴜɴᴛᴇᴇʀ Sᴇʀᴠɪᴄᴇ. The introduction to service learning begins with orientation, during which all new students participate in "Streetfest," an initiative that sends 1,000 students into Grand Rapids to embark on service projects before they have taken their first class. Later, as students mature academically, they offer their expertise through coursework: the accounting class offers free tax assistance to senior citizens, a music class uses the national Education Through Music program to teach parenting to pregnant teens and unwed mothers, and a recreation class works with at-risk teens in an urban high school.

✦ Fɪʀsᴛ-Yᴇᴀʀ Pʀᴏɢʀᴀᴍs. Calvin believes that responsible adulthood begins as students enter its front gate, not as they graduate. Incoming students are immediately introduced to the concept of "responsible freedom," in which Calvin challenges students to make their own decisions, encouraging them to choose wisely. One of their first learning experiences, and one that Calvin students won't likely forget, is the first-year English class. Students meet weekly with senior citizens who provide the stories and wisdom that are the basis for all writing assignments. The senior partners receive bound copies of their life histories at the close of the semester.

"Calvin helped me find out what my gifts are and how they can be used for service in God's world."

—A Cᴀʟᴠɪɴ sᴇᴄᴏɴᴅ-ʏᴇᴀʀ
STUDENT

✦ Cɪᴠɪᴄ Eᴅᴜᴄᴀᴛɪᴏɴ. Calvin's curriculum emphasizes off-campus study to provide students with learning experiences that have unusually deep and long-lasting effects on them spiritually and morally, with a special emphasis on developing a cross-cultural consciousness. Students do development work in Honduras, study language in Spain, and experience both subtle and radical differences in culture in England, Hungary, and China that prepare them to enter society with a breadth of vision and depth of commitment to making life better for all others.

✦ Sᴘɪʀɪᴛᴜᴀʟ Gʀᴏᴡᴛʜ. Programs such as "LOFT" ("Living Our Faith Together"), a Sunday-night worship celebration, combine group Bible studies with a mentoring program to nourish the spirit.

During the college experience, Calvin develops young people who step into the world with values, a sense of integrity, the hope of making a difference, and a deep-seated commitment to the college's mission.

Other Calvin Profiles:

• Academic Honesty Program
• Character & Sexuality Program
• Civic Education Program
• Faculty & Curriculum Program
• Volunteer Service Program

CARROLL COLLEGE

100 NORTH EAST AVENUE
WAUKESHA, WI 53186

414.547.1211
http://www.cc.edu/

UNDERGRADUATES: 2,400

"Carroll helps us develop into well-rounded individuals by exposing us to many frontiers of life. I feel prepared academically, socially, and mentally for the challenges ahead."

—A CARROLL FOURTH-YEAR STUDENT

CARROLL COLLEGE is dedicated to educating students who will become global citizens and who will have the character to lead with integrity and passion. Founded in 1846 as a church-affiliated, liberal arts college, Carroll fosters a learning environment based on seven ideals: valuing human diversity and the dignity of all people and respecting their ideas, opinions, and traditions; practicing personal academic integrity; caring for the physical environment of the campus and its neighborhood setting; supporting and enhancing the development of others; encouraging creativity, artistic expression, and excellence in all areas of their lives; seeking to understand their purpose in the world; and dedicating themselves to exploring personal values and the spiritual quest for meaning.

Turning students into leaders is at the foundation of Carroll's curriculum and cocurricular activities:

✦ STUDENT LEADERSHIP. "Challenge 2000+," a three-part, entirely volunteer program, prepares students to serve as leaders on campus and in their communities. Based on a leadership model, this program proposes that to become effective leaders students must develop organizational skills, clarify their personal values, and become involved in society's most relevant issues. The program offers students many opportunities to lead, such as becoming resident assistants or orientation leaders. It also teaches them the concept of following, emphasizing that by being good followers students will learn the art of cooperation and realize their potential as organizers and workers.

✦ VOLUNTEER SERVICE. The philosophy underlying Carroll's leadership program is that leaders "give back" to the school by serving others. Each year, students participate in more than 100 community service projects, such as serving food at soup kitchens, volunteering for Special Olympics, and tutoring children at local elementary schools.

✦ FIRST-YEAR PROGRAMS. First- and second-year students apply to and are accepted to "Challenge 2000+" based on their commitment to learning. Students in the third phase of the program arrange community service opportunities for first-year students. Students choose to be a part of the leadership program because they want to become leaders in the next century; they do not receive academic credit for participating.

✦ CIVIC EDUCATION. The mission of the service-based student senate is to challenge students to explore the concerns they see on campus and develop their integrity while resolving issues. Students also participate in voter registration drives to support their commitment to civic responsibility.

Carroll encourages students to pursue activities that will help them become leaders in society. As a result, the number of students applying for leadership positions on campus has increased. By assuming such roles early on, students begin to understand their purpose in the world and become caring individuals who encourage development, vision, and creativity in others.

SINCE ITS FOUNDING IN 1854, Central Methodist College has blended a values-based liberal arts tradition with professional preparation to help students develop into "leaders of character." Primarily a residential campus, CMC focuses on the full development of each member of the college community. Through close relationships with faculty, staff, and classmates, students participate in all facets of campus life. As they help shape the future of the college through their broad range of activities, students report that "at CMC, I learned I could do anything." This is achieved through the following programs:

✦ FIRST-YEAR PROGRAMS. Initiated in 1987, CMC's first-year program has increased student retention more than 20%. Faculty advisors teach the course, introducing new students to college life and work and emphasizing issues of character development. Through the current text, *Call to Character* (edited by Colin Greer and Herbert Kohl), as well as discussions and writing assignments, students examine the importance of becoming educated, responsible citizens.

✦ FACULTY AND CURRICULUM. A faculty task force is redesigning CMC's general education requirement around a "Character Core" that includes the first- and senior-year seminars, new required courses in literature and religion, a choice of "character intensive" courses across the curriculum, and a range of courses addressing character and diversity.

✦ VOLUNTEER SERVICE. Through practical internships and participation in service and spiritual organizations, students provide community service that includes urban neighborhood clean up, providing home-based help for people needing assistance, developing library resources at the local jail, working at various community care centers, and initiating a local chapter of Habitat for Humanity. Students may also serve in Rotaract, affiliated with the local Rotary organization.

✦ SPIRITUAL GROWTH. CMC's strong relationship with the United Methodist Church provides much of the college's ethos. Because CMC's educational model promotes intellectual, social, physical, and spiritual development, opportunities for spiritual growth abound. The Wesley Foundation offers weekly student-led chapel services, Bible study groups, covenant and fellowship gatherings, and personal faith discussions. The annual "Christian Perspectives Week" features speakers and worship leaders that engage students in reflection and dialog. Required courses in religion teach students about a range of spiritual traditions and beliefs while helping them clarify their own assumptions and convictions.

✦ SENIOR-YEAR PROGRAMS. CMC's senior capstone course engages students in a collaborative project emphasizing service to the college or community. The current text, *The Moral Compass* (edited by William J. Bennett), stimulates discussion and writing assignments focusing on issues of character and ethical and moral decision-making. This course serves as a corollary to the first-year seminar, especially as some seniors mentor incoming students.

Just as CMC changes the lives of its students, its graduates change the lives of others through professional and civic activities. A strong sense of responsibility is the heart of CMC, and character is its foundation.

CENTRAL METHODIST COLLEGE

411 CENTRAL METHODIST SQUARE
FAYETTE, MO 65248

660.248.3391
http://www.cmc.edu/

UNDERGRADUATES: 1,200

"CMC has changed my life forever. The faculty found something in me that I did not know existed, helping me develop into a better student and person."

—A CMC THIRD-YEAR STUDENT

Other CMC Profiles:

• Faculty & Curriculum Program
• First-Year Program
• Senior-Year Program
• Spiritual Growth Program

CHAPMAN UNIVERSITY

333 NORTH GLASSELL STREET
ORANGE, CA 92866

714.997.6815
http://www.chapman.edu/

UNDERGRADUATES: 2,600

"Chapman's vision of personalized education is more than a mission statement; it's a commitment. Chapman has changed me, and I—like other students—have changed Chapman."

—A CHAPMAN THIRD-YEAR STUDENT

CHAPMAN UNIVERSITY has pursued its mission of "personalized" liberal arts education to prepare students to lead inquiring, ethical, and productive lives as global citizens through active commitment to the Christian Church. Founded in 1861, it gained university status in 1991. Busts of Albert Schweitzer, George Washington, Adam Smith, Martin Luther King, Jr., and others are located throughout campus to encourage students to reflect on the relationship between knowledge, faith, compassion, and service. Chapman demonstrates this commitment throughout its curriculum and activities.

✦ FIRST-YEAR PROGRAM. All new students participate in the Freshman Seminar Program, which helps them develop critical-thinking skills through reflection on values, not only their own, but those of others and of societies past and present.

✦ FACULTY AND CURRICULUM. Required courses in Western Civilization and World Cultures help students understand how ethics and values have shaped our world. The Honors Program encourages students to explore the ideas of great thinkers and challenges them to consider how these ideas apply to their own lives and their role in society.

✦ VOLUNTEER SERVICE. Faculty, staff, and students regularly participate in campus-wide community service projects through the Community Service Council. The faculty encourages and, in some cases, requires service projects to supplement course work. During orientation, new students have the opportunity to engage in service to the surrounding community. They continue to participate in service projects throughout the year through fraternities, sororities, and other student organizations. Through "GIVE" ("Getting Involved in Volunteer Efforts"), students paint classrooms at a local school, refurbish equipment for the local YMCA, organize food donations to the Second Harvest Food Bank, and collect gifts for children with AIDS. A Student Development Transcript provides students with a record of their participation in various service-related projects.

✦ SUBSTANCE-ABUSE PREVENTION. Chapman sponsors activities and provides information to enable students to make responsible decisions about their physical and mental well-being. Students may be trained to serve as peer educators to help fellow students address issues of substance abuse, sexual activity, and conflict resolution.

✦ SPIRITUAL GROWTH. Chapman is dedicated to helping students develop spiritually. Two years ago, the president established the office of Dean of the Chapel to encourage the growth of spiritually/religiously based student organizations, with the objective of having a group for each of the religions represented on campus. The Dean of the Chapel also has assisted in raising funds to build the new campus chapel.

From the moment they arrive at Chapman, students are oriented toward community service and individual spiritual growth. Chapman provides its students with an environment of active learning in which they can develop skills in character building and civic responsibility.

Other Chapman Profiles:

• Spiritual Growth Program

THE GUIDING PRINCIPLES and ethics of Clarke College are derived from the core values of the Sisters of Charity of the Blessed Virgin Mary (BVMs). Since 1843, the BVMs have established a respect for education that is evident in the personal interest that they and a committed lay faculty take in students' potential, progress, and achievements. Respect for education and a dedication to freedom, charity, and justice are evident throughout Clarke's curriculum:

✦ FIRST-YEAR PROGRAMS. The Freshman Seminar enables new students to participate in peer group discussions led by faculty facilitators, in which they focus on issues of personal responsibility as mature, responsible adults who treat others—as well as themselves—with human respect and dignity.

✦ FACULTY AND CURRICULUM. The core of Clarke's liberal arts curriculum is the General Education Program, in which students select courses in religion, the arts, humanities, sciences, and philosophy. Students examine issues critical to the content and discuss ethical and moral responses. Well-respected professors teach first-year students as well as seniors. Faculty and staff share a common optimism about students' potential, demonstrating sensitivity and integrity both in and outside the classroom.

✦ VOLUNTEER SERVICE. During the year, most resident students participate in some volunteer activity coordinated through the Campus Ministry. They may tutor or mentor elementary students as part of their federal work-study programs or volunteer in nursing or physical therapy or at homes for the aged or physically challenged.

✦ STUDENT LEADERSHIP. Clarke is committed to developing students who exhibit a collaborative leadership style and who can be positive role models for their peers. Student leaders are actively involved in organizing student activities, managing residence halls, and programming. They learn practical skills such as budgeting, time management, and team building.

✦ SPIRITUAL GROWTH. Clarke offers many opportunities for students to explore and strengthen their spirituality. Students may participate in Catholic liturgies, nondenominational prayer groups, and Bible study. Two major spiritual retreats are held twice a year—the Antioch Retreat (open to all students) and the Journey Retreat (for students approaching graduation).

✦ CIVIC EDUCATION. Students are encouraged to develop civic responsibility, for example through the Honors Program by conducting research that is related to a need in the community or relevant field of inquiry. This work is compiled and distributed to appropriate agencies that benefit from free, high-quality research that they otherwise would not have been able to afford. Students learn that the more talent they are given, the more they need to give back.

✦ RESPONSIBLE LIVING PROGRAMS. Clarke takes a proactive approach to substance-abuse prevention through education and group and individual counseling. Student-led programs go beyond rule enforcement to help change perceptions and behaviors. Through the Social Action Theatre, students explore real-life issues of alcohol abuse and sexuality to promote responsibility, problem-solving skills, and mutual respect.

Clarke's mission is to guide students toward a larger vision, one that enables them to develop the knowledge, experience, and world perspective to make ethical and moral choices.

CLARKE COLLEGE

1550 CLARKE DRIVE
DUBUQUE, IA 52001

319.588.6300
http://www.clarke.edu/

UNDERGRADUATES: 1,200

"Character building often happens outside the classroom. Faculty and staff promote an environment that fosters respect, responsibility, and a spirit of cooperation."

—A CLARKE THIRD-YEAR STUDENT

COLLEGE OF MOUNT ST. JOSEPH

5701 DELHI ROAD
CINCINNATI, OH 45233-1670

513.244.4200
http://www.msj.edu/

UNDERGRADUATES: 2,300

"I have had the opportunity to become a student leader and to travel to places where I've witnessed the lives of the poor. These experiences have deepened my faith, helped me understand our society, and shown me how I can contribute."

—A MOUNT ST. JOSEPH
FOURTH-YEAR STUDENT

THE COLLEGE OF MOUNT ST. JOSEPH is dedicated to educating good citizens within the framework of its Catholic tradition and mission. Founded in 1920 by the Sisters of Charity, the Mount fosters an environment that challenges students intellectually and spiritually so that they can develop the skills, character, and judgment to become informed citizens. The Mount's Christian philosophy is integrated with the liberal arts and career preparation and is at the heart of its academic programs and cocurricular activities:

✦ FACULTY AND CURRICULUM. Regardless of major, students must fulfill general education requirements in ethics, religion, and philosophy. These courses provide students with the foundation they need to nurture sound judgment; develop a lifelong passion for service; and recognize their obligations to God, themselves, and others. Students with exceptional academic achievement participate in the Mount's Honors Program, through which they take responsibility for their own learning under the guidance of experienced faculty members.

✦ VOLUNTEER SERVICE. The Mount Model of Service Learning helps students reflect on their basic responsibilities as citizens. Students engage in this process through "Plus One Option," the Mount's nationally recognized program in which students are awarded an additional free credit for participating in service projects and assessing their experiences. Through involvement in these activities, students learn about diversity and community building. Faculty and staff accompany students to such destinations as the Lakota Indian Reservation in South Dakota, Tierra Madre Mission in New Mexico, Cincinnati's own impoverished neighborhoods, and to communities in Appalachia and Nicaragua.

✦ SUBSTANCE-ABUSE PREVENTION. The Mount's approach to wellness focuses on providing services and activities that reach out to students and help them integrate spirituality with healthy lifestyle choices. The Peer Educator Program trains students to provide support and practical responses to those learning to resist the use and abuse of alcohol, drugs, and tobacco.

✦ STUDENT LEADERSHIP. "TEAM" ("Together Each Accomplishes More") prepares students for leadership roles. The Student Government Association encourages all students to participate in the Mount's governance process and in student clubs and organizations. Membership and leadership opportunities within these organizations provide students with cocurricular activities that complement educational programs and foster intellectual, spiritual, social, and physical development.

✦ SPIRITUAL GROWTH. The Mount aims to build a Christian community in which students, faculty, and staff deepen their understanding of the Catholic faith. Students plan and take part in liturgies, prayer groups, spiritual retreats, and service activities that promote spiritual development.

The Mount promotes academic excellence while emphasizing Christian values. Through this focus, it prepares students to reach their full potential academically, professionally, and—most important—personally as they become active, involved citizens.

THE COLLEGE OF SAINT BENEDICT for women and Saint John's University for men work in partnership to provide a liberal arts education founded on Benedictine principles. Two of only five Catholic schools recognized as selective national liberal arts colleges, CSB and SJU, founded in 1913 and 1857, respectively, have received national recognition for their unique educational experience. Together, they challenge students to live balanced lives of learning, work, leadership, and service in a changing world.

Faculty and staff believe that moral development and service learning produce students who are able to positively affect their world. To foster emotional, cognitive, spiritual, and social development, CSB and SJU offer the following character-building programs:

✦ STUDENT LEADERSHIP. The goal of the Leadership Initiative is to help develop people who will practice shared ethical leadership over their lifetime. Programs for CSB and SJU students include student employment leadership training, discussions on leadership and ethics, integration of service into leadership activities, and the "Courageous Kids" program.

✦ VOLUNTEER SERVICE. The Benedictine character of service prizes social justice and promotes peace and the common good. To instill CSB and SJU students with an understanding of service remains a primary goal, and 600 students participate in "VISTO" ("Volunteers in Service to Others"), an organization serving the local community. Other initiatives include Spring Break Trips (more than 20 service programs), the Urban Plunge Retreat program (80 students work with inner-city communities), "Hunger and Homelessness Week," "Celebration of Service," "AIDS Awareness Week," and "Martin Luther King Week."

✦ SPIRITUAL GROWTH. At CSB and SJU, the peer ministry model exemplifies focused student leadership in relation to spiritual life. Students shape, plan, and execute spiritual events on campus. "Student ministers" live with students and help articulate the vision of Campus Ministry. Full-time professional staff is minimized to endow students with more opportunities for taking initiative.

✦ SUBSTANCE-ABUSE PREVENTION. The area of health and wellness has been a focus at CSB for more than six years, when the provision of healthcare was changed from an illness model to a wellness model. With that philosophical change, the Health Education Office was created to assist students with their knowledge of their future health, well-being, and use of controlled substances. This office promotes speakers who discuss value systems, personal choices, and potential risks related to sexuality, alcohol, drug usage, diet, exercise, and relationships.

✦ SENIOR-YEAR PROGRAM. The Senior Seminar cultivates in junior and senior CSB and SJU students the ability to make "good moral and ethical judgments" that are "consciously made and defensibly maintained." This seminar examines ethical issues from a wide range of disciplines, leading to integrated ethical reasoning with knowledge and interests.

CSB and SJU help students make "an entry into a heritage of leadership and service." Consequently, graduates take meaningful service experiences into the world with them, and they are ready to be active citizens of the world.

COLLEGE OF SAINT BENEDICT & SAINT JOHN'S UNIVERSITY

COLLEGE OF SAINT BENEDICT
37 S. COLLEGE AVE.
ST. JOSEPH, MN 56374
320.363.5308

SAINT JOHN'S UNIVERSITY
COLLEGEVILLE, MN 56321
320.363.2196
http://www.csbsju.edu/

UNDERGRADUATES: 3,800

"CSB and SJU exemplify character development in a liberal arts setting. Through ethical decision making, leadership, community service, and spiritual development, students form a greater knowledge of themselves and their community in an environment that also supports them mind, body, and soul."

—AN SJU SECOND-YEAR STUDENT

Other CSBSJU Profiles:

• Student Leadership Program
• Substance-Abuse Prevention Program

THE COLLEGE OF ST. CATHERINE

2004 RANDOLPH AVENUE
ST. PAUL, MN 55105

651.690.6000
http://www.stkate.edu/

UNDERGRADUATES: 2,300

"St. Catherine's challenges us to integrate academic study and activist work to bring about a more just world. Although the faculty and staff present us with tough issues, they also give us the tools we need to take appropriate action."

—A ST. CATHERINE'S
THIRD-YEAR STUDENT

THE VISION of the College of St. Catherine is to educate women "to lead and influence." Founded as a Catholic, liberal arts institution for women by the Sisters of St. Joseph of Carondelet in 1905, St. Catherine's has been committed to a mission of social justice by preparing students to lead lives dedicated to leadership and community service.

A call to action, an emphasis on ethics and spiritual growth, and academic excellence are integrated throughout St. Catherine's programs and cocurricular activities:

◆ FIRST-YEAR PROGRAMS. "The Reflective Woman" is a multidisciplinary course offered to first-year students that helps them develop reflective judgment using various frameworks from liberal arts traditions. During their first year, students develop a moral compass with which to navigate between greater personal freedom and new responsibilities at college.

◆ CIVIC EDUCATION. Faculty participate in the interdisciplinary Teaching-Learning Network, a vehicle designed to help students become active citizens by engaging them in significant public work with diverse groups of people. A focus on citizenship and education as the work of democracy encourages students to serve and connects their work to Catholic social teachings. This focus cultivates in students the skills, habits, and outlook to recognize the multiple values of work with public purpose. St. Catherine's sponsors many programs to develop students' sense of personal responsibility as citizens. For example, students and faculty may work at The Jane Addams School for Democracy, which works to strengthen community and advance the understanding that democracy depends on the contributions of diverse people working on projects that are vital to all. Students also participate in the Center for Democracy and Citizenship at the Humphrey Institute of the University of Minnesota.

◆ CHARACTER AND SEXUALITY. Students are encouraged to define themselves independently of the narrow expectations of women that society widely holds. Sensitive to its students' needs, St. Catherine's provides high-quality programs in which they acquire knowledge, gain an understanding of their cultural heritage, develop the ability to make critical judgments, and form a commitment to intellectual inquiry.

◆ VOLUNTEER SERVICE. St. Catherine's offers faculty and students many opportunities to engage in meaningful service work in which they donate time to such service projects as the Neighborhood House, a nonprofit community center.

◆ SENIOR-YEAR PROGRAMS. During the third or fourth year, students concentrate on the issue of justice in the interdisciplinary seminar "The Global Search for Justice," in which they examine their own values and how they apply to the world at large.

St. Catherine's adheres to a conviction that religious and ethical values build a framework for living. The school maintains its commitment to the liberal arts as a foundation for students to develop an appreciation for lifelong learning and the pursuit of excellence.

As they pass through the "Gates of Opportunity" to what the *Wall Street Journal* calls "Hard Work U," students can see that College of the Ozarks is not a typical school. Founded in 1906 as a church-affiliated, liberal arts institution, C of O's original mission of "providing a Christian education to youth . . . found worthy but who are without sufficient means" has never changed. All students work on campus in lieu of paying tuition. The strength of C of O lies in its people—faculty, staff, and students—who are determined to make it one of the best small colleges in the U.S. (as recognized by *U.S. News and World Report*). Through the Keeter Center for Character Education and several other initiatives, C of O offers many character-building opportunities:

✦ **First-Year Programs.** Before enrolling, students participate in the two-week orientation program, "Character Camp," in which students work in groups on service projects both on and off campus. Through case studies, they come to understand how to make informed, responsible decisions. They sign an Honor Code Pledge Card acknowledging that lying, stealing, and cheating are not tolerated and complete brief courses stressing trust, responsibility, and correct social behavior.

✦ **Faculty and Curriculum.** All students take two semesters of "Citizenship and Healthy Lifestyles." Faculty focus on leadership skills, patriotic growth, citizenship, and learning to enable students to develop high standards of personal and civic behavior that they are expected to exhibit as role models.

✦ **Civic Education.** C of O provides "a climate where loyalty to American institutions, ideas, and obligations" is based on the knowledge and understanding of US history and government. This is accomplished through required course work, a variety of extracurricular activities, ROTC, and the encouragement of active citizen participation. The Keeter Center's "Citizen Abroad" program fosters awareness of the global community while strengthening appreciation of America. Students can join the Young Republicans or Young Democrats, participate in student government, travel to Washington, DC, with a political science professor during spring break, and participate in voter registration drives.

✦ **Student Leadership.** C of O sends groups to national conferences and meetings such as the Business Ethics Symposium, the National Leadership Forum on Faith and Values, and the National Student Leadership Conferences so they can interact with their peers. Other students participate in conferences sponsored by the Young America's Foundation.

✦ **Volunteer Service.** Students have ample opportunities for service through the Bonner Community Service program and campus chapters of groups such as Rotoract (Rotary Club) and Habitat for Humanity.

✦ **Senior-Year Programs.** All C of O students take an interdisciplinary capstone course in which they examine people throughout history, especially how their ideas, values, and decisions have shaped the world, for better or for worse.

Spiritual and moral integrity are the measurements by which students live their lives, and C of O inspires students—from first day to last—to become exemplary involved citizens and leaders, lifelong learners, and men and women of responsibility.

COLLEGE OF THE OZARKS

POINT LOOKOUT, MO 65726

417.334.6411
http://www.cofo.edu/

UNDERGRADUATES: 1,500

"As a C of O student, I have learned that the classroom offers only the beginning of education. C of O has strengthened my character, taught me the value of work, and allowed me to graduate debt free."

—A C of O fourth-year student

Other C of O Profiles:

• Profile of President Davis
• Academic Honesty Program
• Civic Education Program

Colorado State University

FORT COLLINS, CO 80523-0015

970.491.1101
http://www.colostate.edu/

UNDERGRADUATES: 18,600

"Colorado State provides us with spiritual guidance and the resources we need to learn how we may serve our communities."

—A COLORADO STATE
FOURTH-YEAR STUDENT

Other Colorado State Profiles:

• Faculty & Curriculum Program
• Volunteer Service Program

SINCE IT WAS ESTABLISHED IN 1870 as a public, land-grant institution, Colorado State University's mission has been to turn students into leaders who can successfully and ethically participate in a complex, global society. Colorado State fosters a comprehensive educational environment to encourage students to participate in academic and cocurricular activities that strengthen their moral reasoning skills:

✦ FIRST-YEAR PROGRAMS. The Key Academic Community, a collaborative effort between Student and Academic Affairs, is a residentially based program for first-year students that promotes respect for self and others, a commitment to academic achievement, an acceptance of diversity, and active cocurricular involvement. The University Honors Program offers first-year Honors students a seminar that combines discussion of current national and global issues with an extended orientation to campus programs and services.

✦ FACULTY AND CURRICULUM. Colorado State has a statement of ethical principles for its academic faculty and professional staff that addresses appropriate behavior, professional responsibilities, and ethical choices. By the 2000 fall semester, a revised core curriculum will offer courses specifically designed to increase students' global awareness and understanding by exploring how personal responsibility affects relationships with others.

✦ VOLUNTEER SERVICE. Colorado State encourages students to engage in meaningful service activities. Through the Service Integration Project, they assist faculty in using service learning as an effective teaching tool. They also may participate in activities and trips sponsored by the Office of Service Learning and Volunteer Programs, as well as in numerous outreach activities organized by student groups.

✦ SUBSTANCE-ABUSE PREVENTION. "BOLT" ("Based on Life Theater") is a peer theater group in which student actors address many issues of personal responsibility. The group presents in classrooms, residence halls, and other areas throughout campus.

✦ STUDENT LEADERSHIP. The "President's Leadership Program" is a year-long, interactive, experimental academic course in which students clarify their personal values and examine the relationship between character development and leadership. The program leads students toward a critical examination of themselves and others to help them become "transformational" leaders.

✦ CIVIC EDUCATION. Three of Colorado State's eight academic colleges incorporate personal and civic responsibility into their special educational missions. Students have the opportunity to research and explore such issues as public policy, social practice, and the historical development of racial and ethnic beliefs.

Colorado State provides an environment in which students can push against the boundaries of what they know and draw conclusions based on their judgment and experience. The school seeks to develop leaders who have clarified their personal values and can reach across cultural boundaries and contribute to society universally.

ESTABLISHED BY NORWEGIAN LUTHERAN IMMIGRANTS in 1891, Concordia College has always been dedicated to its mission of "influencing the affairs of the world by sending into society thoughtful and informed men and women dedicated to the Christian life." The integrating element in the curriculum and campus life is adherence to Christian ideals, which is evident in Concordia's programs and cocurricular activities:

✦ FIRST-YEAR PROGRAMS. During orientation week, new students are introduced to a strong ethic of service. "SOS" ("Sources of Service"), an on-campus student organization, coordinates "Hands for Change," a program in which students donate 2,000 hours of service to the local community.

✦ ACADEMIC HONESTY. Faculty, staff, and students are required to follow specific guidelines for academic integrity. All students sign a pledge to represent their work and the work of others accurately and fairly.

✦ FACULTY AND CURRICULUM. The "Faith, Reason, and World Affairs Symposium" is an annual program that brings together leading thinkers to address issues of ethics and values for the college and local community. During the symposium, classes are suspended so that all students and faculty can participate in the plenary and workshop sessions.

✦ VOLUNTEER SERVICE. Concordia offers courses in 15 academic disciplines that incorporate service learning. Academic goals and community needs determine the type of service activity students pursue. Students may help by staffing after-school programs at local public schools, conducting public policy research for nonprofit agencies, mentoring students in welfare-to-work programs, or participating in other meaningful activities that connect Concordia's mission to the community.

✦ SUBSTANCE-ABUSE PREVENTION. "AWARE" ("Advocates for Wellness and Related Education") is a committee of students who share a common interest in promoting physical and spiritual health to encourage healthy lifestyle choices.

✦ STUDENT LEADERSHIP. The "May Internship Program" affords present and future student leaders the opportunity to develop their leadership skills while also planning and achieving organizational goals. The Cornerstone Programming Center is a leadership development resource that coordinates student involvement in on-campus cocurricular activities.

✦ SPIRITUAL GROWTH. The Campus Ministry provides faculty, staff, and students with leadership and guidance in religious activities. Students assist with worship, plan gatherings, organize relief fund drives, and host Bible study and special retreats.

✦ CIVIC EDUCATION. Students are encouraged to participate in off-campus activities that emphasize civic responsibility. They may intern with members of Congress or federal agencies or travel abroad during the month-long "May Seminar Abroad."

Concordia encourages students to pursue knowledge as a significant form of Christian service and to develop skills that will prepare them for a lifelong process of learning and service to others through faith.

CONCORDIA COLLEGE

901 8TH STREET SOUTH
MOORHEAD, MN 56562

218.299.3004
http://www.cord.edu/

UNDERGRADUATES: 2,900

"Concordia has provided me with opportunities to reach out to the local community and to work with others for the greater good."

—A CONCORDIA THIRD-YEAR STUDENT

Other Concordia Profiles:

• Faculty & Curriculum Program

CONCORDIA UNIVERSITY

1530 CONCORDIA WEST
IRVINE, CA 92612

949.854.8002
http://www.cui.edu/

UNDERGRADUATES: 900

"Faculty, staff, and student leaders understand that more than academics is required to help students mature. Concordia encourages growth and spiritual development by providing us with service opportunities that help us become engaged citizens."

—A CONCORDIA FOURTH-YEAR STUDENT

FOUNDED IN 1976 as a liberal arts institution, Concordia University seeks to develop well-rounded individuals dedicated to lifelong learning and service to others. Guided by the Great Commission of Christ Jesus and the Lutheran Confessions, Concordia emphasizes traditions of faith and academic excellence throughout its curriculum, services, and cocurricular activities:

✦ FIRST-YEAR PROGRAMS. First-year students are introduced to the Concordia community during "Week of Welcome" (orientation), during which such topics as conflict resolution, diversity, student development theory, behavior, and learning styles are discussed.

✦ ACADEMIC HONESTY. Concordia considers honesty to be an important part of character development. Honesty is stressed and conveyed through university policy, a comprehensive student conduct and disciplinary review system, and numerous workshops.

✦ FACULTY AND CURRICULUM. Concordia has seven educational targets for every student: systemic inquiry, clear communication, health and well-being, sociocultural responsiveness, aesthetic responsiveness, Christian values, and professional application. These targets help students to develop competency, mature interpersonal relations, purpose, and integrity, as well as to manage their emotions and work toward establishing a clear identity.

✦ SUBSTANCE-ABUSE PREVENTION. Alcohol and drug awareness weeks, fliers, substance-abuse workshops, convocations, and annual alcohol and drug seminars for athletes promote a drug-free and healthy lifestyle. Project Care team members help struggling individuals to correct negative and self-destructive behaviors.

✦ VOLUNTEER SERVICE. Every cocurricular and student group is expected to participate in one service project per semester. Students may collect clothes for the homeless, build shelters in Mexico, or assist Habitat for Humanity. Additional opportunities for community service exist in neighboring congregations and in private and governmental agencies, which offer a variety of social services.

✦ STUDENT LEADERSHIP. Students can participate in leadership workshops in which they develop and strengthen their communication, management, and leadership skills. Workshops are offered continuously throughout all student government organizations, clubs, and residence hall programming.

✦ SPIRITUAL GROWTH. Weekly chapel and Sunday church services provide ample opportunity for faculty, staff, and students to reflect on their personal values.

✦ SENIOR-YEAR PROGRAMS. "Global Synthesis" is a capstone course that helps seniors integrate the learning aspects of their college experience.

Concordia is dedicated to turning students into world citizens who will proceed in life with integrity, honor, and respect for others.

SERVICE AND FAITH have been recurring themes at Dallas Baptist University since its founding in 1898. As it celebrates more than 100 years as a Christian, liberal arts institution, DBU is committed to offering a sense of mission along with high-quality education to create servant leaders who can integrate faith and learning in their respective callings. A life-sized bronze statue depicting Christ washing the disciple Peter's feet is located at the heart of DBU's campus, reminding the campus community that their lives of personal and civic responsibility must be born of a spirit of service for their neighbors and a relationship with God.

DBU cultivates Christian character and education in numerous programs:

✦ FIRST-YEAR PROGRAMS. A "Foundations for Excellence" class is required of all incoming DBU students to help prepare them spiritually and intellectually for university challenges. Also, first-year students are strongly encouraged to participate in "Spiritual Rush Weekend," when faculty and staff host students in their homes to explore such topics as "integrity" and "community."

✦ FACULTY AND CURRICULUM. Each Friday, the entire campus is invited to participate in the "Friday Symposium" hosted by the philosophy department. This is an opportunity for students, faculty, and invited guests to engage in timely analysis and critical thought on a variety of interdisciplinary themes. DBU also sponsors a Pew College Society to give students an outlet for contemporary exposition on issues of moral ideals and commitments.

✦ VOLUNTEER SERVICE. An emphasis on serving the community begins with service projects during "SWAT" ("Student Welcome and Transition") Week each year. Students then have continuing opportunities to serve together in many meaningful ways, such as in the campus chapter of Habitat for Humanity and for the spring campus-wide service day.

✦ STUDENT LEADERSHIP. The hallmark of student leadership initiatives at DBU is the Christian Leadership Scholars program. In addition to offering a financial scholarship, this program focuses on the personal development of student leaders by outlining the expectations of personal character that they should possess. New students to this program participate in a unique course that challenges them to understand and practice the value of living personally and civically responsible lives.

✦ SPIRITUAL GROWTH. Spiritual growth is a component of most programs at DBU, both academic and extracurricular. Students and faculty also participate in chapel services that provide them with a community worship experience, and the campus community also has an active intercessory prayer ministry.

Through the integration of spirituality and learning across all aspects of the campus, DBU students gain a deeper knowledge of their faith. This knowledge pervades the formation of each student and encourages responsible living. Personal and civic responsibility are the byproducts of the understanding gained through developing a relationship to creation, the primary characteristic of college life at DBU.

DALLAS BAPTIST UNIVERSITY

3000 MOUNTAIN CREEK PARKWAY
DALLAS, TX 75211–9299

214.333.7100
http://www.dbu.edu/

UNDERGRADUATES: 2,900

"The uniqueness of DBU lies in its purposeful mission statement to 'integrate faith and learning.' DBU helped me to see that learning without piety is just empirical fact and that piety without learning is mere sentimentality."

—A DBU FOURTH-YEAR STUDENT

Other DBU Profiles:

• Spiritual Growth Program

DARTMOUTH COLLEGE

6001 PARKHURST HALL
HANOVER, NH 03755

603.646.1110
http://www.dartmouth.edu/

UNDERGRADUATES: 4,300

"Dartmouth has definitely facilitated my development as a thoughtful citizen and compassionate person."

—A DARTMOUTH FOURTH-YEAR STUDENT

Other Dartmouth Profiles:

• Civic Education Program
• Spiritual Growth Program
• Volunteer Service Program

"**BE** NOT CONTENT with the commonplace in character anymore than with the commonplace in ambition or intellectual attainment. Do not expect to make a lasting impression on the world through intellectual power without the use of an equal amount of conscience and heart." These 19th-century words from William Jewett Tucker, ninth President of Dartmouth College, describe the mission of this private, Christian institution founded in 1769 that has grown into a modern liberal arts school. Dartmouth embraces action for the common good, welcomes the diversity of the modern world, and respects religious faith and practice within a secular, pluralistic institution through the character-building attributes of its various programs:

✦ **FACULTY AND CURRICULUM.** Dartmouth emphasizes close contact between faculty and students. One special residential cluster is built around a faculty master, who resides there with family to facilitate intellectual and social integration. Faculty act as advisors for all first-year students, and each upperclassman has a faculty major advisor.

✦ **VOLUNTEER SERVICE.** At some point in their college career, 74% of Dartmouth students participate in community service through the 40 local programs of the Tucker Foundation. Nearly 500 students participate in DarCorps, a twice yearly day-of-service campus event. More than 65 undergraduate students are awarded 10-week community service fellowships and internships each year for off-campus service nationwide and around the world. Career Services, the Dickey Center for International Understanding, the Rockefeller Center, the Ethics Institute, and other programs support numerous public service internships annually.

✦ **SUBSTANCE-ABUSE PREVENTION.** The "DAPA" ("Drug and Alcohol Peer Advisor") program trains Dartmouth students to counsel their peers on substance abuse. The "PEAC" ("Peer Education Action Corps") program provides information and training to campus leaders to effectively influence the opinions of peers and change social norms around substance and sexual abuse, eating disorders, and other health-related issues.

✦ **CHARACTER AND SEXUALITY.** The Dartmouth Chaplaincy, working with religious leaders, administrators, and students, publishes the brochure *Sexuality and the Dartmouth College Community*, which states: "Decisions we make regarding relationships and how to express ourselves sexually have broad moral, social, personal, religious, and even political consequences." To encourage responsible choices, leaders in the Dartmouth community are available for counseling and guidance.

✦ **SENIOR-YEAR PROGRAMS.** Dartmouth's president selects a group of Senior Fellows to pursue individually designed programs of study or research that further their intellectual growth during their final year. The senior honor and advisory group, Paleopitus, advises the president on matters of policy and community. The Senior Symposium, a program of lectures on social issues, is organized each year by the departing senior class as an "intellectual gift" to the college.

Dartmouth inspires graduates to excel in personal and professional endeavors through outstanding strength of character combined with intellectual ability learned at this forward-thinking institution that champions basic values.

THE DEFIANCE COLLEGE, founded in 1850, champions citizenship building through challenging academic coursework and outstanding volunteerism. This liberal arts institution affiliated with the United Church of Christ nurtures individual students by helping them develop the intellectual, emotional, spiritual, social, and physical dimensions of themselves. Defiance students are encouraged to search for truth and develop sensitivity to the world around them through community service and responsible citizenship. Toward that goal, Defiance has incorporated service learning into the curriculum and into the mainstream of campus life:

✦ FIRST-YEAR PROGRAMS. All first-year students are required to participate in a community service project. The Freshman Seminar introduces students to service work and helps them adjust to their new responsibilities. Unique to Defiance is the Faculty-in-Residence program, in which a faculty member lives alongside students in one of the residence halls and works to develop special programming to address such issues as academic performance and personal responsibility.

✦ VOLUNTEER SERVICE. Defiance sponsors numerous service initiatives in which students are encouraged to design their own service projects, such as mentoring or tutoring at-risk youth either through "America Reads" or "DC Connects," a Defiance-sponsored program. Defiance also has collaborated with Defiance City Schools to establish an on-campus, neighborhood learning center where local children are tutored in a student-led, afterschool program.

✦ SPIRITUAL GROWTH. The Office of Campus Ministry provides numerous opportunities for faculty, staff, and students to explore and deepen their faith. Through study, discussion, fellowship, and service, students are encouraged to develop their spiritual lives. Students may participate in Bible study groups or participate in more formal programs such as "Body & Soul," a student fellowship that meets weekly to discuss selected topics.

✦ CIVIC EDUCATION. Defiance seeks to instill in each student an understanding of civic duty. Through "The Program for Responsible Citizenship," a program founded in the arts and humanities, students learn to lead and serve in their communities and beyond, experiencing the positive influence they bring to society as they undertake their civic responsibilities.

✦ SENIOR-YEAR PROGRAMS. As part of the Presidential Service Leadership Scholarship program, senior service leaders accompany Defiance president Dr. James Harris on an international service trip to participate in various economic development projects.

Defiance encourages students to grow beyond boundaries imposed by themselves or by society through service to fellow students, within their chosen fields of endeavor, to their communities, and to the world.

THE DEFIANCE COLLEGE

701 NORTH CLINTON STREET
DEFIANCE, OH 43512

800.520.4632
http://www.defiance.edu/

UNDERGRADUATES: 800

"Defiance's mission is for all students to 'Lead, Know, Serve, and Understand.' As a result, I have developed life-changing qualities that will contribute to our society."

—A DEFIANCE FOURTH-YEAR STUDENT

Other Defiance Profiles:

• Profile of President Harris
• Civic Education Program
• First-Year Program
• Senior-Year Program
• Volunteer Service Program

DePauw
University

313 SOUTH LOCUST STREET
GREENCASTLE, IN 46135

765.658.4800
http://www.depauw.edu/

UNDERGRADUATES: 2,200

*"Students are expected
to step up and be leaders
at DePauw. By taking
on major projects, I've
learned to share myself
with other students, as
well as with the
community."*

—A DePauw second-year
student

PREPARING STUDENTS to take their place as responsible citizens and leaders in both the local and global communities constitutes DePauw University's commitment to instilling moral values while promoting academic success. Founded in 1837 as a private, liberal arts university, DePauw stresses extensive voluntary service as it leads the nation in per capita student internships. Numerous programs highlighting character development include:

✦ **FACULTY AND CURRICULUM.** DePauw faculty incorporate leadership concepts into courses that cross disciplinary lines in such areas as Women's Studies; Conflict Studies; and Asian, Latin American, Caribbean, and Black Studies. Faculty also teach noncredit courses and seminars on topics related to leadership.

✦ **VOLUNTEER SERVICE.** The Grover L. Hartman Center for Civic Education and Leadership serves as a coordinating center for DePauw student volunteer services. More than 75% of the student body participates each year in service capacities such as Saturday work projects, Alternative Spring Break, Winter Term in Service both abroad and in the U.S., leadership training seminars, and volunteer management training. The student-directed DePauw Community Service organization matches students with 25 community agencies. In addition, 21 Civic Fellows help to promote awareness of community through education and service and are required to complete six to eight hours per week in community service and/or leadership training.

✦ **SUBSTANCE-ABUSE PREVENTION.** As a result of a DePauw student proposal, an entire dormitory was designated a substance-free living unit. An upperclass convocation on alcohol awareness targeted first-year students. Other students formed "PARTY" ("Promoting Alcohol Responsibility Through You"), a nonalcoholic event organization. DePauw has also supported recent revision of existing sorority and fraternity policies on social events and alcohol use.

✦ **STUDENT LEADERSHIP.** To put into practice the leadership skills they learn in the classroom, several DePauw student groups joined forces to redesign student government. In their Student Congress message, they stated: "We expect to learn from each other, respect our differences and celebrate our diversity...to work for the betterment of our campus, our community, our nation, and our world."

✦ **SPIRITUAL GROWTH.** DePauw believes that students acquire the abilities they need to face major issues in American today through living faith-centered lives, and it supports more than 21 religious groups on campus. The Religious Life Center offers a series of seminars each semester to discuss contemporary moral and ethical issues from a religious point of view. Also, the Center oversees the "Sunday Celebration" worship service, as well as other faith traditions. The "Theology in Service" program offers a forum for students to reflect on the underpinnings of a life of service.

DePauw's educational ethos fosters a lifelong sense of service and a commitment to society. The *Princeton Review* ranked DePauw among the nation's top 15 colleges, describing it as a place "where students are truly making a difference in terms of service and political/social activism, both on campus and in the surrounding community."

Other DePauw Profiles:

• Volunteer Service Program

EARLHAM COLLEGE provides students with a high-quality undergraduate education in the liberal arts and sciences, shaped by the distinctive perspectives of the Religious Society of Friends (Quakers). Since 1847, Earlham has remained true to the basic tenants of the Quaker faith: Respect for Persons, Academic Integrity, Peace and Justice, and Simplicity. An adherence to the Quaker tradition is evident in Earlham's governance by consensus, its curriculum, and its cocurricular activities:

◆ FIRST-YEAR PROGRAMS. During "New Student Week," all first-year students are introduced to the importance of volunteer community service and perform two hours of assistance to social service organizations. Thereafter, "EVE" ("Earlham Volunteer Exchange"), a student-run volunteer program, places students with community organizations in need of assistance.

◆ FACULTY AND CURRICULUM. The Earlham community remains purposely set apart from the world and seeks to help students integrate the intellectual, emotional, spiritual, and physical aspects of life. In this learning environment, students are encouraged to develop tolerance, civility, and respect for others as major components of their value systems.

◆ ACADEMIC HONESTY. Because Earlham expects students to be honest seekers of ideas and knowledge, it believes that trust is necessary and implicit in a learning community. Consequently, Earlham maintains a policy of not requiring students to sign an oath affirming academic honesty.

◆ VOLUNTEER SERVICE. At the beginning of every semester, 30 community organizations participate in an on-campus Volunteer Activity Fair to attract student volunteers. Students provide free tutoring services to elementary, middle, and secondary school pupils; serve as reading partners to elementary children through "America Reads"; and become pen-pals with area sixth graders.

◆ SUBSTANCE-ABUSE PREVENTION. Earlham believes that substance abuse is not only dangerous and self-destructive, but that it can impair an individual's ability to grasp the truth and live responsibly within a community. Students are held accountable for their personal behavior and are encouraged to personally help others engaged in self-destructive lifestyles.

◆ STUDENT LEADERSHIP. Earlham values the contribution of students in institutional governance. Students are members of all governing committees, including such key panels as the Budget and Faculty Affairs committees. In these roles, students are included in discussions with faculty and staff and are able to observe the honesty and integrity involved in all decisions affecting the college.

Earlham has combined a concern for spirituality with a devotion to academic excellence to foster a learning environment in which students can acquire the knowledge and skills to transform themselves and society. As members of each class have attested to two, five, and ten years after graduation, Earlham has continued to influence the values they apply to their occupational learning experiences and personal lives.

EARLHAM COLLEGE

801 NATIONAL ROAD WEST
RICHMOND, IN 47374

768.983.1200
http://www.earlham.edu/

UNDERGRADUATES: 1,100

"In four years at Earlham, I have learned to see the complexity of human issues with compassion and knowledge. I have learned the skills to make positive changes."

—AN EARLHAM FOURTH-YEAR
STUDENT

Other Earlham Profiles:

• Volunteer Service Program

EASTERN COLLEGE

1300 EAGLE ROAD
ST. DAVIDS, PA 19087-3696

610.341.5803
http://www.eastern.edu/

UNDERGRADUATES: 1,200

"My time at Eastern has taught me that showing Christ's love to the world is not only my choice, but my responsibility. Making this the driving force of my studies has been challenging, yet I know it's preparing me to serve the needs of others through my life's work."

—AN EASTERN THIRD-YEAR
STUDENT

Other Eastern Profiles:

• First-Year Program

"Ethically, strategically, compassionately, and globally" describes how Eastern College prepares students to think and act in their future roles as leaders and people of influence. This private, comprehensive, Christian college of arts and sciences founded in 1952 has developed a number of innovative programs and activities focused on the emerging needs in society, especially those within developing communities. In addition to rigorous academics, character-building courses emphasizing community involvement include:

✦ FIRST-YEAR PROGRAMS. At Eastern, an award-winning first-year program, "Living and Learning in Community," focuses on helping students develop a critical evaluation of their key values and worldviews.

✦ FACULTY AND CURRICULUM. Eastern faculty serve as role models of service, having developed and led numerous schools, organizations, and programs that target the needs of people in developing communities. A core curriculum combines the study of great ideas and biblical perspectives with an examination of critical contemporary issues, such as "Science, Technology, and Values" and "Justice in a Pluralistic World." An alternative core curriculum offered through Eastern's new Honors College combines "Great Books" with significant service in the community. Astronomy and chemistry majors design and deliver supplementary laboratories and programs for grade-school children, including guided observations in Eastern's state-of-the-art observatory. Environmental studies majors participate in the Au Sable Institute and spend a full term in the study of policy issues that affect the environment.

✦ VOLUNTEER SERVICE. An Eastern community service program offers a broad selection of opportunities—including the country's first campus chapter of Habitat for Humanity—through which students can fulfill their service-learning requirement.

✦ STUDENT LEADERSHIP. A leadership program exists to develop Eastern students' potential year by year, and a mentoring program for junior and senior women is offered through the campus Hestenes Center for Christian Women in Leadership.

✦ SPIRITUAL GROWTH. Youth ministry students at Eastern serve as interns in local churches, where they help young people form important life commitments. Social work students focus on issues concerning children and the family, with particular attention given to the transformational effectiveness of community faith-based institutions. A spiritual growth program includes student chaplains and small-group Bible studies in the residence halls, student-led worship teams for weekly chapel services, and a yearly "Spiritual Emphasis" week.

Eastern College graduates make a difference in the world because they are committed to meaningful service as well as personal excellence. According to its mission statement, this college community knows it has successfully fulfilled its mission when students' college experiences motivate them throughout their lives to "participate in opportunities for meaningful service and grow in their love of God and neighbors."

Eastern Mennonite University, a private, church-affiliated, liberal arts school, has focused on character development since its inception in 1917. The Mennonite Church founded the school to promote nonviolence, peace building, service, community, and faith in reconciliation. Ranked as one of *U.S. News and World Report*'s top 10 "Southern liberal arts colleges," EMU champions personal and civic responsibility through the following programs:

✦ First-Year Programs. EMU's First-Year Experience course provides students with a small group experience and the opportunity to relate to a faculty mentor. Students discuss topics such as how to live within a diverse community and how to develop a healthy sexual identity. A service project promotes a sense of responsibility toward others and lifetime volunteerism.

✦ Faculty and Curriculum. The cross-cultural component of the Global Village Curriculum is a life-changing experience. By living in another culture for a time, students are transformed by reflecting on the values of their own culture and the commitments by which they choose to live. "Issues and Values," the final Global Village course, invites students to articulate a worldview based on the ideas and values explored during their university experience.

✦ Student Leadership. The Student Life Division encourages leadership development through course work as well as through numerous opportunities to practice leadership. Leadership roles open to students include resident assistant, pastoral assistant, ministry assistant, student orientation staff, campus activities committee, recreation and sports staff, and Student Government Association member.

✦ Spiritual Growth. Faith development and spiritual growth occur through many activities. EMU's network of spiritual leaders fosters student leadership and expands the possibilities for spiritual growth. The network includes campus pastors, pastoral assistants, and ministry assistants. In the Pastoral/Ministry Assistant Program, 40 students are nurtured as spiritual leaders to other students on campus. Following fall leadership training retreats, ministry assistants lead Bible studies and provide spiritual support to their peers. The ministry assistants themselves meet weekly in small groups with the pastoral assistants for pastoral support and spiritual work. Pastoral assistants in turn receive spiritual guidance from the campus pastors and assist with chapel services.

✦ Healthy Lifestyles. The innovative publication *The Paper* and the "Real World" programs address substance-abuse issues with students to help them make wise lifestyle decisions and take responsibility for their behavior and its effect on the community. Students are also encouraged to explore topics related to sexuality in their first-year small groups and in residence hall discussion groups. These programs go beyond just providing information to encouraging students to choose behaviors leading to well-being for themselves and others. Accountability and self-discipline describe key aspects of the peer judicial system that works with students when they fail to achieve the standards of conduct set by the university.

EMU seeks to empower students to not only develop personal responsibility in their lives, but also to pursue peace and enhance the well-being of others through Christian servant leadership.

EASTERN MENNONITE UNIVERSITY

1200 PARK ROAD
HARRISONBURG, VA 22802-2462

540.432.4000
http://www.emu.edu/

UNDERGRADUATES: 1,000

"Character development at EMU is about people helping each other. We learn how to listen better, and through sharing our stories, we grow holistically."

—AN EMU second-year student

Other EMU Profiles:

• Civic Education Program
• Faculty & Curriculum Program
• First-Year Program

ELON COLLEGE

2700 CAMPUS BOX
ELON COLLEGE, NC 27244-2010

800.334.8448
http://www.elon.edu/

UNDERGRADUATES: 3,700

"Elon helps students to get firsthand experience in service, travel, and leadership. The frame of mind on campus is that you might wake up on a Saturday morning and work on a Habitat for Humanity project, or you might decide to spend a semester in London. It's something that everyone does."

—AN ELON THIRD-YEAR
STUDENT

Other Elon Profiles:

• Volunteer Service Program

AT ELON COLLEGE, students are encouraged—and often required—to test many theories and concepts in real-world situations. Founded as a private college in 1889 by the United Church of Christ, Elon's mission offers students a liberal arts education that enriches them as human beings and prepares them for a life of service through character- and career-oriented programs:

✦ FACULTY AND CURRICULUM. Faculty connect classroom teaching with experiential and service opportunities. Elon's general studies program helps students think critically and constructively, respect other cultures, and develop habits of responsible leadership. Global Studies, the first-year element, is a seminar taught by faculty who draw on their own interests and expertise. Students later take eight liberal studies classes outside their majors linking classroom content with community service or social action, complete three advanced studies courses, and take a final Experiential Learning Requirement. The five Elon Experiences—service, leadership, study abroad, internships/co-ops, and research—develop resourceful, independent, lifelong learners and citizens.

✦ ACADEMIC HONESTY. The Elon Honor System consists of academic and social honor codes, which emphasize ethical, responsible behavior.

✦ VOLUNTEER SERVICE. The Kernodle Center for Service Learning and "Elon Volunteers!" enable students to develop an ethic of service by connecting campus and community. More than 67% of Elon students provided 40,000 hours of service during the 1997–98 academic year by raising alcohol and rape awareness, working for Habitat for Humanity, providing literacy education, and assisting the developmentally disabled.

✦ STUDENT LEADERSHIP. Through the Leadership Development office, 22% of students led 106 groups and organizations during the 1997–98 academic year. Through the Isabella Cannon Emerging Leaders program, first-year students who attend workshops, special programs, and monthly group discussions; participate in 20 hours of service; and become active in at least one campus organization can apply for the three-year Isabella Cannon Leadership Fellows Program to become a Leadership Scholar.

✦ CIVIC EDUCATION. In the Model United Nations club, upperclassmen work with first-year students on a mock Security Council meeting. Students do research, write resolutions, give speeches, and negotiate within a simulated world crisis. During the Semester in Washington program, students learn the inner workings of the political system.

✦ SPIRITUAL GROWTH. The Campus Pastor's office coordinates programs such as "Turning 21," which teams students with a faculty or staff mentor to help them understand that this birthday is more than an opportunity to legally drink; "Hometown Heroes," which allows students to invite mentors from their hometowns to campus for a special banquet and awards ceremony; "Listening Post," in which local senior citizens advise Elon students on life issues and choices; and "Life Stories," an effort to find meaning in memories, write an autobiography, and determine life goals.

Elon combines campus community life with academic and experiential programs to help students develop a strong set of values through contribution.

Founded in 1836 as a college in Oxford, Georgia, by the Methodist Episcopal Church, Emory received university status in 1919 when it moved to Atlanta. Emory University's mission is twofold: To help men and women develop fully their intellectual, aesthetic, and moral capacities and to improve human well-being through the lifelong quest for knowledge and public service. These purposes are at the core of Emory's philosophy that education is a powerful social force that can enable individuals to use knowledge for the common good.

Emory's character-building cornerstones include:

✦ Faculty and Curriculum. CEPPP (the Center for Ethics in Public Policy and the Professions) deepens knowledge of ethics and encourages faculty, students, and staff to pursue lives of moral meaning and ethical practice. CEPPP enriches the faculty's moral sensibilities in teaching and research so that they can, in turn, nurture an ethical foundation in students. Every year, CEPPP sponsors several nationally known scholars to lecture on ethical issues and engage faculty in discussion. The annual Faculty Ethics Seminar offers an additional opportunity for sustained attention to ethics.

✦ Civic Education. Every year in May, students have the opportunity to visit other cultures and participate in community projects to learn about cultural values and social patterns. Through intercultural exchange, students broaden their political, economic, sociological, and spiritual views of the global community.

✦ Substance-Abuse Prevention. ADEC (the Alcohol and Drug Education Committee) strives to educate and make students aware of the effects of alcohol and to encourage responsible decisions involving the use of alcohol. ADEC sponsors "National Collegiate Alcohol Awareness Week" and "Spring Break Week" at Emory, both featuring activities to increase awareness about the dangers of drinking.

✦ Volunteer Service. "Volunteer Emory" is a student-led group that coordinates many on-campus and community service projects. Students work with more than 150 local organizations representing issues such as HIV/AIDS, the environment, women's concerns, homelessness, animal rights, and care for the elderly.

✦ Spiritual Growth. Through worship, service, education, and student organizations, Emory provides numerous opportunities for faculty, staff, and students to nourish their spiritual growth. Emory offers approximately 150 courses that address religious issues and makes the study of religious traditions a valued theme throughout campus.

Emory continues its cherished affiliation with the United Methodist Church and derives from this heritage the conviction that education is a strong, moral force in society and the lives of its individual members. Emory prepares students to use their knowledge and empathy to serve and contribute meaningfully to their local and world communities.

EMORY UNIVERSITY

1380 OXFORD ROAD NE
ATLANTA, GA 30322

404.727.6123
http://www.emory.edu/

UNDERGRADUATES: 6,000

"I hope that everyone will have a good sense of the student involvement here at Emory and our interest in seeing more participation with projects involving service."

—AN EMORY FOURTH-YEAR STUDENT

Other Emory Profiles:

• Faculty & Curriculum Program
• Student Leadership Program

FISK UNIVERSITY

1000 17TH AVENUE NORTH
NASHVILLE, TN 37208-3051

615.329.8500
http://www.fisk.edu/

UNDERGRADUATES: 800

"Fisk has given me a sense of family and community. All students are welcomed with open hearts and minds and are encouraged to choose their own path. At orientation, we are placed in groups of students from all over the world; by commencement, we have made lifelong friends."

—A FISK FOURTH-YEAR
STUDENT

FISK UNIVERSITY, one of the early Black institutions of higher learning established after the Civil War, was founded by the American Missionary Association in 1866. This small, liberal arts institution distinguishes itself by equipping students for intellectual and social leadership in the modern world. Jubilee Hall stands as an historic landmark on Fisk's campus, representing the first permanent structure built for the education of African-Americans. Educational excellence and character development merge to form outstanding programs that include:

✦ **FIRST-YEAR PROGRAMS.** First-year and new students are encouraged to participate in a comprehensive, interactive orientation. Students learn about Fisk's history and academic requirements; they also attend lectures on health care, meetings with alumni, and seminars on alcohol and other substance abuse. First-year males are required to attend discussion sessions focusing on leadership in the Black community, activism, voter registration, etiquette, and Fisk pride and traditions.

✦ **ACADEMIC HONESTY.** During the opening convocation, first-year students pledge their allegiance with a traditional oath to uphold the integrity of Fisk and to conduct themselves according to an honor code.

✦ **FACULTY AND CURRICULUM.** Fisk's core curriculum forms a solid foundation for future citizens through multicultural and interdisciplinary learning experiences that develop communication skills and critical thinking. Young men participate in the "Gentlemen's Lecture Series," designed to introduce them to the qualities of manhood.

✦ **VOLUNTEER SERVICE.** Fisk students serve as community volunteers in the heart of Nashville. Many students become Big Brothers and Big Sisters and volunteer as mentors and tutors for community youth. Other community involvement includes activities such as the annual AIDS Walk, raising funds for Muscular Dystrophy Association and The College Fund/UNCF, building homes for Habitat for Humanity, aiding the National Black Women's Health Project, providing relief efforts for victims of natural disasters, and introducing local and national inner-city youth to Fisk and other higher-education opportunities.

✦ **SPIRITUAL GROWTH.** Fisk seeks to create an environment that examines the spiritual dimension of life and offers religious freedom and expression. Spiritual awareness is fostered through regular Sunday chapel services, the annual baccalaureate address, "Religious Emphasis Week," concerts by The Fisk Jubilee Singers, seminars, and special convocations. Every Friday afternoon, the chapel remains open for "quiet hour," a contemplative pause from hectic schedules for students and faculty.

From the moment new students step onto the Fisk campus to the time they leave its halls, they are treated as adults capable of making important life decisions, guided not only by faculty and staff, but by peers. Fisk students are armed with much more than a highly respected diploma when they graduate. They take with them a code of ethics and values that will serve them as they continue the Fisk legacy of strong leadership and advocacy for political and social change, with an emphasis on serving the needs of the disadvantaged.

Founded in 1946, Franciscan University of Steubenville helps students discover a faith-based context for life through a Catholic, liberal arts education. The intensive academic curriculum and preprofessional experience impart to Franciscan students the moral, spiritual, and intellectual values that establish a sense of service to individuals and to society. The school's mission statement calls on Franciscan students to balance faith and scholarship with maturity and leadership.

An ethos of Christian character development permeates the campus and all Franciscan programs:

✦ Faculty and Curriculum. Franciscan faculty guide students through teaching and personal example, cultivating a strong curriculum that includes a Great Books Honors Program and study abroad at Franciscan's campus in Austria. Each program strives to develop intellectual virtues that nurture students' adaptability in rising to the "most unexpected challenges" and that prepares them to assume "positions of leadership in the Church and in the world."

✦ Volunteer Service. The Works of Mercy Program provides outlets for students to volunteer in the local community by visiting nursing homes and prisons, tutoring children, working in soup kitchens, and helping in downtown homeless shelters.

✦ Student Leadership. The Leadership Project embodies a Christian character-development program that enables students to realize their roles of responsibility in both society and the Church. Also, student leaders can experience hands-on leadership challenges by participating in the Residence Life Programs, run by resident assistants who oversee frequent discussions related to students' spiritual, academic, or physical well-being.

✦ Spiritual Growth. One of Franciscan's principles includes a commitment to stewardship. The Chapel Ministry models this principle by inviting students to share their gifts as lectors, musicians, ushers, servers, or sacristans while challenging them to grow in service to others.

✦ Civic Education. Personal and civic responsibility are stressed at Franciscan's Faith Households, in which small groups of five to 20 students live together to provide mutual support and accountability in fulfilling their academic, social, spiritual, and physical commitments.

The integration of faith and academics in and out of the classroom distinguishes a Franciscan liberal arts education. Its ultimate purpose is to graduate men and women who take a mature, responsible approach to life and become leaders in their careers, communities, families, and churches.

FRANCISCAN UNIVERSITY OF STEUBENVILLE

1235 UNIVERSITY BOULEVARD
STEUBENVILLE, OH 43952-1796

740.283.3771
http://www.franuniv.edu/

UNDERGRADUATES: 1,600

"My education has served a a springboard, giving me both the tools and the skills I need to live a life of academic, relational, and spiritual virtue."

—A Franciscan fourth-year student

Other Franciscan Profiles:

• Faculty & Curriculum Program
• Spiritual Growth Program
• Volunteer Service Program

FURMAN
UNIVERSITY

3300 POINSETT HIGHWAY
GREENVILLE, SC 29613

864.294.2000
http://www.furman.edu/

UNDERGRADUATES: 2,600

"Furman has enabled me to acquire leadership skills and the chance to serve the Greenville community in a very meaningful manner. My experiences have given me a way to demonstrate what I have learned in the classroom."

—A FURMAN THIRD-YEAR
STUDENT

Other Furman Profiles:

• Profile of President Shi
• Volunteer Service Program

BY STRESSING THE ARTS AND SCIENCES, fostering Christian character, and providing a broad foundation for specialized careers, Furman University's goal is to prepare students for living as well as for livelihood. An independent, nonsectarian, liberal arts college founded in 1826, Furman believes in educating the whole person—intellectually, spiritually, physically, and artistically—through these and other programs:

✦ FACULTY AND CURRICULUM. During the year, faculty and students meet at "Values Dinners" to discuss their personal philosophies. In the "What Really Matters" lecture series, professors and administrators discuss their deepest concerns and beliefs. Current and former faculty, along with students, provide intellectual and social programs for senior citizens through the yearlong "Learning in Retirement" program.

✦ VOLUNTEER SERVICE. More than half of the students assist in "CESC" ("Collegiate Educational Service Corps") programs at hospitals, schools, nursing homes, parks, and recreational centers. Students organize and administer the program, work as tutors in schools, run errands for senior citizens or cancer patients, and deliver leftover food from the dining halls to soup kitchens and homeless shelters. CESC has existed for 30 years, sponsors programs in 93 agencies, and has won local, state, and national honors for its work. In the past eight years CESC, working with Habitat for Humanity, has helped build 22 homes. Moreover, as counselors and instructors, students, as well as faculty and staff, contribute to a summer program, "Bridges to a Brighter Future," that in the summer of 1999 brought 60 disadvantaged secondary-school students to Furman for several weeks of academic teaching and enrichment activities.

✦ STUDENT LEADERSHIP. A four-year "Student Leadership Development Program" emphasizes self-knowledge, initiative, commitment, and collaboration while it promotes citizenship and community service.

✦ SPIRITUAL GROWTH. The "Religion-in-Life Lecture Series" features guest speakers who examine the moral and spiritual aspects of such issues as racism and the Holocaust. Students choose the symposium topics, and this series reflects Furman's desire to cultivate in students, faculty, and staff an interest in the world and a commitment to helping others.

✦ CIVIC EDUCATION. Courses include work with nonprofit and community organizations. A medical ethics/medical sociology class, taught by faculty from the philosophy and sociology departments, takes students into the local hospital system to learn about the medical profession. Student and faculty teams have worked with city government to study conditions at the detention center and to recommend changes. Furman students, faculty, and staff, in partnership with several local agencies, tutor at and provide administrative help in a child development and family services center. Internships, research, service learning, and study abroad are encouraged by the Center for Engaged Learning. A class in American government, for instance, participated in a project at the Greenville Literacy Association.

At Furman, civility, concerns of the spirit, and high standards matter. The university encourages civic responsibility and social awareness among students, faculty, and staff. An education at Furman calls for flexibility rather than formulas, creativity rather than constraints.

CHRIST-CENTERED IN ITS TRADITIONS since its founding by Quakers in 1891, George Fox University, a church-affiliated, liberal arts and sciences institution, emphasizes a commitment to prepare students for lives of personal and civic responsibility. For about a decade, *U.S. News & World Report* has recognized George Fox as one of "America's Best Colleges," as evidenced by the following programs developed in the Quaker tradition:

✦ FIRST-YEAR PROGRAMS. During orientation, new students spend an afternoon in community-service projects such as painting, cleaning, or doing yard work for the elderly. In fall 1998, students contributed 1,500 hours of service at 20 sites.

✦ ACADEMIC HONESTY. George Fox requires that all students endeavor "to be honest and of high integrity in all matters pertaining to their University life" (the *Student Handbook*). Penalties for violating the policy range from making restitution, receiving a failing grade on a paper or in a course, or being suspended.

✦ FACULTY AND CURRICULUM. Their Christian lifestyle agreement requires faculty and staff to model personal and corporate responsibility. Integrating faith and learning is the university's first objective, which extends through the core curriculum and all other courses.

✦ VOLUNTEER SERVICE. Each fall, all George Fox students and 350 employees spend a day in service at local social service agencies and churches. Also, through the Student Life Office and the student government, students work in a youth and family services home, help build homes with Habitat for Humanity, assist in two area shelters for abused families, and teach English as a second language in community courses.

✦ SUBSTANCE-ABUSE PREVENTION. The use of tobacco, alcoholic beverages, and illicit or nonprescribed drugs is prohibited for members of the George Fox community, reinforced by education about substance abuse in the annual "Alcohol Awareness Week" and in personal counseling programs.

✦ STUDENT LEADERSHIP. With university assistance, the student government plans, funds, and directs "ELITE" ("Empowering Leaders Through Experience"), an annual conference for student leaders from George Fox and throughout the nation, especially the Northwest.

✦ SPIRITUAL GROWTH. Undergraduates attend twice-weekly chapel services and participate in a "Spiritual Formation" program that features guest speakers, motivators, and lecturers who provide spiritual direction, instruction, and encouragement.

✦ CIVIC EDUCATION. The "May Serve" program offers students and their faculty or staff mentors the opportunity to work with churches in underprivileged and developing countries in ministries with children, unwed mothers, and the poor. During spring break and Christmas vacation, students, faculty, and staff focus on service in areas as diverse as inner cities in the U.S. to Russia, Brazil, Nepal, and Tibet.

Grounded in the basics of their academic disciplines, students are challenged to "be humble in spirit as [they] prepare to serve others with what [they] have learned" at George Fox.

GEORGE FOX UNIVERSITY

414 NORTH MERIDIAN STREET
NEWBERG, OR 97132

503.538.8383
http://www.georgefox.edu/

UNDERGRADUATES: 1,700

"George Fox is full of opportunities for leadership and ministry—it's a great place to get involved! I have grown spiritually through campus worship services, as well as through learning from the personal witness of my professors' lives."

—A GEORGE FOX FOURTH-YEAR STUDENT

Other George Fox Profiles:

• Profile of President Brandt

GORDON COLLEGE

255 GRAPEVINE ROAD
WENHAM, MA 01984

978.927.2300
http://www.gordon.edu/

UNDERGRADUATES: 1,500

"Gordon has challenged me to see my classes and relationships through faith—as well as to wrestle with my identity as a Christian, a student, and a contributor to the world."

—A GORDON FOURTH-YEAR STUDENT

Other Gordon Profiles:

• Profile of President Carlberg
• First-Year Program
• Spiritual Growth Program

THE FIRST LINE of Gordon College's mission statement contains its core purpose: to graduate men and women who are "distinguished by intellectual maturity and Christian character." A college of the liberal arts and sciences with religious orientation founded in 1889, Gordon is the result of a 1985 merger with Barrington College. The goal of the Gordon experience—in the classroom, in the residence halls, on the playing field, or in chapel—is the education of whole, well-rounded people. This fundamental objective informs and enhances various programs and initiatives at Gordon:

✦ FIRST-YEAR PROGRAM. The process starts with First-Year Seminar, a yearlong program required of all first-year and transfer students. Groups of 10 to 12 students are led by a faculty or staff member as they examine their individual character formation through selected readings, short papers, and discussions in the first semester. Students also prepare a longer, reflective "spiritual autobiography" in which they probe and articulate their own personal faith. In the second semester, they explore the connection between personal character and community values.

✦ FACULTY AND CURRICULUM. Institutional leaders at Gordon approach their positions with integrity and act in a way befitting a Christian community and an institution of higher learning. Many faculty and staff serve as personal mentors to students, and students often visit faculty at home for dinners and casual interaction.

✦ VOLUNTEER SERVICE. Gordon offers students a variety of community outreach ministries. Many students forego Christmas or spring break to participate in short-term mission trips in India or Central America.

✦ STUDENT LEADERSHIP. Leadership opportunities on and off campus allow students to learn the meaning of "servant leader." Student leaders, who participate as the orientation staff, resident assistants, and student government, receive training in facilitating a moral community at Gordon.

✦ SPIRITUAL GROWTH. Gordon's sense of Christian community nurtures students' physical, social, and spiritual growth. Required chapel services and several student-led initiatives foster exploration of spiritual issues, as well as encourage spiritual growth and a commitment to putting faith into daily practice. Gordon's "La Vida" program, a structured wilderness adventure, tests personal capabilities—for example, through solo backpacking and rappelling—to encourage reflection and instill perseverance and trust in self, in others, and in God. Hiking is supplemented with personal contemplation time. The program is modeled on biblical history, as God often tested people in the wilderness to prepare them for future service. For many students, "La Vida" is the highlight of their Gordon experience.

Overall, Gordon anticipates moral development as an outcome, and not merely a component, of the curricular and extracurricular educational experience. Gordon's approach to character building consists of more than externally "controlling" behavior through rules and regulations or paying mere lip service to a life of virtue. Gordon's fundamental commitment to placing Christian character at the heart of what the school stands for—and does—brings its goals to life through students' entire educational experience.

T<small>WO</small> PATRIOTS founded all-male Hampden-Sydney in 1776, making it the 10th oldest college in America. Woven into its extraordinary history, Hampden-Sydney students recognize the consistent emphasis on citizenship-building and civic and religious freedoms. James Madison and Patrick Henry were on the first Board of Trustees and serve as timeless models of "good men and good citizens" that Hampton-Sydney continually strives to produce.

Through adherence to the principles of an Honor Code, instruction in the values of the American constitutional system, and active involvement in community affairs, this private, liberal arts institution instills the habit of "character" in all of its students:

✦ A<small>CADEMIC</small> H<small>ONESTY</small>. Known for their zealous preservation of the Honor Code, Hampden-Sydney's students are required to sign a statement certifying commitment to academic integrity. The first evening of orientation includes an Honor Convocation ceremony and group discussions on the precepts of the Honor Code, led by a member of the Student Court. These ceremonies highlight the primacy of character development and honor at Hampden-Sydney.

✦ F<small>ACULTY AND</small> C<small>URRICULUM</small>. Hampden-Sydney professors and students not only study and work together, but live together as well, giving students daily examples of dedication and service. For example, an economics professor who was recently a consultant to nations in Central Europe, an elder in College Church, and a member of the volunteer fire department serves as teacher, mentor, and coworker to students.

✦ S<small>TUDENT</small> L<small>EADERSHIP AND</small> C<small>IVIC</small> E<small>DUCATION</small>. Two initiatives, The Center for Leadership in the Public Interest and "The Society of '91," prepare young men for lives of leadership in service to the public good. The Center for Leadership requires coursework, an internship, and a publicly defended thesis. Graduates have worked in the offices of the U.S. Vice President, as well as in other federal and state offices. The Society educates and motivates students to become leaders by example as well as by action. Through classes, events, and service experiences, young men contribute to and strengthen their community.

✦ V<small>OLUNTEER</small> S<small>ERVICE</small>. Hampden-Sydney encourages students to participate in community activities that build character and reinforce good citizenship. Through the "Good Men and Good Citizens" organization, students perform services throughout the year. Each fraternity and residence hall has at least one service project per semester, such as serving on the volunteer fire department or the local rescue squad.

Educating students in all aspects of leadership and citizenship creates an invigorating atmosphere for the young men of Hampden-Sydney. The mission of building integrity, coupled with Hampden-Sydney's rich history, produces soundly developed leaders for the near future.

HAMPDEN-SYDNEY COLLEGE

PO BOX 667
HAMPDEN-SYDNEY, VA 23943

804.223.6000
http://www.hsc.edu/

UNDERGRADUATES: 900

"A plaque resides at the front gate of our college that proclaims: 'Enter as boys, leave as men.' No statement could be truer about Hampden-Sydney College."

—A<small>N</small> HSC F<small>OURTH-YEAR</small>
S<small>TUDENT</small>

Other Hampden-Sydney Profiles:

• Academic Honesty Program

HAMPTON UNIVERSITY

HAMPTON, VA 23668

757.727.5000
http://www.hamptonu.edu/

UNDERGRADUATES: 5,200

"Hampton provides an education that exceeds beyond excellence in the classroom. Students receive world-class training in leadership, public service, spirituality, and learning how to live lives that promote strong families and vibrant communities."

—A HAMPTON THIRD-YEAR STUDENT

Other Hampton Profiles:

• Profile of President Harvey

"EDUCATION FOR LIFE" describes the rich preparation for personal and civic responsibility that begins for students at Hampton University and continues long after they leave. Founded in 1868, Hampton has always worked to instill values of respect, integrity, and uprightness of character through its academic and service programs, calling on its president, faculty, and staff to exemplify these virtues. President Harvey addresses new students and their parents about the high moral and ethical expectations, leadership, and service required of every Hampton student.

This historically Black, private, liberal arts institution recognizes character formation as a foundational component of its programs:

✦ ACADEMIC HONESTY. The Hampton Code of Conduct forms the basis of the university's ethos. Each student agrees to honor the Code, a comprehensive set of standards from self-respect to a professional work ethic, which is displayed in every campus building and is part of every course introduction. The Code is further elaborated through the required semester-long orientation course.

✦ FACULTY AND CURRICULUM. The Faculty Advisor Program offers intense faculty interaction with Hampton students to help them meet academic and personal challenges. The core curriculum integrates the values prescribed in the Code of Conduct with experiential learning situations, which are frequently presented in a public forum and are overseen by "Breakout Instructors" (course facilitators).

✦ VOLUNTEER SERVICE. Hampton's service-learning initiatives include those designed to better their community. Some efforts demonstrating student dedication to service include "Walk for Breast Cancer Awareness," Bangladesh student support, Big Brother/Big Sister programs, tutoring in local community centers, and mentoring to area youth.

✦ STUDENT LEADERSHIP. Hampton cultivates campus leaders who work constructively for the betterment of society. Faculty, staff, and students led and hosted the first Annual African-American/Jewish Community Relations Symposium, which resulted in an African-American/Jewish Relations Honors course. The Honors College specifically prepares students in leadership and lives of service.

✦ CIVIC EDUCATION. Programs promoting responsible citizenship include "SAILLS" ("Student Athletes Involved in Learning, Leadership, and Service") and the "Expanding Teacher Education Through Service-Learning." In addition, Greek organizations, student Christian groups, and the Honors College offer practical opportunities for personal involvement in community life. Proactive participation with the United Way, Sickle Cell Anemia Foundation, American Diabetes Foundation, and the NAACP help to develop lifelong habits of participation in community affairs in Hampton students.

The Hampton spirit evolves from a deep commitment to serve others, which enables graduates to meet the larger world prepared and inspired.

Founded in 1876, Hendrix College is a church-affiliated liberal arts school that stands as a vibrant community of outstanding students and a distinguished, dedicated faculty. It articulates a clear and compelling mission: "Hendrix is dedicated to the cultivation of whole persons through the transmission of knowledge, the refinement of intellect, the development of character, and the encouragement of a concern for worthy values. In these ways Hendrix prepares its graduates for lives of service and fulfillment in their communities and the world." Student development programs at Hendrix highlight this mission:

✦ First-Year Programs. Orientation combines adventure, discovery, and outreach. A two-day, off-campus excursion begins the experience, with small groups, student peer leaders, and a faculty or staff member leading service trips for Habitat for Humanity, outdoor adventure trips, or educational trips to observe local politics in action in Little Rock. The remainder of the week offers social events and workshops to help students make a successful transition to college. The Council of New Student Advisors, a trained faculty group, provides advising.

✦ Faculty and Curriculum. Hendrix encourages its faculty to provide leadership in appropriate regional and national professional organizations, as well as in community organizations in Central Arkansas. Students often cite the civic work of professors as influential in their own decisions to pursue volunteer service. Also, the Hendrix curriculum weaves issues of personal and civic responsibility into its course work—not only do students in the required Western Intellectual Traditions course analyze the relationship between personal meaning and civic or political engagement, they also read and discuss ancient Greek, medieval, early modern, and contemporary versions of the relationship between individuals and society. Required courses in philosophy or religion extend this discussion.

✦ Volunteer Service. "VAC" (the "Volunteer Action Center") involves more than 80% of Hendrix students in numerous community programs during "Service Saturdays," when Turpentine Creek Animal Refuge, the Arkansas Children's Hospital, Special Olympics, Habitat for Humanity, and Riddle's Elephant Farm provide diverse practical experiences. Summer travel destinations include a medical mission in Haiti, a school in Africa, and a prison in Russia. Nearly 20% of all Hendrix students participate in a Big Buddy program in the public schools. Each spring, students support local charities with a weeklong series of fund-raising activities.

✦ Student Leadership. The Leadership Hendrix Program provides experiential learning opportunities that develop students' leadership skills. Workshops and retreats address leadership styles, characteristics of good leaders, and ethics in leadership. The annual Leadership Summit convenes officers from all student organizations for additional leadership training.

✦ Spiritual Growth. Hendrix understands that opportunities for spiritual growth, theological exploration, moral development, and the growing expression of one's religious faith are central components of a liberal arts education. Religious life includes weekly chapel services, small study groups, meditation, and prayer. As an institution related to the United Methodist Church, Hendrix cultivates future lay and clergy programs.

In its curriculum and cocurricular programs, Hendrix demonstrates a strong commitment to enabling students to develop the competencies, conscience, and compassion required of leaders in a civil society.

HENDRIX COLLEGE

1600 WASHINGTON AVENUE
CONWAY, AR 72032-3080

501.329.6811
http://www.hendrix.edu/

UNDERGRADUATES: 1,000

"At Hendrix, I have come to understand and develop my internal motivation to pursue the truth and seek an ethical and moral lifestyle."

—A Hendrix fourth-year student

HIGH POINT UNIVERSITY

UNIVERSITY STATION
833 MONTLIEU AVENUE
HIGH POINT, NC 27262-3598

336.841.9000
http://www.highpoint.edu/

UNDERGRADUATES: 2,900

"High Point encourages us to assume personal responsibility for our choices and actions by providing opportunities for us to be both leaders and servants."

—A HIGH POINT FOURTH-YEAR STUDENT

Other High Point Profiles:

• First-Year Program

B EGINNING WITH THE RECRUITMENT PROCESS, High Point University emphasizes that an education is incomplete if a student "does not inculcate moral values without which success in life and work is at risk." Faculty are regularly reminded, by both the president and the academic vice president, that every High Point instructor must be a teacher of ethics. Thus, mandatory ethics courses are enhanced by the self-discipline and intentional consideration of self, society, and vocation modeled by High Point's educators.

This church-affiliated, liberal arts institution founded in 1924 gained university status in 1991. It operates under the auspices of The United Methodist Church and strongly promotes character formation through the following programs:

✦ FIRST-YEAR PROGRAMS. Because most entering students preregister, the mandatory, weeklong orientation has been intentionally designed as an instrument of character formation. The Student Handbook, *A Guide to Campus Life,* the Conduct Code, the Honor Code, and the Student Government Association contribute to first-year students' awareness of personal responsibility and academic integrity.

✦ FACULTY AND CURRICULUM. Because High Point encourages teaching ethics across the curriculum, all degree candidates must complete a course and a senior seminar that include consideration of ethical issues related to work in the student's chosen field of study. Also, since 1990, the University has not only established the Culp Chair of Applied Ethics, but has also appointed a Minister to the University and a Bishop-in-Residence as a way of guaranteeing leadership with regard to spiritual programs and character formation.

✦ SPIRITUAL GROWTH. As an alternative to traditional forms of campus ministry, the Cultural Enrichment Series of the University has created a church on campus, High Point Chapel, that the *Greensboro News and Record* has described as "the place to be on Wednesday evenings." Public discussions of moral and spiritual values are often presented by campus members who encourage character formation, enabling those students who previously indicated no religious preference or had never been involved in spiritual formation to pursue moral issues.

✦ STUDENT LEADERSHIP. The North Carolina Center for the Common Good, which will be housed on campus, and the Southeast Center for Organizational Leadership, which was funded through a grant, both offer opportunities for students and faculty to explore aspects of leadership and public service.

✦ VOLUNTEER SERVICE. In addition to maintaining a volunteer center within the Office of Student Life, the University provides administrative space for the United Way Volunteer Center of High Point. The Campus Life Awards Ceremony, established by the Community Affairs Board of the Student Government Association in collaboration with High Point administrators, promotes character formation and servant leadership among both individuals and organizations.

High Point inculcates values to facilitate success in college and in the wider world. As High Point students commit themselves personally to the task of creating a caring community, they inspire and influence those they serve.

HILLSDALE COLLEGE offered liberal arts degrees to women and slaves well before the Civil War—not because they were females and Blacks, but because they were intelligent, capable people. Since 1844, this Midwestern, private institution has integrated academic progress and character development both in and out of the classroom. Hillsdale students immerse themselves in a curriculum designed to pass on the rich legacy of "the American experiment of self-government under law"; for them, learning about the past is what prepares them for the future.

Developing character beyond the college experience includes the following programs and off-campus opportunities:

✦ FIRST-YEAR PROGRAM. The fall 1999 semester launched the Herbert H. Dow II program in American Journalism that trains students in the fundamentals of journalism and prepares them for careers in a field that currently lacks ethical standards. This program is devoted to "the restoration of ethical, high-minded journalism standards, and to the reformation of our cultural, political and social practices."

✦ ACADEMIC HONESTY. Every faculty member makes clear that personal responsibility plays a vital role on Hillsdale's campus. Academic honor policies, outlined every semester, emphasize that cheating and plagiarism will not be tolerated.

✦ VOLUNTEER SERVICE. Extracurricular opportunities abound for Hillsdale students, with 28 volunteer programs contributing to community development. Peer Tutoring and The Writing Center programs pair students with others who require assistance. Coordinated by "GOAL" ("Great Opportunities for Assistance and Leadership"), Habitat for Humanity, Adult Literacy, Girl Scouts, "Kids Need Moms," Big Brothers/Big Sisters, and the Humane Society initiatives involve college students in multiple aspects of community life. More than 16,000 volunteer hours were logged for the 1997–98 school year.

✦ CIVIC EDUCATION. Hillsdale does not accept federal funding, and thus students understand their responsibility for financial aid and learn to honor their obligations. This type of citizenship building is further developed by the broad-based curriculum founded on Greco-Roman and Judeo-Christian thinking and values. The Center for Constructive Alternatives and the Shavano Institute for Leadership strive to provide solutions to many of today's problems through a series of speakers who base their experience with world issues on our rich Western heritage.

✦ SUBSTANCE-ABUSE PREVENTION. Hillsdale has a "zero-tolerance" drug policy. Students found using, possessing, or in the presence of drugs are immediately placed on a one-semester suspension. Counseling for those who admit dependency is available.

Through its curriculum, activities, policies, and external programs, Hillsdale College remains true to the mission of its founders from 150 years ago: "By training the young in the liberal arts, Hillsdale College prepares students to become leaders worthy of that legacy."

With its steadfast adherence to traditional values, Hillsdale keeps alive a treasured past and lays the path toward a brighter future.

HILLSDALE COLLEGE

33 EAST COLLEGE STREET
HILLSDALE, MI 49242-1298

517.437.7341
http://www. Hillsdale.edu/

UNDERGRADUATES: 1,200

"Hillsdale prepares us to live life virtuously, with a foundation in the Western tradition. Such an education, to me, is beyond priceless; it is essential."

—A HILLSDALE FOURTH-YEAR STUDENT

Other Hillsdale Profiles:

• Civic Education Program

HOUGHTON COLLEGE

1 WILLARD AVE.
HOUGHTON, NY 14744

800.777.2556
http://www.houghton.edu/

UNDERGRADUATES: 1,200

"Through student leadership, rigorous academics, and cross-cultural study, Houghton's Christian community propels us to explode preconceptions and realize our potential, becoming determined scholar-servants."

—A HOUGHTON FOURTH-YEAR STUDENT

Since 1883, young adults have been attracted to Houghton's Christian, liberal arts education. Today, students from 40 states and 20 countries grow academically and spiritually with the help of the committed faculty and staff at this Wesleyan Church–affiliated school. Houghton routinely receives national recognition for the quality of its faculty and facilities, and the school dedicates many programs and initiatives to character development:

◆ **First-Year Programs.** Based on academic achievement and commitment to Christian living, a select group of Houghton students are invited to study in London during the spring semester of their first year. Houghton also offers "Highlander," a ropes course and wilderness adventure program that challenges new students physically, emotionally, and spiritually.

◆ **Volunteer Service.** Many Houghton students are involved in ministries ranging from church choirs and youth groups to weekly visits to nearby nursing homes. Several faculty and students recently went to Honduras to help relieve the devastating destruction of Hurricane Mitch.

◆ **Substance-Abuse Prevention.** Houghton forbids the use of tobacco, illegal drugs, and alcoholic beverages. Students willingly sign a statement of community expectations, committing themselves to abiding by these and other standards of Christian conduct. The Counseling Center is available to students who need help to overcome an addiction.

◆ **Student Leadership.** Houghton cultivates leadership by placing a student representative on almost all governing committees. Houghton's Student Life Office recently initiated "Impact '99," a national leadership conference designed to enhance the leadership skills of young people across the nation's campuses.

◆ **Spiritual Growth.** Houghton provides many opportunities for students to grow spiritually. Chapel is held three times a week with inspiring speakers and inspirational music. "Christian Life Emphasis Week" occurs each semester at the college and is often a time of spiritual renewal for students and faculty alike. "TREK," a recently added program, encourages students to share their "journey" as committed Christians.

◆ **Civic Education.** Cosponsored by the business department and the IRS, Houghton accounting students volunteer to prepare taxes for the local community through "VITA" (the "Volunteer Income Tax" program). Now in its seventh year, the program offers students who have taken the Federal Income Taxation course at Houghton face-to-face interaction with local community members and experience with IRS policies and regulations.

◆ **Character and Sexuality.** Most Houghton students seek to honor their commitment to campus expectations and their own value systems by not engaging in sexual intimacy until they marry. Courses help students formulate and articulate their beliefs about the sacredness of marriage.

Houghton faculty and staff strive to prepare students to exhibit the scholar's passionate yet humble commitment to a chosen academic discipline, as well as the servant's qualities of serving enthusiastically and unselfishly wherever called—all within the context of a lifelong commitment to Christian faith.

HOWARD PAYNE UNIVERSITY, founded in 1889, promotes academic excellence and faith-based commitment in and out of the classroom. This private, Christian, coeducational liberal arts institution prizes service and student leadership, integrating practical vocational training and spiritual learning. Programs challenge students socially, spiritually, emotionally, intellectually, and physically. Beginning with orientation week for first-year students, Operation Sting highlights the expectations and responsibilities of college life, and the University Transition program continues to help students develop these critical-thinking skills. Other HPU character-building initiatives include:

✦ FACULTY AND CURRICULUM. Highly qualified faculty members demonstrate a commitment to academic excellence as well as Christian principles. HPU's Integration of Faith and Discipline Task Force ensures that faith and learning are woven throughout the curriculum, especially in such courses as the nationally recognized Douglas MacArthur Academy of Freedom honors program.

✦ VOLUNTEER SERVICE. Both HPU and its students have been recognized for volunteerism, including a recent state Governor's Award. "Operation Christmas Child" and "S.W.A.R.M." ("Serving With A Right Motive") Day bring together faculty, staff, and students in service. Students participate in a number of mission trips and service projects throughout the year.

✦ STUDENT LEADERSHIP. HPU educators desire that students become effective leaders, strengthening such values as commitment, calling, character, competency, and community. A Servant Leadership pilot program develops student leaders who can apply spiritual principles along with practical and professional skills.

✦ CIVIC EDUCATION. Through courses, internships, and community projects, students gain an understanding of the ways their education, faith, talents, and gifts can transform our culture.

✦ SUBSTANCE-ABUSE PREVENTION. The emphasis on faith and values at HBU provides a strong foundation for coping with the moral and ethical decisions of college life and beyond. In addition to faculty and staff, Student Mentors help guide students to campus resources when personal issues arise. HPU participates in such programs as National Collegiate Alcohol Awareness Week to reinforce the importance of a healthy lifestyle.

✦ SPIRITUAL GROWTH. Students receive spiritual guidance through campuswide prayer ministries, Ministerial Alliance, Fellowship of Christian Athletes, Fall Revival, and Resurrection Week. In chapel, students explore ways to integrate their beliefs with everyday issues. The Baptist Student Ministry helps students turn beliefs into action within a practical ministry.

✦ CHARACTER AND SEXUALITY. Plans are under way for Impact Weekend, when students stay in faculty and staff homes to discuss such topics as integrity and relationships. The purpose of this program is to strengthen the family setting and to build a support system for students.

Throughout its history, HPU has produced students who have learned that leadership is not about being served, but about serving. Students develop into citizens who know that what really matters in life is simple: committing themselves to helping others.

HOWARD PAYNE UNIVERSITY

1000 FISK AVENUE
BROWNWOOD, TX 76801

915.646.2502
http://www.hputx.edu/

UNDERGRADUATES: 1,500

"Colleges and universities cannot disregard the truth found in the Bible and still say they offer an education."

—AN HPU FOURTH-YEAR STUDENT

JOHN BROWN
UNIVERSITY

2000 WEST UNIVERSITY STREET
SILOAM SPRINGS, AR 72761-2121

501.524.9500
http://www.jbu.edu/

UNDERGRADUATES: 1,400

"The education I have received at JBU goes far beyond what I could learn from a textbook. The professors are open with students about their personal life experiences, struggles, values, beliefs, and philosophy. This kind of education is not about head knowledge; it is about life."

—A JBU SECOND-YEAR
STUDENT

Other JBU Profiles:

• Character & Sexuality Program
• Senior-Year Program
• Volunteer Service Program

EVANGELIST JOHN E. BROWN, SR., founded John Brown University in 1919, focusing on a Christ-centered education that stresses faith-based character development and strong academics. The faculty, staff, and trustees of JBU believe it is imperative that this private, liberal arts institution remain true to its core mission that integrates classroom and service experience. The three-pronged philosophy practiced at JBU, "Head, Heart, and Hand," refers to the pursuit of intellectual growth, the pursuit of Christian character, and the pursuit of service in the workplace. JBU prizes personal development and civic responsibility, championing Christian character formation in its programs:

✦ FIRST-YEAR PROGRAMS. The "Day of Caring" is the aspect of orientation that helps to establish community service as part of the JBU experience. Students work closely with city officials to complete community projects, such as washing windows for the elderly, painting park benches, and helping in the United Way agencies.

✦ FACULTY AND CURRICULUM. The JBU student/faculty ratio is 16:1, and this close proximity fosters mentoring relevant to educational and spiritual growth. The General Education Capstone supports personal wholeness, where the classroom environment intentionally stresses holistic education.

✦ VOLUNTEER SERVICE. Opportunities are plentiful at JBU for faculty and students to work together in service-learning organizations. Habitat for Humanity and The Eagle Construction Company (a student-run initiative) build housing for the needy. The Big Brother/Big Sister program enables JBU students to adopt local children who benefit from college-age mentors. Created by JBU students, The Multi-Cultural Center reaches out to the Hispanic community. Also, students can serve as interns and volunteers in the New Life Ranch, an outreach program for troubled youth.

✦ STUDENT LEADERSHIP. The JBU Student Government Association and faculty volunteers organize a Student Leadership Summit annually to discuss service and effective leadership in personal and community life.

✦ CIVIC EDUCATION. The JBU Community Service Outreach team matches students with work project needs in the Siloam Springs community. More than 55% volunteer in community projects at JBU, such as "ACTS," a local, national, and international service program that addresses needs ranging from soup-kitchen work to drug rehabilitation center involvement. The "IMPACT" program at JBU targets the impoverished town of Watts, Oklahoma, where students travel to mentor disadvantaged youth.

✦ CHARACTER AND SEXUALITY. A new Center for Marriage and Family Services provides professional Christian counseling to JBU students and community members, offering corporate Employee Assistance Programs and monthly "Life-Solutions" Seminars.

John Brown students establish a deep understanding of Christian character that leads to a personal sense of responsibility and service to the world.

KING'S COLLEGE, founded in 1946 by the Congregation of the Holy Cross, provides students with a Catholic, liberal arts education. In its mission statement, King's articulates a compelling commitment to prepare students for responsible living. Educators emphasize a personalized process of intellectual, moral, and social growth and urge students to understand ethical issues and moral implications of practices and policies through the following programs:

✦ FACULTY AND CURRICULUM. Through its integrated core curriculum, the King's faculty strives to encourage educational standards that stress an understanding of history; an appreciation of great works of art and literature; a global awareness of diverse cultures; and familiarity with science and technology. Faculty develop and insert ethics across the curriculum to help students nurture mature moral reflection. The "Recovering the Moral Dimensions of Collegiate Education Program" began in 1994 and has several facets, including faculty development, that offer intensive study of the moral traditions in philosophy and theology. Special issues such as communitarian ethics, assisted suicide in a medical context, matters of race and poverty, and capital punishment have been analyzed and used in upperclass coursework.

✦ VOLUNTEER SERVICE. One of King's goals is to have every student participate in service projects as part of his or her undergraduate experience. One-third of the students serve in various organizations, such as in Habitat for Humanity, the Commission on Economic Opportunity, and Junior Achievement, as well as in various nonprofit businesses, the local conservancy project, and soup kitchens. The Patron's Day celebration includes a full day devoted to hands-on service for new students.

✦ STUDENT LEADERSHIP. Noncredit retreats and workshops integrate learning and leadership experience for King's students. These programs focus on the seven core values of the Social Change Model of Leadership Development: consciousness of self, congruence, commitment, collaboration, common purpose, controversy with civility, and citizenship.

✦ CIVIC EDUCATION. Acting as a catalyst for integrating serious ethical study and reflection on the various professional and business programs offered at King's College, the Center for Ethics and Public Life seeks to transform the public and personal dimension of students' lives. The Center oversees the moral and intellectual purpose of King's, fostering dialog on ethical dimensions in academic fields, developing student courses in professional programs, sponsoring faculty programs to address ethical concerns, arranging lectures on timely ethical topics, and serving as a resource for reflection on moral life.

✦ SPIRITUAL GROWTH. The Campus Ministry provides various activities that assist students in developing their belief system. Retreat programs encourage community building and develop a deeper relationship with God. The student-led "LIFE" organization educates the college community about supporting life at all levels, in the womb and on death row.

King's prepares its students for a satisfying and purposeful life through carefully crafted character-forming courses and service-learning opportunities.

KING'S COLLEGE

133 NORTH RIVER STREET
WILKES-BARRE, PA 18711-0801

570.208.5900
http://www.kings.edu/

UNDERGRADUATES: 1,700

"At King's College, I received all the educational advantages found at a larger institution, as well as the personal attention and commitment to character development that a smaller school has to offer."

—A RECENT KING GRADUATE

Other King's Profiles:

• Faculty & Curriculum Program

LYNCHBURG COLLEGE

1501 LAKESIDE DRIVE
LYNCHBURG, VA 24501

804.544.8664
http://www.lynchburg.edu/

UNDERGRADUATES: 1,700

"Through the many community service projects sponsored by Lynchburg, I have learned that I can make a difference in the world. The faculty and staff set an inspiring example by working side by side with students on service projects."

—A LYNCHBURG THIRD-YEAR
STUDENT

Other Lynchburg Profiles:

• Volunteer Service Program

LYNCHBURG COLLEGE, rated among the best of the small, liberal arts colleges in the country by publications such as *U.S. News & World Report,* was founded in 1903 as a church-affiliated institution that prizes character development through education. As Lynchburg President Charles Warren wrote: "In this complex and rapidly changing world, our mission is to develop the whole person—as critical thinker, principled leader, and community servant." From the moment prospective students visit Lynchburg until they graduate, they learn the importance of personal and civic responsibility, modeled by faculty and staff. Five Centers of Distinction and a nature study center provide interactive learning and community service experiences beyond the classroom.

✦ **FIRST-YEAR PROGRAMS AND RESPONSIBLE LIVING.** As soon as first-year students arrive on campus, they participate in the mandatory "OCTAA" ("On Campus Talking About Alcohol") program, which teaches individual responsibility for alcohol use and related lifestyle choices. Also, they become aware of academic integrity through Lynchburg's Honor Code and Student Judicial System traditions. Connection Leaders is a program that pairs first-year students with upperclassmen, who then serve as peer mentors.

✦ **ACADEMIC HONESTY.** Since 1934 the Lynchburg Honor Code has been part of student life and before attending classes all students sign pledges to adhere to a strict standard of academic integrity. Also, the Student Judicial System upholds standards of behavior on its three student-run boards: Honor, Student Conduct, and Appeals.

✦ **FACULTY AND CURRICULUM.** In the Lynchburg College Symposium Readings (LCSR) Program, students study, discuss, and write about life lessons based on classical readings that include tyranny, freedom, science, and morality. Ethics education and service-learning components are part of the business and education curricula.

✦ **VOLUNTEER SERVICE.** Through "SERVE" ("Students Engaged in Responsible Volunteer Service"), nearly 500 students, faculty, and staff volunteer more than 15,000 hours annually to more than 200 college and community organizations. These include the Battered Women's Shelter, Hunger Task Force, Adult Literacy Corps, College Rescue Squad, and Habitat for Humanity.

✦ **STUDENT LEADERSHIP.** Students develop leadership skills through participation in the annual Anderson Leadership Conference, Student Government Association (SGA), and Student Activities Board (SAB). SGA appoints students to serve on faculty/staff standing committees charged with college governance. Both the SGA and the SAB are recipients of the National Association for Campus Activities awards for excellence in programming and leadership. The Blue Key National Honor Fraternity selects junior and senior men who have made outstanding contributions to campus life through leadership, scholarship, and service.

✦ **SENIOR-YEAR PROGRAMS.** The Senior Symposium features lectures on current issues related to the LCSR selections. Small group discussions provide an atmosphere in which students grapple with issues facing humanity within Western civilization as well as within other traditions.

In their personal lives, future careers, and as servant leaders in their communities, Lynchburg students receive the tools to succeed in personal and professional development to meet their world.

"TO PREPARE STUDENTS for lives of civic responsibility" is the central tenet of a Manchester College education. The encouraging environment has created a sense of self-identity, strong personal faith, and a dedication to service in students since 1889, when Manchester was founded as a church-affiliated, independent, liberal arts college. As its mission statement reads: "We seek to graduate persons who possess ability and conviction."

When Manchester students graduate, they enter the marketplace with both personal convictions and career abilities, learned through focused programs:

✦ FIRST-YEAR PROGRAMS. Incoming first-year students who have demonstrated outstanding commitment to service during their high-school years are eligible for Service Scholarships. These students maintain high academic standards, continue to volunteer in service organizations, and lead others to develop a strong sense of commitment.

✦ FACULTY AND CURRICULUM. Manchester is home to the nation's oldest peace studies major. The Peace Studies Institute plans conferences and workshops around individual and global conflict-resolution strategies. Faculty model their own convictions in ways that inspire students to do likewise—in January, faculty and students travel to Nicaragua to care for rural communities, and in the spring they organize trips to support Habitat for Humanity. The environmental studies major also emphasizes ethical concerns, and the Koinonia Environmental Center provides educational opportunities for elementary school children through mentoring.

✦ VOLUNTEER SERVICE. Manchester's religious affiliation with the Church of the Brethren highlights its "faith, learning, and service" motto. Service organizations such as Americorp, through which students work as tutors in local elementary schools, and Habitat for Humanity, through which students concentrate on local community improvements, are overseen by the Office of Volunteer Service, a student-run organization.

✦ STUDENT LEADERSHIP. The Manchester College Reconciliation Service trains student residence hall assistants in conflict-resolution. The general education program has offered courses in human conflict since 1970.

✦ CIVIC EDUCATION. Programs such as the Model United Nations and the Mock Trial Team develop students' abilities to articulate their beliefs. With clear intentions, Manchester students serve their community in many ways: accounting students assist the elderly with tax returns, the women's basketball team "adopts" retirement community residents and brings them to games, and students help ensure that local children have what they need to enjoy holidays such as Halloween and Thanksgiving.

Manchester students wear green ribbons at graduation indicating their commitment to civic responsibility and pledge to "explore and take into account the social and environmental consequences of any job I consider or any organization for which I work." Because Manchester students excel in dedication to personal integrity and civic responsibility, they eagerly enter the world ready to serve others creatively, intellectually, and practically.

MANCHESTER COLLEGE

604 EAST COLLEGE AVENUE
NORTH MANCHESTER, IN
46962-1225

219.982.5000
http://www.manchester.edu/

UNDERGRADUATES: 1,000

"It gives me hope to know that schools like Manchester are committed to teaching others the importance of peaceful conflict resolution."

—A MANCHESTER FOURTH-YEAR STUDENT

Other Manchester Profiles:

• Civic Education Program

MARIST COLLEGE

290 NORTH ROAD
POUGHKEEPSIE, NY 12601-1387

914.575.3000
http://www.marist.edu/

UNDERGRADUATES: 4,100

"My Praxis and Global Outreach experiences provided a bridge between in-class learning and hands-on service at Marist. By pulling academics and community service together, this gave a fuller dimension to my education and expanded my sensitivity to those in need."

—A MARIST FOURTH-YEAR STUDENT

Other Marist Profiles:

• Civic Education Program
• First-Year Program

MARIST COLLEGE has a proud history of helping students attain a lifelong commitment to moral and ethical values. Founded in 1905 by the Marist Brothers, a Catholic teaching congregation, Marist College evolved into a Normal Training School by 1929 and into a four-year college by 1946. Today, this private, liberal arts college articulates a clear goal of personal and intellectual development that emphasizes students' civic responsibility. A Marist education, as described in its mission statement, supports the "pursuit of higher human values and dedication to the principle of service," as demonstrated by its dedication to character-building education:

✦ FIRST-YEAR PROGRAMS. At Marist, the Introduction to Philosophy course encourages reflection about different fields of study and on decision-making strategies. "Self-Management" aims to teach students responsibility and its application to everyday life issues.

✦ FACULTY AND CURRICULUM. Marist students experience a core curriculum that strives to integrate personal and civic responsibility. Students are asked "to reflect on and act on the Judeo-Christian ideals of love, justice, and compassion as the foundation for a good life and a good society."

✦ VOLUNTEER SERVICE. Dedication to the pursuit of higher values is complemented by a commitment to service through programs for the disadvantaged. A wealth of community projects, such as Global Outreach Spring Break (serving the poor in Mexico and Puerto Rico), Habitat for Humanity (serving the poor in Poughkeepsie), Grace Smith House (for battered women), and Hillcrest House/Shelter (for the homeless), involve more than 700 students and faculty, who work closely to combine social research, hands-on personal experience, and critical reflection. Also, in affiliation with the New York Theological Seminary, Marist faculty provide college courses (such as the Spirituality Today Workshop) in a local correctional facility and recently received an Outstanding Community Service citation by the Seminary.

✦ SPIRITUAL GROWTH. Developing moral integrity through spiritual growth includes the annual Effron Lecture in Jewish Studies, the annual Holocaust Memorial Program, an Ethics and Society lecture series, and a Strategic Choices for Peace and Social Justice series.

✦ CIVIC EDUCATION. The interdisciplinary minor Public Praxis strives to inspire students to live and work with a civic-minded code of conduct. With a view to fully engage learning with a commitment to social transformation, the course work requires students to integrate at-site experience with scholarship, critical reflection, and rigorous analysis.

✦ SENIOR-YEAR PROGRAMS. In the senior-year Ethics course, students undertake a retrospective analysis of ethical self-understanding in the Judeo-Christian and secular humanist traditions, as well as an assessment of the new ethical demands prompted by a technological culture.

Marist students strive to find particular ways to integrate the enduring value of our heritage with the constantly evolving needs of the larger society.

LEADERSHIP, character, and intellect—these are the touchstones of education at Mary Baldwin College. Since its founding in 1842, this Christian liberal arts college for women has focused not just on strong academics and career preparation, but on creating an environment in which young women learn leadership with a strong ethical component. Residence hall life, athletics, arts, student government, curriculum, clubs, and special programs all combine to help each student develop into the best person she can be.

✦ **ACADEMIC HONESTY AND RESPONSIBILITY TO THE COMMUNITY.** On Charter Day every fall, all new students sign the Honor Pledge. Mary Baldwin's student-administered Honor Code—which prohibits lying, cheating, and stealing—and Judicial Code—which governs how students live together respectfully in a diverse community—are respected by the entire college community. Debate and focus sessions ensure that these time-honored codes continue to be relevant to new students.

✦ **FACULTY AND CURRICULUM.** The nationally recognized Virginia Women's Institute for Leadership (VWIL) is the best known source of leadership development at Mary Baldwin, increasing the school's traditional strength in this area. Courses such as "Ethics, Community and Leadership" are built into VWIL's curriculum and are open to all undergraduates. PEG (the Program for the Exceptionally Gifted) is a program that enables girls as young as 14 to pursue college degrees.

✦ **CIVIC EDUCATION.** Mary Baldwin's student government system, through which young women learn to work with others and make their voices heard, prepares students for active, responsible citizenship.

✦ **STUDENT LEADERSHIP.** Leadership is woven into all aspects of life at Mary Baldwin. Students have great authority in governing their own affairs. By being accountable to their peers, they learn responsibility to the larger community. In addition to learning by doing, students take part in formal leadership training programs, such as Emerging Leaders and outdoor challenge programs. Mary Baldwin was the first women's college to be granted a chapter of Omicron Delta Kappa, the prestigious honorary leadership society.

✦ **VOLUNTEER SERVICE.** Mary Baldwin's long tradition of service to others manifests itself in volunteer programs such as the student chapter of Habitat for Humanity, tutoring programs for at-risk children in the community, blood drives, and many other activities. Faculty and staff often work alongside students in such projects.

✦ **SPIRITUAL GROWTH.** The Carpenter Quest Program is a unique two-year course combining academic study of religion, exploration of the role of faith in daily life, and community service. Courses such as "Faith, Life and Service" are built into the curriculum.

Mary Baldwin has evolved into a multifaceted institution with strong traditions and progressive opportunities for young women preparing to make their way in the world—and to make it a better place for others.

MARY BALDWIN COLLEGE

PO BOX 1500
STAUNTON, VA 24401

540.887.7000
http://www.mbc.edu/

UNDERGRADUATES: 1,300

"Mary Baldwin students learn about leadership as we grow intellectually and spiritually. Caring teachers and friends, as well as unique opportunities such as Quest, hold our campus community together."

—A MARY BALDWIN FOURTH-YEAR STUDENT

Other Mary Baldwin Profiles:

• Profile of President Tyson
• Spiritual Growth Program
• Student Leadership Program

MESSIAH COLLEGE

COLLEGE AVENUE
GRANTHAM, PA 17027-0800

717.766.2511
http://www.messiah.edu/

UNDERGRADUATES: 2,700

"Messiah looks at higher education as much more than a classroom experience. Students are challenged to view their college experience as a time to holistically develop themselves as unique and special persons in service to society."

—A MESSIAH THIRD-YEAR STUDENT

DISTINCTIVE CHRISTIAN ETHICS characterize the educational mission of Messiah College, a private, church-affiliated, liberal and applied arts school. Steeped in character formation since it was founded in 1909, Messiah's educational objectives for its undergraduates are to develop understanding of the interdependent nature of human society, cultural diversity, and the importance of moral and spiritual regeneration in society, as well as the practice of good stewardship of economic and natural resources and the willingness to work for reconciliation at both global and personal levels. Each Messiah student is assigned a faculty advisor who emphasizes reflection on these objectives and encourages students to read widely in relevant areas.

The values inculcated by faculty mentoring are further enhanced by Messiah's purposeful student development programs:

✦ FACULTY AND CURRICULUM. In addition to high-quality academics, Messiah's curriculum is infused with core requirements in non-Western perspectives and ethics. To simultaneously strengthen individual students' commitments and broaden their understanding of others remains a primary goal of interdisciplinary core requirements. Faculty members engage student advisees in going beyond the classroom to pursue Messiah's objective of "being prepared to act as servants in the world."

✦ VOLUNTEER SERVICE. To develop voluntary service into a life "habit," the Agape Center for Service Learning provides and coordinates a variety of Messiah programs such as working for Habitat for Humanity, preparing tax returns for the elderly and low-income adults, and teaching English as a second language to recent immigrants in Harrisburg.

✦ STUDENT LEADERSHIP. The Emerging Leaders program guides Messiah students over four years in numerous activities and discussions about leadership, responsibilities, and opportunities. Students learn to identify their leadership potential and, with help from campus mentors, participate in college activities as practice for the future. The Center for Leadership Development also helps students develop into community leaders.

✦ CIVIC EDUCATION. Messiah offers students the opportunity to study at its Philadelphia campus, where students have been equipped to improve and transform a contemporary urban environment. A nationally recognized internship program provides workplace experience as a complement to classroom content.

Programs such as these reflect the powerful ethos created at Messiah and echo the reason for its educational mission: "To educate men and women toward maturity of intellect, character, and Christian faith in preparation for lives of service, leadership, and reconciliation in church and society."

Founded in 1847 as a school for orphan girls, Midway College, a private, church-affiliated liberal arts school and Kentucky's only college for women, provides a nurturing learning environment that enables students to assume roles of responsibility and leadership. Midway assists students in the development of personal integration and self-sufficiency through a strong commitment to the intellectual, moral, and spiritual components of a true education. Faculty and staff encourage these young women to become productive participants in society and responsible citizens in democracy. Midway also supports men and women who are employed and of nontraditional college age to earn undergraduate degrees through evening and extension programs.

Midway's commitment to community service and a rich liberal arts education is evident in the following programs:

✦ Faculty and Curriculum. A longstanding "family atmosphere" encourages the development of mentor-student relationships, enabling students to examine moral lessons from the past and establish appropriate moral ideals for today. Required religion and ethics courses are useful in defining ethical principles and applying them to daily experiences. Faculty and staff exemplify service to students and the community by initiating service projects within local elementary and middle schools, as well as by coordinating college participation in national efforts such as the Empty Bowl Project and the observance of Martin Luther King, Jr. Day.

✦ Volunteer Service. The entire Midway family, including students, combine fundamental values and commitment by actively contributing to their community at multiple levels. The Kentucky Watershed Watch educates citizens on water quality and campus environmental issues; the Empty Bowl Project, a nationwide program, feeds the hungry through help from college students, elementary schools, and community leaders.

✦ Student Leadership. A number of student initiatives provides an atmosphere for fellow students to develop as leaders, including the Center for Women, Diversity, and Leadership; the Commonwealth/Conquest, a program designed to increase citizen participation in the public policy process; a Career Series for Women; and the Midway Orientation Program, in which returning students organize and plan for orientation, working with faculty and hosting new students. The Ruth Slack Roach Leadership Scholarship Program strengthens students' leadership potential through a variety of service-based projects both on and off campus.

✦ Spiritual Growth. A longstanding covenant between Midway and the Christian Church exists and supports the Midway College Fellowship, an ecumenical campus organization that works in conjunction with the Office of the College Minister. This program fosters friendships and provides Bible study, prayer groups, worship, and community service.

✦ Civic Education. Course work is complemented by appropriate "real life" involvement in civic, religious, and work activities. These include an Arts and Leisure series, the Kentucky Association of Student Professionals, the Midway Association of Student Nurses, the Midway College Fellowship, and the Psychology/Sociology Club.

Midway College encourages spiritual values in order to build a community of responsible contemporary women who serve as leaders in their personal and professional lives.

MIDWAY COLLEGE

512 EAST STEPHENS STREET
MIDWAY, KY 40347-1120

606.846.4421
http://www.midway.edu/

UNDERGRADUATES: 9,000

"Before Midway, I wasn't very self-confident. Now I've improved as a student and have even become a leader. I've gained a strong voice here."

—A Midway fourth-year student

MILLSAPS COLLEGE

1701 NORTH STATE STREET
PO BOX 150556
JACKSON, MS 39210

601.974.1000
http://www.millsaps.edu/

UNDERGRADUATES: 1,200

"I cannot fathom the idea of an education that does not intertwine all elements of knowledge. By being exposed to multiple perspectives at Millsaps, we find those things that we truly love."

—A RECENT MILLSAPS
GRADUATE

ENABLING STUDENTS TO THINK FOR THEMSELVES has inspired the educational ethos at Millsaps College since 1890. Critical reasoning is prized at this private, liberal arts school affiliated with The United Methodist Church, and faculty strive to engender clear thinking in Millsaps students. Believing that a college must do more than educate, Millsaps rigorously pursues civic and personal responsibility through the following programs:

✦ **FIRST-YEAR PROGRAMS.** Millsaps first-year students participate in a required student- and faculty-planned 10-week program that addresses attitudes and expectations regarding the Honor Code and the Code of Student Behavior, as well as sexual relations, ethnic diversity, and conflict management.

✦ **CIVIC EDUCATION.** Relationship-building results when faculty, staff, and Millsaps students volunteer in community programs such as Junior Achievement and Midtown Redevelopment Efforts. Millsaps' Campus Link Chapter (Americorps) focuses on literacy work in public schools and other community centers. Practical hands-on lessons are then complemented by Millsaps' 10-course core curriculum that fosters competency in reasoning, global awareness, civic duties, and communication.

✦ **STUDENT LEADERSHIP.** The "LEAD" program works with first-year students and student leaders to refine, build, and create awareness of leadership and service opportunities on campus. Twice-yearly leadership retreats foster unity among leaders and the many groups on campus. "Project Lead" promotes civic responsibility with semester-long service commitments in the Millsaps and Jackson community.

✦ **VOLUNTEER SERVICE.** Students may tap into "Circle K" (a branch of Kiwanis International) and commit to three hours of community work per semester. In 1996, the Millsaps student body was recognized as having the second largest Circle K participation worldwide. In partnership with Galloway Memorial United Methodist Church, the Millsaps chapter of Habitat for Humanity provides housing for urban Jackson. Also, the Catholic Campus Ministry "Saltillo Trip" provides civil services and ministry to a local Mexican population.

✦ **SPIRITUAL GROWTH.** The Millsaps Campus Ministry Team coordinates events for personal development on and off campus. The "Seeking and Understanding Series" raises issues related to the moral and spiritual health of society and campus life. Panels of faculty, students, and off-campus leaders launch discussions on diverse topics such as race relations, faith and science, and human rights issues abroad.

✦ **SENIOR-YEAR PROGRAMS.** The capstone course "Reflections on Liberal Studies" enables all graduates to reflect on the four-year college experience and address how they will assume their roles in society.

Millsaps provides the small class size, strong core curriculum, and challenging academic endeavors and service opportunities that prepare its graduates for world citizenship.

Other Millsaps Profiles:

• Academic Honesty Program
• Faculty & Curriculum Program
• Senior-Year Program

MISSISSIPPI COLLEGE, an academic community where faith and learning have been encouraged and cherished since 1826, promotes the pursuit of Christian responsibility and service among its faculty, staff, and students. Mississippi's president, Howell Todd, emphasizes to prospective students and their parents that character development and the cultivation of personal values, based on a genuine concern for others, stand at the center of "who we are and what we do."

The ideals of Christian responsibility and service, faith and learning, care and compassion, and character development describe the core of Mississippi's curriculum and cocurricular activities:

✦ FIRST-YEAR PROGRAMS. "Freshman Experience" is a required program in which students gather with faculty and staff for an extensive process of personal reflection, orientation, and education. During the semester-long program, groups of 15 first-year students, led by two upperclass mentors, one faculty member, and one staff member, meet weekly to discuss issues of civic duty, personal responsibility, and the purpose of higher education.

✦ FACULTY AND CURRICULUM. Mississippi seeks to integrate moral reasoning and values development into the core curriculum, which is divided into three general learning areas: Analytical Reasoning and Effective Communication, Personal Values and Attitudes, and Social and Cultural Understanding.

✦ VOLUNTEER SERVICE. Mississippi's Service Center identifies areas of need in the community and matches them with student volunteers. Each semester, students participate in food and blood drives; tutor peers; mentor and befriend community children at the Baptist Children's Village; participate in charity-sponsored athletic events; and volunteer in nursing home ministries. They also help build homes for the needy through the campus chapter of Habitat for Humanity.

✦ SUBSTANCE-ABUSE PREVENTION. The Student Government Association sponsors "Drug Awareness Week," during which students learn about the risks of drugs and alcohol abuse. Success in drug awareness heightens university sensitivity to other addictive behaviors such as eating disorders and smoking. Faculty members strive to integrate health-related concepts into the core curriculum and address issues dealing with substance abuse.

✦ SPIRITUAL GROWTH PROGRAMS. Students are required to participate in Mississippi's Chapel Program, where at least half of the services are of a religious nature. The Honors Program, offered to students who have maintained an exceptional academic record, explores Christian ethics and values and encourages students to reflect on some of the complex ethical issues they will face in the future.

Mississippi encourages students to use their skills and abilities to pursue lifelong learning and to dedicate their lives in service to God and others in their communities.

MISSISSIPPI COLLEGE

200 WEST COLLEGE STREET
CLINTON, MS 39058

601.925.3000
http://www.mc.edu/

UNDERGRADUATES: 2,300

"What sets Mississippi apart is the desire to instill and develop character in students, which seems to permeate the campus at all levels. Dedication to character building is the reason that this institution will always hold a special place in the hearts of its students."

—A MISSISSIPPI FOURTH-YEAR STUDENT

MOREHOUSE COLLEGE

830 WESTVIEW DRIVE SW
ATLANTA, GA 30314

404.681.2800
http://www.morehouse.edu/

UNDERGRADUATES: 3,000

"The Morehouse environment does not allow us to ignore the distressing conditions in some of our communities. Believe me, whether it is through the Crown Forum lectures or in our classes, we are going to be encouraged and challenged to respond."

—A MOREHOUSE THIRD-YEAR STUDENT

ONE OF THE MOST DISTINGUISHED INSTITUTIONS of higher education, Morehouse is the nation's only historically Black, liberal arts college for men. Founded in 1867, this highly competitive school attracts only the most motivated high-school students from across the U.S. Although small, the college's commitment to excellence in scholarship, leadership, and service has resulted in extraordinary contributions to professions, communities, the nation, and the world by illustrious alumni such as Nobel Peace Prize laureate Martin Luther King Jr.; former Secretary of Health and Human Services Louis Sullivan; MacArthur Fellow Donald Hopkins; Olympian Edwin Moses; filmmaker Spike Lee; and a number of congressmen, federal judges, and college presidents. The following programs all focus on encouraging students to understand and affirm the responsibilities attendant with being a "Morehouse Man":

◆ FIRST-YEAR PROGRAMS. Each new student is required to participate in "Rites of Passage" activities designed to bring about a "spirit of brotherhood" and provide dynamic opportunities for new students to learn about the Morehouse mission and purpose. Alumni play a key role, including participating in "Alumni Interaction/Spirit Night," when alumni share personal experiences from their student days and explain what it means to be a "Morehouse Man." The alumni also introduce students to the traditional Morehouse spirit songs and chants.

◆ ACADEMIC HONESTY. Each student signs a Student Creed that affirms the Morehouse ideals and practices of personal and academic integrity. By signing the Creed, a student declares publicly that he has freely chosen to follow a code of "civilized behavior." Allegiance and obligation to the Creed discussed annually at campus-wide forums attended by the entire student body.

◆ VOLUNTEER SERVICE. The service ethic is a significant part of the Morehouse experience. A large number of Morehouse men recently spent their spring break in Chicago tutoring and mentoring students from Sojourner Truth Elementary. Morehouse has also established "Technology and the Morehouse Learning Community" to train local churches on how to use computer software to improve church operations. Morehouse also organizes "Operation Olive Branch," an annual conference that brings together six local colleges to discuss ways to improve the Atlanta community through campus-based service activities.

◆ STUDENT LEADERSHIP. At the heart of Morehouse's mission is preparing and training tomorrow's world leaders. The objective of the new seven-year, three-part strategic plan (education, research, and service) is to establish a leadership studies program that will be added to the list of major/minors. The goal of the new Leadership Center at Morehouse will be to inspire a new generation of leaders through programs and activities that draw on and extend Morehouse's traditions and rich heritage. One activity already in place is required student attendance at 24 Crown Forums. These sessions expose students to a series of lectures on ethics, character development, and leadership. Guest lecturers have included baseball great and entrepreneur Reggie Jackson and motivational speaker Les Brown.

Guided by a commitment to excellence, Morehouse seeks to develop men with a zest for learning, a concern for the welfare of others, and a commitment to lead. Morehouse also assumes a special responsibility for teaching its students about the history and culture of Black people.

MOUNT ST. MARY'S COLLEGE, a private, liberal arts institution primarily for women, promotes critical thinking, leadership development, and compassionate faith through intelligent service to others. Founded in 1925 by the Sisters of St. Joseph of Carondelet, Mount St. Mary's Catholic tradition fosters a values-based learning environment in which students can realize their potential and acquire the skills to become proactive citizens. Dr. Cheryl Mabey, who has gained national recognition for the Women's Leadership Program, states: "The concept of service learning throughout the curriculum provides a totally different understanding of our academic task."

Mount St. Mary's commitment to leadership and character-building includes the following programs:

✦ **FACULTY AND CURRICULUM.** Service learning at Mount St. Mary's begins in the core curriculum, continues in courses designed for departmental majors, and culminates with internships. By taking the ideas, concepts, and theories presented in their course work and applying them to the real world, students learn that they can make a difference and become active and engaged citizens in society.

✦ **VOLUNTEER SERVICE.** Mount students can participate in the Center for Urban Partnerships that joins faculty and students with community service agencies, grass roots organizations, K–12 educators, government officials and policy makers, and businesses to form strategic partnerships to better serve the community. The Student Ambassadors Program sends students back to the urban high schools from which they graduated to act as counselors, mentors, and role models for high-school youth. Currently, 40 ambassadors serve in 35 high schools, two housing projects, one middle school, and a transition home for homeless women and children.

✦ **SUBSTANCE-ABUSE PREVENTION.** Mount St. Mary's fosters an environment that promotes personal growth and emotional and physical well-being. Counseling services exist on-campus to offer students constructive and positive ways to deal with issues of drug and alcohol abuse, as well as eating disorders, anxiety, and depression.

✦ **STUDENT LEADERSHIP.** The Leadership Studies Minor and the Leadership Portfolio integrate study with practical opportunities. Students study models and values of leadership through specific analysis of policies and issues affecting society; identify their own leadership abilities; and refine their leadership skills by participating in departmental clubs, student, and service organizations.

✦ **SPIRITUAL GROWTH.** The Campus Ministry promotes spiritual growth with numerous opportunities for faculty, staff, and students to participate in religious services and reflect on scripture. In addition to weekly religious and prayer services, the Campus Ministry sponsors Bible studies, retreats, and special observances such as Hanukkah Night, Advent Dinners, and Holocaust Remembrance Week.

At Mount St. Mary's a values-based academic program prepares students to occupy significant leadership and service roles in society. As they recognize their leadership potential, Mount graduates claim lifelong habits of civic responsibility that will enrich their own lives while serving others.

MOUNT ST. MARY'S COLLEGE

12001 CHALON ROAD
LOS ANGELES, CA 90049

310.954.4000
http://www.msmc.la.edu/

UNDERGRADUATES: 1,700

"The Mount has helped me on my journey to better serve God and my family. It has been the ideal environment to grow intellectually and spiritually and has helped me define and strengthen my position in life."

—A MOUNT THIRD-YEAR STUDENT

Other Mount Profiles:

• Profile of President Kennelly
• First-Year Program
• Student Leadership Program

NAZARETH COLLEGE OF ROCHESTER

4245 EAST AVENUE
ROCHESTER, NY 14618

716.389.2525
http://www.naz.edu/

UNDERGRADUATES: 1,800

"Nazareth has fostered a strong dedication to service and leadership within me. The value it places on community activism has helped to shape my work and success. I will always carry Nazareth's staff and faculty support, encouragement, and commitment with me."

—A NAZARETH THIRD-YEAR STUDENT

FOSTERING A STRONG SENSE OF SERVICE and a commitment to a life informed by intellectual, ethical, and aesthetic values is part of the mission of Nazareth College, an independent, liberal arts school founded in 1924 by the Sisters of St. Joseph. Nazareth has earned national recognition for its focus on responsibility to the community, exemplified in these programs:

✦ **FIRST-YEAR PROGRAMS.** New students, along with Nazareth's president, faculty, staff, and student orientation leaders participate in a half day of community service as part of "Orientation Weekend."

✦ **VOLUNTEER SERVICE.** The Center for Service Learning coordinates resources and helps students, faculty, and staff to explore and arrange for community service. Twenty-one faculty members teach 28 service-learning courses to 570 students. In celebration of Nazareth's 75th anniversary, April 15, 1999, was designated a "Day of Service" to thank Rochester for its support. More than 1,000 Nazareth students joined 160 faculty and staff in performing 4,000 hours of service at 100 sites throughout Rochester.

✦ **STUDENT LEADERSHIP.** In September, student leaders receive training that clarifies their roles and responsibilities; in January, they take part in another weekend of training and workshops led by Nazareth faculty and staff. Diversity and peer mediation training are also provided for student leaders.

✦ **CIVIC EDUCATION.** In the "Learning Styles and Strategies Specialist" program, Nazareth faculty instruct education students on-site in public schools; the students also volunteer to assist teachers. About 75 Nazareth students participate each semester, providing 20,200 hours of service yearly in approximately 20 elementary, middle, and senior high schools.

✦ **SPIRITUAL GROWTH.** Campus Ministry offers opportunities for prayer and worship, retreats, prayer/study groups, and programs on moral issues such as the death penalty and genetic engineering. Religious studies courses give students a global perspective, allowing them to learn about and reflect on their own faith tradition, as well as on the religious traditions of others.

✦ **SUBSTANCE-ABUSE PREVENTION.** A full-time specialist offers educational programs campus-wide, provides information, and counsels individuals. A Substance Abuse Committee works with the specialist to plan "Alcohol Awareness Week" before spring break.

✦ **CHARACTER AND SEXUALITY.** Male and female peer educators work with faculty and staff to provide a special program about sexuality and responsible decision making. These peer educators receive training from the staff of Health Services and Counseling Services, and staff also talk with individuals and offer other presentations and information.

In their years at college, 91% of Nazareth students participate in community service, and the percentage of alumni volunteers is higher than the national average. Nazareth hopes that graduating students take with them not only knowledge, but the ability to think critically; not only memories, but wisdom, understanding, compassion, generosity, and respect for diversity.

Founded in 1887 by Nebraska Methodists as a private school, Nebraska Wesleyan University is dedicated to intellectual and personal growth within the context of liberal arts education and Christian concern. NWU has gained recognition as a top college by the Carnegie Foundation for the Advancement for Teaching and by *U.S. News & World Report*. The university seeks to integrate questions about meaning and value with the pursuit of learning and understanding through these vigorous programs:

✦ **First-Year Program.** The "Liberal Arts Seminar," required for all first-year students, introduces study skills, research, group collaboration, and responsibility to the community.

✦ **Faculty and Curriculum.** The general education curriculum requires courses in Western values and traditions, diversity, and global issues, and students serve on the President's Council on Cultural Diversity. Faculty can undertake international projects or study trips that enhance their ability to encourage international perspectives in the classroom through the sabbatical program.

✦ **Volunteer Service.** NWU students, in partnership with an elementary school in Lincoln, volunteer to read, supervise games and study sessions, and tutor. Elementary-school students come to campus for Halloween or Valentine's Day and are paired with NWU students at athletic events. In May 1990, NWU received an award from the Lincoln Public Schools for this program. Also, each fall, 400 students, faculty, and staff take part in "Lend a Hand to Lincoln Day," in which teams of 20 people work in nursing homes, hospitals, retirement homes, and the Hispanic Center. Also, during an ice storm in October 1997, the NWU field house served as a Red Cross shelter for thousands of Lincoln residents who had no electricity or heat. For their work in supervising games and activities for children and adults, NWU students received awards from the Red Cross.

✦ **Student Leadership.** Students serve on campus committees, including the NWU's Board of Governors, where two students have full voting privileges. Also, the annual "LEAD" retreat develops leadership skills and strategies for collaboration.

✦ **Spiritual Growth.** Campus Ministry provides regular chapel programs, along with work projects in neighborhood centers in Lincoln, East Los Angeles, and the Dominican Republic.

✦ **Substance-Abuse Prevention.** NWU participates in "SCIP" ("School Community Intervention Program"), which addresses drug, alcohol, and behavioral problems in junior-high and high-school students.

✦ **Senior-Year Program.** "Attitudes and Values," a required senior seminar, encourages students to reflect on and analyze interrelationships among humanistic, artistic, social, scientific, and technological aspects of contemporary life.

From the beginning to the end of their experience, NWU students develop a sense of self-worth, personal responsibility, intercultural sensitivity, and commitment to community service.

NEBRASKA WESLEYAN UNIVERSITY

5000 SAINT PAUL AVENUE
LINCOLN, NE 68504-2796

402.465.2217
http://www.nebrwesleyan.edu/

UNDERGRADUATES: 1,700

"My experience at NWU has expanded my mind, matured my person, and instilled within me a sense of reverence and illumination that cannot be described."

—An NWU fourth-year student

NIAGARA UNIVERSITY

NIAGARA UNIVERSITY, NY 14109

716.285.1212
http://www.niagara.edu/

UNDERGRADUATES: 2,300

"At Niagara, I learned that our greatest gift to others is love and kindness without regard for personal gain. Giving of oneself captures the warmth of humanity."

—A NIAGARA FOURTH-YEAR STUDENT

NIAGARA UNIVERSITY prizes ethical and social values that enrich student lives and strengthen society. Founded in 1856, Niagara is a private, comprehensive institution that adheres to the altruistic tradition of the Vincentian Fathers and Brothers—the religious community founded by St. Vincent de Paul, the universal patron of all charitable deeds. Niagara's mission seeks to instill in students a deep concern for the rights and dignity of human beings, especially the poor, the suffering, the handicapped, and the outcast.

Outreach concerns distinguish Niagara's curriculum and are evident in the following programs:

✦ **FIRST-YEAR PROGRAMS.** Niagara introduces new students to the campus, faculty, staff, and other students through two orientation programs. "CARE" ("Collegiate Advisement, Registration, and Expenses") is a two-day summer program in which students and their parents attend seminars about the university and experience campus life. The student-run New Student Orientation program takes place a few days before upperclassmen return to campus and combines numerous activities and events to welcome Niagara's freshmen.

✦ **FACULTY AND CURRICULUM.** Niagara integrates its service-learning program into the classroom to expose students to practical experience in serving others. "Learn and Serve Niagara" encourages an academic approach to service learning, in which students donate time and talent to a specific community agency or group where the service becomes part of a class grade. Last year, more than 1,800 students donated more than 33,000 hours of their time to community service through this program.

✦ **VOLUNTEER SERVICE.** "NUCAP" ("Niagara University Community Action Program"), cofounded by faculty and students, sponsors numerous, one-day activities for inner-city children, senior citizens, and physically and mentally challenged individuals. Students arrange parties and sports events for local children and the handicapped and sponsor dinners for residents of nursing homes. NUCAP also sponsors a sleep-out to bring attention to the plight of the homeless.

✦ **SUBSTANCE-ABUSE PREVENTION.** Niagara takes a visible role in challenging students to be responsible decision-makers and to make healthy and positive lifestyle choices. Niagara partners with local law enforcement agencies in presenting educational programs for students that address alcohol and drug abuse and sexual assault.

✦ **SPIRITUAL GROWTH.** The Campus Ministry assists faculty, staff, and students to grow in their own faith. Students participate in liturgies and retreats that help them explore their spirituality as part of the institution's holistic approach to education.

Niagara's mission encourages students to become responsible, caring citizens who value service to others as a way of life. By educating men and women to develop sensitivity and compassion for others, Niagara graduates those who effectively serve their communities.

THE 1804 CHARTER that established Ohio University as the first such school in the Northwest Territory states that education of youth is "important to morality, virtue and religion," as well as "friendly to the peace, order and prosperity of society." OU has a 200-year-old legacy of character- and community-building education, and students on the classic residential campus enjoy the opportunity and diversity of a large institution that still manages to have a "small college" feel. The "Ohio Experience" includes these distinctive features:

✦ FIRST-YEAR PROGRAMS. Students are welcomed into "A Community of Values" that includes respect, diversity, involvement, learning, and commitment. Opening weekend features the President's Convocation, which focuses on ethical principals and learning habits.

✦ ACADEMIC HONESTY. The Office of Judiciaries establishes "climates of integrity" on campus, encouraging students to be forthright and honest in all aspects of their university and personal lives.

✦ FACULTY AND CURRICULUM. Faculty contribute to students' personal as well as intellectual development. Ethical analysis and conduct are strengthened by service learning and a commitment to incorporating ethical issues across the curricula and through Student Affairs programming.

✦ STUDENT LEADERSHIP. OU student and alumni leaders are found in nearly all aspects of professional and scholarly life. This is achieved in part through peer leadership, organization opportunities, and collaborative academic work, enabling students to develop the competency, sense of conscience, and compassion required of leaders in a civil society.

✦ CIVIC EDUCATION. Civic and community education are emphasized in several programs and institutes, including "A Community of Values" and campus-wide ethics presentations by top teacher-scholars. Students also learn through "ILGARD" (the "Institute for Local Government Administration and Rural Development"), which helps them learn civic education by working with local governments.

✦ SPIRITUAL GROWTH. The nondenominational Galbreath Chapel is open to students of any faith. Other organizations promoting spiritual growth include United Campus Ministry, Catholic Student Foundation, Hillel Foundation, and the Muslim Student Association.

✦ SUBSTANCE-ABUSE PREVENTION. OU emphasizes physical and moral wellness through a variety of programs, services, and organizations, among them the "Binge Drinking Prevention Coalition" and "PATH" ("Personal Accountability, Trust, and Honor").

✦ CHARACTER AND SEXUALITY. Through "POWER," whose motto is "Respect Yourself, Respect Others, Protect Yourself and Others," students examine personal values associated with sexuality and sexual assault.

✦ SENIOR-YEAR PROGRAMS. Capstone "Tier III" courses offer seniors the chance to synthesize their learning with classmates from a wide cross-section of majors, helping them address interdisciplinary problems.

From convocation to commencement, students travel their own unique path at OU, immersing themselves in character- and community-building education.

OHIO UNIVERSITY

ATHENS, OH 45701

740.593.1000
http://www.ohiou.edu/

UNDERGRADUATES: 24,000
(16,000 MAIN CAMPUS)

"OU is a blend of the best a large university has to offer and the intimacy of a close-knit community. It is big enough to be diverse, attract excellent faculty and students, and offer modern facilities, yet small enough to feel like home."

—AN OU FOURTH-YEAR STUDENT

Other OU Profiles:

• Profile of President Glidden
• Character & Sexuality Program
• Student Leadership Program
• Substance-Abuse Prevention Program
• Volunteer Service Program

ORAL ROBERTS UNIVERSITY

7777 SOUTH LEWIS AVENUE
TULSA, OK 74171

918.495.6161
http://www.oru.edu/

UNDERGRADUATES: 3,400

"ORU teaches us how to live, learn, and lead. It inspires us to become positive, intelligent, effective leaders in our communities."

—AN ORU FOURTH-YEAR STUDENT

In 1963, evangelist Oral Roberts established Oral Roberts University with the purpose of graduating individuals who are spiritually and intellectually alive. Since 1993, President Richard Roberts has continued to uphold this private, charismatic Christian, liberal arts university's founding principles while advancing ORU to the forefront of faith-based higher education through the following programs:

✦ **FIRST-YEAR PROGRAMS.** "Wing" chaplains, academic peer advisors, and "wing-backers"—adults in the community who serve as mentors—assist first-year students in making a successful transition to university life. The Freshman Council encourages students to participate in campus and community activities, while the University Success course prepares them for the rigors and challenges of academic life.

✦ **ACADEMIC HONESTY.** All faculty, staff, and students sign the ORU Code of Honor Pledge in which they promise to adhere to Christian principles, apply themselves wholeheartedly to their intellectual pursuits, and uphold all standards of academic honesty.

✦ **FACULTY AND CURRICULUM.** Each course within ORU's curriculum addresses at least one of the 10 general objectives that all students achieve by graduation: (1) spiritual development, (2) physical development, (3) communication, (4) analysis, (5) problem-solving, (6) values in decision making, (7) social interaction, (8) global perspectives, (9) effective citizenship, and (10) aesthetic responsiveness. The required curriculum includes three courses for spiritual development.

✦ **VOLUNTEER SERVICE.** ORU's Community Outreach Department provides volunteer assistance to areas of need in Tulsa and its surrounding communities. Each year, more than 600 students contribute 26,000 hours of service to 40 nonprofit organizations and schools. During the annual one-day event in 1999, about 800 students, staff, and faculty cleaned yards, painted homes, distributed food and clothing, and held a carnival in a low-income Tulsa housing development.

✦ **STUDENT LEADERSHIP.** Numerous programs offer opportunities for students to develop their leadership skills. They may serve as academic peer advisors and dorm "wing" chaplains or assume various leadership positions in student government, student groups, and academic departments. Twenty VIP students build a bridge with alumni and serve as active ambassadors for ORU in the community.

✦ **SPIRITUAL GROWTH.** ORU encourages students to enrich their spiritual lives by participating in required chapel services, devotions, retreats, missions, and music ministries. Each year, ORU students touch the lives of more than 60,000 people through work in mission projects in 25 nations.

ORU challenges students to enter the marketplace by developing their minds and spirits to initiate change. Consequently, graduates fulfill ORU's spiritual vision of healing society's wounds through touching the mind and heart of each individual.

Paramount among Pepperdine's distinctions is its values-based approach to higher education, which fosters students' spiritual and ethical development as they advance intellectually. This approach honors George Pepperdine's vision of the school he founded in 1937 to "help young men and women to prepare themselves for lives of usefulness . . . and to help them build a foundation of Christian character and faith which will survive the storms of life." Accordingly, this private arts and sciences university's mission statement affirms that as a Christian university Pepperdine is committed not only to high standards of academic excellence, but to Christian values to prepare students for "lives of purpose, service, and leadership."

The vision of George Pepperdine and the university's mission are demonstrated through the core values that underlie the school's programs:

✦ **Faculty and Curriculum.** Pepperdine encourages character development beginning with orientation, which all incoming undergraduates attend. Throughout the orientation, students participate in lectures and group discussions on issues such as race relations, eating disorders, date rape, alcohol abuse, and AIDS awareness. All faculty support Pepperdine's mission by encouraging moral, ethical, and spiritual growth in their classes by addressing the moral and ethical issues of each discipline. Also, the required first-year seminar course introduces and applies critical-thinking and problem-solving skills to a specific content area.

✦ **Civic Education and Spiritual Growth.** Liberal arts undergraduates are required to attend a weekly convocation, which features a variety of formats and programs that promote the mission of Seaver College. Topics include community building, personal and social issues, faith development, worship, arts and entertainment, and cultural enrichment.

✦ **Volunteer Service.** Approximately 400 student volunteers serve the greater Los Angeles area through Pepperdine's Volunteer Center, providing 35,000 hours of ongoing community service. Students offer tutoring to underprivileged and homeless children; help aspiring U.S. citizens pass their citizenship test; serve as mentors to children at a juvenile detention center; form friendships with senior citizens and people with cerebral palsy; serve meals to the homeless; and conduct Bible studies for inner-city youth. In addition, the curriculum-based Service Learning Program integrates community service with academic course work. Students gain training in their major field while donating their expertise to not-for-profit organizations by assisting greater Los Angeles communities in the areas of education, human services, and public safety.

Pepperdine University's emphasis on character development is clearly stated in its *1998–99 Annual Report:* "It is our belief that only leaders of character will be capable of addressing the problems of cynicism, alienation, immorality, and crime in our communities, as well as the economic, environmental, political, and other problems that plague us. In the face of such challenges, it gives us great hope for the future as we see the academic and moral quality of the students who enroll at Pepperdine." Students graduate from the university as fully prepared citizens who help their communities improve and progress as they pursue values-based lives established through Pepperdine's academics and spiritual education.

PEPPERDINE UNIVERSITY

24255 PACIFIC COAST HIGHWAY
MALIBU, CA 90263

310.456.4000
http://www.pepperdine.edu/

UNDERGRADUATES: 2,900

"Pepperdine has enabled me to view life through ethical eyes, preparing me to enter the world and make a positive contribution, both professionally and spiritually."

—A Pepperdine second-year student

PRESBYTERIAN COLLEGE

503 SOUTH BROAD STREET
CLINTON, SC 29325

864.833.2820
http://www.presby.edu/

UNDERGRADUATES: 1,100

"Presbyterian instills moral values and teaches us that the true purpose of education is to serve society and others."

—A PRESBYTERIAN SECOND-
YEAR STUDENT

FOUNDED IN 1880, Presbyterian College offers students a liberal arts education within a community of faith, learning, and intellectual freedom. In its statement of purpose, Presbyterian defines itself as a place where integrity and values matter. Two of its eight stated goals are "to acquaint students with the teachings and values of the Christian faith" and "to help students develop moral and ethical commitments that include service to others."

Accordingly, Presbyterian integrates aspects of personal and civic responsibility into its curriculum and cocurricular activities:

✦ ACADEMIC HONESTY. For more than 80 years, Presbyterian has emphasized the Codes of Honor and Conduct that encourage an atmosphere of mutual respect and trust. A commitment to honor promotes respect for the ideas, values, and property of others; a readiness to subordinate one's own interests to the interests and well-being of the college community; and a dedication to abide by the rules of the college. All students who pledge to uphold the Codes of Honor and Conduct sign the Honor Roll.

✦ FACULTY AND CURRICULUM. Presbyterian's core requirements are designed to instill compassion in students and elevate their social conscience. Courses such as Media and Society, Ethical Theory, Professional Ethics, and the American Religious Experience help students explore their values and develop personal responsibility.

✦ VOLUNTEER SERVICE. *"Dum vivimus servimus"* ("While we live, we serve") is Presbyterian's motto describing its commitment to service. Student Volunteer Services coordinates a wide range of opportunities for students to serve others; more than half of Presbyterian's 1,100 students participate in more than 30 service programs. Such programs as Big Brothers/Big Sisters, "Adopt-a-Grandparent," Habitat for Humanity, Meals-on-Wheels, and the annual Area Five Special Olympic Games offer hands-on service experiences. Also, the Office of Volunteer Services sponsors a holiday gift drive for the Salvation Army during Christmas and Thanksgiving. "Into the Streets" describes a program in which faculty, staff, and students go into the streets of Laurens County for a day to work on various community projects.

✦ SPIRITUAL GROWTH. Five recognized student religious groups meet weekly on campus for spiritual fellowship. These groups include the Westminster Fellowship, Newman Club, Baptist Student Union, Canterbury, and Fellowship of Christian Athletes. The annual Winter Conference Retreat, held in January, provides an opportunity for faculty, staff, and students to interact with the Thomas F. Staley Distinguished Christian Scholar and hear other prominent religious leaders during the course of the year.

Presbyterian champions an educational ethos that develops the entire person, stressing character formation in both academic and volunteer service. For Presbyterian graduates, how they make their life is more important than how they make a living.

Other Presbyterian Profiles:

• Academic Honesty Program
• Senior-Year Program

SINCE 1746, Princeton University has been dedicated to intellectual freedom, academic integrity, and service to the community. A private, liberal arts, research institution, Princeton celebrated its 250th anniversary in 1996. Princeton's president, Harold Shapiro, states: "It is incumbent upon universities to prepare students to live in a society where they will have to make their own moral choices and have the ability to address such issues honestly, thoughtfully, and with full respect for the worth and dignity of all people." It is this belief in education as a vehicle for moral reasoning that Princeton emphasizes throughout its curriculum and cocurricular activities:

◆ **ACADEMIC HONESTY.** Students abide by an honor system, established in 1983, that governs all written examinations. Tests are not supervised, and students are required to write and sign the following statement on every examination paper: "I pledge my honor that I have not violated the honor code during this examination."

◆ **FACULTY AND CURRICULUM.** Princeton places special emphasis on undergraduate education—in and outside the classroom. Undergraduates work closely with some of the most distinguished members of the faculty, beginning with Freshman Seminars and ending with the Senior Thesis. Community-based learning enriches course work by encouraging students to apply the knowledge and analytic tools gained in the classroom to the pressing issues that affect local communities.

◆ **VOLUNTEER SERVICE.** Students work on numerous service projects both on and off campus. Community House, a student-run service organization founded in 1969, addresses specific needs of residents in the local community and the greater Princeton and Trenton areas. Students tutor adults in literacy programs; help mothers prepare young children for preschool; and provide companionship to the elderly. The Student Volunteers Council, the largest on-campus student organization, also coordinates many local service opportunities for students.

◆ **CIVIC EDUCATION.** The Community Based Learning Initiative, a collaborative effort of students, faculty, administration, and community experts, provides students with opportunities for community involvement and hands-on research in the classroom. Students may participate in projects with such organizations as the John S. Watson Institute for Public Policy, a research organization that provides research data to decision-makers, and Coalition for Peace Action, a grassroots organization that brings together people of all ages and backgrounds to promote peace.

◆ **SPIRITUAL GROWTH.** The Office of Religious Life creates and coordinates many opportunities for students to explore and express their faith, working closely with chaplains from many religious organizations on campus and in the surrounding community. Interfaith initiatives, presentations on spirituality and the arts, and choral groups describe spiritual opportunities for Princeton students.

Princeton students benefit from an environment that enables them to explore their personal beliefs and moral convictions and prepares them to take their place in society, creating citizen leaders for their communities and beyond.

PRINCETON UNIVERSITY

PRINCETON, NJ 08544

609.258.3000
http://www.princeton.edu/

UNDERGRADUATES: 4,600

"Students at Princeton are constantly challenged to become better citizens and better human beings. I can think of no environment more conducive to or nurturing of moral and intellectual growth."

—A PRINCETON THIRD-YEAR STUDENT

Other Princeton Profiles:

• Academic Honesty Program

RAMAPO COLLEGE OF NEW JERSEY

"Leadership and Learning are Indispensable to Each Other."
John F. Kennedy, 19

505 RAMAPO VALLEY ROAD
MAHWAH, NJ 07430

201.529.7500
http://www.ramapo.edu/

UNDERGRADUATES: 4,700

"Ramapo has prepared me not only to start my career, but also to appreciate cultural differences within the U.S. This gives me a better understanding of the ethics and values of other cultures."

—A RAMAPO THIRD-YEAR STUDENT

FROM ITS ESTABLISHMENT IN 1969 as a state-supported, liberal arts college, Ramapo College of New Jersey has emphasized thematic learning and innovative interdisciplinary programs. International and intercultural education involve students in the cultural diversity of U.S. society and the world, as exemplified by these programs:

✦ FIRST-YEAR PROGRAM. In the required "College Seminar," faculty, staff, and upper-division peers introduce first-year students to college life, learning, and responsibilities.

✦ FACULTY AND CURRICULUM. Each semester, more than 20 faculty incorporate service learning into their courses. As part of the "Living and Learning Program," faculty members spend time in dormitories to provide intellectual and social role modeling on topics from travel to social issues.

✦ VOLUNTEER SERVICE. The service-learning program, based in the Division of Student Affairs, provides Ramapo students with two alternative spring breaks—in Appalachia or on a reservation in the Southwest—where they work to improve lives of people in those communities.

✦ STUDENT LEADERSHIP. Ramapo is the only higher-education institution in New Jersey with an Omicron Delta Kappa circle. This national leadership honor society for college students, faculty, staff, and alumni is based on the idea that leaders of "exceptional quality and versatility" should cooperate in "worthwhile endeavors" and that outstanding students, faculty, staff, and alumni should meet on a basis of "mutual interest, understanding, and helpfulness." In addition, "EDGE" ("Extracurricular Dimension of Growth Experiences") supplies an extracurricular transcript to students who lead in the intellectual and cultural life of the community.

✦ SPIRITUAL GROWTH. "The Heroes of Conscience" lecture series explored the lives of people who demonstrated moral courage in adversity and risked their lives or careers to help others. Intended to improve moral reasoning skills, the series attempted to answer questions such as: What gives some of us the capacity to stand up for principles and beliefs? Can the acts of such individuals inspire us all? Also, Ramapo's Council of International Education sponsored the series "Human Rights: Human Responsibilities," which commemorated the 50th anniversary of the Universal Declaration of Human Rights in 1998. The 11 lectures and complementary reader addressed political, economic, cultural, and social rights in a global context.

✦ SUBSTANCE-ABUSE PREVENTION. The "Curriculum Infusion Project" of the Center for Health and Counseling Services is based on collaborations among faculty members who are willing to introduce topics related to alcohol and drug prevention into their course curricula.

Ramapo students seek the meaning of their beliefs for their lives and build value systems that enable them to become effective leaders and citizens. As Dr. Robert Scott, Ramapo's president, writes, "To us, education is as much about character and citizenship as it is about careers and commerce."

Other Ramapo Profiles:

• Faculty & Curriculum Program
• Substance-Abuse Prevention Program

FOUNDED IN 1877 as a college for men, becoming coeducational in 1968, and gaining university status in 1991, Regis University seeks to develop "men and women in service of others." Consistent with its mission as a private, Jesuit, comprehensive institution, Regis encourages students to develop the skills and leadership abilities necessary not only for distinguished professional work, but also for improving and transforming society. Members of the Regis community examine and attempt to answer the basic question, How ought we to live?

Students at Regis learn to establish their framework of values for making ethical and responsible personal choices through these programs:

✦ FACULTY AND CURRICULUM. Regis faculty and staff, challenged by the university's president, inspire students to understand and practice personal and civic responsibility through the service components incorporated in regular course work—as well as in all aspects of university life. The liberal arts curriculum integrates service in several disciplines, examining values and empowering students to positively influence society as an educational goal.

✦ VOLUNTEER SERVICE. The Center for Service Learning recruits students to serve in the community, as well as integrates these experiences into courses across disciplines. Service-learning experiences encourage students to reflect on and explore economic, social, and political issues within society. In addition, athletes and student clubs are required to participate in direct service opportunities or fund-raising initiatives.

✦ SPIRITUAL GROWTH. Campus Ministry provides activities that enable members of the Regis community to respond to Ignatius Loyola's invitation to find God in all things—including liturgical services, weekend retreats and days of reflection, spiritual direction and advising, Scripture study, community celebrations, and reflection on justice issues.

✦ CIVIC EDUCATION. Through public forums, the Institute on the Common Good enables students to participate in dialogs that seek common ground on community issues. Through contact with community leaders who represent a range of viewpoints, the institute aims to engage students in an atmosphere of mutual respect. In 1998, the institute sponsored the appearance of Archbishop Desmond Tutu—the fifth Nobel Peace Prize recipient to speak at Regis in the past three years—who talked about "Making a Friend Out of an Enemy." Also, Father David Hollenbach, SJ, the Margaret O'Brien Flatley professor of Catholic Theology at Boston College, spoke about "The Choice America Faces Today: The Common Good or The Death of Public Life?"

As a consequence of Ignatius Loyola's vision, Regis University encourages all members of its community to learn proficiently, think logically and critically, identify and choose personal standards and values, and be socially responsible. Proud of its history of Jesuit Catholic education, Regis University is committed to continuing that tradition of excellence in the future.

REGIS UNIVERSITY

3333 REGIS BOULEVARD
DENVER, CO 80221-1099

303.458.4100
http://www.regis.edu/

UNDERGRADUATES: 7,600

"Regis has created an atmosphere made up of community service, spirituality, education, family, and camaraderie to give me a well-rounded college experience."

—A REGIS THIRD-YEAR
STUDENT

Other Regis Profiles:

• Civic Education Program

St. Bonaventure University

PO BOX D
ST. BONAVENTURE, NY 14778

716.375.2000
http://www.sbu.edu/

UNDERGRADUATES: 2,200

"University Ministries at St. Bonaventure, and the many special people there, have shared with me many valuable insights into becoming a better Christian. They have taught me how to have compassion for everyone, while at the same time standing up for my values and beliefs."

—A St. Bonaventure
FOURTH-YEAR STUDENT

During the Middle Ages, Franciscans helped establish the great universities of Europe—including Oxford and Cambridge. In 1856, they came to Western New York and founded St. Bonaventure University, a Catholic, comprehensive institution. In a curriculum shaped by eight centuries of spiritual and intellectual heritage, St. Bonaventure offers students much more than academic excellence. For more than 140 years, a commitment to Franciscan values has shaped the foundation of a St. Bonaventure education through many challenging programs:

✦ **Faculty and Curriculum.** The new core curriculum implemented through Clare College helps students to begin forming and assessing the intellectual, cultural, moral, and spiritual foundations of their lives. The other schools reflect these values throughout their curricula based on the guiding principles of educating students, enriching faculty through intellectual challenges, and providing service to others. A typical mission statement reads, "The School of Business promotes an environment characterized by the Franciscan values of compassionate service, contemplation, love, joy and peace, respect and dignity for all."

✦ **Volunteer Service.** To enhance students' moral development, University Ministries offers numerous voluntary social service programs, such as linking students with area children who are at risk or with "adopted" grandparents. The oldest student-run soup kitchen in the nation involves 275 students and other campus members each year.

✦ **Student Leadership.** University Ministries also offers leadership roles in the campus retreat ministry, the on-campus Respect Life committee, and on service trips for Habitat for Humanity or to Jamaica or Mexico. Other programs include Peer Educators, who provide informational programs on alcohol and drug abuse, HIV/AIDS, and other campus life issues; Student Government, which provides a holiday celebration for 30 needy area families with the help of the campus and community; Alpha Phi Omega, a national service fraternity that assists with numerous projects; and "MERT" ("Medical Emergency Response Team"), which responds to on-campus medical emergencies with oversight by Health Services.

✦ **Spiritual Growth.** Students may choose to explore and enrich their faith through a number of opportunities, including attending a mountain retreat that offers peaceful "re-creation," prayer, and family-style hospitality to all students and community members.

✦ **Civic Education.** The new Franciscan Center for Social Concern will combine academics with service by educating students about the issues of the poor and marginalized and teaching them to advocate for justice. First-year students will take part in local service programs. Sophomores will participate in a program focusing on human rights, Catholic social teaching, and the Franciscan understanding of the "human person"; direct service to the poor; an advocacy agency visit; and a week of reflection and analysis. Juniors will become organizers or student leaders and participate in a summer experience of peace and advocacy work. Seniors will be encouraged to commit to a year as a lay volunteer after graduation.

Students leaving St. Bonaventure are no ordinary graduates; they are committed citizens and servant-leaders who actively work to improve the world.

FOUNDED IN 1847 as a church-affiliated school of liberal arts and sciences, St. Francis College is the oldest Franciscan college in the U.S. It clearly articulates its commitment to providing not only intellectual development, but to stimulating moral, spiritual, and social growth; instilling a lifelong love for learning; and promoting opportunities for helping people, recognizing that higher education is a means to improve society. This mission, combined with the eight Franciscan Goals of Higher Education—which include creating "a humble and generous attitude toward learning," providing "service to the poor and the needy," and committing to "a community of faith and prayer"—provide a foundation for the college's nationally recognized general education program. Under the leadership of the Franciscan Friars of the Third Order Regular, the college's curricular and cocurricular programs stress the value of Franciscan ideals:

✦ FACULTY AND CURRICULUM. St. Francis' curriculum, introduced in 1994, includes specific outcomes, emphasizing ethics and values, multicultural and global awareness, and basic skills—writing, critical thinking, use of technology, use of primary source materials, verbal communication, and quantitative reasoning. Faculty, staff, and administrators also explain, model, and inspire students to understand and practice the virtues and standards of personal and civic responsibility.

✦ FIRST-YEAR PROGRAM. St. Francis pays special attention to the issues of personal and civic responsibility in its Freshman Year Experience Program, which focuses students' attention on moral and intellectual decision-making as it promotes Franciscan values.

✦ CIVIC EDUCATION. St. Francis educates students in the responsibilities of democratic citizenship, from both theoretical and experimental perspectives. The 20-year-old Dorothy Day Center is woven into campus life as faculty, staff, campus ministers, and others work with students to integrate community service, faith and character formation, and academic excellence. In this context, students consider questions of citizenship: What does it mean now? What ought it mean? How does it relate to justice, community, diversity? What are the ideals to which democratic citizens are called? What are essential values for responsible citizenship? What are the skills needed to be a socially responsible citizen?

✦ VOLUNTEER SERVICE. The Franciscan goal of "service to the poor and needy" is partially met through the Dorothy Day Center and also through the 10-hour service-learning component of the required sophomore-level Faith and Franciscanism course. More than teaching what is good, such programs enable students to learn to *do* what is good.

The St. Francis community recognizes that knowledge is not a personal possession intended solely for self-advancement, but rather something that must be shared generously with others. The campus community strives for "excellence without arrogance," and all members willingly learn from one another. Other values that shape the St. Francis experience and build community include reverence for all life and for the goodness of all humanity, respect and tolerance for all persons and an appreciation for diversity, and a global vision and stewardship of the world's resources. St. Francis students have abundant opportunities to learn about personal responsibility so that they can exercise high ethical standards in their personal and professional lives.

ST. FRANCIS COLLEGE

PO BOX 600
LORETTO, PA 15940

814.472.3100
http://www.sfcpa.edu/

UNDERGRADUATES: 1,500

"As a nontraditional student, I have encountered many challenges trying to balance family, work, and studies. The faculty at St. Francis has helped to ease these burdens, and I came to realize that I, in turn, enjoyed helping those who are less fortunate. This has helped me to better appreciate my own blessings."

—A ST. FRANCIS THIRD-YEAR STUDENT

Other St. Francis Profiles:

• First-Year Program

St. John Fisher College

3690 EAST AVENUE
ROCHESTER, NY 14618

716.385.8000
http://www.sjfc.edu/

UNDERGRADUATES: 1,600

"Fisher has provided me with the maturity to be responsible for myself and my own actions. It helped reinforce my existing strength and converted it into an undying spirit that allows me to advocate for positive change."

—A FISHER FOURTH-YEAR
STUDENT

Other Fisher Profiles:

• Volunteer Service Program

"TEACH ME GOODNESS, discipline, and knowledge." In keeping with the motto of the Basilian Fathers who founded it, St. John Fisher College is committed to the development of values in the Fisher community, including a commitment to the lifelong search for truth, a belief in the dignity of every individual, and an affirmation that service to others is a worthy expression of our humanity. These values serve as the guiding principles in both academic and student life programs at this church-affiliated, liberal arts school founded as a men's college in 1948 and coeducational since 1971.

The Basilian tradition is especially emphasized in programs for new students:

✦ FIRST-YEAR PROGRAM. The First-Year Program is designed not only to assist students in the transition to college, but also to orient them to the history and values of the Fisher community. Underlying all aspects of the first-year experience is the "Fisher Creed," an expression of Fisher's vision and mission statements in the form of a campus compact that all students sign, signifying their commitment to respect, open-mindedness, integrity, diversity, responsibility, education, leadership, and growth.

The program is divided into four major components:

• "Great Beginnings," a one-day academic orientation for students and their parents, not only covers the practical issues of academic procedures and finances, but also introduces Fisher's core values.

• "Orientation" includes academic, social, cultural, and religious activities to help students make a successful transition to college.

• "Learning Community," required of all first-year students, gives them the opportunity to take courses in "clusters" focused on a central theme. This format enables students to learn cooperatively and to develop close working relationships with other students and faculty.

• "Freshman Seminar," the final element of the program, provides not only an orientation to college life, but a support system to foster their academic success and personal growth. The goals are to help students become responsible campus citizens, develop independent learning skills, and explore their educational and career aspirations. First-year students also explore the "Fisher Commitment," a nationally recognized four-year career success program.

✦ VOLUNTEER SERVICE. To encourage and reward students who have demonstrated a commitment to community service while in high school, Fisher established the Fisher Service Scholars Program. Students are expected to commit 100 hours per semester to community service in addition to carrying a full academic courseload and, often, maintaining other campus commitments and jobs. Their ability to manage competing demands helps students understand the virtues of personal responsibility. The Service Scholars Program joins other campus traditions of community service, which collectively enrich campus life at Fisher.

Fisher's formula of blending theory with day-to-day living provides students with multiple avenues for reinforcing core moral values that guide them as they prepare for lives of personal and civic responsibility, in keeping with the tradition of its Basilian founders.

BASED ON THE NORBERTINE TRADITION OF LEARNING AND SERVICE, St. Norbert College, a private, Catholic, liberal arts and sciences institution founded in 1898, strives to provide a superior education that encourages both intellectual and spiritual development. Ranked among the best liberal arts colleges in the Midwest by *U.S. News & World Report,* St. Norbert has created a sense of community based on common prayer, service, cooperation, and collegiality. From this environment emerge young men and women who become servant-leaders through St. Norbert's various service- and leadership-based programs:

✦ FIRST-YEAR PROGRAMS. Four transitional programs target incoming St. Norbert students: "New Student Summer Orientation," "The Freshman Year Experience," "Freshman Seminar," and "For Freshmen Only." These programs welcome new members into the community and strengthen relationships among first-year students, faculty, and upperclassmen.

✦ ACADEMIC HONESTY. The Academic Honor Code defines academic dishonesty and describes the Academic Court that judges transgressions. Students are required to sign a pledge stating that they fully understand the code and intend to abide by it before they can register for courses.

✦ FACULTY AND CURRICULUM. The General Education courses at St. Norbert require students to "examine and critically reflect upon value statements and consider the implication of those values." The "Praxis: Social Justice and Homelessness" class connects classroom learning with community work. Likewise, the Peace and Justice Center promotes curricular and cocurricular programs and events for students who focus on the practical application of social justice.

✦ VOLUNTEER SERVICE. The Mary Minahan McCormick Service and Leadership Hall directs the 190 residents who contribute 6,000 hours of community service each semester. Students provide ongoing services such as tutoring, mentoring, and coaching youth, as well as supplying food to the needy. The Service Learning Clearinghouse encourages students to become involved locally and globally, while the Volunteer Fair matches students with long-term service groups such as AmeriCorps, the Peace Corps, and Jesuit Volunteer Corps.

✦ SUBSTANCE-ABUSE PREVENTION. "PEERs" ("Peer Educators for Effective Relationships") are dedicated volunteers who raise awareness about difficult topics by bringing powerful interactive performances to student audiences. Date rape, alcohol use, sexually transmitted diseases, and abstinence are a sampling of some subjects presented. Also, student-designed initiatives such as The Risk Management Program and The Alcohol Task Force address risks and strategies related to alcohol usage.

✦ STUDENT LEADERSHIP. St. Norbert offers the Leadership Studies Academic Minor that focuses on the ethical dimensions of leadership and the global common good. The Leadership Resource Library contains 400 works on leadership and service. Norbertine Leadership Awards capture community spirit by recognizing exceptional student and staff leadership and service.

Many instances of pain, despair, aloneness, and hopelessness exist in the world. St. Norbert graduates leave its halls to become effective teachers of hope and powerful servant-leaders in their communities.

ST. NORBERT COLLEGE

100 GRANT STREET
DEPERE, WI 54115

920.403.3020
http://www.snc.edu/

UNDERGRADUATES: 1,900

"St. Norbert's deep dedication to peace and justice—not just in mission, but in practice—is what makes it truly unique."

—A ST. NORBERT FOURTH-YEAR STUDENT

Other St. Norbert Profiles:

• Student Leadership Program

St. Olaf College

1520 ST. OLAF AVENUE
NORTHFIELD, MN 55057-1098

507.646.2222
http://www.stolaf.edu/

UNDERGRADUATES: 2,900

"St. Olaf succeeds in building character because it allows students the opportunity to pursue it themselves. The size and spirit of the community enable students to explore options in life, while strong guidance helps them focus on worthwhile goals."

—A St. Olaf third-year
student

COMMITTED TO THE LIBERAL ARTS, rooted in the gospel, and drawn to a global perspective, St. Olaf's College fosters an enriching environment for providing a broad character-building education. Affiliated with the Evangelical Lutheran Church since its founding in 1874, St. Olaf educates students to understand that life is more than a livelihood—rather, it reflects the development of the whole person in mind, body, and spirit. Part of the educational ethos at St. Olaf's highlights service, which "stimulates students' critical thinking and heightens their moral sensitivity; it encourages them to be seekers of truth, leading lives of unselfish service to others; and it challenges them to be responsible and knowledgeable citizens of the world."

With a view toward these goals, St. Olaf provides a number of character-building programs:

✦ **ACADEMIC HONESTY.** For 88 years, the St. Olaf Honor System has continuously set classroom standards of integrity for its students. Violations are reviewed and judged by a student-elected Honor Council.

✦ **VOLUNTEER SERVICE.** At St. Olaf, the Student Network offers students more than 35 different volunteer service programs and logged more than 10,000 hours of community work last year. A national leader in sending graduates to careers in the Peace Corps, St. Olaf emphasizes a sense of mission not only locally, but also globally.

✦ **SPIRITUAL GROWTH.** The St. Olaf Student Congregation oversees various student initiatives for spiritual growth. One of its four commitments is to benevolence—more than 90% of generated income goes to charitable causes, such as churches and schools in Tanzania. "Bread for the World," Fellowship of Christian Athletes, and the Christian Outreach Team are some of the campus programs that promote spiritual reflection for students and hands-on servant-leader experiences.

✦ **SENIOR-YEAR PROGRAMS.** "SALT" ("Senior Administrative Leadership Team") works in partnership with the St. Olaf local community to prepare its senior-year students as day-to-day stewards of St. Olaf's mission to serve. These students exemplify cooperation, interdependence, and leadership as they work with the Northfield community.

Each student receives a yellow card on their first day that portrays the campus culture and character-building aspects of a St. Olaf education with an affirmation that reads: "I will strive to practice and encourage among my colleagues: RESPECT for the dignity of others, despite differences in our beliefs; INTEGRITY in action and and intent; CELEBRATION of the gift of community by becoming engaged in it; HONESTY in all aspects of life, in and out of the classroom. Recognizing that community has no boundaries, I will carry these values with me as I travel, work, study, and serve."

By instructing students in leading lives with such expectations, St. Olaf prepares its graduates to enter the workplace as leaders of virtuous citizenship.

Other St. Olaf Profiles:

• Academic Honesty Program
• Spiritual Growth Program

FOUNDED IN 1872 and becoming coeducational in 1966, St. Peter's College is a private, independent, liberal arts school that educates students in personal and civic responsibility through dynamic programs in the Jesuit tradition:

✦ FIRST-YEAR PROGRAMS. All students meet with their faculty advisor before starting their first year. The "Emerging Leaders Program" identifies first-year students with outstanding leadership potential who are then paired with faculty and administrators who mentor them throughout the year.

✦ FACULTY AND CURRICULUM. The core curriculum requires courses intended to foster responsibility and to develop moral reasoning skills. Through the service-learning program, an option offered in selected courses from various departments, students volunteer at least two hours a week at a local school or social service agency. In 1997–98, seven faculty members and 160 students contributed 3,200 hours of community service through these academic courses.

✦ VOLUNTEER SERVICE. St. Peter's encourages students, faculty, and administrators to work in surrounding communities. In 1997–98, *more* than 500 students contributed 9,000 service hours to more than 30 Hudson county religious and nonprofit organizations and social service agencies.

✦ STUDENT LEADERSHIP. All students serving as club leaders, peer counselors and mentors, and student government leaders are required to participate in leadership-development training. St. Peter's regularly sends students to several state and national leadership training programs.

✦ CIVIC EDUCATION. Since 1984, St. Peter's has been associated with The Washington Center in Washington, DC, through which students participate in semester-long, for-credit internships with legislators and governmental agencies. Also, St. Peter's Guarini Center for Governmental Affairs sponsors seminars and conferences that feature a panel of speakers who discuss national and global issues. The Ambassadors' Program brings United Nations ambassadors to campus to lecture, share a "diplomatic dialog" with faculty and students, and meet with business leaders.

✦ SPIRITUAL GROWTH. The Office of Campus Ministry arranges for worship, prayer, reflection, education, and dialog about fundamental issues of faith. It sponsors several retreats and discussion groups that focus on life choices, spiritual direction, and contemporary moral and social justice issues.

✦ SUBSTANCE-ABUSE PREVENTION. The Wellness and Peer Education Center provides a comprehensive, holistic approach to promoting wellness, health education, and drug and alcohol education. Student Wellness Education Leaders, selected and trained through the Center, assist other students and provide programs on wellness topics.

Drawing on the 450-year-old Jesuit philosophy of education that seeks to prepare people for a lifetime of learning, leadership, and service in a diverse society, St. Peter's is committed to educating students to become "men and women for others."

ST. PETER'S COLLEGE

2641 KENNEDY BOULEVARD
JERSEY CITY, NJ 07306-5997

201.915.9000
http://www.spc.edu/

UNDERGRADUATES: 2,400

"Faculty at St. Peter's do not just teach or instruct; rather, they serve as mentors to students. They empower us to believe in ourselves and our ability to be contributing members of society."

—A ST. PETER'S FOURTH-YEAR STUDENT

SEATTLE PACIFIC UNIVERSITY

3307 THIRD AVENUE WEST
SEATTLE, WA 98119

206.281.2000
http://www.spu.edu/

UNDERGRADUATES: 2,600

"In my SPU classes, I've been introduced to the lives of people such as Desmond Tutu and Mohandas Gandhi, who demonstrated how a person's beliefs, integrity, and determination can make a profound difference in the world—and inspire others to strive to do the same."

—AN SPU FOURTH-YEAR STUDENT

Other SPU Profiles:

• Profile of President Eaton
• Character & Sexuality Program
• First-Year Program
• Spiritual Growth Program
• Student Leadership Program

SEATTLE PACIFIC UNIVERSITY is a Christian, liberal arts institution established in 1891 by the Free Methodist Church of North America. SPU educates individuals who learn to understand their talents, exhibit honesty and integrity, and value serving others. Combining thoughtful scholarship with prayerful faith prepares students for leadership and service. Promoting understanding, instilling compassion, and developing an appreciation for ideas are central components of SPU's character-building programs:

✦ FIRST-YEAR PROGRAM. SPU's first-year, core program, the Common Curriculum, focuses on encouraging Christian formation; developing critical-thinking, speaking, and research skills; and connecting liberal arts to real-life, human issues.

✦ FACULTY AND CURRICULUM. The University Core sequence of the Common Curriculum introduces the relevance, unity, and life-changing properties of knowledge in three classes: "Character and Community," "The West and the World," and "Belief, Morality, and the Modern Mind." Through these courses, students learn that ideas matter and are instruments of change.

✦ VOLUNTEER SERVICE. Urban Involvement organizes many opportunities for students to serve in the local community by tutoring children, assisting the homeless, befriending at-risk youth, and distributing food at food banks. Several times a year, Urban Involvement sponsors "Urban Plunge," a four-day program in which students live on the streets of Seattle and experience the life of the homeless.

✦ SPIRITUAL GROWTH. Campus Ministries offers numerous activities to nourish the spiritual life of the campus community. Chapel/Forum is an accredited program that integrates faith and learning to equip students to become world citizens. Campus Ministries sponsors weekly meetings and Bible studies in which students discuss various spiritual topics. "SPRINT" ("Seattle Pacific Reachout International") is a student organization that encourages mission activity on a worldwide scale. Throughout the year, SPRINT sponsors chapel programs, mission conferences, and prayer meetings to raise awareness of the Christian mission. During Christmas holidays, spring breaks, and summers, students participate in cross-cultural ministries in such countries as Mexico, Romania, Sierra Leone, Uganda, Nicaragua, and Bangladesh.

✦ CHARACTER AND SEXUALITY. The Center for Relationship Development helps students build positive and meaningful relationships with their families, educators, employers, potential marriage partners, and each other. The Center promotes solid commitments, lasting love, and a Christian approach to sexuality.

SPU believes faith, engagement, and service play an integral part in educating individuals to become leaders in their faith and communities. Students learn that a cultivated mind can lead to understanding and bring about positive change.

Southwest Missouri State University educates students to think critically and exercise intellectual judgment about the cultures and institutions of the larger world. SMSU achieves this objective through its distinctive public affairs mission, which seeks to develop citizens of enhanced character who are committed to contributing to society. Founded in 1905 as a public, comprehensive state school, SMSU received a statewide mission in public affairs from the Missouri Legislature in 1995 and is the only institution in Missouri with this designation.

Character development is supported in SMSU's far-reaching curricular and cocurricular activities:

✦ **First-Year Programs.** Introduction to University Life explores responsible citizenship. Faculty and students discuss the moral challenges they face and the characteristics and qualities associated with academic and personal achievement.

✦ **Faculty and Curriculum.** SMSU's public affairs focus is the integrating principle for the entire curriculum. Knowledge in biology, for example, has implications for ethical issues such as eligibility for organ transplants or limits placed on cloning. Similarly, chemistry has implications for public environmental concerns, including water quality and the diminishing ozone layer. Programs such as the Environmental Sciences and Policy minor and the Chemistry for the Citizen course develop students' academic expertise and civic responsibility.

✦ **Volunteer Service.** SMSU's Campus Volunteer Center links students with areas of community need. Students participate in food drives for the Ozarks Food Harvest, build homes with Habitat for Humanity, assist with Special Olympics, and work with children in the Head Start program. The Student Community Action Team and Campus Ministries also coordinate meaningful community service programs for faculty, staff, and students.

✦ **Student Leadership.** The SMSU Residence Hall Association (RHA) works to communicate students' needs regarding residence life services and policies, increases student involvement on campus, and promotes a high quality of community living. Every year, RHA actively participates in the state, regional, and national associations, sending student delegates to the fall, winter, and summer conferences. This year, RHA and the SMSU Residence Hall Conference staff will host a residence life leadership conference to enable students to enhance their leadership skills.

✦ **Civic Education.** Citizenship and Service Learning (CASL) is an experiential learning program that links a discipline-based course with related service work to benefit an external government or service organization. The CASL staff develops service placements with organizations and agencies designated as "Community Partners," some of which include the Springfield Police Department, the Salvation Army, and the Department of Family Services.

SMSU's dedication to public affairs creates a community of principled scholars and citizens who have the sensitivity and character to become instruments of positive change for their local communities and in the world beyond.

SOUTHWEST MISSOURI STATE UNIVERSITY

901 SOUTH NATIONAL
SPRINGFIELD, MO 65804

417.836.5000
http://www.smsu.edu/

UNDERGRADUATES: 14,000

"At SMSU, students receive an outstanding level of personal attention from faculty and staff, which helps us determine who we are and how we can contribute to our communities and to the world."

—AN SMSU FIFTH-YEAR STUDENT

Other SMSU Profiles:

• Profile of President Keiser
• First-Year Program
• Senior-Year Program
• Substance-Abuse Prevention Program
• Volunteer Service Program

SOUTHWESTERN COLLEGE

100 COLLEGE STREET
WINFIELD, KS 67156-2499

316.221.8236
http://www.sckans.edu/

UNDERGRADUATES: 1,000

"SC has greatly impacted my life. Everyone here challenged me to find my role in ministry outreach teams and other organizations and programs. SC gives all students the chance to explore their niche and develop into 'responsible citizens in a world without boundaries.'"

—A SOUTHWESTERN FOURTH-
YEAR STUDENT

Other SC Profiles:

• Spiritual Growth Program
• Student Leadership Program

FOUNDED IN 1885 as a private school affiliated with the United Methodist Church, Southwestern College serves students in both a residential setting and in professional studies programs for working adults. Southwestern weaves service learning and character development throughout its curriculum, as demonstrated by these programs:

✦ FACULTY AND CURRICULUM. The integrative studies program encourages students to apply knowledge and ethical considerations to real-life situations. The student-faculty ratio of 13:1 ensures hands-on learning that focuses on solving problems, applying critical-thinking skills, exploring creative expressions, learning to communicate ideas, making connections between disciplines, and integrating ideas into experiences. Making up the general education component of SC's graduation requirements, integrative studies is composed of 33 credit hours spread out over four years, with the highest concentration of courses taken in the first year.

✦ CIVIC EDUCATION. During their undergraduate years, hundreds of students are involved in SC's four service-learning programs—Conocer Southwestern, Discipleship Southwestern, Leadership Southwestern, and Share Southwestern. Although all are designed to encourage students' development as mature citizens, the programs appeal to individual interests and preferences. For example, now in its first year, Conocer (Spanish for "to know or to experience something unfamiliar") stresses diversity and cross-cultural experience and describes the process students use as they explore the Spanish language and Hispanic culture.

✦ SPIRITUAL GROWTH. Discipleship provides a holistic approach to Christian faith through Bible study, involvement in local churches, and interaction with other Christians, helping students to grow in their faith.

✦ STUDENT LEADERSHIP. The nationally recognized Leadership program combines classes in which high-level communication skills and theory are explored with projects to give students opportunity for teamwork, skills development, and real-life experience.

✦ VOLUNTEER SERVICE. Share is designed for students who have the creativity and initiative to be agents of change in areas about which they are passionate, whether in environmental restoration, mentoring, elder care, or many other fields. Volunteers can serve individually or in groups.

✦ SENIOR-YEAR PROGRAM. All students at Southwestern, whether on campus or in the professional studies centers, finish their academic studies by participating in Responsibility for the Future, Southwestern's capstone course. Seniors from all academic majors deal with issues that shape the future as they integrate disciplines to synthesize their learning experiences and how to apply them.

Southwestern believes that college sets the course for the rest of a student's life. Citizens who succeed in our society are shaped not only by the need for technological skills, but also by the contributions of citizens with high ethical and moral standards. Graduates of Southwestern exemplify this learning.

ONE OF THE MOST PRESTIGIOUS INSTITUTIONS within higher education, Spelman College, founded in 1881, remains one of only two historically Black, liberal arts schools for women in the U.S. Highly selective, the mission of Spelman is to train women for positions of leadership. Graduates often remark how the "Spelman experience" offered them a supportive yet challenging environment in which they developed the skills and confidence to pursue their dreams. The many programs at the core of the "Spelman experience" provide the opportunity for young women to develop and apply moral and ethical values:

✦ ACADEMIC HONESTY. Each year, the entire campus revisits the basic philosophy underlying the "Standard of Conduct Expected of a Spelman Woman." Learning to comply with the required standards is an integral part of the Spelman experience.

✦ VOLUNTEER SERVICE. The Office of Community Service is the campus-wide clearinghouse for all volunteer activities. During their four years at Spelman, all students are strongly encouraged to participate in at least one ongoing service project. Comprehensive community outreach is centered in two local communities, Harris Homes, a public housing community, and West End, a historic African-American community. Spelman also participates in the Bonner Scholars program, a national initiative to reward high-school students with full scholarships based on their commitment to volunteer service.

✦ STUDENT LEADERSHIP. Every three years, a second-semester first-year student is selected by her peers to serve a three-year term on the Board of Trustees at Spelman. The student trustee is expected to serve as role model for other students. This unique student leadership opportunity is only one example of the numerous opportunities for Spelman women to take on leadership responsibilities during their undergraduate years.

✦ SPIRITUAL GROWTH. Spelman encourages each student to make college a time of spiritual exploration and development. The College Minister oversees the spiritual life of the campus community, and students of all faiths are invited to attend the interdenominational Christian worship services held each Sunday in Sisters Chapel. One of the popular student groups on campus is "Movements of Praise," which provides opportunities for Spelman women to praise and worship God through various forms of dance, concentrating on the biblical significance of liturgical dance.

✦ SUBSTANCE-ABUSE PREVENTION. Spelman is committed to maintaining a drug-free environment. The campus does not permit alcoholic beverages on Spelman property or at any college-sponsored event. The college offers a wide range of educational programs on the effects and dangers of alcohol and drug abuse, and campus administrators meet annually to review all drug- and alcohol-abuse prevention policies and programs.

Spelman is a major resource for educating Black women leaders, striving to maintain an environment that nurtures self-confidence, pride, hope, strength of character, and a love of learning while encouraging and challenging students to take personal responsibility for bringing about positive change in their communities and in the world.

SPELMAN COLLEGE

350 SPELMAN LANE SW
ATLANTA, GA 30314-4399

404.681.3643
http://www.spelman.edu/

UNDERGRADUATES: 2,000

"Spelman teaches students to have self-confidence. We realize how much we can accomplish through the examples of the successful women who have attended Spelman before us."

—A SPELMAN SECOND-YEAR STUDENT

STATE UNIVERSITY OF NEW YORK COLLEGE AT ONEONTA

ONEONTA, NEW YORK 13820

607.436.3500
http://www.oneonta.edu/

UNDERGRADUATES: 5,000

"Learning about another culture, another way of life, is just a fraction of what we have to do. I believe that we are our brothers' and sisters' keepers, and SUNY-Oneonta gave us our opportunity to show it."

—A SUNY-ONEONTA FOURTH-YEAR STUDENT

F ROM ITS FOUNDING IN 1889 as a teacher-training institute through its growth to a public, comprehensive college of the liberal arts and sciences, the State University of New York College at Oneonta has remained committed to its mission statement, which articulates "a concern for students' personal, cultural, and ethical development." The entire SUNY-Oneonta community—president, faculty, staff, and students—is actively involved in developing, communicating, and practicing personal and civic responsibility, as demonstrated through numerous SUNY-Oneonta programs:

✦ **FACULTY AND CURRICULUM.** Service-learning opportunities are an integral component of the curriculum across disciplines, with more than 2,000 students participating annually. The General Education requirement includes three courses with "perspectives on human value and expression." Oneonta is the only SUNY institution to offer certification through American Humanics, an alliance dedicated to preparing students for careers with human services organizations. Specific academic programs such as "Learn and Serve in India," established in 1980, enable students "to learn about India and then to continue learning by giving services back to its people." Students in the SUNY-Oneonta program founded and continue to support the Indo-International School for lower-caste children in Dundlod through the "Children's India Fund."

✦ **STUDENT LEADERSHIP.** Founded in 1988, the Student Leadership Institute offers students opportunities to develop leadership skills through workshops in ethics, communication, and leadership styles. In 1999, SUNY-Oneonta offered its first Presidential Undergraduate Leadership Forum, designed to help undergraduates develop and improve their leadership skills, prepare them to accept leadership assignments after graduation, and establish their personal leadership philosophies.

✦ **VOLUNTEER SERVICE.** The nationally known Center for Social Responsibility and Community links academic study and volunteer service, instilling in students a sense of social responsibility to build strong communities. The entire campus gets involved in the annual "Into the Streets" day of service to the community. The Center, begun with grant funding, now assists other colleges in developing similar volunteer service programs.

✦ **SUBSTANCE-ABUSE PREVENTION.** "CHOICES" ("Choosing Healthy Options in the College Environment Successfully") is a comprehensive alcohol and drug-abuse prevention program that helps students empower their peers to adopt a "developmental" rather than a "crisis" model of behavior with regard to the use of alcohol and other drugs. SUNY-Oneonta also initiated and hosted the area's first "Community Forum on Alcohol and Other Drug Prevention," which brought together students, representatives from three area colleges, community leaders, school district representatives, and business owners to share ideas about preventing substance abuse and developing alternative youth activities.

In addition to the institutional and programmatic manifestations of civic and personal responsibility, a more personal demonstration occurred in 1977 when more than 200 members of the faculty and staff offered a unique gift to President Alan Donovan on his birthday: a pledge from each to perform one hour of community service. The entire campus proves that dedication to service is what the SUNY-Oneonta community is all about.

Other SUNY-Oneonta Profiles:

• Substance-Abuse Prevention Program

FOUNDED IN 1948 by the Congregation of Holy Cross, Stonehill is a Catholic liberal arts college (coeducational since 1951) that views the spiritual and moral development of its students as a vital part of the educational process. Following in the Holy Cross educational tradition, Stonehill believes that the mind cannot be cultivated at the expense of the heart. In particular, it works to cultivate in its students concern for the dignity of every person and a desire to create a more compassionate and just world. Stonehill endeavors to develop a quality of campus life that forges strong bonds of community, as well as a tradition of service that reaches beyond the campus to other communities—especially those in need. This commitment is demonstrated in Stonehill's others-oriented programs:

✦ **VOLUNTEER SERVICE.** Committed to developing volunteer opportunities that invite students to share their good fortune with others, at orientation Stonehill introduces first-year students to its motto of "Light and Hope" and the significance those words have for its educational mission. Students are encouraged to have the competence to see the world as it is ("Light") and the courage to act with justice in response ("Hope"). Stonehill students accordingly participate in a variety of service opportunities, chiefly:

• "Into the Streets," which begins at orientation when new students engage in direct community service. Many students participate throughout their four years at Stonehill.

• "Stonehill Gives Back," which sends more than 200 seniors, faculty, and staff into local neighborhoods to perform community service.

• "Alternative Spring Break," during which Stonehill students and administrators have renovated schools in Lima, Perú; built a medical center in Nicaragua; built homes in Appalachia; and taught children in the Bronx, New York.

✦ **SPIRITUAL GROWTH.** In addition to developing service opportunities, Stonehill challenges students to establish their religious faith as a more coherent influence in their lives. Campus Ministry calls on students to reflect on their religious and moral values and to develop a plan for their own spiritual growth while in college.

✦ **SENIOR-YEAR PROGRAMS.** Stonehill believes that students who show initiative and demonstrate responsibility while at college are better prepared for the challenges they face after graduation. Whether participating in the "Senior Transition Conference," which assists students with a host of practical issues as they prepare for post-college life, or organizing "Fear No People," a student-sponsored and -operated schedule of lectures and special events held every November to promote the acceptance and understanding of diversity, Stonehill students are engaged in proactive, constructive projects and events.

In 1998–99, Stonehill used its 50th anniversary celebration to reflect on the importance of character building in its educational mission. Proud of its past, but eager for the future, Stonehill's commitment to educating the whole person has been reinvigorated.

STONEHILL COLLEGE

320 WASHINGTON STREET
EASTON, MA 02357

508.565.1000
http://www.stonehill.edu/

UNDERGRADUATES: 2,700

"The Stonehill community has supported my academic pursuits and guided me in my spiritual life. I thank God and my parents for these opportunities every day."

—A STONEHILL THIRD-YEAR STUDENT

Other Stonehill Profiles:

• Character & Sexuality Program
• Senior-Year Program
• Spiritual Growth Program

TEXAS CHRISTIAN UNIVERSITY

2800 SOUTH UNIVERSITY DRIVE
FORT WORTH, TX 76129

817.257.7000
http://www.tcu.edu/

UNDERGRADUATES: 7,200

"My time at TCU has helped me to become a global citizen. I've learned that I must take responsibility for myself in order to be a productive citizen in a global society."

—A TCU THIRD-YEAR STUDENT

Other TCU Profiles:

• Spiritual Growth Program
• Substance-Abuse Prevention Program

SINCE 1873, Texas Christian University has maintained traditions derived from its historic ties to the Disciples of Christ Church. Through its respect for the tenets of a Christian value system, TCU promotes an environment of diversity and acceptance, reasoned faith, and individual religious preference. TCU believes that thoughtful, probing questions are valuable and vital and that exploring the moral and religious dimensions of human existence is essential to a high-quality, liberal arts education.

This deep philosophy underlies TCU's curricular and cocurricular programs:

✦ FIRST-YEAR PROGRAMS. Students participate in several orientation programs that introduce them to the values of civic and personal responsibility. "Examining Perceptions in a Global Community" is a first-year course that engages students in group consensus activities to explore and discuss their perceptions of themselves and others. "Frog Camp," another orientation program, addresses student participation in a diversified community on campus and beyond. The program encourages first-year students to share with one another, keep a journal, and broaden their ideologies to include their new experiences.

✦ VOLUNTEER SERVICE. "Making Voluntary Service Happen" is a workbook that guides the service activities of all student organizations. The workbook helps students see that effective service begins with self-assessment and concludes with personal evaluation. Students participate in such service events as "Hunger Week" and "Day of Caring," as well as volunteer with numerous community service organizations throughout the year.

✦ STUDENT LEADERSHIP. "PRISM" ("Purpose, Responsibility, Integrity, Service, Mentoring") is a four-year leadership-development program in which students develop personal values through active community involvement. During the program's third year, classes use such service as the foundation for learning about ethics. Recently, PRISM IV students developed a leadership curriculum that focuses on ethics and character development for elementary school children, and this program has been presented to and accepted by the Fort Worth Independent School District. The Campus Leadership Forum is designed for those students with limited time who want to participate in leadership activities such as hearing nationally recognized speakers, attending community leadership dinners, and participating in a leadership-development conference.

✦ SUBSTANCE-ABUSE PREVENTION. "ADE," Texas Christian's "Alcohol and Drug Education" Center, incorporates personal and community wellness into student development. The Center promotes healthy lifestyles and responsible decision-making by offering programs, training, and alternative activities. The Center also collaborates with "Students Reaching Out," a student-directed program that helps students develop personal responsibility for themselves, for others, and for their university by setting positive examples.

TCU fosters the development of mature individuals who respect others, feel passionate about a free and just society, and are prepared to serve that society as responsible citizens.

"SINCE THE DAY WE OPENED OUR DOORS, we have been at least as concerned about the character development of our students as we have about their intellectual development." The words of Brigadier General Malham M. Wakin, USAF, Retired, and Professor Emeritus state the core philosophy of the U.S. Air Force Academy. Although the Academy has been in the business of building character in male cadets since its inception in 1955 and in male and female cadets since 1976, the commitment to character development was made explicit in 1993 with the establishment of the Character Development Commission (CDC) and the Center for Character Development.

The head of every major organization at USAFA serves on the CDC, which is chaired by the Dean and meets monthly to serve as a board of directors for character-development efforts, including authoring and implementing a comprehensive plan of vigorous programs of substantial breadth and depth:

✦ FACULTY AND CURRICULUM. The Center for Character Development, directed by Colonel Mark Hyatt, is staffed with 21 full-time professionals engaged in developing, instituting, and administering character programs in the areas of Character and Ethics, Honor and Integrity, and Human Relations. The key to the involvement of institutional leaders and all staff and faculty revolves around the "ACES" ("Academy Character Enrichment Seminars") Program, which strives to impart the importance of character development and the role of Academy personnel in that process.

✦ ACADEMIC HONESTY. Honesty is emphasized through the Academy's Honor System and Code: "We Will Not Lie, Steal, or Cheat, Nor Tolerate Among Us Anyone Who Does." Honor in academics is specifically addressed through the Academics with Honor program.

✦ STUDENT LEADERSHIP. Academy cadets learn, understand, and practice the virtues associated with good leadership through their immersion in a 4,000-member leadership laboratory. Each semester, cadets rotate among significant leadership roles. The Academy also sponsors the annual National Character and Leadership Symposium, to which expert speakers and undergraduate students from around the nation are invited.

✦ SPIRITUAL AND ETHICAL GROWTH. The spiritual growth initiatives, which are not necessarily faith-centered, are integral to the Academy's programs. The institution's values and the notion of wholehearted devotion residing deep within are offered to inspire students to develop moral and ethical integrity. "EATC" ("Ethics Across the Curriculum") attempts to address prominent ethical issues in each academic discipline, approaching moral education as a dimension, and not just a block, of the curriculum.

The President's commission outlines the qualities and service required of U.S. military officers, mandating the "special trust and confidence in the patriotism, valor, fidelity and abilities" that Americans can place in the leaders of their armed forces. The USAFA is committed to graduating officers with the knowledge and character necessary to fulfill their commission to the U.S. Air Force, becoming trusted representatives of their country as they support and defend the Constitution as distinguished military leaders.

UNITED STATES AIR FORCE ACADEMY

USAF ACADEMY, CO 80840-6260

719.333.4904
http://www.usafa.af.mil/

UNDERGRADUATES: 4,100

"Here at the Academy, cadets, officers, airmen, and staff all work together to produce graduates of integrity."

—A USAFA SENIOR CADET

Other USAFA Profiles:

• Profile of Superintendent Oelstrom
• Academic Honesty Program
• Spiritual Growth Program
• Student Leadership Program

606 THAYER ROAD
WEST POINT, NY 10996

914.938.4041
http://www.usma.edu/

UNDERGRADUATES: 4,000

*"The Academy develops
leaders who are focused
on selfless service to
others. The consequences
of a lack of character in
the military are severe—
in few professions does
the ability to make
correct decisions under
the most adverse
circumstances determine
the safety of lives and
the security of nations."*

—A USMA FOURTH-YEAR
CADET

Other USMA Profiles:

• Academic Honesty Program
• Faculty & Curriculum Program
• Student Leadership Program

THE MISSION OF THE U.S. MILITARY ACADEMY, the nation's oldest service academy dating back to 1802, is to develop commissioned officer *leaders of character* to serve in the U.S. Army. Having adopted coeducation in 1976, West Point prepares all of its cadets for lives of service through rigorous programs:

✦ STUDENT LEADERSHIP. At West Point, character development spans all three formal programs that make up the Cadet Leader Development System—Academic Program, Military Program, and Physical Program. The 47-month cadet experience mandates character as the seminal trait of an Academy graduate. This comprehensive approach to character development has been in place at West Point for more than 150 years.

✦ ACADEMIC HONESTY. Cadets and faculty are expected to be persons of character in every setting. The Cadet Honor Code ("A cadet will not lie, cheat, steal, or tolerate those who do") governs all aspects of cadet life, whether in the barracks, in the classroom, on the athletic field, or away from the Academy. From their first day at West Point, cadets learn to live by the Honor Code and are expected to confront and, if necessary, report other cadets who violate its precepts.

✦ CIVIC EDUCATION. All cadets participate in two separate, but complementary programs that relate directly to character development. Administered by the Commandant of Cadets through the Academy's Center for the Professional Military Ethic, teams of cadets and faculty provide small-group instruction within the Honor Education and Respect Education Programs. Cadets devote more than 50 hours during their four years at the Academy to these programs that foster the essential values of integrity and respect.

✦ FACULTY AND CURRICULUM. The unifying principle behind the academic curriculum is the intellectual development required of commissioned officers. Courses develop individual moral awareness, the ability to apply ethical considerations in decision-making, and the skill to promote ethical conduct within organizations. The core curriculum includes courses in general psychology, military leadership, philosophy (ethics), history of the military art, constitutional and military law, American politics, and international relations. The Academy's predominantly military faculty serve as professional role models and mentors who help cadets understand and accept West Point's core values, which will guide their careers as Army officers. Faculty also coach and advise cadets involved in intercollegiate athletics and extracurricular activities, focusing on matters of integrity.

The Military Academy's integrated approach to leadership and character development is recognized worldwide. For the past 13 years, West Point has hosted the National Conference on Ethics in America, which brings together students from colleges and universities throughout the nation to discuss character development on college campuses; 130 students from 62 colleges participated in the most recent conference.

All West Point offerings and activities address the many values and tenets of the military professional ethic to prepare leaders as commissioned U.S. Army officers who serve and protect their nation.

THE PURPOSE OF THE U.S. NAVAL ACADEMY is "to produce leaders of character to lead the nation in peace and war." Since its founding in 1845, the Academy has produced great leaders in all walks of life—from the battlefield, high seas, and outer space to the boardroom and the White House. The deep commitment to prepare all midshipmen—the Academy adopted coeducation in 1976—for leadership roles begins when each new Academy member takes the solemn oath " . . . to support and defend the Constitution. . . . " Midshipmen then spend the next four years preparing to become leaders in the military and the nation through a number of substantive, character-building programs:

◆ FIRST-YEAR PROGRAMS. The first-year program enables midshipmen to build character and develop a sense of personal and civic responsibility. Extensive training in human relations, leadership, and the Navy's Core Values—Honor, Courage, and Commitment—lays the foundation.

◆ ACADEMIC HONESTY. The Honor Concept of the Brigade of Midshipmen states: "Midshipmen are persons of integrity: They stand for that which is right." Through an Honor Education Program that calls on midshipmen to enforce this concept and hold their peers accountable, graduates leave the Academy with a true sense of the importance of integrity.

◆ FACULTY AND CURRICULUM. The importance of integrity is addressed across all academic fields, but more significantly is demonstrated through the actions and example of the faculty. The monthly Integrity Development Seminar is an Academy-wide program in which 240 seminar groups focus on a specific ethical topic. Faculty and staff volunteer to facilitate discussions on ethical reasoning and decision making in areas of personal, civic, and military responsibility. Each year, midshipmen are required to take core curriculum courses that emphasize leadership, law, American government, moral reasoning, and Naval Heritage.

◆ STUDENT LEADERSHIP. Leadership and character development separate the Naval Academy from most other academic institutions. All students graduate to become leaders of integrity in the Navy and Marine Corps, so they must develop and refine their leadership skills while at the Academy. Initially, midshipmen must take orders—knowing that learning how to follow is learning how to lead. With each year, midshipmen gain increased responsibility and practical experience in leadership. Finally, in senior year, midshipmen become responsible for military training and conduct.

◆ VOLUNTEER SERVICE. The student-run Midshipmen Action Group is a volunteer civic and charitable service organization that averages about 18,000 volunteer hours per year in numerous local community projects, including education, environment, and social services. This group has been nationally recognized for its efforts on "Make a Difference Day."

◆ SPIRITUAL GROWTH. In addition to the regular religious services available, midshipmen actively participate in eight religious activity groups that offer further fellowship and worship opportunities.

The Naval Academy develops midshipmen who graduate with the highest standards of integrity, character, and leadership. Its most important obligation is to ensure that future leaders possess the personal integrity to discern right from wrong—and the courage to do what is right.

UNITED STATES NAVAL ACADEMY

121 BLAKE ROAD
ANNAPOLIS, MD 21402-5000

410.293.1000
http://www.usna.edu/

UNDERGRADUATES: 4,000

"The Academy is a place where leadership is not just taught, but lived; where the friends you make may someday be the ones who lay down their lives for you; and where strength of character is a measure of success."

—A USNA FOURTH-YEAR MIDSHIPMAN

Other USNA Profiles:

• Academic Honesty Program
• First-Year Program
• Student Leadership Program

UNIVERSITY OF DAYTON

300 COLLEGE PARK
DAYTON, OH 45469

937.229.4411
http://www.udayton.edu/

UNDERGRADUATES: 6,700

"My experience in service, such as in the Christian Appalachia Project, has opened my eyes to the difficulties that job-seekers face when opportunities are scarce. Witnessing this has strengthened my convictions about social justice and enabled me to appreciate the value of community."

—A UD THIRD-YEAR STUDENT

Other Dayton Profiles:

• Volunteer Service Program

THE UNIVERSITY OF DAYTON'S MISSION embodies a spirit of service that is distinguished by its Catholic, Marianist tradition. Founded in 1849, UD educates students to lead by influencing the affairs of the world and to serve by enriching the lives of individuals and communities. Challenging students to make a difference is at the core of UD's curriculum and cornerstone programs:

✦ FIRST-YEAR PROGRAMS. A three-day orientation engages new students in a range of academic and community activities that familiarize them with university life. The "New Student Convocation," Academic Deans' addresses, and advising sessions are designed to help students understand the purpose of a college education. Community activities such as residence hall and orientation meetings help students feel at home on campus.

✦ FACULTY AND CURRICULUM. Service learning plays an important role in UD's curriculum. The Provost's office supports "CLASP" ("Community Leadership and Service Program"), a faculty initiative that began by bringing together groups of students led by a faculty member to discuss the merits of service learning. It has evolved into an organization that sponsors numerous service-learning activities for faculty members: it sponsors and organizes service-learning minicourses; secures speakers for faculty events; organizes faculty surveys, panels, and workshops on service learning; and promotes many other events and activities.

✦ VOLUNTEER SERVICE. Campus Ministry has a 30-year tradition of providing voluntary service opportunities for more than 1,000 UD students through 29 service clubs. The Center for Social Concern, a division of Campus Ministry, sponsors such events as urban plunges, "Into the Streets," "Summer in Appalachia," and "Summer of Service." The Center also organizes "WISH" ("Week in Solidarity with the Homeless"), "Hunger Awareness Week," and numerous programs on justice education and service learning. "Christmas on Campus" is an annual, campus-wide event at which UD celebrates Christmas with children in the Dayton community.

✦ STUDENT LEADERSHIP. "LTLT" ("Leadership Today for Leaders of Tomorrow") is a program designed by the Office of Student Activities to teach students leadership skills, meet the needs of current student leaders, and provide the next generation of student leaders with support. Through LTLT, students participate in such events as "Think Lunch on Thursdays!," a series of monthly, lunchtime programs on leadership; "Leadership Now," seminars to help students enhance self-confidence; and "Leadership for Tomorrow," two weeklong programs designed to enhance skills that student leaders can draw on beyond their undergraduate experience.

✦ SPIRITUAL GROWTH. Campus Ministry reaches out to members of the university community to help them develop in their faith. "FISH" ("Faith in Sharing") are small, faith-sharing communities of four to six members who gather to pray and share together on a regular basis.

Learning through service is at the core of UD's mission. UD seeks to educate individuals who will make service and learning lifelong pursuits and who will use their skills and education to make meaningful contributions to society.

THE UNIVERSITY OF MARY is a Catholic, Benedictine, liberal arts institution established in 1955 on the principles of service and leadership. The Rule of Benedict provides a guiding framework to introduce values that develop character, enhance relationships, and build community. To achieve these goals, Mary emphasizes the Benedictine values of service, community, hospitality, respect, prayer, and moderation in its curriculum and cocurricular activities:

✦ FIRST-YEAR PROGRAM. "Lifejackets, Parachutes, and Armor" is a first-year, required course in which moral and ethical decision-making skills are introduced with the Benedictine values as a foundation. During the seminar, students develop a sense of community, explore career opportunities and lifestyle choices, and experience volunteerism.

✦ FACULTY AND CURRICULUM. Mary's curriculum ensures that when students graduate they are proficient in seven areas that are essential for functioning in careers and leading full lives: (1) communication, (2) effective thinking and problem-solving, (3) valuing, (4) aesthetics, (5) social environment, (6) physical environment, and (7) professional development. Mary also has completed its sixth year of implementing a campus-wide project to incorporate the Benedictine values into classrooms of every discipline.

✦ VOLUNTEER SERVICE. More than 500 students are involved in the Student Volunteer Program, which links students with such agencies as Big Brother/Big Sister, Habitat for Humanity, and Special Olympics. Through Campus Ministry, students have the opportunity to work with the North Dakota State Penitentiary and the Cheyenne River Youth Project on a reservation in South Dakota. Four academic divisions require service hours as a prerequisite for admission.

✦ STUDENT LEADERSHIP. Through the Harold Schafer Leadership Center, the Emerging Leaders Program sponsors student internships and mentoring by business leaders throughout the Midwest. The concept of servant-leader is a core element of all programs offered by the Center.

✦ SUBSTANCE-ABUSE PREVENTION. Mary's Assistance Program involves faculty, staff, and students in prevention, detection, and referral for any university member with substance abuse, emotional, or other problems. The staff collaborates with student counselors to increase awareness on campus and provide assistance in recovery.

✦ SPIRITUAL GROWTH. Required courses in philosophy and theology enable students to become lifelong learners in issues of faith, effective thinking, and valuing. Campus Ministry sponsors an annual ecumenical Prayer Day, Benedictine Awareness Week, youth retreats, spiritual search weekends, weekly liturgical celebrations, and Bible studies.

University of Mary's philosophy states that "all students are encouraged to seek the truth; see themselves as whole and unique individuals responsible to God; and become leaders in the service of truth." Students learn that they are responsible for the progress of society and are encouraged to become decision-makers, problem solvers, and agents of positive change.

UNIVERSITY OF MARY

7500 UNIVERSITY DRIVE
BISMARCK, ND 58504

800.288.6279
http://www.umary.edu/

UNDERGRADUATES: 2,100

"The Benedictine values at Mary have helped me grow in my faith and develop stronger relationships."

—A MARY SECOND-YEAR STUDENT

UNIVERSITY OF MIAMI

PO BOX 248025
CORAL GABLES, FL 33124

305.284.2211
http://www.miami.edu/

UNDERGRADUATES: 8,000

"As a Miami senior, both my academic and leadership experiences have become extraordinary assets on my personal journey to establishing my values."

—A MIAMI FOURTH-YEAR STUDENT

Other Miami Profiles:

• Academic Honesty Program
• Substance-Abuse Prevention Program

THE UNIVERSITY OF MIAMI, founded in 1925, articulates its commitment to preparing students for lives of personal and civic responsibility in many ways. As a guiding principle, this private, comprehensive liberal arts institution concentrates on the personal growth of its students and an institutional pledge to "respect the differences among people." Ranked fifth nationally for the diversity of its students, Miami is in a position to encourage cross-cultural perspectives in student life.

Some of the character-development programs that highlight Miami's ethos of a value-based education include:

✦ FIRST-YEAR PROGRAMS. First-year students instantly become aware of the university's dedication to service through the orientation outreach program, in which 100 students are placed at 10 volunteer sites. The "First Year Insight" program offers faculty and staff time to mentor new students. Classroom assignments and dialog embrace issues such as college transition, peer influence, diversity, alcohol/drug use, and leadership.

✦ ACADEMIC HONESTY. On their arrival, Miami students are introduced to the student-designed Honor Code that calls for high standards of academic integrity. The Student Honor Council prepares students to hear cases of alleged violations and oversees programs on the topics of academic integrity and ethics.

✦ FACULTY AND CURRICULUM. Innovative "Learning Communities" distinguish Miami's progressive teaching methods, which integrate two or more courses through a common, interdisciplinary focus. Faculty coordinate readings, assignments, field trips, and social activities in small classes to promote interaction among and between the students and faculty.

✦ VOLUNTEER SERVICE. Last year, more than 18,000 hours of community service work was reported through the Butler Volunteer Services Center. By actively including community service in every facet of the university experience, students develop a keen interest in the power of social action and responsible citizenship.

✦ STUDENT LEADERSHIP. The Leadership Institute champions character, integrity, and competence in its students, bringing faculty, staff, alumni, and civic and corporate leaders together to cultivate leaders through a 45-hour certification program. Facilitators encourage students to challenge conventional thinking, take risks, and strive for personal excellence.

✦ SPIRITUAL GROWTH. Miami's Chaplains Association gathers nine religious organizations under the "Many Paths, Common Purpose" program. This on-campus religious system brings a unique collaborative quality to the university's spiritual life.

✦ SENIOR-YEAR PROGRAM. The "Senior Reflection Seminar" enables seniors to examine their leadership experiences and look to the importance of a lifetime commitment to service beyond graduation.

From new-student orientation to capstone seminar, Miami students enjoy both the breadth and depth of character-building experiences that prepare them for lives of civic responsibility and personal development.

FOR MORE THAN 155 YEARS, the University of Notre Dame has pursued its mission of creating an environment of teaching and learning that fosters disciplined habits of mind, body, and spirit essential to the development of educated, skilled, and free people. Established in 1842 as a church-affiliated, comprehensive university, UND seeks to cultivate in its students not only an appreciation for great human achievements, but also a disciplined sensibility to the poverty, injustice, and oppression that burden the lives of so many. UND's programs endow students with personal development-based sensibilities:

✦ **FIRST-YEAR PROGRAMS.** "First Year of Studies" is a required program designed to relieve the uncertainty that first-year students often feel regarding college and their choice of major by allowing them to tentatively declare an intended major. The curriculum allows first-year students to focus on honing their learning skills and developing time management strategies through UND's Learning Resource Center.

✦ **ACADEMIC HONESTY.** Adopted in 1987, the Academic Code of Honor facilitates moral education to help students develop personal conduct standards for their lives beyond UND. All undergraduate students are required to sign the code.

✦ **FACULTY AND CURRICULUM.** The Center for Ethics and Religious Values in Business and The Erasmus Institute were established in 1981 and 1997, respectively, to promote social justice and ethical behavior. The Ethics Center at the College of Business Administration is designed to strengthen the Judeo-Christian ethical foundations in business and public policy decisions. The Erasmus Institute fosters general scholarship through research and courses informed by Catholic thought.

✦ **VOLUNTEER SERVICE.** For more than 11 years, the Center for Social Concerns has been at the heart of service and social awareness for UND. Every year, 2,000 students volunteer for center-sponsored community service projects, ranging from low-income housing rehabilitation to tutoring developmentally disabled children. Many of the programs feature learning components directed by the Department of Theology.

✦ **SUBSTANCE-ABUSE PREVENTION.** The Office of Alcohol and Drug Education promotes and implements educational programs on alcohol and other drugs. Staff members provide in-depth assessments of students seeking or in need of assistance. The office also sponsors "SADD" ("Students Against Drunk Driving") and "Flip Side," a club that organizes nonalcoholic social activities.

✦ **SPIRITUAL GROWTH.** Campus Ministry sponsors numerous programs devoted to spiritual and character development. The "Notre Dame Encounter with Christ" is a two-day retreat offered five times a year focusing on sustained prayer and personal reflection. Mass is celebrated daily in each of UND's 27 residence halls.

UND encourages students to develop human solidarity and a concern for the common good by furnishing them with the opportunity to use their skills and knowledge to serve and promote a just society.

UNIVERSITY OF NOTRE DAME

NOTRE DAME, IN 46556

219.631.7505
http://www.nd.edu/

UNDERGRADUATES: 7,800

"Through Notre Dame's Center for Social Concerns, I developed my consciousness as a Christian and a citizen about the struggles faced by the poor, the oppressed, and the marginalized—and I learned how I can work to change those conditions."

—A UND FOURTH-YEAR STUDENT

Other UND Profiles:

• Portrait of President Malloy
• Academic Honesty Program
• Faculty & Curriculum Program
• Volunteer Service

UNIVERSITY OF OKLAHOMA

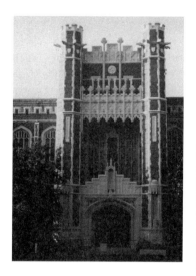

NORMAN, OK 73019

405.325.0311

http://www.ou.edu/

UNDERGRADUATES: 16,200

"It takes only a few hours to fall in love with the people, the traditions, and the atmosphere at OU. After four years, I am still just as passionate about my college experience and the 20,000-plus members of the 'Sooner Family' as the day I arrived."

—AN OU FOURTH-YEAR STUDENT

Other OU Profiles:

• First-Year Program
• Volunteer Service Program

ACADEMIC EXCELLENCE and a strong sense of community distinguish the University of Oklahoma. Established in 1890 as a public, comprehensive institution, OU promotes a learning environment that actively incorporates a variety of extracurricular activities to help students develop personal, social, intellectual, and occupational skills in addition to the ethical values essential for success. OU's character-building programs, activities, and services are designed to foster personal development and enhance the overall quality of campus life:

✦ FIRST-YEAR PROGRAMS. "New Sooner Orientation" introduces first-year students to OU through programs and activities such as "Convocation," "Academic Success," "Campus Resources," "Recreation & Health," "Getting Acquainted," and many others. "Gateway to College Learning" helps students make a successful transition to a university learning environment by teaching them to use specific academic skills, helping them acquire the life skills necessary for citizenship in a diverse community, and learning about the history and traditions of campus life at OU.

✦ FACULTY AND CURRICULUM. The "Faculty-in-Residence" and "Adopt-a-Faculty" programs promote teacher-student interaction beyond the classroom and build community experiences. The Phillips Scholars Program targets underrepresented minority students for intensive mentoring, helps students acclimate to corporate America, and encourages participation in community service.

✦ VOLUNTEER SERVICE. OU Volunteers, the community service center, encourages and facilitates volunteerism by providing resources and information on local, national, and international service programs. The "Adopt-an-Area" program allows student living groups to designate campus areas as litter free. National Arbor Day is recognized and honored with an Arbor Week celebration of activities, including a joint beautification project of planting trees in the city of Norman.

✦ STUDENT LEADERSHIP. The President's Leadership Class was established in 1961 as a first-year scholarship-leadership program designed to cultivate leadership abilities through diverse activities and interaction with many university, state, and national leaders. Student-leader retreats with university administrators are designed to emphasize current campus issues. To maximize student communication among various organizations, a new Student Leadership Wing is being designed to include a resource center, consulting services, and workshop opportunities to study effective leadership skills and civic responsibility.

✦ CIVIC EDUCATION. The "OU Cousins" program matches international and exchange students with American students to create meaningful relationships among these communities on an individual basis. The program provides numerous venues for social interaction and opportunities for cultural exploration. "Bridges," a small, multicultural leadership group made up of staff and students, builds community through understanding.

OU recognizes, appreciates, and actively pursues its commitment to educating students through excellence in teaching, creative activity, and service to the community and larger society.

THREE CENTRAL TENETS—fine teaching, vigorous service to others, and spiritual discovery—form the core of the University of Portland's commitment to building student character. This private, Catholic institution, founded in 1901, has always prized the ideals of personal and civic responsibility. Since UP's inception, the Holy Cross Order has supported its educational objectives, service-learning programs, and annual themes (social justice for the year 1999; world hunger for the year 2000) that challenge UP students to think emotionally, spiritually, and with maturity about significant ways to improve the world in which they live.

UP emphasizes a character-building ethos in its comprehensive programs:

✦ **FACULTY AND CURRICULUM.** Since 1997, a refocused curriculum has actively stressed character development. An ethics component exists in all business and nursing courses, and a Chair of Ethics has been recently established. Philosophy and theology courses are core requirements for all students, as are service-learning projects across all disciplines.

✦ **FIRST-YEAR PROGRAMS.** "Freshman Plunge" orients new students with a three-day program of service learning that includes housing renovation in low-income neighborhoods, tending to the homeless, and investigating the volunteer service needs of the Portland community. Plans for a Freshman Resource Center target character-shaping programs for incoming students.

✦ **VOLUNTEER SERVICE.** UP promotes far-reaching service programs that challenge students to invest personal time and effort in serving others. UP now offers 32 volunteer service programs encompassing a wide range of community involvement. "Christmas in April" includes neighborhood repair work, "Rural Plunge" targets renovations for migrant farm workers in rural Oregon, and "Urban Plunge" undertakes projects in a low-income area of Portland. UP students also visit the elderly, work in local jails, and volunteer in soup kitchens and local elementary schools.

✦ **STUDENT LEADERSHIP.** The president, deans, directors, and faculty encourage students in overseeing and directing community service projects to develop their leadership skills. Students also participate in local Oregon political campaigns. Serving as peer models, they have helped to significantly reduce student drunkenness through a five-year program.

✦ **SPIRITUAL GROWTH.** Spiritual retreat programs and campus ministry activities promote UP's education of the mind, heart, and soul and reinforce the spiritual life, which is central to the Congregation of the Holy Cross.

Commitment to preparing students for civic and personal responsibility defines UP's educational goals. Graduates enter the workplace with confidence and skills to serve others effectively, genuinely, and thoughtfully.

UNIVERSITY OF PORTLAND

5000 NORTH WILLAMETTE BLVD
PORTLAND, OR 97203-5798

503.943.7202
http://www.uofport.edu/

UNDERGRADUATES: 2,200

"UP changes us—better said, we are moved to grow here in many ways. Students are stimulated to be the best we can be—to explore; to dig deeper; to chase after knowledge, substance, and soul."

—A UP THIRD-YEAR STUDENT

Other UP Profiles:

• Profile of Father Tyson
• Spiritual Growth Program

UNIVERSITY OF RICHMOND

28 WESTHAMPTON WAY
RICHMOND, VA 23173-1903

804.289.8000
http://www.urich.edu/

UNDERGRADUATES: 4,400

"My service-learning experience at UR has been the single most defining aspect of my education. UR has helped me develop a better understanding of who I am and what I can do to bring about positive change in my community."

—A UR FOURTH-YEAR STUDENT

Other UR Profiles:

• Character & Sexuality Program

COMMUNITY SERVICE and service learning are distinguishing characteristics of a University of Richmond education. Founded in 1830 by the Virginia Baptist Education Society, UR has evolved from a small, Baptist college to a liberal arts institution that is committed to serving individuals of all faiths. Personal and civic responsibility and moral leadership play valued roles in UR's curriculum and cocurricular activities:

✦ FIRST-YEAR PROGRAMS. The spirit of community service is introduced to new students during UR's formal Orientation Program, during which a community service fair communicates that expressing concern for others through volunteerism is an important campus value. Also, when fraternities and sororities hold their information sessions for new members, each chapter stresses its philanthropic effort as an integral part of its tradition.

✦ STUDENT LEADERSHIP. The Jepson School for Leadership Studies requires all students to complete service-learning assignments in which they are challenged to connect leadership to practice. In real-world settings, students test the theories and principles of leadership, as well as their own attitudes toward moral leadership and responsibility. The Coston Family Chair in Leadership and Ethics is an endowed faculty position that ensures a focus on business ethics, the moral challenges of leadership, the role of values and ethics in organizational cultures, and the place of values and ethics in the development of institutional and public policy. "COMPS" ("Community Problem-Solving Seminar") is a summer program that combines a seminar on social analysis and policy with an internship in a public or community agency dealing with a related social problem.

✦ VOLUNTEER SERVICE. "VAC" ("Volunteer Action Council") is a student-run organization that links students with numerous area agencies in need of assistance. Students may volunteer with such Richmond-area agencies as AIDS Information and Support, Boys Club, Animal Welfare, nursing homes, Richmond City Schools, Central Virginia Food Bank, Earth Action, and many others. Faculty, staff, and students work together to build homes and contribute to Habitat for Humanity. To date, 12 Richmond area homes and 12 homes overseas carry UR's name.

✦ CIVIC EDUCATION. Students have ample opportunity to develop civic responsibility by participating in service-learning assignments. "LINCS" ("Learning in Community Settings") develops new and existing research opportunities and relationships with local community agencies and provides students with a broad range of credit-bearing, service-learning opportunities. UR's School of Law strongly encourages pro-bono work among its students. Third-year law students, for example, work directly with clients, under the supervision of licensed attorneys, to represent indigent individuals in the criminal and civil court system.

UR believes in educating students intellectually and spiritually and instilling in them freedom of thought and expression. Students learn that, by assuming moral leadership and demonstrating compassion for others, they are able to make significant, long-lasting contributions to society.

"**W**HAT IS AN URBAN UNIVERSITY? It is one that is not just *in* or *near* the city, but *of* the city." These words by the Rev. Dennis Dease, president of the University of St. Thomas, enunciate the rich opportunities for students to engage in community experience at this private, Catholic, liberal arts institution founded in 1885. St. Thomas, which adopted coeducation in 1976 and gained university status in 1990, enables students to address community problems within their fields of learning, not only to gain deeper insight into them, but to "create the solutions that have eluded the present generation of leaders." The university has created a fertile environment for character building through its programs:

✦ **FACULTY AND CURRICULUM.** St. Thomas welcomes students of all faiths and backgrounds and emphasizes values-centered education. Students are required to complete at least two courses in moral and philosophical reasoning and three courses in faith and the Catholic tradition. The "Senior Citizens Go to College" program allows people 55 or older to attend classes at St. Thomas at no cost; these students often enrich the class by sharing their wisdom and experience. Faculty are increasingly integrating course-related community service into their curriculum. For example, St. Thomas geography students have researched low-income mortgage-lending patterns, local bus routing, and the frequency of lead water pipes in neighborhoods with many children.

✦ **VOLUNTEER SERVICE.** About 350 St. Thomas students in the Tutoring Program volunteer to help youths at two local homeless shelters and 25 public and private schools. The university requires all undergraduate business majors to take a noncredit course in community. "Volunteers in Action," part of Campus Ministry, coordinates the efforts of several hundred students involved in nine programs, including helping at the Shriner's Hospital for children and at "Listening House" for homeless people. The related "VISION" program organizes service trips nationally and internationally for 200 students, staff, and faculty. Hundreds of St. Thomas students, staff, and faculty turn out each fall and spring to clean the banks of the Mississippi River, and the 75 clubs and student organizations on campus must perform an annual service project to maintain their official standing.

✦ **CIVIC EDUCATION.** Undergraduates volunteer at two St. Thomas programs— the "Hispanic Pre-College Project" and "Bridge for Success" for single parents and those on welfare—that help economically disadvantaged people enter or continue college.

✦ **SPIRITUAL GROWTH.** St. Thomas has two seminaries, one undergraduate and one graduate, and the Jay Phillips Center for Jewish-Christian Learning. The John A. Ryan Institute for Catholic Social Thought recently launched the Catholic Education Program and Catholic Social Teaching to integrate Catholic social thought and education. Christian Social Thought and Management works to integrate faith and business management.

St. Thomas students apply what they learn in the classroom. In one difficult incident, a first-year student wrote anti-Semitic and anti-Hispanic hate messages in one of the residence halls. The student-led response included organizing prayer vigils, creating posters in opposition to the graffiti, and holding campus forums to discuss and learn more about issues of hate. The messages stopped, and the student left the school. St. Thomas students turn learning into positive change.

UNIVERSITY OF ST. THOMAS

2115 SUMMIT AVENUE
ST. PAUL, MN 55105

651.962.5000
http://www.stthomas.edu/

UNDERGRADUATES: 5,300

"Education at St. Thomas takes us back to our core values—our works and actions define who we are, and we take what we learn in church and in the classroom and put it to work in the community."

—A ST. THOMAS FOURTH-YEAR STUDENT

UNIVERSITY OF SCRANTON

800 LINDEN STREET
SCRANTON, PA 18510-4699

570.941.7400
http://www.uofs.edu/

UNDERGRADUATES: 4,000

"The Scranton community is one in which students learn about themselves through their relationships and contact with other students and faculty. The primary focus helps us learn not only the curriculum, but who we are as individuals."

—A SCRANTON SECOND-YEAR STUDENT

BY TRADITION, choice, and heartfelt commitment, the University of Scranton, a Jesuit, comprehensive institution, provides an environment in which students are challenged to develop "a commitment to the value system contained in the Gospels, a principled respect for the dignity of the human person, a devotion to justice, a dedication to the service of the poor, a love of truth, and a restless passion for learning." Founded in 1888 as Saint Thomas College by the Diocese of Scranton, it achieved university status in 1938 and was entrusted to the care of the Society of Jesus (the Jesuits) in 1942; it adopted coeducation in 1970.

The Jesuit ideal of *cura personalis* (care for the whole person) is expressed in "seamless learning"—integration of academic and student life—as expressed in Scranton's curriculum and cocurricular activities:

✦ FACULTY AND CURRICULUM. The general curriculum requires courses in theology, religious studies, philosophy, natural sciences, humanities, cultural diversity, and social/behavioral sciences to enable Scranton students to acquire an understanding of the world and an awareness of themselves and others. The "Task Force on Ignatian Identity and Mission" and the Center for Mission Reflection equip staff as mentors and models.

✦ FIRST-YEAR PROGRAMS. The general education curriculum, which requires mastery of written, oral, and electronic communications skills, builds on a first-year seminar that helps students make the transition to college life.

✦ VOLUNTEER SERVICE. "Collegiate Volunteers" links all Scranton students with volunteer opportunities in the community. In 1997–98, students contributed 165,424 student volunteer hours to 110 nonprofit agencies. In the Panuska College of Professional Studies, one of the five principal academic units at the university, students complete 80 hours of service (20 per year) as a requirement for graduation.

✦ SPIRITUAL GROWTH. University Ministries prepares students as leaders for parish and community life through liturgical life on campus and weekend retreats and evenings of renewal, reflection, and prayer. In 1997–98, 42 student leaders, 50 volunteer service leaders, and 128 liturgical ministers were trained. To accommodate the demand for student retreats, a second building has been opened at the University Conference and Retreat Center at Chapman Lake.

✦ SUBSTANCE-ABUSE PREVENTION. Peer counseling and education programs focus on spiritual and emotional wholeness. These programs include "Drug and Alcohol Information Center and Educators," student educators who encourage responsible, no-risk decision making about the use of alcohol and other drugs; "SART"(the "Sexual Assault Response Team"), composed of students, faculty, and staff who assist victims of sexual assault; and the HIV/AIDS Peer Educators, certified Red Cross HIV instructors who encourage students to make responsible decisions.

Since its founding by the Most Reverend William O'Hara, the first bishop of the Roman Catholic Diocese of Scranton, the university has never lost sight of its original goal: offering a values-based education to the students it serves.

"QUALITIES OF VIRTUE AND SOCIAL WORTH." This is what education should instill, stated the founder of the public, comprehensive University of Virginia in 1819. Thomas Jefferson wrote that only "educated citizens" could make "profound and lasting contributions to society." UVA emphasizes its message of the rights and responsibilities of citizenship to students *and* their parents before and during their UVA years. Faculty and staff serve as mentors and advisors to 350 student organizations and councils and live among students, modeling ethical standards and responsible decision-making. The education-for-life message is also delivered by upper-class students who mentor first-year students the moment they arrive on campus. Striving toward self-governance, students help determine residential policies; elect a First-Year Council representative; and establish student committees to plan programs, events, and First-Year groups. Students are involved in a wide range of UVA activities that develop an informed, active, and responsible citizenry, including:

✦ VOLUNTEER SERVICE. During their first week on campus, new students volunteer through SERVE. Student volunteerism continues through Madison House—3,000 students in 16 programs now contribute 100,000 service hours each year. Named a "Point of Light" by President Bush in 1990, Madison House also won an award from the U.S. Department of Housing and Urban Development. UVA also sends the region's largest number of volunteers to the Peace Corps.

✦ ACADEMIC HONESTY. New students are inducted into UVA's Honor System, the nation's oldest student-run honor code that affirms personal freedom, respect, and trust.

✦ STUDENT LEADERSHIP AND ETHICS EDUCATION. Faculty, staff, and students plan courses and seminars on ethical decision making, and UVA's nine schools all offer leadership and ethics courses. The hundreds of students elected to campus leadership positions are supported by year-round ethics workshops.

✦ SUBSTANCE-ABUSE PREVENTION. Listed in *Promising Practices: Campus Alcohol Strategies, 1996–97* as one of 12 leaders in alcohol education, UVA's faculty, staff, and student leaders model responsible personal behavior through credit courses and a variety of campus-run programs, many geared toward athletes.

✦ CIVIC EDUCATION. The Internship Program offers academic credit for civic and community work: architecture students work on design projects for local neighborhoods, arts and sciences and law students work in local civic and social organizations, and nursing students work in volunteer clinics. Education students work with local schools in various programs, and a recent study showed that many UVA graduates teach overseas or in at-risk public schools.

UVA was cited in 1993 by the American Association of University Administrators for "exemplary practice in achieving campus diversity." With help from its 15-year-old Peer Advisors Program, the university was recognized for graduating 89% of its African-American students, the highest rate in the country. Spiritual life also constitutes an important element of a UVA education. Each year, UVA honors a male and a female student, as well as a faculty member, who exhibit "fine spiritual qualities practically applied to daily living." UVA is committed to providing an undergraduate education that instills in its students the importance of making a difference in their community, bringing to life the Jeffersonian ideal of a responsible and informed citizenry.

UNIVERSITY OF VIRGINIA

PO BOX 9017
CHARLOTTESVILLE, VA 22906-9011

804.982.3200
http://www.virginia.edu/

UNDERGRADUATES: 12,400

"Thomas Jefferson's ideal in creating the University of Virginia was that to have a functional democracy, the citizens who participate in it must be educated. UVA carries on that ideal in grand fashion."

—A UVA FOURTH-YEAR
STUDENT

Other UVA Profiles:

• Profile of President Casteen
• Academic Honesty Program
• First-Year Program
• Volunteer Service Program

VITERBO COLLEGE

815 NINTH STREET SOUTH
LA CROSSE, WI 54601-8802

608.796.3000
http://www.viterbo.edu/

UNDERGRADUATES: 1,700

"Viterbo has enabled me to experience leadership in ways I could not have done elsewhere. I have learned more from my extracurricular activities than I could have from classwork alone."

—A VITERBO FOURTH-YEAR STUDENT

ESTABLISHED BY THE FRANCISCAN SISTERS of Perpetual Adoration in 1890, Viterbo College began as a preparatory school to train elementary school teachers. This private, church-affiliated, multipurpose school is named for the 13th-century Franciscan, Saint Rose of Viterbo, Italy. Viterbo provides a nationally recognized values-based education that adheres to the spirit of its original Franciscan mission: to learn truth, build unity, and spread hope. To that end, Viterbo embraces persons of all faiths and prepares students to be leaders and servants in their communities.

Several noteworthy Viterbo programs emphasize service and ethics:

✦ **FIRST-YEAR PROGRAMS.** First-year students can enroll in "Person, College, Community," a course that teaches how to balance freedom and responsibility. Part of the course requires students to examine case studies of community challenges and use an ethical decision-making process to resolve those problems.

✦ **FACULTY AND CURRICULUM.** Every course in Viterbo's curriculum has a moral or value component that relates to course content. The D.B. Reinhart Institute for Ethics in Leadership is a campus institution that was officially chartered in April 1999. Its mission is to promote the concepts of ethics and leadership as integral components of courses, conferences, workshops, and public forums for the college and local community. One program, "Bringing Ethics to Life," covers the challenges faced by healthcare providers and consumers. Other programs have been scheduled to address ethics in education, business, the arts, and culture.

✦ **VOLUNTEER SERVICE.** Many opportunities to serve the needs of people are available through the Campus Ministry and the La Crosse Volunteer Center. Service projects are limited only by the imagination of volunteers who see a need and want to make a difference in the lives of others. Students volunteer with such organizations as Habitat for Humanity and "Place of Grace," a Catholic worker house. Many students take spring and summer trips to Appalachia to assist as tutors in literacy programs. Viterbo also offers students a course on homelessness, which ends with a class trip to the homeless shelters of Omaha.

✦ **SPIRITUAL DEVELOPMENT.** The Campus Ministry coordinates religious activities to assist faculty, staff, and students in praying, reflecting, and growing in their faith. It organizes and implements weekly services, liturgies, Bible studies, and spiritual retreats.

✦ **SUBSTANCE-ABUSE PREVENTION.** Viterbo's student-directed "CONNECT" program is the centerpiece of campus chemical-abuse prevention. Students produce videos, stage mock DWI arrests, promote alcohol-free alternatives, and use a variety of creative methods to illustrate that "living it up on campus" can be fun and fulfilling without the use of alcohol and drugs.

Viterbo seeks to position students on a path toward promoting the common good. Service to others and the Franciscan heritage are central to its mission: to encourage students to use their education to promote Franciscan values of human dignity and respect for the world.

Other Viterbo Profiles:

• First-Year Program
• Substance-Abuse Prevention Program

WAKE FOREST UNIVERSITY is a private, coeducational institution whose mission is to educate with "goodness and intelligence." Founded in 1834 by the North Carolina Baptist Convention, Wake nurtures and challenges students in the liberal arts tradition, seeking to instill in them moral, academic, and personal values. These values are the legacy of three traditions: the Judeo-Christian and Baptist heritage, political democracy, and liberal education. These values are embodied in Wake's curriculum and cocurricular activities:

✦ FIRST-YEAR PROGRAMS. First-year seminars are designed for new students to develop critical-thinking skills and engage in rigorous intellectual exchange. Groups of 15 students are enrolled in each section and are taught by faculty from all academic divisions. Seminars address ethical issues in medicine, the arts, politics, and science. The annual new student leaders retreat provides an additional opportunity to analyze and discuss moral reasoning as it applies to popular culture.

✦ ACADEMIC HONESTY. Faculty, staff, and students are expected to abide by Wake's Honor Code. First-year students attend a special assembly during orientation where the Honor Code is explained and during which they are expected to sign the "Book of Honor."

✦ VOLUNTEER SERVICE. The "ACE" Fellows Program assists faculty members in integrating service-learning components into existing classes. More than half of all Wake undergraduate students make volunteerism part of their educational experience. The Volunteer Service Corps provides opportunities for nearly 1,000 students to regularly perform community service, placing volunteers in such service programs as "America Reads," Habitat for Humanity, and the Honduras Outreach Project. Wake's "Alternative Spring Break" provides numerous service opportunities to students who choose to spend their spring break volunteering to help with problems ranging from urban poverty to environmental degradation.

✦ SPIRITUAL GROWTH. Bible study, weekly worship, and community outreach provide students with ample opportunity to develop spiritually and morally. Campus ministers serve as counselors for students and help them address a variety of moral concerns. By participating in activities that promote spiritual growth, students learn tolerance and gain respect for one another.

✦ HEALTHY LIFESTYLES. A mandatory health class devotes three class periods to alcohol and substance abuse, sexually transmitted diseases, and rape prevention. "Alcohol 101" is an interactive CD-ROM that is installed on all new students' computers to increase awareness of alcohol abuse. Students interested in promoting healthy living can be trained as Peer Health Educators and, with student organizations, educate fellow students about substance abuse, stress, sexual health, and violence prevention.

Wake is dedicated to carrying on its tradition of preparing individuals for personal enrichment, enlightened citizenship, and professional life. Students develop a critical appreciation of moral, aesthetic, and religious values that will help them make meaningful contributions to the well-being of society.

WAKE FOREST UNIVERSITY

1834 WAKE FOREST ROAD
WINSTON-SALEM, NC 27106

336.758.5255
http://www.wfu.edu/

UNDERGRADUATES: 3,900

"My experience at Wake has been rich and varied, from the rigors of the classroom to the packed streets of Calcutta, India, as a City of Joy Scholar. Looking back, I realize how fortunate I am to have had all of the opportunities afforded to me as a Wake student."

—A WAKE FOURTH-YEAR STUDENT

Other Wake Profiles:

• Profile of President Hearn
• Academic Honesty Program
• Student Leadership Program
• Substance-Abuse Prevention Program

WASHINGTON AND LEE UNIVERSITY

LEXINGTON, VA 24450-0303

540.463.8400
http://www.wlu.edu/

UNDERGRADUATES: 1,700

"Washington and Lee requires a sincere commitment to excellence. Those of us who have made the commitment received rewards and benefits for our effort."

—A W&L FOURTH-YEAR
STUDENT

Other W&L Profiles:

• Academic Honesty Program
• Civic Education Program

FOR 250 YEARS, Washington and Lee University has helped shape men and women and lead them into a life of service. This small, private, liberal arts college is named for two of America's most influential people—George Washington, its first major benefactor, and Robert E. Lee, president of the college immediately following the Civil War.

W&L's numerous character-development programs include:

✦ **ACADEMIC HONESTY.** Since Lee's presidency, honor has been the moral cornerstone on campus. As the legend goes, in 1865 a young student from Tennessee approached Lee to ask for a copy of "the rules." General Lee replied, "We have but one rule here, and it is that every student must be a gentlemen." Lee's concept of honor, that students will not lie, cheat, steal, or violate trust, is so deeply rooted in the school's history that it is woven into almost every element of academic life. Students are free to schedule their own unproctored exams, and professors frequently give take-home closed-book tests. The undergraduate library and most academic buildings are left unlocked 24 hours a day, and no electronic devices are installed at the entrance to catch book thieves.

✦ **CIVIC EDUCATION.** New at W&L is the Shepherd Poverty Program, which offers course work, seminars, lectures, and subsidized summer-service projects that enable students to work with poor people in the U.S. and in developing countries. The program grew out of W&L's mission "to serve society through the productive use of talent and training."

✦ **VOLUNTEER SERVICE.** W&L's impact on the local community is immense. Students volunteer with organizations such as Habitat for Humanity and Big Brothers/Big Sisters, as well as help raise funds for area food banks. Students also serve as tutors at local schools and volunteer in the emergency room at the local hospital and for Red Cross blood drives. A program of particular note is "WITS" ("Women in Technology and Science"), a student-initiated organization that reaches out to area middle-school girls to encourage them to pursue math and science.

✦ **STUDENT LEADERSHIP.** Student autonomy is one of the hallmarks of a W&L education. The student-elected Executive Committee and its appointed official committees are responsible for administering the Honor System and nearly all student-related campus activities.

✦ **SUBSTANCE-ABUSE PREVENTION.** W&L's "LIFE" ("Lifestyle Information for Everyone") program educates the student community about the dangers of using alcohol and drugs. It produces literature, sponsors speakers, hosts seminars, and provides counseling services to help students steer away from choices that might result in personal and academic problems.

W&L students stand on the shoulders of its founding giants as they strive to continue a long tradition of service to the nation. The university has provided America with four Supreme Court justices, 27 U.S. senators, 31 governors, and 65 U.S. congressmen. As the ninth oldest college in America, W&L will continue to draw on its rich past and legacy of service to help shape the future of the nation and the world.

THE MISSION OF WESTMONT COLLEGE, a liberal arts school with a religious orientation established in 1937, is to assist "college men and women toward a balance of rigorous intellectual competence, healthy personal development, and strong Christian commitments." The institution's goal is to equip graduates who will become "global leaders." The objectives outlined in its *Viewbook* include preparing students to enter the world not only as leaders, but as followers of Christ "who are mature and thoughtful about the world and their role in it—truly prepared for significant service to their families, communities, professions, churches, and the world."

Students are also significantly influenced through the words and actions of Westmont's president, Dr. David Winter, who encourages prospective and new students to consider who they want to become—and then to view Westmont as a valuable resource for helping them develop their abilities through its various programs:

✦ FACULTY AND CURRICULUM. Westmont's liberal arts program is designed for students to learn about and discuss aspects of personal and civic responsibility in such areas as philosophy, literature, and the behavioral, natural, and social sciences. Its "Vision Statement" asserts that "the goal of all meaningful learning, and of liberal education in particular, is to inform the way we live." In classrooms, athletic fields, residence halls, and other areas, faculty and staff are influential in helping Westmont students develop a healthy philosophy of life that reflects a concern for others. Through the chapel program, speakers share and model for Westmont students lives of service and significance.

✦ VOLUNTEER SERVICE. Dr. Winter encourages all students to become actively involved in college life and to pursue a variety of ministry projects in the local community and throughout the world. Westmont students have a long history of service to those around them through "Christian Concerns," a student-run organization that oversees and coordinates more than 30 ministries that serve the Westmont and Santa Barbara communities, as well as people outside of the U.S.

✦ CHARACTER AND SEXUALITY. During the 1998–99 school year, Westmont sponsored a 12-part series on sexuality, "And God Created . . . Sex." Programming included well-attended discussions about sexuality; the impact of entertainment and advertising on student views about their gender roles and bodies; gender differences in communication; body image/eating disorders; and pornography. A Westmont faculty member recently developed a brochure on pornography that calls for both personal and social responsibility and that has been used in residence hall discussions and in training resident assistants.

Westmont's commitment to promoting personal and civic responsibility is also evident throughout a "Community Life Statement" that includes a variety of behavioral expectations for all college members. The goal is to provide an environment conducive to developing character in future generations of "global leaders of core convictions, broad sympathies, and Christian service."

WESTMONT COLLEGE

955 LA PAZ ROAD
SANTA BARBARA, CA 93108-1089

805.565.6000
http://www.westmont.edu/

UNDERGRADUATES: 1,400

"Westmont develops 'complete graduates' who create positive change. The rigorous academics, strong but gentle emphasis on spiritual formation, inspirational relationships with faculty and staff, and deep relationships with fellow students have helped make me a better person."

—A WESTMONT THIRD-YEAR STUDENT

Other Westmont Profiles:

• Profile of President Winter

WHEATON COLLEGE

501 COLLEGE AVENUE
WHEATON, IL 60187

630.752.5000
http://www.wheaton.edu/

UNDERGRADUATES: 2,300

"At Wheaton, character development is driven by our mission; it is not limited to classrooms or programs, but is emphasized through every aspect of campus life."

—A WHEATON FOURTH-YEAR STUDENT

Other Wheaton Profiles:

• Profile of President Litfin
• Faculty & Curriculum Program

SINCE 1860, the core of Wheaton College has been its people—the dedicated men and women who intentionally integrate their *faith* with their *work*. This private, Evangelical (nondenominational) Christian, liberal arts college helps build the mission of the church and improve society around the globe by promoting the development of "whole and effective Christians" through excellence in Bible-based education. Central to Wheaton's longstanding mission is developing character and competence in future servant-leaders who choose to live lives of personal and civic responsibility in their communities and in the wider world. *The Idea of a Christian College,* by Wheaton Professor Emeritus Arthur Holmes, captures the college's spirit and is now required reading throughout the 91 member schools of the Coalition of Christian Colleges and Universities. Wheaton's character-building cornerstones include:

✦ FACULTY AND CURRICULUM. The Faith and Learning Program encourages all professors to contemplate ways of incorporating the tenets of Christian doctrine into their academic disciplines. Not merely educators, Wheaton faculty teach and mentor students by word and example to approach their careers and lives with thoughtfulness and intentionality. The Center for Applied Christian Ethics sponsors on-campus seminars on ethical issues in which Wheaton faculty and students join distinguished experts and community leaders in armchair considerations of the importance of personal responsibility in social, professional, and spiritual life.

✦ CIVIC EDUCATION. The Urban Studies Program engages Wheaton students in various dimensions of urban life and culture in nearby Chicago by combining Christian teachings with economics, political science, and sociology to foster social change. Students gain an interdisciplinary perspective on the problems and causes of poverty, hunger, and oppression in developing nations through the Human Needs and Global Resources Program, which also encourages them to seek effective responses to these conditions based on biblical principles and sound socioeconomic theory and practice. Wheaton's Honduras Project provides opportunities for learning, leadership, and service in a developing country.

✦ STUDENT LEADERSHIP. Character-building and leadership development are the main objectives of the High Road Wilderness Programs offered at Wheaton's Honey Rock Camp in northern Wisconsin.

✦ VOLUNTEER SERVICE. Through the Office of Christian Outreach, Wheaton students touch the lives of those at home and abroad. The Christian Service Council sends more than 600 students into the Chicago community to tutor children, work in boys and girls clubs, and participate in correctional, immigrant, and visitation ministries. The Student Missionary Project sends 35–40 students on short-term assignments to such countries as Bulgaria, India, Namibia, Nepal, and Senegal. The nine-week summer program National City Ministries engages students in church-centered work in large cities, and the Youth Hostel Ministry is an evangelism program aimed at young people traveling throughout Europe.

✦ SPIRITUAL GROWTH. Programs include the Small Group Discipleship Program and Residence Hall Spiritual Life Committee. On-campus World Christian Fellowship coordinates small groups, retreats, prayer groups, services, and celebrations.

Wheaton students are inspired to deepen and fulfill their commitment of service to the world through profound dedication to their faith—the clear and consistent message of the Wheaton experience.

WILMINGTON COLLEGE, founded in 1870, is a church-affiliated school that helps students develop a strong sense of personal and civic responsibility. The foundation of Wilmington's commitment to preparing students for their future lives is founded on the Quaker traditions of concern for the individual, the equality of all people, and the belief in social justice. As stated in its Mission Statement and Goals, Wilmington "seeks to develop in each student . . . the value of truth and justice." This commitment is most clearly demonstrated by the "Wilmington College Testimonies," a statement that all entering students sign, affirming their commitment to abide by Wilmington's standards of conduct. Numerous academic and extracurricular programs demonstrate Wilmington's commitment to responsibility standards:

✦ FACULTY AND CURRICULUM. The Quaker precepts of conduct and mission inform the ways in which campus community members interact with one another. The president, faculty, and staff work together in teaching, modeling, and inspiring students to understand the virtues of civic and personal responsibility. The president teaches an Honors Seminar on the topic of Community, and faculty and staff are actively involved with students in the broader community. Every student must take courses in Global Issues and Awareness.

✦ FIRST-YEAR PROGRAMS. On their first day on campus, students, their families, faculty, and staff attend New Student Convocation, which sets the moral tone for the year. During their first night on campus, new students meet with their Resident Assistant and agree to acceptable standards of behavior to reaffirm their commitment to a moral community.

✦ STUDENT LEADERSHIP. Wilmington offers a Leadership Minor to enable students to "set goals and develop strategies to achieve them; to make carefully considered and ethical decisions; to lead as if people really mattered; and to engender positive changes." The Leader Scholars program, with more than 70 students, provides training in leadership styles, opportunities for leadership development, and encouragement to become servant leaders. In addition, a Peace Studies Minor and an Applied Peace Studies Certificate are available. The Peace Resource Center and Office of Campus Ministry collaborate in training students in mediating on-campus disputes, and students in turn train public school students in peer mediation. The director of the Center uses student facilitators in "Project TRUST," a diversity program in the local middle school.

✦ VOLUNTEER SERVICE. The Center for Service Learning places student volunteers with eight different social service or nonprofit agencies and also sponsors "plunge" activities at least once a month. Each Christmas break, 10 to 20 students work for Habitat for Humanity in Mississippi. Faculty and staff are actively involved on the YMCA Board of Directors, the Chamber of Commerce, the Emergency Food and Shelter Board, the School Board, Leadership Clinton, the Clinton County Community Action Board, and the Regional Planning Commission. Wilmington employees contributed nearly 10,000 hours of community service in 1998.

At Wilmington College, as former president Benjamin F. Trueblood said, "Education is for use" in transforming students and their communities—"not just for display."

WILMINGTON COLLEGE

251 LUDOVIC STREET
WILMINGTON, OH 45177

800.341.9318
http://www.wilmington.edu/

UNDERGRADUATES: 1,100

"Wilmington has given me a broad understanding and appreciation for more than just class work. It enabled me to become a leader, taught me the importance of building and maintaining quality relationships, and proved how individuals can make a difference in their community."

—A WILMINGTON FOURTH-
YEAR STUDENT

Other Wilmington Profiles:

• Student Leadership Program

XAVIER UNIVERSITY

3800 VICTORY PARKWAY
CINCINNATI, OH 45207

513.745.3000
http://www.xu.edu/

UNDERGRADUATES: 3,900

"Xavier taught me the importance of looking beyond myself to see what an integral role each of us can play in the world around us. I stepped off campus with tools that not only allowed me to compete in the 'real world,' but also to succeed and find fulfillment in my life."

—AN XAVIER FOURTH-YEAR
STUDENT

Other Xavier Profiles:

• Faculty & Curriculum Program
• Spiritual Growth Program

XAVIER UNIVERSITY remains true to its Jesuit heritage of educating the whole person. Founded in 1831 as a seminary for men, Xavier gained university status in 1930 and became coeducational in 1969. President James Hoff, SJ, carries on the Xavier tradition of "educating the head, the heart, and the hand." Following the goals exemplified by Ignatius of Loyola, founder of the Society of Jesus, Xavier emphasizes knowledge and compassion for others and incorporates these values in its curriculum and cocurricular activities:

✦ FIRST-YEAR PROGRAMS. Several first-year programs are administered through Xavier's Office of Retention Services. "PREP" ("Priority Registration Experience Program") helps incoming students register for fall classes with their academic advisors and learn more about university life. Freshman Seminars teach new students practical skills such as note taking, time management, and reading comprehension. Xavier's Parent Participation Program maintains communication among students, parents, and the university and helps parents stay informed of important first-year issues and activities

✦ FACULTY AND CURRICULUM. Xavier's core curriculum challenges students to examine, develop, and exercise moral reasoning. Every student is exposed to an intense curricular focus on ethics, religion, and society through a four-course program that encourages students to evaluate the ethical and religious undertones of socially significant issues. Small classes, mentoring relationships with faculty, and service-learning opportunities also create an environment in which students can explore values that will help them become significant contributors to society.

✦ VOLUNTEER SERVICE. The Office of Spiritual Development, instituted in 1992, sponsors numerous programs to help students develop personal and social responsibility and deepen their compassion for others. It coordinates and implements academic service-learning semesters that take place among the poor in Nicaragua and in disadvantaged neighborhoods in urban Cincinnati. It also assists "Xavier Action," a student-directed organization that pairs student volunteers with community service projects.

✦ CIVIC EDUCATION. Xavier is dedicated to developing students' knowledge and values to instill in them a personal commitment to helping society. The Dorothy Day House sponsors several Peace and Justice programs in which students can learn about civic leadership and peaceful social action. Programs such as Amnesty International, Habitat for Humanity, *Pax Christi*, "St. Vincent DePaul," "Earthbread," "Earthcare," and "Students for Life" are based at Dorothy Day House, where lectures, discussions, and theme weeks promote greater awareness of community and global issues.

✦ SPIRITUAL GROWTH. Campus Ministry, a division of the Office of Spiritual Development, promotes activities that encourage students to integrate their minds, bodies, and spirits and to respond to the invitation of St. Ignatius Loyola "to find God in all things." Prayer, scripture study, and discussion groups challenge students to expand their spiritual horizons. Retreats provide time for students to reflect on their life experiences.

Xavier helps students to become intellectually, spiritually, and morally prepared to assume their place in a rapidly changing global society and to have a positive influence on the lives of others.

Since 1701, Yale University's mission has been to educate men and women (it adopted coeducation in 1969) to serve the public good through the study of liberal arts and sciences so that they "may be fitted for Publick employment in both Church & Civil State," according to its charter.

Yale's founders recognized that for education to lead to public virtue, it must transcend the mere accumulation of facts, and this philosophy continues to guide university life today, as demonstrated by its curriculum and programs:

✦ FIRST-YEAR PROGRAMS. Aware that first-year students may have special needs for social and academic orientation, Yale offers several programs that include: "FOOT" ("Freshman Outdoor Orientation Trips"); the Dwight Hall Freshperson Conference; and "PROP" ("Pre-Registration Orientation Program"), a weeklong orientation for minority students. These programs encourage new students to meet the faculty and staff and adjust to university life. A central figure for new students is the Freshman Counselor, a senior who lives alongside new students and advises them with course selection and personal concerns.

✦ FACULTY AND CURRICULUM. Many Yale courses are devoted to issues that address personal and civic responsibility. In every department, courses are available that explore moral and ethical problems facing the world today. For example, a new program in bioethics features seminars and lectures that examine ethical issues in medicine, public policy, business, and general scientific research.

✦ VOLUNTEER SERVICE. Approximately half of all undergraduate students participate in local community service. Students are actively encouraged to tutor elementary and secondary school children, serve as "big siblings," work in soup kitchens, volunteer at Yale–New Haven Hospital, and renovate low-income housing. Many students participate in service work through Dwight Hall, a nonprofit network of students, citizens, and leaders who promote community service and social justice. The organization coordinates the activities of more than 2,000 undergraduates in community-service projects in the greater New Haven area.

✦ SPIRITUAL GROWTH. The Chaplain's Office collaborates with Yale Religious Ministry (YRM) to foster an appreciation for religious diversity and spiritual life. Both organizations serve the spiritual and personal needs of the Yale community by providing counseling, student program support, and pastoral care. YRM cosponsors such events as Religious Awareness Days, Chaplain Teas, and Religious Forums.

Yale graduates possess the skills and convictions to become valued citizens and active members of society. Repeatedly, Yale students use the citizenship-building opportunities with which their education has provided them to support the democratic institutions of justice and individual liberty.

YALE UNIVERSITY

PO BOX 208234
NEW HAVEN, CT 06520-8234

203.432.9300
http://www.yale.edu/

UNDERGRADUATES: 5,400

"Yale is very supportive of students who engage in volunteer service, providing opportunities and encouraging connections with the community. The experiences I've had at Yale as a mentor, teacher, helping hand, and citizen of New Haven have been invaluable."

—A YALE FOURTH-YEAR
STUDENT

Other Yale Profiles:

• Spiritual Growth Program
• Volunteer Service Program

IDENTIFICATION PROCESS

THE JOHN TEMPLETON FOUNDATION sent a nomination packet to the president, public information officer, and vice president for academic affairs and vice president for student life at all four-year accredited colleges and universities in the United States. Institutions were invited to nominate character-development programs that deserved special recognition. Each college and university was also encouraged to nominate its president for distinguished leadership in the field of character development, as well as to nominate itself for the Templeton Honor Roll designation. In addition, the nomination packet was sent to a wide range of higher-education associations and centers that promote character development as an important aspect of the undergraduate experience.

Each program, institution, and president nominated was promptly mailed an extensive application form that required the contact person to respond in writing to a list of questions that addressed specific selection criteria.

At the same time that the Foundation was receiving nominations and applications, we recognized that some exemplary programs would not receive or return a nomination form to us. Therefore, the Foundation asked the Institute on College Student Values at Florida State University, under the direction of Dr. Jon Dalton, to conduct an exhaustive and comprehensive proactive search to identify additional exemplary programs, presidents, and institutions. Between the nomination process and this proactive search, the researchers at the Institute on College Student Values reviewed more than 2,500 programs and 1,000 institutions.

SELECTION PROCESS

In collaboration with members of the project's Advisory Board, the Institute on College Student Values developed a set of rigorous selection criteria for each of the 10 Exemplary Program categories, the Presidential Leadership recognition, and the Templeton Honor Roll designation. The Institute's research team read, reviewed, and rated each application. Although Florida State University is very committed to character development and has received national recognition for its programs, the University was excluded from consideration in any category to avoid any perception of conflict of interest.

INSTITUTE ON COLLEGE STUDENT VALUES

The Institute on College Student Values at Florida State University was established in 1991 to provide a forum for college and university educators to explore more effective ways to promote ethical development as an integral part of the undergraduate experience. The Institute's annual conference brings together researchers and educators to exchange ideas and perspectives on character-development programs for college students.

Jon C. Dalton, Ed.D., director of the Institute on College Student Values, is a past president of the National Association of Student Personnel Administrators; in that capacity, he also served as a member of the board of directors of the American Council on Education. Dr. Dalton is Vice President for Student Affairs and Associate Professor of Higher Education at FSU.

ADVISORY BOARD

A distinguished advisory board* assisted the John Templeton Foundation in establishing the program categories, criteria, and selection process used in preparing *Colleges That Encourage Character Development*. The advisory board was not responsible for selecting the exemplary programs, presidents, and Honor Roll schools profiled.

FIRST-YEAR PROGRAMS
M. LEE UPCRAFT
Professor Emeritus, Center for the Study of Higher Education,
The Pennsylvania State University

ACADEMIC HONESTY PROGRAMS
SALLY COLE
Executive Director, The Center for Academic Integrity, Duke University

FACULTY AND CURRICULUM PROGRAMS
ANNE COLBY
Senior Scholar, The Carnegie Foundation for the Advancement of Teaching

VOLUNTEER SERVICE PROGRAMS
ELIZABETH L. HOLLANDER
Executive Director, Campus Compact, Brown University

SUBSTANCE-ABUSE PREVENTION PROGRAMS
RICHARD A. YOAST
Director, Office of Alcohol and Other Drug Abuse, American Medical Association

STUDENT LEADERSHIP PROGRAMS
HELEN S. ASTIN
Associate Director, Higher Education Research Institute,
University of California, Los Angeles

SPIRITUAL GROWTH PROGRAMS
SHARON DALOZ PARKS
Associate Director, Whidbey Institute

CIVIC EDUCATION PROGRAMS
BENJAMIN R. BARBER
Director, The Walt Whitman Center for the Culture and Politics of Democracy,
Rutgers, The State University of New Jersey

CHARACTER AND SEXUALITY PROGRAMS
RICHARD P. KEELING
Academic Program Director, University Health Services,
University of Wisconsin–Madison

SENIOR-YEAR PROGRAMS
GRETCHEN VAN DER VEER
Director, Office of Leadership Development and Training,
United States Corporation for National Service

PRESIDENTIAL LEADERSHIP
ROBERT H. ATWELL
President Emeritus, American Council of Education

* affiliation for identification purposes only

Glossary

Binge Drinking
Defined by most experts as having five or more drinks in a row for men and four or more drinks in a row for women. According to research from the Harvard School of Public Health, binge drinkers are 10 times as likely to drive after drinking and 11 times as likely to fall behind in class work. Half of all college binge drinkers start in high school.

Campus Crime
Recent studies reveal that 80% of campus crime turns out to be student-on-student; 90% involves drugs or alcohol.

Campus Ethos
The distinguishing attitudes, beliefs, and values of a campus community. The term also refers to the spirit of a campus. While not directly observable, the ethos of a college campus can be a formidable force in shaping the minds and hearts of students. The root meaning of the Greek word for ethics, *ethikos*, signifies an ethos that is rooted in community and transmitted through customs.

Capstone Course
In the 19th century, this senior-year course usually was taught by the college president to provide a moral context for the student's education and graduation. Today, "Senior-Year Courses," usually aligned with the student's major, are dramatically increasing on college and university campuses.

Character
Rooted in the Greek word *charakter*, the term "character" has come to mean the constellation of strengths and weaknesses that form and reveal who we are. Our character does not consist of a single statement or a random act but of those qualities and dispositions that we place consistently—both good and bad. Assessing our character means taking an inventory of our dominant thoughts and actions. As Aristotle once said, "We are what we repeatedly do." Character, as a concept that explains personality and behavior, is neither liberal nor conservative because it is not primarily about politics or policy.

Civic Education
An education that provides students in the U.S. with the skills, knowledge, and conviction to participate in our democracy. A civic education focuses on teaching the "democratic virtues," those principles, beliefs, and practices such as voting and joining associations, that support a democratic society. Sadly, recent findings from an annual survey of first-year college students reveal record-low levels of student interest in keeping up to date with political affairs, discussing politics, or working on political campaigns.

Civil Society
This term has many meanings. Some use it to describe the combination of decency, civility, and manners that are adopted as an antidote to the harsh edge of public debate. Others consider the term to be synonymous with private charity, volunteerism, and service. For most, maintaining a civil society means affirming and strengthening the community-based, voluntary, religious, and civic institutions in our society that sustain our democracy.

Cocurricular Activities
Student activities on the campus and in nearby communities that are independent of a college or university's formal academic program of courses and classes. These activities usually are associated with student organizations, clubs, and other student-life groups.

Conscience
The term literally means "with knowledge." Thomas Aquinas considered conscience a "sacred and sovereign monitor" that governs our moral decisions. Kant emphasized the judicial aspect of conscience, "duty's inner citadel." Many college educators believe that helping students develop a strong conscience—a desire to do what's right—is at the heart of a character education.

Core Curriculum
A set of courses that form the core of every student's education at a particular college or university; a defined group of specific courses required to graduate. Until the middle of the 20th century, nearly all colleges and universities had a core curriculum; however, since the 1960s, core requirements have become less rigid at most institutions of higher education.

Critical Thinking
The careful observation of a problem followed by a thoughtful and reasoned response. One outcome of the college experience is to foster a more systematic, thorough, and focused mode of thinking.

ETHICAL DEVELOPMENT
The ability to grow in awareness of what is right and wrong. On many college and university campuses, administrators are establishing centers and offices that focus on how best to design classroom and cocurricular activities to foster students' ethical development.

ETHICS
From the Greek word *ethikos;* a systematic study of morality; a branch of philosophy. On a practical level, 84% of North American companies have a corporate ethics code.

ETHICS-ACROSS-THE-CURRICULUM
A comprehensive effort being undertaken at some colleges and universities to institute and integrate a broad-based ethical component to the entire curriculum of an institution.

FRESHMAN ORIENTATION
A program of academic advising, tours, and other educational and social activities designed to help incoming students acclimate to college life. Sometimes referred to as the "First-Year Experience," this program offers a comprehensive introduction to a college or university. Orientation programs range from a single day to an entire semester and include a wide variety of activities and goals, sometimes including a volunteer service project.

GREEK ORGANIZATIONS
Fraternities or sororities on a campus whose names usually are composed of Greek letters. Greek organizations consist of four basic types: social, service, professional, and honorary. Greek life on college and university campuses is as healthy as ever.

HONESTY
From the Latin *honor* ("a mark of respect"), the term refers to truth-telling and trustworthiness. According to recent studies, more than 75% of students on most campuses admit to some cheating, whereas 24% admit that they would lie to get or keep a job. Many colleges and universities have instituted Honor Codes or campus compacts to set a clear standard of honesty related to academic work.

HONOR CODE
An Honor Code usually includes one or more of the following elements: a written pledge in which students affirm that their work will be or has been done honestly; unproctored examinations with a clause obligating students to report any cheating they learn about or observe; and a requirement that students form most of

the judiciary that hears alleged violations of the Honor Code. Research shows that students at Honor Code institutions are far less likely to cheat than are those students who attend a school that does not have an Honor Code.

HONORS PROGRAMS
An honors program is a sequence of courses designed specifically to encourage independent and creative learning. For more than three decades, "honors" education has been an institution on American campuses. To give them additional prominence, honors programs sometimes evolve into honors colleges, depending on the focus, resources, and commitment of the institution. In such cases, the name of the honors college may be different from that of the institution. Admission to honor programs or honors colleges within a university is usually highly selective.

IDEALISM
A state of mind that carries the desire to recognize and aim for the best in our own life and for the life of the community of which we are a part. The pursuit of a great vision, a dream, a hope for a better future.

IN LOCO PARENTIS
Literally, "in place of the parent." With regard to education, the term refers to the supervision of a minor by a school when a parent is not present. Throughout the 19th and 20th centuries, colleges and universities supervised students *in loco parentis;* in recent decades, institutions of higher education have been moving increasingly away from this responsibility, in part because of recent Supreme Court decisions.

INTEGRITY
Strength and firmness of character; utter sincerity and honesty. A person of integrity keeps his or her word. This quality includes the ability to articulate deeply held values and principles and the ability to resist betraying those values.

JUSTICE
Fairness or equality in apportioning advantages and rewards, as well as punishing wrong conduct. We need justice in order to protect the rights of everyone. The quality of justice means standing up for our own rights and the rights of other people.

LEARNING COMMUNITIES
Currently a popular term in higher education, a learning community generally consists of two or more courses that students take together as part of a group. Often designed for incoming students in their first and second

semesters, small learning communities enable students to get to know their classmates more quickly. Students who are involved in learning communities report that they feel more comfortable participating in class.

MISSION STATEMENT
A statement of purpose, intent, and goals that defines the ideals of a college or university. Many current character-development initiatives in higher education are born when the college president or board of trustees expresses the conviction that the institution must return to its "historic mission."

MORALITY
A system of rules or principles prescribing how we should act and defining what our rights and obligations are. A moral person is one who is capable of distinguishing right from wrong and demonstrates a predilection for what is right.

NATIONAL ALCOHOL AWARENESS WEEK
Generally takes place in October. This event provides the entire campus with the opportunity to educate students about issues of alcohol use and abuse. Students, faculty, and administrators take part in various activities designed to inform young people about the dangers of alcohol to self and others.

PARTY SCHOOL
A college or university that is perceived to have an atmosphere more conducive to social interaction than to academic rigor. This term is often used to denote a school where alcohol consumption is widely prevalent.

PEER CULTURE
The habits and concepts accepted by a specific group. Studies by the Higher Education Research Institute (HERI) show that a student's peer group is the single most potent source of influence on growth and development during the undergraduate years. Furthermore, HERI found that students' values, beliefs, and aspirations tend to change in the direction of the dominant values, beliefs, and aspirations of their peer culture.

PEER EDUCATORS
Usually upperclass students who have been trained to educate their peers about issues related to personal and civic responsibility. Peer educators often lead small group discussions or organize formal presentations related to policies and issues of alcohol misuse, sexual harassment, sexual health, and academic honesty. Both qualitative and quantitative analyses confirm that college students prefer learning about these issues from their peers.

PERSONAL RESPONSIBILITY
This term signifies being dependable and displaying integrity. Personal responsibility means being accountable to ourselves and others by fulfilling obligations and keeping promises.

PHILOSOPHY OF LIFE
Recent studies indicate that whereas 85% of American undergraduates in 1968 expected college to help them develop a philosophy of life, in 1998 less than half did. The college experience, both in and out of the classroom, historically has been thought of as a "search for meaning." Developing a philosophy of life means exploring such perennial and seminal questions as: Who am I? Where am I going? What is the purpose of life? Interestingly, studies reveal that participating in volunteer activities during the undergraduate years helps students develop a meaningful philosophy of life.

RESPECT
Showing regard for one's own worth and the worth of others. This includes treating our own lives as having inherent value, treating others as having dignity and rights equal to our own, and treating property as an extension of a person.

SELF-CONTROL
The ability to delay gratification or to make decisions based on meeting long-term goals. Self-control enables a person to avoid at-risk activities (such as binge drinking), which often have harmful consequences. Historically, learning to practice and display self-control or self-discipline has been an essential aspect of the undergraduate experience. It is arguable that the majority of personal and social problems in society today—drug abuse, violence, school failure, alcoholism, unwanted pregnancy, debt, and poor eating habits—involve deficiencies or failures in self-control.

SERVICE LEARNING
A popular term in higher education today, service learning is a balance between service to the community and academic learning. Linking the terms "service" and "learning" symbolizes the central role of reflection (often through journal writing or small group discussions) as integral to the process of learning through a service experience. According to recent studies, 61% of all college students received academic credit for service work, 11% of all colleges and universities have a graduation requirement related to public service, and 17% of all institutions consider service experience during the admission process.

Spiritual Growth

A process by which a person searches for meaning, connectedness, and significance, often within the context of religious belief and understanding. An outcome of spiritual growth during the college years is a vision of moral integrity that coheres and connects our beliefs to our behavior.

Standards of Behavior

Refers to principles or ideals of human conduct. Many institutions of higher education institute and affirm standards of behavior to guide their students. Standards of student behavior include student rights, expectations, and institutional rules.

Student Leadership

Almost all colleges and universities aspire to prepare students for positions of leadership both inside and outside the campus community. However, a growing number of colleges have established programs dedicated to providing high-quality educational experiences that help students develop the competencies, conscience, and compassion required of leaders in a civil society.

Values

What we judge worth having (a job, wealth, wisdom), worth doing (helping others, enjoying family time, planning a vacation), or worth being (honest, happy, successful). Values can be considered nonmoral (such as the benefits of exercising, gardening, reading) or moral (such as the rewards of self-discipline, fairness, compassion). Some personal moral values (serving those less fortunate) are those that certain individuals freely accept without imposing their strong sense of obligation on others.

Virtues

Lived moral values; objectively good moral qualities or attributes (patience, prudence, compassion, courage). A virtues-infused character education has become very popular in colleges and universities.

Resource Directory of Higher-Education Organizations

This Resource Directory profiles 70 higher-education organizations that encourage—through programs or publications—one or more dimensions of character development.
— Editors

American Association for Higher Education (AAHE)
One Dupont Circle, Suite 360
Washington, DC 20036-1110
202.293.6440
http://www.aahe.org

AAHE is an individual membership organization that promotes change and reform in higher education to ensure its effectiveness in a complex, interconnected world. Consisting of more than 9,000 professors, college administrators, students, and individuals concerned about the future of higher education, AAHE recently initiated a Service Learning Project. The project is anchored by an 18-volume series designed to provide resources to faculty wishing to explore community-based learning in and through the academic disciplines. The organization will also be convening a series of meetings to promote service-learning collaboration across the disciplines.

American Association of State Colleges and Universities (AASCU)
1307 New York Avenue NW, Suite 500
Washington, DC 20005-4701
202.293.7070
http://www.aascu.org

AASCU promotes a broad understanding of the essential role of public higher education in our society. Among its many programs is the Academic Leadership Institute, which provides professional development opportunities for newly appointed chief academic officers at AASCU-member institutions.

American College Health Association (ACHA)
P.O. Box 28937
Baltimore, MD 21240-8937
410.859.1500
http://www.acha.org

ACHA is the principal advocate and leadership organization for college and university health professionals. The organization provides advocacy, education, and services for its members to enhance their ability to improve the health of all students and the wider campus community.

American College Personnel Association (ACPA)
One Dupont Circle, Suite 300
Washington, DC 20036-1110
202.835.2272
http://www.acpa.nche.edu/

ACPA is a professional association that offers student-affairs professionals educational programs, services, and other professional development opportunities to enhance the quality of the learning environment on college and university campuses.

American Council on Education (ACE)
One Dupont Circle, Suite 800
Washington, DC 20036-1193
202.939.9300
http://www.acenet.edu

ACE is the nation's principal higher-education association. Dedicated to the belief that equal educational opportunity and a strong higher-education system are essential cornerstones of a democratic society, ACE recently established an initiative to strengthen the role of colleges and universities in promoting civic responsibility among students.

American Medical Association (AMA)
Office of Alcohol and Other Drug Abuse
515 North State Street
Chicago, IL 60610
312.464.4202
http://www.ama-assn.org/special/aos/alcohol1/

In response to the alarming statistics on alcohol use on college campuses, the AMA and The Robert Wood Johnson Foundation are collaborating on two national efforts. *A Matter of Degree: The National Effort to Reduce High-Risk Drinking Among College Students* seeks to confront the issues and problems associated with youth and alcohol and to create solutions through environmental changes. *Reducing Underage Drinking Through Coalitions* brings together 12 broad-based coalitions to reduce alcohol abuse among minors and create healthier communities.

ASSOCIATION FOR COLLEGE AND UNIVERSITY RELIGIOUS AFFAIRS

Alice Millar Chapel
Northwestern University
1870 Sheridan Road
Evanston, IL 60208-1350
847.491.7353
chaplain@nwu.edu

A professional association of chaplains and directors of religious affairs.

ASSOCIATION FOR MORAL EDUCATION

http://www.wittenberg.edu/ame

AME was founded in 1976 to provide an interdisciplinary forum for professionals interested in curriculum development and research that links moral theory with educational practice. Through its program of conferences and publications, AME serves as a resource to educators, practitioners, and the public in matters related to moral education and development.

ASSOCIATION FOR PRACTICAL AND PROFESSIONAL ETHICS (APPE)

Indiana University
618 East Third Street
Bloomington, IN 47405
812.855.6450
http://www.php.ucs.indiana.edu/~appe

APPE is committed to encouraging and developing high-quality interdisciplinary scholarship and teaching within the fields of practical and professional ethics. At its annual meeting, APPE hosts the Intercollegiate Ethics Bowl, a competition among college students that focuses on responding adroitly to complex ethical questions and dilemmas.

ASSOCIATION FOR RELIGION AND INTELLECTUAL LIFE (ARIL)

College of New Rochelle
New Rochelle, NY 10805
914.235.1439
http://www.aril.org

ARIL is a global network of people from various religious traditions who share a commitment to bringing the passions of the heart into closer relationship with the life of the mind. In the year 2000, ARIL is celebrating the 50th anniversary of its magazine, *Cross Currents*.

ASSOCIATION FOR STUDENT JUDICIAL AFFAIRS (ASJA)

P.O. Box 2237
College Station, TX 77841-2237
http://www.asja.tamu.edu

ASJA encourges the development and enforcement of standards of conduct for students in an educational endeavor that fosters students' personal and social development. Students must assume a significant role in developing and enforcing such regulations so that they can be better prepared for the responsibilities of citizenship.

ASSOCIATION OF AMERICAN COLLEGES AND UNIVERSITIES (AAC&U)

1818 R Street NW
Washington, DC 20009
202.387.3760
http://www.aacu-edu.org

AAC&U is an institutional membership association that works to advance the aims of liberal education. Strengthening the undergraduate curriculum is one of five priority areas the organization will focus on in the coming years.

ASSOCIATION OF AMERICAN UNIVERSITIES (AAU)

1200 New York Avenue NW, Suite 550
Washington, DC 20005
202.408.7500
http://www.tulane.edu/~aau/

The AAU consists of more than 60 universities concerned with undergraduate education and related higher-education policy issues.

ASSOCIATION OF CATHOLIC COLLEGES AND UNIVERSITIES (ACCU)

One Dupont Circle, Suite 650
Washington, DC 20036
202.457.0650
http://www.accunet.org

ACCU is an association of more than 200 colleges and universities in the U.S. interested in advancing the importance and contributions of Catholic higher education. The organization publishes the semi-annual journal *Current Issues in Catholic Higher Education*.

ASSOCIATION OF COLLEGE AND UNIVERSITY HOUSING OFFICERS–INTERNATIONAL (ACUHO-I)

364 West Lane Avenue, Suite C
Columbus, OH 43201-1062
614.292.0099
http://www.acuho.ohio-state.edu

ACUHO-I provides technical support to college personnel involved in student housing. Its new magazine, *Talking Stick*, contains reports and programming ideas on timely subjects related to the field of college and university resident halls and student housing.

ASSOCIATION OF COLLEGE UNIONS–INTERNATIONAL (ACUI)

One City Centre, Suite 200
120 West Seventh Street
Bloomington, IN 47404
812.855.8550
http://www.acuiweb.org

ACUI brings together college student-union and student activities professionals from nearly 1,000 schools worldwide. It is dedicated to enhancing campus life through programs, services, and useful publications. ACUI currently has a special initiative to integrate civic values into its core programs and activities.

ASSOCIATION OF GOVERNING BOARDS OF UNIVERSITIES AND COLLEGES (AGB)

One Dupont Circle, Suite 400
Washington, DC 20036
202.296.8400
http://www.agb.org

AGB's mission is to advance the practice of citizen trusteeship and help ensure the quality and success of the nation's colleges and universities. AGB has developed programs and services that strengthen the partnership between president and governing board, define the responsibilities of governing board members, and provide guidance to regents and trustees.

THE BACCHUS AND GAMMA PEER EDUCATION NETWORK

P.O. Box 100430
Denver, CO 80250-0430
303.871.0901
http://www.bacchusgamma.org

The network is an association of college- and university-based peer-education programs that focus on alcohol-abuse prevention and other related student health and safety issues. The network operates on the philosophy that students can play a uniquely effective role, unmatched by professional educators, in encouraging their peers to consider, talk honestly about, and develop responsible habits, attitudes, and lifestyles regarding alcohol and related issues.

THE BONNER SCHOLARS PROGRAM

10 Mercer Street
Princeton, NJ 08540
609.924.6663
http://www.bonner.org

The foundation provides four-year community-service scholarships to approximately 1,500 students annually (known throughout higher education as "Bonner Scholars"). The scholarship supports those young men and women who have high financial need and a commitment to volunteer service.

CAMPUS COMPACT

Brown University
Box 1975
Providence, RI 02912
401.863.1119
http://www.compact.org

Campus Compact is a national membership organization of college and university presidents committed to helping students develop the values and skills of citizenship through participating in public and community service.

CAMPUS CRUSADE FOR CHRIST

100 Lake Hart Drive
Orlando, FL 32832
407.826.2000
http://www.ccci.org

Campus Crusade is an interdenominational Christian ministry and student organization that provides information, training, relationships, opportunities, and environments conducive to the spiritual growth of college students.

CAMPUS OUTREACH OPPORTUNITY LEAGUE (COOL)

1531 P Street NW, Suite LL
Washington, DC 20005
202.265.1200
http://www.cool2serve.org

COOL, founded in 1984, is a national organization dedicated to the education and empowerment of college students through community service. It aims to mobilize and connect students of all backgrounds to lead a movement that promotes student activism and fosters the civic responsibility necessary to build a just society.

The Carnegie Foundation for the Advancement of Teaching
555 Middlefield Road
Menlo Park, CA 94025
650.566.5100
http://www.carnegiefoundation.org

The foundation is a major national center for research and policy studies about teaching. Its reports and publications have addressed the most serious challenges facing the undergraduate education experience. The foundation is currently engaged in an initiative titled Higher Education and the Development of Moral Character and Civic Responsibility.

The Center for Academic Integrity
Box 90434
Duke University
Durham, NC 27708
919.660.3045
http://www.academicintegrity.org

The center provides a forum to identify, affirm, and promote the values of academic integrity among students. By encouraging and supporting research on factors that affect academic integrity, the center hopes not only to help students and faculty develop curricular models that address issues of ethical choice, but also to make business and government leaders more aware of the impact their decisions can have on the moral development of college students. The center holds an annual conference and is currently developing an Academic Integrity Assessment and Action Guide designed to be used by colleges and universities interested in strengthening their academic integrity systems.

The Center for Campus Organizing (CCO)
165 Friend Street
M/S #1
Boston, MA 02114-2025
617.725.2886
http://www.cco.org

CCO is an educational organization that helps students on college campuses learn the leadership skills necessary for grassroots community organizing. Its mission is to promote the principles and practices of participatory democracy on campuses and within society at large. The center publishes articles, booklets, and a quarterly newsletter highlighting the state of student and campus activism.

The Center for Ethical Leadership
464 12th Avenue, Suite 320
Seattle, WA 98122
206.328.3020
http://www.halcyon.com/cel

The center provides training and education in ethical leadership, civic responsibility, and collaborative problem solving to promote the common good. It has active programs involving youth, neighborhood, religious, corporate, government, nonprofit, and education leaders.

Character Education Partnership (CEP)
918 16th Street NW, Suite 501
Washington, DC 20006
800.988.8081
http://www.character.org

CEP is a nonpartisan coalition of civic organizations, schools, businesses, and individuals dedicated to developing the character of our youth for a more compassionate and responsible society. CEP maintains a national resource center on character education and sponsors conferences, research, and publications.

Council for Advancement and Support of Education (CASE)
1307 New York Avenue NW, Suite 1000
Washington, DC 20005-4701
202.328.5900
http://www.case.org

CASE is an international association of alumni administrators, fund-raisers, public relations managers, publications editors, and government relations officers. CASE believes that institutional advancement officers have a special duty to exemplify and observe the highest standards of personal and professional conduct.

Council for Christian Colleges and Universities (CCCU)
329 8th Street NE
Washington, DC 20002
202.546.8713
http://www.cccu.org

The council focuses on helping Christian colleges and universities better fulfill their mission to effectively integrate biblical faith, scholarship, and service. Since 1994, the council has been involved in the comprehensive assessment project *Taking Values Seriously*, which examines the values of students as they enter CCCU institutions, as they graduate, and after they have been out of college for two years.

Council for Higher Education Accreditation (CHEA)

One Dupont Circle, Suite 510
Washington, DC 20036-1135
202.955.6126
http://www.chea.org

A membership organization of more than 3,000 colleges and universities, CHEA serves as a national voice for accreditation through voluntary self-regulation and as a policy center and clearinghouse for the higher education community.

Council of Independent Colleges (CIC)

One Dupont Circle, Suite 320
Washington, DC 20036-1110
202.466.7230
http://www.cic.edu

CIC is an association of more than 460 independent colleges and universities that work together to enhance educational programs and increase the visibility of private higher education's contributions to society.

The Education as Transformation Project

Wellesley College
The Office of Religious and Spiritual Life
Wellesley, MA 02181
781.283.2659
http://www.wellesley.edu/RelLife/project

The project is a multiyear organizing effort begun in 1996 to initiate a dialog about religious pluralism and spirituality in higher education. It is working with more than 250 colleges and universities to develop new models and strategies to support religious diversity on campus and explore how spirituality can serve as a web that interconnects educational initiatives such as college student values, moral and ethical development, experiential education, health, and community service.

Ethics Resources Center (ERC)

1747 Pennsylvania Avenue NW, Suite 400
Washington, DC 20006
202.737.2258
http://www.lmco.com/erc

The mission of the ERC is to enhance understanding of business ethics through dialog, research, publications, and collaboration. In 1992, ERC launched its Campaign for Character, an initiative that includes the dissemination of high-quality teacher training seminars and video-based learning programs on character education.

The Higher Education Center for Alcohol and Other Drug Prevention

Education Development Center, Inc.
55 Chapel Street
Newton, MA 02158-1060
800.676.1730
http://www.edc.org/hec

The center provides support to colleges and universities to develop strategies for changing campus culture related to alcohol abuse and drug use. The center offers technical assistance, develops publications, and conducts training workshops on college campuses throughout North America.

Higher Education Research Institute (HERI)

University of California, Los Angeles
3005 Moore Hall, Box 951521
Los Angeles, CA 90095-1521
310.825.1925
http://www.gseis.ucla.edu/heri

HERI is one of the leading centers for higher-education research and evaluation in North America, with a special emphasis on how the college experience affects the cognitive and ethical development of students. HERI conducts an annual survey of first-year college students. The results are published each year in *The American Freshman*, which examines the norms held by first-year college students. The institute is currently researching the cognitive, behavioral, and affective outcomes among college students who participate in service-learning courses. This study will also examine the effects of service learning on faculty.

Hispanic Association of Colleges and Universities (HACU)

8415 Datapoint Drive, Suite 400
San Antonio, TX 78229
210.692.3805
http://www.hacu2000.org

HACU is a national association of more than 200 colleges and universities that collectively enroll two-thirds of all Hispanics in higher education. HACU has initiated a number of educational projects to address and improve Hispanic graduation rates, including linkages between colleges and universities and precollegiate school systems.

INSTITUTE FOR GLOBAL ETHICS
11 Main Street
P.O. Box 563
Camden, ME 04843
207.236.6658
http://www.globalethics.org

The institute is an independent, nonpartisan organization dedicated to elevating public awareness and promoting the discussion of ethics in a global context. As an international, membership-based think tank, the institute focuses on ethical activities in education, the corporate sector, and public policy.

INSTITUTE ON COLLEGE STUDENT VALUES
Florida State University
313 Westcott Building
Tallahassee, FL 32306-1340
850.644.5590
http://www.fsu.edu/~staffair/institute

The institute conducts an annual conference for student-affairs professionals, educators, campus ministers, and other individuals interested in character development during the college years. It is designed to be a think tank for those who wish to explore more effective ways to promote the ethical development of college students.

INTERCOLLEGIATE STUDIES INSTITUTE (ISI)
P.O. Box 443
Wilmington, DE 19807
800.526.7022
http://www.isi.org

ISI is an educational organization whose purpose is to convey to successive generations of college youth a better understanding of the values and institutions that sustain a free society. To accomplish this goal, ISI has established an integrated program of lectures, conferences, publications, and fellowships that reaches thousands of college students and faculty across the country.

JOSEPHSON INSTITUTE OF ETHICS
4640 Admiralty Way
Suite 1001
Marina del Rey, CA 90292-6610
310.306.1868
http://www.jiethics.org

The mission of the institute is to improve the ethical quality of society by advocating principled reasoning and ethical decision-making. One of the institute's programs is the Character Counts! Coalition, a wide-ranging alliance of schools, youth organizations, and civic groups that supports the ethical development of young people through programming that focuses on practicing the Six Pillars of Character: trustworthiness, respect, responsibility, fairness, caring, and citizenship.

THE KENAN ETHICS PROGRAM
Duke University
Box 90432
102 West Duke Building
Durham, NC 27708
919.660.3033
http://www.kenan.ethics.duke.edu

The program supports the study and teaching of ethics and promotes moral reflection and commitment in personal, professional, community, and civic life. It encourages moral inquiry across intellectual disciplines and professions, within the context of campus life, as well as across interdependent local, national, and global communities. The program sponsors the annual conference Moral Education in a Diverse Society.

KETTERING FOUNDATION
200 Commons Road
Dayton, OH 45459
513.434.7300
http://www.kettering.org

The foundation is rooted in the American tradition of "inventive research," embodied by its founder, Charles F. Kettering, holder of more than 200 patents and best known for his invention of the automotive self-starter. Today, the foundation conducts research and publishes educational and community resources to help citizens act responsibly and effectively on the challenges facing our society. The foundation recently developed and widely disseminated civic education study guides and activities for use in college and university classrooms.

LEADERSHAPE
1801 Fox Drive
Suite 101
Champaign, IL 61820
217.351.6200
http://www.leadershape.org

The mission of LeaderShape is to offer the highest quality, state-of-the-art leadership programs that improve society by inspiring, developing, and supporting college student leaders. The W. K. Kellogg Foundation recently named The LeaderShape Institute an "exemplary program."

MEDICAL INSTITUTE FOR SEXUAL HEALTH
P.O. Box 162306
Austin, TX 78716-2306
800.892.9484
http://www.medinstitute.org

Driven by medical, educational, and other scientific data, the institute informs, educates, and provides solutions to medical professionals, educators, government officials, parents, and the media about problems associated with sexually transmitted disease and nonmarital pregnancy. It recently published an information packet titled National Guidelines for Sexuality and Character Education.

NATIONAL ACADEMIC ADVISING ASSOCIATION (NACADA)
Kansas State University
2323 Anderson Avenue, Suite 225
Manhattan, KS 66502-2912
785.532.5717
http://www.ksu.edu/nacada

NACADA is an association of professional advisors, faculty, administrators, and students who do academic advising or work to promote the highest quality academic advising on college and university campuses. The organization has a core values statement that provides a framework against which those who advise can measure their own performance. Among its many educational materials, NACADA recently published a monograph titled *First-Year Student Academic Advising*.

NATIONAL ASSOCIATION FOR CAMPUS ACTIVITIES (NACA)
13 Harbison Way
Columbia, SC 29212-3401
803.732.6222
http://www.naca.org

NACA is a member-based association of colleges and universities, talent firms, artists and performers, student programmers and leaders, and professional campus activities staff. It serves as a clearinghouse and catalyst for information, ideas, and campus-based leadership opportunities.

NATIONAL ASSOCIATION FOR COLLEGE ADMISSION COUNSELING (NACAC)
1631 Prince Street
Alexandria, VA 22314-2818
703.836.2222
http://www.nacac.com

NACAC is an association of more than 6,600 members who work with students as they make the transition from high school to postsecondary education. The school counselor and the college admission counselor are most often the primary sources of information about the transition process. NACAC has established a Statement of Principles of Good Practice, the code of ethical conduct for all individuals and institutions involved in the admission process.

NATIONAL ASSOCIATION FOR EQUAL OPPORTUNITY IN HIGHER EDUCATION (NAFEO)
8701 Georgia Avenue, Suite 200
Silver Spring, MD 20910
301.650.2440
http://www.nafeo.org

NAFEO is a national umbrella and advocacy organization for 118 of the nation's historically and predominantly Black colleges and universities. Its mission is to articulate the need for a system of higher education in which race, ethnicity, socioeconomic status, and previous educational attainment levels are not determinants of either the quantity or quality of higher education.

NATIONAL ASSOCIATION FOR WOMEN IN EDUCATION (NAWE)
1325 18th Street, NW, Suite 210
Washington, DC 20036
202.659.9330
http://www.nawe.org

NAWE addresses issues related to the interests, scholarship, and advancement of women educators and college students. The organization holds an annual conference designed for women who aspire to or who are currently in leadership roles on campus and in their community.

NATIONAL ASSOCIATION OF COLLEGE AND UNIVERSITY CHAPLAINS (NACUC)
c/o Office of the Chaplain
Williamette University
900 State Street
Salem, OR 97301

NACUC is a multifaith professional organization concerned with the religious life of the entire college or university. The organization publishes *NACUC NEWS*, a publication of articles, reviews, and news, and *Ailanthus*, a semiannual journal of professional and scholarly papers related to religious life in higher education. NACUC also convenes an annual meeting.

National Association of Independent Colleges and Universities (NAICU)

1025 Connecticut Avenue NW, Suite 700
Washington, DC 20036-5405
202.785.8866
http://www.naicu.edu

Made up of more than 900 private colleges and universities, NAICU's primary objective is to inform the public and government about the accomplishments and concerns of independent higher education.

National Association of State Universities and Land-Grant Colleges (NASULGC)

1307 New York Avenue NW, Suite 400
Washington, DC 20005-4701
202.478.6040
http://www.nasulgc.org

NASULGC is an association of 202 land-grant colleges and universities that supports high-quality public education. The organization is initiating a public education campaign to raise awareness about the dangers of excessive alcohol consumption by college students.

National Association of Student Personnel Administrators (NASPA)

1875 Connecticut Avenue NW, Suite 418
Washington, DC 20009
202.265.7500
http://www.naspa.org

With more than 8,000 individual members and more than 1,175 member campuses, NASPA provides support to senior student-affairs officers and administrators. One of its most recent initiatives is to develop a set of principles to promote student learning that should guide the cooperation and collaboration of all academic and student-affairs professionals on a college or university campus.

National Campus Ministry Association

2 Ocean Dune Circle
Palm Coast, FL 32137
904.446.8066

An association of campus ministry professionals that provides networking and resources for personal and professional growth to those who are engaged in ministry in higher education.

National Clearinghouse for Leadership Programs (NCLP)

1135 Stamp Student Union
University of Maryland
College Park, MD 20742-7174
301.314.7164
http://www.inform.umd.edu/CampusInfo/
Departments/OCP/NCLP

NCLP provides a central clearinghouse of leadership materials, resources, and assistance to leadership educators. Its members receive publications, assistance, consultation, access to leadership resource files, and networking opportunities with other professionals engaged in leadership education.

National Collegiate Honors Council (NCHC)

Radford University
Radford, VA 24142
540.831.6100
http://www.runet.edu/~nchc

NCHC seeks to enhance the academic, cultural, and social opportunities available to exceptionally motivated undergraduate students. Specifically, its purposes are to stimulate development of new honors programs in colleges and universities, promote an awareness of honors learning within higher education, and help honors programs improve intellectual discourse on campuses in ways advantageous to all students and faculty.

National Hillel/The Foundation for Jewish Campus Life

1640 Rhode Island Avenue NW
Washington DC 20036
202.857.6560
http://www.hillel.org

Hillel cooperates with a vast array of Jewish organizations to bring to campuses across the U.S. the broadest range of social, educational, cultural, and religious programs for Jewish students of all backgrounds.

National Interfraternity Conference (NIC)

3901 West 86th Street, Suite 390
Indianapolis, IN 46268-1791
317.872.1112
http://www.nicindy.org

A federation of 67 men's national and international fraternities, NIC provides a variety of services to support and enhance the fraternity movement throughout the U.S. and Canada. It offers educational materials on "Alcohol-Free Housing," "Adopt an Elementary School," "Leadership Development," and "The Crime of Hazing."

NATIONAL PANHELLENIC CONFERENCE
3901 W. 86th Street, Suite 380
Indianapolis, IN 46268
317.872.3185
http://www.greeklife.org/npc

The mission of the National Panhellenic Conference is to support and promote women's sororities and fraternities as a positive element of the higher-education experience. The organization works closely with colleges and universities to maintain and advance high standards of conduct and scholarship for women in Greek-letter societies.

NATIONAL PAN-HELLENIC COUNCIL, INC. (NPHC)
Memorial Hall West, Room 108
Bloomington, IN 47405
812.855.8820
http://www.nphc.org

NPHC is a national coordinating body for the nine historically African-American fraternities and sororities on American college and university campuses. Alumni chapters across the country are highly active in civic and community-service initiatives.

NATIONAL SOCIETY FOR EXPERIENTIAL EDUCATION (NSEE)
1703 North Beauregard Street
Alexandria, VA 22311
703.575.5475
http://www.nsee.org

NSEE is a membership association and national resource center that promotes experienced-based approaches to teaching and learning. For more than 25 years, NSEE has developed best practices for effectively integrating experience into educational programs.

NATIONAL WOMEN'S HEALTH RESOURCE CENTER (NWHRC)
120 Albany Street, Suite 820
New Brunswick, NJ 08901
877.986.9472
http://www.healthywomen.org

NWHRC is the national clearinghouse for women's health information. It has a popular Web site and publishes the award-winning National Women's Health Report.

SOCIETY FOR VALUES IN HIGHER EDUCATION (SVHE)
Portland State University
633 SW Montgomery Street
Portland, OR 97207
503.721.6520
http://www.adm.pdx.edu

SVHE is a fellowship of faculty members and others who care deeply about ethical issues facing higher education and the wider society. Members of SVHE conceive and carry out national projects that focus on issues such as integrity and civic responsibility in higher education.

UNITED NEGRO COLLEGE FUND (UNCF)
8260 Willow Oaks Corporate Drive
Fairfax, VA 22031
800.331.2244
http://www.uncf.org

A consortium of 39 private, accredited, four-year historically Black colleges and universities, UNCF is the nation's oldest and most successful African-American higher-education assistance organization. It was recently awarded a major grant from the Ford Foundation to support changes in the curriculum at UNCF colleges designed to successfully institutionalize service-learning opportunities.

THE WALT WHITMAN CENTER FOR THE CULTURE AND POLITICS OF DEMOCRACY
Rutgers, The State University of New Jersey
409 Hickman Hall
New Brunswick, NJ 08903
732.932.6861
http://www.wwc.rutgers.edu

The center is dedicated to sustaining democratic theory and extending democratic practice. It approaches democracy in the spirit of Walt Whitman — as a mode of living rather than as a set of strictly political arrangements. The center sponsors research, conferences, and empirical studies of democratic theory.

WOMEN'S COLLEGE COALITION
125 Michigan Avenue NE
Washington, DC 20017
202.234.0443
http://www.womenscolleges.org

The coalition is an association representing the 79 women's colleges in the U.S. and Canada. It makes the case for single-sex education for women to the higher-education community and policy makers, as well as to the media and the general public. One of its areas of focus is the development of women leaders in society.

LISTING OF PROFILED SCHOOLS ALPHABETICALLY

Listing of Profiled Schools by Category